Structural - Strategic - Solution-Focused/Solution-Oriented Models

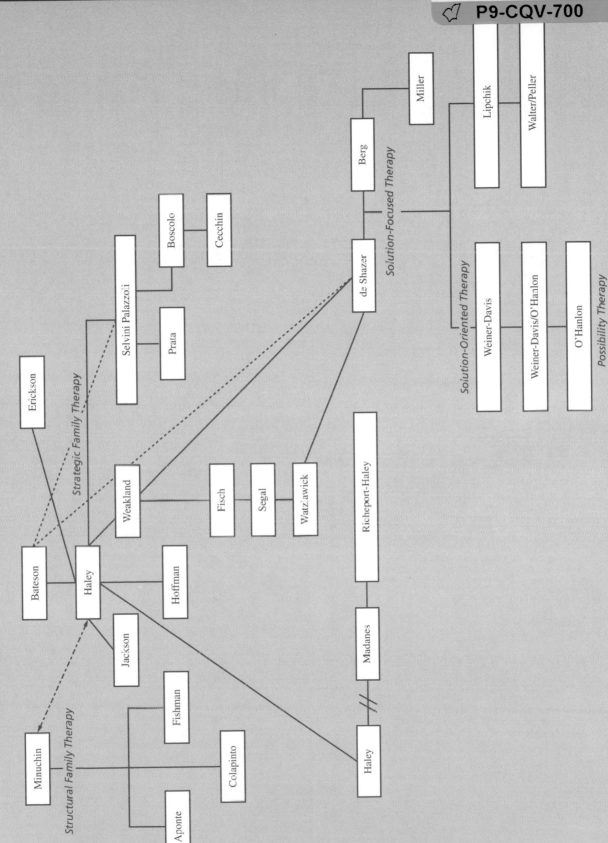

Strategic Family Therapy

Structural Family Therapy

Solution-Focused Therapy

Solution-Oriented Therapy

Possibility Therapy

Direct Influence = ——————

Indirect Influence = ············

Reciprocal Relationship = ‹----›

Philosophical/Theoretical Divorce = //

A GENOGRAM OF FAMILY THERAPY

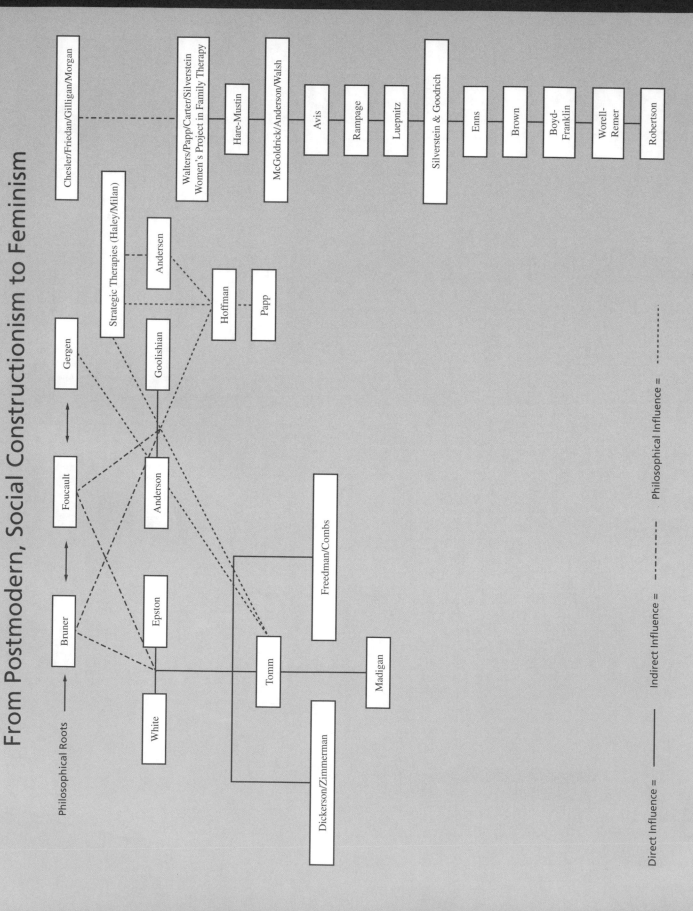

From Postmodern, Social Constructionism to Feminism

Philosophical Roots ⟶

Direct Influence = ———————

Indirect Influence = — · — · — · — ·

Philosophical Influence = - - - - - - -

Chesler/Friedan/Gilligan/Morgan

Walters/Papp/Carter/Silverstein
Women's Project in Family Therapy

Hare-Mustin

McGoldrick/Anderson/Walsh

Avis

Rampage

Luepnitz

Silverstein & Goodrich

Enns

Brown

Boyd-Franklin

Worell-Remer

Robertson

Strategic Therapies (Haley/Milan)

Andersen

Hoffman

Papp

Gergen

Goolishian

Foucault

Anderson

Bruner

Epston

Freedman/Combs

Tomm

White

Madigan

Dickerson/Zimmerman

A GENOGRAM OF FAMILY THERAPY

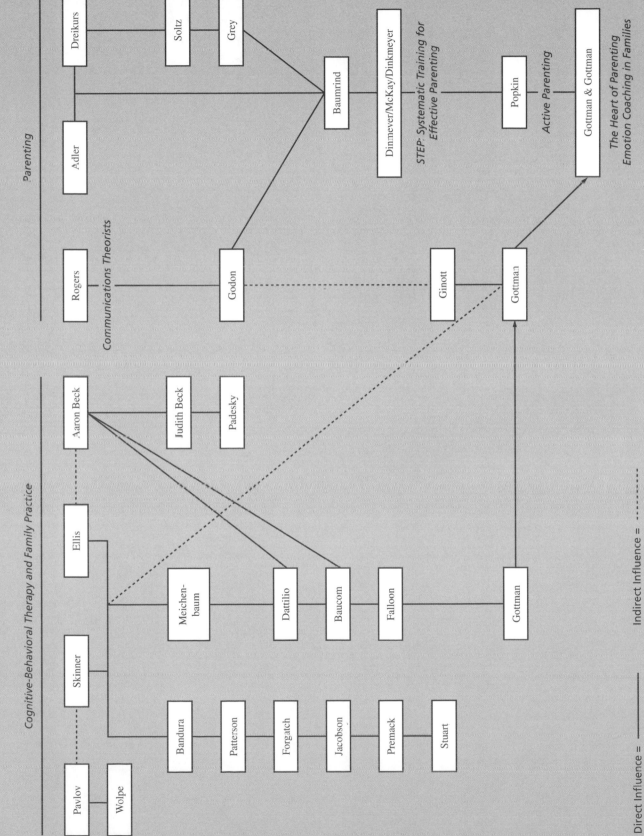

Cognitive-Behavioral Family Therapy and Parenting

Parenting

Communications Theorists

Cognitive-Behavioral Therapy and Family Practice

STEP: Systematic Training for Effective Parenting

Active Parenting

The Heart of Parenting Emotion Coaching in Families

Dreikurs — Soltz — Grey

Adler

Baumrind

Dinmeyer/McKay/Dinkmeyer

Popkin

Gottman & Gottman

Rogers — Godon — Ginott — Gottman

Aaron Beck

Judith Beck — Padesky

Ellis

Meichen- baum — Dattilio — Baucom — Falloon — Gottman

Skinner

Bandura — Patterson — Forgatch — Jacobson — Premack — Stuart

Pavlov — Wolpe

Direct Influence = ————

Indirect Influence = ‑ ‑ ‑ ‑ ‑

Theory and Practice *of* Family Therapy and Counseling

James Robert Bitter
East Tennessee State University

BROOKS/COLE
CENGAGE Learning™

Australia • Brazil • Japan • Korea • Mexico • Singapore • Spain • United Kingdom • United States

**Theory and Practice of Family Therapy
and Counseling**
James Robert Bitter

Acquisitions Editor: Seth Dobrin

Development Editor: Tangelique Williams

Assistant Editor: Christina Ganim

Editorial Assistant: Ashley Cronin

Technology Project Manager: Andrew Keay

Marketing Manager: Karin Sandberg

Marketing Coordinator: Ting Jian Yap

Marketing Communications Manager:
Shemika Britt

Project Manager, Editorial Production:
Rita Jaramillo

Creative Director: Rob Hugel

Art Directors: Vernon Boes, Caryl Gorska

Print Buyer: Linda Hsu

Text Permissions Editor: Roberta Broyer

Image Permissions Editor: Deanna Ettenger

Production Service: Matrix Productions

Text Designer: Cheryl Carrington

Photo Researcher: Cheri Throop

Copy Editor: Ellen Brownstein

Cover Designer: Cheryl Carrington

Cover Image: Getty Images

Compositor: International Typesetting and
Composition

For product information and technology assistance, contact us at
Cengage Learning Customer & Sales Support, 1-800-354-9706

For permission to use material from this text or product,
submit all requests online at **cengage.com/permissions**
Further permissions questions can be emailed to
permissionrequest@cengage.com

Library of Congress Control Number: 2007936243

Student Edition:

ISBN-13: 978-0-534-42178-6

ISBN-10: 0-534-42178-4

Brooks/Cole
10 Davis Drive
Belmont, CA 94002-3098
USA

Cengage Learning is a leading provider of customized learning solutions
with office locations around the globe, including Singapore, the United
Kingdom, Australia, Mexico, Brazil, and Japan. Locate your local office at
international.cengage.com/region

Cengage Learning products are represented in Canada by Nelson
Education, Ltd.

For your course and learning solutions, visit **academic.cengage.com**

Purchase any of our products at your local college store or at our
preferred online store **www.ichapters.com**

Printed in Canada
1 2 3 4 5 6 7 12 11 10 09 08

Dedications

For my loving wife and partner, Lynn Williams, and our wonderful children, Alison and Nora—the real gifts of love that I have in my life.

In loving memory of my parents, Greg and Betty Bitter, who adopted me when I was six months old and gave me a foundation that has sustained me for sixty years.

For the family therapists who nurtured me as a person and a professional: Manford A. Sonstegard and Virginia Satir

Brief Contents

PART 1

Basic Issues in the Practice of Family Therapy and Counseling   2

Chapter One: Introduction and Overview   5

Chapter Two: The Family Practitioner as Person and Professional   24

Chapter Three: Virtue, Ethics, and Legality in Family Practice   43

PART 2

Theories and Techniques of Family Therapy and Counseling   67

Chapter Four: Multigenerational Family Therapy   72

Chapter Five: Adlerian Family Therapy   97

Chapter Six: Human Validation Process Model   121

Chapter Seven: Symbolic-Experiential Family Therapy   145

Chapter Eight: Structural Family Therapy   166

Chapter Nine: Strategic Family Therapy   189

Chapter Ten: Solution-Focused and Solution-Oriented Therapy   217

Chapter Eleven: Postmodernism, Social Construction, and Narratives in Family Therapy   239

Chapter Twelve: Feminist Family Therapy   268

Chapter Thirteen: Cognitive-Behavioral Family Therapy   300

Chapter Fourteen: Parenting for the 21st Century   328

PART 3

Integration and Application   357

Chapter Fifteen: Integration I: From Self-Discovery to Family Practice— Forming a Relationship and Family Assessment   359

Chapter Sixteen: Integration II: Shared Meaning, Facilitating Change, and Tailoring Interventions   378

Appendix: Summary and Review of Family Models   391

Glossary   411

Name Index   433

Subject Index   436

Contents

Foreword by Gerald Corey   xi

Preface   xiii

PART 1   Basic Issues in the Practice of Family Therapy and Counseling   2

CHAPTER 1   Introduction and Overview   5
Introduction   5
Why I Became a Family Counselor and Therapist   6
Overview of This Book   10
Suggestions for Using the Book   15
The Family Systems Perspective   16
    Family Systems and Cybernetics   17
Differences Between Systemic and Individual Approaches   20
References   22

CHAPTER 2   The Family Practitioner as Person and Professional   24
Introduction   24
The Family of the Family Practitioner   25
    "Hanging Hats" and Clearing the Mind and Heart to Focus   28
Personal Characteristics and Orientations of Effective
    Family Practitioners   30
The Process of Change and Therapeutic Process   32
Beginning Your Work as Family Practitioners   33
The Scholar/Practitioner in Family Counseling and Therapy   37
Toward a Foundation for Integration   39
Gender and Multicultural Lenses   40
Summary   41
References   41

CHAPTER 3   Virtue, Ethics, and Legality in Family Practice   43
by David Kleist and James Robert Bitter
Introduction   43
A Consideration of Virtue   44

Ethical Codes and Standards of Professional Practice   46
    Perspectives on Ethics   47
Ethical Decision Making   53
    Models of Ethical Decision Making   53
Commonly Discussed Ethical Dilemmas in Family Practice   58
Professional Regulations and Legal Requirements   61
Conclusion   62
Recommended Readings   63
References   63

PART 2   Theories and Techniques of Family Therapy and Counseling   67

Introduction to the Case of the Quest Family   68
The Biography of the Quest Family   69
Quest Family Genogram   70
References   71

CHAPTER 4   Multigenerational Family Therapy   72

Introduction   72
Key Concepts   81
    Differentiation of the Self and Emotional Cutoff   82
    Triangulation and the Nuclear Family Emotional System   82
    The Family Projection Process and Multigenerational
        Transmission   83
    Sibling Position   83
    The Societal Projection Process or Societal Regression   84
Therapy Goals   84
The Therapist's Role and Function   85
    Therapist Self-Awareness   85
    Implications for Training of Family Therapists   85
Techniques   86
A Bowen Therapist With the Quest Family   88
Summary and Multicultural Evaluation   92
    Contributions to Multicultural Counseling and Gender Issues   92
Recommended Readings   94
References   95

CHAPTER 5   Adlerian Family Therapy   97

Introduction   97
Key Concepts   101
    Family Atmosphere   101
    The Family Constellation   102
    Mistaken Goals: An Interactional View   104
Therapy Goals   106

The Therapist's Role and Function   107
Techniques   107
An Adlerian Therapist With the Quest Family   109
Summary and Multicultural Evaluation   114
    Contributions to Multicultural Counseling and Gender Issues   115
Recommended Readings   118
References   119

CHAPTER 6   Human Validation Process Model   121

Introduction   121
Key Concepts   124
    Family Life   124
    Functional versus Dysfunctional Communication in Families   125
    Defensive Communication Stances in Coping With Stress   126
    Family Roles and Family Triads   129
Therapy Goals   130
The Therapist's Role and Function   131
Techniques   132
A Satir Therapist With the Quest Family   134
Summary and Multicultural Evaluation   137
    Contributions to Multicultural Counseling and Gender Issues   138
Recommended Readings   143
References   144

CHAPTER 7   Symbolic-Experiential Family Therapy   145

Introduction   145
Key Concepts   151
    Subjective Focus   151
    An Almost Atheoretical Stance   151
    Being Is Becoming   151
    Intimacy: The Desired Outcome   151
    The Dialectics of a Healthy Family   152
Therapy Goals   153
The Therapist's Role and Function   153
Techniques   154
A Symbolic-Experiential Therapist With the Quest Family   156
Summary and Multicultural Evaluation   160
    Contributions to Multicultural Counseling and Gender Issues   160
Recommended Readings   163
References   164

CHAPTER 8   Structural Family Therapy   166

Introduction   166
Key Concepts   171
    Family Structure   171
    Family Subsystems   172
    Boundaries   173

Therapy Goals   174
The Therapist's Role and Function   175
Techniques   175
A Structural Family Therapist With the Quest Family   178
Summary and Multicultural Evaluation   182
    Contributions to Multicultural Counseling and Gender Issues   182
Recommended Readings   186
References   187

CHAPTER 9   **Strategic Family Therapy**   189
Introduction   189
    The MRI Model   194
    The Milan Model   195
Key Concepts   197
Therapy Goals   199
    The MRI Model   199
    The Washington School   199
    The Milan Model   200
The Therapist's Role and Function   200
Techniques   201
    Process and Techniques at MRI   202
    Process and Techniques at the Washington School   203
    Process and Techniques in Milan   204
A Strategic Family Therapist With the Quest Family   206
Summary and Multicultural Evaluation   209
    Contributions to Multicultural Counseling and Gender Issues   210
Recommended Readings   214
References   215

CHAPTER 10   **Solution-Focused and Solution-Oriented Therapy**   217
Introduction   217
Key Concepts   222
Therapy Goals   223
The Therapist's Role and Function   223
Techniques   224
A Solution-Oriented Therapist With the Quest Family   227
Summary and Multicultural Evaluation   231
    Contributions to Multicultural Counseling and Gender Issues   232
Recommended Readings   235
References   236

CHAPTER 11   **Postmodernism, Social Construction, and Narratives in Family Therapy**   239
Introduction   239
Key Concepts   246

The Linguistic Approach: Harlene Anderson
and Harold Goolishian 247
The Reflecting Team: Tom Andersen 248
The Narrative Approach: Michael White and David Epston 249
Therapy Goals 251
The Therapist's Role and Function 252
Techniques 252
A Narrative Therapist With the Quest Family 257
Summary and Multicultural Evaluation 259
Contributions to Multicultural Counseling and Gender Issues 260
Recommended Readings 264
References 265

CHAPTER 12   Feminist Family Therapy 268

Introduction 268
Key Concepts 276
Honoring the Experiences and Perceptions of Women 276
The Personal Is Political 277
Social Transformation and Advocacy 277
Therapy Goals 278
The Therapist's Role and Function 279
Techniques 279
A Feminist Therapist With the Quest Family 283
Summary and Multicultural Evaluation 287
Contributions to Multicultural Counseling and Gender Issues 287
Recommended Readings 292
References 293

CHAPTER 13   Cognitive-Behavioral Family Therapy 300

Introduction 300
Key Concepts 307
Therapy Goals 310
The Therapist's Role and Function 310
Techniques 311
A Cognitive-Behavioral Therapist With the Quest Family 315
Summary and Multicultural Evaluation 319
Contributions to Multicultural Counseling and Gender Issues 320
Recommended Readings 324
References 325

CHAPTER 14   Parenting for the 21st Century 328

Introduction 328
A Short History of Parenting 329
Key Concepts 332

Techniques   336
    Positive Parenting for Functional Families   336
    A Word or Two About Blended Families and Step-Families   339
    Parenting Difficult Children   339
Summary and Multicultural Evaluation   346
    Contributions to Multicultural Counseling and Gender Issues   347
Recommended Readings   349
References   350

PART 3   Integration and Application   357

CHAPTER 15   Integration I:

From Self-Discovery to Family Practice—Forming a Relationship
and Family Assessment   359
Discovering a Model or Set of Models for Professional Use   359
Videotaping Your Work and Taking Time for Reflection   360
A Process for Family Therapy Across Models   361
    Forming a Relationship   361
    Conducting an Assessment   362
    Eight Lenses   362
    Formal Assessments   373
    Case Conceptualization   374
Summary   375
References   375

CHAPTER 16   Integration II:

Shared Meaning, Facilitating Change, and Tailoring Interventions   378
Hypothesizing and Shared Meaning   378
    Describing the System   379
    Integrative Models   379
Facilitating Change   380
    Resilience   381
Tailoring Treatment   383
Ensuring Therapeutic Efficacy: Treatment Adherence
    and Relapse Prevention   384
An Integrative Therapist With the Quest Family   385
Some Final Thoughts   388
References   389

Appendix: Summary and Review of Family Models   391

Glossary   411

Name Index   433

Subject Index   436

Foreword

When I was pursuing my doctoral studies in counseling in the 1960s, I never had a course in family therapy and I can never recall hearing any mention of the family systems approach in any of my courses. I went through my entire program thinking that the only way to study counseling was to understand the dynamics of the individual. My friend and colleague, Dr. Jim Bitter, was one of the key people to introduce me to a family and systemic approach to counseling and psychotherapy. Being exposed to a systemic perspective broadened my view of individual counseling and working with individuals in group therapy. Indeed, I learned how essential it is to know something about an individual's family-of-origin if we hope to counsel a person effectively.

I am guessing that there will be many readers of *Theory and Practice of Family Therapy and Counseling* who will be very much unaware of the family systems perspectives. If you are one of the readers who is just learning about family systems therapy, let me assure you that this book will be a comprehensive overview of the field, and there will be more here than you can grasp in a single course during one semester. However, this book will serve as a splendid introduction to the field of family therapy. Not only will you learn about 10 different theories of family therapy, but Jim Bitter will be your guide and mentor in assisting the beginning development of your personal integrative approach to working with families. It is almost as if Jim is your personal tutor as you are learning about the many different approaches to family systems therapy.

There are a number of features that make this book a unique one in family therapy textbooks. First of all, the author uses a common format for organizing each of the theory chapters, which will make your job of comparing these approaches realistic. The first two chapters give you a fine introduction to the rest of the book, and in these two chapters you get a real sense of Jim Bitter, the person, the author, the teacher, and the family therapist. Each of the theory chapters has exceptionally clear sections on key concepts, goals, and techniques. You will be introduced to the Quest family and then follow this family through each of the theory chapters. This case example gives a concrete illustration of how each theory can be applied to counseling the same family. The personal exercises that appear at the end of each chapter will assist you in personalizing your learning and help you to apply what you are reading to a fuller understanding of how your family background has a current influence on you personally and professionally. There are two chapters on integrative approaches, which aim to assist you in thinking about your own personal synthesis. Jim does a nice job of guiding you through the process of learning how to focus on aspects of various theories that fit for the person you are.

I found the summary sections to be most helpful in pulling together the key ideas of the chapter; further, the sections on contributions to multicultural and gender concerns are most useful in seeing practical applications. You will find plenty of suggestions on where to go beyond the chapter if you want to learn more about any theory. Make no mistake: This is not always easy reading, and you will be challenged to think and to reflect on what you are reading. One reading of the chapter will not result in total comprehension. However, I trust that you will feel encouraged as you read this book in your own quest to better understand how your family history has a current impact on you and becoming a family practitioner.

I have read this book several times, and it has been instrumental in helping me to get a better sense of what family therapy is all about. My hope is that you also will be encouraged to do what it takes to become an effective family practitioner—and that this book can be a part of the experience.

Gerald Corey, Ed.D., ABPP
Professor Emeritus, Human Services and Counseling
California State University, Fullerton

Preface

This book is intended for undergraduate and graduate students interested in the fields of family therapy and family counseling. This book is designed to accommodate multiple perspectives, including those represented by the American Association for Marriage and Family Therapy (AAMFT), the International Association of Marriage and Family Counselors (IAMFC), and the fields of counseling, human services, nursing, pastoral counseling, psychiatry, psychology, and social work. It surveys the major theories and practices of contemporary family systems and seeks to support the development of personal, professional, and ethical family practice. Most importantly, the book provides a model for a successful integration of multiple points of view.

I had several goals in writing this book. I wanted to:

- address the use of theoretical models across several fields, giving as much consideration to health, growth, and resiliency as I did to assessment and to remediation;
- present some models that were absent in other texts;
- provide real examples of quality work for each approach, as well as work with a single family that could be used for comparison across models;
- focus on personal development, as well as professional development; and
- I wanted to write in the kind of conversational tone that has made other textbooks so successful.

This book is divided into three parts. Part 1 deals with the language, conceptualizations, and issues that are the foundation for family practice. Chapter 1 provides an overview of the book and of the fields of family therapy and family counseling. It defines the language and thinking associated with family systems theory. In Chapter 1, I also tell the reader a little bit about my own family history and how it relates to both my personal and professional development. I hope this brief biography can serve as a model for students who may be starting their own personal explorations in preparation for a career in the helping professions.

Chapter 2 addresses personal and professional development more directly. In this chapter, I use some of the processes I learned from 10 years of training with Virginia Satir, a late, great pioneer of family therapy. They are designed to help the reader discover self in family context and to consider the tremendous influence family systems have had on each of us as growing counselors and therapists. I also list some of the personal and professional characteristics that are particularly useful in family practice; some ideas for how to get started with families; the relationship of scholarship to practice in the fields of family therapy and family counseling; and a first look at a model for integration that will be more fully developed in Part 3.

Chapter 3 introduces the reader to the ethical, professional, and legal issues that have shaped the development of family practice. This chapter on *applied ethics* is co-authored with my friend and colleague, David Kleist. We focus on learning to think about ethical issues from the perspectives of virtue, professional ethical codes, and legal requirements in the field. This chapter takes into account the guidance and mandates of multiple ethical codes, including those developed by the American Association for Marriage and Family Therapy (AAMFT), the American Counseling Association (ACA), the American Psychological

Association (APA), the International Association of Marriage and Family Counselors (IAMFC), the National Association of Social Workers (NASW), and the National Board for Certified Counselors (NBCC).

Part 2 is devoted to a consideration of 10 models of family therapy and counseling, plus a special chapter on effective parenting for the 21st century. It starts with a presentation of the biography and genogram of the Quest family, a family that will be part of each of the theory chapters. The 10 theory chapters have a consistent organization so that students can compare and contrast the various models. Each of the theory chapters starts with an introduction to the model that defines its major characteristics and identifies its founders. The introduction is followed by a transcript of an actual family counseling or family therapy session, usually featuring a major contributor to that approach. I want the reader to have these sessions in mind when they consider the *key concepts, therapy goals, therapist's role and function,* and *techniques* that follow. Toward the end of each chapter, I present another therapy session with the *Quest family*, using the model presented in that chapter. I end each of the theory chapters with a summary of the chapter, an experiential exercise for personal development, a consideration of gender and cultural issues, suggested readings, an introduction to the accompanying video, and references. Although an emphasis has been placed on creating a conversational tone in these chapters, each chapter is referenced fully with the most current articles and books.

Part 3 addresses the integration and application of models. There are two chapters on integration. Chapter 15 is designed to help the reader discover a model or set of models that fits the individual's worldview and perspectives on family practice. An emphasis is placed on assessing personal values and beliefs and using videotapes of initial work for reflection and development as a family counselor or therapist-in-training. A four-stage process for conducting family sessions also is described, including processes for *forming relationships, family assessment, hypothesizing and shared meaning,* and *facilitating change*. The first two parts are developed fully in this chapter while the last two parts are presented in Chapter 16.

Chapter 16 focuses on the processes of collaboration and change. An emphasis is placed on resiliency work, tailoring treatment to individual families, and methods for ensuring treatment adherence and relapse prevention. Finally, the integrative model presented in Chapters 15 and 16 is applied one last time to the Quest family. The Appendix is a short summary, reviewing the theories and practices presented in this book; included in the Appendix is a set of comparative tables related to the main points presented in each model. At the end of the book, I have provided a glossary of terms that is comprehensive across the fields that comprise family practice.

With this structure in place, we are now ready to begin a journey together. It is my hope that you will enter into the field of family therapy and find an exciting place for yourself as a family practitioner. Family practice is very much a growing and developing field. Only 60 years ago, the field was still in its infancy. I hope you will feel yourself grow into family practice as you consider the different models presented in this book.

Acknowledgments

No one writes a textbook like this without a lot of help, and I have had wonderful support from the very beginning. Starting with Julie Martinez and Marquita Flemming, my first editors, then Christina D. Ganim and Tangelique Williams, the people associated with Brooks/Cole and Cengage Learning have provided me with a team of consultants and experts who have made every part of this book possible. First and foremost among them is Sherry Cormier, who served as a developmental editor, friend, and confidant. Her wisdom is in every chapter. Amy Lam and Ashley Cronin provided excellent help in their roles as editorial assistants. Seth Miller and his team at Matrix Productions handled copy-editing, enhancing both the accuracy and clarity of the book. Karin Sandberg and her team developed and implemented a marketing plan that supported the delivery of the book to you. And of course, this book would not ever have been started without the kindness, support, and constant encouragement of Jerry Corey.

Special thanks are extended to the chapter reviewers, who provided consultation and detailed critiques. Their recommendations have been incorporated into this text:

- Chapters 1 and 2: Gerald and Marianne Corey
- Chapter 3: David Kleist and I co-wrote this chapter, but he is the expert in this area.
- Chapter 4: Betty Carter
- Chapter 5: Jon Carlson, Governors State University; William G. Nicoll, Florida Atlantic University; and Richard E. Watts, Sam Houston State University
- Chapter 6: Jean McLendon, Satir Training Institute of the Southeast; John Banmen, Satir Training Institute of the Northwest
- Chapter 7: J. Graham Disque, East Tennessee State University
- Chapter 8: Harry Aponte
- Chapter 9: Madeleine Richeport-Haley
- Chapter 10: Jane Peller
- Chapter 11: Don Bubenzer and John West, both from Kent State University; J. Graham Disque, East Tennessee State University
- Chapter 12: Roberta Nutt, Texas Women's University; Patricia E. Robertson, East Tennessee State University
- Chapter 13: Frank Dattilio, Harvard Medical School and University of Pennsylvania School of Medicine.
- Chapter 14: Michael Popkin, Active Parenting, Atlanta, Georgia; Sherry Cormier and Cheryl McNeil, West Virginia University
- Chapters 15 and 16: Gerald and Marianne Corey

I also want to thank the students in the Marriage and Family Therapy concentration of the Counseling Program at East Tennessee State University who gave this text an initial trial run and offered many helpful additions and corrections. Candace Park was my executive assistant during the development and taping of the video segments associated with each of the theories in the book, and she also introduces the theory in each video segment. The following students, friends, family, and colleagues were involved in the actual therapy or role-playing of families and therapists for the video segments: Jessica Adesuyi, Lea Brown, Trish Clybern, Steve Cockerham, Graham Disque, Ed Dwyer, Stacy Foster, Aaron

Gilly, Linda Good, Doug Fox, John Lawson, Beverly Leigh, Jeanie Livingston, Emily Long, Jean McLendon, Meghan Noble, Betty Ann Proffitt, Cassandra Pusateri, Patricia Robertson, and Joel Tramel and his children Seth and Abby. I especially want to thank my family—Lynn, Alison, and Nora Williams—for their participation in various video segments. A special thanks to Daniel Santiago and his wonderful crew at the video studio at East Tennessee State University.

Thank you to all of those who reviewed the manuscript: Jack Presbury, James Madison University; John Barlow, University of Central Arkansas; John Barletta, Australian Catholic University; Carolynn Kohn, University of the Pacific; Catherine B. Roland, Montclair State University; Taranum Chaudry, Lewis and Clark College; Bill McHenry, Shippensburg University of Pennsylvania; Phillip W. Henry, Shippensburg University of PA; Ray Wooten, St. Mary's University, San Antonio; Gerald T. Moote, Jr., State University of New York at Buffalo; Charlotte Daughhetee, University of Montavallo; Jill M. Thorngren, Montana State University; Brian Wlazelek, Kutztown University of Pennsylvania; Jay H. Fast, West Virginia University; Debra L. Stout, California State University, Fullerton; Dan Wulff, University of Louisville; John K. Mooradian, Michigan State University; Marla J. Muxen, South Dakota State University; Lisa Langfuss Aasheim, Portland State University; Kelly M. Burch-Ragan, Western Kentucky University; Stephen T. Fife, University of Nevada, Las Vegas; Brian Sullivan, University of Queensland; Eagle Desert Moon, California State University, Northridge Thomas Burdenski, Tarleton State University; Trude D. Hendrickson, University of Minnesota Willie V. Bryan, University of Oklahoma; Glen A. Eskedal, Suffolk University; Edward P. Cannon, Marymount University; Richard D. Recor, Webster University; Michael Leftwich, Emporia State University; Donald Loffredo, University of Houston, Victoria; Carol Messmore, Florida Atlantic University; Anita Moreno, Case Western Reserve University; Todd Kates, Northeastern University; Touwanna Edwards, Lewis University; Nina Hamilton, Illinois State University; Olga L. Mejía, California State University, Fullerton; Ruth Paris, Boston University Paul Smokowski, University of North Carolina, Chapel Hill; Karen Kayser, Boston College Karen Greving, Arizona State University; Dennis Frank, Roosevelt University.

To each and every person who contributed to the completion of this book and the accompanying video, my heartfelt thanks.

—James Robert Bitter

About the Author

James Robert (Jim) Bitter is Professor of Counseling in the Department of Human Development and Learning at East Tennessee State University in Johnson City, Tennessee. He is a nationally certified counselor and family therapist, and a former officer of the North American Society of Adlerian Psychology (NASAP). He is also a former editor of the *Journal of Individual Psychology* and a Diplomate in Adlerian Psychology. He is on the editorial board of *The Family Journal*, and has served in the past in a similar role on the *Journal of Counseling and Development*. He received his doctorate in Counselor Education from Idaho State University in Pocatello, Idaho.

Jim received awards for *Outstanding Teaching* in the College of Human Development and Community Service at California State University at Fullerton, and for *Outstanding Scholarship* in the Clemmer College of Education at East Tennessee State University. He has taught in the graduate Counseling programs of three universities, has co-authored two books, and has published more than 50 articles.

Together with Oscar Christensen, Bill Nicoll, and Clair Hawes, Jim is a co-founder and core faculty member of the Adlerian Training Institute (ATI) in Boca Raton, Florida. He has contributed to the development of Adlerian Brief Therapy with individuals and families. He is the featured expert for Adlerian Family Therapy (Bitter, 1998) in the Allyn and Bacon series *Family Therapy with the Experts*, and he has offered workshops in Canada, England, Greece, Ireland, Korea, New Zealand, and Peru, as well as throughout the United States. He was introduced to Adlerian Family Therapy and Counseling by Manford A. Sonstegard, with whom Jim has worked for more than 30 years.

Jim studied and worked for 10 years with one of family therapy's pioneers, Virginia Satir. He was a trainer in her Process Communities for 3 of those years, and published an article and a number of chapters with her before her death in 1989. He is a past-President of AVANTA, Satir's training network.

Jim currently sees couples and families, together with graduate students at East Tennessee State University's Community Counseling Clinic. Together with his ATI colleagues, he continues to develop Adlerian Brief Therapy with individuals, groups, couples and families. His focus on a fully present relationship in all forms of therapy is an integration of Adlerian counseling with the work of Virginia Satir and Erv and Miriam Polster.

Jim has been married to Lynn Williams for almost a quarter of a century; they have two daughters, Alison and Nora Williams. In his leisure time, Jim likes to travel, collect stamps, play basketball, and read.

Theory and Practice *of* Family Therapy and Counseling

PART

1

Basic Issues in the Practice of Family Therapy and Counseling

Chapter 1 Introduction and Overview

Chapter 2 The Family Practitioner as Person and Professional

Chapter 3 Virtue, Ethics, and Legality in Family Practice

Introduction and Overview

Introduction

Why I Became a Family Counselor and Therapist

Overview of This Book

Suggestions for Using the Book

The Family Systems Perspective

Differences Between Systemic
   and Individual Approaches

[handwritten annotation: middle child → ridiculed → theory of individual psychology + self-esteem. rickets]

Introduction

Working with families has been part of therapeutic practice for almost 100 years. Starting with **Alfred Adler's** family and community interventions in Vienna, systemic perspectives have gradually taken hold in almost all of the helping professions. In the last thirty-five years, the fields of family counseling, family therapy, social work with families, family psychology, psychiatric nursing with families, and family psychiatry have really come into prominence. Thirty-five years ago, family practice promised greater effectiveness than had been achieved with either individual or group counseling and therapy. Because these relational approaches sought to change the very systems in which individuals actually lived, many professionals hoped that the changes enacted would endure and that both individual and system relapse would disappear. Although these hopes have not been fully realized, family practice has had enormous success, and it is now a fully integrated part of most treatment programs.

Family practice is fundamentally different from individual counseling and therapy. Although it shares some similarities with group interventions, the intimacy and intensity of couples and **family systems** make it a treatment unit unlike any other. Perhaps the hardest task for those trained to work with individuals is learning assessment and interventions with families from multiple systemic perspectives. I will say more about this later. This book provides you with an invitation to experience the thinking of the pioneers and leaders who have shaped systemic approaches in the fields of family practice.

This book surveys 10 approaches to family counseling, therapy, and practice, highlighting key concepts, therapy goals, techniques, process, and application. There is an additional chapter devoted to effective approaches in parenting. I hope you will read these chapters with the goal of learning the breadth and depth of each therapy orientation. The models presented here will sometimes have a great deal of similarity and will sometimes be quite different and even contradict each other. Consider not only the ideas and interventions of each model but also the worldview espoused by both the founders of the theory and the practitioners who currently contribute to its development.

Each of these models will, most likely, have some relevance to your own **family-of-origin**. This is often a good place to start. It is almost axiomatic these days that family practitioners-in-training must consider the impact that their families-of-origin have had on their personal development. If we do not make this journey into our own histories, we are in danger of trying to work out our personal family issues with every new family we encounter.

Over time, various ideas and models will start to appeal to you: They will fit with your values and beliefs and, in some cases, they will even enhance or broaden your worldview. You will start to create a foundation for your work, and you will find that parts of different models will integrate into that foundation. This is not a process that happens quickly. It will certainly not happen at the end of a course or two on the theories and practices of marriage and family therapy. This is a lifetime journey.

You might start by asking yourself the following questions:

- What beliefs do these theorists and practitioners have about families in general?
- Do I hold to the same beliefs, ideas, or values—or are there other values and positions that seem to be more important to me?
- If I were bringing my family-of-origin and/or my current family members to therapy with me, would I want to come to a family practitioner, counselor, or therapist using this approach? Why or why not? What would my expectations be? What goals would I have for the work I was contemplating in therapy?
- What kind of relationship would I want to have with the family practitioner? What would contribute to my trust, comfort, willingness to work, determination to change, and feeling of accomplishment at the end?

There are useful parts to every theory and model we will consider in this book. None of the approaches considered here holds a claim to absolute "truth," however, or even to the "right" way to do family practice. Each theory is built on a perspective and provides a different kind of **lens** through which families may be viewed and understood. And each of these perspectives inevitably leads to continually developing implications for family practice.

Finding a model or models that work for you is an important first step as a professional. Such a discovery provides a framework for working with the multitude of diverse families you will encounter, families who are often facing very complicated and even severe problems. Family practice is supposed to be a challenge. It is supposed to engage your mind and your heart. It will endlessly change you as a person, and it will require you to reflect on your use of self in counseling and therapy as much as your use of skills and techniques. Family counseling, therapy, and practice will test your strengths, poke at your weaknesses, and enlarge your view of life. Ultimately, it can be one of the most rewarding careers in the helping professions.

Why I Became a Family Counselor and Therapist

Like most people who are attracted to the helping professions, I came from a family that had its happy times and its struggles. You can probably say the same thing about your family. In my particular case, my father was a man who kept a lot inside himself and was somewhat aloof and distant, not really knowing what to do with children and leaving us to be raised by my mother. My mother was a warm, gregarious woman who loved her life as a homemaker and a community volunteer. My mother and father were both devout Catholics; they also believed that they were soul mates; and they were committed to a marriage that was to last forever. They adopted me when I was 6 months old. Two years later, they would adopt my 6-week-old sister, Jo Ellen. We were a working-class, nuclear family of the 1950s, seeking the promise of a better life through hard work and dedication. We lived in a small town in central Washington, known for its production of apples and its traditional values—with little or no diversity acknowledged or appreciated in the community. In short, we were what the world called a "normal" family. Manners were important; faith was important; hard work was important; extended family and community were important and intertwined. Contributing to others and making a difference in the world was expected and valued.

My grandfather died when I was 9, and my grandmother came to live with us. She and my mother were very close, and they loved being together. My grandmother was respectful of the relationship between my father and mother, and she helped everyone when she could, but she also had her own life and interests. I remember having long talks with my grandmother and being amazed by her stories of being a schoolteacher in Wisconsin before she met and married my grandfather. Having Grandma with us in the family seemed as natural to me as having parents. In a short period of time, it was as if she had always been in our home.

Then, when I was 14, my mother died from cancer. Both of my parents were heavy smokers, and both were addicted to it long before the surgeon general started putting warnings on the sides of cigarette packages. My mother's death turned everything upside down. Both my father and my grandmother met my basic needs and those of my sister, but both were grieving, crying with a sadness that seemed as though it would never end. Within a year, I would distance myself from the pain in the family by heading off to a Catholic boarding school. My sister would not be able to find such a convenient way out: She led a troubled life throughout high school and, as soon as possible, she started a life-long search for her "real" parents.

This is a relatively short synopsis of my early life. When you read it, what issues do you think have been part of my own development as a person and as a counselor or therapist? What is emphasized in my life? What do you think I left out? Do you have any guesses about how I have approached women and men? Do you think the limited experience and traditional values that were part of my upbringing had an effect on how I viewed race, diverse cultures, **gender** issues, and roles and functions in the family? Do you think that coming-of-age in the 1960s had any effect on how I saw people and life? What effect do you think adoption has had on me—and on my sister? Do you think the two of us are more alike or different? What would lead you to your conclusions? If you had to write your own autobiography, what facts, interpretations, values, and beliefs would you emphasize? What parts would you choose to forget or simply not mention?

Here's a little more information about how my educational and professional experiences began. My father dedicated the proceeds from my mother's life insurance to sending his children to college. I was blessed with a great education (academically as well as in life) at Gonzaga University in Spokane, Washington. I majored in English literature with a minor in philosophy. It turned out, however, that my father was right: There really weren't any jobs waiting for a person with a degree in English literature and philosophy. For a year after I graduated, I worked in a gas station and tried to figure out what I wanted to do with my life.

I had many of the common developmental difficulties that occur in late adolescence and early adulthood. If it was possible to engage in life the hard way, I usually did. It was the counselors at Gonzaga who really helped me begin the process of growing up. They were the people who, it seemed to me, had a handle on kindness, caring, and stability, as well as a moral and ethical life. It was their modeling of effective engagement that led me to want to become a counselor.

In 1970, I headed off to Idaho State University in Pocatello, Idaho, to get a master's degree in counseling. At that time in the history of the counseling profession, the skills and interventions associated with Rogerian or person-centered therapy made up the majority of our training. We spent hours learning to do reflections and active listening, continually paraphrasing content and feelings, hoping that it would all become second nature to us. For many of my peers, it did become second nature, but I struggled. I always had more questions I wanted to ask: How everything fit together? Who said what to whom? How did people react when my clients did one thing or another? What were the different parts that made up the personalities of the individuals I was seeing, and how did those parts work *for* people or *against* them? I was also far more directive in my interventions than would make any of my supervisors comfortable, because I genuinely wanted to help people find solutions to their problems. In the early days of my training, I seldom felt that I was effective and, in truth, I am sure that I wasn't.

In early 1971, one of my professors went to a conference in which a man named **Ray Lowe** demonstrated **Adlerian family counseling**. My professor brought back tapes and books, and later he even brought Ray Lowe himself to our campus. I absorbed everything I could about the Adlerian model. The more I read about Adlerian psychology, the more I felt at home. Alfred Adler was systemic before we even had such a word in our professions. He saw people as socially embedded; took into account the effects of **birth order**, **family constellation**, and **family atmosphere**; and considered interaction and "doing" central to understanding human motivation and behavior. Discovering the works of Adler and **Rudolph Dreikurs** helped me to make sense out of my own life as well as the lives of the clients entrusted to my care.

I was part of a team who opened up the first public (open-forum) family education center at Idaho State University. I even conducted the first family counseling interview ever done there. I had lots of support and was given lots of room to make mistakes—and to learn. But I had found "my" approach. As graduate students, we ran parent study groups, held weekly family counseling sessions, and carried what we were learning into local area schools and community agencies. I stayed at Idaho State University to get my doctorate in Counselor Education. In 1974, we held a Conference on Adlerian Psychology that featured, once again, Ray Lowe and such masters as **Heinz Ansbacher**, **Don Dinkmeyer**, and the man who was to become my best friend and colleague for the second half of my life, **Manford Sonstegard**.

Sonstegard was simply the best family and group counselor I had ever seen in action. He had an enormously calm manner that reflected what **Murray Bowen** called a **"differentiated self."** He listened very carefully to the positions and counter-positions taken in families and groups, and he always stayed focused on re-directing motivation. When I graduated later that year (1974), I was able to get a position in the counseling program for which Sonstegard was the chair. Over the next thirteen years, we established and conducted Adlerian family counseling sessions in multiple states in the mid-Atlantic region of the United States from our base in West Virginia.

Adler (1927/1957) had called his approach **individual psychology**, but it was anything but oriented toward the individual. He used the term *individual* to emphasize the necessity of understanding the whole person (rather than just parts of people) within that person's social contexts. Adler focused on the individual's movement through life (one's style of living) and how that style was enacted with others. He spoke of having a **psychology of use**, rather than possession. From Adler's perspective, people had a purpose and use for the symptoms he encountered in therapy. Others in the client's life generally reacted in ways that maintained the very problems for which individuals sought help. Without any question, Adler was a systemic thinker, and working with systems was part of his therapy back in the 1920s. A fuller presentation of Adler's model will be presented in the second theories chapter, but I mention his work here because it fit so well with how I saw individuals, groups, couples, and families. I didn't have the language of systemic therapy when I first read Adler, but the ideas were all there, and his psychology has served as a wonderful foundation for me for more than 30 years.

In 1979, I had the opportunity to attend a month-long training seminar called a Process Community led by **Virginia Satir** and two of her trainers. The training program focused on applications of her **human validation process model** to individuals, groups, couples, and families. Centered in her now-famous focus on communication and self-esteem, it was as much a personal growth experience as it was a learning experience for family practitioners. More than 100 participants were accepted for the program held just north of Montreal, Quebec, in Canada. Half of the participants spoke only English, and half of the participants had a primary language of French, so that every word was offered in both languages. The power of Satir's work in this cross-cultural experience was overwhelming. I came away from the month with a new dedication to experiential teaching and learning, and a determination to integrate Satir's communication, human validation, process model with the Adlerian principles I used in clinical practice (see Bitter, 1987, 1988, 1993; Satir, Bitter, & Krestensen, 1988).

In 1979, I became a member of the AVANTA Network, an association of Satir-trained practitioners who used her methods and processes, and were engaged in training others to do the same. For the next 10 years, until her death, I was privileged to work with Satir during three more Process Communities, to coauthor an article and a chapter with her, and to spend at least a week each year learning the newest ideas, hopes, and dreams of one of the most creative family systems therapists ever to have graced our planet.

Virginia Satir taught me the power of **congruence** in communication as well as the forms that **metacommunications** often take in therapy. She introduced **sculpting** to my work and gave me processes for creating transformative experiences with families. Her emphasis on touch, nurturance, presence, and vulnerability put my heart as a person and a counselor on the line, but it also opened up avenues of trust and caring that had been missing before. Satir taught me how to join with families and still not get lost in them. When she died, it was as if I had lost a mother, a father, a sister, and a brother all rolled into one. I had certainly lost one of the best teachers in my life.

In the 1990s, I had two opportunities to do month-long training programs with **Erving and Miriam Polster**, the master **Gestalt therapists**. Their emphasis on awareness, contact, and experiment in therapy fit wonderfully with the decade's worth of knowledge I had received from Satir. They also had the same kind of great heart that Satir had. Whether working with individuals, couples, or families, both Satir and the Polsters demonstrated the importance of an authentic and nurturing relationship in facilitating change. At the heart of both models was a dedication to **experiential therapy** and learning through **experiment** and **enactment**. Even today, when I walk into a room to meet a family, I feel the wisdom of these great therapists with me (see Bitter, 2004).

As you can see, I have been given the gift of great teachers in my lifetime. I have been welcomed by them into learning situations that I wouldn't trade for anything in the world. Watching great masters at work has provided me with ideas and models for effective interventions that I never would have discovered on my own. To tell the truth, I often found myself imitating them initially in very concrete ways, sometimes using the exact words and interventions that I had seen them create spontaneously. Over time, I would begin to feel a more authentic integration of their influences in my life and work—and I let these influences inform my own creativity in family practice.

I have become fascinated by the flow and rhythms of therapeutic relationships. The two most important aspects of family practice are still the client(s) and the practitioner, with the latter being in the best position to influence the process. I currently think in terms of four aspects to therapeutic movement: **Purpose, Awareness, Contact**, and **Experience** (Bitter 2004; Bitter & Nicoll, 2004). You may already have noticed that the acronym for these words spells the word *pace*. In both my personal and professional life, paying attention to purpose, awareness, contact, and experience brings a useful *pace* to human engagement and provides me with enough structure to support creativity in my interventions.

Purposefulness has always been a central aspect of Adlerian therapy and provides a sense of directionality and meaning to life. Awareness and contact are most clearly defined in the Polsters' Gestalt practice. I consider both of these aspects to be critical to an enlivened and energized life. They make *being present* sufficient as a catalyst for movement and change. Awareness and contact are also essential to more fully realized human experiences. They allow both the client(s) and the practitioner to touch the authentic within them and to find expressions that flow from their hearts. Such experiences are a natural part of Virginia Satir's work. The therapeutic experiments and enactments common to systemic family therapy are just one form of such experiences.

Although I like the integration of thinking and practice that currently marks my own work, I began by absorbing as much of the great masters as I could, often imitating them until their processes became natural within. I would recommend a similar process to all of you who are reading this book. If family systems theory and practice is what you want to do, find a model or set of models that seem to fit you. Then watch as many of the tapes and DVDs that feature your chosen approach(es) as you can.[1]

Each of the theory chapters in this book will have an actual family counseling or therapy session right after the model has been introduced. I have tried to pick family practitioners who represent the most current development of each approach and who are still working and clinically active today. I also have created a ficticious family I call the Quest family that is a conglomerate of several real families I have worked with over the years. I use this created family to demonstrate how each theoretical perspective might work with them. As you read about both of the families in each chapter, think about which approach you like best, what you would want to do or use yourself, and what you cannot imagine yourself doing. This is one way to begin to narrow down the choices to the systems perspectives that will best fit you.

Thinking systemically about clients is one perspective—or I should say, set of perspectives—that provides a framework for therapeutic practice. For me, thinking systemically just fits the way I see human process and the social world in which we all live. We are social beings. We interact with others every day. We are influenced by the people in our lives, and we return that influence to them. In truth, we are very seldom alone and, even when we are, we are often thinking about and reflecting on life with others. Even the act of giving help involves at least two people and, in my mind, counselors and therapists join with even single clients to form a new system. I believe in family systems therapy because it is a reflection of the way we live. And, at its best, intervening in systems increases the likelihood that, when change is enacted, it will be supported and maintained.

Overview of This Book

Family counseling and therapy was initiated in the early part of the 20th century, but it is in the latter half of that century that the practice of working with families really came into its own. That is when the masters of family theory and practice—**Nathan Ackerman, Gregory Bateson, Murray Bowen, Oscar Christensen, Richard Fisch, Jay Haley, Lynn Hoffman, Don Jackson, Cloe Madanes, Monica McGoldrick, Salvador Minuchin, Virginia Satir, Maria Selvini Palazzoli, Paul Watzlawick, John Weakland,** and **Carl Whitaker**—developed ideas and models that would serve as the foundation for the family practice professions. Now, after some 50 years of substantial growth and development, the field has begun to incorporate the postmodern, social constructionist positions of **Tom Andersen, Harlene Anderson, Insoo Kim Berg, Steve de Shazer, David Epston, Kenneth Gergen, Harold Goolishian, William O'Hanlon, Michele Weiner-Davis,** and **Michael White**. Race, **culture**, gender, and **family life-cycle** development are now central considerations in family therapy (Carter & McGoldrick, 2005; Luepnitz, 1988; McGoldrick, 1998). More than ever before, family practice is poised to offer multiple models of integration (see Breunlin, Schwartz, & MacKune-Karrer, 1992; Gehart & Tuttle, 2003; Hanna, 2007). It is also ready to offer guidance on tailoring treatment to the needs of clients (Carlson, Sperry, & Lewis, 2003) as well as to the unique therapeutic voices of emerging practitioners (Simon, 2003).

Family practitioners come in many different forms and represent similar, if distinct, orientations. There are the marriage and family therapists who receive their training in programs that are now largely autonomous and accredited by the Commission on Accreditation for Marriage and Family Therapy Education (COAMFTE), the accrediting body for the American Association for Marriage and Family Therapy (AAMFT). There are marriage and family counselors who receive their training in counselor education programs, sometimes accredited by the Council for Accreditation of Counseling and Related Educational Programs (CACREP), and who belong to the International Association of Marriage and Family Counselors (IAMFC), a division of the American Counseling Association (ACA). Clinical family practitioners also are trained in schools of social work. Since the 1960s, courses in clinical family practice have expanded from elective offerings to become a core training focus in many social work programs. And both psychiatry and psychology now have divisions devoted to family practice.

In general, those who have been associated with AAMFT and family practice in psychiatry and psychology have tended to focus on psychopathology—both how it is maintained and what effects it has on family systems. There is a real emphasis within these disciplines on intervening in family process to enact changes that will solve problems, alleviate symptoms, and return the family to health.

Those associated with IAMFC, counseling programs in general, and social work programs have tended to focus more on family growth and development, resource identification, and what is now considered resiliency practice (Simon, Murphy, & Smith, 2005). Here, the emphasis is on normalizing family process, activating ignored or denied individual and family skills and abilities, and focusing on what works and avenues to desired solutions. To be sure, these are not dichotomous positions, and many family therapy models can be embraced by both orientations.

The theories chapters in this book have a relatively consistent format to aid you in comparing and contrasting the various approaches. Each chapter begins with a short introduction that introduces the founders and major contributors to the theory as well as its main emphasis. This introduction is followed by an actual therapy session conducted by one of the main contributors to the model. Within the presentation of this therapy session, I ask you to consider certain questions that relate to understanding the model, its application, and how it relates to your own values and beliefs about helping others and family practice. The therapy session is followed by a section that highlights key concepts of the model: Here, the heart of the theory is presented for your consideration. Somewhat shorter sections on therapy goals and the therapist's role and function follow so that an emphasis is placed on the purpose and the person of the therapist. The Techniques section in each chapter is designed to provide you with the process, skills, and interventions most associated with the theory. In this section I address how to use the model with families. The techniques section is followed by an application of the model to the Quest family, a fictitious family I created from various families I have seen over the years. A full description of the Quest family is presented at the beginning of Part Two. Again, the purpose of presenting the Quest family is to allow you to compare and contrast the different theories in actual practice. Each theory chapter ends with a summary of the approach, the gender and cultural contributions associated with practitioners of the theory, and a list of suggested readings and references. Although the word *therapist* is used throughout this text, it is intended to include all family practitioners from the fields of counseling, marriage and family therapy, psychiatry, psychiatric nursing, psychology, and social work.

Table 1.1	Overview of Contemporary Family Counseling and Therapy Models
Bowen's Multigenerational Family Therapy	***Key figures:*** Murray Bowen, Betty Carter, Thomas Fogarty, Phillip Guerin, Michael Kerr. A multigenerational approach that looks for problem patterns across at least three generations and focuses on the difficulties associated with triangulation and failure to achieve a differentiated self. This model employs a type of coaching that aims to strengthen the strongest, most differentiated members on the belief that changing any part of the system will change the whole system.
Adlerian Family Therapy	***Key figures:*** Alfred Adler, Rudolf Dreikurs, Oscar Christensen. A teleological approach that focuses on the purposes of adult-child interactions and makes use of family constellation and birth order, interactive patterns, a typical day, and goal disclosures in redirecting and reorienting families.
Satir's Human Validation Process Model	***Key figures:*** Virginia Satir, John Banmen, Jean McLendon. Originating as a communications-experiential model, this approach focuses on the ways in which people communicate under stress, often adhere to inflexible family rules, and engage in the process of change. Satir therapists use reframing, congruent communication, and sculpting to highlight good intentions, validate individual feelings, and engage families in the discovery and practice of new possibilities.
Whitaker's Symbolic-Experiential Family Therapy	***Key figures:*** Carl Whitaker, William Bumberry, David Keith, Thomas Malone, Gus Napier. An existential model of family therapy that seeks to create new experiences in families through play, seeding the unconscious, evolving family crises, and even creating anxiety. Whitaker approaches family therapy as a coach who is always willing to consider possibilities that are even more outrageous and anxiety-provoking than the family has experienced together so far.
Structural Family Therapy	***Key figures:*** Salvador Minuchin, Harry Aponte, Jorge Colapinto, Charles Fishman, Patricia Minuchin. The first model to consider the importance of structure in families and to create ways to assess and change systems, subsystems, power, boundaries, and alignments through the interventions of joining, reframing, and enactments. Structural family therapists give directives and take an active stance in relation to changing family dynamics.
Strategic Family Therapy	***Key figures:*** Jay Haley, Cloe Madanes, Maria Selvini Palazzoli, Paul Watzlawick, John Weakland. Three family therapy models that treat stated problems as real and set about helping the family to solve them. Highly influenced by Milton Erickson, these models use paradox, counter-paradox, double binds, circular questioning, and reframing to maneuver family members into desired solutions for their problems.
Solution-Focused and Solution-Oriented (possibility) Therapies	***Key figures:*** Insoo Kim Berg, Steve de Shazer, Eve Lipchick, Bill O'Hanlon, Jane Peller, John Walter, Michele Weiner-Davis. Growing out of and away from the strategic family therapy models, the "solution" approaches joined the postmodern movement and developed questions of difference (including exception questions, the miracle question, and scaling questions) to orient clients toward preferred outcomes and desired possibilities.
Postmodern, Social Constructionist, and Narrative Approaches to Family Therapy	***Key figures:*** Tom Andersen, Harlene Anderson, David Epston, Kenneth Gergen, Harold Goolishian, Stephen Madigan, Michael White. These models that ushered in the postmodern era in family therapy—Narrative approaches to family therapy—were first introduced "down under" when White and Epston began to think of families as living out narratives often imposed on the system. Using externalization, unique events, and re-authoring interventions, narrative therapists seek to separate clients from problem-saturated stories and to co-create stories

(Continued on next page)

Table 1.1 (Contd.)	
	of competence and capabilities. Therapists using postmodern, social constructionist approaches often adopt what Anderson and Goolishian called a "not-knowing" position, characterized by interest, curiosity, and inquiries about the next most interesting development. Reflecting teams have been used in each of these models to add diverse, multiple voices and perspectives to the process of therapy.
Feminist Family Therapy	*Key figures:* Carol M. Anderson, Judith Myers Avis, Laura Brown, Betty Carter, Phyllis Chesler, Barbara Ehrenreich, Carolyn Enns, Carol Gilligan, Rachel T. Hare-Mustin, bell hooks, Deborah Anna Luepnitz, Dell Martin, Monica McGoldrick, Jean Baker Miller, Peggy Papp, Pam Remer, Patricia Robertson, Olga Silverstein, Lenore Walker, Froma Walsh, and Judith Worell, to name a very few.
	Growing out of the feminist revolution of the 1960s and 70s, feminist family therapists challenged patriarchy and the acceptance of white, male, heterosexual privilege inherent in the field of family therapy. They then went on to place gender-role and power assessments, egalitarian relationships based on informed consent, consciousness raising, assertiveness training, gender issues, and cultural diversity at the center of family therapy.
Cognitive-Behavioral Family Therapy	*Key figures:* Frank Dattilio, Albert Bandura, Aaron Beck, Albert Ellis, John Gottman, Neil Jacobson, Donald Meichenbaum, Gerald Patterson, Ivan Pavlov, B. F. Skinner, John Watson, and Joseph Wolpe.
	An application of behavioral learning theory and evidence-based practice to family therapy. This model blends the work of cognitive therapists, confronting irrational beliefs, with methods for shaping and reinforcing desired behaviors and interactions in families that research has shown to be effective. This model is preferred by most managed-care facilities, because it develops client actions and problems; it designs specific, often time-limited, interventions enacted in the service of ending identified dysfunctions or pathologies.
Parenting	*Key figures:* Alfred Adler, Diana Baumrind, Don Dinkmeyer, Rudolf Dreikurs, Haim Ginott, Thomas Gordon, John Gottman, Gary McKay, Michael Popkin.
	A review of the major parent-education programs and models currently used in the United States. These models focus on democratic or authoritative-responsive parenting that employ encouragement, active listening, reflective practice, natural and logical consequences, choices, and coaching in the service of building self-esteem in children and understanding and redirecting their mistaken goals. Emotion coaching and emotional intelligence are at the heart of raising competent, self-reliant kids and preparing them to cope with the challenges they will face throughout their development.

The theories chapters start with the systemic approach of Murray Bowen. Sixty years ago, the models that would become the foundation for the field of marriage and family therapy began to emerge. These models included the multigenerational approach taken by Murray Bowen with his emphasis on **differentiation of self**, the problems of **triangulation**, and the passing of problems from one generation to the next. Murray Bowen also emphasized that the personal development and the professional development of the therapist were linked and were essential to the practice of family therapy.

Adler was the first practitioner-theorist to speak of social embeddedness, family atmosphere, family interactions, family constellation, and birth order, and he was the first psychologist to engage in systemic practice and interventions.

Ninety years ago, Adler was already meeting with families, children, and teachers in front of local communities at one of his 22 child guidance centers in Vienna in an effort to understand and redirect mistaken interactions. His initial work with families and communities was systematized and expanded by Rudolf Dreikurs, who was, during his lifetime, the most prominent of Adlerian practitioners in the United States. Adler's focus represented a huge paradigm shift in the development of psychodynamic theories—just as the general field of family therapy and practice would be another paradigm shift away from a focus on private, individual work.

Perhaps no family practitioners emphasized the use of self in therapy more than Virginia Satir and Carl Whitaker. Although both are considered experiential therapists, they have very different styles.

A pioneer in the field of family therapy, Satir brought her background as a clinical social worker to her understanding of family process. She emphasized self-esteem and communication as avenues for understanding and intervening in family dynamics, and she provided us with a process for change that included human contact, touch, caring, and nurturance. Her career began with the families she saw in her private, clinical practice, but it ended with a focus on impacting large groups and systems, whole cultures, and even governments.

Although Satir was highly experiential in her approach, it was really Carl Whitaker who introduced the symbolic (with all of its existential meaning) to experiential therapy with families. Whitaker gave a whole new meaning to the process of **coaching** in family therapy. He stretched the boundaries of creativity and innovation when he danced with families; in contrast to Satir's nurturing presence, Whitaker often provoked anxiety in an effort to promote change. He also demonstrated the value of working with co-therapists in family sessions.

One of the family practitioners who both influenced and was influenced by Carl Whitaker was the great master of structural family therapy, Salvador Minuchin. Minuchin helped the field of family therapy understand the **organization** of families through the **sequences of interactions** and the boundaries (or lack of them) that existed in **subsystems**. Using **joining, reframing**, and enactment, Minuchin and his followers provided the early foundation for systemic work with families, especially poor families.

By the 1980s, Minuchin's work was often integrated with the problem-solution focus of the strategic therapists. Strategic therapists focused on the possibilities for change in systems that they understood to be hierarchies of **power** and **function**. Many of these practitioners were influenced by the theories and systemic thinking of Gregory Bateson as well as the indirect messages and trance work of Milton H. Erickson. This was especially true for **Jay Haley**, who also worked with Minuchin for a while. Similarly, it was true for the people at the Mental Research Institute (MRI) in Palo Alto, California, where the focus on brief family therapy was first introduced. In turn, the strategic therapists in the United States would also influence the strategic model in Milan, Italy, where Maria Selvini Palazzoli and her associates would focus on **paradox, counterparadox**, and **circular (or relational) questioning**.

By the 1990s, the field of family therapy itself began to experience a paradigm shift. Most of the approaches mentioned above fell into what we would now call a **modernist** perspective in that they all searched for the essence of what comprised family process and sought to change the family in more functional and useful ways. The **postmodern perspective** challenged the idea of essences and a *true* knowing of the family system, suggesting that knowing a family depended as much on the perspective of the knower as the family. In this sense, if we were to replace any family practitioner with any other family practitioner, a whole new understanding of the family would emerge. If there were multiple therapists working with a family, there would be multiple perspectives on both understanding and helping the family. In this sense, most postmodern practitioners adopt a collaborative, **social constructionist** approach to family therapy. They believe that families are literally co-constructed in the language, stories, and processes that make up their lives and even in the process of therapy itself.

The bridge between modern and postmodern family therapies is really in the solution-focused and solution-oriented therapies of Steve de Shazer/Insoo Kim Berg and Bill O'Hanlon/Michele Weiner-Davis, respectively. Each of these approaches adopt a postmodern, social constructionist perspective on therapy and turn the strategic focus on solving problems on its head, preferring to focus on strategies for enacting **preferred solutions**.

Today, the heart of the social constructionist approaches to family therapy comes in the form of challenging dominant cultural and social positions and taking a stance against the ways in which such dominance constricts and restricts individuals and families. The work of Michael White and David Epston focuses on the narratives that families have developed in relation to social norms, and works through **externalization** to free people up to create **preferred stories**. Their style of therapy is often called de-centered and reflects the **not-knowing position** favored by the linguistic therapists, Harlene Anderson and the late Harold Goolishian. In addition, most of the social constructionist models now employ some form of what Tom Andersen from Norway calls a **reflecting team**. The purpose of the reflecting team is to provide an audience to therapy that will respond from multiple perspectives and give families many different lenses from which to view their struggles and successes.

The goals and aims of the social constructionists are often shared by feminists who led the way in considering gender issues and cultural diversity in family practice. Feminist family therapists understand **patriarchy** to be the dominant cultural and social stance of almost all societies, and they have critiqued family systems theory for its lack of focus on gender and multicultural issues. Feminists demanded that a gender perspective and cultural diversity become frameworks for understanding and working with families.

I have saved the chapters on cognitive-behavioral family therapy (CBT) and parenting until last. Most of family systems therapy is descriptive and relational. The ideas and models covered in these two chapters are pragmatic and are often featured in hospitals, community agencies, and outpatient programs that are governed by managed-care systems. Both CBT and parenting programs focus on change in families' and children's behaviors that is evidence-based and scientifically determined. Social constructionists would ask: "Whose science? Whose evidence?" And to be sure, almost all of the change advocated by CBT and modern parenting programs reflect a unitary set of ideal values, a perspective taken as "final truth" in what represents the culture of any given country.

As you read these differing approaches to family practice, it will be impossible to integrate all of them. Some ideas and conceptualizations fit together better than others. It is enormously hard, for example, to see how the social constructionist models and structural-strategic models might merge when the roles and functions of the family practitioners are so different. Similarly, it is hard to imagine how structural-strategic models might be integrated with cognitive-behavioral family therapy. But perhaps these last two statements only reflect my lack of imagination. Maybe one of you will see the thread that can be used to stitch such an integration into your own personal tapestry of family therapy.

Suggestions for Using the Book

I have attempted to write this book as if we are having a conversation. It still contains all the references you will need for further consideration of each topic, but its most important function is to invite you into the world of family therapy and for you to consider whether this kind of work is right for you. Any kind of work in the helping professions, whether it be counseling, therapy, or family practice, requires a development of the person as well as professional skills. There are many professions in which it is at least possible to be competent without addressing who we are as people—for example, engineering, visual arts, mathematics, or the sciences—although even these career fields are enhanced by personal development and growth. In the helping professions, and especially in family practice, who you are as a person is central to everything you do: You are the instrument that provides the catalyst for change.

As you read each chapter, consider how it applies to your own life, your own experiences, and your own worldview or perspectives. Can you see yourself approaching clients in the way that each of the models in this book suggest? Which techniques would you find comfortable and which would be a stretch for you? What can you learn about your own family-of-origin from studying each of the theories in this book? Do they help you change any of the ways in which you approach family members now? What would it be like for you, as a client, to go see each of these family practitioners? And most importantly, what would it say about you as a person and as a professional to be part of a profession in family therapy?

Before you study each approach in depth, I recommend that you look at the comprehensive review that is provided in the integration chapters. In addition to looking briefly at the key concepts associated with each therapeutic model, I also highlight the different perspectives or lenses with which families can be viewed. These lenses [sometimes called **metaframeworks** (Breunlin, Schwartz, & MacKune-Karrer, 1992)] allow you to consider a family from many angles and to develop a more holistic, context-embedded view of the family and its members. Different approaches will help you assess and understand the purposes for which families interact, their communication processes, the sequences or patterns of interaction, the organization and rules that govern the family, the developmental stages of the family, and the gender, cultural, and societal issues that may be affecting the family. And all of them will have some impact on how you develop your own self-awareness.

I often think of multiple perspectives in the same way I might look at a tree—or any object for that matter. At a great distance, the tree almost looks flat as if it were painted against some pastoral background on a canvas. As I approach the tree, it begins to take on shape and texture; I can see the cylindrical roundness of its trunk and limbs, the shape of the leaves, and even the texture of bark. When I get close enough to touch the tree, I can feel the differences in these textures, imagine its history, how long it has been here, and what it has been through to attain the shape and posture that it currently holds. I can walk around the tree and, in some cases, I can even crawl up into it. I can feel the muscles in my own body stretch and contract as I pull myself up from limb to limb. I can feel the wind blowing through the tree and over my face and hands. For a while, I am part of the tree and, still, I am different and not part of the tree.

Although this metaphor works for me in terms of thinking about the many perspectives that can aid me in knowing and understanding a family, it also invites me to consider my relationship to the tree in terms of change. Should I simply get to know the tree and then let it be? Do I think of it as a tree I just happened to encounter or is it a tree placed in my care? Does it need pruning and, if so, in what way? Does it need fertilizer and, if so, what kind and how much and at what time in its development? Is it a tree indigenous to the area in which it is rooted and in the company of other trees just like it? Or has the tree been transplanted from another place, another climate, another context? Would I see this tree differently if I were different—for instance, if I were not a man, but a woman; or if I were not oriented toward an individual tree, but rather saw this tree in relation to all other trees in the area or that had ever been? Am I stretching this metaphor too far?

I wonder what metaphor for working with families each of you could generate? I also wonder if the metaphor will be the same or different when you finish reading the various theories presented in this book. Imagination is not such a bad way to start any journey. What do you imagine families and family practice might be like?

The Family Systems Perspective

For those counselors and therapists living in Western cultures, perhaps the most difficult adjustment they will make is adopting a "systems" perspective, which goes against all of the values and experiences associated with individualism, autonomy, independence, and free choice. In the more collectivist cultures of Asia, interdependence, family "embeddedness" and connectedness, hierarchies of relationship, and multigenerational—even ancestral— perspectives inform the daily experiences and cultural views in many countries: A systems perspective seems "normal" there. Yet even in Western cultures—indeed, in all parts of the world—humans are born into families, and most people spend their lives in one form of family or another. It is in these families that individuals discover who they are. Families and systems are where people grow and develop, survive tragedies, and celebrate accomplishments and good times. Few of us do any of these things alone.

As we get older, we move into other systems (the school, the church, the community, and society in general). For most of us, the family still serves as home base, the place to which we constantly return and from which we evaluate people and processes in the other systems we encounter. The often unspoken rules and routines of the family give us a sense of constancy and familiarity in life; hopefully, they also provide us with a feeling of safety and a sense of what it means to be functional and capable of handling the tasks and challenges of life.

Family Systems and Cybernetics

Perhaps I should warn you ahead of time about this next part of the chapter: *It is not going to be easy to understand immediately*. So why am I going to talk about systemic thinking and cybernetics at all? Part of the answer is that these concepts, both historically and in current practice, inform the way family practitioners approach their work. Part of the answer is that it will challenge you to move from an individual focus to an interactive one. And part of the answer is also that having this knowledge may create new possibilities for the ways in which you will choose to make a difference in the families you see.

Focusing on the family as a unit rather than focusing on the individual brings about an entirely new way of considering what is going on. Such a focus moves us away from evaluating individual actions toward an understanding of interaction—and even sequences of interaction. When an individual behaves in a certain way, especially one that seems peculiar to a large part of the community or culture, we have a tendency to ask *why*? The answers we posit are usually in the form of cause and effect: B happened because of A; A caused B to happen. It might be diagrammed like this:

When we think in terms of interaction, however, we can never really know *why* or what caused the interaction. We can describe the interaction and note *what* is happening, *how* it is going, and maybe even *what purpose* the interaction seeks or serves but, in an interaction, A and B occur in relation to each other. A and B may not have caused each other, but they certainly were an influence on each other. If we diagrammed a relational interaction, it might look like this:

If we replace any part of the interaction with someone or something else, the interaction would be different. If Ann says to Bob, "You never pick up around the house," and Bob responds with irritation, "I like it messy; it has a lived in look," that's one interaction, and it is characteristic only of Ann and Bob at that moment in time and in that context. Let's say, however, that we replace Ann with Arthur and that Arthur and Bob are gay men who own a home together. Arthur says, "We're having people over tonight. Maybe we should clean the place up." Bob responds, but with a bemused tone in his voice: "I like it messy; it has a lived in look." Notice that Bob has not changed a thing about the content of his response: He has used exactly the same words. Still the meaning is different because his tone carries a **meta-message**. Meta-messages are directions about how the content is to be taken. It may be tempting to say that Bob responds with a different meta-message because of *who* is speaking: that is, whether it is Ann or Arthur. But such a simplification would not take into account a real difference in relationship, the impact of gender issues or being **gay** men in a heterosexist society, or even the choices Bob makes in how to focus his attention on what Ann or Arthur might say. Indeed, the minute we try to imply linear cause and effect, we are forced into a thin description that all but loses real meaning.

Okay, here comes the really hard stuff. Anthropologist, Gregory Bateson (1972) adopted the term **cybernetics** from the work of Norbert Wiener (1948) Cybernetics is an **epistemology** of systems, a way of thinking and conceptualizing how systems work, how they self-regulate, and how they remain stable. Wiener was a mathematician, and he primarily applied his ideas to machines and the development of computers. He was interested in the ways in which feedback could be used to correct and guide a system in its effort to be effective in different contexts. Among other things, feedback made it possible for systems to use past performance to regulate current processes. It also became possible for systems to anticipate and influence future changes by choosing and selecting feedback to pass along now. Family members are constantly engaged in feedback, in maintaining family routines and rules, and in communications that will affect the ways in which the family operates and faces future challenges. Each action or communication from an individual family member affects all others in the family and, in turn, the responses from other family members also affect the individual in a kind of circular fashion. It is from cybernetics that we get the concept of **circular causality** and **feedback loops**.

Circular causality is the idea that A causes B, which causes C, which causes D, etc., and each of these entities (letters) acts upon and is affected by every other entity in the system. In a car, which is a **closed system**, the ignition of gasoline may cause pistons to pump, which generates power for a host of other mechanical parts to move in line with directions received from shifting gears. But at the simplest level, the size of the piston also influences how much gasoline enters the chamber, and a breakdown in any part of the car's system generally shuts down the whole system. Today, modern cars are so complicated that they literally are regulated and checked by computers, the very machines that first benefited from the development of feedback loops.

A feedback loop is the process that any system uses to assess and bring correcting information back into the system: These feedback loops either initiate change (called a **positive feedback loop**) or deter change (called a **negative feedback loop**). Positive and negative, in this sense, are not used to indicate good and bad or right and wrong, which are evaluations that can be asserted only through linear causality. Rather, these terms relate only to whether they promote change (positive) or not (negative).

In families, a bad or wrong individual behavior may lead to either a positive or negative feedback loop. For example, an adolescent uses cocaine (a bad behavior), is caught by the police in a public setting, and is charged with possession and use. His father declares that "he cannot handle this crazy family anymore" and disappears, leaving the mother and son to cope on their own. Change has occurred as a result of a positive feedback loop—even though all of the people in this system may feel that nothing positive is going on at all. In a different family system facing the same problem with their adolescent, two parents who are on the verge of divorce may pull together enough to focus on and try to address their child's problems. In this case, the system maintains itself through a negative feedback loop—even though we may think that staying together for the adolescent is really a positive thing. Cybernetics, therefore, is actually the science of communication, and it can be applied to machines or humans with equal success.

Gregory Bateson (1972) was the first person to outline the ways in which cybernetic thinking could be applied to human communications and psychopathology. Bateson suggested that very often superficial changes, what we would now call **first-order changes**, were simply ways in which the family system stayed the same, "an effort to maintain some constancy" (p. 381) or **homeostasis** and balance in the system. He was more concerned with the possibility of **second-order changes** or changes in the family system that endured and transformed family process altogether. Even though Bateson would never practice family therapy himself, he joined with therapists Don Jackson, Jay Haley, and John Weakland in founding the Mental Research Institute (MRI) in Palo Alto, California. There they would study families that included **identified patients** with schizophrenia. Applying the principles of cybernetics to the family system, they came to see schizophrenic families as locked in transactional no-win/no-escape processes they described as **double binds** (Bateson, Jackson, Haley, & Weakland, 1956). Bateson et al. described a mother's visit to her hospitalized, schizophrenic son: The mother's body tightened up when the boy attempted to hug her. When he withdrew, the mother asked: "Don't you love me anymore?" The boy's face reddened, and the mother said: "Dear, you must not be so easily embarrassed and afraid of your feelings." The mother–son relationship is a no-escape relationship, and this interaction constitutes a set of directives in which the boy cannot win. One such experience can be tolerated or dismissed; however, the MRI group posited that schizophrenic families were engaged in relatively constant double binds. Indeed, they were characterized by them.

Double-bind theory would prove inadequate in addressing schizophrenia as a whole. It launched the field of family therapy, however, through its attempt to understand symptoms as meaningful within the systems that support and maintain them.

Because cybernetics grew out of the structures applied in mathematics and the computer sciences, there has been a tendency to look at systems mechanically. Machines are almost always closed systems: They have a certain structure, function in a certain way, and produce a given and predicted outcome. Biologist **Ludwig von Bertalanffy** (1968) developed **general systems theory** from his study of living systems, a systems model that describes families and human systems as both open and contextual. Living systems develop and grow. They act in an effort to become, rather than merely to exist, and to resist or initiate change. Almost every living system is made up of subsystems. Similarly, every system is a subsystem to larger systems.

Most families have spousal, parental, and sibling subsystems, which we shall consider more fully in the chapter on structural family therapy. A nuclear family is also a subsystem of extended families, ancestral families, churches, communities, cultures, governments, and the global community. Families also act in and interact with the physical and social environments they encounter. Like all living systems, families are by definition **open systems** in which all of the parts will contribute to all of the rest of the parts. Family members are not locked into a singular outcome by a fixed structure (as machines are), but have the capacity for what von Bertalanffy (1968) calls **equifinality** or the ability to achieve a desired end in many different ways. Children bring new ideas and resources to family life and can enrich parents as much as parents can anticipate children's needs and provide care and developmental opportunities for their youngsters. Personal growth doesn't really exist because the growth in any one person almost always affects the growth of everyone else in the system. Parents may have a significant influence in the development of their youngest child, but it is equally possible that the influence of siblings is more important and/or has made a major contribution to the growth of that child. This is equifinality within a family system: two or more ways to get to or account for the same observable end.

Von Bertalanffy reminded family therapists who focused on the nuclear family and the principle of homeostasis that they were, in effect, reducing the family system to a closed machine (Davidson, 1983). In addition to the concept of equifinality, von Bertalanffy's theory insisted that systems were more than the sum of their parts; that systems should be viewed holistically, having systems within and interacting with larger systems in the environment; that human (living) systems were ecological, not mechanical; and that living systems engage in spontaneous activity rather than merely reacting.

When cybernetics is applied to machines, a kind of first-order cybernetic stance is actually possible: Structure, patterns of interaction and organization, feedback, and systemic function all can be observed objectively without necessarily affecting the performance of the inanimate object. The observer and that which is being observed are separate; the observer can carry out changes in the system without becoming part of the system. This is called **first-order cybernetics**. The principles of general systems theory applied to living organisms called into question the possibility of an independent observer. Indeed, anyone attempting to observe and change a family participates in it and becomes part of an actual living system: The observer both influences and is influenced by the family. This is called **second-order cybernetics** (Goldenberg & Goldenberg, 2007). As we shall see in the chapter on social constructionism, some postmodern therapists have come to distrust the power imbalance inherent in modernism and first-order cybernetics. They have adopted a *not-knowing* or **decentered position** in an attempt to focus on the client as expert and all but remove the therapist from imposing personal/professional influence on the family. von Bertalanffy, however, believed that it was impossible for therapists to *not* influence the family system; he noted that not all values, positions, and perspectives were of equal value; indeed, some positions—even those held by the family—can cause damage to the system and the environment. It is, therefore, essential that therapists study and understand the values, assumptions, and convictions that have been adopted in their own lives, and to evaluate their theories and practices in relation to the impact these will have on the family, the community, and the culture. This is a position that we shall consider further when we look at Bowen's multigenerational family therapy.

How are you doing so far? The good news is that the hardest concepts in this chapter are now behind us. You may occasionally need to review the meaning of these concepts and many others as you go through this book. I have placed a glossary at the end of the book as an aid in remembering what different ideas and concepts mean. The names and terms included in the glossary are in bold type the first time they appear in the book.

Differences Between Systemic and Individual Approaches

As you have probably seen by now, there are some significant differences between systemic approaches and those associated with individual therapy. To be sure, there are some similarities too, but it is the differences that set the orientation of the helper toward those who are served.

Individual therapy tends to focus on the development of the individual's self, coping responses, and problem solving. People are seen in isolation from the systems in which they live, and the counselor or therapist is betting that the one hour of influence she or he has each week will be greater than the influences in the rest of the client's life. In individual therapy, clients are assessed against fixed norms, and their symptoms are considered in relation to standard descriptions of psychopathology. In many therapeutic models, the therapist is still expected to be objective, to discover the cause of painful emotions or disruptive behavior, and, having found the cause, to do something to fix it. It is not uncommon in these same approaches for close attention to be paid to the content of what people say, and constant judgments must be made about the functionality or improvement of the client.

Modern systems therapists tend to want as many members of the family as possible in the room—often including friends and other members from the family's community. It is not, however, how many people are in the room that counts: It is how the family practitioner thinks about the people in the room. It is about focusing on transactions, sequences of interaction, interdependence, recursion, and mutual influence (concepts more fully defined in subsequent chapters): It is about process. It involves seeing the purpose and systemic logic in what often appear to be paradoxical processes. It is accepting the subjectivity of the family practitioner, studying it, knowing it, watching for its impact on the therapy session, and working to place it in the service of clients' well-being. It is learning to see how a problem affects the family and how the family maintains the problem. It is understanding that each individual has an internal system (Schwartz, 1995), and it is learning to consider the impact of larger systems on the family, especially the politics that relate to race, gender, culture, sexual/affectional orientation, age, socioeconomic status, and creed. And most recently, it also includes listening to the stories within families, and the stories about these stories, and the ways in which each person participates in creating their own realities as well as the stories about these realities.

In short, family practitioners seek to address systems embedded in systems that are embedded still further in other systems. They seek to explore the meaning and purpose of interactions and transactions, and engage in processes that support the kinds of solutions that individuals and families seek for their own lives. In *Theory and Practice of Counseling and Psychotherapy* (Corey, 2005), Gerald Corey and I use the case of Ann to illustrate the differences between what an individual practitioner and a systemic practitioner might do:

> Ann, age 22, sees a counselor because she is suffering from a depression that has lasted for more that 2 years and has impaired her ability to maintain friendships and work productively. She wants to feel better, but she is pessimistic about her chances.
>
> Both the individual therapist and the systemic therapist are interested in Ann's current living situation and life experiences. Both discover that she is still living at home with her parents, who are in their 60s. They note that she has a very successful older sister, who is a prominent lawyer in the small town in which the two live. The therapists are impressed by Ann's loss of friends who have married and left town over the years while she stayed behind, often lonely and isolated. Finally, both therapists note that Ann's depression affects others as well as herself. It is here, however, that the similarities tend to end:

The individual therapist may:	The systemic therapist may:
Focus on obtaining an accurate diagnosis, perhaps using the *DSM-IV-TR* (American Psychiatric Association, 2000).	Explore the system for family process and rules, using a genogram.
Begin therapy with Ann immediately.	Invite Ann's mother, father, and sister into therapy with her.
Focus on causes, purposes, and cognitive, emotional, and behavioral processes involved in Ann's depression and coping.	Focus on the family relationships within which the continuation of Ann's depression "makes sense."
Be concerned with Ann's individual experiences and perspectives.	Be concerned with transgenerational meanings, rules, cultural, and gender perspectives within the system, and even the community and larger systems affecting the family.
Intervene in ways designed to help Ann cope.	Intervene in ways designed to help change the transactions and familial patterns that maintain the depression in Ann's contexts.

> Systemic therapists do not deny the importance of the individual in the family system, but they believe an individual's systemic affiliations and interactions have more power in the person's life than a single therapist could ever hope to have. (Bitter & Corey, 2005, pp. 424–425)

Finally, I want to reemphasize that practice with family systems is not merely a set of interventions used with multiple family members. It is a way of thinking and understanding human process that is applied even when family practitioners choose to see individual clients (individuals are sometimes called **monads** in family literature). In most texts, working with coupled relationships (or **dyads**) is addressed as part of the various family models discussed. Couples are certainly subsystems within most families, but the emphasis in couples work is most often related to intimacy and focusing on the dyadic relationship.[2] Family counseling and therapy, on the other hand, must address multiple relationships as well as multiple systems and subsystems. Further, family practice often works with the loss or diffusion of intimacy involved in triadic relationships. Becvar and Becvar (2003) have suggested that "family therapy" is really a misnomer: They prefer the term relationship therapy (p. 12). I agree with the use of this language, but I believe that the relationship work that is needed in families is often quite different from the relational work in couples therapy. In this book, we will focus on families in all of their forms. I believe it is in the multigenerational contexts of family life that we can see the effects of structure, rules, boundaries or their lack, and the positive and negative influences of **triads**.

References

Adler, A. (1957). *Understanding human nature* (W. B. Wolfe, Trans). New York: Fawcett Premier. (Original work published in 1927)

American Psychiatric Association. (2000). *Diagnostic and statistical manual of mental disorders* (4th ed., text translation). Washington, DC: Author.

Bateson, G. (1972). *Steps to an ecology of mind.* New York: Dutton.

Bateson, G., Jackson, D. D., Haley, J., & Weakland, J. (1956). Toward a theory of Schizophrenia. *Behavioral Sciences, 1,* 251–264.

Becvar, D. S., & Becvar, R. J. (2003). *Family therapy: A systemic integration* (5th ed.). Boston: Allyn & Bacon.

Bitter, J. R. (1987). Communication and meaning: Satir in Adlerian context. In R. Sherman & D. Dinkmeyer (Eds.), *Systems of family therapy: An Adlerian integration* (pp. 109–142). New York: Brunner/Mazel.

Bitter, J. R. (1988). Family mapping and family constellation: Satir in Adlerian context. *Individual Psychology, 44*(1), 106–111.

Bitter, J. R. (1993). Satir's parts party with couples. In T. Nelson & T. Trepper (Eds.). *101 interventions in family therapy* (pp. 132–136). New York: Haworth.

Bitter, J. R. (2004). Two approaches to counseling parents alone: Toward a Gestalt-Adlerian integration. *The Family Journal, 12*(4), 358–367.

Bitter, J. R., & Corey, G. (2005). Family systems therapy. In G. Corey, *Theory and practice of counseling and psychotherapy* (7th ed., pp. 420–459). Belmont, CA: Brooks/Cole.

Bitter, J. R., & Nicoll, W. G. (2004). Relational strategies: Two approaches to Adlerian brief therapy. *Journal of Individual Psychology, 60*(1), 42–66.

Breunlin, D. C., Schwartz, R. C., & MacKune-Karrer, B. (1992). *Metaframeworks: Transcending the models of family therapy.* San Francisco: Jossey-Bass.

Carlson, J., & Kjos, D. (Producers). (1998). *Demonstration video for Family Therapy with the Experts video series.* Boston: Allyn & Bacon/Longman. [ISBN #0-205-30673-X]

Carlson, J., Sperry, L., & Lewis, J. A. (2003). *Family therapy techniques: Integrating and tailoring treatment.* New York: Brunner Routledge.

Carter, B., & McGoldrick, M. (Eds.). (2005). *The expanded family life cycle: Individual, family, and social perspectives* (3rd ed.). Boston: Pearson.

Corey, G. (2005). *Theory and practice of counseling and psychotherapy* (7th ed.). Belmont, CA: Brooks/Cole.

Davidson, M. (1983). *Uncommon sense.* Los Angeles: Tarcher.

Gehart, D. R., & Tuttle, A. R. (2003). *Theory-based treatment planning for marriage and family therapists.* Pacific Grove, CA: Brooks/Cole.

Goldenberg, I., & Goldenberg, H. (2007). *Family therapy: An overview* (7th ed.). Belmont, CA: Brooks/Cole.

Hanna, S. M. (2007). *The practice of family therapy: Key elements across models* (4th ed.). Belmont, CA: Brooks/Cole.

Luepnitz, D. A. (1988). *The family interpreted: Feminist theory in clinical practice.* New York: Basic Books.

McGoldrick, M. (Ed.). (1998). *Re-visioning family therapy: Race, culture, and gender in clinical practice.* New York: Guilford.

Satir, V. M., Bitter, J. R., & Krestensen, K. K. (1988). Family reconstruction: The family within—a group experience. *Journal of Specialists in Group Work* (special issue), *13*(4), 200–208.

Schwartz, R. C. (1995). *Internal family systems therapy.* New York: Guilford.

Simon, G. M. (2003). *Beyond technique in family therapy: Finding your therapeutic voice.* Boston: Pearson.

Simon, J. B., Murphy, J. J., & Smith, S. M. (2005). Understanding and fostering family resilience. *The Family Journal, 10*(13), 427–436.

Sperry, L., Carlson, J., & Peluso, P. (2006). *Couples therapy: Integrating theory and practice* (2nd ed.). Denver, CO: Love Publishing.

von Bertalanffy, L. (1968). *General systems theory.* New York: Braziller.

Wiener, N. (1948). Cybernetics. *Scientific American, 170*(5), 14–18.

Endnotes

[1] I especially like the series of videotapes produced by Jon Carlson and Diane Kjos (1998) under the title *Family Therapy with the Experts.* Also, many of the master family therapists are on videotapes produced by AAMFT through their website, which you can access by going to: **http://www.aamft.org/FamilyTherapyResources/index_nm.asp**. Similarly, IAMFC has a Distinguished Presenter Video Series that is excellent and often has multiple therapists seeing the same family or couple. You can access this site by going to: **http://www.iamfc.com/videos.html**.

[2] For an excellent resource on couples therapy, the reader is referred to Sperry, Carlson, and Peluso (2006).

CHAPTER 2

The Family Practitioner as Person and Professional

Introduction

The Family of the Family Practitioner

Personal Characteristics and Orientations of Effective Family Practitioners

The Process of Change and Therapeutic Process

Beginning Your Work as Family Practitioners

The Scholar/Practitioner in Family Counseling and Therapy

Toward a Foundation for Integration

Gender and Multicultural Lenses

Summary

Introduction

In the fields that engage in family practice, it is really impossible to separate the person from the professional. Every part of becoming a family counselor, therapist, or practitioner requires you to engage in new ways of thinking, seeing, and conceptualizing. Personal reflection is a constant part of being fully human and present with your clients. Systemic theories and intervention techniques are certainly important, but being able to form and maintain an effective therapeutic relationship is more important than any of the other skills you will acquire (Blow, Sprenkle, & Davis, 2007; Carlson, Sperry, & Lewis, 2005). I will talk about some of the qualities and traits that seem to facilitate constructive relationships in family practice later in this chapter. Most of these qualities can be learned, but they work best when they are fully integrated into the practitioner's way of being.

Family counselors and therapists simply cannot divorce who they are from the work that they do. Like everyone else in life, we have "triggers," buttons that seem to get pushed regularly and that bring out the kinds of automatic responses that sometimes leave us asking, "Wow, what was that?" Such automatic responses usually come from unmet needs, unconscious motivations, challenged values or personality traits, or unfinished business, especially unfinished business with our family-of-origin. Our choice is either to be aware of our family issues and concerns or not. When we try to ignore our own issues and concerns, they commonly re-emerge in therapy as **emotional reactivity** (or **countertransference**), strong positive or negative feelings that are triggered automatically. Such automatic responses are usually not helpful in family practice. They lack clarity and authenticity. We are left to ask, "With whom is the practitioner working: The family in front of them, themselves, or their own family-of-origin? If you are going to choose a profession in family counseling or therapy, it will also be important to be open to self-evaluation; to expanding your awareness about your own family experiences and the meaning associated with them; and to the personal development of what Murray Bowen calls a *differentiated self*. You will have to learn to recognize what triggers you, to challenge the automatic responses you have to old issues and concerns, and to find alternatives to the emotional reactions that have been with you for a long time. Choosing to become a professional family practitioner is also choosing to work on and develop yourself as a person.

The Family of the Family Practitioner

Virginia Satir used to say that if she walked into a room with 12 people in it, she would meet everyone she ever knew (Satir, Banmen, Gerber, & Gomori, 1991). When family counselors, therapists, or practitioners meet new families, the people from their past whom they are most likely to reexperience come from their own families-of-origin. So how can you come to understand your own family well enough that you can know what will push your buttons and then how to challenge your automatic responses?

There are several avenues that you may find useful. The first is to create a **genogram** of your family, going back at least three generations (counting your own) to the families of your parents' parents. Getting this information will probably require you to interview people in your family and perhaps to ask questions that are personal and that you never would have dreamed of asking before. Even if this is difficult to do, push yourself farther than you would normally. Call people up. Go home for a visit. Send letters seeking information. Teach yourself to just listen and consider information without reacting as you normally might.

Genograms are explained in more detail in the Bowen chapter on **multigenerational family therapy** (Chapter Four). They are essentially a structural map of at least three generations of your family's life. Creating a personal structural map, however, is just the beginning. Within the map, there will be room to note all of the relational connections that happened in your family and to indicate the emotional ties and reactions too. Do not be surprised when old emotions surface just from the process of creating your own genogram. This happens quite often; it is supposed to happen. Take careful note of the people and situations that trigger these emotional responses in you.

Use the genogram to tell a story that is representative of each of the relationships in your family-of-origin, as well as significant relationships between you and members of your extended family. What themes run through these stories? What can you learn about your cultural affiliations from these stories? What have you learned about men and women? What meanings are attached to these stories that still seem to permeate your life?

Take some time to put an adjective next to each person in your genogram: Choose an adjective that represents the quality that the person brings to your life. Next to your parents and your siblings, put three adjectives instead of one. Think of the adjectives you assign to your parents as relational (Bitter, 1988). If you give your father the adjective critical, ask yourself in what way was he critical of you and how did you feel? If you say your mother was loving, in what way did you feel loved by her? What tones of voice did each parent use? How did they phrase their criticism or offer their love? What meaning did these experiences have when you were little? What meaning do they have now?

We often find an initial place in the world in relation to our siblings. Which of your siblings was most different from you? In what ways? Which of your siblings was most like you? Again, in what ways? Have these relationships stayed the same or changed over the years? What meaning do you associate with the adjectives that you assigned to yourself and each of your siblings?

You can take the adjectives that are part of your three-generation genogram and think of them as a **wheel of influence** (Satir et al., 1991). Put yourself in a circle in the middle of large piece of paper. Draw spokes out from that circle, leading to each of the adjectives and the people who represent those adjectives. Make the spokes of the wheel of varying lengths to indicate which of the qualities, traits, or descriptions you want to keep close to you and which ones you want to keep at a distance. What influence do the various adjectives actually have in your life? My wheel of influence is at the bottom of this page.

Another tool you may want to create is a historical timeline of your family-of-origin. Starting with the birth of your oldest grandparent, mark by year all the comings and goings in your family up to the present time. When were all of the people in your family born? When did they go to school, change schools, or graduate? When did each family member marry, move into a new home, have children, launch children, start jobs, change jobs, or retire? Who died and when? Put all of this information on top of a year-by-year line. Below the line, note what else was happening in history during the various periods of your family's

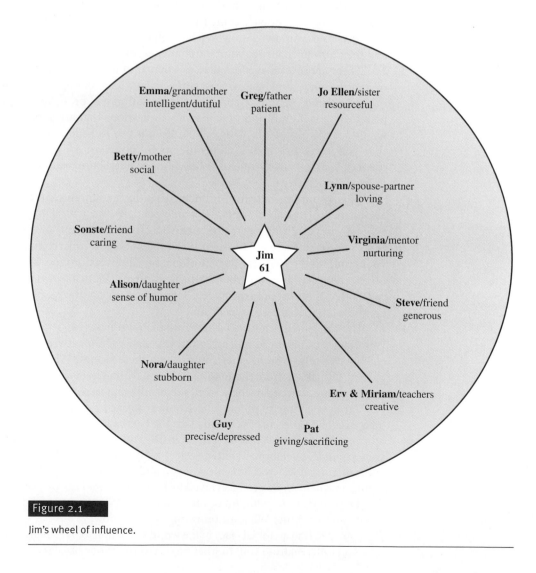

Figure 2.1

Jim's wheel of influence.

Jim's family moves to Columbine Street in Wenatchee, WA, during the summer.	Jim's grandfather dies in Yakima, WA. Grandmother comes to live with his family.	Steve Bruno moves in next door. Becomes Jim's best friend.	Jim is suspended from school for 3 days for not telling on boys in his class. He has to write-out the *Book of John* to return to school.	Jim's mother dies in Wenatchee, WA in February (cancer). Jim is altar boy at funeral.
1957	**1958**	**1959**	**1960**	**1961**
President Eisenhower's second inauguration on January 21; he sends troops to Central High School in Little Rock to enforce integration on September 24.	*Explorer I*, first American satellite is launched on January 31.	Alaska becomes the 49th state in the union on January 3. Hawaii becomes the 50th state in the union on August 21.	Kennedy/Nixon Debates	U.S. severs relations with Cuba on January 3. John F. Kennedy is inaugurated as 35th President of the U.S. on January 20. *Bay of Pigs* invasion of Cuba fails in April (17–20). Freedom Riders travel through South on buses to protest segregated interstate bus facilities (May).

Figure 2.2

A small segment of Jim's family timeline: 1957–1961 (ages 10–14).

chronological development. To give you an idea of how this might look, I have included a small section of my own family timeline (see above).

Putting together all of this information may, in and of itself, raise all sorts of emotions and old memories. We are all human. So were all of our family members. Some did better with us; some did worse. We were all imperfect. Having the courage to be imperfect is also having the courage to be more fully human—and to validate and respect the humanness of others. If you are in a course on family counseling or therapy, you may find it useful to share what you learn about yourself with your classmates. Sometimes, telling your story to others helps you organize it and own it. Sometimes the questions that others ask open up new avenues of investigation.

As you begin to learn more about yourself and your family-of-origin, you may want to explore your life through personal counseling or therapy. Although I believe that family practitioners can gain a great deal from being a client, I am not in favor of requiring personal therapy for all trainees. Such a requirement flies in the face of freedom and is inconsistent with the democratic ideals that are part of my own life. Still, it is hard for me to understand how anyone can flourish in the helping professions without a dedication to self-reflection, self-awareness, and personal/family explorations.

Counseling and therapy should not be limited to those who suffer from pathology or dysfunction. Some of the field's most important work has been in supporting the growth and development of those who help others. Counseling can help you examine your own attitudes, values, convictions, beliefs, and needs. Counseling can help you understand yourself and your own family so that you won't inadvertently impose your own values on the families you see in practice. And as you begin to practice, ongoing personal counseling and supervision can offer you chances to understand and reconsider the issues in your own life that occasionally interfere with your ability to help others. The more we can learn about ourselves, the less likely we will be to enter into countertransference—and the more likely we will be fully present with the families we meet in therapy.

give client the power when you do this hanging your hat on your first judgment First impressions

"Hanging Hats" and Clearing the Mind and Heart to Focus

Virginia Satir was one of family therapy's great models of **presence** when working with families. Her full focus was on the family and each of its members. Her focus was characterized by *congruence* and allowing the full use of her senses from seeing and hearing to touch and intuition. Her clarity of heart and mind is not something that everyone seems capable of achieving, but she always claimed it could be learned: It did not have to be innate. Here is an exercise she called "Hanging Hats" that she used to help people become more fully present (see Satir et al., 1991). She used this name for the exercise to emphasize the natural human tendency to project internal images onto others, to hang old hats on the new people that we meet.

She would start by asking those who wanted to be family practitioners to close their eyes. This was not an attempt to shut out the outside world; rather, it was a decision to focus internally. She wanted those who would help others to start with themselves, focusing on what was natural and even physical. Her first suggestion was almost always to "pay attention to your breathing; just notice that air, which gives us life, comes easily in and out of our bodies, supporting us, nurturing us, and requiring nothing beyond what is already natural for us to do." Then, she would often ask us to extend that natural function, to see what it would be like to take a little more air into the center of our bodies, and not hold it but release it easily back into the environment. To be sure, there is all sorts of evidence that this kind of breathing releases tension (Kabat-Zinn, 2005) and distress (especially the act of breathing out), but this was also just her first step in preparing counselors and therapists to be present.

She often mixed this first focus on the physical with visualizations that were designed for health and enhancement of self-esteem (see Banmen & Banmen, 1991; Banmen & Gerber, 1985). She might ask people to visualize looking up toward the sun, and heads would almost automatically tilt upward, a physical act that we now know will also tend to release individuals from feelings of fear. Within the visualization, she might wonder whether people could feel the warmth of the sun flowing over them. She might also wonder whether people could open themselves up to an appreciation of changes that being in the sun brings to one's life, bringing all the value of the sun into the very center of their being. And could we appreciate ourselves for all that we have been through to become the people that we have become, an acceptance of who we are as human beings? Satir would often suggest that this was preparation for becoming more fully human: "Very little change goes on without the patient and therapist becoming vulnerable" (Baldwin & Satir, 1987, p. 22).

When people, listening to her voice, were centered in rest, their heart rates slowed and their breathing calm, she would ask them to open their eyes and look at the people with them, perhaps an individual, a couple, or a family. Satir would often have participants in triads, which she considered the basic unit of the family. She would ask people to use their eyes to take a picture of each person in front of them, placing the pictures on the otherwise blank screen in the participants' minds. Then, she might suggest that participants go back inside themselves, letting any other picture from the family practitioner's past or present come forward, placing it on the mind's screen right next to the initial pictures. All sorts of questions might arise from this experience: Whose picture comes forward? What relationship did the person in the picture have to the family counselor or therapist? How did the family practitioner feel about the person who came to mind? What issues, if any, still exist between the family practitioner and the person who came to mind in this process? Each of these questions were important in their own right, but they also helped to clarify and answer a larger question: Who is the family practitioner having the pleasure of meeting: The person, couple, or family, or pictures the therapist is about to associate (impose) on his or her clients?

Satir would then ask people to open their eyes once more and really look at the people with whom they were sitting. What did people notice about others? What part of every other person *stands out*? What meaning does the person associate with a chosen part or trait? Here is a processing that involved me when I attended a Satir conference in 1979.

Satir: Okay, Jim has curly hair, and you notice it: What do you think about curly hair?

Participant: It's soft.

Satir: And what meaning do you associate with softness?

Participant: I feel that he is probably kind.

Satir: Now isn't that interesting: There's a bit of a leap there from softness to kindness, isn't there? (Turning to me) And are you kind?

Jim: I try to be.

Satir: And sometimes, are you also grumpy and not in the mood to be kind?

Jim: Yes.

Satir: But you have curly hair: Isn't that a permanent contract for unlimited kindness?

Virginia knew that everything we notice is meaningful. If we attend to something, we attach meaning to it. Our only choice is whether we will be conscious (aware) of the meanings we are making or not. Projection (seeing ourselves in others), of course, goes hand-in-hand with introjection (or an internalization of others), so Satir would often ask family practitioners to imagine what observers thought would *stand out* in them. That is, what do you think stands out to others in you and what meaning do you think they attach to it? What is it like to have this fantasy about yourself? How does your body respond? How do you wind up feeling?

Satir was also interested in what our first experiences with each other were. First impressions are hard to change, so taking time to reflect on our first impressions is an important step in defusing their power and becoming present. Let's say that my first impression of you is that you are a bright, intelligent, interesting person whose company I enjoyed, but the next time I see you, you seem lost, distracted, and not very coherent. Rather than change my mind about you, I am likely to say that you were not having a very good day: My first impression still holds. If you're distracted and incoherent again, I might still say, "Wow! Two bad days in a row." It isn't until the third similar experience that I actually decide my first impression was mistaken. Now, if it takes me three new experiences to change a positive first impression, what is going to happen with a negative first impression? It is very likely that it will be so strong that I won't even give you a chance for a second impression. Reflecting on first impressions allows us to set our expectations aside and see who we are really with at this time in this space.

Finally, Satir would ask us to remember any third-party information we had about the people we were meeting—any gossip or rumors we had heard about the people with whom we were about to make contact. In clinical and school settings, this often includes information that is part of the files kept on individuals, couples, or families. It is a far different thing to meet people as they are than to meet a "schizophrenic," "a failing child with ADHD," or "a batterer." Labels, as we shall see, carry a lot of power, and one of the great misuses of this power is to eliminate the real person or people sitting right in front of us.

So before you ever meet your first family—and just before you meet every other family you will ever see—I would highly recommend that you start by *centering* yourself, by becoming present. In order to be worth something to others, you have to start with your own self-worth. Take a moment to breathe and to release yourself from distress and distractions. Appreciate who you are and who you are becoming. Allow yourself to have access to all of your senses and to use them appropriately: What will you see when you walk in the room? What will you hear? What are you feeling? When you extend your hand in greeting and receive the hands of others, how will you experience this touch? What messages do you want your touch to send and what messages are you open to receiving? Smell and taste will probably be least useful in meeting a person or family but, on occasion, even these senses can help you be more fully present.

As you meet the members of a family for the first time, be aware of any stress you may feel in your body. This is often a first clue that the exercise of hanging hats is necessary. Ask yourself: What pictures come to mind, what traits in others stand out, what do you think people attend to in you, what first impressions are involved, and what third-party information do you have? Is any of this getting in your way? What will help to clear your heart and mind? What will help you set projections, introjections, and outside information aside for the time being and allow you to meet the people right in front of you?

Being present is the first step in making contact and in engaging a family. Both *presence* and *contact* happen in the here and now. They are facilitated by a decision to be aware of self, others, and the context in which you are meeting. Family practitioners remove themselves from good contact when they ask distracting questions, such as "How am I doing?" or "What will others think of my work?" or "Can I do this *right*?" Our first questions ought to be: Who am I meeting at this moment in time? What do these people want to convey to me about their thoughts, feelings, and behaviors? What interests me about them? Indeed, what fascinates me about them? What do I need to do to welcome them, create some safety, and validate the effort it took for everyone to get to the session? While presence and contact are essential to a therapeutic relationship, there are other personal and professional attributes that also contribute to successful family practice—and we will consider these next.

Personal Characteristics and Orientations of Effective Family Practitioners

In this section, I will describe the values, traits, attributes, characteristics, and orientations that are commonly associated with effective family counseling and therapy. No one has all of the characteristics mentioned here. There is also no ideal combination of characteristics because, in reality, a wide range of people and personalities have become very successful family practitioners. For those of you who may be just starting in the field, however, it may be useful to consider the following attributes and their importance to you as a person and to your work as a facilitator of family growth and development.

- **Presence.**   Of all the qualities listed here, none is more important than the ability *to be present* in counseling and therapy sessions. To be present is to focus on the clients with interest and even fascination, which means bringing all of our senses to bear in meeting the people with whom we will work.
- **Acceptance, Interest, and Caring.**   Human beings spend most of their lives in systems and institutions permeated with criticism and authoritarian structures. Effective family practitioners position themselves as antidotes to such negative experiences and situations. They seek to replace critical, negative judgments with understanding, reframing, and acceptance. They set a tone from the very first session that allows anything to be expressed and to be heard with interest.
- **Assertiveness and Confidence.**   Although there is no specific personality type that a family practitioner must *be*, it is difficult to imagine a shy or reticent person achieving any measure of success. Family counseling and therapy, especially when the families include young children and teenagers, require a certain degree of assertiveness. Assertiveness is related to confidence. It is speaking in a clear, even voice and communicating without defensiveness. It includes setting boundaries in the service of psychological freedom. It is being comfortable as a leader of the process without taking over for the family itself.
- **Courage and Risk**.   Courage is usually the foundation for assertiveness and confidence. Courage walks hand-in-hand with respect. It starts with faith in oneself as well as the processes involved in family practice. Courage frees family practitioners to

listen and allows them to stay calm and relaxed while observing family dynamics and interactions. There is always a risk in any new therapeutic relationship; family counseling and therapy involves taking reasonable risks in the service of better or preferred lives.

- **Adaptability (openness to change).**   Family counseling and therapy rarely progresses in a linear fashion. Families move forward and then fall back; they take in, but they also block. Family systems are like any living organisms: They require constant adaptation within the process of change. Effective family practitioners come to expect the ebbs and flows of therapeutic process. Adapting to the needs of the situation is not just an option in family counseling and therapy: It is a necessity.

- **Listening Teleologically.**   **Teleology** is the study of final causes, an intended future, or purposes and goals. Both human beings and families intend the future. Everything that people do is in the service of some envisioned end or goal. Knowing the goals and desired outcomes of a person or a family directly impacts the process of therapy. As Satir and Baldwin (1983) note, every complaint also contains a hope: This is the basis for reframing, which we will consider in later chapters.

  Adlerians are perhaps the most teleologically oriented (Carlson, Watts, & Maniacci, 2006; Christensen, 2004). They tend to transform all problem statements into interactions by asking, "When was the last time this problem occurred? How did it go?" It is in the interaction that Adlerians discover the goals, motives, and purposes that individuals and families intend with their behaviors.

- **Working in Patterns and Holism.**   **Patterns** occur across the human experience. Both individuals and families establish patterns to organize their lives and bring a certain level of consistency and predictability to what they do. To understand individuals and families is to understand the patterns that they have chosen to enact. **Holism** is an understanding of human patterns and processes within the social contexts that support them (Smuts, 1996). Individuals grow and function within family systems, and family systems exist within communities and cultures that are further influenced by nations and even global considerations. Getting to know people and their families requires a very wide focus that includes an assessment of the impact that larger systems play in the lives of clients.

- **Appreciating the Influence of Diversity.**   Most of us grow up in a given part of the world in a certain community within a family that has influencing, if unrecognized, cultures and a socioeconomic status. We absorb both the attributes and the evaluations of the life situations in which we grow up. Slowly, we come to recognize that other people in other parts of the world are different than we are. Family practitioners, like other members of the helping professions, realize that tolerance of differences is not enough; today's counselors and therapists need to be sensitive to and actually understand and appreciate differences in social class, race, ethnicity, creed, gender, health/ability and sexual/affectional orientation, and to bring this understanding and appreciation right into the middle of our work.

- **Having a Sincere Interest in the Welfare of Others.**   What effective family practitioners initially bring to counseling and therapy is a focused interest in the family and its members. They want to get to know the family, "to feel their way in" as Carl Whitaker suggests (Whitaker & Bumberry, 1988). Eventually, they may come to care about the family members they see but, even before that caring develops, they are interested in the welfare of their clients. Effective family practitioners know that the kind of relationship they form with the family and its members has a greater impact than whatever techniques or interventions are used (Carlson, Sperry, & Lewis, 2005).

- **Tending the Spirit of the Family and Its Members.**   Tending the spirit is about the creation and maintenance of meaning and the connections among family members that supports that meaning. **Harry Aponte** (1994) has most directly integrated meaning, spirit, and family systems interventions, but we can also find an emphasis on tending the spirit of the family in the family violence work of Cloe Madanes (1990). Adlerians emphasize the development of a community feeling and social interest in families. Feminists remind us of the importance of the female spirit, and social constructionists emphasize the meaning that is co-constructed in counseling and therapy as well as in family life. Tending to the spirit of the family is part of the evolution of the field that has re-inserted human issues in the processes of family systems work.

- **Involvement, Engagement, and Satisfaction in Working With Families.** Effective family practitioners love the involvement and engagement of working with the family as a unit. They find satisfaction is working with the issues of intimacy, contact, **rituals**, and routines of family life. They see families and the world in terms of the interactions and transactions that take place. They see family life as developmental and are prepared to facilitate family transitions. In short, family practitioners are effective, because they are interested in and excited about the possibilities for wellness and resilience that family work provides.

The Process of Change and Therapeutic Process

In one sense, change is inevitable: It is life. From the moment we are conceived until long after we die, we change. Where there is no change, there is simply no life. Change is also something that happens both internally and externally. When we talk about changing internally, we are considering the human capacities for adaptation, adjustment, and taking a different stance. But change also happens *in* the world, and it has real effects on the lives of people. External change and its effects may be easiest to see in natural disasters where, for example, certain structures or places we have come to know and trust are simply wiped out of existence (as in a tornado or a hurricane). In families, loss of a job, divorce, adding children, moving to a new location, starting school, and leaving home are all examples of changes that affect the family and its members.

Each of the models we will study approaches the process of change somewhat differently. All of them contribute something to an understanding of how change occurs and how people adapt to changes in their lives. For now, however, let me use Satir's description of the process of change to orient us to what can happen in family counseling and therapy. Satir believes that the patterns and routines people create to make their lives functional achieve a kind of normalcy she calls the family's **status quo**. People tend to stay in their patterns and routines until their lives are disrupted by an outside force she calls a **foreign element**. It is the disruption of our patterns and routines that sends both the family and its members into **chaos**, the feeling that comes with being disoriented and unable to focus. In chaos, everything seems overwhelming, unsafe, and out of balance. If people are able to regain a sense of balance and safety, if they are able to right themselves and feel their feet back on the ground, they often are able to create or discover **new possibilities**, to change course, or to adapt. Whatever works will, over time, become a **new integration**, a new set of patterns and routines, and a new status quo (Satir & Baldwin, 1983; Satir et al., 1991; Pelonis, 2002).

Of course, family practitioners tend to meet families when they are in chaos. The family may want to make major decisions in an effort to reduce the pain of the problems they face, but this is usually a mistake. In the beginning, exploration is usually a much more important intervention than problem solving. Discovering who the people are and why they are seeking help provides focus as well as goals for counseling and therapy. I believe the single most important thing that you can do when a family is in chaos is stay *present* and *listen*. The first tasks of family practice are almost always to form a relationship with the family and begin an assessment.

Although the ultimate end of counseling and therapy may be the facilitation of change, each model will have different ways of achieving that end. In the chapters that follow, you will read about change processes that involve coaching, nurturing, sculpting, educating, experiencing, enacting, directing and indirecting, focusing on solutions, co-constructing preferred outcomes, and even training for more effective living. Almost none of the models we will study advocate change for the sake of change. The ends these approaches seek may be varied in description and process, but there are some general guidelines:

- It is better for families to rediscover their connections than to be left in disarray and disengagement;
- It is better to remove constrictions from systems and allow people to experience life more fully than to leave them in protective states;
- It is better for systems to be organized than disorganized;
- It is better for communication to be open, congruent, and responsive than to be closed, defensive, or dismissive;
- It is better to say what we think and feel about things that matter than to be lost in silence;
- It is better to set limits, define a bottom line, and clarify what we can do and give than to be controlled by others;
- It is better for people to think rationally than irrationally;
- It is better to know than not to know;
- It is better for people to feel something than to feel nothing at all;
- It is better for people to act and take a chance than to become immobilized and constricted;
- It is better to have goals and hope than to be discouraged;
- It is better to have access to a greater number of internal parts than just a few;
- It is better to be appreciative of one's gender, culture, and ethnicity than to reject it or be cut off from it; and
- It is better for people to risk optimism, faith, and courage than to live in fear.

Of course, there are exceptions to every one of these generalities. But taken together, they point toward growth, development, organization, meaningfulness, increased opportunities, wider and varied experiences, and augmented capacities and strengths. Which of these guidelines might inform your goals in working with families? Are there additional guidelines you could offer? Are there some that don't fit for you at all. Envisioning where you are going with a family is essential to getting there.

Beginning Your Work as Family Practitioners

There are actually some people who seem to be *born* counselors and therapists when they are working with individuals. Such people listen extremely well, bring a focused interest to most of their therapeutic relationships, and have what appears to be a natural capacity for expressing empathy. When working with families, however, we all tend to have difficulties when we first get started. Listening well to family members without paying attention to family process can actually get us lost. Disorganized families often seem chaotic. Learning to think and work systemically is not easy: It takes time and practice.

The first family you see will probably be in a practicum or internship, and you will be under supervision. Being observed when you see your first family is often an added distraction, but it is also an essential safeguard for you and the family. It is not uncommon for the concerns, issues, and problems in the family to trigger unresolved, unfinished, or unaddressed issues in your own relationships. Knowing that you have an experienced practitioner backing you up can help turn initial anxiety into excitement. Here are a few guidelines that may support your development as a family practitioner.

Getting Started.   It is normal to feel a little anxious when you go to meet your first family. It may help you to remember that the family is probably nervous too. So are all of your fellow practicum students or interns. Start with your courage. You have met people before, and you know how to bring forth your interest, your friendliness, and your warmth. Think about what you do when you want to welcome someone into your home. The same qualities will serve you well when you meet families for the first time. Take a deep breath and use your eyes and ears to really take in each person.

At first, be willing to listen and engage the family without having to change it. Be patient. If you get too concerned about what theories or techniques might inform your work, you will lose contact with the family. Start by being as fully present as possible. Ask yourself what you are hearing and what you are seeing. Respond empathically. Let each person know that you hear and understand them. You can trust things to unfold.

Have the Courage to Be Imperfect.   The **courage to be imperfect** is a phrase coined by Sofie Lazersfeld and used extensively by Rudolf Dreikurs and other Adlerians (Terner & Pew, 1978). This kind of courage comes from accepting ourselves as human beings who are not perfect and who make mistakes. Effective counselors and therapists often trust their intuition or make guesses and observations that they hope will be useful in family work. Reasonable risks are part of the work we do. They are also the foundation for the mistakes we make. If you are going to learn to be an effective family practitioner, you are going to make mistakes. They can't be avoided. Having the courage to be imperfect is having the courage to be human—and to be ourselves. It is the courage to be wrong and admit error; to experience the disagreement of others; and to reconsider and correct faulty impressions, interpretations, or the language of our interventions.

Study Your Own Work.   Much of the coursework you will have before you see your first family will have addressed your personal development and the way you think and conceptualize family process. When you start to practice family counseling and therapy, you begin what I hope will be a lifelong commitment to skills development. Nothing will serve this process more than videotaping as much of your work as possible. Be willing to spend the hours necessary to watch these tapes and reflect on what worked well for you and what you want to change in the future.

It may take you a few times to get beyond being concerned about the way you look or the way your voice sounds, but even these observations can begin to give you some information about what works and what doesn't. Be patient with yourself and just notice what you actually do: This also will help you be patient with families. What you actually *do* in family practice will say more about your family practice than what you *think* you should be doing. What are the underlying beliefs and values that seem to be the foundations for the choices you make in your work? How did family members respond to you and to your interventions? What goals and objectives seem to be present in your efforts? Studying your own work will make the difference between one day having twenty years of experience or having one year of experience twenty times over.

Cultivate Silence and Reflection.   Dealing with silence can sometimes be one of the hardest things for new practitioners to learn. We are used to conversational engagement, and we may have a desire to fill gaps with any comments that come to mind. Silence in our clients can be a sign that they are thinking about themselves or others in the family, thinking about what just occurred in the session, or simply not knowing what to say. Silences in family work tend not to last very long, but they can *feel* twice as long as they are in actual time.

Learn to tolerate quiet times. Use the time to observe and to reflect. What has just been happening? What are the people in the room feeling? Who is doing what with whom? What are you feeling at this moment in time? You don't want your reflections to distract you from staying present but, with practice, you will be able to check in with yourself without losing contact with the family.

For most of us, reflecting on our work will occur after the session is over. I encourage family practitioners to write their reflections in a journal as a regular part of their practice. Think about what happened in the session. What were you feeling and experiencing? What did you consider saying that went unsaid? What did you say or do that you wish you hadn't or that needed better timing? What issues came up for you? How do they relate to your own family or relational experiences? What part of your self-reflection would be important to discuss with your supervisor or peers? Is there anything within your reflections that you think would be useful to share with the family? Keeping a journal of these reflections is one way to mark your growth and development over the span of your career.

Think About Your Evolving Role as a Family Practitioner.   One of your most important reflections will be on your evolving role as a family practitioner. What does it mean to you to be a family counselor or therapist? What do the processes and activities in your work say about you as a professional? As you read about the different theories and models of family counseling and therapy, you will have to consider a wide range of roles and functions. Some roles will include directive interventions; some will be more collaborative. Some roles will focus on assessment of dysfunction and change; some will focus on strengths and resiliency. Some will be interested in communication and meaning; others will be primarily interested in behaviors. Which of these roles and functions are a good fit for you?

Salvador Minuchin (2005b) has suggested that his role as a family therapist has evolved over thirty years of practice. He is not the same structural family therapist he first described in the 1970s. His style and process have changed as he has grown older. He has learned from the families he has interviewed, and he has learned from his peers. He notes that he has "copied" many aspects of style from fellow therapists like Carl Whitaker, Jay Haley, and Michael White. When he copies these people, he may borrow a way of phrasing a question, giving a directive, or engaging certain family members, but he uses these interventions "with a Spanish accent"; that is, he integrates new and different styles and makes them his own.

You cannot define your professional role once and for all. It will evolve and change, depending on the clients with whom you work, the services you provide, the location and setting of your practice, and the training and collaborations in which you engage. My own work has led me to a belief in encouragement, a focus on strength and resiliency in families, the dismantling of constraints and restrictions, and the facilitation of change through enactments and the development of new experiences.

Develop a Sense of Humor.   A sense of humor is one of the most important tools that a family practitioner can have. A sense of humor starts with our capacity for enjoyment and enriches human contact. The work that we do is important. It requires that we approach it in a responsible manner, and it often starts with matters that need our most serious attention. Still, nothing is serious forever, and humor and laughter, when appropriate and well-timed, can lighten relational encounters and add an almost transcendent perspective. In this sense, real humor never puts anyone down. Like laughter, it lifts us up and invites us closer. Humor reminds us that we are not alone—that we have a common humanity. Having a sense of humor is probably the greatest safeguard against therapist fatigue and burnout.

Consider Collaborative Practice.   The different approaches we will study in this book will present a wide range of therapeutic relational stances. Some will be exploratory in nature; others will be nurturing. Some will see the therapist as a coach, and others will approach family process as a conductor or a director. Still others will engage families in play. The distinctive styles of the masters of family therapy can be both magical and entertaining. While it is important for each person to find and develop an individualized style, professional styles will change many times over the course of a career. Even the most innovative masters of therapy tended to approach their first family sessions carefully, allowing themselves time to observe and learn. I think this is a good way for most new practitioners to start.

Enter into your first family sessions from a position of respect. Let the family members you meet instruct you about their lives together. Start with interest, friendliness, and observation, the tools of an explorer. Don't rush the process of change. Even if you are limited to only one session lasting only one hour with the family, spend 45 minutes getting to know the family and its members. Consider the possibility that the family really does know what it needs and that its members can share in the process of setting goals for your work together. Consider the possibility that family members have many, if not all, of the resources they need to handle the challenges they face. Inviting families to be partners in the experience of counseling or therapy increases safety, reduces resistance, and leads to empowerment.

From such a foundation of respect, it is possible over time to integrate other skills, techniques, and interventions. It is not uncommon for even very experienced family practitioners to borrow skills and styles from each other. When I first started, I copied people I thought were effective, often using the very words and actions I had seen them use with their families. Some of the things I borrowed worked well for me too, and I made them part of my own style. Some things did not work so well, and I eventually let them go. Developing your own style involves trying things out, occasionally trusting your intuition, and experimenting with interventions. Innovation seeks what is fresh and lively, and its effectiveness is supported by the respectful connections we form with our clients.

If you have no other way to begin, consider saying, "I would like to get to know a little bit about each of you. What would be important for me to know?" Later you might also ask, "What did each of you hope would happen in our work together?" Such a start focuses the process on engagement and collaboration. It begins with an exploration of people and relationships and highlights the wishes and hopes that are often hidden in complaints and problems. It also tends to generate new information and allow family members to consider different perspectives. A collaborative relationship with clients may include the feedback of families as part of one's own supervision. In the last five minutes of a session, I often ask families about what has worked for them: "How did this session go for you today? What was helpful? What is still missing for you?"

No matter how directive family counselors and therapists have been during their careers, many of them become increasingly collaborative as they age (Aponte, 1994; Hoffman, 2002; Minuchin, 2005a; Selvini, 1988). They become more patient in their approach. Their timing is more precise, and interventions seem to arrive in a style that is more easily received. Their work extends the capacity for joining throughout the session. If you want an effective process with which to get started, a collaborative stance will serve you well.

Be Careful With Advice.   Families that are suffering often come to counseling or therapy seeking a quick solution to their problems. They are hoping that a wise counselor will give them some advice or direction that will change their lives and make things better. Such a wish can be very seductive to a new family practitioner. After all, many of us approach this work with the hope that we can help people, make a difference in their relationships, and set them on a course that will lead to greater harmony and happiness.

The paradox is that advice, when it is useful at all, is more easily accepted when it comes from someone who is older and has the kind of life experiences that suggest wisdom—and these are the very people who are less prone to dispensing advice. I am not saying that advice should never be given: This chapter is loaded with advice. Nor am I saying that suggestions and directives are inappropriate. They all have their place depending on the models from which you choose to work. This is just a caution: When you are first getting started, be careful with interventions based on giving advice. Advice-giving is not the same as counseling or therapy.

Have a Life of Your Own.   Family counseling and therapy is intense relational work. It is easy to get absorbed in the problems and lives of the families we see. We feel responsible for them and, at the same time, we know that they are the ones who must cope with and handle the challenges they face. If we get lost in our work, we may begin *to take our work home with us:* This is a sure way to experience professional burnout. The most effective family practitioners I know have lives of their own. They may have their own families and be raising their own children, but they are also interested in history, culture, music, art, and theater, to name a few possibilities. They may exercise or play sports. They may read, write poetry, collect stamps, cook, or have hobbies. They may belong to a church, engage in politics, or coach a little league team. In short, they have lives of their own. More importantly, they seek to live enriched lives.

Family practitioners, like other members of the helping professions, cannot divorce who they are from what they do. Who we are and the relationships we form are two of the most important aspects of therapy. How we choose to live has a great deal to do with the kinds of personal and interpersonal support we bring to our work. It is important to ask yourself periodically if you are living the way you want to live. Do you have more interests than your work? Are the relationships you have with family and friends meaningful? Are you contributing to your community and society in ways that fit you? Do you experience growth and development in your own life? Your life and your work can be **recursive**, each affecting and supporting the other and providing balance to your life and the experience of being grounded when you work.

The Scholar/Practitioner in Family Counseling and Therapy

With few exceptions, the models of family therapy presented in this book emerged from the efforts of clinicians who wanted to understand family practice through engagement and action. Bowen at the National Institute of Mental Health (NIMH) and Georgetown University; Bateson, Jackson, and associates at the Mental Research Institute (MRI) in Palo Alto, California; and Minuchin and colleagues at the Philadelphia Child Guidance Center studied families in an effort to see what worked. These men were, for the most part, scholar-practitioners determined to discover or create the interventions that would make a difference with some of the most severe problems encountered in physical and mental health. In many ways, they were qualitative and action researchers embedded in and connected with the very systems they sought to know and study.

Even private practice practitioners such as Dreikurs, Satir, and Whitaker brought an investigative orientation to their clinical work that focused on personal and professional-skills development as well as family growth and development. In more recent years, Monica McGoldrick and her many associates have focused on developing theory and practice that seeks to articulate the relationship of race, ethnicity, culture, gender, and sexual orientation to families and family therapy (see McGoldrick, 1998).

Starting in 1942 with the formation of the American Association for Marriage and Family Therapy (AAMFT), there has been a concerted effort to demonstrate the efficacy and effectiveness of family practice through the *Journal of Marital & Family Therapy*. In 1995, meta-analyses of effectiveness studies concluded that:

- Marriage and family therapy worked better than no psychotherapy at all;
- Marriage and family therapy did not appear to have negative or harmful effects;
- Marriage and family therapy was more efficacious than individual therapy when working with adult schizophrenia, marital distress, depressed women in distressed marriages, adult alcoholism and substance abuse, adolescent conduct disorders, anorexia in teenage women, childhood autism, and a variety of physical illnesses in both adults and children;

- No particular model of marital and family therapy was superior (more effective) to any other approach;
- There was some evidence that marital and family therapy was more cost effective than in-patient or residential treatment for schizophrenia and severe conduct disorders or delinquency in adolescents; and
- While marriage and family therapy is a critical and necessary component in the treatment of severe problems, the most effective programs also include psychoeducational therapies, individual or group counseling, and/or medication. (Pinsof & Wynne, 1995)

Southern (2005) noted that four marriage and family therapy journals, publishing 131 articles between 1980 and 1999 contained the results of mostly quantitative studies. Even though qualitative research was increasing, it accounted for a very small percentage of the articles. For a field that still feels it must validate and justify its methods, such a finding is perhaps not surprising. This same study also noted that articles addressing diversity issues in the *Journal of Marital & Family Therapy* nearly doubled in ten years to 31% of the articles during the last five years leading up to 2000.

Toward the end of the 1980s, the International Association of Marriage and Family Counselors (IAMFC) established *The Family Journal* in an additional effort to provide a forum for "groundbreaking, innovative scholarship for counseling researchers, educators, and practitioners." For more than fifteen years, this journal has provided space for both qualitative and quantitative research; the development of theory and practice; the relationship of personal exploration and growth to professional development; considerations of race, culture, and gender in family counseling; and efficacy studies for the training of family practitioners.

In a content analysis of *The Family Journal*, Southern (2005) listed the main themes addressed as "techniques, training, & supervision, assessment & diagnosis, children at risk, multicultural issues, family issues, ethics, sexual issues, marital & couple issues, addiction, and healthy relationships" (p. 8), with an increase in articles dealing with ethics, addiction, and work and socioeconomic issues. Southern also noted a trend toward increased coverage of sexual issues, training and supervision, marital and couples issues, family issues, and health.

In spite of its openness to qualitative design, such articles still make up a relatively small amount of the total number of articles. Still, I believe qualitative investigations and action research methods hold the greatest promise for an integration of scholarship and clinical practice (see Sprenkle & Piercy, 2005).

Qualitative research embeds the knower (all of us as practitioner-scholars) within the experiences of the known (the family) and asks us to consider what effects our presence and observations have on the people and systems we are investigating. Isn't this what all of us have to do in clinical practice anyway? Is it not important to regularly reflect on who we are, what we are experiencing, and what kinds of recursive effects we are having with the families we serve? Qualitative research engages us in a search for patterns and themes, and the more formal processes of continual categorization, sorting and resorting, and coding and recoding have the potential to orient and train the practitioner's mind for receiving and making meaning out of the stories and experiences in therapy (Echevarria-Doan & Tubbs, 2005). Qualitative research can be phenomenological and supports efforts to study families in natural contexts (Dahl & Boss, 2005). It reminds us that meaning can be different to various members of families and systems; that there are multiple ways of knowing; and that the language and meanings of everyday life are socially constructed and significant. Most importantly, qualitative research emphasizes that we are not separate from the people and families we study and serve: The knowledge we have is shared and held by practitioners and families alike. These assumptions provide a significant bond between clinical practice and clinical research with the strengths of each informing and enhancing the other.

Action research offers practitioners still another model for assessing and evaluating our effectiveness in therapy (Mendenhall & Doherty, 2005). Again, action research is a methodology that can train and orient the minds of family practitioners in useful ways. It emphasizes democratic partnership (or collaboration); problem solving in context; cyclical processes of interventions and evaluations; adjustments, humility, and adaptability. In action research, participants engage in corrective and evaluative processes that guide the changes in approach and intervention, the very same guidance that the early masters of family therapy sought in their developmental work.

For too many years, the very word *research* has led to resistance in those who are training for the helping professions. Required courses in statistics, empirical and experimental design, and controlled studies seemed to be disconnected from the rest of professional training in family practice. With the emergence of qualitative and action research methods, it is possible for scholarship to be reconnected and indeed fully integrated with clinical practice.

Toward a Foundation for Integration

What I will suggest in this book is that each theory or model brings certain perspectives to the practice of family counseling and therapy. One way to create a foundation for the integration of these models is to look at what we can learn by developing perspectives, assessments, and interventions across the various approaches. In 1992, Breunlin, Schwartz, and MacKune-Karrer (1997) introduced the concept of metaframeworks as a method for transcending the various approaches to family therapy. They identified 6 metaframeworks that they treated as core perspectives. The original 6 were:

1. internal family systems (a systemic conceptualization of individuals);
2. sequences (or patterns of interaction);
3. organization of systems;
4. developmental processes (in individuals, families, and macro-systems);
5. multicultural perspectives; and
6. gender perspectives

With these 6 perspectives, Breunlin and associates provided a means for assessing families across models and developing multiple avenues for intervention in their "blueprint for therapy" (p. 281). I like to think of each metaframework as a different lens through which I can meet, learn about, and come to understand the family. In 2005, Gerald Corey and I added 2 additional perspectives to the original 6. They were (a) teleological lens (or goal-orientation) and (b) a process lens (see Bitter & Corey, 2005). We will consider these 8 lenses in more detail in the integration chapter toward the end of the book. I recommend that you now read that part of the integration chapter that provides a description for each of the 8 lenses. You can read the chapter for detail later on.

As you read the theory chapters in this book, think about what the various models might contribute to each of the 8 lenses. I occasionally note certain contributions to these perspectives in the theory chapters, but you may discover contributions I have not mentioned. In my own work, these 8 lenses provide me with richer understandings and family descriptions than I would have using only 1 perspective. At various times, I use some lenses more than others. In most cases, the family members and the issues presented just seem to fit 1 subset of perspectives better. It is not uncommon, however, for me to consider all 8 lenses at least initially. Any or all of them may have meaningful applications during the therapy process. As Breunlin et al. (1997) note, there is a *recursiveness* to these perspectives with each lens influencing and being influenced by the rest. The advantage of using these lenses in family practice is that they provide the practitioner with multiple perspectives for assessment as well as the means for **tailoring** therapeutic interventions to the specific needs of the family (Carlson, Sperry, & Lewis, 2005; Goldenberg & Goldenberg, 2002). I believe these 8 lenses provide a foundation for integrating the ten approaches that make up this book.

Gender and Multicultural Lenses

Because the early years of family counseling and therapy almost completely ignored the lenses of gender and culture, I believe that it is important to highlight these perspectives here. Like other institutions and practices in society, family counseling and therapy has all too often reflected and supported the dominant value system, ignoring the effects of oppression based on class, race, ethnicity, gender, health/ability, and sexual/affectional orientation. The very definition of family in the United States is based on a nuclear, middle-class family that is white, of mixed-European cultures, Protestant, healthy and able, and heterosexual; the father is an "absent" breadwinner and the mother stays at home, raising two children (preferably one of each gender with the oldest being male). This description accounts for only 3% of the actual population in the United States (McGoldrick, 1998). It is also an ideal that has not served women well, rendering the "mother perpetually on call for everyone both emotionally and physically" (p. 4). It is a patriarchal arrangement that reinforces gender stereotypes while minimizing or eliminating much needed alternatives for the other 97% of the population.

Race, class, ethnicity, culture, gender, health/ability, and sexual/affectional orientation are dynamic parts of individuals and family systems. To know ourselves as individuals and family practitioners requires that we investigate our families-of-origin for the cultural experiences that relate to these dynamics. Before we can know the richness and diversity of other families, we must come to know our own heritage. Whether we are part of the dominant culture or of one or more marginalized cultures, both our values and our families have been organized in ways that shape these meanings in our lives.

Of all the discriminations people face in the world, sexism and the oppression of women are the oldest and most pervasive. Indeed, one of the most difficult aspects of working with multicultural families is balancing the need to be sensitive and appreciative of cultural differences when those differences still involve discrimination against women. Still, there is no society or culture that lacks feminist voices. In this first decade of the 21st century, we have truly become a global village: Television and mass communication are joining people across borders. Women all over the world are supporting each other in their acquisition of freedom and equality.

What meanings do you attach to being male or female? What is your cultural heritage? How have these two perspectives shaped your life when you were young and now? Who benefits from the definitions you attach to gender and culture? Who is privileged by these definitions? Who is marginalized? If you were going to make a special effort to be sensitive to and appreciate diversity, how would that effort affect your family practice? How would it affect your role with others? How would your words reflect your sensitivity and appreciation?

Because gender and cultural perspectives are so important to the field today, I will give special consideration to these lenses at the end of each theory-based chapter—in addition to considering the lenses in more detail in the integration chapter. The most effective models and practitioners tailor their approach to fit the unique needs of families with a wide range of structures, cultures, economics, and genders. Family practitioners today are required to possess the knowledge for working with various cultures; called to a personal and professional consideration of their own gender heritage and cultural experiences; and, in an effort to prevent harm, must learn the culturally sensitive skills needed to assist families with the realities of their individual cultures.

Summary

One of the most important issues in family practice is the attention that must be given to personal growth and development. Working with families is both complicated and exciting: It appeals to those who like challenges, who look forward to engaging with others, who see life in relational terms, and who want to make a difference in human systems. The work is personal; it happens up close. It is the kind of work that touches our own life experiences and all too easily reminds us of our own family concerns and issues. Sorting through our life experiences, personal concerns, and family issues is essential to meeting families in an open and grounded manner.

There will be many things that you learn throughout your training as a family counselor or therapist. Asking families to see themselves in a new way starts with the requirement that we are able to see our own families in a new way. Helping families through the change process is more easily facilitated when we have engaged in purposeful changes ourselves. Developing our professional processes in a therapeutic relationship is just part of the larger experience of paying attention to the relationships we have in the rest of our lives.

References

Aponte, H. J. (1994). *Bread and spirit: Therapy with the new poor—Diversity of race, culture, and values.* New York: Norton.

Baldwin, M., & Satir, V. M. (1987). The use of the self in therapy. *Journal of Psychotherapy, 3*(1), 17–25.

Banmen, A., & Banmen, J. (Eds.). (1991). *Meditations of Virginia Satir: Peace within, peace between, and peace among.* Palo Alto, CA: Science and Behavior Books.

Banmen, J., & Gerber, J. (Eds.). (1985). *Meditations and inspirations of Virginia Satir.* Milbrae, CA: Celestial Arts.

Bitter, J. R. (1988). Family mapping and family constellation: Satir in Adlerian context. *Individual Psychology, 44*(1), 106–111.

Bitter, J. R., & Corey, G. (2005). Family systems therapy. In G. Corey, *Theory and practice of counseling and psychotherapy* (7th ed., pp. 420–459). Belmont, CA: Brooks/Cole.

Blow, A. J., Sprenkle, D. H., & Davis, S. D. (2007). Is who delivers the treatment more important than the treatment itself? The role of the therapist in common factors. *Journal of Marital & Family Therapy, 33*(3), 298–317.

Breunlin, D. C., Schwartz, R. C., & MacKune-Karrer, B. (1997). *Metaframeworks: Transcending the models of family therapy* (rev. ed.). San Francisco: Jossey-Bass. (Original work published 1992)

Carlson, J., Sperry, L., & Lewis, J. A. (2005). *Family therapy techniques: Integrating and tailoring treatment.* New York: Routledge.

Carlson, J., Watts, R. E., & Maniacci, M. (2006). *Adlerian therapy: Theory and practice.* Washington, DC: American Psychological Association.

Christensen, O. C. (Ed.). (2004). *Adlerian family counseling* (3rd ed.). Minneapolis, MN: Educational Media Corp.

Dahl, C. M., & Boss, P. (2005). The use of phenomenology for family therapy research: The search for meaning. In D. H. Sprenkle & F. P. Piercy (Eds.), *Research methods in family therapy* (2nd ed., pp. 63–84). New York: Guilford.

Echevarria-Doan, S., & Tubbs, C. Y. (2005). Let's get grounded: Family therapy research and grounded theory. In D. H. Sprenkle & F. P. Piercy (Eds.), *Research methods in family therapy* (2nd ed., pp. 41–62). New York: Guilford.

Goldenberg, H., & Goldenberg, I. (2002). *Counseling today's families* (4th ed.). Pacific Grove, CA: Brooks/Cole.

Hoffman, L. (2002). *Family therapy: An intimate history.* New York: Norton.

Kabat-Zinn, J. (2005). *Coming to our senses: Healing ourselves and the world through mindfulness.* New York: Hyperion.

Madanes, C. (1990). *Sex, love, and violence: Strategies for transformation.* New York: Norton.

McGoldrick, M. (1998). *Re-visioning family therapy: Race, culture, and gender in clinical practice.* New York: Guilford.

Mendenhall, T. J., & Doherty, W. J. (2005). Action research methods in family therapy. In D. H. Sprenkle &

F. P. Piercy (Eds.), *Research methods in family therapy* (2nd ed., pp. 100–118). New York: Guilford.

Minuchin, S. (Speaker). (2005a). *Family assessment: Seven steps model* (Cassette Recording No. EP05-WS24ab). Phoenix, AZ: Milton H. Erickson Foundation.

Minuchin, S. (Speaker). (2005b). *Family therapy: New developments* (Cassette Recording No. EP05-P/CP8). Phoenix, AZ: Milton H. Erickson Foundation.

Pelonis, P. (2002). *Facing change in the journey of life.* Athens, Greece: Fytraki Publications.

Pinsof, W. M., & Wynne, L. C. (1995). The efficacy of marital and family therapy: An empirical overview, conclusions, and recommendations. In W. Pinsof & L. Wynne (Eds.), *Family therapy effectiveness: Current research and theory* (pp. 585–613). Washington, DC: American Association for Marriage and Family Therapy.

Satir, V. M., & Baldwin, M. (1983). *Satir: Step-by-step.* Palo Alto, CA: Science and Behavior Books.

Satir, V. M., Banmen, J., Gerber, J., & Gomori, M. (1991). *The Satir model: Family therapy and beyond.* Palo Alto, CA: Science and Behavior Books.

Selvini, M. (Ed.). (1988). *The work of Mara Selvini Palazzoli.* Northvale, NJ: Jason Aronson.

Smuts, J. C. (1996). *Holism and evolution.* Highland, NY: The Gestalt Journal Press. (Original work published 1926)

Southern, S. (2005). Themes in marriage and family counseling: A content analysis of *The Family Journal. The Family Journal, 20*(10), 1–9.

Sprenkle, D. H., & Piercy, F. P. (Eds.). (2005). *Research methods in family therapy* (2nd ed.). New York: Guilford.

Terner, J., & Pew, W. L. (1978). *The courage to be imperfect: The life and work of Rudolf Dreikurs.* New York: Hawthorn.

Whitaker, C. A., & Bumberry, W. M. (1988). *Dancing with the family: A symbolic-experiential approach.* New York: Brunner/Mazel.

CHAPTER 3

Virtue, Ethics, and Legality in Family Practice

by David Kleist and James Robert Bitter

Introduction

A Consideration of Virtue

Ethical Codes and Standards of Professional Practice

Ethical Decision Making

Commonly Discussed Ethical Dilemmas in Family Practice

Professional Regulations and Legal Requirements

Conclusion

Recommended Readings

References

Introduction

As you read this chapter, we are going to consider three aspects of professional work that should be related, but often are not even complementary to each other: **virtue** or goodness, professional ethical codes, and legal conduct.

First, we want you to think about what constitutes personal and relational virtue—a good life—and the morality that supports these two. In recent years, virtue has become almost exclusively the domain of religion, but it once was a matter of public discourse (Aristotle, 350 B.C.-1985; Cicero, 44 B.C.-1991; Plato, 380 B.C.-1992; and more recently, Bellah, Madsen, Sullivan, Swidler, & Tipton, 1985/1996, 1991)—and it needs to be again. We also will look at what the masters of family counseling and therapy might contribute to this discussion.

David Kleist is a colleague from Idaho State University. Since David actually teaches a course in legal and ethical issues in family counseling and therapy, and I (Jim Bitter) don't, I asked him to help me present the issues and processes that are essential to our work.

Second, although professional ethics can serve as guidelines for appropriate conduct with clients, as well as provide opportunities for the personal learning and growth for the professional helper (Corey, Corey, & Callanan, 2007; Sperry, 2007), it too often has been addressed simply as a way to avoid malpractice lawsuits (Austin, Moline, & Williams, 1990). Real ethical questions in family practice are almost never easy to answer, and even the principles that underlie our professional codes often need adjusting for application across cultures, locations, and with each gender (Wilcoxon, Remley, Gladding, & Huber, 2007).

Third, there are the legal requirements of each state that define our responsibilities in relation to professional practice. This is especially true in the areas of confidentiality; child and elder abuse; harm to self, others, and sometimes property; informed consent; dual relationships; professional identity and competence; and education and training. In additional, there are federal requirements to consider, such as HIPAA[1] and *Jaffee* vs. *Redmond* (Supreme Court of the United States, No. 95-266), which deal with federal validation and limitations on confidentiality in psychotherapy. Although personal virtue and professional ethics ought to be foremost in our relationships with clients, it is the laws of each state and the federal government that ultimately dictate these standards in our work.

A Consideration of Virtue

Within Western cultures, most discussions of virtue have yielded relatively common themes. Although Aristotle (350 B.C.-1985) chose happiness as the highest good, it was never to be achieved in isolation. Indeed, happiness was the result of virtuous actions that were conducted with moderation; bravery (or courage); temperance; generosity; mildness and friendliness; truthfulness; wit; justice and fairness; consideration and considerateness; and rational thought, intelligence, and even wisdom. To this list, Cicero (44 B.C.-1991) added orderliness, goodwill, honor, faithfulness, and service. We find many of these same themes in the thoughts of Plato (380 B.C.-1992) and most subsequent philosophers in western societies. These western traits were formulated for and assigned to individuals who sought to live a good life in relation to others of similar status and condition.

As Aristotle (350 B.C.-1985) noted, there are certain preconditions to such virtuous action and, again, each of these preconditions must be held by the individual or they invalidate virtue. Included in the preconditions are free will and voluntary action, the capacity for rational decision making, the intention of achieving rational ends, and choice (or the power to enact either good or evil). These individual conditions have, for the most part, been enshrined in each of the codes of ethics that address professional practice in the helping professions. But what does this mean for cultures and societies in which the individual is not the most important character in the determination of moral action—as is true for many Asian countries? And what does it mean for the systemic therapies that choose to work *relationally* rather than *individually*? Do systemic therapy masters have anything to add to a conversation about individual virtue or goodness and a good society (or system)?

Systemic Perspectives.   Perhaps the most fully developed individual and systemic positions on virtue comes from Adler (1927/1946, 1933/1938). Adler posited that the nature of human beings was to be connected to and in relationship with others. He called the capacity for such connectedness a **community feeling**. The enactment of a community feeling was characterized by the taking of an active **social interest** in the well-being of others. Not only was this the basis for virtue but, by extension, it was also the basis for individual and family mental health.

Heinz Ansbacher (1992) addressed and clarified community feeling and social interest, noting that having a community feeling is related to the feeling of being in harmony with the universe and with the development of life throughout time. He called social interest "the action-line of the community feeling" (p. 405): the practical implementation of an interest in the well-being of others. What are people and families with a community feeling and social interest like?

They are more relaxed, having a sense of humor about the whole situation and about themselves. They will make a contribution when in a group, will be the better followers and the better leaders. They will be interested in the interests of others. They will be more mature and more reliable. They will be the better cooperators. (Bitter & West, 1979, pp. 96–97)

To Ansbacher's description of people with social interest above, we would add that the following traits can be found in the writings of many Adlerians: cooperation, contribution, caring, connectedness, **courage**, confidence, and competence (what might be called the 7 Cs).

Although Adler may have had the most developed perspective on what constituted a good life, he was not the only systemic thinker to contribute to this discussion. Other family therapists have developed models that directly or indirectly suggest a diversity of values, virtues, and qualities of a good life.

Kerr and Bowen (1988) highly valued rational thought and placed it in opposition to emotional reactivity, but the true test of a differentiated self was the ability to stay calm and observant in the midst of often emotionally charged personal family systems. It was in elevating one's rational responsiveness that whole systems had a chance to change.

Satir (1983) wrestled with the same concerns for the individual in relation to the system. For her, however, the answer was not in rational thought, but in emotional honesty communicated congruently in the present moment. The mark of maturity could be seen in "one, who having attained his (sic) majority, is able to make choices and decisions based on accurate perceptions about self, others, and the context . . . ; who acknowledges these choices and decisions . . . ; and who accepts responsibility for their outcomes" (p. 118).

One of the virtues that emanates from the work of both Bowen and Satir is the value of clarity in both mind and heart. Both masters knew that such clarity came from reflection and from a refusal to act based on automatic reactions. Although Whitaker (1976) appeared to value spontaneity of experience over all else, including reflection, in practice his interventions were designed to do many of the same things that Bowen and Satir valued: (a) release the family from self-imposed constrictions; (b) augment freedom of movement and expression; and (c) help family members find a balance between individuation and connectedness, dependence and independence, and personal needs and family requirements.

Similar dialectical themes are reflected in the structural work of Salvador Minuchin (1974, 2004) and most of the strategic therapists. In these models, a diversity of resources and cultures is valued over limited perspectives and options; order and boundaries facilitate openness and freedom, including the right of an individual or system to close down periodically; the individual and the system are structurally and developmentally interdependent; flexibility and adaptability are valued over rigidity; and leadership is better when it is balanced and seeks harmony. To these values, Adlerians, Satir, **solution-focused therapists**, social constructionists, and **feminist therapists** would add the value of **social equality**, and the importance of **collaboration**. Feminists would further note that the valuing of the right, just, or principled action may be the valuing of an illusion: That relational morality calls on all of us to care for others as well as ourselves (Gilligan, 1982). Feminist research echoes Adler's call for community feeling and social interest.

Both the global village and systems orientations reframe individual virtue within communal contexts. Quality connections with others are increasingly valued over individual, even heroic, action—although the goal is always for both the individual and the system to grow and develop. In this sense, words like caring, clarity, cooperation, courage, confidence, and competence take on a relational focus. Freedom for the individual is balanced with the survival needs and development of the whole. Individual capacities are contextualized as one set of resources among many that may be available to the group, the family, or the relationship. Difference and diversity are valued over sameness and routine. This valuing and appreciation of multiple perspectives (Breunlin, Schwartz, & MacKune-Karrer, 1997; Lum, 2003) is key to reshaping what constitutes virtue in an increasingly intimate world with diverse and interdependent cultures.

■ Ethical Codes and Standards of Professional Practice

As everyone who has ever read their profession's ethical codes soon learns, ethical codes primarily provide guidance, rather than absolute directives, for professional activity. Almost every family counselor has wished, at one time or another, to find a clear and concise answer to an ethical dilemma carefully defined in our profession's codes of ethics. Having such a definition would make clinical life so much easier. Ethical dilemmas would surface and answers would be found in some section of a code of ethics; further, a concrete requirement for action would be immediately clear. And, once in a while, we actually can find clear directives in our standards of practice: Don't have sex with your clients; do not let clients harm self or others; and provide informed consent are a few examples. Most ethical dilemmas, however, are much more difficult to understand and resolve.

Those who have chosen to work in the helping professions, particularly with families, find themselves working with what Donald Schön (1983) refers to as ill-defined problems. Ill-defined problems occur when human beings frame a given experience as a problem. Conducting a family counseling or therapy session with a family that has a member who serves as your mechanic is simply an experience that has to be addressed. Most, if not all, helping professions would frame this experience as a potential problem because of the dual or multiple relationships involved. Jensen (2005) defines a dual relationship as "a separate and distinct relationship that occurs between the therapist and a patient, or a patient's spouse, partner, or family member, either simultaneously with the therapeutic relationship, or during a reasonable period of time following the termination of the therapeutic relationship" (p. 17). In the example above, there is the "customer–mechanic" relationship, the "family counselor–client" relationship, the "family counselor–other family member" relationship, and the "family member–family member" relationship.

Let's see what help various codes of ethics may provide. The *ACA Code of Ethics* [American Counseling Association (ACA), 2005] encourages counselors to avoid nonprofessional relationships, except when "the interaction is potentially beneficial to the client" (p. 5). Similarly, the *IAMFC Code of Ethics* [International Association of Marriage and Family Counselors (IAMFC), 2005] encourages family counselors to "avoid whenever possible multiple relationships, such as business, social, or sexual contacts with any current clients or family members" (p. 5). The AAMFT Code of Ethics [*American Association for Marriage and Family Therapists* (AAMFT), 2001a] also requires that therapists:

> . . . make every effort to avoid conditions and multiple relationships with clients that could impair professional judgment or increase the risk of exploitation. Such relationships include, but are not limited to, business or close personal relationships with a client or the client's immediate family. When the risk of impairment or exploitation exists due to conditions or multiple roles, therapists take appropriate precautions. (principle 1.3)

We find similar language in the *NASW Code of Ethics* [National Association for Social Workers (NASW), 1996]:

> Social workers should not engage in dual or multiple relationships with clients or former clients in which there is a risk of exploitation or potential harm to the client. In instances when dual or multiple relationships are unavoidable, social workers should take steps to protect clients and are responsible for setting clear, appropriate, and culturally sensitive boundaries. (principle 1.06c)

So now what? Let's say you are a family counselor, and you are a member of both IAMFC and ACA. IAMFC suggests avoiding business relationships, whereas ACA's code would allow such a relationship *if* it is beneficial to the client. To which code are you bound: the one for a division of ACA that represents your counseling specialty or the one for the entire counseling profession? Another difficult question is how would you determine what might be a beneficial relationship? That's apparently not so easy to answer, because the ACA goes on to suggest that potentially beneficial interactions "may include purchasing a service or product provided by a client" (ACA, 2005, p. 5).

AAMFT (2001a) lists two highly problematic concerns with dual relationships that could result: impaired professional judgment and client exploitation. Okay, so that's easy. If I think that a dual relationship with my mechanic could impair my professional judgment or result in exploitation, I just don't take that person or family on as a client: That's nice and clear. But what if I don't live in a big city? What if I live in a small town in a rural state or up in the northern territories of Canada? What if I am the only therapist for miles around? How can I avoid dual relationships then? Well, if I can't, I am directed to take appropriate precautions. I wonder what those are.

If it all comes down to my professional judgment, what will motivate my actions: a duty to respectfully follow perhaps multiple codes of ethics; a desire to avoid legal problems; or a desire to do what I think is best, based on my personal virtue, morality, and character? Welcome to the world of ethics in family practice.

We began this chapter by noting that professional ethics provide not only guidance but also opportunity for personal learning and growth. Ethical decision making—especially when dealing with conflicting professional ethical codes—moves you into the realm of ambiguity and uncertainty. It becomes the practitioner's responsibility, hopefully with consultation from experienced professionals, to make clinical choices that promote the well-being of clients. So, what do "beneficial" or "promote" or "well-being" really mean in action? *How* are these terms defined? *Who* has a role in defining these terms? Even though these are difficult questions to address, some of your most meaningful moments as a family practitioner may occur in the uncertain struggles with professional ethics.

Any consideration of professional ethics is fuzzy, and the phrase, "it depends" will emerge more often than a definitive answer. A dilemma is a dilemma because it is not easily solved, and wrestling with it often raises more questions than it answers.

Perspectives on Ethics

There are multiple ways to address ethics, moral action, and professional practice. In this section, we will discuss two of the most salient and familiar perspectives on ethics as applied to our work with families: **principle ethics** and **virtue ethics**. We then will discuss an emergent perspective on ethics, firmly grounded in postmodern thought, called **participatory ethics** (McCarthy, 2001).

Principle Ethics.   Principle ethics can be seen as preexisting obligations a family practitioner embraces prior to any interaction with clients (Meara, Schmidt, & Day, 1996). The most commonly mentioned principles in the fields of counseling, psychology, and social work reflect the western values and themes first articulated by Plato, Aristotle, and Cicero: **autonomy, beneficence, nonmaleficence, fidelity, justice**, and **veracity** (Remley & Herlihy, 2005).

Autonomy is the principle underlying the individual's freedom of choice. There are many ways the principle of autonomy can play out in family practice. At the outset of family consultation, you will describe to your client your preferred approach or model as part of what is called **informed consent**. Families have the right to say "no" to the services you offer if those services do not fit them. The principle of autonomy also favors the individual over the family or the group. In many Asian cultures, however, what is best for the individual is never considered above what is best for the family. It is important to keep in mind that autonomy is a decidedly western value. Even in Western cultures, the principle of autonomy forces family practitioners to articulate who they see as their client(s): Is it each individual in the family or is it the family as a whole? Will the practitioner support the needs and development of individuals, of the family, or attempt to do both? And how will conflicts in these areas be resolved?

Beneficence means to promote the client's welfare and well-being. Family practitioners take steps to consciously and consistently work toward the betterment of the families with whom they work. Sounds simple, doesn't it?

Let's imagine a family who has come to you for support and guidance. We will use this family throughout the rest of this chapter to consider other ethical questions and concerns. The family has recently been charged with child neglect. The specific charge of neglect involves the family's 14-year-old child, who is suffering from leukemia. The parents hold religious beliefs that do not allow medical intervention to be given for any illness, even cancer. The parents want to gain your support for their freedom to choose the health care interventions they deem appropriate within their religious system. Prayer is their preferred form of intervention.

Supporting their freedom sounds like the right thing to do, but there in front of you is their 14-year-old child, suffering—and most likely dying—from cancer. So what actions do you take that would be seen as promoting the client's welfare? And who, exactly, *is* your client: the parents, the child, the family as a whole? The answer to this question will be central to every move you make.

Let's say that promoting the 14-year-old child's welfare seems clear to you, but then you are viewing the child's problem from the perspective of what's possible using western medical procedures, a perspective clearly outside of the religious values that are informing the parents' actions. As it turns out, even the child espouses the same religious convictions. So if you support the family's perspective, are you prepared to watch this young person die when everything within your own value system tells you the child has a chance with what you might deem "proper medical care"?

The third ethical principle is nonmaleficence. This is the classic credo of doctors since the days of Hippocrates: Do no harm. This directive seems so simple, but the meaning of "harm" can be individual, contextual, cultural, or even historical. What the family practitioner means by harm can be quite different from the family's definition and, even within the family, differences may exist as to what constitutes harm for each family member.

In the early days of family therapy, Jay Haley (1963) used **paradoxical interventions** when certain client symptoms were thought to be maintaining a family's problems: Haley would sometimes prescribe and augment the symptom as opposed to working directly to relieve it. For example, a father might exhibit great anxiety and worry about his family's welfare, checking on his kids at school 3, 4, or 5 times a day. Haley might tell the father that he is not worrying enough. What about all the hours of the night when other family members are asleep? Haley might even instruct the father to set his alarm clock to wake him on the hour, every hour. Upon awakening, he is to get out of bed and wake each of his children and ask if they are okay. For 5 nights in a row, the father is directed to carry out this task.

We already have noted that the definition of *harm* can differ across different periods in history. During the 1960s and 1970s, paradoxical interventions might have caught the scorn of some, but they would have been allowed to continue. Such interventions certainly brought about sudden, beneficial changes at times, even though their use raised the issue of whether the end justified the means. Today, standing up in your agency's case meeting and describing this intervention might very well lead to charges of an ethical violation.

Fidelity refers to the responsibility to maintain trust in the therapeutic relationship. Family practitioners must remain faithful to the promises they make to clients, especially when maintaining the client's right to privacy. What does this principle mean in relation to family secrets? Building and maintaining trust is the cornerstone to an effective therapeutic alliance with clients. The codes of ethics for all of the helping professions recognize the importance of keeping individual family members' private conversations with their counselor or therapist confidential unless that individual has given consent to share the content of the conversation. This right to privacy also is codified in law through the current HIPAA regulations and requirements.

Let's say the 16-year-old daughter of a family speaks to you one-on-one prior to a family session about her recent experimentation with marijuana and her fear of her parents' potential response. You listen intently and affirm the confidentiality of the conversation. During the family session, the father and the mother both indicate that they are worried about their daughter. Her grades in school are getting worse ("She has always been a good student."); she is hanging out with a different set of friends, and she sneaks out to see them at night, but she won't introduce any of her friends to them; and she is dressing differently. The parents ask her: "Are you doing drugs?" The girl denies that she is. The parents look to the counselor: "Do you think she is doing drugs?" How do you reconcile the principles of beneficence, nonmaleficence, and fidelity in this case? What affect would disclosing this **family secret** have on the 16-year-old daughter? How might she view the counseling process and you as a family counselor? If you think this dilemma is hard, what will you do when you know that one of the parents is having an extramarital affair that is directly harming other members of the family? With each additional ethical principle, the professional waters muddy even more.

Justice refers to fairness, including equitable service for all clients. As of 2004–2005, Counselors for Social Justice (CSJ), a new division of the ACA, has a website that specifically targets issues of equity, oppression, discrimination, and injustice (see **http://www. counselorsforsocialjustice.org**). Such a development highlights how valued this principle is within the counseling profession:

> Counselors for Social Justice is a community of counselors, counselor educators, graduate students, and school and community leaders who seek equity and an end to oppression and injustice affecting clients, students, counselors, families, communities, schools, workplaces, governments, and other social and institutional systems. (CSJ mission statement)

In the teaching of ethics, the principle of justice has been the most misunderstood and debated principle. For many, equality and fairness mean equal treatment or the same treatment. For us, equality means that all people have an equal right to be valued and respected even when they are different from one another. Both philosophy (Aristotle, 350 B.C.-1985) and systems theory (Bateson, 1979) have noted that *differences* cannot be ignored: justice means treating similar people similarly and different people differently.

For example: Is working with a family with an only child and an income of more than $100,000 the same as working with a family of eight whose income is less than $25,000? Is the difference in incomes different enough to warrant a different way of providing family counseling or therapy? Do you think poverty has real effects on family life? If you are in private practice and you have set a rate for your services at $100 per hour, will you even see the poorer family? How will you bill them? Will you see them for free or on a sliding scale—and how many poor families will you be able to accept in your practice and still make a living yourself? Justice requires that you wrestle with these issues before you even see your first family. It also has a place in your consideration of whether you work with oppressed families as if they have control over their own lives or work with the macro-systems to change society, as feminist family therapists (Silverstein & Goodrich, 2003), among others, would recommend.

Veracity is the implementation of truthfulness: It is intimately related to personal and professional integrity. It is only recently that veracity has been included in major ethical texts (Corey, Corey, & Callanan, 2007). One reason for the inclusion of veracity on the list of ethical principles is the increasing requirements of **managed care**. Managed care not only dictates the treatment people receive from medical doctors, but also the services delivered to individuals and families for mental health problems. In the name of controlling health care costs, managed care companies limit the type and duration of services offered to clients. For family practitioners to remain on a preferred provider list, they must agree to abide by the parameters set by such companies. Managed care means that family practitioners within that system must wrestle with split loyalties. Being truthful, an essential part of informed consent, is essential for resolving professional conflict in the managed worlds of hospitals and community agencies.

These six common ethical principles do not exist independent of one another. Hill (2004) has suggested that these ethical principles are present in any ethical dilemma; the family practitioner, however, needs to assess which principles are most relevant to any given situation and how other principles might also be addressed. Deciding which ethical principle is most pertinent in any given situation can be a difficult task. The decision often depends on your in-the-moment interpretation of the ethical principles, consultation with other professionals, and guidance from your profession's code(s) of ethics. What would be an action that you would define as promoting the clients' welfare in the case of the 14-year-old child with leukemia?

In reviewing your profession's codes of ethics, you find no statement that begins with "when counseling a family whose child has leukemia and whose religious beliefs do not support medical intervention, you must . . . ." What you will find in the codes of ethics are statements such as, "The primary responsibility of counselors is to respect the dignity (of clients) and to promote the welfare of clients" (ACA, 2005, p. 4); "Marriage and family counselors do not engage in activities that violate the legal standards of their community" (IAMFC, 2005, p. 11); or "Marriage and family therapists participate in activities that contribute to a better community and society" (AAMFT, 2001a, Section 6.6); and "Social workers may limit clients' right to self-determination when, in the social workers' professional judgment, clients' actions or potential actions pose a serious, foreseeable, and imminent risk to themselves or others" (NASW, 1996, 1.02).

So what can we glean from these statements that might help? The ACA's Code of Ethics makes beneficence the primary ethical responsibility. Okay, what action(s) serve(s) to promote the family's welfare? Respecting their welfare may mean respecting their autonomy to make decisions on their own. Yet respecting autonomy may contribute to the parents ending up in court either facing jail time or the removal of their child from their custody. Whose welfare is served then?

IAMFC's Code of Ethics asks you to ponder the legal standards of the community within which you practice. At issue here is the community's definition of "child neglect" (probably a state statute). For example, the state of Wisconsin defines child neglect as:

> Any person who is responsible for a child's welfare who, through his or her actions or failure to take action, intentionally contributes to the neglect of the child is guilty of a Class A misdemeanor or, if death is a consequence, a Class D felony. (State of Wisconsin, 2005)

So, if you are practicing in Wisconsin, respecting the parents' autonomy may contribute to the death of their child, a Class D felony. A similar statute exists in the state of Idaho. It appears that in both states the most relevant principle is beneficence, particularly the beneficence of a child.

The AAMFT code of ethics is more utilitarian, asking the marriage and family therapist to consider which course of action brings about the greatest good. In our family example, promoting the welfare of the child, who may not be fully informed about her own best interests, probably meets this ethical standard. This position is also supported by the NASW code of ethics and seems to align with community and state laws.

This family example shows the constructivist nature of ethical decision making when viewing problems through principle ethics. The words and intent of the codes, together with relevant legislation, all carry variations of meaning. In such cases, the local interpretation of ethical principles significantly influences a family practitioner's actions.

Freeman and Francis (2006) note one significant problem with principle ethics: They have been given relevance and authority separate from and prior to their actual use in ethical decision making. Autonomy, for example, is important in any given case, because autonomy is valued as a principled guide to action. In theory, it supercedes localized interpretations and applications of ethical standards. To be sure, principle ethics in some cases can remind family practitioners to be sensitive to diverse cultures when local interpretations and laws are not (for example, in supporting the welfare of gay and **lesbian** clients). In some cases, however, the principles themselves may not be culturally sensitive (for example, autonomy in relation to an Asian culture), and the practitioner is left to adapt the principle to fit the needs of the culture, thereby challenging the very foundation on which principle ethics is based (Dubois, 2004).

The family case we have presented highlights the potential impact of religion on the application of the ethical principles. Other cultural influences include race, ethnicity, nationality, age, gender, sexual/affectional orientation, ability and disability, and poverty. Dubois (2004) suggests that ethical principles may have universal relevance, but the focus should be on how the specific principles are enacted within a given culture. That is, the question is not whether autonomy is a relevant principle in Sri Lanka; rather it is how Sri Lankans perform respect for autonomy.

Virtue Ethics.   Where principle ethics focuses on actions and choices based on predetermined values (Corey, Corey & Callanan, 2007), virtue ethics focuses on the character traits of individuals or the profession (Kleist & White, 1997). Principle ethics asks, "What shall be *done*?" Virtue ethics asks, "What kind of person shall the family practitioner *be*?" What do you think? Is it possible that your ethical behavior as an emergent family counselor or therapist is more about personal moral being than a mere understanding and application of a set of ethical principles?

There are multiple positions on virtue ethics just as there are on principle ethics. Jordan and Meara (1990) define virtue as "nurtured habits grown mature in the context of a formative community and a shared set of purposes and assumptions" (p. 110). Virtue in this sense is not innate: It is learned. Although principle ethics can be taught, it is not as easy to teach integrity, courage, and humility. And if these are important virtues to have, how does one measure these virtues? Advocates of virtue ethics argue that family practitioners should not merely seek the safety of ethical behavior, as in principle ethics, but should aspire to an ethical ideal. At the beginning of this chapter, we considered some of the virtues that might serve as ethical ideals in family practice. Cohen and Cohen (1999) and Vasquez (1996) have long argued for ethical decision making based on principle ethics, but grounded in a virtue ethic foundation. For Vasquez, virtue ethics can facilitate multicultural practice in the same way that flexibility is enhanced by boundary setting.

For example, you are seeing a Native American family in counseling at a local agency that offers free counseling for those families with limited means. You have successfully guided the family to a place at which they would like to terminate the counseling relationship. At your final session, the family presents you with a blanket that they have made together. To them, the blanket represents a "thank you" for the services provided. Typically, great caution is suggested in all professional codes when considering the acceptance of a gift or bartering for therapeutic services. Vasquez suggests that the virtue of respect may contribute to understanding that the blanket is offered as a cultural means for expressing appreciation. Emphasis on the character of the individual and the profession provided by virtue ethics adds a sense of personal responsibility to the more external guidelines of principle ethics.

That said, virtue ethics has plenty of detractors. Like the challenge to principle ethics, virtue ethics can be challenged for their cultural relevance. Bersoff (1996) acknowledges the social construction and social embeddedness of virtues and community wisdom, the very foundation of a virtue ethics perspective. Think of the virtues that you hold dear. Where did they come from? Do you have any idea of the history of these virtues in your own cultures? The very nature of multiple cultures means that their will be a diversity of perspectives on what is defined as virtue and virtuous behavior.

The teachability of virtue ethics is an additional dilemma (Bersoff, 1996; Kitchener, 1996). Can the virtues of the helping professions be taught within a two- to three-year program? What about the nurtured habits that you developed within your family-of-origin? Assuming that some values were nurtured in you from the time you were an infant, what if these values do not fit well with the virtues of the helping professions? Would you be willing to give up values you have held all your life and adopt the values supported by your profession? What would that mean for you within your own family life? If professionally congruent virtues cannot be taught and learned during a graduate program, those programs may have to adopt the difficult position of choosing candidates who already possess professionally desirable attributes and values (Bersoff, 1996). What are the problems that accompany this idea? The problems would be even more complex if members of a profession had to agree on a set of professional virtues and then create a means of assessing candidates during the interview process. Impossible, you say! Maybe, but some preparational programs are currently attempting to do exactly that.

Participatory Ethics.   A third perspective on ethics is grounded in postmodern philosophy, thought, and sensibilities: It is called participatory ethics. Postmodernism believes in a multiplicity of realities and truths; it values people's meaning-making processes as they create narratives of experience; and it examines dominant cultures that impede the self-agency of people whose voices have had only marginal participation in society. Feminism, social constructionism, and **multiculturalism** all have embraced this shift away from the modern to the postmodern. Participatory ethics invites families to be co-contributors to the ethical decision-making processes in family practice (Rave & Larsen, 1995). Postmodernists have critiqued family counseling and therapies based in modernist philosophy as colonizing clients by viewing family practitioners as the keepers of knowledge and the people responsible for any decision related to counseling or therapy (see Hoffman, 1985). Participatory ethics seeks to include and value the knowledges brought to counseling or therapy by families. Client feedback on the processes of family practice is encouraged. That is, client input is valued as "expert" in relation to how individuals and families experience their own lives, and practitioner "expertness" is related to leadership of the therapeutic process.

For our family with the 14-year-old child, how might their stories of lived experience be prized? How, if at all, has the dominant discourse in which this family is situated oppressed their self-agency, their self-determination? A family practitioner adopting participatory ethics might invite and emphasize the family's experience and meaning-making processes in interactions with the dominant culture or the stories told by the court system about child neglect and how such stories influence the preferred view of their family. As participatory ethics attends to the marginalized, the voice of the 14-year-old child might be encouraged and amplified. The family counselor could work with the parents to help them imagine themselves through the eyes of their child, to imagine what the experience of the situation might be like and what the child's preferred choices might be. The postmodern shift to participatory ethics can be quite powerful: In this model, the family practitioner's position of power is counterbalanced by honoring the family's own power in their process of living.

We have introduced three perspectives on ethics: principle, virtue, and participatory. Take a moment to reflect on the essence of each of these perspectives and your emotional reaction to them. With principle ethics, you have externally derived guidelines based on at least six principles to guide your professional actions. Virtue ethics calls on you and the helping professions to examine the character traits essential to family practice and how these characteristics may impact ethical processes. Last, participatory ethics takes you to the space between you and your clients, to the relationship in which clinical decisions are co-constructed and negotiated with families. What are the potential positives in each that you see? What are the problems? What does your "gut" tell you about your thoughts and feelings about each? Now look at your answers to these questions. What do they say about you and your work with families? If you are not satisfied by one and only one perspective on ethics, then which blend fits for you? How would you integrate that blend? Continue to ponder such questions as we now move through various decision-making models.

Ethical Decision Making

Understanding principles and virtues alone does not resolve an ethical dilemma. Some process is necessary that utilizes these principles and virtues. What follows are descriptions of three ethical decision-making models related to the three ethics models we have already presented. These three models do not constitute all available ethical decision-making models. They are simply used to demonstrate how different perspectives might be applied.

Models of Ethical Decision Making

The ACA Code of Ethics (2005) states that "when counselors are faced with ethical dilemmas that are difficult to resolve, they are expected to engage in a carefully considered ethical decision-making process" (p. 3). This same code goes on to note that ". . . counselors are expected to be familiar with a credible model of decision making that can bear public scrutiny and its application" (p. 3). None of the other helping profession codes state the importance of understanding and utilizing ethical decision-making models so explicitly. Because no decision-making model has been shown to be better than any other, the responsibility is on the practitioner to demonstrate and justify publicly the value of solving an ethical dilemma in a particular way. What follows are brief descriptions of three ethical decision-making models.

Critical-Evaluation Model.   Kitchener's (1984) **critical-evaluation model** is based on the ethical principles of autonomy, beneficence, nonmaleficence, and justice. Today, we would include the principles of fidelity and veracity in this list, and use 8 steps in the critical-evaluation model (Corey, Corey, & Callanan, 2007). They are:

1. Identify the problem or dilemma: ethical, moral, and legal dimensions.
2. Identify potential issues, stakeholders, stakeholders' responsibilities, and the competing principles involved in the situation.
3. Review ethical guidelines of the profession against your own moral perspective on the situation.
4. Know the applicable laws and regulations of the state in which you practice.
5. Consult.
6. Consider possible courses of action, and the actions of all parties involved.
7. Enumerate possible consequences of various decisions for all stakeholders.
8. Decide which option is the best choice. (p. 21–23)

Let's walk through each step of this model with the family whose child has leukemia that the parents are addressing with prayer, using the critical-evaluation model. We provide only brief examples and not the complete process.

Step 1: Identify the problem: From an ethical standpoint, we have concerns regarding breaching client confidentiality and the welfare of the clients, including the child. Morally, you may be wondering about the safety and welfare of the child and about our tolerance for the parents' autonomous decision making.

Step 2: Identify potential issues involved: Do the parents know the potential legal conse-quences of their actions? Equally important, do you know the potential legal consequences of your actions as a family counselor or therapist? What legal responsibility do you have for any harm that befalls the child? Legally, are there any other stakeholders? What about grandparents? The state is a stakeholder because they are acting on behalf of the welfare of the child. What legal duty do you have as a family practitioner to the state?

The principles of autonomy, beneficence, nonmaleficence, justice, fidelity and veracity all seem pertinent here. Obviously autonomy is very pertinent as it relates to the princi-ple of beneficence and the duties imposed by mandatory reporting laws in various states. Nonmaleficence is a primary concern in relation to the child. Justice is also a concern: What is fair and to whom? If fairness implies affirming that both parents have an equal say in the medical decision, does the child have a say? Would that not be fair? What actions might you take that demonstrates fairness in relation to the state's interest? Who is involved in these discussions? In regard to fidelity, you have duties to both the parents and the child. As a licensed family practitioner, you also would have duties to the state. Feeling stretched in multiple directions yet? Veracity would require that you provide informed consent that spells out the relationships among the various constituents whom you must serve, including the family; its individual members, especially the child; and the state.

Step 3: Review ethical guidelines of profession: As we noted much earlier, ethical codes and standards of practice contain often conflicting guidelines and little that might help to resolve such a case easily. Family practitioners must respect the dignity and promote the wel-fare of the family; maintain cultural sensitivity, confidentiality, and privacy while respecting differing views toward disclosure of information; and uphold the professional laws of the state. In the end, it comes down to a very complex question: How does the family practi-tioner work with the family, demonstrate sensitivity for the family's perspective, and decide what constitutes the family's welfare?

Step 4: Know the applicable laws: From the *legal* standpoint, which again depends spe-cifically on various state laws, the parents' withholding of medical care for a life-threatening condition can be viewed as child neglect. If the child were to die, child abuse leading to death would most likely lead to a legal indictment. For the purpose of this example, let's make this step easy: The laws of your state define the parents' religious beliefs as harmful to the child and, therefore, require the family practitioner to report the parental position as intended child abuse.

Step 5: Obtain consultation: This step is by far the easiest and most often-used step by students engaged in family practice. It is also the first step to go once a person is working full-time in private practice or in agencies. Failure to seek consultation will almost always have negative results if an ethical decision is ever challenged within a professional associa-tion or in a court of law. Obtaining consultation can provide an opportunity to get feedback and recommendations regarding your decision-making process. The more uncomfortable you are in sharing your decision-making process in consultation, the more likely you are to be taking actions that you already know are not the best for your clients. Legal consultation is vital for any family counselor when considering the case above.

Step 6: Consider possible courses of action: At this step, creative thinking is necessary. This is the time for reflective processes. You want to take enough time to complete this step with the confidence that you have explored solutions from many angles. Your solutions also should address the actions of all of the people involved in a solution.

You decide to tell the parents that your primary obligation is to their 14-year-old child due to the state's interest in protecting children. You provide them with the options of either taking their child to a doctor or preparing to have the state remove their child from the home because you are required by law to call the child-protection agency to advise them of the parents' decision to avoid medical intervention. Your actions and words are firm and deliberate, but friendly. What are your reactions to such a course of action? To what principles are you paying primary attention? Whose interests have been protected?

A second option is to remain loyal to your clients' religious beliefs. You understand the legal requirements placed on you and the legal context in which the family is embedded. Autonomy and cultural sensitivity are your main reasons and, although the results of such actions may lead to harm for the child, you believe that promoting the family's welfare is best served by promoting its autonomy. The idea that not all laws are ethical is central to your reasoning. In addition, you believe that the laws of the state are secondary to the larger laws set forth by the family's religious "higher power." Although such actions may not be what the majority of family practitioners would do in a similar situation, you believe that at times civil disobedience truly provides the best ethical action.

What other ethical stances are possible and what principles support these stances?

Step 7: Enumerate possible consequences of the various options.   For the first option, the child probably would receive the medical care indicated. The parents might be placed on probation and mandated to a parenting program, after which they might regain custody of their child. The parents themselves might be bitter and even more distrustful of both the government and family counseling or therapy. There is very little chance that the parents will ever consider therapeutic interventions of any kind again. Imagine this case for a moment. Given today's world, the media already will have attended to this story, and your actions now are known to thousands. These thousands will now take in this event and connect it to their attitudes toward the helping professions. Should the awareness of the public nature of your decision factor into your decision-making process?

The second option will invariably lead the parents to respect your ability to honor the family's right to make decisions regarding their child. It is still uncertain as to whether your actions will lead to further involvement with the authorities—either for the parents or for you. Quite likely, the child's condition will worsen and may lead to death. How will you feel about your decision then? This action, too, will catch the attention of the public. How might the public view family practitioners with this option?

Step 8: Choose what appears to be the best course of action.   Hopefully you see the two options described here as only two of many more options that might be available. The very application of this model based solely on principle ethics demonstrates how often no-win possibilities occur. Let's see if virtue ethics adds anything to our considerations.

A Virtue-Ethics Model.   Most professional codes are based on principle ethics. Except for a few aspirational statements in some codes, there is very little in the documents themselves that pertains to virtue ethics. As we have noted before, virtue ethics requires the professional to look inward and make space for a self-reflective process. Attending to oneself in ethical decision making opens the door for the emotional experiences of empathy and compassion. Cohen and Cohen (1999) view the role of emotion in decision making as a legitimate component of a "morally good motive . . . (and) that moral action is no mere affair of rules but is instead infused with emotion, human relatedness, and sensitivity to the nuances of individual context" (p. 24). A decision-making process based on virtue ethics would include many of the questions below:

- What is my "gut" telling me about the family's situation?
- If I were in these parents' shoes, what might I feel or want to do? How would I answer the same question for the child(ren), extended family members, family friends, or the community?
- How important is my own spiritual/religious value system to me, and how hard might I fight to have it respected? Does this tell me anything about what the family is experiencing?

- How open am I to accepting that my view of the "right" choice might be different from the view of the "right" choice held by various family members?
- How open am I to accepting that my view my might be different from the state's view? Am I willing to be courageous and stand up for my view or for the clients' views if they are different from what the law requires?
- Do I agree with what the codes suggest I do in this situation? Do the codes help me to be the preferred family practitioner I want to be?
- Which possible courses of action best fit my preferred view of myself as a family practitioner? Which personal and professional values are activated in me as I face this dilemma: caring, compassion, judgment, courage, humility, connectedness? Other values or virtues?
- Which choice am I willing to live with? How ready am I to make a choice and live with the uncertainty of its outcome?

When infusing your ethical decision making with virtue ethics, you bring yourself deeply into the ethical decision-making process. How central to the decision-making process are you willing to place yourself as a family practitioner? Is it possible to be too central? What would that look like for you?

Participatory Ethics.   What might an ethical decision-making model based on participatory ethics look like? The specific process we will propose here is based on the **feminist ethical decision-making model** constructed by Rave and Larsen (1995) and the model for *the vulnerable therapist* described by Coale (1998). Participatory ethics retains much of the structure of a rational-evaluative process and still requires the self-reflection of a feeling–intuitive process. But instead of leaving ethical decisions completely in the hands of the family practitioner, participatory ethics focus on the relational, co-constructed knowledge that comes from active involvement of clients in the decision-making process. The model may be applied as follows:

1. Recognizing a problem: Problem recognition comes from a combination of perspectives. The family practitioner's personal and professional knowledge, competence, and "gut" feelings are combined with the clients' local knowledge and "gut" feelings in an effort to understand and clarify the ethical dilemma. The family practitioner's task is to open space within the counseling or therapy sessions for the clients to inform the ethical process. Space is opened by actively encouraging input, feedback, and the sharing of client perspectives on the counseling process.

2. Defining the problem: Once you and your clients come to an understanding of the ethical dilemma that is present, each party contributes to a conversation about how to define and frame the problem. All the questions posed during the virtue ethics model related to stakeholders and feelings are relevant here. What extends the virtue ethics model is the inclusion of the clients in defining the problem as well as understanding the cultural values that you as family practitioner bring to the process. From a postmodern perspective, the cultural "selves" of family practitioners are not simply acknowledged and managed, but are embraced and brought into the conversations with clients. In this way, the emphasis is on situating our "selves" as cultural beings within the decision-making process, highlighting, not hiding, such influences. The family practitioner trusts the family to handle the very human, ethical struggle in which the practitioner and all other parties are engaged.

3. Developing solutions: This step of the participatory ethics model is very similar to steps 5 and 6 of the virtue ethics model. Again, the defining element for the participatory model is valuing the client's conceptualizations of solutions and their reaction to each possibility.

In developing solutions, consultation is integral to the process and may involve inviting still other voices into the collaborative conversations held with clients.

Even though we are presenting the participatory ethics model in linear steps, in this model, like most approaches to family systems, the steps are recursive—with each step influencing and being influenced by the others. Further, it is not uncommon for each additional step to require adjustments and reconsiderations in earlier steps. All of this is especially true when integrating consultation into the process. Consultation may require circulating back to previous conversations as well as being integrated throughout the rest of the process. In participatory ethics, no single step can be a one-time occurrence in the process of ethical decision making.

4. Choosing a solution: Just as the virtue ethics model values self-reflections at both the rational and emotional levels, participatory ethics values conversations with clients about their processes and reactions, rationally and emotionally, to possible solutions. Respect for self-agency is central to the dialogue and the goal is to select a solution that all parties, including the family practitioner, can support.

5. Reviewing the process: This step starts with the family practitioner openly reflecting on all aspects of the ethical decision-making process in which she or he is engaged.

- Would the family practitioner want to be treated this way?
- How are the values and personal characteristics of the family practitioner influencing the choices that have been made?
- What has been the effect of the family practitioner's power in these ethical conversations?
- Have the clients' perspectives been taken into account? (Rave & Larsen, 1995)

To open oneself to deliberate reflection may serve to "check" the credibility and trustworthiness of the constructed solution. It also models for clients the importance of self-reflection in this participatory process.

6. Implementing and evaluating the decision: Participatory ethics recognizes that ethical dilemmas force everyone into a state of vulnerability and sometimes anxiety (Coale, 1998). It is a model in which all parties participate in both the decision making and the consequences of the decisions made. The process cannot end with implementation of a decision: Evaluation and regular reevaluation are essential.

- Does the outcome continue to feel right?
- How has the decision affected the therapeutic process?
- Is the solution we chose the best we can do?

7. Continuing reflection: The last step in the participatory ethics model returns the family practitioner to self-reflection and a consideration of the ethical decision-making process in a removed or disengaged space.

- What did I learn from the process about myself and about the participatory process?
- How might this experience affect me in the future?
- How, if at all, have I changed as a result of my participation in the process?

Not only is examination of the outcome for the client required, but so is reflection on the decision's impact in relation to the family practitioner. Each and every decision made extends into the future, well beyond the current clients' situation. Valuing personal/professional experience of the process through continued reflection facilitates greater awareness and learning for you as a family practitioner and enhances the ethical process with future clients.

We have presented only three ethical decision-making models. What reactions do you have to each of them? What feelings surface? Your thoughts and feelings are speaking to the kind of person you want to be as a family practitioner.

Commonly Discussed Ethical Dilemmas in Family Practice

We will now shift to a discussion of some of the most commonly encountered, or constructed, ethical dilemmas when working with families and family members. Whole texts have been written addressing ethics in family practice (AAMFT, 1998, 2001b; Golden, 2004; Herlihy & Corey, 2006; Vesper & Brock, 1991; Wilcoxon, Remley, Gladding, & Huber, 2007; Woody & Woody, 2001): The most common dilemmas that surface are related to confidentiality, multiple clients, informed consent, and gender and multicultural issues. We now will delineate some of the issues that family practitioners have faced in these four areas. This is not a comprehensive list and there are no easy answers to propose. We note these issues so that you will know that you are not alone when you are confronted with similar ethical problems.

A Learning Challenge

Family practitioners actually have very little time to reflect on their place in ethical decision-making processes. Managed care has not found a way to reimburse self-awareness. Here's a challenge for you: Take a practicing family counselor or therapist to lunch and ask her or him some of the questions we have asked you to consider. When finished, ask your companion what it was like to spend 30 to 60 minutes in conversation with you about such topics? Now, if you succeed in being genuinely curious during your questioning, we are willing to bet that the majority of family practitioners will say something like, "You know, I don't get to do this very often: This was great! I wish I could find more time to do this." Reflective conversations like this engage professionals in self-care, help to prevent burnout, and encourage ethical practices. ●

Confidentiality.   Trust in any therapeutic relationship is intimately tied to the guarantee of **confidentiality**. The ability to speak openly and with emotional honesty is supported by a trusting relationship that ensures a respect for privacy. This right to privacy in psychotherapy is recognized in all fifty states and by the federal government in HIPAA standards and Supreme Court decisions. But what degree of privacy can a family counselor or therapist truly uphold? Confidentiality can be an enormous responsibility for a practitioner working with just one person. When working with multiple people in one room, the challenges to confidentiality increase exponentially. It is in the subtexts of confidentiality and family practice that the ethical issues become extremely difficult, especially in conceptualizing the client(s) served; providing informed consent; and handling relational matters in an individual context.

Conceptualizing the Client(s).   If one's practice consists solely of individual clients, the definition of client is clear: It is the person sitting across from you in a counseling or therapy session. The more systemically oriented therapies, however, embraced the family-as-a-whole as *the* client—with many, like Whitaker, insisting that all members of the family be present before therapy begins. The first practitioners of **Bowen family therapy, structural family therapy**, and the various strategic models emphasized family dynamics in which individuals were little more than parts of an interaction or actors in a systemic drama. In the last decade, there has been a concerted effort to reinstate the individual into family systems theories, with the postmodern models tending to conceptualize families and clients as those individuals who are in conversation about any given problem. In these later models, those in conversation about a problem determine who needs to be involved in "family" sessions.[2] What happens to confidentiality in these shifting conceptualizations of family is at the heart of one whole set of ethical concerns? Even within systemic orientations, there are those who choose to approach families not as one client but as multiple clients, a perspective that is assumed in most state laws.

Remley and Herlihy (2005) indicate that laws hold individuals, not the collection of people called a "family," accountable for actions that may violate the freedom of others. This should not be surprising in a society that values individualism over collectivism. But it also has a similar impact on the more practical standards of practice involved in professional codes.

A clear example relates to the use of case notes in family practice. If the client is *the family*, there is *one* client. Logically, the family practitioner would write *one* set of case notes for the *one* client. This is not necessarily so: IAMFC (2005), for example, suggests that "in situations involving multiple clients, couple and family counselors provide individual clients with parts of records related directly to them, protecting confidential information related to other clients who have not authorized release" (p. 6). In both the law and this professional code, one family of five equals five individuals. To meet HIPAA standards, each individual has to have his or her own records, notes, consent, and other individual data. Having multiple clients in counseling or therapy has a direct impact on informed consent.

Informed Consent.   AAMFT (2001a, 2001b) notes that confidentiality and informed consent are interrelated. Specific applications of confidentiality and its limitations need to be discussed early and often in treatment. Further, the family practitioner and the clients need to agree not only on those limitations mandated by law, but also those that the therapist may set for effective treatment.

ACA (2005) echoes this position, calling on

> . . . counselors [to] clearly define who is considered "the client" and discuss expecta-tions and limitations of confidentiality. Counselors seek agreement and document in writing such agreements among all involved parties having capacity to give consent concerning each individual's right to confidentiality and obligations to preserve the confidentiality of information known. (p. 8)

IAMFC (2005) supplements the ACA code, suggesting that "marriage and family coun-selors have an obligation to determine and inform counseling participants who is identi-fied as the primary client . . . (and) make clear when there are obligations to an individual, couple, family, third party or institution" (p. 5).

Even if you are successful in negotiating a contract that identifies the client as the whole family, issues of confidentiality still persist. The limits on confidentiality with a whole family are the same as those that exist in group counseling or therapy: The practitioner cannot guarantee that members of the family won't disclose essentially private information to others outside of the session. This potential dynamic also weakens, if not removes, the legal benefit of privileged communication (Remley & Herlihy, 2005). In short, communica-tion between a client and yourself as counselor is valued legally, in that a court of law may find the benefits of protecting privacy outweighs the public's need to know the content of therapeutic conversations. However, once another person is present in the room, as with couple and family work, the legal protection of privileged communication no longer exists. If clients viewed their individual rights and protections from a legal perspective, agreeing to family counseling might not be in their individual best interest.

Handling Relational Matters in an Individual Context.   Given the propensity of both the law and professional codes to designate the client as each individual, there are a host of relational concerns that must be clarified and addressed before counseling or therapy can begin. Among these issues are: "extramarital affairs, commitment to the relationship, sexual activities/preferences/orientations, criminal activities, substance use, and mental states suggesting the risk of violence and dangerousness to self or others" (Woody & Woody, 2001, p. 31). Similar issues for children and adolescents must be considered, as well as "behaviors that pose potential risk to the child's health and welfare, e.g., truancy, substance use, gang affiliations, etc." (p. 31).

From the IAMFC (2005) Code of Ethics: "Marriage and family counselors inform clients that statements made by a family member to the counselor during an individual counseling, consultation, or collateral contact are to be treated as confidential" (Section B-7, pp. 8–9). If both your professional approach and your personal values are grounded in the idea that joining with "family secrets" does not promote the welfare of the family, what do you do with this predicament? Again, from IAMFC (2005), Section B-7:

> . . . the marriage and family counselor should clearly identify the client in counseling, which may be the couple or family system. Couple and family counselors do not maintain family secrets, collude with some family members against others, or otherwise contribute to dysfunctional family system dynamics. (p. 9)

All of the family practice codes support individual confidentiality, but only if such actions do not contribute to maintaining unhealthy family dynamics. There is not a great deal of direction in these guidelines for handling ethical dilemmas related to the common issues we have discussed. In holding to individual confidentiality within the context of family counseling or therapy, obvious concerns surface with the principle of beneficence and your obligation to promote client welfare.

Gender and Cultural Issues.   Feminists long have noted that the *normal* family, across cultures, has not always been so good for women. A gender perspective in ethics reminds us that patriarchy has real effects on both genders and has to be taken into account when people are engaged in ethical decision making. Feminists also remind us that patriarchy is just one form of oppression and that discrimination on the basis of race, gender, disability, religion, age, sexual orientation, cultural background, national origin, marital status, and political affiliation still have to be factored deliberately into ethical stances.

Because discrimination, oppression, and marginalization have been such a strong part of the social contexts in which we live, a consideration of gender and cultural perspectives in ethical decision making is essential. In spite of what may be codified in law, there are, indeed, multiple perspectives on "the family" that emanate from various cultures. Western cultures tend to portray the nuclear family as normal, limiting it to parents and their children. If the law and Western culture want to recognize aunts, uncles, cousins, grandparents, and ancestors as part of a family system, these family members are called **extended family**. Such languaging, easily as much as physical separation, distances individuals from their natural support systems. In cultures in Africa, Asia, the Middle East, and South America, as well as in some Native American societies, many different members—and sometimes multiple wives—and multiple generations are included in the conceptualization of family. Such a conceptualization of family often can bridge the physical distance between individuals and create a very different ethical stance in the world.

Even in Western cultures today, the forms that constitute family vary widely from the nuclear model that has been enshrined as normal. Functional families are led by single mothers, single fathers, grandparents, single gay fathers, single lesbian mothers, gay co-parents, lesbian co-parents, and cohabiting parents who have never married. Any of these families may also include biological children, children in foster care, children from surrogate parents, or adopted children. In the United States, we are experiencing a cultural war in relation to the debate about what constitutes marriage and the family. It is a war that recognizes that the definitions of both have already changed. Because there is no evidence of inherent harm in any of these different couple and family arrangements, family practitioners have an affirmative moral and ethical responsibility to support and care for families in all of their diverse forms (Dworkin, 1992).

Think about your own family-of-origin. What perspectives on family, culture, and gender were contained in your upbringing? What were the virtues and limitations contained in your family's worldview? How many kinds of families and cultural perspectives have you encountered in your lifetime? What experiences, if any, did your family-of-origin have of discrimination or oppression based on cultural differences or because your family had a different structure than the heterosexual nuclear family that has been declared "normal" in the dominant culture?

Professional Regulations and Legal Requirements

Stukie and Bergen (2001) note that:

> Professional regulation has to do with two things. The first is licensure or certification, which involves deciding who is allowed to perform a certain function and, of all those performing it, who can use a particular title. The second involves setting the standards of acceptable practice. (p. 2)

Although we tend to associate professional regulations with the professional boards of each state, there are actually many groups that get involved in the process of safeguarding both the public and the profession. Among these groups are voluntary professional organizations, state regulatory agencies, federal regulatory agencies, the judicial system, third-party payers (that is, insurance companies and managed care companies), national regulatory associations, and sometimes international regulatory entities. Again, each of these groups has a recursive influence on the others: We often find, for example, that there is very little difference between the legal requirements for the practice of marital and family therapy and the certification requirements of various professional organizations. Indeed, it is not uncommon for licensure requirements to include specific professional certifications as a first step toward licensure.

All of the professional regulation agencies attempt to address three questions related to family practice: What is family counseling or therapy? How is competence as a family practitioner assessed and measured? How valid and relevant are those competency measures for the protection of consumers?

Stukie and Bergen (2001) suggest 10 principles that should be considered in the development of professional regulations in the field. Among their recommendations are a comprehensive model based on effective professional development and growth, rather than minimal competence; fully funded, staffed, and empowered regulatory boards; integrated regulatory boards that address all aspects of psychotherapy, rather than separate disciplines; ongoing competency assessments that are demonstrable in spite of the costs and logistical problems that may be involved; standards of practice that detail requirements related to advertising, record keeping, informed consent, and other legal expectations for practitioners; disciplinary procedures that are immediately responsive to the needs of clients and practitioners; and the right of consumers to choose the mental health providers of their choice.

The field of psychotherapy in general, and couple and family therapy in particular, is no longer dominated by psychiatrists and doctoral-level psychologists. By far, most of the couple and family practitioners are now trained at the masters level and have completed approximately two years of supervised practice before being evaluated and obtaining a license. This dramatic change has taken place in just the last 30 to 40 years. The number of people seeking psychotherapeutic services is also on the rise. To protect consumers and define professional identities and competence, professional regulations and state laws will become increasingly specific in their definitions and requirements for practice. Although it is impossible to legislate virtue, morality, good judgment, or clinical skills, state laws and professional regulations forge a professional covenant with the public. These regulations always are based on the application of principle ethics—and the principles always reflect the dominant community standards of the state or organization enacting them.

Indeed, state and national laws often take certain moral, ethical, and professional issues out of the hands of the practitioner. Helping professionals in most states, for example, are mandated to break confidentiality and take affirmative, prescribed actions if (a) clients are dangerous to self, to others, and, in some states, to property; (b) clients engage in or suffer child or elder abuse; or (c) the helping professional is otherwise required to do so by courts in the administration and application of specific laws. Such mandates are considered in law to be so serious that the covenant with consumers requires a consistent outcome every time (that is, reporting)—even if the outcome can be demonstrated to create more problems than it solves.

State and federal legal requirements also have created standards of care for psychotherapeutic practice. This is especially true for those professions and professionals who must operate under HIPAA requirements and standards. Failure to meet professional standards of practice is the most common grounds for malpractice and incurred liability. It is what makes professional liability insurance a necessity these days and increasingly expensive to purchase.

▪ Conclusion

Ethical practice is supported by an understanding of ethical principles, virtues, the law, professional codes of ethics, ethical decision-making models, and you. If you are in the presence of your client(s), you are engaged in an ethical encounter—from the time you prepare for an upcoming session through completion of your weekly case notes. During all aspects of the encounter, you have the potential to harm or promote the well-being of your client(s). An ethical practitioner recognizes the subtle, nuanced ways in which counseling or therapy influences our clients. Ethical encounters highlight the importance of personal awareness and presence in therapeutic relationships.

Where to Go From Here

You can access the main ethical codes related to counseling, psychotherapy, and family practice at the following websites:

American Association for Marriage and Family Therapy:

http://www.aamft.org/resources/LRMPlan/Ethics/ethicscode2001.asp

American Association of Pastoral Counselors:

http://www.aapc.org/ethics.cfm

American Counseling Association:

http://www.cacd.org/codeofethics.html

American Psychological Association:

http://www.apa.org/ethics/code2002.html

International Association of Marriage and Family Counselors:

http://www.iamfc.com/ethical_codes.html

National Association of Social Workers:

http://www.socialworkers.org/pubs/code/code.asp

Recommended Readings

American Association for Marriage and Family Therapy. (1998). *A marriage and family therapist's guide to ethical and legal practice: Answers to questions on current ethical topics and legal considerations in MFT practice.* Alexandria, VA: Author. This short booklet, part of AAMFT's legal and risk-management program, uses the AAMFT code of ethics to address many of the current issues in the practice of marriage and family therapy.

American Association for Marriage and Family Therapy. (2001). *User's guide to the AAMFT code of ethics.* Alexandria, VA: Author. This book provides vignettes and commentary for each part of the AAMFT code. For programs based on an AAMFT model, this is an excellent casebook.

Coale, H. W. (1998). *The vulnerable therapist: Practicing psychotherapy in an age of anxiety.* New York: Haworth Press. Helen Coale has written a compelling ethical text on the value of virtue and participatory ethics. Her foundation in postmodern, social constructionism places her work on the cutting edge of family practice ethics.

Cohen, E. D., & Cohen, G. S. (1999). *The virtuous therapist: Ethical practice of counseling and psychotherapy.* Pacific Grove, CA: Brooks/Cole-Wadsworth. This is the single best book available on virtue ethics. For those who want to review the essential virtues for professional helpers as well as consider applications in practice, Cohen and Cohen have covered the waterfront.

Corey, G., Corey, M. S., & Callanan, P. (2007). *Issues and ethics in the helping professions* (7th ed.). Belmont, CA: Brooks/Cole-Thomson. This is the most used teaching text in the counseling profession. It is also the most comprehensive, covering ethical practice with individuals, groups, couples, and families.

Golden, L. B. (2004). *Case studies in marriage and family therapy* (2nd ed.). Upper Saddle River, NJ: Pearson, Merrill, Prentice-Hall. This book presents 19 cases covering a broad range of issues and applying an equally broad range of family-practice models.

Stukie, K., & Bergen, L. P. (2001). *Professional regulation in marital and family therapy.* Boston: Allyn and Bacon. This is a book for those who want to consider best practices in the development of professional regulations. All students and family practitioners, however, will find the state-by-state listing of legal requirements and regulations in marriage and family therapy extremely helpful.

Wilcoxon, S. A., Remley, T. P., Gladding, S. T., & Huber, C. H. (2007). *Ethical, legal, and professional issues in the practice of marriage and family therapy.* Columbus, OH: Pearson/Merrill/Prentice-Hall. A comprehensive text that addresses contemporary ethical issues, family law, and professional identity, as well general ethical and legal requirements for family practice.

Woody, R. H., & Woody, J. D. (Eds.). (2001). *Ethics in marriage and family therapy.* Washington, DC: American Association for Marriage and Family Therapy. This AAMFT-sponsored manual covers the ethical landscape and provides commentary and references that are extremely useful in considering various aspects of professional practice.

References

Adler, A. (1938). *Social interest: A challenge to mankind* (J. Linton & R. Vaughan, Trans.). London: Faber & Faber. (Original work published 1933)

Adler, A. (1946). *Understanding human nature* (W. B. Wolfe, Trans.). New York: Greenberg. (Original work published 1927)

American Association for Marriage and Family Therapy. (1998). *A marriage and family therapist's guide to ethical and legal practice: Answers to questions on current ethical topics and legal considerations in MFT practice.* Alexandria, VA: Author.

American Association for Marriage and Family Therapy. (2001a). *AAMFT code of ethics.* Alexandria, VA: Author.

American Association for Marriage and Family Therapy. (2001b). *User's guide to the AAMFT code of ethics.* Alexandria, VA: Author.

American Counseling Association. (2005). *ACA code of ethics.* Alexandria, VA: Author.

Ansbacher, H. L. (1992). Alfred Adler's concepts of community feeling and of social interest and the relevance of community feeling for old age. *Individual Psychology, 48*(4), 402–412.

Aristotle. (1985). *Nicomachean ethics* (T. Irwin, Trans.). Indianapolis, IN: Hackett. (Original work written 350 B.C.)

Austin, K. M., Moline, M. E., & Williams, G. T. (1990). *Confronting malpractice: Legal and ethical dilemmas in psychotherapy.* Newbury Park, CA: Sage.

Bateson, G. (1979). *Mind in nature.* New York: Dutton.

Bellah, R. N., Madsen, R., Sullivan, W. M., Swidler, A., & Tipton, S. M. (1991). *The good society.* New York: Random House.

Bellah, R. N., Madsen, R., Sullivan, W. M., Swidler, A., & Tipton, S. M. (1996). *Habits of the heart: Individualism and commitment in American life* (rev. ed.). Berkeley, CA: University of California Press. (Original work published 1985)

Bersoff, D. N. (1996). The virtue of principle ethics. *The Counseling Psychologist, 24*(1), 86–91.

Bitter, J. R., Robertson, P. E., Roig, G., & Disque, J. G. (2004). Definitional ceremonies: Integrating community into multicultural counseling sessions. *Journal of Multicultural Counseling and Development, 32,* 272–282.

Bitter, J. R., & West, J. (1979). An interview with Heinz Ansbacher. *Journal of Individual Psychology, 35*(1), 95–110.

Breunlin, D. C., Schwartz, R. C., & MacKune-Karrer, B. (1997). *Metaframeworks: Transcending the models of family therapy.* San Francisco: Jossey-Bass. (Original work published 1992)

Cicero, M. T. (1991). *On duties* (M. T. Griffin & E. M. Atkins, Eds.). Cambridge, England: Cambridge University Press. (Original work written 44 B.C.)

Coale, H. W. (1998). *The vulnerable therapist: Practicing psychotherapy in an age of anxiety.* New York: Haworth Press.

Cohen, E. D., & Cohen, G. S. (1999). *The virtuous therapist: Ethical practice of counseling and psychotherapy.* Pacific Grove, CA: Brooks/Cole-Wadsworth.

Corey, G., Corey, M. S., & Callanan, P. (2007). *Issues and ethics in the helping professions* (7th ed.). Belmont, CA: Brooks/Cole-Thomson.

Dworkin, S. D. (1992). *Counseling gay men and lesbians.* Alexandria, VA: American Counseling Association.

DuBois, J. M. (2004). Universal ethical principles in a diverse universe: A commentary on Monshi and Zieglmayer's case study. *Ethics and Behavior, 14,* 313–319.

Freeman, S. J., & Francis, P. C. (2006). Casuistry: A complement to principle ethics and a foundation for ethical decisions. *Counseling Values, 50,* 142–153.

Gilligan, C. (1982). *In a different voice.* Cambridge, MA: Harvard University Press.

Golden, L. B. (2004). *Case studies in marriage and family therapy* (2nd ed.). Upper Saddle River, NJ: Merrill/Prentice-Hall.

Haley, J. (1963). *Strategies of psychotherapy.* New York: Grune & Stratton.

Herlihy, B., & Corey, G. (2006). *ACA ethical standards casebook* (6th ed.). Alexandria, VA: American Counseling Association.

Hill, A. (2004). Ethical analysis in counseling. *Counseling and Values, 48,* 131–148.

Hoffman, L. (1985). Beyond power and control: Toward a 'second order' family systems therapy, *Family Systems Medicine, 3*(4), 381–396.

International Association of Marriage and Family Counselors. (2005). *IAMFC code of ethics.* Alexandria, VA: Author.

Jensen, D. (2005). So, what exactly is a dual relationship? *The Therapist, 17*(4), 16–19.

Jordon, A. E., & Meara, N. M. (1990). Ethics and the professional practice of psychologists: The role of virtues and principles. *Professional Psychology: Research and Practice, 21,* 107–114.

Kerr, M., & Bowen, M. (1988). *Family evaluation.* New York: Norton.

Kitchener, K. S. (1984). Intuition, critical evaluation, and ethical principles: The foundation for ethical decisions in counseling psychology. *The Counseling Psychologist, 12*(3), 43–55.

Kitchener, K. S. (1996). There is more to ethics than principles. *The Counseling Psychologist, 24,* 92–97.

Kleist, D. M., & White, L. J. (1997). The values of counseling: A disparity between the philosophy of prevention in counseling and counselor practice and training. *Counseling and Values, 41,* 128–140.

Lum, D. (2003). *Culturally competent practice: A framework for understanding diverse groups and justice issues* (2nd ed.). Pacific Grove, CA: Brooks/Cole-Thomson.

McCarthy, I. C. (2001). Fifth province re-versings: The social construction of women lone parents' inequality and power. *Journal of Family Therapy, 23,* 253–277.

Meara, N. M., Schmidt, L. D., & Day, J. D. (1996). Principles and virtues: A foundation for ethical decisions, policies, and character. *The Counseling Psychologist, 24,* 4–77.

Minuchin, S. (1974). *Families and family therapy.* Cambridge, MA: Harvard University Press.

Minuchin, S. (Speaker). (2004, June). *New developments: 40 years later.* Presentation at the annual meeting of the South Carolina Association for Marriage and Family Therapy, Mount Pleasant, SC.

National Association of Social Workers. (1996). *NASW code of ethics*. Washington, DC: Author.

Plato. (1992). *The republic* (G. M. A. Grube, Trans.; C. D. C. Reeve, 2nd ed., rev.). Indianapolis, IN: Hackett. (Original work written 380 B.C.)

Rave, E. J., & Larsen, C. C. (1995). *Ethical decision making in therapy: Feminist perspectives*. New York: Guilford.

Remley, T. P., & Herlihy, B. (2005). *Ethical, legal, and professional issues in counseling* (2nd ed.). Upper Saddle River, NJ: Merrill/Prentice-Hall.

Satir, V. M. (1983). *Conjoint family therapy* (3rd ed.). Palo Alto, CA: Science and Behavior Books.

Schön, D. A. (1983). *The reflective practitioner: How professionals think in action*. New York: Basic Books.

Silverstein, L. B., & Goodrich, T. J. (Eds.). (2003). *Feminist family therapy: Empowerment in social context*. Washington, DC: American Psychological Association.

Sperry, L. (2007). *The ethical and professional practice of counseling and psychotherapy*. Boston: Allyn & Bacon.

State of Wisconsin. (2005). Chapter 948:21. *Wisconsin penal code* (revised). Madison, WI: Author.

Stukie, K., & Bergen, L. P. (2001). *Professional regulation marital and family therapy*. Boston: Allyn and Bacon.

Vasquez, M. J. T. (1996). Will virtue ethics improve ethical conduct in multicultural settings and interactions? *The Counseling Psychologist, 24,* 98–104.

Vesper, J. H., & Brock, G. W. (1991). *Ethics, legalities, and professional practice issues in marriage and family therapy*. Boston: Allyn and Bacon.

Wadsworth. (2007). Codes of ethics for the helping professions (3rd ed.) Belmont, CA: Author.

Whitaker, C. A. (1976). The hindrance of theory in clinical work. In P. J. Guerin (Ed.), *Family therapy: Theory and practice* (pp. 154–164). New York: Gardner Press.

Wilcoxon, S. A., Remley, Jr., T. P., Gladding, S. T., & Huber, C. H. (2007). *Ethical, legal, and professional issues in the practice of marriage and family therapy*. Columbus, OH: Pearson/Merrill/Prentice-Hall.

Woody, R. H., & Woody, J. D. (Eds.). (2001). *Ethics in marriage and family therapy*. Washington, DC: American Association for Marriage and Family Therapy.

Endnotes

[1] HIPAA stands for the *Health Insurance Portability and Accountability Act* of 1996 and, among other things, it sets very strict standards for how patients' medical records may be used. By extension, these requirements apply to any licensed person or group accepting third-party payments and/or filing reports with third-parties.

[2] For an example of such a session in action, see Bitter, Robertson, Roig, and Disque (2004).

PART 2

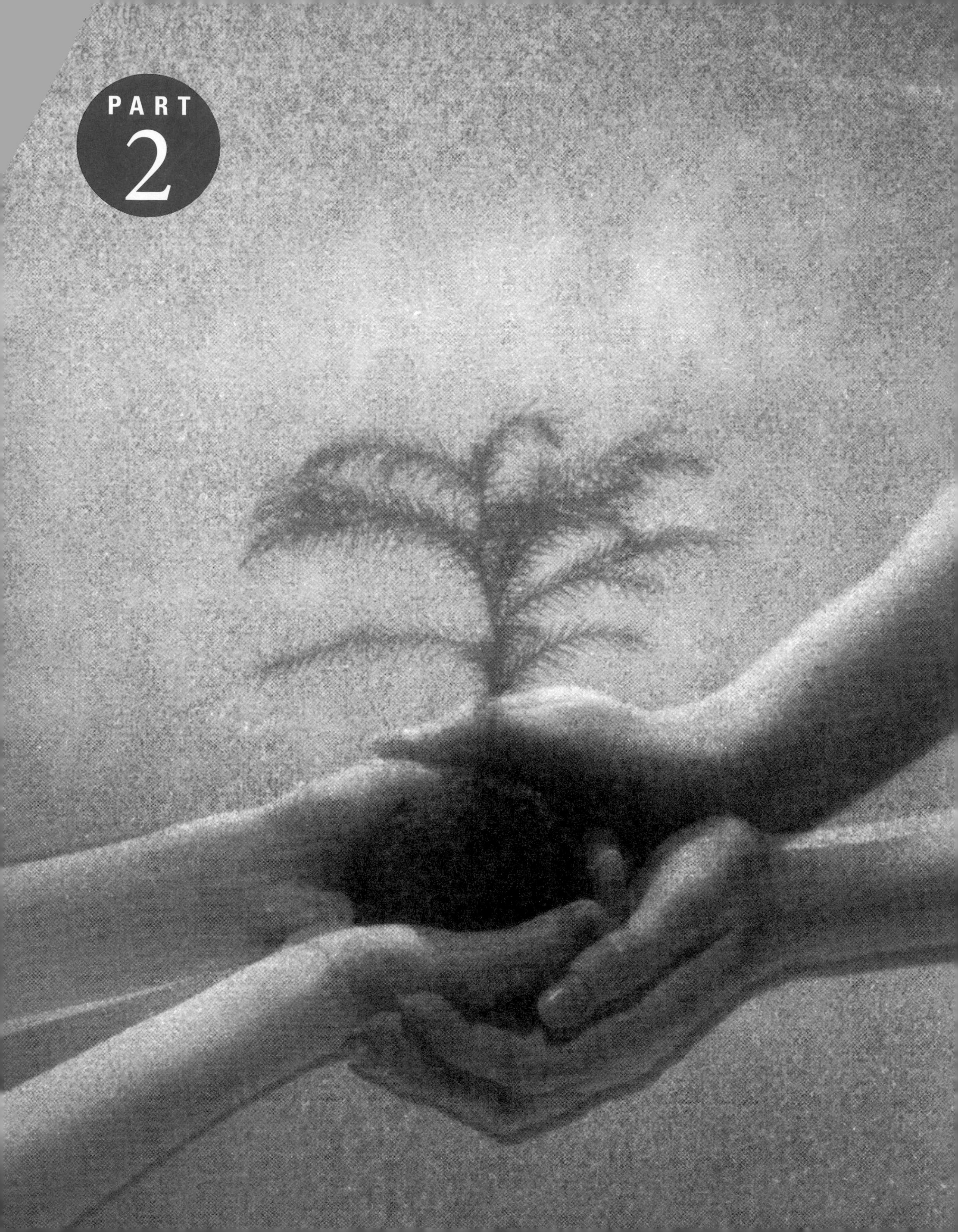

Theories and Techniques of Family Therapy and Counseling

Introduction to the Case
of the Quest Family

Chapter 4 Multigenerational Family
Therapy

Chapter 5 Adlerian Family Therapy

Chapter 6 Human Validation Process
Model

Chapter 7 Symbolic-Experiential Family
Therapy

Chapter 8 Structural Family Therapy

Chapter 9 Strategic Family Therapy

Chapter 10 Solution-Focused and
Solution-Oriented Therapy

Chapter 11 Postmodernism, Social
Construction, and Narratives
in Family Therapy

Chapter 12 Feminist Family Therapy

Chapter 13 Cognitive-Behavioral Family
Therapy

Chapter 14 Parenting for the 21st Century

Introduction to the Case
of the Quest Family

The Biography of the Quest Family

Quest Family Genogram

References

One of the best ways to learn about a theory is to see it in action. Live demonstrations are often the best way to make initial observations about therapeutic process with families. There are also many useful videotapes and DVDs that will allow you to "sit-in" with master therapists at work.[1] I have also created a short video segment for each of the theories covered in this book, which will demonstrate one of two interventions associated with each model.

I have attempted to give you some of the same kind of demonstration experience through the creation of the Quest family. Toward the end of each theory chapter, I will present the Quest family case as if they were seeing a therapist who uses that chapter's approach. Each example includes dialogue that I hope will give you another opportunity to experience the model in action.

When you read about each theory and practice as it is applied to the Quest family (and to the case presented toward the beginning of each chapter), there are several questions you might want to ask yourself:

- What kind of relationship does the therapist form with the family, and what skills are employed to establish that relationship?
- What sequences or patterns do you notice both in the descriptions of how the family interacts at home and within the sessions themselves?
- How is the family organization affecting their ability to cope with life and handle the challenges they face?
- How do family members communicate with each other, and how do their communications reflect family roles and rules?
- Where is the family in terms of both individual and family life cycle development? That is, are individual adults facing the world on their own; coupling; forming a family with young children; adjusting to family life with adolescents;

launching young adults; coping with divorce, remarriage, or blending families; or handling the issues related to aging, later life, and death? Each of these normal developmental experiences tend to cause stress and challenge the family's resources. How well is the family coping with change?

- What parts of each individual are employed or ignored in the way people cope? Given the family dynamics, what purpose might individuals have for behaving and interacting the way they do?
- How do culture and gender issues affect our understanding of the family, its members, and the ways in which the practitioner intervenes in family process?
- What goals are established for therapy and which skills, techniques, and interventions are employed in the service of those goals?
- How would you proceed if you were working with the Quest family within the various models presented?
- How would you evaluate the process and success of your therapeutic interventions?

These questions invite you to think about the Quest family and other demonstrations of the models from many different perspectives. Each perspective is like a different pair of glasses with different sets of lenses. What do you see if you actively choose to look at the family differently? Of course, no amount of thinking about a family or even watching the masters at work can substitute for actual practice under supervision. If you are not already engaged in seeing families, that will happen soon. During this first exploratory stage, however, I urge you to let your mind and heart become engaged with the ideas and processes of family counseling and therapy. Imagination can be the start of actualization: Visualizing yourself in action is great preparation for your first counseling sessions with families.

Examining the various approaches to working with the Quest family will allow you to compare and contrast different stances in relation to family practice. It will also give you a chance to decide which aspects of family practice fit for you and which parts seem foreign or unacceptable to you. I would urge you to continually consider how you might plan to integrate the approaches you like into a coherent whole?

Below, I have presented the story of the Quest family that will be constant for all the family counseling and therapy models in this book. When you finish reading about the Quest family, ask yourself whether you think the family is functional or dysfunctional, healthy or unhealthy, in need of minor adjustment or a major restructuring. What do the answers to these questions say about your initial approach to and contact with the family? Then, allow yourself to ask different kinds of questions: What are you curious about? What do you want to know next? What metaphor comes to your mind about providing therapy for this family? Do the considerations of curiosity and metaphor lead to different perspectives than the questions about functionality? Welcome to the journey.

The Biography of the Quest Family

Paul and Jane Quest have been married for twenty years. They were married on her birthday in 1985. Paul often jokes that he married her on her birthday to keep down the number of presents he has to buy each year, but, in fact, he always gets her very nice gifts—and gets them often. He also works hard to keep Jane's birthday celebration with the family and their anniversary remembrances separate.

Paul's father, James, came from a fairly well-to-do Boston family, described by him as WASP (White, Anglo-Saxon, and Protestant). Paul's mother, Karen, was from a poorer, working class, Irish family. James did not marry until he was in his late 30s. He had always wanted to be a surgeon and although he had dated—occasionally even seriously—he was dedicated primarily to his work and his specialty in oncology. He met Karen, who was a new surgical nurse, when he was 35 years old. She was 23 years old, 12 years younger, but she was, with her soft red hair and almost crystal green eyes, the most beautiful woman he had ever seen. She was the daughter of an Irish beat cop, and the only person in her family to ever finish college. She had a B.A. in nursing from Boston College. They were married in 1958, after two years of courtship. James converted to Catholicism in order to marry Karen, and he promised to raise his children in the Catholic Church and send them to Catholic schools.

Paul was born two years later, in 1960, and he was named after James' father. He was a bright, beautiful baby boy, 7 lbs, 3 oz., 21 inches long. Karen stopped working outside of the home in order to raise their son, a decision that James fully supported. Two years later, Karen was pregnant again, but miscarried in her fourth month. Karen was certain that the miscarried child was a little girl, whom she called Katherine to herself. They were never able to have another child, which Karen called "God's will." Paul was, therefore, a pampered and somewhat spoiled child.

Still, Paul did very well in school and, from an early age, he wanted to follow in his father's footsteps. He was interested in everything his father did and he loved being at the hospital. By the time he was ten years old, he already had observed one of his father's surgeries and knew that was what he would do when he finished college.

Jane's father, Joseph, was the eldest son and first grandson of Boston police officers. He knew from the time he was a young child that he, too, would be a police officer in Boston one day. Jane's mother, Amy, was the eldest daughter of a Boston beat cop and Joseph seemed to be a man "just like her father." Both families were Irish and Catholic. Joseph and Amy met in high school, but waited to marry until Joseph finished the police academy and was on the job. They dated for more than five years, and both Joseph and Amy took pride in the fact that she was still a virgin on her wedding night. Amy was pregnant almost immediately, and their first child, Laura, named for Amy's grandmother, was born a year later.

Although both Joseph and Amy wanted a large family, it took almost four years for Amy to get pregnant again. She blamed it on the stress of Joseph's job, her worry for him, and the long hours that he put in. Still, in 1960, Amy gave birth to her son, named after his father, and called Joey by everyone in the family. Amy's devotion to her son was endless and Laura, the daughter, soon felt that she was on her own. She became very independent and very close to her grandmothers. Two years later, Jane was born.

Jane would turn out to be the "star" of the family: She was good at school; she was cute and charming; she had a flair for acting; she loved animals; she was an artist; she played the violin; and she seemed to bring energy and fun to almost everything she did. She would eventually graduate from Boston College, on scholarship and magna cum laude with a degree in psychology.

Jane's older sister, Laura, on the other hand, had a rough period during her late teens and young adulthood. She felt distant from her father and mother and, in any case, did not like police officers or anything about them. She had gotten pregnant in high school and arranged for an abortion without her parents' consent. After high school, she moved out. She worked as a salesperson at Filenes, a department store in Boston, and she was a friend with almost anyone her parents would not like. When she was

24, Laura married a construction worker outside of the church. His name was John Westin, and he was a "good-time boy." He drank a lot and was in almost constant verbal fights with Laura's father, who considered him "scum." When he hit Laura in a drunken rage, Joseph beat him to within an inch of his life and then put him in jail. John and Laura were divorced in 1984—with her father's blessing. She began to get along with her father much better after that.

Joey, Jane's only brother, was much loved by his mother, but seemed almost incapable of doing anything for himself. He was still living at home in his early 30s, and his mother cooked for him and cleaned his clothes. She liked having two men around the house. Although Joey did not join the police, his father did manage to get him a job with the city for a while. Joey later passed a civil service examination, got on "the list," and went to work for the post office. He never married.

Jane met Paul in 1983. She was completing her degree in psychology and taking a graduate course in psychopathology as part of her undergraduate degree. Paul had finished his undergraduate work in pre-med in only 3 years: He was 20 years old and he started in medical school immediately. Paul saw Jane across the room in the university library, and it was all over for him. He walked up to Jane, introduced himself, asked her if she would like to get a cup of coffee with him, and they were a couple from that point on.

They married 2 years later and their first child was born on schedule as Paul finished his first residency in internal medicine. She was named Amy after Jane's mother and at Paul's suggestion. There was very little conflict between Paul and Jane—nothing that anyone really would notice. They were very happy with Amy: She was healthy, interested in others, kind, and intelligent. Two years later, Ann was born and now Paul and Jane had two beautiful daughters. Except for some relatively early childhood bickering, the two girls settled into sisterhood and even seemed to like each other and get along.

When Amy and Ann reached their teenage years, both were gone a lot with various activities. With Amy driving, Jane did not see the girls as much as when she was chauffeuring them around town. It seemed as though the empty nest had arrived early for her, and Jane decided to do volunteer work at a woman's shelter. It was there that she met a young woman with two small boys.

The boys were named Jason and Luke, and they were 4- and 2-years-old, respectively, when Jane first met them. They had been terribly abused by their father: They had been burned with cigarettes, had broom straw pushed under their nails, and had been hit in the head and spanked mercilessly. Their mother, too, had been abused and there was a court order keeping the father away from all of them. Shortly after Jane met them, the mother disappeared, leaving a note that asked Jane to look after her boys. The mother was found dead a few weeks later. By that time, Jane had taken the boys in as foster children and, after their mother's death, Paul and Jane started the process of adoption, which took a little over a year.

Jane had hoped that love would make the difference in the boys' lives, but they were twenty times more difficult than her daughters had ever been. They liked to hurt things and each other. They fought physically, kicking, biting, and hitting all the time. They beat the neighbor's dog with a stick. They stole within the family and without—food, money, clothes—and recently Jane had stopped Jason from setting Luke on fire. She always felt in conflict with them. Paul, too, felt the change in the house and, to Jane, he seemed to withdraw further into his work. Amy was heavily involved in the last of her high school days and she was dating a young man she would stop seeing when she went to college. Only Ann was available to help her mother with the boys. She cut back on her activities at school and after school. She did the best she could, but the boys never listened to her.

Quest Family Genogram

At the time of therapy, Paul is 45, Jane is 43, and Amy and Ann are 18 and 16, respectively. The two boys, Jason and Luke, are 6 and 4. A genogram of the Quest family appears on the following page. A genogram is a family map that indicates both the structure and emotional relationships of the family and its members. We will take a closer look at genograms in the chapter on Bowen's multigenerational family theory. For a complete guide to genograms, see McGoldrick, Gerson, and Shellenberger (1999).

In all of the theory chapters that follow, you can assume that the practitioners have access to this background information on the Quest family. Each practitioner will apply the theory and techniques of the model as it would be adapted to the Quest family information. You may find it useful from time to time to refer back to this family data and genogram as you note how each theory addresses various aspects of the case.

I realize that there is a lot of information contained in the story of the Quest family. This amount of information is uncommon in therapeutic practice. It constitutes the raw data that will be the foundation for the qualitative analysis and action research that will inform future therapeutic practice in the field of family counseling and therapy. How each model chooses to sort

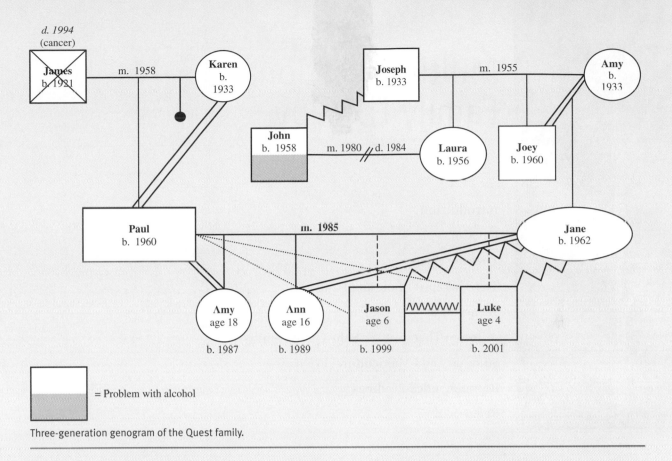

Three-generation genogram of the Quest family.

through the data, identify significant themes, and decide on therapeutic interventions says something about both the model and its practitioners. As you sort through the information contained in the story of the Quest family, what themes stand out to you? How do you prioritize the themes you identify? How would you verify that the themes you have identified as significant are also important to the family? In what ways does an identification of themes, sequences, and processes inform your understanding of the family? Are you aware that just answering these questions engages you in qualitative research (Dahl & Boss, 2005; Echevarria-Doan & Tubbs, 2005)? When your understanding is translated into interventions and you assess the effectiveness of those interventions, you are also engaged in action research (Mendenhall & Doherty, 2005). Like all areas of the helping professions, evidence-based practice is essential to the future development of family counseling and therapy.

References

Dahl, C. M., & Boss, P. (2005). The use of phenomenology for family therapy research: The search for meaning. In D. H. Sprenkle, & F. P. Piercy (Eds.), *Research methods in family therapy* (pp. 63–64). New York: Guilford.

Echevarria Doan, S., & Tubbs, C. Y. (2005). Let's get grounded: Family therapy research and grounded theory. In D. H. Sprenkle, & F. P. Piercy (Eds.), *Research methods in family therapy* (pp. 41–62). New York: Guilford.

McGoldrick, M., Gerson, R., & Shellenberger, S. (1999). *Genograms: Assessment and intervention* (2nd ed.). New York: Norton.

Mendenhall, T. J., & Doherty, W. J. (2005). Action research methods in family therapy. In D. H. Sprenkle & F. P. Piercy (eds.). *Research methods in family therapy* (pp. 100–118). New York: Guilford.

[1] I also recommend that you attend a convention or workshop where a great master who interests you is presenting. The *Evolution of Psychotherapy* conferences are some of the best. They are held once every five years and are sponsored by the Milton H. Erickson Foundation. The last one was held in December, 2005. You can find more information about these conferences at **http://www.erickson-foundation.org**.

CHAPTER 4

Multigenerational Family Therapy

Introduction

Key Concepts

Therapy Goals

The Therapist's Role and Function

Techniques

A Bowen Therapist With the Quest Family

Summary and Multicultural Evaluation

Recommended Readings

References

 ## Introduction

Murray Bowen was one of the original developers of mainstream family therapy. His approach is often referred to as multigenerational (**transgenerational** or **intergenerational**) family therapy. His approach is more theory-based than any other model we will consider. For Bowen, effective clinical practice followed from an effective theoretical orientation. Bowen and his associates introduced much of the mainstream language for family systems therapy, including concepts and clinical practice related to multigenerational assessment, family life cycle development, **ordinal birth position**, genograms, triangles and triangulation, **emotional cutoff**, and differentiation of self: We will address all of these ideas later in this chapter.

Bowen began his training in a psychoanalytic model and some of his ideas can be traced to that background. In fairness, Bowen would have seen his approach as a departure from psychoanalytic therapy. His approach operates on the premise that a family can best be understood when it is analyzed from at least a three-generation perspective, because a predictable pattern of interpersonal relationships connects the functioning of family members across generations. According to Bowen, the cause of an individual's problems can be understood only by viewing the role of the family as an emotional unit. A basic assumption in Bowen family therapy is that unresolved **emotional fusion** (or **attachment**) to one's family must be addressed if one hopes to achieve a mature and unique personality.

Murray Bowen

Betty Carter

Betty Carter is both a Bowen family therapist, now retired, and a feminist. She has an M.S.W. and was the Director of the Family Institute of Westchester in Mount Vernon, New York.[1] Betty Carter's contributions to Bowen therapy include an integration of gender issues as a part of family therapy, an appreciation for diversity of culture, differentiation in the consideration of death and loss, and, together with Monica McGoldrick, the development of the family life cycle perspective (Carter & McGoldrick, 2005). In a consultation session she conducted at the 1997 annual conference of AAMFT, Betty worked with a bicultural couple in relation to blending their two families (Carter, 1997).

In this session, Tito, age 40, a Puerto Rican who was raised in New York, is married to Diana, age 27, a Caucasian who was raised in south Florida after her parents moved there from the northern part of the United States. Tito had a previous marriage to Mary, who also came from Puerto Rico. Tito and Mary had a difficult and painful divorce, partly because Tito was already seeing Diana. Diana also had been married before, to a man who divorced her when their children were born. One of her children died at 2 months of age. Her only son is Robin, age 6. Tito's children include Lenny, age 19, who is currently in the Air Force; Tammy, age 18, his only daughter; Andre, age 15, who assumed the role of peacemaker for a while; and Isaac, age 13. Isaac lived with his mother, Mary, in Puerto Rico after the divorce, but returned to the United States and to Tito, because he does not read or write Spanish well enough to participate effectively in Puerto Rican schools.

A genogram is a family map that outlines both the structure and the emotional processes of the family. Figure 4.1, provides a guide to the symbols used in a genogram.

A partially completed genogram of Tito and Diana's blended family appears on p. 76.

A host of questions and possibilities may come to your mind when you look at this genogram. What are the issues surrounding the blending or merging of families, and how might they be present here? Should the role of a stepparent be different from that of a biological parent? If so, in what ways? How important is it for the therapist to have resolved issues with her own family-of-origin before she works with this family? How might the therapist's own life experiences become involved in this therapy session?

In addition, there is another set of important questions that address cultural issues in the family. What effect will different cultures have on this family's interactions? What place will issues related to being male from a Hispanic culture have in the family: Will these issues affect Tito's relationship with his sons and daughter, with Mary, with Diana, or with Robin? Will the culture in some way define Isaac's relationship with his mother? What might you expect from the different cultures in terms of emotional expression? What do you think about children being removed from their culture-of-origin, no longer knowing the language or customs that were part of their parents' or grandparents' lives? What effects do differing cultures of a therapist and her clients have on the counseling relationship?

In reviewing Tito and Diana's genogram, Carter offered the following hypotheses based on Bowen theory:

- The goal of therapy seems to be for the new family to accomplish a more effective blending, to live happily together, or at least not be in turmoil all the time;
- The attitude of Tito's four children toward the situation most likely reflects the unresolved attitudes that Tito and Mary still express toward each other;
- To the degree that the old marriage is unresolved, it is dead baggage in the new marriage;

(*Continued on p. 76*)

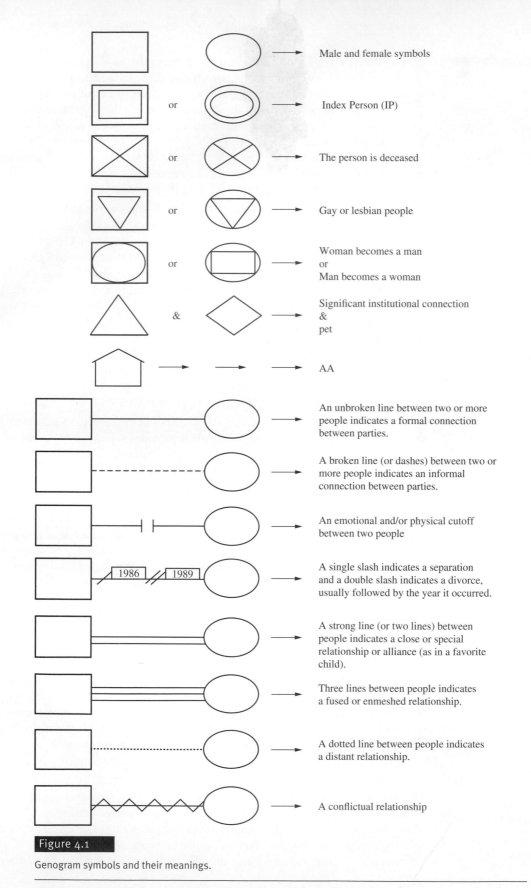

Figure 4.1

Genogram symbols and their meanings.

Adapted from McGoldrick, Gerson, & Shellenberger (1999) & McGoldrick (2005).

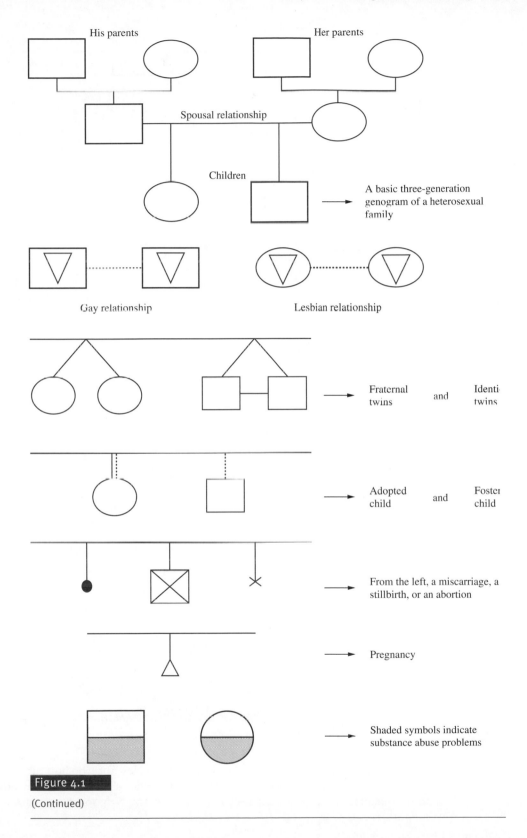

His parents

Her parents

Spousal relationship

Children

→ A basic three-generation genogram of a heterosexual family

Gay relationship

Lesbian relationship

→ Fraternal twins   and   Identi twins

→ Adopted child   and   Foster child

→ From the left, a miscarriage, a stillbirth, or an abortion

→ Pregnancy

→ Shaded symbols indicate substance abuse problems

Figure 4.1

(Continued)

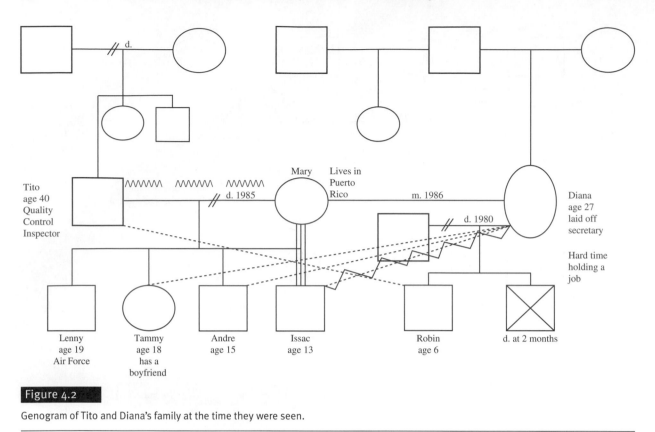

Genogram of Tito and Diana's family at the time they were seen.

- There hasn't been enough time and space for Tito and Mary to achieve joint parenting for their children;
- In this situation, Diana becomes the scapegoat, Mary stays in a victimized position, the children defend and stay loyal to their mother, and it is hard for everyone to move on.

Betty: Okay, let's work. We're just going to jump right in, right off the diving board and right in. I'm visiting from New York, so I am going to swim into your lives and swim right out.

Tito: From New York City?

Betty: In Westchester, just above New York City.

Tito: I grew up in the Bronx.

Betty: Oh, you did? We are definitely neighbors, definitely neighbors. So you're a New Yorker?

Tito: Well, yes and no.

Betty: What does that mean?

Tito: I wasn't born there, but I lived there a good deal of my life.

Betty: You're from Puerto Rico originally?

Tito: Si.

Betty: Si. My Spanish isn't as good as it should be coming from New York. So how did you get mixed up with a Southerner? You see, that's a story I should tell too, because my husband is from Tennessee, so I am interested in how we native New Yorkers get mixed up with Southerners.

Diana: I'm from Orlando.

Tito: She's a native Orlandoan, but her parents are from Michigan and Canada.

Betty: I see. I guess everyone in Florida comes from out of town. (Pause) Now, here is what I [want you to] know. I really want to be, first of all, helpful to the two of you. It is sort of like a little opportunity to get together and talk. I work with lots of stepfamilies, families who are mixing and blending like your [family] is trying to do.

Tito: Ours is mixing like oil and water.

Betty: Like oil and water, huh? Well, I've heard that story before too. What I have here, what I'm looking at—have you seen this before?—is a genogram. It's a family diagram, and it gives the basic facts of your family. (Showing the genogram to Tito and Diana) So this diagram, Tito, shows me that you were divorced from a woman named Mary, who's now in Puerto Rico. And you've got four kids: the oldest, Lenny, 19, going down to Isaac, 13. Okay, and Diana, you were divorced in about 1980, right?

Diana: Right.

Betty: And you have one living son, Robin, age 6. And all of you together (Lenny is in the Air Force, right?), so it's the other three kids and Robin and the two of you, trying to figure out how to make that into a family, I guess. Were you divorced, Tito, in September, 1985? Is that right? [Tito: Yes.] So that's very recent. (Pause) I have a lot of questions, and there's a lot of information I want to hear [about] how you are handling this stuff, which is very complex. But first, I would like to hear what you think is the most important thing that you can talk to me about. What would be helpful to you today—each of you? It may be different things.

> Tito says that Isaac's rejection of Diana is most on his mind, and he goes on to explain that Isaac is the youngest, very loyal to his mother, and that accepting Diana would be, for him, an act of disloyalty. Diana agrees that her main concern is with Isaac, because he also seems to be an influence on the other children. Initially, Tammy was quite hostile toward Diana, but Diana has noticed in recent months that Tammy is being nicer to her. And Lenny, who is away, has always accepted her as his father's spouse. Andre, the middle boy, seemed to be more like Lenny in attitude, but since Isaac's return, he has started to follow Isaac's lead. Mary told Isaac that if he came to live with his father and Diana, it would mean that he didn't love her anymore. And, since he returned anyway, if he did anything to upset Diana, Mary told Isaac that Tito would beat him. Diana feels that Mary sets all of the kids against her, and that she cannot win.

Betty: It sounds to me as if Mary doesn't feel adjusted yet, huh, hasn't accepted the divorce?

Tito: I think she has. I think she's accepted it.

Betty: As a fact, yes, but emotionally?

Diana: I think you're right there. I don't think she's accepted it emotionally.

Betty: What about you, Tito? Do you think that you had enough time to finish your first marriage before the two of you started? It sounds like maybe you were going in two directions at the same time for a while.

Tito: Yes. That's when I first [went to see a counselor].

Betty: You were torn and were going in both directions there. One of the complications may be that there wasn't enough time for Mary. The divorce wasn't her idea, I guess. Maybe she hasn't had enough time to get over it or something . . . to be more supportive about moving on.

Tito: Even though she is the one who divorced me.

Betty: Was it her idea to get divorced? Well, it's an upsetting process even if you are the one who decides. But she's the one who decided. And what do you think was the cause of that? Why do you think she decided that? Because of the relationship you had with Diana?

Tito: Yes. And because we had had long talks, and she knew our relationship was breaking up. Definitely.

Betty: Now, what kind of communication do you have with her? With Mary.

Tito: I talk to her on the phone.

Betty: You do. And how does that go? I mean, fighting . . . or . . . ?

Tito: It's down to business now.

> Betty goes on to explore the reasons that Mary returned to Puerto Rico. Mary seems to have felt that it was too hard to make it financially in America. She incurred a $2,000.00 debt on a Visa card before she left that Tito and Diana are trying to handle. She took a number of trips before leaving, but mainly her return seems to have been to regain the support of family and friends in Puerto Rico.

Betty: As you go through the ordinary day-by-day, who's mostly in charge of the children?

Tito: I am.

Betty: You are. So it's not a problem then where Diana has to come in and do disciplining or . . .

Diana: I'm not even allowed to do that. And that's one thing I don't like about it. When Isaac tells me to "shut up," I can't say anything, because I don't want to start anything. So in order to avoid it, I just ignore it.

Betty: I see.

Diana: But the bad thing about it is that I'm worried about [the influence on] my son, because he's treating his peers badly at school. He's not respected in the home. Isaac's always making fun of him and calling him names, and telling him to "shut up," and nobody says anything about it. And I can't.

Betty: When you say, "you can't," [is it that] Tito has asked you not to do the disciplining?

Diana (nodding): I can't say anything. If he swears in front of me or if he wants to disobey in front of me—even for what his father's told him to do—I'm just totally not allowed to do anything. And I feel like a child myself.

Betty: I see. So you feel kind of undermined by having no authority.

Diana: Well, I don't really want to have authority a lot. I just want to be able to correct, when necessary, and say, "Don't tell me to shut up." Or "Show a little respect, please!"

Betty: So what do you do about that when they're disrespectful to you?

Diana: When it gets really bad and keeps on getting out of hand, I wind up running to him, as if a tattle-tale child would run to him, and say, "Daddy, would you please tell him not to tell me to shut up." And I feel like that. I don't like being in that position, because he [Isaac] can do the same thing, and then it's my word against his.

Betty: So, it's like you're the oldest daughter, running to complain about the other kids.

Diana: Yes. And he will actually pick on me to make me get upset.

Betty: Who will? Isaac?

Diana: Isaac.

Betty: So he baits you.

Diana: He does. Like he'll be doing his homework, and it's 8:30 at night—he usually doesn't go to bed until 1:00 A.M.—and all of a sudden, he'll want me to get off the couch, so he can make up the bed and go to sleep. And he's in the middle of doing homework, and he has dishes to do after that, and all of a sudden, he wants to uproot me and make me go somewhere else. And he'll say things, like "Get up!" It just starts getting to me sometimes.

I've lived there since June, and there's been a lot of hate and a lot of hardship, but I've very rarely even stood up for myself. I've always been patient. I've tried. It's been hard, especially with that kind of baiting going on.

Betty: Well, it sounds like it's been hard. . . . Do you feel that Tito appreciates how difficult it is for you?

Diana: I think he does more now, but I don't think he was aware of it.

Betty: What do you mean by "now"?

Diana: He still thinks I have total control over the situation. By leaving the room, I am in total control by not letting him get to me, not letting him bait me. Well, that's hard to do over and over again, when you keep on getting tried. It's hard to do. He still sometimes blames me and thinks I have control.

Betty: So you don't feel entirely supported by him. Maybe, at least, he doesn't appreciate how hard your position is. It's not simple.

Diana: I guess I don't feel entirely supported. Also, my son needs to be supported. I need to be supported so that I can give support. My son is going through as much of that as I am. It kind of bothers me, because I don't know what to say or what to do. And I don't want my son to cry on my shoulder every time [Isaac] does it, because then he will be a mama's boy.

Betty: You mean you don't know how to handle it when Robin complains?

> Diana then goes on to explain that she is afraid that Robin comes to her too often, seeking comfort. She notes that Isaac calls Robin a mama's boy, and Robin doesn't seem to say anything about it.

Betty: Of course, society tells you, right, that a mother has to be very careful or you'll ruin your son. Do you believe that nonsense?

Diana: I know it's happened in the past. I didn't let Robin play outside until he was three or four, because I was scared of him getting hit by a car. We lived on a dead-end road. I was over-protective.

Betty: So you buy some of it.

Diana: Yeah. . . . Well, when he was three years old, he said things like, "When I grow up, I'll be a big girl, and I'll put make-up on." And I said: "No, you won't be a big girl. You'll be a big boy."

Betty: So you're afraid he's going to be gay?

Diana: Oh, yes.

Betty: Are you? Really?

Diana: Yes, sometimes. Because he's interested in make-up and . . . things like that, because that's what I do.

Betty: Well, I never heard of a situation where a child became gay, because he was raised by a parent of the opposite sex. [Betty later explained to some gay students that she didn't say this because she (Betty) thought it was a problem, but because she could see that Diana did.]

Diana (relieved): Okay.

Betty: So I wish you could stop worrying about that. I mean, there are a lot of things to worry about. I wish you'd at least stop worrying about that. I've never heard of that happening. Would you try to let go of that one?

Diana: Okay. He doesn't have a lot of security. He doesn't have a lot of confidence in himself.

Betty: That may be, but that can happen to men and women. I thought you seemed like a pretty nice person and, if he turned out like you. . . . (pause) After all, Tito picked you

	out. (turning to Tito) There must be something okay about her. Would you think Robin would be so bad off if he turned out like her?
Tito:	No, I wouldn't.
Diana (moved):	Oh.
Betty:	Well, the other thing, too: I want to congratulate you, Tito. I think that the direction you're going in is a good one. It's difficult, but it's better than what usually happens. In other words, the idea that you're going to be in charge of your kids and not expect Diana to step in and become their mother or take charge of them or something like that. However many problems you have, you [saved] yourself about 150 others by not falling into that one. And that's a very common one, where men expect their new wives to sort of step in with the kids and take over. And that . . . really . . . doesn't . . . work!

> Some discussion about the pressures of parenting follows, and then Betty introduces the problem of triangulation in the family system. Triangulation occurs anytime that two people in conflict pull a third person into the relationship to defuse the anxiety or difficulties present.

Betty:	Now, Tito, I'm interested in your position in the middle. Diana says that you're not firm enough with the kids regarding how they treat her and Robin. How do you plead to that one?
Tito:	I could be a little stronger. What keeps me from being as strong as I should be, maybe, is a combination of feelings of guilt and not wanting to alienate them more than they already are. I don't want the feelings of hostility to become intensified and I think they would be if I took a real hard stand.
Diana:	Every time he asserts himself, Isaac says he doesn't care, he doesn't love him. Everybody says that. So he just feels like he shouldn't say anything because of that. (turning to Tito) What do you think?
Tito:	I do. I do. I do tell them how I feel. And when they say I don't love them, I tell them, "Yes, I do." When they say I don't care for them, I show them how I care for them.
Betty:	But still, it gets through to you in a certain way. I mean, I think you're very tender-hearted. (Diana nods.). . . She's nodding. She's agreeing. I suppose you think you are supposed to look tough or something, but I think we've got your number. Maybe you're too tenderhearted, Tito, and that's why you're caught in the middle. You can understand that Diana's in a tough spot and you sympathize with her; but, on the other hand, you feel deeply for your children.
Tito:	I do.
Betty:	So you're caught in the middle, trying to understand both sides and make them happy. (Tito nods.) They end up shooting you. If they're shooting each other, you're in the middle getting it, huh?
Tito:	I think sometimes I'm standing with one foot on an elevator going up and the other on an escalator going down.
Betty:	Yes. Well, you see, it probably is a little bit out of guilt. I mean in the sense that because of the divorce, the children are upset, and therefore you're trying to make it up to them in some way, trying not to alienate them further. But you know what? I think that you can be firmer with them without really alienating them—even though it will hurt you. It hurts you to hear them complain or be upset. But probably they need a stronger message from you about how they have to act toward Diana and Robin. . . . Probably, they need a stronger message and, you see, your tenderheartedness prevents you from doing it. You don't have to be mean about it, but I would probably be more persistent about it—and even if they complain. . . . (pause) They're not

going anywhere. They know you care about them. [But] I think the whole message about how they have to act toward Diana and Robin has to come from you in the beginning.

> The discussion turns toward the protests that Isaac and the other kids might put up if Tito were to send a stronger message about what he expected of them in terms of behavior toward Diana and Robin. The main focus is still on Isaac, his baiting of Diana and his selfishness, which Betty reframes as part of being the baby of the family. In the course of talking about how Tito winds up in the middle between his spouse and his kids, Diana notes that Tito sometimes threatens to leave when the going gets tough. This is especially hard on her since that is what her first husband did.

Betty: Well, Tito, did you know that she takes this seriously? That she gets so scared when you make threats like that, that she's afraid you're really going to do it? Did you know that she takes it this seriously?

Tito: I didn't really think about it much. It's just that sometimes you say things that you wish you didn't say.

Betty: Do you mean it?

Tito: No.

Betty: No. But now you see that she thinks you do, and she gets scared to death. So now there's a new piece of information for you.

> The substance of the session concludes with Betty offering some coaching to Tito regarding his place in the middle.

Betty: I agree with you [Tito] that you need to be the person in charge, and you need to do the discipline. I agree with you. I think that's the wisdom of you having so much experience. It would never work for Diana to be trying to discipline them. But some relationship, she needs to have with them. It's going to take time. But with you in the middle, explaining each of them to the other, you're going to get killed by both of them, and they're going to have a harder time getting there.

Diana: That's what happened the last time [between Isaac and me]. We both got mad at him.

Tito: This is when I say I want to throw in the towel.

Betty: Sure. That's when you feel "I spend all this time trying to help these people understand each other, and they're both mad at me." Yeah. I think you ought to resign from that job of explaining both of them to each other. To hell with that.

Key Concepts

Bowen emphasized the role of theory as a guide in practicing family therapy. For him a well-articulated theory is essential in remaining emotionally detached as a family therapist. "He has been accused of being 'against emotion,' which is ridiculous to people who have done work on their own family. But he [did want] clients to think in their sessions" (Betty Carter, personal communication, April 22, 2005). Bowen (1975) believed that the absence of a clearly articulated theory had resulted in an unstructured state of chaos in family therapy. This approach offers a method for organizing data, explaining past events, and predicting future events. It contributes to an understanding of both the causes and control of events.

Bowen's theory and practice of family therapy grew out of his work with schizophrenic individuals in families. He was much more interested in developing a theory of family systems therapy than in designing techniques for working with families. In two major articles, Bowen (1966, 1976) identifies eight key concepts as being central to his theory that can be grouped into five areas of assessment: differentiation of the self and emotional cutoff, triangulation and the **nuclear family emotional system**; the **family projection process** and the **multigenerational transmission process; sibling position**; and **societal regression**. Of these, the major contributions of Bowen's theory are the core concepts of differentiation of the self and triangulation. In this section, we also deal with the importance of self-awareness on the part of the family therapist, especially with reference to understanding how experiences in the family-of-origin are likely to affect clinical practice.

Differentiation of the Self and Emotional Cutoff

The cornerstone of Bowen's theory is differentiation of the self, which involves both the psychological separation of intellect and emotion, and independence of the self from others. Differentiated individuals are able to choose to be guided by their thoughts rather than their feelings. Undifferentiated people have difficulty in separating themselves from others and tend to fuse with dominant emotional patterns in the family. These people have a low degree of autonomy, they are emotionally reactive, and they are unable to take a clear position on issues: They have a **pseudo-self**. People who are fused to their families-of-origin tend to marry others to whom they can become fused; that is, people at similar levels of differentiation tend to seek out and find each other when coupling. One pseudo-self relies on another pseudo-self for emotional stability. Unproductive family dynamics of the previous generation are transmitted from one generation to the next through such a marriage (Becvar & Becvar, 2003). In family systems theory, the key to being a healthy person encompasses both a sense of belonging to one's family and a sense of separateness and individuality.

Differentiation from the family-of-origin allows one to accept personal responsibility for one's thoughts, feelings, perceptions, and actions. Simply leaving one's family-of-origin physically or emotionally, however, does not imply that one has differentiated. Indeed, Bowen's phrase for estrangement or **disengagement** is emotional cutoff, a strong indication of an undifferentiated self. Individuation, or psychological maturity, is a lifelong developmental process that is achieved relative to the family-of-origin through reexamination and resolution of conflicts within the individual and relational contexts.[2]

The distinction between emotional reactivity and rational thinking can be difficult to discern at times. Those who are not emotionally reactive experience themselves as having a choice of possible responses; their reactions are not automatic but involve a reasoned and balanced assessment of self and others. Emotional reactivity, in contrast, is easily seen in clients who present themselves as paranoid, intensely anxious, panic stricken, or even head-over-heels in love. In these cases, feelings have overwhelmed thinking and reason, and people experience themselves as being unable to choose a different reaction. Emotional reactivity in therapists almost always relates to unresolved issues with family-of-origin members. For example, the sound of a man's voice in a family session reminds the therapist of his father and immediately triggers old feelings of anger and anxiety, as well as an urgency to express them. Clarity of response in Bowen's theory is marked by a broad perspective, a focus on facts and knowledge, an appreciation of complexity, and a recognition of feelings, rather than being dominated by them: Such people achieve what Bowen sometimes referred to as a **solid self** (Becvar & Becvar, 2003).

Triangulation and the Nuclear Family Emotional System

Bowen (1976) notes that anxiety can easily develop within intimate relationships. Under stressful situations, two people may recruit a third person into the relationship to reduce the anxiety and gain stability. This is called triangulation. Although triangulation may lessen the emotional tension between the two people, the underlying conflict is not addressed and, in the long run, the situation worsens: What started as a conflict in the couple evolves into a conflict within the nuclear family emotional system. Triangulation was central to the therapy session we looked at earlier conducted by Betty Carter. Because Tito and Mary had unresolved and intense conflicts, the focus of their attention became Isaac, the now problematic son: Isaac was triangulated into Tito and Mary's relationship. Instead of fighting with each other, they are temporarily distracted by riveting their attention on their son. Similarly, the conflict between Diana and Isaac also involved the triangulation of Tito as an interpreter of one to the other. Unlike Satir, Bowen almost never envisioned a triad that was functional.

Thomas Fogarty introduced a distinction between triangles and triangulation to Bowen theory (Guerin, 2002). For him, the former was a structure that existed in all families while the latter was an emotional process. His focus on couples led him to believe that there was directional movement within family triangles that almost always included a pursuer and a distancer. These were complementary relational positions with the pursuer characterized as someone who wants lots of relational contact, especially during times of stress while the distancer is less expressive of thoughts and feelings, and often finds comfort in necessary tasks rather than relationship.

The Family Projection Process and Multigenerational Transmission

The most common form of triangulation occurs when two parents with poor differentiation fuse, leading to conflict, anxiety, and ultimately the involvement of a child in an attempt to regain stability. When a parent lacks differentiation and confidence in her or his role with the child, the child also becomes fused and emotionally reactive. The child is now declared to "have a problem," and the other parent is often in the position of calming and supporting the distraught parent. Such a triangle produces a kind of pseudo-stability for a while: The emotional instability in the couple seems to be diminished, but it has only been projected onto the child. This family projection process makes the level of differentiation worse with each subsequent generation (Papero, 2000). When a child leaves the family-of-origin with unresolved emotional attachments, whether they are expressed in emotional fusion or emotional cutoff, they will tend to couple and create a family in which these unresolved issues can be reenacted. The family projection process has now become the foundation for multigenerational transmission.

Sibling Position

Bowen adopted Toman's (1993) conceptualization of family constellation and sibling (or birth) position. Unlike Adler, Toman's birth positions are fixed and ordinal in nature. A phenomenological perspective does not really enter into it. Toman believed that position determines power relationships, and gender experience determines one's ability to get along with the other sex. In addition to noting the unique positions of only children and twins, Toman focused on 10 power/sex positions: the oldest brother of brothers; the youngest brother of brothers; the oldest brother of sisters; the youngest brother of sisters; the male only child; and the same five configurations for females in relation to sisters and brothers. Under this conceptualization, the best possible marriage, for example, is hypothesized to be the oldest brother of sisters marrying the youngest sister of brothers. In this arrangement, both parties would enter the marriage with similar expectations about power and gender relationships. Conversely, the worst marriage would occur between the oldest brother of brothers and the oldest sister of sisters. In this case, both parties would seek and want power positions, and neither would have had enough childhood experience with the other sex to have adequate gender relationships.

Toman supported his hypothesis by noting that the divorce rate among couples comprised of two oldest children was higher than any other set of birth positions. The absence of divorce, however, is not the same as a happy marriage. When we consider the critical traits in a happy marriage, his predictions based on birth order start to lose credibility. Happiness in coupling or marriage is demonstrably more related to attitudinal and behavioral interactions within the spousal system—especially during periods of family stress—than to birth order (Gottman, 1994, Walsh, 2003).

Bowen, however, accepted what appeared to be the "science" of Toman's theory of family constellation and birth order. Using this ordinal approach, Bowen believed he could predict the role that children would play in the emotional life of the family. He also thought it would greatly determine which family patterns would be projected into the next generation.

Guerin (2002) discussed the importance of what he called the "sibling cohesion factor" (p. 135), especially when there were more than two children in the sibling subsystem, allowing for triangles to form. The sibling cohesion factor is the capacity of the children within the sibling subsystem to meet without their parents and discuss important family issues, including their evaluations of their parents. Healthier families tend to have this factor as part of the family process; the lack of it suggests to Guerin that there is intense triangulation between the parents and children.

The Societal Projection Process or Societal Regression

Bowen (1976) also applied his theory to an assessment of societal process. He believed that under circumstances of chronic societal stress, public anxiety would increase, and government leadership would abandon rational considerations in favor of emotionally driven decisions designed to bring about short-term relief. The most common process would involve two groups joining together to preserve their own positions at the expense of a third (Papero, 2000). Such societal projection processes tend to result in laws that do little to affect the chronic problem, bring relief to very few, and generate helplessness in many. In short, the result is a societal regression quite similar to family dysfunction. I believe that the issues in the United States related to abortion or same-sex marriage are good examples of this societal regression. For example, we have recently seen economic conservatives and Christian conservatives join together to take a stand against same-sex marriage, enacting state constitutional laws that declare marriage to be only between a man and a woman—a law that affects very few people, but leaves many with feelings of helplessness.

Because the family is not a static entity, a change in one part of the system affects the actions of all others involved. In his therapy, Bowen sometimes worked with one member of a conflictual dyad (or couple). He did not require that every family member be involved in the therapy sessions. Bowen tended to work from the inside out: Starting with the spousal relationship, he helped the two adults establish their own differentiation. As a therapist, he attempted to maintain a stance of **neutrality**. If the therapist becomes emotionally entangled with any one family member, the therapist loses effectiveness and becomes part of a triangulated relationship. Bowen maintained that, to be effective, family therapists have to have a very high level of differentiation. If therapists still have unresolved family issues and are emotionally reactive, they are likely to revisit those difficulties in every family they see.

Therapy Goals

Although all family therapists are interested in resolving problems presented by a family and decreasing their symptoms, Bowen therapists are mainly interested in changing the individuals within the context of the system. They contend that problems that are manifest in one's current family will not significantly change until relationship patterns in one's family-of-origin are understood and addressed. Emotional problems will be transmitted from one generation to the next until unresolved emotional attachments are dealt with effectively. Change must occur with other family members and cannot be done by an individual in a counseling room.

The practice of Bowen family therapy is governed by the following two goals: (1) the lessening of anxiety and symptom relief and (2) an increase in each family member's level of differentiation of the self (Kerr & Bowen, 1988). To bring about significant change in a family system, it is necessary to open closed family ties and to engage actively in a detriangulation process (Guerin, Fogarty, Fay, & Kautto, 1996). Although problems are seen as residing in the system rather than in the individual, the route to changing oneself is through changing in relation to others in the family-of-origin.

The Therapist's Role and Function

Bowen viewed himself as an objective researcher who aimed to help individuals in the family assess and understand their relational styles within the family system. Bowen therapists function as teachers, coaches, and neutral observers who are responsible for establishing the tone of family therapy. Bowen taught individuals or couples about triangulation and then expected them to go back to their family-of-origin to extricate themselves emotionally from these triangular patterns. The purpose of going home again is not to confront family members, or even to establish peace and harmony, but to encourage clients to come to know others in their family as they are (Bowen, 1976).

Bowen helped individuals or couples gather information, and he coached or guided them into new behaviors by demonstrating ways in which individuals might change their relationships with their parents, **siblings**, and extended-family members. He instructed them in how to be better observers and also taught them how to move from emotional reactivity to increased objectivity. He did not tell clients what to do, but rather asked a series of questions that were designed to help them figure out their own roles in their family emotional process. Although he provided guidance for how they could free themselves from fused emotional relationships, he saw it as their responsibility to take the steps necessary to bring about self-differentiation. According to Bowen, this occurs through a rational understanding of the nuclear family emotional system, the family projection process, and the transmission process over several generations (Kerr & Bowen, 1988). Bowen therapists maintain that therapy sessions can be viewed as rehearsals for becoming differentiated; the main therapeutic work of relating to members of their family in new ways happens outside the therapy session.

Therapist Self-Awareness

As a prerequisite to practicing effectively with families, therapists must be aware of how they have been influenced by their own family-of-origin. If a family therapist overly identifies with one family member in the therapeutic encounter, it is likely that his or her own childhood issues have been triggered. The therapist will probably not be objective or open to understanding certain clients. It is inevitable that we will encounter aspects of our family in the families with whom we work. The premise underlying the significance of understanding our family-of-origin is that the patterns of interpersonal behavior we learned in our family-of-origin will be repeated with clients unless the practitioner has achieved differentiation.

Implications for Training of Family Therapists

Bowen (1978) developed a method for training family therapists that aimed at helping them differentiate themselves from others in their families-of-origin and that reduced their inclination to become involved in triangulated relationships. There are four steps in Bowen's training method:

1. Trainees are encouraged to construct comprehensive family diagrams (called genograms) in order to identify key turning points in their families. It is essential that trainees learn information about their family relational systems.
2. Trainees are given the task of making visits to their families-of-origin for the purpose of becoming a keen observer of their families' processes. During this time, it is crucial that they learn how to identify and control their own emotional reactivity to members in their families.
3. Bowen also encouraged trainees to visit their families in times of high tension, such as a serious illness or imminent death of a family member, because it is at these times when change is most likely. Their task is to keep free from entering into old triangular patterns. In essence, they are to detriangulate themselves from emotionally reactive situations.
4. Instead of getting trapped into old patterns of emotional reactivity, they are expected to develop person-to-person relationships with as many family members as possible. The members should strive to relate to one another, rather than to talk about others. In many Bowen-oriented institutes, trainees must join a "therapist's own family" group to work on family-of-origin issues and reactions.

In Chapter Two, I talked about the importance of family therapists doing their own family-of-origin work: This is one of many ways in which such work gets done.

Techniques

Bowen's theory describes how individuals function within a family system, how they develop dysfunctional patterns, and how they can repair and enhance their relationships with members of their family. The transgenerational approach focuses on emotional sequences with one's family-of-origin, spouse, and children. Bowen therapists believe that understanding how a family system operates is far more important than using a particular technique. They tend to use interventions such as process questions, tracking sequences, teaching, coaching, and directives with a family. They value information about past relationships as a significant context from which they design interventions in the present.

Genogram Work.   Bowen assumes that multigenerational patterns and influences are central in understanding present nuclear family functioning. He devised a "family diagram," later developed into what is now called a genogram (McGoldrick, Gerson, & Shellenberger, 1999), as a way of collecting and organizing important data over at least three generations. A family genogram consists of a pictorial layout of each partner's three-generational extended family. It is a tool for both the therapist and family members to understand critical turning points in the family's emotional processes and to note dates of births, deaths, marriages, and divorces. The genogram also includes additional information about essential characteristics of a family: cultural and ethnic origins, religious affiliation, socioeconomic status, type of contact among family members, and proximity of family members. Siblings are presented in genograms horizontally, oldest to youngest, each with more of a relationship to the parents than to one another. By providing an evolutionary picture of the nuclear family, a genogram becomes a tool for assessing each partner's degree of fusion to extended families and to each other. Bowen also integrates data related to birth order and family constellation. These family maps have a structural consistency and are, therefore, used by multiple family systems models—especially structural and strategic therapies, and many adaptations in form have been made.

The symbols used in genograms and their meaning are presented in Figure 4.1 on pages 74 and 75. Using this figure, you may want to review the partial genogram used by Betty Carter in meeting with Tito and Diana on page 76. And I would also suggest that this would be a good time to take another look at the Quest family genogram presented with the case as conducted by a Bowen therapist toward the end of this chapter.

Asking Process Questions.   The most common Bowen technique consists of asking process questions that are designed to get clients to think about the roles they play in relating with members of their family. Bowen's style tended to be controlled, somewhat detached, and cerebral. In working with a couple, for example, he expected each partner to talk to him rather than to talk directly to each other during the session. His calm style of questioning was aimed at helping each partner think about particular issues that are problematic with their family-of-origin. One goal is to resolve the fusion that may exist between the partners and to maximize each person's self differentiation both from the family-of-origin and the nuclear family system.

A Bowen therapist is more concerned with managing his or her own neutrality than with having the right question at the right time. Still, questions that emphasize personal choice are very important. They calm emotional response and invite a rational consideration of alternatives. A therapist attempting to help a woman who has been divorced by her husband may ask:

- Do you want to continue to react to him in ways that keep the conflict going, or would you rather feel more in charge of your life?
- What other ways could you consider responding if the present way isn't very satisfying to you and is not changing him?
- Given what has happened recently, how do you want to react when you're with your children and the subject of their father comes up?

Notice that these process questions are asked of the person as part of a relational unit. This type of questioning is called circular, or is said to have **circularity**, because the focus of change is in relation to others who are recognized as having an effect on the person's functioning.

Relationship Experiments.   "Relationship experiments are behavioral tasks assigned to family members by the therapist to first expose and then alter the dysfunctional relationship process in the family system" (Guerin, 2002, p. 140). Most often, these experiments are assigned as homework, and they are commonly designed to reverse pursuer–distancer relationships and/or address the issues related to triangulation. Relationship experiments are incorporated within Guerin's five-step process for neutralization of symptomatic triangles in which he (1) identifies the triangle, (2) delineates the triangle's structure and movement, (3) reverses the direction of the movement, (4) exposes the emotional process, and (5) addresses the emotional process to augment family functionality.

Coaching.   Bowen used coaching with well-motivated family members who had achieved a reasonable degree of self-differentiation. To coach is to help people identify triggers to emotional reactivity, look for alternative responses, and anticipate desired outcomes. Coaching is supportive, but is not a rubber stamp: It seeks to build individual independence, encouraging confidence, courage, and emotional skill in the person.

I-Positions.   **I-positions** are clear and concise statements of personal opinion and belief that are offered without emotional reactivity. When stress, tension, and emotional reactions increase, I-positions help individual family members step back from the experience and communicate from a more centered, rational, and stabilized position. Bowen therapists model I-positions within sessions when family members become emotionally reactive and, as family members are able to take charge of their emotions, Bowen therapists also coach them in the use of I-statements.

Displacement Stories.   Displacement stories are usually implemented through the use of film or videotape, although storytelling and fantasized solutions also have been used. The function of a displacement story is to provide a family or family members with an external stimulus (film, video, book, or story) that relates to the emotional process and triangulation present in the family, but allows them to be considered in a less defensive or reactive manner. Films such as "I Never Sang For My Father," "Ordinary People," or "Avalon" all have been used by Bowen therapists to highlight family interactions and consequences, and to suggest resolutions of a more functional nature.

A Bowen Therapist With the Quest Family

Paul and Jane Quest have a first meeting without their children with a Bowen therapist. The Bowen therapist began the session by welcoming Paul and Jane and asking them what they hoped would happen during therapy. Both Paul and Jane identified trouble in adjusting to life with their two boys as the core reason for therapy.

In order to get a better picture of the family, the Bowen therapist helped Paul and Jane to construct a genogram that resulted in the diagram in Figure 4.3.

Paul noted that their life was much different since the boys had joined the family and he suggested that although the boys were part of the family, he was not sure he had become their father yet. He felt drawn to spending more time with Amy and Ann than with the boys, who in many ways still seemed like visitors to him. Tears came to Jane's eyes as she listened to Paul talk. She was not sure whether the tears were about Paul's hesitancy with the boys, frustration she herself felt, or just simple exhaustion. She did feel as though she had lost Paul a little bit since the boys came to the family, and she felt a good deal of sadness about that.

Addressing Paul and Jane together, the therapist began the session.

Therapist: Here's what I believe I understand about your life at the moment. This diagram indicates that the two of you have been married for twenty years, and you started having children about two years into your marriage. As often happens in families, one parent seems to have felt closer to the first child, and the other to the second. In this case, Paul, you indicated a closer relationship to Amy, and Jane seems to have been closer to Ann. Is that right?

Paul: Well, I love both of my girls, and I know Jane does too.

Therapist: Yes. Of course. This isn't about loving them. It's just about closeness and how that develops. You may have had a closer relationship, Paul, with your mother than your father: Would you say that's true?

Paul: Yes. I loved my father; he was a good man. But I have always been closer to my mother.

Therapist: How was it in your family, Jane?

Jane: Well, my mother was quite close to Joey, but my father had a hard time with him. He worked a lot and he wasn't always with us. He seemed to feel less stress around Laura, my sister, and around me as I got older. But Joey, even though my father really wanted a boy, is my mother's son. Still is.

Therapist: And now you both have two sons. So how is that going?

Jane: It has been a lot harder than I thought it would be. When I first brought the idea up, I had this vision of the boys just fitting into our family and everyone getting along. But they have had such problems in their lives—before and with us.

Therapist: And they brought those problems with them.

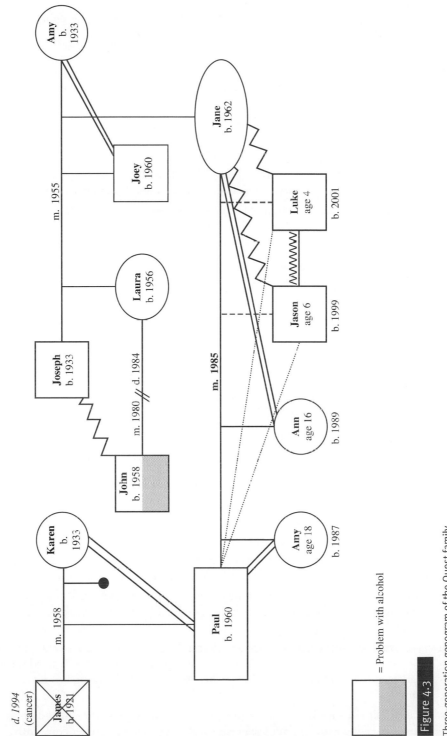

Figure 4.3

Three-generation genogram of the Quest family.

= Problem with alcohol

Jane:	Yes. They fight with each other. They fight Ann . . . me. If it were not for Ann, I would really feel alone in all of this.
Therapist:	So Ann is your support in taking Jason and Luke on?
Jane:	Yes. But it's hard on her. She's only sixteen. She is a teenager and should be with her friends more.
Therapist:	Paul, where are you in all of this?
Paul:	I try to be available when I am home, but my load at work has increased in the last couple of years. I am there a lot. I really rely on Jane to be the central figure at home. I also don't know what to do with the boys. Even when I am home, it is like I am not ready for them to be there too. I miss the life we had when it was just Amy and Ann. It is also Amy's last year with us before she leaves for college. I want to spend as much time with her as possible.
Therapist:	So you feel yourself less involved, even withdrawing from Jason and Luke. [Paul: Yes.] Did you know that Jane felt as lonely in raising these young men as she does?
Paul:	I think I try to ignore it, because I don't want to feel like I have deserted her, but I know it's hard for her. It's hard for all of us.
Therapist:	Paul, how was it for you with your father?
Paul:	My father was a great man. He was a surgeon and he was very good. Like I am now, he was very busy, much in demand, and spent a lot of time away from home. He relied on my mother to raise me.
Therapist:	And how did that go?
Paul:	My mother? Well, she was wonderful: A bit smothering as I got older, but she did everything for me. She loved my father and understood his need to work.

> The therapist took the next few minutes to ask about Paul's feeling of being smothered, to explore what Paul knew about the baby that had miscarried in his family, and how his mother had felt about that. He then turned to Jane, asking her how her mother had been with her son. Jane's entire body seemed to tighten as she talked about Joey. She did not want Jason or Luke to grow up to be like Joey, unable to take care of himself, still relying on her mother for everything, over-protected and pampered.

Therapist:	And how does your father, Jane, get along with Paul?
Jane:	They get along very well. My dad hated my former brother-in-law.
Therapist:	Laura's husband . . . John?
Jane:	Yes. And he was happy when they divorced. Paul doesn't drink. He is ambitious and hardworking. He takes care of all of us and we are even able to help my parents out when they have needs. So my father thinks Paul is terrific.
Therapist:	So at least you don't experience much difficulty or stress in relation to your in-laws: Is that right, Paul? [Paul: Yes.] Your father, though, died in 1994. What was that like for you?
Paul:	Well, that was really hard too. He had cancer: lungs, pancreas, and eventually the liver. He suffered quite a bit for a while, because he wanted to stay alert. Toward the end, I had him on morphine constantly, but there wasn't really anything I could do to save him.
Jane:	Paul and I also take care of his mother now. She lives independently, and doesn't want anyone staying with her. But she needs someone looking in on her constantly.
Therapist:	And who mostly does that?
Paul:	Well, I see her at least once a day. And Amy or Ann drop in on her at least once or twice a week, but . . .

| Jane: | Mostly, I have to take care of mom-Quest. |

The therapist noted that in the course of the last ten years or so, Jane has had to support her husband through his father's death, take on the responsibility of caring for his mother, watch her children transition from childhood into more independent teens, provide volunteer help in the community, and also experience the loss of her husband to his work. Just saying this out loud brought tears to Jane's eyes, which she wiped away with her hand before reaching for a tissue that she held in her hands.

| Therapist: | What were you hoping would happen when you adopted Jason and Luke? That is, did you think it would bring you and Paul closer together? |

| Jane: | Well, yes. I thought it would be like it was when Amy and Ann were young. We were happier then. And we did things with each other. |

| Paul: | I want to do things together again. I just don't know how. I have no idea what to do with them. |

| Therapist: | Paul, what did your father do with you? |

| Paul: | We didn't do a lot. Well, that's not true really. He would let me come to the hospital. I even watched him do surgery when I was just a little older than Jason. And he would take me to a baseball game now and then. I guess we went for walks at night when I was little. |

| Therapist: | I really think that doing something like that is part of the answer. I think that if these boys are going to become part of the family, it's you, Paul, who has to take charge and find a way to incorporate them into your life. What are you feeling as I say that? |

| Paul: | I guess I want to know: Why me? I mean I know what to do with Amy . . . and with Ann. |

| Therapist: | I sense that. You seem to know how to be with one woman at a time. At first, it was being with your mother, then with Jane, and now you seem to focus on Amy. But a family is more than one person at a time. You must feel caught sometimes between the needs of your mother and the needs of your family—especially Jane's needs. Is that true? |

| Paul: | Yes, definitely. |

| Therapist: | And what do you do when you feel pulled in two directions? My guess is that you withdraw into work. [Paul nods.] And that is also what you want to do when you feel that Jane wants more of you than you can give or Jason and Luke seem to be taking over and demanding total attention. You feel the need to distance yourself, even as Jane is pursuing you even harder. I really feel that we have to reverse that. It's the only way we are going to know what else needs to be addressed and handled in this family. |

| Jane: | Are you saying that Paul needs to be home more? |

| Therapist: | Probably, but it's more a matter of taking responsibility for raising these kids, just as he did with Amy and Ann. Paul, I really think you need to be the man in charge of Jason and Luke. They need time with you, but they also need you to help them with their behavior: to lay down the rules and handle it when they break them. And Jane needs to help this process by stepping back and letting you be in charge. |

For the next few sessions, Paul was coached about how he could become more engaged with Jason and Luke, and his time in the boy's life did increase. Both Jason and Luke responded over several months with gradual improvements in behavior. They still fought, but their fighting was not as rough and they began to learn how to fix things. Paul showed them how to care for a hurt bird they found. He helped them to repair some things they had broken.

Jane, however, started to show signs of depression, often crying for no reason. The Bowen therapist noted that Jane's depression had been with her a long time, but had been kept at bay through her volunteer work, the raising of her older children, and now taking care of the boys. Another reversal of the pursuer–distancer relationship put Paul in the position of seeking relationship time with Jane in an effort to discover what really was happening with her. Paul was guided not to try to fix anything, but to listen and to simply understand what she was feeling. This process revealed problems in the triangle between Paul, his mother, and his wife. Dealing with this triangulation was the focus of therapy for quite a while.

Summary and Multicultural Evaluation

Bowen's approach to family therapy can be characterized as the application of rational thinking in emotionally saturated systems. His core concepts of differentiation of self and triangulation have become central both to understanding family systems as well as training future family counselors and therapists. His emphasis on the separation of thought and feeling, as well as therapeutic detachment, has been criticized by some feminists as another case of elevating rationality and autonomy over connectedness, integration, and interdependence (Luepnitz, 1988). And, indeed, Bowen's model, although supporting personal presence and involvement, puts greater emphasis on emotional neutrality and objective observation than on personal connection and conjoint family process. The current feminist emphasis on collaboration, involvement, and connection places most feminist therapists at the opposite end of the continuum from Bowen's personal emphasis on detachment theory.

Still, no other model has generated as many scholar-practitioners dedicated to re-visioning family therapy with the intent of making race, culture, and gender central to clinical practice (McGoldrick, 1998). Bowen therapists also have made significant contributions to concepts related to **tracking sequences**, family and marital structures, and leadership in family systems. Sometimes called "natural systems therapy or family systems therapy" (Becvar & Becvar, 2003, p. 145), Bowen's model was one of the first to develop and provide the language and conceptualizations that now dominate family therapy.

Contributions to Multicultural Counseling and Gender Issues

Monica McGoldrick and her colleagues and associates are probably the most prolific and dependable sources addressing multicultural and gender issues in family therapy. Her work with Carol Anderson, Betty Carter, Peggy Papp, and Froma Walsh, to name a few, literally forced the field of family therapy (and especially AAMFT) to integrate culture and gender as significant perspectives in therapeutic work. Starting in 1982 with the original publication, McGoldrick, Giordano, and Garcia-Preto (2005) set about the task of delineating family characteristics in a wide range of cultures from Africa, the Americas, Asia, Europe, and the Middle East. Their original belief that culture was almost biologically transmitted from one generation to the next has become more fluid and dynamic over the years, and there simply would not be a multicultural perspective (or lens) in family therapy without their work. This multicultural work, along with the work of the Women's Project (Walters, Carter, Papp, & Silverstein, 1988), also has integrated the perspectives of women and a consideration of gender issues in family therapy (see McGoldrick, Anderson, & Walsh, 1989). Beginning in 1980, Carter and McGoldrick (2005) also created a systemic, family life cycle developmental perspective in family therapy that has become the framework for considering families from their inception to their rituals for loss and death (Walsh & McGoldrick, 1991).

Boyd-Franklin (2003) notes that the use of genograms with African-American families is important, but must be reserved for the middle part of therapy—after trust in the therapist has been developed. Genograms started in the first session often trigger suspiciousness and resistance in African-American families, who may feel that the counselor or therapist is prying. Once trust is established through successful problem solving, the genogram can be instrumental in discovering the often permeable relationships in the family and the family projection processes that may be tied to the identified patient.

Boyd-Franklin also likes the use of coaching as a means of offering "family therapy with one person" (p. 211). Based on the idea that a change in any part of the system will cause adjustments in the rest of the system, this model is especially effective with single parents and others who only can be seen individually. A systemic exploration of the life of a single individual can unlock the family history and point out both the internal and external family stressors that have been present.

Boyd-Franklin stresses that African-American families are part of a **collectivistic culture**—as are most Asian families. In these families, differentiation must be balanced with a need for continued connection and interdependence. Too much differentiation can lead to both emotional and literal cut offs with other members of the family.

Still, there are very few limitations related to this approach in multicultural settings. Falicov (1998) noted that triangles had cultural meaning and warned that triangles could not be "isolated from their cultural context, reified, and assumed to have the same universally problematic implications in all cases" (p. 46). The fact that culture is becoming a central metaphor in Bowen therapy and is viewed both developmentally and dynamically is a testimonial to how far the theory and, indeed, the field has advanced.

Exercises for Personal and Professional Growth

The exercise I propose here for your consideration will, perhaps, take less space to describe than any other exercise in this book—and the rest of your professional life to work on and develop fully. It is based on Bowen's early use of family maps and their development by Monica McGoldrick and her associates into genograms.

- Using at least three generations from your own family, begin the process of constructing your personal genogram.
- Use the genograms that appear in this chapter as a guide—as well as the figure that gives you the structural and emotional symbols that will be needed to represent your family.

In order to get the information you will need, I recommend that you return to your family-of-origin and that you bring a tape recorder to interview older family members. Such an oral history-taking is an excellent way to gather family stories and practice the nonreactive demeanor that is required for a differentiated self. For many of you, this will be your first trip into family background, **family rituals**, gender and cultural processes in the family, and the rest of life that make up the contexts of our lives. This genogram exercise often catches young practitioners by surprise: It has all the appearance of a simple diagram but, when it is done properly, it is often an emotional journey that serves as the beginning of the personal work that must be completed if one is to become an effective family counselor, therapist, or social worker.

- When you have your genogram completed, use your colleagues or fellow trainees to form triads.
- After sharing some of the stories associated with each of your genograms, start to draw the triangles that existed in your family. Pay special attention to the ones in which you were triangulated into other people's relationships. How were you induced into the triangle? What were the triggers that started the process? What were the results?
- Are there still triangles in your life that pull you in? Does such triangulation extend across multiple generations?

- Have there been any changes? Who was successful at handling them?
- If you are currently in an intimate relationship, does triangulation ever enter into your interactions?
- What stances (verbal and non-verbal) could you take to detriangulate yourself? What do you think would happen if you took those stances? What are your worst fears about detriangulation? What is the best that could happen?

For more help with the process of constructing genograms, see McGoldrick, Gerson, and Shellenberger (1999). For help with applying Bowen theory to current relationships, see Gilbert (1992).

Where to Go From Here

Bowen, structural, and strategic therapists are still central contributors to AAMFT, as well as to journals such as *Family Process*, the *Journal of Marital and Family Therapy*, and the *Family Therapy Networker*. Bowen therapists also contribute to the *Journal of Feminist Therapy* and *The Family Journal* (developed by IAMFC). Attending state and national AAMFT meetings and reading mainstream journals are the best ways to access current developments in this model.

Michael Kerr took over as Director of the Bowen Center at Georgetown University after Dr. Bowen died. Kerr's 20-year relationship with Bowen and his writings make him the heir apparent for the Bowen model. He can be reached at:

Bowen Center for the Study of the Family Georgetown Family Center
4400 MacArthur Blvd NW, Suite 103
Washington, DC 20007-2521
Phone: 800-432-6882 or 202-965-4400; fax: 202-965-1765
E-mail: **info@thebowencenter.org** or **mekerr@thebowencenter.org**

Recommended Readings

Bowen, M. (1978). *Family therapy in clinical practice.* New York: Jason Aronson. After Bowen had published many articles and led the development of his model through NIMH and into Georgetown University, he published this book as his signature position in the field.

Carter, B., & McGoldrick, M. (Eds.). (2005). *The expanded family life cycle: Individual, family, and social perspectives* (3rd ed.). Boston: Allyn & Bacon. This is the most comprehensive and detailed text available on the family life cycle and how this developmental perspective is integrated in clinical practice.

Gilbert, R. M. (1992). *Extraordinary relationships: A new way of thinking about human interactions.* New York: John Wiley. Gilbert's book is an excellent presentation of Bowen theory applied to couples, and it teaches his principles in language that reaches both lay family members and professionals.

Guerin, P. J., Jr., Fogarty, T. F., Fay, L. F., & Kautto, J. G. (1996). *Working with relationship triangles: The one-two-three of psychotherapy.* New York: Guilford. This book features the Bowen work of Phillip Guerin and Thomas Fogarty, two of the most prominent Bowen therapists practicing today. This is must reading for modern Bowen therapists.

Kerr, M. E., & Bowen, M. (1988). *Family evaluation.* New York: Norton. Michael Kerr completed this book, which is one of the last works on which Bowen would collaborate, and it brings Bowen's earliest work into full fruition.

McGoldrick, M., Gerson, R., & Shellenberger, S. (1999). *Genograms: Assessment and intervention* (3rd ed.). New York: Norton. Anyone who studies and uses genograms starts with this book and refers to it often. It not only demonstrates a dynamic use of genograms, but also offers enormous insight into the founders of modern psychology, celebrity families, and the personal/professional development of therapists.

McGoldrick, M., Giordano, J., & Garcia-Preto, N. (Eds.). (2005). *Ethnicity and family therapy* (3rd ed.). New York: Guilford. This is the most comprehensive work available on race, culture, and ethnicity within the context of family therapy. This book is often the central multicultural text in the preparation of family counselors and therapists.

Finally, if you are interested in an in-depth study of this approach, I recommend the following sources as must reading: Bowen (1966, 1971, 1975, 1976, 1978), Guerin, Fogarty, Fay and Kautto (1996), Kerr and Bowen (1988), and Papero (2000). In addition to Bowen, James Framo (1992) has made significant contributions to multigenerational family therapy, integrating perspectives from object-relations theory.

 # DVD Reference

The video segment that accompanies Bowen's theory is based on a case by Phillip Guerin. Dr. Bitter works with a family in which the mother feels that her daughter's friend and the friend's mother are bad influences on her child; the father in this family is largely absent or *cut off* from the family process. Dr. Bitter demonstrates how a Bowen therapist might work with triangles in a family and coach the various family members toward a more reasonable solution.

References

Becvar, D. S., & Becvar, R. J. (2003). *Family therapy: A systemic integration* (5th ed.). Boston: Allyn & Bacon.

Bowen, M. (1966). The use of family theory in clinical practice. *Comprehensive Psychiatry, 7*, 345–374.

Bowen, M. (1971). Family therapy and family group therapy. In H. Kaplan & B. Saddock (Eds.), *Comprehensive group psychotherapy* (pp. 384–481). Baltimore: Williams & Wilkins.

Bowen, M. (1975). Family therapy after twenty years. In J. Dyrud & D. Freedman (Eds.), *American handbook of psychiatry* (vol. 5, pp. 367–392). New York: Basic Books.

Bowen, M. (1976). Theory in the practice of psychotherapy. In P. J. Guerin, Jr., (Ed.), *Family therapy: Theory and practice* (pp. 42–90). New York: Gardner Press.

Bowen, M. (1978). *Family therapy in clinical practice.* New York: Jason Aronson.

Boyd-Franklin, N. (2003). *Black families in therapy: Understanding the African American experience* (2nd ed.). New York: Guilford.

Carter, B. (Speaker). (1997). *On not becoming a wicked stepmother* (AAMFT videotape #V009). Palm Desert, CA: Convention Cassettes Unlimited/Landes Slezak Group.

Carter, B., & McGoldrick, M. (2005). *The expanded family life cycle. Individual, family, and social perspectives* (3rd ed.). Boston: Allyn & Bacon.

Falicov, C. J. (1998). *Latino families in therapy: A guide to multicultural practice.* New York: Guilford.

Fogarty, T. F. (1976). Systems concepts and dimensions of self. In P. J. Guerin (Ed.), *Family therapy: Theory and practice* (pp. 144–153). New York: Gardner.

Framo, J. (1992). *Family-of-origin therapy: An intergenerational approach.* New York: Brunner-Mazel.

Gilbert, R. M. (1992). *Extraordinary relationships: A new way of thinking about human interactions.* New York: John Wiley.

Gottman, J. M. (1994). *What predicts divorce: The relationship between marital processes and marital outcomes.* Hillsdale, NJ: Erlbaum.

Guerin, P. J., Jr. (2002). Bowenian family therapy. In J. Carlson & D. Kjos (Eds.), *Theories and strategies of family therapy* (pp. 126–157). Boston: Allyn & Bacon.

Guerin, P. J., Jr., Fogarty, T. F., Fay, L. F., & Kautto, J. G. (1996). *Working with relationship triangles: The one-two-three of psychotherapy*. New York: Guilford.

Kerr, M. E., & Bowen, M. (1988). *Family evaluation*. New York: Norton.

Luepnitz, D. A. (1988). *The family interpreted: Feminist theory in clinical practice*. New York: Basic Books.

McGoldrick, M. (Ed.). (1998). *Re-visioning family therapy: Race, culture and gender in clinical practice*. New York: Guilford.

McGoldrick, M. (2005). Powerpoint Presentation on Genograms. In Milton H. Erickson Foundation, *Evolution of Psychotherapy Handout CD*. Phoenix, AZ: Author.

McGoldrick, M., Anderson, C. M., & Walsh, F. (Eds.). (1989). *Women in families: A framework for family therapy*. New York: Norton.

McGoldrick, M., Gerson, R., & Shellenberger, S. (2005). *Genograms: Assessment and intervention* (3rd ed.). New York: Norton.

McGoldrick, M., Giordano, J., & Garcia-Preto, N. (Eds.). (2005). *Ethnicity and family therapy* (3rd ed.). New York: Guilford.

Papero, D. V. (2000). The Bowen theory. In A. M. Horne (Ed.), *Family counseling and therapy* (3rd ed., pp. 272–299). Itasca, IL: F. E. Peacock.

Toman, W. (1993). *Family constellation: Its effects on personality and social behavior* (4th ed.). New York: Springer. (Original work published 1961)

Walsh, F. (Ed.). (2003). *Normal family processes: Growing diversity and complexity* (3rd ed.). New York: Guilford.

Walsh, F., & McGoldrick, M. (Eds.). (1991). *Living beyond loss: Death in the family*. New York: Norton.

Walters, M., Carter, B., Papp, P., & Silverstein, O. (1988). *The invisible web: Gender patterns in family relationships*. New York: Guilford.

Endnotes

[1]Elliott Rosen became director when Betty Carter retired and the Family Institute of Westchester has moved to Harrison, New York. The training programs remain based on Bowen theory and therapy.

[2]Thomas Fogarty (1976) introduced a structural approach to differentiation with his concept of the *four-dimensional self:* The four dimensions, lateral, vertical, depth, and temporal, provide four perspectives from which individual development can be assessed. The lateral dimension addresses the individual's typical movement toward or away from others when engaged in interaction. It is this dimension that is involved in pursuer–distancer relationships considered later in this chapter. The depth dimension contains the emotional reactions developed over time as a result of being in relationships. The vertical dimension addresses what people do in life: how they occupy themselves, develop a career or profession, and become productive. The temporal dimension incorporates the individual's experience of time and the rhythm of life; it also assesses whether, in times of stress, the person develops anxiety over the future or stays stuck in past difficulties and failures. Each of these four dimensions, for Fogarty, has to be in rational balance for the individual to engage in functional living. His concept introduces a more fluid, developmental conceptualization to the differentiation process.

CHAPTER 5

Adlerian Family Therapy

Introduction

Key Concepts

Therapy Goals

The Therapist's Role and Function

Techniques

An Adlerian Therapist With the Quest Family

Summary and Multicultural Evaluation

Recommended Readings

References

Introduction

Alfred Adler was the first psychiatrist of the modern era to do family therapy. His approach was systemic long before systems theory had been applied to psychotherapy (Carich & Willingham, 1987). After World War I, Adler set up more than 30 child-guidance clinics in Vienna, where he conducted therapy sessions in an open forum before parents, teachers, and members of the local community. All of these clinics were eliminated by Hitler's Nazi Party by 1934 (Christensen, 2004). Rudolf Dreikurs brought the process to the United States in the form of family-education centers. He systematized and refined Adler's early work with family constellation and purposeful behavior, delineating the goals of children's misbehavior and developing an interview and goal-disclosure process that produced a **recognition reflex** in children (Terner & Pew, 1978).

A basic assumption in Adlerian family therapy is that both parents and children often become locked in repetitive, negative interactions based on mistaken goals that motivate all parties involved. Further, these negative interactions and patterns are a reflection of the autocratic/permissive dialectic that has permeated much of the Euro-American social heritage. In most cases, therefore, the problems of any one family are common to all others in their social and ethnic community. Although much of Adlerian family therapy is conducted in private sessions, Adlerians also use an educational model to counsel families in public, in an open forum at schools, community agencies, and specially designed family-education centers. At these centers, the therapist engages both a family-in-focus

Alfred Adler

Oscar Christensen

and the audience in an exploration of **motivations** and a reorientation of the family based on encouragement and the use of natural and logical consequences (Bitter, Roberts, & Sonstegard, 2002; Christensen, 2004; Sherman & Dinkmeyer, 1987).

Oscar Christensen, Professor Emeritus from the University of Arizona and one of America's foremost Adlerian family counselors, used an open forum when he met with the Lohman family (Christensen, 1979). Joyce and Tim Lohman were the parents of four children: David (age 14), Michael (age 12), Donna (age 10), and Nick (age 8). David and Donna were African-American children adopted by Joyce and Tim—both of whom were Caucasian. Michael and Nick came to the family by birth.

During the initial interview, the parents were asked to help the counselor learn about each of the children. David was described as "bossy, bright, but not a hard worker." Michael was described as "hard working, responsible, and the 'good' child." Given Adler's focus on the influence of psychological birth order, which I will develop more fully later, it is interesting to note that Michael seems to have found an area of weakness in David ("not a hard worker") and capitalized on it. Donna was presented as "liking to be the center of attention, thriving in a social context; happy at times, but also competitive and not so easy going." Nick is the "baby of the family, shy, quiet, and needing people to do things for him." Joyce further noted that Donna probably didn't have a special place as the "only girl," because both parents tended to see boys and girls as pretty much the same.

The presenting issues for the Lohman family start with a problem regarding lost or stolen money in the home. Michael has a paper route and he has kept the money he collects in a jar on the bookshelf in the living room. His money is now missing, and there has been a lot of accusing going on. Everyone in the family denies taking the money and Michael has now taken to locking his money up in the trunk of the family car. The parents also are concerned about the fighting that seems to happen most often between David and Donna. Tim believes that they seem to enjoy it, but that "the rest of the family does not."[1] And finally, there is some concern about Nick in relation to doing work around the house. He may have the job of sweeping, but he "forgets," has to be reminded by David or mom, and sometimes even gets others to do his work.

Listening to the descriptions and issues offered by the parents, Dr. Christensen (1979) described the family system in the following manner:

> I think we really have two oldest children in this family: Dave finds his place by being the leader, the responsible person, and many things in that direction. Mike's power, I think, is in his goodness. He gets an awful lot of mileage out of the missing money, and all the rewards and the good-guy things he was trying to do with the money. Donna finds her place by being the one nobody loves; she feels left out, and she creates a lot of situations in which people prove that she is right. And Nick, of course, is the super baby, whose greatest strength is putting others in his service. It's as if his great power over people, really, is in being helpless or needing assistance.

What do you think of Dr. Christensen's summary of the family system? Is that how you would describe these children or do you have a different picture? What influence do you think the attitudes, values, beliefs, and convictions of the parents have on the family unit? Do you think, in general, that parents or siblings have a greater influence on individual personality development? What role do you think race or **ethnicity** play in this family and the difficulties that are reported here? What effect do you think adoption has in this family? David and Donna were adopted when they were younger than 5 years old: Would it have made a difference in the development of the family system if they had been older when they were adopted? Are you concerned at all with the idea that parents within the dominant culture in the United States are raising children from a discriminated and marginalized culture? Do you think David and Donna will lose a significant part of their heritage and culture being raised by the Lohmans? How might a consideration of race, ethnicity, and culture inform and structure this family counseling session?

In this initial session, Dr. Christensen was interested in getting to know the children psychologically, paying special attention to the mistaken goals that might be motivating the problem behaviors described by the parents. Here is the interview that he conducted with the four children in relation to the first issue the parents raised.

Christensen:	Mike, mom tells me that there's some money missing at your house that you had. Can you tell me a little bit about it?
Mike:	Quite a bit of money was missing. I had it on a shelf, and then I noticed it was missing the next day. This was my money from collection when I do my route.
Christensen:	How does that make you feel?
Mike:	I don't like it at all: Distrustful of the kids in my family. Since it was taken, I don't let them use any of my stuff or go in my room.
Christensen:	That's kind of sad, isn't it? You don't feel like you can trust them. Did you ask the other kids who did it? You don't think they did—or do you?
Mike:	Yes, I think so, because no one else came in the house.
Christensen:	So who do you think it is?
Mike:	Well, Donna's taken some money before, and Nick has. But I don't think it's Nick, because I threatened that no one could use stuff in my room, and Nick, he likes to use stuff, like my football. So Donna could have done it.
Christensen:	Maybe Donna, huh? Donna, it looks like you might want to say something to that. Do you want to say something?
Donna:	(head slightly down with no eye contact) Yeah. I wouldn't do it, because before Mike offered us each a dollar if any of his stuff wasn't stolen. So, I am trying not to go in his room at all or steal anything from anybody in the family.
Christensen:	Well, that's pretty neat. And how do you "try" hard?
Donna:	I try by not thinking of money anymore.
Christensen:	Okay, do you have any idea why you maybe stole money before?
Donna:	I don't know.
Christensen:	Could it have been your way to show everybody you're the boss?
Donna:	I don't think so.
Christensen:	I don't think so either. Could it possibly be that this is your way of kind of getting even with everybody?
Donna:	Might have been.
Christensen:	Might have been. That's a possibility, huh? So sometimes you like to hurt other people's feelings, because your feelings are hurt?
Donna:	Yes.
Christensen:	Could it be that sometimes Mike and Dave hurt your feelings?
Donna:	Yeah.
Christensen:	Could you tell me how they do it?
Donna:	They call me names! Saying I'm stupid.

Christensen:	That would hurt anybody's feelings, I suspect. Why do you suppose they do that?
Donna:	I don't know.
Christensen:	I'm not sure either, but do you suppose you sometimes do something to make them call you stupid?
Donna:	Sometimes. Because they think I'm trying to be better than they are, and they just want to try to make me feel bad, because my feelings get hurt easy.
Christensen:	And when your feelings get hurt easy, what do you make them do?
Donna:	I don't know.
Christensen:	Could it be that sometimes you feel sad, because this is a way you have to feel a little bit sorry for yourself? And when you feel sorry for yourself, what does that give you a right to do . . . when you're feeling oh-so-sad?
Donna:	(shrugs) I don't know.
Christensen:	Sometimes, does it let you kind of get even with the boys? (pause) So what do you do when you are really mad at the boys? Sometimes, do you think about taking something of theirs that means a lot to them? Maybe really get even with them? [Donna's face suggests a recognition reflex as described later in this chapter.] That's a possibility.

> Dr. Christensen turns the conversation toward Nick in an effort to help him understand the motivation for his forgetfulness. Adlerian family counselors and therapists use a tentative goal-disclosure process to see if the child will indicate through a little smile and a twinkling in the eyes (what Dreikurs called a recognition reflex) that the purpose has been revealed.

Christensen:	Nick, mom tells me that you have some difficulty getting the sweeping done. In fact, you've had the sweeping job for a couple of weeks now and still haven't gotten around to it. How come you do that?
Nick:	Because I keep forgetting.
Christensen:	How come you're such a good forgetter?
Nick:	I don't know.
Christensen:	I just don't know if I've ever met anybody who has such a good forgetter as you do. Are you probably the best in the whole family at forgetting?
Nick:	(shrugs) Un-huh.
Christensen:	Must take a lot of skill to be able to forget that well: Do you have any idea why you forget so good?
Nick:	Nope.
Christensen:	I'm not sure either, but could it be that this is a good way for you to have people help you—and take care of you?
Nick:	Maybe. (with a recognition reflex)
Christensen:	Maybe. And could it be your way to have mom and dad treat you a little extra-special . . . because you're the baby.
Nick:	Un-huh.
Christensen:	Would you like to change that? (Nick: Un-huh.) Nick, one thing I'm going to tell your mom and dad—and I think your big brothers and big sister, too—is that in order to show you how much we respect you, we're going to quit doing so much for you. That's how we allow you to grow up. And that's where big guys in the family, like Dave, come in: Dave is an important person in your life, and I'd like to ask Dave to not help Nick so much. Let him be the person who helps for a change.

Dr. Christensen then engages Dave and Mike in a conversation about the ways in which they become involved in fighting with Donna, their younger sister. Donna sometimes may provoke one of them into fights that go on until one of the parents gets upset. This happens most often with Dave. Mike, on the other hand, has such an investment in being the "good guy" that he sits back and smiles when Donna gets in trouble. This encourages Dave to keep Donna down. It is suggested that both of them sometimes work at keeping Donna the "bad one." Dr. Christensen wonders if it might be possible for the boys to walk away when provoked and for them to refuse to fight with her.

Children most often misbehave in direct relation to the **parent value system**. Here, the parents value harmony and cooperation, so fighting is a response that both gains attention and demonstrates power.

Christensen: I think most people would perceive Donna to be the problem child. I don't think she is. I think she has perceived that the best way to fit into this family is through her sadness. I'm not impressed with her sadness, and I would like to see [the rest of the family] become less impressed with it. She's much too strong a child to feel sorry for her. She can handle these three boys and any other six just like them.

Staying out of the children's fights will minimize the first-child dominance of Dave, as well as the moral superiority of Michael, the former demonstrating power through bossiness and the latter through moral goodness. Nick demonstrates his power by being helpless and putting others in his service. The recommendation for the family is to never do things for Nick that he can do for himself.

Key Concepts

Adlerians believe that human beings are essentially social, purposeful, subjective and interpretive in their approach to life (Sweeney, 1998). These attributes are no accident. They are required at least in part from the moment of birth. Without the social, physical, and emotional nurturing provided in the family, no infant would survive. Within the family, children quickly become active agents, defining and redefining the family constellation or system; striving for growth, significance, and meaning; and acting in line with their subjective, and too often mistaken, interpretations of life.

Parents should be the natural leaders of families. They are older, more experienced, and carry societal mandates for rearing the next generation. Too often, however, children have a far greater impact on the development and interactions of the family than do the parents. Even in functional families, children seem more capable of influencing adult behavior than the other way around. In part, this is because most adults have very little effective preparation for parenting. When push comes to shove, most parents reenact the **autocratic** or **permissive** upbringings that they experienced themselves.

Family Atmosphere

"The conjunction of all the family forces—the climate of relationships that exist between people—is termed family atmosphere" (Sherman & Dinkmeyer, 1987, p. 9). Because the family is a system, each member exerts an influence on every other member. In each family, an atmosphere or climate develops that can be said to characterize how the family members relate to each other. We already have noted that both autocratic and permissive atmospheres are common in western Euro-American culture and easily become incorporated in family life as a need for power and control.

Family atmosphere, however, is unique to each family. The relationship between the parents is often the clearest indication of what will constitute the family's way of being and interacting. Parents are the models for how one gender relates to the other, how to work and participate in the world, how to get along with other people. Children may experience these models as joyful, angry, loving, frightening, strict, easy-going, involved, indulgent, protective/ overprotective, hostile, nurturing, challenging, or respectful, to name a few. What the family comes to value plays a significant role in the development of children and family life. When both parents maintain and support the same value, Adlerians call it a **family value**: It is a value that cannot be ignored and that will require each child to take a stand in relation to it. Common family values emerge around education, religion, money, achievement, right and wrong.

> An essential ingredient in family atmosphere is the manner in which the members communicate. Who speaks to whom? Do they tend to be hostile, critical, command-ing, direct, indirect, attentive, preoccupied, active, passive, cooperative, competitive? Are they warm, caring, and able to negotiate differences? Do they utilize double mes-sages, create openness or rigidity, fear or seriousness? Is there a sense of tension, chal-lenge, or ease? (Sherman & Dinkmeyer, 1987, p. 10)

Each person within the system learns to negotiate within the limitations of the climate established. With rare exceptions, the atmosphere in which we are raised tends to become the model for how we expect life and the world to be.

The Family Constellation

Adler (1930, 1931, 1938) often noted that the family system or constellation consisted of the parents, children, and even extended family members, but then he would immediately shift to a discussion of birth order. Adler made reference to essentially five birth positions: only, oldest, second-of-only-two, middle, and youngest.

Both only children and oldest children have their parents all to themselves at least for a short period of time, and parents seem to have a strong influence on their early development. Only and oldest children will tend to have a high achievement drive, regardless of whether they actually do succeed in achieving, and both will be interested in continuing what the family values. Only children, however, will never be dethroned by the birth of another sibling. They will remain the center of the adult world. They may develop adult language sooner than other children, and they will be almost forced to take a stand for or against the parents' value system: They either embrace it or fight it, but seldom take a middle ground. If only children are pam-pered or overprotected, they easily can become spoiled, but they also can respond to care, affection, and additional resources with a high degree of success.

It is hard for oldest children not to become impressed with the position of being "first" or "on top," and they will do almost anything to stay in that position. When this position is threatened, oldest children may seem timid, extremely sensitive, or easily hurt. Many oldest children are dependable, serious, responsible, "good" individuals who seek adult approval. They may tend toward perfectionism and can sometimes want to do only those things at which they already know they can succeed. They often are expected by their parents to "set a good model" for their siblings, and younger children will consider them bossy.

The child who is the second-of-only-two is extremely focused on the oldest child. Indeed, the oldest child has far more influence on the child in the second position than the parents ever will have. In most cases, the second-of-only-two will decide to be the opposite of whatever she or he believes the firstborn to be. It is as if the second born is in a race, always trying to catch-up, and in constant competition. The second-of-only-two will never have the parents' undivided attention, so children in this position seek to be different: The things at which the oldest child excels, the second child will avoid—and vice versa.

When a third child is born, second children become middle children. They quickly learn that they are squeezed between an oldest child, who always seems to be on top, and a young-est child, who seems to be able to get privileges and service from the parents. Life seems unfair to middle children. They also may believe that the oldest and the youngest align against them, leaving the middle child to take the blame for problems or simply leaving them out altogether. They are sensitive to criticism and easily angered when being bossed around. They may seek a peer group to whom they give more allegiance than the family. They even may rebel against expectations and traditions. But they never stop comparing themselves to others: Suffering by comparison too often becomes a constant in life.

Youngest children will never be dethroned. A true youngest is always the baby of the family. Typically, youngest children use helplessness and dependent behaviors to put others—especially parents—in their service. They also can be good entertainers and good observers. Often, they will use their observations to develop in areas and ways that none of their siblings have attempted and often they will outshine all of their brothers and sisters. Being the baby can lead them to the conclusion that they are special, but they also can decide they are unwanted. Those who believe they are special may seek pampering or overprotection: They can become easily spoiled. Those who think that they do not have a place may begin to feel hated or neglected.

These five positions represent vantage points from which children view the world. It is not the position, however, that counts, but rather the meaning and interpretation the child gives to that position. In this sense, every person's birth position is unique and uniquely defined. Adler's (1931) emphasis on **phenomenological** interpretation of family position (or perceived place within the family) was so strong that, even when he talked about parents in an unhappy marriage, he believed children would intervene as active agents. Although he acknowledged the dangers of raising children in a disruptive marriage, he also thought that the children would become skilled at reading dissension and play one parent against the other. Adlerians believe that children do not merely react: They interact, often having more influence on the responses of parents than the other way around.

In addition to a phenomenological assessment of birth position, Adlerians consider a number of additional variables in describing the family constellation. How many years are there between the siblings? Is a child the only boy or girl in the family? What are the effects of being special (for example, being twins; being the favorite of a parent or grandparent; being ill, physically challenged, traumatized, or facing death; or being talented or beautiful)? What are the effects of **family structure** (for example, being in a single-parent home or in a blended family, or being part of an extended family)? Taken together, each of these considerations contributes to the development of a pattern that indicates how family members fit into the system and how each is likely to act and interact. "It is the actions and interactions within the family and the interpretations that each person assigns to these that give initial meaning to children's lives and to the family as a whole" (Bitter, Roberts, & Sonstegard, 2002, p. 46).

Adlerian family therapists view the family constellation as a description of how each person finds a place within the system. How does each child relate to the parents, guardians, or extended family members? How does each child relate to and define "self" in relation to the other children? Who is most different from whom? Which children have aligned with each other? Against whom? Which parents have aligned with which children? Toward what end? How does each child address family values; negotiate within and influence the family atmosphere; or handle the impact of culture, age and gender differences, and the demands of school and society?

A typical investigation of a family constellation may start by asking the parents to describe each of the children. These descriptions often reveal both the effects of birth order and the unique ways in which each child has adapted behaviors to engage or challenge what is important to the parents. Many Adlerians use genograms to develop a graphic picture of the family system (Bitter, 1988, 1991a; Sherman & Dinkmeyer, 1987). A phenomenological perspective can be gained by asking family members, especially the index person or a child the family identifies as having difficulties, to provide three adjectives for each person in the genogram. In 1932, Adler noted that descriptions of family members reveal a statement about self within various relationships. He stated:

> . . . there is no character trait without a relationship to others. When the patient says, "My father was kind," this means "he was kind to *me*." When he says his mother was critical, the idea which penetrates is that he attempted to keep at a distance from his mother. (Ansbacher & Ansbacher, 1979, p. 194)

Although descriptions of parents tend to reveal essential information about the describer's sense of belonging, adjectives assigned to siblings require a knowledge of the relationship the person has with each of the siblings. Knowing that my sister is "happy, achieving, and pleasing" is only useful if the therapist knows whether the describer is similar to or the opposite of this sister. In the Adlerian model, a genogram says nothing in and of itself. It is a starting point from which clients communicate the meaning in their lives. When whole families construct a genogram, there are often as many interpretations as there are family members.

Mistaken Goals: An Interactional View

Adlerians make a distinction between the life goals that account for the development of lifestyles and the more immediate goals that account for everyday behavior. Dreikurs (1940a, 1940b) first delineated four goals of children's misbehavior as a motivational typology for the everyday behaviors of children. These goals are **attention getting, power struggle, revenge**, and a **demonstration of inadequacy** (also called an **assumed disability**). They act as "shorthand explanations/descriptions of consistent patterns of misbehavior in children" (Bitter, 1991b, p. 210), and they reflect increasing levels of discouragement with each additional goal.

Dreikurs (1950) and Dreikurs and Soltz (1964) also developed a systematic approach to goal recognition based on (a) descriptions of the child's misbehavior, (b) the parents' reactions to the misbehavior, and (c) the child's reaction to the parents' attempts at discipline. The goal recognition criteria can be summarized using the following chart (Figure 5.1):

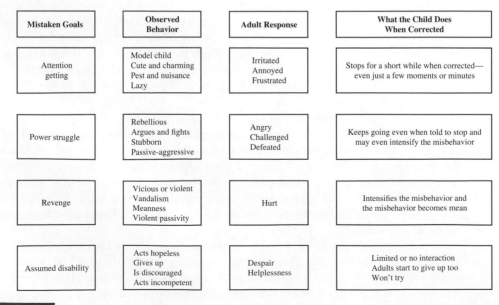

Mistaken Goals	Observed Behavior	Adult Response	What the Child Does When Corrected
Attention getting	Model child Cute and charming Pest and nuisance Lazy	Irritated Annoyed Frustrated	Stops for a short while when corrected—even just a few moments or minutes
Power struggle	Rebellious Argues and fights Stubborn Passive-aggressive	Angry Challenged Defeated	Keeps going even when told to stop and may even intensify the misbehavior
Revenge	Vicious or violent Vandalism Meanness Violent passivity	Hurt	Intensifies the misbehavior and the misbehavior becomes mean
Assumed disability	Acts hopeless Gives up Is discouraged Acts incompetent	Despair Helplessness	Limited or no interaction Adults start to give up too Won't try

Figure 5.1

Identifying the mistaken goals of children's misbehavior.

Using these four goals as tentative hypotheses, Dreikurs found that he could suggest mistaken goals to children, and that a recognition reflex (a smile or a twinkle in the eyes) would indicate which goals the children sought. Let us say that two children are constantly fighting in the family, often drawing one or both parents in as referees. Dreikurs' goal disclosure process would take the following form:

Therapist:	Do you know why the two of you fight all the time?
Child:	(shrugging shoulders) Well, he starts it.
Therapist:	Maybe, but I have a different idea. Would you like to hear it?
Children:	(shrugging shoulders again, but looking attentive)
Therapist:	Could it be that the two of you fight all the time to see if you can get your mom or dad to tell you to stop?

In this example, the goal of attention getting has been suggested in terms that the children will understand. The other three goals might be tentatively advanced in the following manner:

Power:	Could it be that you want to show your parents that you are the boss or that they can't make you stop?
Revenge:	Could it be that you feel hurt, and this is a way to get back at them, to get even?
Assumed disability:	Could it be that you want to be left alone?

I have added three additional goals to this Adlerian conceptualization that I believe act as conscious motivations for some behaviors, especially in very young children. These goals are **getting, self-elevation,** and **avoidance** (Bitter, 1991b). For example, some children simply operate on the mistaken notion that they should get whatever they want, no matter what it is or to whom it belongs. Because the child has no prohibition against taking what he or she wants, the motivation of getting can be wholly conscious. Adults may call the misbehavior "stealing," but the child is simply getting what is wanted. Another example of a conscious motivation is lying. In order to lie, a child must know the truth and consciously choose to say something that is false. If the child does not know a statement is false, she or he is mistaken, but not lying. When we ask, "What is the purpose of lying?", two immediate goals tend to account for this misbehavior: Self-elevation or avoidance. In the case of self-elevation, children tell stories that make them feel or appear more important than they really are. By far, however, the most common goal for lying is avoidance in all of its various forms: avoidance of punishment or criticism; avoidance of embarrassment or humiliation; avoidance of responsibilities or commitments; or even avoidance of hurting other people's feelings or disappointing others.

Again, these three conscious goals can be disclosed to children in a manner similar to the Dreikursian process I described earlier:

Getting:	Could it be that you believe you should get whatever you want when you want it?
Self-elevation:	Could it be that you want people to know how good or important you are?
Avoidance:	Could it be that you don't like _____, and you will do anything to avoid it?

In addition to delineating the mistaken goals of children, several Adlerian writers have suggested interactional, mistaken goal patterns between adults and children (Bitter, Roberts, & Sonstegard, 2000; Main, 1986). In one of Dreikurs' (1948) early books, he suggested that parents had mistaken goals that often aligned with the mistaken goals of children. Based on Dreikurs' suggestion, I developed the chart, shown in Figure 5.2, that outlined this interactional goal process (Bitter, Roberts, & Sonstegard, 2002). Adults tend to create a picture of themselves as *good parents* (adult goal #1). This picture includes certain attributes, ways of being, and desired child behaviors that are deemed essential to being a good parent. Children see this picture and read its meaning in everything the parent does, and they use it as a button

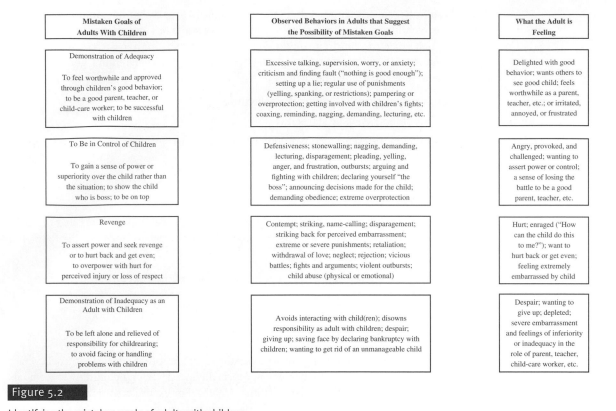

Mistaken Goals of Adults With Children	Observed Behaviors in Adults that Suggest the Possibility of Mistaken Goals	What the Adult is Feeling
Demonstration of Adequacy To feel worthwhile and approved through children's good behavior; to be a good parent, teacher, or child-care worker; to be successful with children	Excessive talking, supervision, worry, or anxiety; criticism and finding fault ("nothing is good enough"); setting up a lie; regular use of punishments (yelling, spanking, or restrictions); pampering or overprotection; getting involved with children's fights; coaxing, reminding, nagging, demanding, lecturing, etc.	Delighted with good behavior; wants others to see good child; feels worthwhile as a parent, teacher, etc.; or irritated, annoyed, or frustrated
To Be in Control of Children To gain a sense of power or superiority over the child rather than the situation; to show the child who is boss; to be on top	Defensiveness; stonewalling; nagging, demanding, lecturing, disparagement; pleading, yelling, anger, and frustration, outbursts; arguing and fighting with children; declaring yourself "the boss"; announcing decisions made for the child; demanding obedience; extreme overprotection	Angry, provoked, and challenged; wanting to assert power or control; a sense of losing the battle to be a good parent, teacher, etc.
Revenge To assert power and seek revenge or to hurt back and get even; to overpower with hurt for perceived injury or loss of respect	Contempt; striking, name-calling; disparagement; striking back for perceived embarrassment; extreme or severe punishments; retaliation; withdrawal of love; neglect; rejection; vicious battles; fights and arguments; violent outbursts; child abuse (physical or emotional)	Hurt; enraged ("How can the child do this to me?"); want to hurt back or get even; feeling extremely embarrassed by child
Demonstration of Inadequacy as an Adult with Children To be left alone and relieved of responsibility for childrearing; to avoid facing or handling problems with children	Avoids interacting with child(ren); disowns responsibility as adult with children; despair; giving up; saving face by declaring bankruptcy with children; wanting to get rid of an unmanageable child	Despair; wanting to give up; depleted; severe embarrassment and feelings of inferiority or inadequacy in the role of parent, teacher, child-care worker, etc.

Figure 5.2

Identifying the mistaken goals of adults with children.

they can push to get attention. Either constant button pushing or power struggles can lead parents to seek **control** (adult goal #2), which in turn invites more power struggles. When parental control is constantly challenged or the child acts in ways designed to get even, parents may resort to seeking *revenge* (adult goal #3). When this happens, the family usually has developed an interactive process that is pathological. In rare cases, parents become totally discouraged and give up, seeking to *demonstrate that raising this child is hopeless* (adult goal #4).

By keeping these interactive goal patterns in mind, Adlerians are able to make sense of both the children's behaviors and the parental actions and reactions reported in family process. Goal recognition and disclosure is central to Adlerian family counseling and therapy (Bitter, Christensen, Hawes & Nicoll, 1998; Christensen, 2004). It systematizes the interviewing process and allows parents and children to back away from mistaken behaviors in favor of more functional and effective approaches.

Therapy Goals

Adlerian family therapists want to engage parents in a learning experience and a collaborative assessment. Part of this assessment includes an investigation of the multiple ways in which parents function as family leaders—or lose the ability to do so. Under most conditions, a goal of therapy is to establish and support parents as effective leaders of the family.

Using the information gathered during assessment, Adlerians explicate the systemic process in the family by describing the place that each person has assumed and the interactive processes that are repeated in daily living. Goal disclosure also is used to facilitate an under-standing of the motivations involved. These interventions serve another goal of therapy: to replace automatic, often non-conscious, negative interactions with a conscious understand-ing of family process.

Adlerian family therapists characterize their approach as **motivation modification** rather than behavior modification. The therapist develops with families specific changes in process that are designed to replace mistaken goals with those that favor functional family interactions. During the last half of the 20th century, Adlerians developed a wide range of parenting skills and interventions that constitute what is now called **authoritative-responsive parenting** or **democratic child-rearing** (Dinkmeyer, McKay & Dinkmeyer, 1997; Lew, 1999; Popkin, 1993). Based on an understanding of the family's specific motivational patterns, parents often leave the therapy session with suggestions designed to initiate a reorientation of the family.

The Therapist's Role and Function

Adlerian family therapists function as collaborators who seek to join the family from a posi-tion of mutual respect. Within this collaborative role, Adlerians stress the functions of sys-temic investigation and education (Bitter et al., 1998; Bitter, Roberts, & Sonstegard, 2002). The systemic investigation focuses on (a) the family constellation or system, (b) the motiva-tions behind problematic interactions, and (c) the family process throughout a typical day. The results of this investigation are used to disclose and discuss the mistaken goals or ideas that may be involved in problematic parent–child interactions. In raising mistaken goals to a conscious consideration, the therapist is able to develop with the family interventions and rec-ommendations designed to correct mistaken goals and provide parents with an understanding of parenting skills associated with more effective and harmonious living.

Adlerian family therapists often use a public therapy process they call **open-forum family counseling** (Bitter et al., 1998; Christensen, 2004). Similar to the process first used by Adler in Vienna, the therapist counsels a family in front of a group of parents, teachers, and other community members. The counselor in these sessions has two clients: the family-in-focus and the audience. The process emphasizes interactions within the family. Very little is disclosed that could not be observed by anyone watching the family in public. By working with the commonalities between the family and the audience, the therapist educates many families through one. It is not uncommon for families in the audience to get more out of the session than the family-in-focus.

Techniques

The open-forum process used by Adlerians has been delineated in several texts over many years (Christensen, 2004; Dinkmeyer & Carlson, 2001; Dinkmeyer, & Sperry, 2000; Dreikurs, Corsini, Lowe, & Sonstegard, 1959). More recently, the process has been incorporated as part of **Adlerian brief therapy** (Bitter et al., 1998). In this model, the parents generally are interviewed initially without the children, a process that supports the establishment of parents-as-leaders in the family. The therapist joins with the parents and the audience through an exploration of the family constellation. The experience of parent–child relationships held in common between the family and the audience links the two, allowing members of each system to have a therapeutic influence on the other.

Problem Descriptions and Goal Identification.   Adlerian therapists use specific examples to understand the concerns that parents present. While listening to a description of specific prob-lem incidents, the counselor often asks the parent(s): "When was the last time that this problem happened? What did you do about it?" These questions help to establish the negative interaction pattern that is likely to be repeated many times during the day. The therapist also asks the parent(s): "How did you feel (or react) when . . . ?" Parents' feelings and reactions are often the most reliable clue to both mistaken goals in children and adults. (See the earlier discussion of mistaken goals for the relationship between child motivation and parental response.)

Typical Day.   Adlerians often assess the family atmosphere and family interactional patterns by asking the family to describe a typical day. An exploration of a typical day will reveal repeated patterns of interaction and the ways in which children meet their immediate goals—as well as the atmosphere and family values supported by the parents' approach to each other and to child-rearing. An investigation of a typical day is especially useful when parents are unable to present specific incidents of concern. Adlerians expect that the same parent–child interactions reported while trying to wake up the children will be repeated a number of times before bedtime.

The Child Interview and Goal Disclosure.   Parent interviews generally yield tentative hypotheses about the goals of children's misbehavior. These guesses are shared with the parents, but they remain only possibilities until they are confirmed in an interview with the child(ren). Goal disclosure with children works best in relation to a specific event or misbehavior, rather than a general discussion. When such an event or misbehavior has been clarified with the child, goals are suggested tentatively. Using Dreikurs' intervention model, Adlerians often ask: "Do you know why you do . . . ?" Children's answers are neither accepted nor rejected, but are acknowledged as a transition to disclosure: "That's a possibility. I have another idea. Would you like to hear it?" As much as possible, goals are suggested in language that has meaning for the child. Again, using Dreikurs' four goals with a child who skips school:

- "Could it be that you skip school to keep dad busy with you?" (attention)
- "Could it be that you skip school to show mom that you're the boss and that no one can make you go?" (a power struggle)
- "Could it be that you skip school to get even with dad?" (revenge)
- "Could it be that you skip school because you want to be left alone?" (an assumed disability)

If the therapist is correct with any of these guesses, the child often will exhibit a recognition reflex. This reflex is a confirmation of the motivational diagnosis. Without a recognition response, the counselor's original assessment of the purposes for misbehavior is suspect and a reevaluation must be considered based on the development of new data.

Reorienting and Reeducating the Family.   Adlerians use the concept of **reorientation** to suggest that most families merely need to be redirected toward a more useful path. In the rare situations in which families seem to need restructuring, Adlerians would seek to help parents become effective leaders of the family, working in cooperation with each other for the welfare of the children. Family reorientation requires an understanding of the essential needs and purposes of the system, as well as the individuals within the system. The first essential needs are safety and encouragement. Caring about the welfare of the family is a foundation for meeting this need. People and systems grow, adapt, and change when strengths are appreciated and the individuals involved have faith in each other, are able to choose among options, and realize their hopes for happiness. Reframing and **normalizing family experiences** are two interventions that support the development of hope.

Families can change dysfunctional interactions when even one person is able to disengage from repetitive, negative patterns. In general, Adlerians believe parents are more likely to disengage when they understand the mistaken goals of their children's misbehavior and, perhaps, even their own mistaken goals in relation to raising the children. It is extremely difficult to maintain useless interactions when purposes have been disclosed and unconscious processes have been made conscious. Because Adlerians want parents to be the natural leaders of the family, helping parents exercise self-control in their adult–child interactions is an essential step.

Leadership in families is supported when each parent feels like a valued team member, and there is a sense of trust and mutual respect between them. This does not mean that both parents need to handle the children in exactly the same way. Indeed, each parent may approach the children differently as long as the other parent is not undermined in the eyes of the children. In many instances, Adlerians simply charge each parent to "mind your own business": When one parent is handling a situation, the other one stays out of it—or even supports it. In cases in which there is a lot of dissension between the parents, work on the couple's relationship is necessary before family work can continue.

When parental leadership seems sound, Adlerian counselors and therapists will tend to engage in some form of parent education, co-developing recommendations for change specifically designed to redirect mistaken goals or interactions. Effective recommendations are based on the implementation of **natural and logical consequences, encouragement**, and **emotional/psychological support** (see Dinkmeyer et al., 1997; Dreikurs & Grey, 1968; Gottman, 1997; Popkin, 1993). Adlerians believe that effective parent education is based on democratic living and real, **social equality** with children.

Neither individuals nor families change in therapy sessions. Change is enacted between therapy sessions. Because nothing succeeds like success, Adlerians often will tailor recommendations to address one issue at a time—and often the problem addressed may be the easiest of the parent's essential concerns. Encouragement of parents is an important part of the reorientation process: In an open forum, both ideas for change and encouragement most often come from audience members. In private sessions, therapists help the family generate their own options for change.

Once a process for change has been identified, the Adlerian family therapist or counselor always seeks a commitment from the parents to engage the children differently. When a parent says that she or he will "try," the therapist knows that some reevaluation of the commitment to change is needed. Sometimes, the planned changes are too much for one or both of the parents to handle. Sometimes the relationship between redirecting mistaken goals and the parent recommendation is unclear. And sometimes parents simply find it hard to rely only on self-control and give up their more familiar attempts to control the child. When parents are able to commit to change, especially in front of an audience in an open forum, change in the family will be noticeable generally within a week.

An Adlerian Therapist With the Quest Family

Paul and Jane Quest bring all four of their children to the first meeting with an Adlerian therapist. Jane had initially come to a family education center where she watched another family counseled in an open forum. Although she felt encouraged by attending the session, she still felt that her family needed more privacy than an open forum would allow, and she made arrangements for private therapy with the therapist. The Adlerian therapist began the sessions by welcoming everyone and by meeting and greeting each family member. She noted that she knew very little about the family, but that she had met Jane a few days earlier, and Jane had given her a brief idea of the family history. Starting with Paul, she asked each family member how he or she felt about coming to the session.

Paul noted that he was very busy at work and always had been. He felt he relied on Jane to handle matters at home, but he also wanted to be involved. He was excited about having the boys join the family, but the changes had been hard on everyone, and he wanted whatever help the family could get. Jane said she was relieved to be there. She felt the family she had seen counseled at the center had really been helped, but she felt her family had more serious problems. Amy and Ann both indicated that they were there because their parents wanted them to come. They were okay with their parents' decision to add the boys to the family, but they didn't really feel connected to them yet. "The boys can be difficult," Amy noted. The boys were very talkative, interrupting often, and in constant motion.

In the therapy room, Jane tried to corral the boys once or twice and tried to make them sit down. Sometimes they would sit briefly, but then they would be on the move again. The therapist asked her how she felt trying to get the boys to sit down. Jane said that they did this all the time. They exhausted her. She felt irritated with them at the moment, but she thought she would be feeling angry quite soon. "What would happen for the time being if we just let them do what they want to do?" the therapist asked. "There is really nothing they can hurt in here or that will hurt them." Jane thought that would be okay, if the therapist didn't mind.

Amy and Ann sat together next to their father and across from the two empty chairs placed close to their mother for the boys. Addressing Paul and Jane first, the therapist began the session.

Therapist:	Could the two of you describe your family for me. What are all of you like—maybe three adjectives for each person? Something like that.
Jane:	Well, Paul is a doctor, very dedicated to his work and gone a lot. Is that what you mean? [therapist nods] He's very intelligent, very goal-oriented, very dedicated to his patients.
Therapist:	And Paul, how would you describe Jane?
Paul:	Jane is really the head of our household. Without her, nothing works. She has done a terrific job raising Amy and Ann, and she is doing the best that anyone could do with the boys at this point.
Therapist:	So tell me about each of the children.
Paul:	Amy is bright, but doesn't pay attention to details. She is messy, but if I ask her to do something, she is very dependable. Ann works hard at everything. She, too, is very dependable. And she is our neat one. Like her mother, she likes everything just so.
Therapist:	Can you tell me about Jason and Luke now?
Jane:	Both of the boys were terribly hurt in their young lives, and they often seem intent on hurting each other even more. Jason likes to be the boss of Luke, and Luke sometimes goes along with it and sometimes not. Jason is very loud. Luke is quieter. Jason doesn't like to be held. Luke would sit in my lap all day if I let him. Luke can play by himself pretty well. Jason can't handle playing alone. He always needs someone interacting with him.

Just as the therapist is about to ask another question, a small fight breaks out between the boys. Jane immediately gets up and makes both of the boys sit down in the circle.

Jane to Jason:	I don't care if he did push you, we don't hit your brother.
Jason:	I didn't hit him.
Jane:	No. You kicked him.
Jason:	Well, I didn't mean to.
Therapist:	Jason, can I tell you a short story my father told me once?
Jason:	No!
Therapist:	Okay, would anyone else like to hear it?
Luke:	Me!
Therapist:	Okay, Luke, I will tell you the story, and if Jason doesn't want to hear it, he can cover his ears. [Jason covers his ears, but looks very intently at the therapist.]

Therapist:	There once was a boy who lived in the woods. His best friend was a big, kind, gentle bear. One day, the boy was sleeping on the ground, and a fly came along and landed on the boy's nose. The bear thought: "That fly will bother my friend, the boy, and wake him up. I have to get rid of the fly." So the bear got up from the rock he had been sitting on, picked up the rock, and dropped it on the fly that was still sitting on the boy's nose. Do you think the rock hurt the boy?
Luke:	The rock hit the boy?
Jason:	The bear dropped the rock on the boy hard.
Therapist:	Yes, but you can't be mad at the bear, Jason; after all, the bear didn't mean to hurt the boy, did he?
Jason:	No.
Jane:	But the boy was still hurt by the rock.
Therapist:	Jason, do you ever feel hurt? [Jason shakes his head, no.] But sometimes you fight with your brother. Do you ever hurt him? [Again, Jason shakes his head, no.]
Luke:	Yes, he does.
Therapist:	[to Jane] When they fight, do they cause bruises, draw blood, anything like that.
Jane:	No, not really.

The therapist now asks Paul and each of the older girls if anyone can remember the boys doing serious damage to each other and no one can. They have done damage to the neighbor's dog; Luke has taken things from each of the older girls; and both boys have taken food and money from neighbors as well as family members. But no one can remember a time when they did serious damage to each other.

Ann:	They are just very loud when they fight. You can hear them all over the house.
Therapist:	Give me an example. When was the last time this happened?
Jane:	They were fighting this morning over the television. One of them wanted it on the Disney channel, and the other wanted it on Nickelodeon. When I came into the television room, Jason had Luke pinned to the floor, hitting him in the chest and on the shoulders.
Therapist:	And what did you do?
Jane:	I pulled them apart. I told Jason again that he was not allowed to hit his brother. I swatted Jason on the bottom, I turned the television off, and I sent them to their rooms.
Therapist:	Did they go?
Jane:	Yes.
Therapist:	Did that stop the fight?
Ann:	Not for long. We maybe had five minutes of peace, before something else got started, and I had to go break them up again.
Therapist:	Jane, how do you feel when you are breaking up these fights?
Jane:	Exhausted. Frustrated. Angry at Jason most of the time.

The therapist shifts the interview toward an investigation of how a typical day goes in their home. Both Amy and Ann have to catch a school bus before 7:00 A.M. Even though they try to be quiet, because their "father has worked late and mother is exhausted," the two boys are almost always awake before they go. Amy fixes them something to eat, and Ann gets them settled in front of a video with admonitions to be quiet so "mom and dad can rest." Paul gets up about the time that Amy and Ann leave for school. He shaves and showers before coming downstairs. He finds that he can talk to the boys early in the morning, although only Jason responds. Luke holds a blanket and sucks his thumb. He stays quiet. When Paul starts to fix breakfast and coffee for himself and coffee for Jane, Luke scrambles upstairs to get in bed with Jane. She usually wakes shortly after Luke arrives, and they snuggle for a while.

Jane: In the morning, it is like herding cats. I get up too late, I know, and I am always in a hurry. I can get Jason dressed if I keep on him, although it is always an argument about what he will wear. Luke just doesn't move. I have to do everything for him. And sometimes, when I get him dressed and go to get dressed myself, he actually takes all his clothes off again and sits in front of the television in just his underwear. It makes me so mad. I generally have yelled at least once before we leave for school. That's another thing: Jason is due at school at 8:20. We are lucky to leave for the 10 minute drive before 8:15. Often we are right down to the tardy wire when we arrive at his school. Then I drop Luke at pre-school.

Jane goes on to say that she picks Luke up at 1:00 P.M. from pre-school and Jason at 3:00 P.M. The girls arrive home on the bus about 3:45. Amy has extracurricular activities, and sometimes gets home later. Ann has cut back on almost all of her outside activities to help with the boys. It is after school when the real fighting occurs, and either Ann or Jane is constantly separating the boys. If the boys are outside playing, Ann has to go check on them at regular intervals to make sure they are not hurting someone's pet or another child. Either Ann or Jane will make dinner. Amy and Paul are often gone. Paul usually gets home after Jane has spent almost 2 hours trying to get the boys to bed. She starts trying to get Luke in bed at 7:30, and they are usually both down by 9:30 or a quarter to ten.

Therapist: I think I have a pretty good picture of how things go. Jane and Paul, I would like to start by acknowledging the obvious. You really have two families. Amy and Ann constitute your first family and Jason and Luke are your second family. And as such, psychologically, you have two oldest children in the family and two children who are the second of two. The four of them really haven't integrated into a family of four, nor are they likely to do so. There is also a framework developing around each set of children: Amy and Ann are the "good" kids, and Jason and Luke are the "difficult" or "bad" kids. Further, it is clear that Paul favors the first set, and you, Jane are working hard to make room for the second set, but you wind up feeling pretty much alone—which you would be if it were not for Ann's help.

Paul: I think you have described it perfectly.

Therapist: I want to talk to just the boys for a moment, but my general feeling, Paul, is that both Jane and the boys need you to be more involved with them. The boys need a father to show them how gentle men act and behave. And Jane, I believe, needs to feel that the two of you are in this together. How does that sit with you?

Paul: I think you are probably right. It has been hard for me to do that, because I don't know what to do often, and I often feel like I just get in Jane's way.

Therapist: Okay. Let me talk with the boys for a minute.

The therapist moves her chair to form a triangle with Jason and Luke. She starts very directly and concretely, mentioning that fighting seems to happen quite a lot between the two of them. She asks them if they know why they fight, to which Jason points out several things that Luke does "wrong."

Therapist: That may be, but I have another idea. Would you like to hear it?

Jason & Luke: [heads nod]

Therapist: Could it be that you fight to see how many times you can get your mother to tell you to stop? [Jason shakes his head, no; but Luke gets a twinkle in his eyes and a little smile across his face, a recognition reflex: then he says, "No."] Could it be that the two of you fight to show your mom that she can't make you stop? [A recognition reflex appears on Jason's face.] Maybe that's it.

The therapist now turns her attention back to the whole family. She acknowledges that bringing two new people into the family has been difficult—for the boys as well as everyone else. Blending a family with large age differences, different genders, different histories, and different developmental needs is a daunting task, and she commends everyone for being willing to create a better world for these young boys. "It may be useful, however, not to think of them as "the boys" so much and to begin to see each of them as individuals trying to find a place in the family and in the community."

The therapist goes on to note that Jason seems to feel that he counts only when he is in a power struggle with adults. He wants to feel big and important, but both his age and life experience negate this. He compensates by getting bigger people to fight with him. Luke, on the other hand, feels his smallness and wants someone to take care of him. He requires service in the morning and he expects so many extras at night that it takes hours to get him to bed. Any time the parents or the young women in the family try to control Jason or give in to Luke, the first family merely proves to "the boys" that their interpretations of self and life are correct.

Therapist: Fighting is a perfect example. Luke does something to irritate Jason. Jason starts to fight with Luke. Luke screams. Someone comes running, usually mom or Ann. Jason gets scolded and punished, but the power struggle is on. And Luke gets saved, keeps older people in his service, and reinforces his helplessness.

Jane: So what can we do when they start fighting?

Therapist: What would work for you that would basically keep you out of it and let them handle it? Keeping in mind that they don't seem to really want to hurt each other: If they did, it would have happened by now. Is it possible to ignore it?

Ann: Not really.

Jane: I could if it weren't in the house.

Therapist: Okay. So the next time they start to fight, you might go to them without talking, take them by the hands, and deposit them outside.

The therapist concludes this session by noting that there is room in this family for four "good" kids. She suggests to Jane that telling the boys not to fight—or not to do anything—only feeds a power struggle in Jason and tells Luke what to do to get attention. It is important to talk when she is encouraging any of the children (five times a day at least) or when she is listening to them and using **active listening** to paraphrase what they say and reflect what they feel. When it is time to correct a problem, however, the therapist suggests to Jane, Paul, Amy, and Ann that they need to act, and not talk. If they need to remove something dangerous from one of the boys, do it pleasantly but without talking. If they need to protect one from the other, separate them without talking. If they need to have the boys go outside to finish a fight or argument, take them there without talking. Talking only gives the boys a clue as to how to respond: It does no good anyway, because the boys are becoming selectively deaf to others in the family.

Through all of this discussion, Paul nods. He seems to understand what is being proposed and, when asked for his reaction, he says, "I think I just needed a plan, and to know what to do." The therapist continues with Paul, asking if he can arrange to come home earlier to be with the boys before they go to bed, as well as spend some special time each week with each of his new children alone, so that he gets to know them individually. He agrees to do this, and the session ends.

Summary and Multicultural Evaluation

Adler was the first psychiatrist to focus on the goal orientation of human beings and human movement or process. His student/colleague, Rudolf Dreikurs, systematized this teleological perspective, creating a foundation for Adlerian family therapy and the development of open-forum family education centers. In open-forum family counseling centers, as opposed to the private session used by the Quest family, the therapist asks the parents and the audience to generate new approaches that will end mistaken interactions and lead to more democratic, harmonious, and effective family living (Evans & Milliren, 1999). Recommendations that come from the audience are often more easily received by the family-in-focus than those that come from the counselor. Families-in-focus often experience the audience as peers in the therapy process. In the final phase of counseling, therefore, the therapist serves as a leader and educator, helping the family and the audience make the best use of the ideas that are generated. In private sessions, the therapist often serves in place of the audience, validating a change in perspective as well as useful and effective approaches to redirecting children's mistaken goals. Adlerian family therapists also use a lot of *encouragement* to strengthen parents in their resolve and help children find new purpose in life.

Adlerians note that confidentiality is impossible in an open-forum setting, and the therapist cannot guarantee it. The process relies on families to self-monitor what they say and what they present. Most of the Adlerian family interview focuses on information that is already public—that almost anyone could see if they followed the family around for a short period of time. Christensen (2004) suggests that what is lost in confidentiality is gained in accountability, since every part of the change process must "make common sense" to the members of the audience. Based on Dreikurs (1971) original formulations, most Adlerians seek to develop *social equality*—the sense that everyone has an equal right to be valued and respected—in the family. This is a development welcomed by feminists and much needed at a time when abuse of power in families is at such high levels.

Although it is probably not true of all Adlerians, it is clear from their writings that both Adler and Dreikurs were pro-feminist. Indeed, Adler was married to and collaborated with a woman from Russia, Raissa Epstein Adler, who was heavily involved in feminist causes at the beginning of the 20th century (Balla, 2003). His early writings on the myth of masculine superiority refuted the alleged inferiority of women and called for new relationships based on mutual respect and social interest. Adler's position was both echoed and developed in the more pragmatic writings of Rudolf Dreikurs (1948, 1971), who called for an end to the war between the sexes and between the generations.

Adlerians add a **teleological lens** to family therapy and counseling that helps clinicians discover and understand the purposes, goals, and private logic (ideas or notions) that motivate problem behaviors and useless interactions. Adlerians remind us that individuals, couples, and families are always in movement toward a desired end, and it is the intended goal that unifies movement and makes sense out of family process. Adlerian family therapy provides clinicians with a structure for discovering the goals behind parent–child and spousal interactions. It also values therapeutic guessing as a means of suggesting goals and purposes to both adults and children. Dreikurs' discovery of the recognition reflex in children made it possible for Adlerians to confirm their teleological hypotheses and effectively guide the redirection of families.

From teleology to social equality, the principles and ideas espoused by Adlerian family practitioners are now eagerly embraced in many psychology, counseling, and social work programs. Indeed, a strong case can be made for infusing the Adlerian model into introductory marriage and family courses (LaFountain & Mustaine, 1998).

If you are interested in a more in-depth study of this approach, we recommend the following sources: Bitter, Christensen, Hawes and Nicoll (1998); Bitter, Roberts, and Sonstegard, (2002); Christensen (2004); Sherman (1999); and Sherman and Dinkmeyer (1987).

Contributions to Multicultural Counseling and Gender Issues

Adlerians approach culture phenomenologically. Similar to birth order, culture becomes a vantage point from which individuals and families view life. It is not the vantage point that determines the individual's position, but rather the interpretation the individual gives it. Indeed, in any given family, there may be multiple interpretations that individual members assign to their culture. This is especially true in families that are experiencing acculturation. Older members may hold to the values of their culture-of-origin with as much or more dedication than they would have done in their home country, while older children who come to a new host culture may try to bridge both worlds. Often complicating family values further, children born in the new or host country may adopt the perspectives of that country through their interactions with the school system and other children. Adlerians believe that the interpretation each family member gives to the culture will be a very strong factor in how the person sees self and life, and interacts with other people. Sometimes, the most effective initial intervention is to listen carefully to all family members and to help them sort out the various positions that each person has adopted.

Many Adlerians have made contributions to multicultural perspectives, with some exceptional work by Miguel Arciniega and Betty Newlon (1995). In 7 of 11 multicultural categories, ranging from being competent in the individual's or family's language-of-origin to considerations of oppression and racism, they noted that Adlerian theory and practice rates positively. The next closest rating—with 5 positives—is Ivey's developmental theory. Corey (1991) echoed this positive assessment of Adlerian theory, noting "Adler's ideas are certainly compatible with many of the macrostrategies for future delivery of services to a culturally diverse population" (p. 54).

For more than 30 years, Adlerians have conducted an international summer school called ICASSI, a two-week Adlerian international convocation, held each summer. Over the years, both trainers and participants have come together from every continent on Earth. This international symposium seeks to develop Adlerian ideas through a professional and cultural interchange both in established centers and new, often underdeveloped countries. In the last decade, ICASSI has been held in Canada, the Czech Republic, Lithuania, Latvia, Romania, Israel, England, and Ireland, to name a few. Smaller programs have been offered in Malta, parts of the old Soviet Union, Greece, Hungary, Italy, Peru, New Zealand, Australia, and Japan. Manford Sonstegard and Oscar Christensen have instituted family-education centers throughout the world, and Bill Nicoll has established certification programs in more than eight countries outside of the United States.

There are very few limitations related to this approach in multicultural settings. One limitation may exist in using a public setting for some cultures: Such cultures may prefer private sessions to ones held in an open forum. A sensitive interest in and valuing of the extended family and culture are, however, part of the Adlerian model. The focus on parents as leaders, as well as an understanding and redirecting of mistaken notions in children, fit well with both individualistic and collectivist cultures. Learning to control oneself in the face of provocation also can be effectively incorporated into a broad range of cultures. But the single most effective intervention in diverse cultural families is an investigation of birth order, a phenomenological understanding that holds across cultures.

As I have already noted, the Adlerian perspective on social interest and social equality goes a long way toward creating a foundation for effective relationships. Adler (1931) believed that true safety for all couples was guaranteed when each partner treated the welfare of the other as more important than their own.

> The fundamental guarantee of marriage, the meaning of marital happiness, is the feeling that you are worthwhile, that you cannot be replaced, that your partner needs you, that you are acting well, and that you are a fellow [hu]man and a true friend. (p. 267)

This same focus on mutual respect and the feeling of belonging has been translated into the most used Adlerian parent–child training programs in the world [*STEP* (Dinkmeyer, McKay, & Dinkmeyer, 1997) and *Active Parenting* (Popkin, 1993)]. It is also the foundation for the collaborative relationship that Adlerian therapists seek to bring to their work with families.

Although most feminist commentaries ignore the Adlerian model, I believe they would find strong support for valuing the voice and perspectives of women and children in the writings of Adler, Dreikurs, Carlson, Christensen, Sperry, Bitter, Nicoll, and others. Adler's early pro-feminist positions, including his belief in the right of women to choose whether or not to have children (Ansbacher & Ansbacher, 1978) and his call for equality between the sexes are foundational elements in both feminist and Adlerian theory.

Exercises for Personal and Professional Growth

You can use an Adlerian phenomenological approach in assessing the family constellation to gain a greater understanding of who you are and what influences have made an impact on your life. Start by identifying your mother and father by name. If you came from an extended family and had lots of contact with other family members (grandparents, aunts, uncles, etc.), list all of them too. If you came from single-parent family, were there other people who served as significant others for you? If you came from a blended family, list all of the adults associated with your family. A drawing of my parents would look like this:

Now list three adjectives for each of your parents and/or the significant others in your life. For Greg, I might list the words conservative, religious, and dedicated. For Betty, I might list the words fun, loving, and social. These words say more about me than they do about my parents. My sister, for example, might list completely different characteristics for our parents. Adler, in 1932, suggested that descriptions of family members always revealed a statement about self within the relationship.

> . . . there is no character trait without a relationship to others. When the patient says, "My father was kind," this means "he was kind to *me.*" When he says his mother was critical, the idea which penetrates is that he attempted to keep a distance from his mother. (Ansbacher & Ansbacher, 1979, p. 194)

So when I say my mother was fun and loving, I mean she was fun and loving with me, which is not a bad way to start life. She was also social, and not just with me, but with everyone; she made a place for people in our home, and people always felt that they could come to visit. My description of my father suggests more distance between us and the importance to him of doing things the right way: I still can hear him telling me to do it right the first time so I wouldn't have to do it over. If I were to use words to describe the relationship between my father and my mother, I would say close and loving. Taken together, these traits and attributions added up to what I felt was a stable life and world.

- What words characterized your parents as individuals?
- Were there other people who were significant to your early life? What words or traits would you assign to them?
- What do these assigned words suggest about your relationships to these people?
- Do you have any of the traits you have assigned to others?

- Are you like your mother or father or both? In what way?
- What words characterize your parents' relationship? What does that tell you about the kind of atmosphere in which you were raised? Was it safe? Was it fun? Or, perhaps, was it more like a jungle, with lots of anger outbursts and aggression?
- Does this say anything to you about what you expect when you raise children?

Now let's look at your siblings and birth order from a phenomenological (subjective) point of view. Name them, oldest to youngest, on a piece of paper, like this:

Oldest—Age	Second—Age	Etc.—Age	Youngest—Age
Adjectives	Adjectives	Adjectives	Adjectives

- If you were an only child, what are three adjectives that describe you when you were little, say 9 years old or less? What are three of your strengths and three of your weaknesses now? Given what you said earlier about your parent(s), do these childhood traits and current strengths and weaknesses make sense to you now?
- If you had one or more siblings, which one was most different from you? In what way? Which one was most like you? In what way? And again, what are three adjectives that describe you when you were little?
- Was there a large age gap (6 or more years) between any of the siblings? Was it like having more than one family in the same house?
- How did you and your siblings align and individuate? Do you still have the same kind of relationships now that you did when you were children?
- Are there patterns to your life that started long ago in your family that you can see operating today? What cognitions and emotions go along with these patterns?

Finally, think back again to when you were little, before the age of 9. Think of something that happened at one time. "One time, something happened." Write down this memory. Then look at it and answer the following questions:

- What part of it stands out? What were you feeling at that exact moment?
- If this were a newspaper story, what would the headline be?
- Is there a moral to the story, a lesson, or a conviction? Does the moral, lesson, or conviction tell you something about how you see life right now?

Now repeat the process, gathering two to three more memories. Adlerians believe that we select these memories to guide us in our daily living now. Does this have any meaning for you as you look at your memories?

Taken together, family constellation, birth order, family atmosphere, and early memories form the basis of what Adlerians call a lifestyle assessment. For a more in-depth look at what this process can tell you about yourself, see either Powers and Griffith (1987) or Shulman and Mosak (1988).

Where to Go From Here

Adlerians in New York, led by the children of Alfred Adler, and Dreikurs in Chicago started a national Adlerian society more than 50 years ago. Today that organization is called the North American Society of Adlerian Psychology (NASAP). NASAP is responsible for the publication of a quarterly journal called the *Journal of Individual Psychology*. It conducts an annual meeting that rotates between Vancouver, British Columbia, Tucson, Arizona, Chicago, Illinois, and specially selected sites in the eastern part of the United States and Canada. Information about the conventions and training programs offered by NASAP is available at:

North American Society of Adlerian Psychology®
50 Northeast Drive, Hershey, PA 17033
Phone: 717-579-8795
Fax: 717-533-8616
Website at: **http://www.alfredadler.org**

For those interested in the Adlerian international summer training community, information can be found at:

International Committee of Adlerian Summer Schools and Institutes
Michael Balla, Director
257 Billings Avenue
Ottawa, ON K1H 5L1
Canada
Fax: 613-733-0289
E-mail: **mjballa@sympatico.ca**
Website at: **http://www.icassi.net**

Recommended Readings

Ansbacher, H. L., & Ansbacher, R. R. (Eds.). (1956). *The individual psychology of Alfred Adler*. New York: Basic Books. The "Bible" of Adlerian psychology: Ansbacher and Ansbacher were introduced to each other by Alfred Adler and spent their highly productive careers organizing, translating, and integrating Adler's most important writings.

Ansbacher, H. L., & Ansbacher, R. R. (Eds.). (1978). *Alfred Adler: Cooperation between the sexes: Writings on women, love & marriage, sexuality & its disorders*. Garden City, NY: Anchor/Doubleday. A comprehensive presentation of Adler's most important works related to women, coupling, and family life.

Ansbacher, H. L., & Ansbacher, R. R. (Eds.). (1979). *Superiority and social interest: Alfred Adler, a collection of later writings* (3rd rev. ed.). New York: Norton. This is a follow-up edition to their 1956 book in which some longer pieces by Adler and his associates are presented with commentary.

Carlson, J., Sperry, L., & Lewis, J. A. (2003). *Family therapy techniques: Integrating and tailoring treatment*. New York: Brunner Routledge. This comprehensive family therapy book uses Adlerian principles to guide the counselor/therapist in the tailoring of treatment to a wide range of families that we currently meet daily in practice. If I were going to keep only one book on my shelf, this is the one I would keep.

Christensen, O. C. (Ed.). (2004). *Adlerian family counseling* (3rd ed.). Minneapolis, MN: Educational Media Corp. This manual is designed to teach the structure and process of Adlerian family counseling, whether enacted in private or in an open forum. This is the book that guides all Adlerian family counselors and therapists when they first get started.

Dreikurs, R. (1958). *The challenge of parenthood*. New York: Plume. (Original work published 1948) This is one of Dreikurs' first works on parenting, and it lays the foundation for seeing parent–child interactions as purposeful exchanges.

Dreikurs, R. (1999). *The challenge of marriage*. Philadelphia, PA: Accelerated Development. (Original work published 1946) Dreikurs presents the basis for social equality in couples and marriage, and provides a blueprint for effective relationships.

Dreikurs, R., & Soltz, V. (1964). *Children: The challenge*. New York: Hawthorn. This is one of the most-used texts on childrearing in the history of publishing, with more than 600,000 copies in print and still available (through Plume) almost 40 years after it was first published. This is a step-by-step guide to effective parenting, and it is the basis for both the **STEP program** and *Active Parenting*.

Hoffman, E. (1994). *The drive for self: Alfred Adler and the founding of individual psychology*. Reading, MA:

Addison Wesley. The most-complete biography of Adler ever written, completed with a psychological historian's eye for detail and accuracy. It is the most-beneficial glimpse into the life and work of one of psychology's great geniuses.

Oberst, U. E., & Stewart, A. E. (2003). *Adlerian psychotherapy: An advanced approach to individual psychology.* New York: Brunner/Routlege. This book devoted to the overall practice of Adlerian counseling and psychotherapy, with excellent chapters related to family counseling, family therapy, and parent education.

Sherman, R., & Dinkmeyer, D. (Eds.). (1987). *Systems of family therapy: An Adlerian integration.* New York: Brunner/Mazel. A thorough presentation of Adlerian family therapy with additional chapters integrating

the work of Satir, Minuchin, Haley, Ellis, and the people at MRI.

Sweeney, T. J. (1998). *Adlerian counseling: A practitioner's approach* (4th ed.). Philadelphia, PA: Accelerated Development. This is the most comprehensive text available on Adlerian theory, counseling, and psychotherapy.

Terner, J., & Pew, W. L. (1978). *The courage to be imperfect: The life and work of Rudolf Dreikurs.* New York: Hawthorn. This superb biography also presents the ideas, principles, and practice of a man whose writings included more than 300 articles and books, as well as countless training programs, institutes, lectures, presentations, and courses.

DVD Reference

Rudolf Dreikurs systematized Adler's approach to families and provided a teleological framework for understanding adult-child behaviors. Teleology is the study of final causes, and in the case of families, it involves the discovery of what purposes or goals might be motivating the behaviors and interactions in the family system.

In the video that accompanies this theory, Dr. Bitter interviews Joel and his two children. Joel is married, but his wife is unable to be present due to her work schedule. Dr Bitter first gets a sense of the family constellation from the father and then proceeds to focus on problem interactions in an effort to discover the mistaken goals that might be operating in both the children and the parents.

References

Adler, A. (1930). *The education of children.* New York: Greenberg.

Adler, A. (1931). *What life should mean to you.* Boston: Little, Brown.

Adler, A. (1938). *Social interest: A challenge to mankind.* London: Faber & Faber.

Ansbacher, H. L., & Ansbacher, R. R. (Eds.). (1956). *The individual psychology of Alfred Adler.* New York: Basic Books.

Ansbacher, H. L., & Ansbacher, R. R. (Eds.). (1978). *Alfred Adler: Cooperation between the sexes: Writings on women, love & marriage, sexuality & its disorders.* Garden City, NY: Anchor/Doubleday.

Ansbacher, H. L., & Ansbacher, R. R. (Eds.). (1979). *Superiority and social interest: Alfred Adler, a collection of later writings* (3rd rev. ed.). New York: Norton.

Arciniega, G. M., & Newlon, B. J. (1995). Counseling and psychotherapy: Multicultural considerations.

In D. Capuzzi & D. R. Gross (Eds.), *Counseling and psychotherapy: Theories and interventions* (pp. 557–587). Englewood Cliffs, NJ: Merrill.

Balla, M. (2003). Raissa Epstein Adler. In Adlerian Society of the United Kingdom and the Institute for Individual Psychology (Ed.), *Yearbook, 2003* (pp. 50–58). Chippenham, Wiltshire: Author.

Bitter, J. R. (1988). Family mapping and family constellation: Satir in Adlerian context. *Individual Psychology, 44*(1), 106–111.

Bitter, J. R. (Speaker). (1991a). *Adlerian family mapping* [video cassette TRT: 105:00]. Villa Park, IL: Copymaster Video.

Bitter, J. R. (1991b). Conscious motivations: An enhancement to Dreikurs' goals of children's misbehavior. *Individual Psychology, 47*(2), 210–221.

Bitter, J. R., Christensen, O. C., Hawes, C., & Nicoll, W. G. (1998). Adlerian brief therapy with individuals, couples, and families. *Directions in Counseling and Clinical Psychology, 8*(8), 95–111.

Bitter, J. R., Roberts, A., & Sonstegard, M. A. (2002). Adlerian family therapy. In J. Carlson & D. Kjos (Eds.), *Theories and strategies of family therapy* (pp. 41–79). Boston: Allyn and Bacon.

Carich, M. S., & Willingham, W. (1987). The roots of family systems theory in individual psychology. *Individual Psychology, 43,* 71–78.

Carlson, J., Sperry, L., & Lewis, J. A. (2003). *Family therapy techniques: Integrating and tailoring treatment.* New York: Brunner Routledge.

Christensen, O. C. (Speaker). (1979). *Adlerian family counseling* [Educational Film]. (Available from Educational Media Corp., Box 21311, Minneapolis, MN 55421-0311.)

Christensen, O. C. (Ed.). (2004). *Adlerian family counseling* (3rd ed.). Minneapolis, MN: Educational Media Corp.

Corey, G. (1991). Invited commentary on macrostrategies for delivery of mental health counseling services. *Journal of Mental Health Counseling, 13,* 51–57.

Dinkmeyer, D., Jr., & Carlson, J. (2001). *Consultation: Creating school-based interventions.* New York: Brunner Routledge.

Dinkmeyer, D., Jr., & Sperry, L. (2000). *Counseling and psychotherapy: An integrated individual psychology approach* (3rd ed.). Upper Saddle River, NJ: Merrill/Prentice Hall.

Dinkmeyer, D., Sr., McKay, G., & Dinkmeyer, D., Jr. (1997). *STEP: The parent's handbook.* Circle Pines, MN: American Guidance Service.

Dreikurs, R. (1940a, November). The importance of group life. *Camping Magazine, 27,* 3–4.

Dreikurs, R. (1940b, December). The child in the group. *Camping Magazine,* 7–9.

Dreikurs, R. (1948). *The challenge of parenthood.* New York: Duell, Sloan, & Pearce.

Dreikurs, R. (1950). The immediate purpose of children's misbehavior, its recognition and correction. *Internationale Zeitschrift fur Individual-Psychologie, 19,* 70–87.

Dreikurs, R. (1971). *Social equality: The challenge for today.* Chicago: Adler School of Professional Psychology.

Dreikurs, R., Corsini, R., Lowe, R., & Sonstegard, M. A. (1959). *Adlerian family counseling.* Eugene, OR: University of Oregon Press.

Dreikurs, R., & Grey, L. (1968). *Logical consequences: A new approach to child discipline.* New York: Hawthorn.

Dreikurs, R., & Soltz, V. (1964). *Children: The challenge.* New York: Hawthorn.

Evans, T. D., & Milliren, A. P. (1999). Open-forum family counseling. In R. E. Watts & J. Carlson (Eds.), *Interventions and strategies in counseling and psychotherapy* (pp. 135–160). Philadelphia: Accelerated Development/Taylor and Francis.

Gottman, J. (1997). *The heart of parenting: Raising an emotionally intelligent child.* New York: Simon & Schuster.

LaFountain, R. M., & Mustaine, B. L. (1998). Infusing Adlerian theory into an introductory marriage and family course. *The Family Journal, 6,* 189–199.

Lew, A. (1999). Parent education: Selecting programs and current and future needs. In R. E. Watts, & J. Carlson (Eds.), *Interventions and strategies in counseling and psychotherapy* (pp. 181–191). Philadelphia: Accelerated Development/Taylor and Francis.

Main, F. (1986). *Perfect parenting and other myths.* Vermillion, SD: Main Press.

Oberst, U. E., & Stewart, A. E. (2003). *Adlerian, psychotherapy: An advanced approach to individual psychology.* New York: Brunner/Routledge.

Popkin, M. (1993). *Active parenting today.* Atlanta, GA: Active Parenting.

Powers, R. L., & Griffith, J. (1987). *Understanding lifestyle: The psycho-clarity process.* Chicago: Americas Institute of Adlerian Studies.

Sherman, R. (1999). Family therapy: The art of integration. In R. E. Watts, & J. Carlson (Eds.), *Interventions and strategies in counseling and psychotherapy* (pp. 101–134). Philadelphia: Accelerated Development/Taylor and Francis.

Sherman, R., & Dinkmeyer, D. (Eds.). (1987). *Systems of family therapy: An Adlerian integration.* New York: Brunner/Mazel.

Shulman, B. H., & Mosak, H. H. (1988). *Manual for lifestyle assessment.* Muncie, IN: Accelerated Development.

Sweeney, T. J. (1998). *Adlerian counseling: A practitioner's approach* (4th ed.). Philadelphia, PA: Accelerated Development

Terner, J., & Pew, W. L. (1978). *The courage to be imperfect: The life and work of Rudolf Dreikurs.* New York: Hawthorn.

Endnote

[1]Christensen (1979) notes that the idea of no one else in the family enjoying the fighting cannot be true; children don't fight unless it engages others and draws attention to themselves.

CHAPTER 6

Human Validation Process Model

Introduction

Key Concepts

Therapy Goals

The Therapist's Role and Function

Techniques

A Satir Therapist With the Quest Family

Summary and Multicultural Evaluation

Recommended Readings

References

Introduction

At about the same time that Bowen was developing his multigenerational approach to family therapy, Virginia Satir (1983) began emphasizing family connection in a model she called **conjoint family therapy**. Satir believed true connection started with enhanced self-esteem, helping individuals to connect to the strengths and internal resources that were part of being more fully human. Connection became contact when two people really engaged each other, and communication was both the expression and enactment of that contact—what Buber (1996) had called an **I-thou relationship**. The quality of communication always reflected the level of self-esteem that each individual brought to any given contact. Satir often noted that "a full contact" could truly happen only between two people. She suggested metaphorically that humans were not like fish: We do not have eyes on the sides of our heads so that we can focus our attention in two directions at once. Still, Satir recognized that systemic process happened among people, and that family triads and triangles were a natural and even essential part of life.

The **human validation process model** (Satir & Baldwin, 1983; Satir & Bitter, 2000) grew out of her mission to release the potential that she saw in every family. A Satir therapist had to be a model of congruent communication, and much of the therapist's work would involve *teaching* when the family members were available to learn. Her approach started and ended with a validation of each family member—and the system in which they lived.

Virginia Satir

It emphasized communication as well as emotional experiencing. Satir was highly intuitive, and she believed that spontaneity, creativity, self-disclosure, and risk-taking were central to family therapy. In her view, techniques were always secondary to the relationship that she, as a therapist, was able to establish with the family. For Satir, it was not techniques, but rather the personal involvement of the therapist with the family that made the therapeutic difference. I continue to use the term human validation process model to describe her work, because it was the last term that Satir used before she died. Today, however, her trainers tend to refer to this approach as the Satir growth model. John Banmen (personal communication, January 9, 2006) prefers Satir transformational systemic therapy, a title that certainly reflects both Satir's work and his own work based on her teachings.

In a family therapy demonstration Virginia Satir conducted for Golden Triad Films (1968a), a blended family came to talk with her about a 16-year-old, troubled boy named Tim. His mother, Elaine, was 34. She was divorced from Tim's father, Buddy, and was remarried to Jerry, age 46, who also had assumed the role of stepfather. Tim's sister, Tammy, was 12 years old, and she was also the daughter of Elaine and Buddy. Elaine, Jerry, Tim, and Tammy participated in this session with Satir.

> A year prior to this interview, the family decided to send the son [Tim] to live with his biological father [Buddy]. His situation deteriorated to the point where he got all F's academically. The parents decided to bring the son back to the family unit. At the time of the interview, the new school year had been in progress for a month and a half. The boy refused to go to school or, when forcibly dropped at school, he refused to stay. The family was in the early stages of therapy at the time Virginia saw them. (Golden Triad Films, 1968b, p. 11)

When you think about this case, what issues or concerns come to your mind related to this family system? What do you think the mother, Elaine, was hoping would happen in relation to her children when she married Jerry? How is the role of a stepfather different from the role of a biological father? What purpose does Tim have for his troubled behavior? What is Tammy's relationship to her brother as well as to her mother, father, and stepfather? What is the relationship of Tim to his school and the school with the family? Most importantly, how would you structure the session? What focus do you think would be essential if you are to help this family cope with their worry about Tim and how he is leading his life? Should helping Tim go to school or get a job be part of the therapist's goals? Before you read about how Satir approached this case, you might want to think about how you would start a session with this family—and what your therapeutic goals might be.

In this session, Satir immediately sensed the pressure that was on this teenage boy and felt the resistance he had even to being part of the family therapy session. She saw the boy as being similar to a crack in a vase, and she did not want to push on that crack in a way that would cause the whole vase to break apart. So she used reframing to develop a focus that would engage the whole family. In Satir's model, reframing is the process of either highlighting the good intentions behind difficult interactions or, as in this case, reorienting a session away from an individual to the system as a whole.

Satir: [to Jerry] Could you tell me as explicitly as possible what it is that you see Tim doing or not doing that gives you a problem?

Jerry: Well, number 1: not going to school. Number 2: not wanting to work. And number 3: I can't . . . beyond my wildest dreams, I can't believe a boy not wanting a car. He had the opportunity to have a car if he went to school, but he chose not to do that. The only other way to have a car is to work, but he chose not to do that. . . .

Satir: Let me see if I can understand Tim not wanting a car. Were you saying that if he wanted a car badly enough that he would work or go to school? And since he isn't working or going to school, he must not want a car?

Jerry: Yes.

Satir: Well, the two might be related or not, but I think you are asking for something that you would like to see Tim have for his life somehow, that you feel he isn't doing. Is that right?

Jerry: Absolutely.

Satir: What would you like to have him have in his life that you are afraid he isn't going to get?

Jerry: I'm not sure what makes him happy, but you have to have a minimum of comforts to make you happy. Given the route he's going right now, he's not going to be able to afford them. In fact, he's not going to be able to support himself.

Satir: I picked up that you said you didn't know what made him happy. You've known Tim about 6 years? And what I hear you say is, "I haven't learned yet or found out how Tim lives inside himself, what has meaning to him."

Jerry: That's correct. I haven't.

Satir: Would you like to know that?

Jerry: I sure would. (Satir & Bitter, 2000, pp. 85–86)

For the next 20 minutes, Satir turned her attention to Tammy, Elaine, and lastly Tim, to see if each family member knew what made other family members—not just Tim—happy. This reframing had the effect of restructuring the session so that everyone had a part to play in a joint task. It also sent the message to Tim that Satir was not going to let him become the scapegoat, or even the major focus, of this family therapy session. It is Satir's gentle inquiries of Tim, however, that let him know that he would be understood and protected by her.

Satir: Well, Tim, when you came here today, what did you want for you?

Tim: I didn't want to come.

Satir: You didn't want to come. But you got here.

Tim: I had to.

Satir: Somebody would be angry if you didn't come? Who would be angry?

Tim: Them . . . all of them.

Satir: And if somebody in the family gets angry at you, what happens for you?

Tim: I won't be able to go anywhere?

Satir: So if you can learn how to do what people in the family ask you to do, you'll get some privileges. Is that kind of how it goes?

Tim: I guess.

Satir: How does that feel to you? To feel that the only way you'll be able to get something is to do what other people tell you to do? It never went over very well with me when I was a kid. How does it feel for you? (pause) Maybe these are too hard to talk about. (Tim makes no response.) So at this point in time, am I to understand that you would like to work it out some way so that you could be more a part of the family and have more things to say about what happens to you? (Tim shrugs his shoulder slightly.) From the way you lifted your shoulder, I have a hunch that you feel it wouldn't matter what you wanted. There wouldn't be any use; it wouldn't matter. That's the feeling I got. (Satir & Bitter, 2000, pp. 89–90)

In this intervention, Satir risks speaking for the self-esteem and inner world of the teenage boy. Her tremendous empathy allows her to "feel" what it is like to be him, even when he is not speaking for himself. Her communication lets him know that she understands him without taking over for him.

In the next part of the session, it becomes clear that Elaine, as a divorced, single parent, married Jerry and very much wanted him to enter the family as a disciplinarian and to help her with the children who felt "out of hand" to her. For the rest of the session, Satir uses sculpting, humor, and touch to facilitate clearer communication, first between Jerry and Elaine, strengthening the bond in the leadership dyad of the family, and then between each parent and the two children. In the process, **family rules** are acknowledged and transformed; reasonable and flexible **boundaries** are named and established; and individual self-esteem is raised through therapist validation and renewed connections with others. In the end, even Tim was engaged in learning new ways to be present within his family.

Satir ends the session by expressing the closeness she's feeling for the family and asking if she could share a hug with them. When she comes to Tim at the end, she asks:

Satir: I would like to hug you too, Tim. Are you ready for that? (Tim smiles and gets up slowly to hug Virginia.) I really appreciate that. (Satir & Bitter, 2000, p. 95)

Satir met more than 5,000 families in therapy during her lifetime. She worked with families from around the world: families of every kind and form; of every nationality, culture, and race; and families of every income level, religious orientation, and political persuasion. She worked phenomenologically and often intuitively. Her personal presence and ability to make full human contact allowed her to engage even the most reluctant and fearful of families in therapy, and her persistent search for and enhancement of self-esteem led to an extremely high rate of families completing therapy.

Key Concepts

Satir's human validation process stresses enhancement and validation of self-esteem, family rules, congruence versus defensive communication patterns, sculpting, nurturing triads and **family mapping**, and **family life-fact chronologies**. It emphasizes factors such as making contact, metaphor, reframing, emotional honesty, congruent communication, creating new possibilities, drama, humor, and personal touch in the therapy process. Like Bowen, Satir believed in looking at three generations of family life. Unlike him, she worked to bring those patterns to life *in the present*, either by having families develop maps (her word for genograms) and life-fact chronologies or by creating a group process in which family patterns and experiences could be reconstructed.

Family Life

Children always enter the world as part of preexisting systems, with the family being the most common and central one. Their early experience is a constant transition from what is known and familiar to what is unknown and unfamiliar, the movement from the womb to the outside world being but the first of many such transitions. These transitions often leave children with feelings of fear, helplessness, and even anger as they struggle for competence and security in a challenging and often difficult new environment. Children enter families that already are loaded with rules and, as they grow, more rules are developed to help the system function and prosper. Rules can pertain to any part of human living and interaction, but the most important rules, according to Satir, are the ones that govern communication: who says what to whom under what conditions. Rules may be spoken or unspoken, embedded in the behavioral responses and interactions of the system. These rules, which are often couched in terms of "shoulds" or "should nots," become strong messages that govern interactions within a family. When parents feel worried or helpless, they tend to set rules in an attempt to control a situation. These family rules may assist children initially in handling anger, helplessness, and fear. They are intended to provide a safety net as children venture into the world (Satir, Bitter, & Krestensen, 1988).

It is impossible for children to grow up without such rules. Unfortunately, they often receive these rules in forms that quickly lose their effectiveness; that is, the rules are perceived to be absolute and too often impossible. Examples are: "Never be angry with your father." "Always keep a smile on your face." "Don't bring attention to yourself." "Never let people see your weaknesses; show neither affection nor anger." "Don't confront your parents; always try to please them." "Don't talk to outsiders about your family." "Children are to be seen but not heard." "Have fun only when all the work is finished." "Don't be different from other family members." Children have to make early decisions about whether to accept these rules or to fight against them.

As children, we learn rules by observing the behavior of our parents. When rules are presented without choice and as absolutes, they typically pose problems for us. As small children, we may have decided to accept a rule and live by it for reasons of both physical and psychological survival. When we carry such a pattern into our adult interactions, rules can become self-defeating and even dysfunctional.

Rather than trying to get people to give up these survival rules in their lives, Satir would assist them in transforming those that were extreme into something useful and functional. For example, if she were working with a person's rule "You must never get angry!", she would broaden the range of choice and transform the impossibility of living up to "always" and "never" standards. "What would it be like for you to say, 'I can sometimes be angry?' because that is a true and more realistic statement, isn't it?" To make the element of choice more salient, she would ask clients to think of three times that they could imagine getting angry and to list these situations. Through this process, a dysfunctional survival rule can be transformed rather than attacked (Satir & Baldwin, 1983).

In healthy families, rules are few and are consistently applied. They are humanly possible, relevant, and flexible depending on changing situations (Bitter, 1987). According to Satir and Baldwin (1983), the most important family rules are the ones that govern individuation (being unique) and the sharing of information (communication). These rules influence the ability of a family to function openly, allowing each member new possibilities in the process of change. Satir (1988) noted that many people develop a range of communication styles as a means for coping with the stress that results from the process of change and the inability of family rules to meet the demands of that change.

Functional versus Dysfunctional Communication in Families

Satir's approach to family therapy distinguishes between functional and dysfunctional communication patterns, as well as between the functional and dysfunctional family processes that evolve from these communication patterns (Bitter, 1987). In families that are functioning relatively well, each member is allowed to have a separate life as well as a shared life with the family group. Different relationships are allowed and are nurtured. Change is expected and invited, not viewed as at threat. When differences lead to disagreements, the situation is viewed as an opportunity for growth rather than as an attack on the family system. The structure of this family system is characterized by flexibility with freedom and open communication. All the members within the family have a voice and can speak for themselves. In this atmosphere, individuals feel support for taking risks and venturing into the world.

A healthy family encourages the sharing of experiences; the members are secure enough to be themselves and to allow others to be who they are.

By contrast, a dysfunctional family is characterized by closed communication, by poor self-esteem of one or both parents, and by rigid patterns. This kind of family resists awareness and blunts responsiveness. There is little support for individuality, and relationships are strained. In a family that exhibits dysfunctional patterns, the members are incapable of autonomy or genuine intimacy. Rules serve the function of masking fears over differences. Rules are rigid, many, and frequently inappropriate for meeting given situations. The members are expected to think, feel, and act in the same way. Parents attempt to control the family by using fear, punishment, guilt, or dominance. Eventually, the system breaks down because the rules are no longer able to keep the family structure intact.

Defensive Communication Stances in Coping With Stress

When stress increases, threatening a breakdown of the family system, members tend to resort to defensive **communication stances**. Satir (1983, 1988) and Satir and Baldwin (1983) identify four universal **defensive communication patterns** that express these defensive postures, or stress positions: **placating**, **blaming**, being **super-reasonable**, and being **irrelevant**. Each of these four stances tends to deny, distort, or eliminate one or more of three elements that are present in every interaction: the self, others, and the context in which the interaction takes place. These elements can be represented as follows:

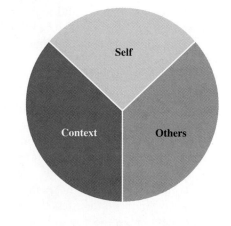

Figure 6.1

Self, others, and context: The necessary elements of interaction, all of which are taken into account in congruent communication.

1. Family members who use placating behaviors as a style for dealing with stress pay the price of sacrificing themselves in their attempt to please others. They may seem weak, tentative, and self-effacing. Because they do not feel an inner sense of value and because they feel helpless without others, such people say and do what they think others expect of them. Out of their fear of being rejected, they strive to be too many things to too many significant others. They often say "yes" when they mean "no." Their responses may include statements such as, "I don't know what I did to mess this up" or "I just want everyone to be happy" and they will sacrifice any or all of themselves to make that happen.

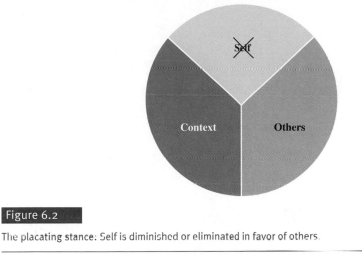

Figure 6.2

The placating stance: Self is diminished or eliminated in favor of others.

2. People who adopt a blaming posture will sacrifice others to maintain a sense of self. They assume a dominating style and find fault with others. As they point the finger of blame at others, they avoid responsibility for mistaken actions and the perceived loss of self-worth and meaning. In their hearts, they want to be significant, even superior, and they want to be appreciated for it. They may feel overburdened by life and, when things start to go wrong, they frequently say, "If it weren't for you . . . ." or "What's the matter with you . . . ." or "I can't believe you . . . ." They attribute responsibility to others for the way they are.

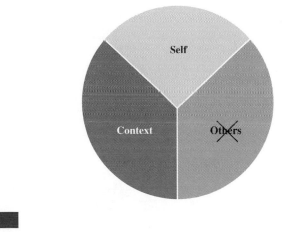

Figure 6.3

The blaming stance: Others are sacrificed to preserve self.

3. People who become super-reasonable tend to function much like a computer. They strive for complete control over themselves, others, and their environment by living a life governed by principle. In their attempt to avoid humiliation and embarrassment, they keep their emotions tightly in check. Of course, the price they pay for being overly controlled and rigid is distance and isolation from others. The super-reasonable communication seeks to establish the right principle by which to handle any stressful situation. Both the self and others are sacrificed to the "right way" to address the needs of any given context. Sentences that start with the word "it" are common: "It's important to . . . ." or "It occurs to one in situations like this that . . . ." or even "It doesn't really matter, does it?"

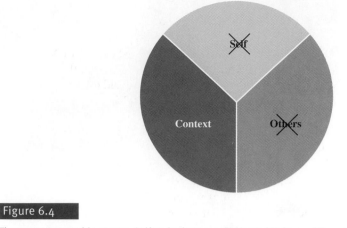

The super-reasonable stance: Self and others are eliminated in favor of the principles that govern the context.

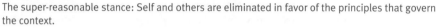

4. Irrelevant communication is manifested by a pattern of distractions in the mistaken hope that hurt, pain, or stress will then diminish. The irrelevant person is unable to relate to what is going on. He or she appears to be in constant motion, seemingly going in different directions at the same time. Because people who rely on this style of behavior are afraid of stress, they avoid taking a clear position, lest they offend others. They may answer a question with a question, change the subject, or attempt to infuse humor into a stressful situation in an effort to cope. Words such as "I don't know" or "I don't get it" or "What's going on anyway?" may reflect this irrelevant stance during times of stress.

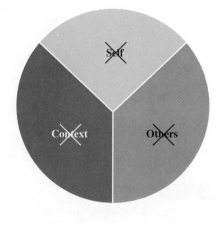

The irrelevant stance: Self, others, and context are denied or distorted in an effort to reduce stress, pain, or hurt.

Let's assume that a 17-year-old high school student comes home to tell her parents some difficult news that she knows will upset everyone in the family. She has decided that she can't wait a minute when she gets in the house. Wherever her parents are, she will have to find them and almost blurt it out; otherwise she may lose her courage and not be able to tell them at all. She is pregnant, and she is frightened both of what is about to happen to her life and what her parents will think, feel, and do. She finds them in the kitchen together, talking. "Mom. Dad. I have something I have to tell you. I don't know how to say this. I know you are going to be mad. I'm pregnant."

What are the possible responses her parents might make to this declaration? Her mother might adopt a blaming stance: "No, Ann. What's the matter with you? You have no business having sex at your age, and now you're pregnant?!? What were you thinking? How could you do this to us?" The other side of blaming would be placating. Her father, for example, might say, "Oh, sweetheart, this is not your fault. I feel like I have failed you somehow. Everything will be okay. I don't want you to be upset. I want you to be happy again. Maybe, maybe, you'll like the baby."

How do you think a super-reasonable parent might respond? I think that she or he might swing into action, trying to handle the situation quickly: "Okay, now there are certain things we are just going to have to do. It's important to decide whether you are going to keep the baby or not, and then there will be people to contact. And if you keep the baby, then we have to figure out what that will mean in terms of your school." You almost can hear the desperate attempt to regain control of the situation in this response. The irrelevant communication, on the other hand, acknowledges with its very utterance that the situation is out of control, and seeks to avoid it. Imagine a response that starts with "Ann, your mother and I were just discussing what we should have for dinner tonight. I just don't know. Maybe, we should go out . . . or stay in."

Is there an alternative to dealing with family life by taking one of these four defensive postures? How does a healthy person deal with the stresses of life? Satir and Bitter (2000) describe how congruent people cope with this stress. They do not sacrifice themselves to a singular style in dealing with it. Their words match their inner experience, and they are able to make direct and clear statements: They are congruent. A congruent response from Ann's mother might go something like this: (taking Ann in her arms) "I know you are feeling scared right now—of what is going to happen to you and probably of having to tell us. I'm scared too, but we have each other, and I just have to believe that we can figure out what to do."

To paraphrase Hans Selye (1974), congruent communication does not turn stress into distress. Instead, people who are congruent transform stress into a challenge that is met in a useful way. Such people are centered, and they avoid changing their colors like a chameleon. They face stress with confidence and courage, because they know that they have the inner resources to cope effectively and to make sound choices. The congruent communicator is alert, balanced, sensitive, and real—and she or he sends clear messages. Through congruence, the needs of self, others, and context all are considered, and the communication is infused with tact and timing. There is power in this kind of communication. It is hard to ignore, and it invites respect for all of the people involved in the interaction.

It is possible to use more than one communication style, even in a single interaction. Batterers, for example, often go from super-reasonable (emphasizing their need for control) to blaming (the actual explosion) to placating (expressing a remorse that is neither real nor prolonged). And although there are some people whose communication style remains relatively constant throughout life, most people will use different styles at different times or in different contexts.

Family Roles and Family Triads

Various members also assume roles that influence family interaction. For instance, a youngest brother assumed the role of victim, whereby he typically felt picked on and constantly sought protection. His sister assumed the role of keeping peace within the family. Even at an early age, other members looked to her as their counselor or expected her to take care of family difficulties. Her father took on the role of the stern taskmaster and disciplinarian, and her mother assumed a hard-working, caregiver role. In this family, each member learned a role that characterized his or her behavior.

The **family roles** that the parents play in relation to each child are especially important, because children always see their parents as essential to their survival. Like Bowen, Satir acknowledged that a child can be brought into the parents' relationship and that the resulting triadic process can be dysfunctional for everyone involved. Unlike Bowen, however, Satir also saw the possibility of two parents forming a **nurturing triad** with each of the children—or, in a single-parent family, a *nurturing dyad*. In such dyads and triads, roles become flexible and open to change. Children are encouraged to make a place for themselves that fits the various situations they are in; they are supported, allowed to make mistakes, and engaged in congruent communication; most importantly, each child's self-esteem is tended and enhanced. They are heard, acknowledged, appreciated, allowed to complain, and given the information they need to handle life both within and outside of the family. Rather than the "two against one" that Bowen noted in triangulation, Satir's nurturing triad can be characterized as "two for one."

As part of the conjoint family therapy with Elaine, Jerry, Tim, and Tammy that was presented at the beginning of this chapter, Satir sculpted dyads and triads to help the family members develop more-flexible boundaries and learn the limits of contact and communication. She demonstrated that Elaine can choose to be fully with Tim (in a dyad), and that Tammy and Jerry could choose to form their own dyad for communication—or each could have some time and space alone. It is even possible that functional communication can be stretched so that three people can be in contact. Satir demonstrated this by having Elaine take one of Jerry's hands and one of Tammy's hands, leaving their other hands free to make another connection. By simply shifting their heads and taking turns, this triad can communicate, but then the fourth person is left out. Indeed, it is impossible for all four of them to be in contact at the same time. Satir noted that it is in Elaine's heart that they are all together, but a four-way communication cannot happen at a single moment in time in real life.

Therapy Goals

The key goals of Satir's approach to family therapy are clear communication, expanding of awareness, enhancing potentials for growth, especially in self-esteem, and coping with the demands and process of change. Each of these processes in therapy is recursive; that is, an enrichment of one tends to enhance the others. Satir et al. (1991) linked self-esteem to the virtues of optimism (hope and desire), courage, congruence, curiosity, and the wisdom that comes from within. Further, each of these elements was supported by opportunity and what Satir called the *five freedoms:* the freedom to see and the freedom to hear in the present; the freedom to speak one's truth; the freedom to think and feel independently of others; the freedom to ask for what you want; and the "freedom to take risks on our own behalf" (p. 62).

Satir believed that families, like all systems, tend to establish a relatively constant state that she called the *status quo*. The *status quo* is made up of more or less constant roles and routines that facilitate everyday living. As such, each family's *status quo* is familiar and known. It is maintained by the family even if there are problems, because it is less threatening than what is new or different and, therefore, unknown and unfamiliar. When a foreign element, or outside stressor, is introduced into the system, change is required and the family system is thrown into **chaos** while the members try to adapt. Chaos is the experience of being lost, of everything spinning out of control, of losing one's balance and equilibrium. In this state, Satir and Baldwin (1983) warned, no decision should be made that cannot be implemented within a few seconds. To the extent that family members can access both internal and external resources (one of which is the therapist) and can be helped to identify new possibilities and practice them, it is possible for the process of change to reach an effective resolution. When change is integrated as a new way of being in the family, a new *status quo* emerges and growth occurs (Pelonis, 2002).

In facilitating families through the process of change, Satir also sought to change the way individuals experienced and understood life. Roles, to her, became adjectives that described various aspects of a person's activities. These descriptions could change. New ones could be added. Old roles could be discarded, because they no longer had to be tied to one's self-esteem. Power, hierarchies, and positions were transformed into interactive collaborations. Each part of the family had to be nurtured and tended, because each part affected every other part. In this atmosphere, change no longer had to be resisted. It was simply what happened in life.

In this sense, the human validation process model is concerned with the growth of individuals and the family, rather than merely stabilizing the family. The aim is for individual members of the family to become more sensitive to one another, to share their experiences, and to interact in new and genuine ways. The task of therapy is to transform defenses and dysfunctional rules, opening people to new possibilities and an integration of nurturing family-life experiences.

The general goal, and process, of therapy is the facilitation of desired change in the family system. The specific goals, which are related to this change process, are:

- generating hope and courage in family members to formulate new options;
- accessing, strengthening, enhancing, or generating coping skills in family members; and
- encouraging members to exercise options that will result in health as opposed to the mere elimination of symptoms. (Satir & Bitter, 2000)

Satir (1988) identified three goals of family therapy: (1) each individual within a family should be able to report honestly about what he or she sees, hears, feels, and thinks; (2) decisions in a family are best made through exploring individual needs and negotiating, rather than through power; and (3) differences should be acknowledged openly and used for growth within the family.

> The central core of my theory is self-esteem. I now clearly see that without a direct link to the experience of the senses, there would be little change in feelings. Consequently, there would be little change in self-esteem, and therefore little, dependable change in behavior. (Satir & Bitter, 2000, p. 71)

The Therapist's Role and Function

The therapist's role and function are to guide family members through the change process. Who the therapist is as a person is far more important than specific intervention techniques. Therapists are best conceived of as facilitators in charge of the therapeutic process; they do not have the task of making change happen or curing individuals. The therapist's faith in the ability of family members to move toward growth and actualization is central to this approach. This attitude infuses the therapy experience with nurturance, support, safety, and human validation (Satir & Bitter, 2000).

Satir (1983) viewed the therapist as a resource person who has a special advantage in being able to observe the family situation. She used the analogy of a camera with a wide-angle lens, which allows the counselor to see things from each person's vantage point. As an official observer, the therapist is able to report on what the family cannot see. Satir (1983) described many roles and techniques that family therapists employ in helping a family achieve its goals. Several of these are listed below. The therapist:

- creates a setting in which people can risk looking clearly and objectively at themselves and their actions;
- assists family members in building self-esteem;

- helps clients identify their assets;
- takes the family's history and notes past achievements;
- decreases threats by setting boundaries and reducing the need for defenses;
- shows that pain and the forbidden are acceptable to explore;
- uses certain techniques for restoring the client's feeling of accountability;
- helps family members see how past models influence their expectations and behavior, and looks for change in these expectations;
- delineates roles and functions;
- completes gaps in communication and interprets messages;
- points out significant discrepancies in communication; and
- identifies nonverbal communication.

The flow of therapy in this model parallels the needs highlighted in the process of change. The initial movement revolves around **making contact** with each of the people in the family session. It is physical as well as emotional, intellectual, and spiritual. It starts with a warm physical greeting and interest that may include taking each person's hand, making eye contact, and bringing one's full attention to each individual. It involves the processes of seeing and listening, interest and fascination, warmth and caring. It is collaborative and engaging. There is openness in the therapist both to the people and the experience of being together. Those who come to therapy feel both welcome and safe.

Families often present themselves when they are already in *chaos*. Naming the experience already starts to settle it. The therapist asks about feelings and thoughts, not about decisions or outcomes. The therapist listens and validates. Fear rises and falls in family members, and the therapist stays present and steady. In this stance, there is a faith that emanates from the therapist: a faith that anything can be faced, anything can be said, and anything can be experienced in the safety of the session. The process is often slow, as if the therapist were working on a tapestry, one stitch at a time.

As family members become available for learning, the therapist creates experiences in which **new possibilities** are considered and tried. New possibilities lead to hope and, when they are practiced, they often become a **new integration** for the family. In this model, the therapist celebrates change and new achievements. It is not uncommon for them to be anchored by appropriate touch and sealed in a new connection that the therapist has with the family and that they have with each other. Validation permeates this model from start to finish.

Although Satir's therapeutic style was quite different from Carl Whitaker's approach, which I will present in the next chapter, both emphasized the role of the therapist as a person. Whereas Whitaker developed his methods out of existential and psychoanalytic roots, Satir was influenced by the thinking of Carl Rogers. Along with Rogers, she based her practice on the notion that we have an inner striving toward fulfillment (self-actualization) and that we have the resources to reach our full potential. Just as in the person-centered perspective, it is the quality of the relationship between the therapist and client that stimulates growth and change in the client. In Satir's view, the therapist is a model of effective communication and a resource person for developing it in a family. Regardless of the counselor's theoretical orientation, it is possible to utilize many of the concepts of Satir's model in working with families.

Techniques

Change occurs in the session and healing occurs in the family's relationships largely as a function of the relationship and climate created by the therapist. It is the individual family member, not the therapist, who is responsible for change. Within the therapy session, the focus of techniques is on emotional honesty, congruence, and systemic understanding. McLendon and Davis (2002) use the acronym **R.E.C.I.P.E.** to remember six ingredients important to therapeutic change: **resourcefulness**, **empowerment**, **congruence**, **inner system**, **pattern**, and **externalization**. Although Satir developed a number of techniques aimed at facilitating the change process, most of her interventions grew out of her intuition about what a given family or member needed. Some of the techniques for assessment and intervention that she developed or employed are family maps (similar to genograms), family life-fact chronology (a listing of a family's three-generation history), family sculpting, drama, reframing, humor, touch, **parts parties**, and **family reconstruction** (Satir & Bitter, 2000).

I now will present some of the more important therapeutic interventions that Satir brought to her work with families. Some of these process interventions have been developed and used in other models, but Satir's use of them always flowed from a growth orientation that bordered on the spiritual. "For me, vitality and self-worth are related to health. That is the manifestation of our spirituality" (Satir as cited in Kramer, 1995, p. 10).

Family Sculpting.   One of Satir's best known techniques is called **family sculpting**, which may be used to increase family members' awareness of how they function and how they are viewed by others in the system. Satir would actually position each family member physically in relation to the whole, often using her communication stances when she wanted to emphasize how members were coping. Through the use of this technique, the family process, boundaries, and interactions became evident, yielding significant information about each member. Family sculpting gives family members an opportunity to express how they view one another in the family structure and also to express how they would like their relationships to be different. By asking family members to assume a physical position that represented how they experienced themselves currently and then asking them to unfold these positions into a sculpting of how they would like to be, Satir was often able to access feeling, desires, and movement all at the same time.

Family Reconstruction.   As a form of psychodramatic reenactment in a group counseling experience, family reconstruction enables clients to explore significant events in three generations of family life. Satir's distinctive use of family maps (similar to genograms), her family life-fact chronology, and her wheel of influence serve as the foundation on which a reconstruction is built (Satir, Bitter, & Krestensen, 1988).

Like Bowen, Satir used a three-generation family map to look at development across one's extended family. Satir believed in representing all people with circles to indicate wholeness. She also listed the children's births in descending order, which allowed the various family dyads and triads to be recognized immediately.

The family life-fact chronology was a presentation of family history across a time line of real events. Starting with the birth of the individual's or family's oldest grandparent and proceeding through to the present, every birth and death, every coming and going, every achievement or defeat, and any individual or family movement was noted. Although such a chronology takes time to prepare, once it is finished, it is easy to see when the family was under extreme stress and what members did to cope.

The wheel of influence was a simple diagram that starts with each person in the center, like the hub of a wheel. Spokes were drawn from that person to significant family members, friends, school and work associates, acquaintances, and others who had an impact on the individual. By assigning adjectives to each person on the wheel, the individual's internal and external resources were immediately manifest.

In a family reconstruction, a focus-individual (whom Satir called "the star") picked people from a group to play significant members of the family. These people then reenacted experiences that had led to the development of the person. This technique guided clients in unlocking dysfunctional patterns that stemmed from their families-of-origin. Family reconstruction took members through different stages of their lives, and it had three goals: (1) to enable family members to identify the roots of old learning; (2) to help individuals formulate more-realistic pictures of their parents; and (3) to assist them in discovering their unique personalities (Nerin, 1986, 1993; Satir & Baldwin, 1983; Satir, Bitter, & Krestensen, 1988).

Although Satir occasionally would use reconstruction with whole families who were stuck in a closed system, the real advantage of this approach is for individuals who have family issues but little or no access to their families-of-origin. By using a group to simulate three generations of family life, clients are able to make sense out of past experiences that otherwise would continue to mystify them. The experience of reenacting and observing significant life events in a focused group process often gives the protagonist a new starting point and the opportunity to interrupt old and entrenched family patterns in favor of more useful processes. For those who would one day be family therapists and who want to identify significant issues that might interfere with their clinical work, family reconstruction is a very useful tool, one Satir always hoped would be a basic part of all training programs.

Parts Parties.   Just as Satir saw a family as a system, she saw each person as a system of parts, both positive and negative. She said that people often distort, deny, or disown parts that are less useful in adolescent and adult life but that served the younger child's need for survival. A parts party is another psychodramatic process, often used in groups, to help individuals acknowledge and integrate multiple aspects of the self. Used with couples or families, it is a means of showing family members what is happening when they interact (Bitter, 1991; Satir & Baldwin, 1983). A simple parts party with a couple, for example, might invite each partner to list six well-known public figures and the characteristic that the person associates with each public figure. Each public figure chosen is really just a projection of an internal attribute of the individual. One partner might choose Abraham Lincoln (to represent integrity), Robert Redford (sexiness), Meryl Streep (talent), Hillary Clinton (leadership), Charles Manson (evil), and Roseanne Barr (bossiness). The other partner might pick Ralph Nader (activism), Robin Williams (humor), Maya Angelou (creativity), Martin Luther King, Jr. (strength), Archie Bunker (grouchiness), and Albert Einstein (intelligence). One way to show the couple why they have difficulty communicating at home some nights and not others would be to put the two sets of parts (played by group members) on either side of a sheet, partition, or wall. As one part for each partner comes out randomly from behind the wall, it is possible that the Robert Redford character will run into Archie Bunker, and the couple won't get very far. On the other hand, Meryl Streep and Albert Einstein might do very well. The process of seeing and experiencing one's parts played by others often adds real dimension to people's lives and facilitates a new integration of and respect for our strengths and weaknesses.

A Satir Therapist With the Quest Family

Paul and Jane Quest bring all four of their children to the first meeting with a Satir therapist. It is Jane who made the initial phone call to the therapist. Jane asked about getting help for the two boys, but she was encouraged to bring the entire family to the session. Paul agreed to come when a time could be arranged that fit with his schedule. Although the Satir therapist knew a little bit about the family from the initial phone call, she wanted to free herself to meet each person as if he or she were brand new. She met Jane first, who seemed warm, friendly, and relieved to be there. Jane introduced her to each of the children, starting with Amy and Ann, both of whom were polite but didn't have much to say. By contrast, the boys were very talkative, interrupting often, and in constant motion. Luke asked her if he got to sit on her lap, to which, the therapist smiled and said, "Maybe for a few minutes. And then I am sure you will be able to find your own special way of being here." Finally, the therapist looked at Paul, standing behind everyone else, extended her hand, and said: "I'd like to meet you, too."

In the therapy room, the family sat in a circle. Luke did start on the therapist's lap, but he was soon up and moving around. His mother tried to corral the boys once or twice, but the therapist assured her that there was nothing they could hurt in the office and that it was okay for them to move around. Amy and Ann sat together next to their father and across from the two empty chairs placed close to the mother for the boys.

Looking at the two young women, the therapist began the session.

Therapist:	What is it like for the two of you to have brothers now? I imagine there have been some major changes at your house.
Amy:	I'm not sure I think of them as brothers yet. They have been in the house for over a year, but I don't know that I feel very close to them. I spend most of my energy around them protecting my things, making sure they can't get into my stuff.
Therapist:	So they don't feel like real family members to you at the moment, maybe someday. But right now, you feel like you have to pay attention to them and what they might do around your belongings.
Ann:	Amy really isn't around them that much. She's finishing high school. It's mostly mom and me who watch the boys.
Therapist:	And do you have the same feeling that Amy has that the boys require a lot of attention?
Ann:	Absolutely. They're exhausting. They are into everything. I think of them as Catholic birth control.
Therapist:	Jane and Paul, what are your feelings about all this?

Just as Paul is about to say something, a small fight breaks out between the boys. It starts with Luke pushing Jason and grabbing a toy that Jason has in his hand. Jason then strikes back, kicking his younger brother. Jane immediately gets up and makes both of the boys sit down in the circle.

Jane to Jason:	I don't care if he did push you, we don't hit in this house.
Jason:	I didn't hit him.
Jane:	No. You kicked him.
Jason:	Well, I didn't mean to.
Therapist:	[talking directly and quietly to Jason] Well, now, let's see. This is your foot (she reaches down and gives his foot a gentle squeeze), and it is attached to your leg. It was your leg that was moving, wasn't it?
Jason:	I guess so. . . . I know how to play soccer!
Therapist:	And you like to play soccer. It makes you happy to kick the ball and run up and down the field. (Jason smiles.) Tell me, how do you like your new home? How do you like your family?
Jason:	I like everyone fine. It's Luke who does bad things and doesn't like people. He wants his real mother.
Therapist:	I see. So sometimes Luke feels a bit lost and wants your first mother and, when he realizes he misses her and feels bad, he sometimes does bad things. But you don't feel that way. You don't miss your real mother.
Jason:	(Jason seems very quiet now. He almost whispers.) No.

The therapist now turns her attention to Jane. She notes that the boys must be quite a change from raising two girls. Jane says that she and Ann are both very tired at the end of the day. She feels as though she has to be correcting the boys all the time, punishing them more than she ever did with the girls, and it is not what she expected. Jane tells some of the history of how the boys came to be part of the family. She knew that their history would have a negative effect on them and that they would be a greater challenge than Amy and Ann were, but she never dreamed how really hard it actually was.

Jane: I feel afraid most of the time. I never know whether they are going to hurt each other or hurt someone else, a baby in the neighborhood or a younger child. I have seen what they sometimes do to cats and dogs, and it is awful.

Therapist: [to Paul] Do you share your wife's fears about the boys?

Paul: I don't know that I am afraid. I feel more lost. I am at work much of the time when Jason and Luke do one thing or another. I don't know what to do, so I generally do nothing. To me, Jane is a hero. She saved Jason and Luke when they had no one, and she tries to make a better life for them every day. (Paul takes Jane's hand.) All I do is earn money. She makes a life for them. She makes a life for all of us.

Therapist: [to Jane] What is it like for you to hear what your husband has to say about you.

Jane: I know Paul loves me, and I know he wants to love all of our children.

Therapist: But you're not sure he loves Jason and Luke enough?

Jane: I just wish he would find time to do more with them. They need a man in their lives. And Ann and I need a break now and then.

Therapist: [to Paul] Well, I am hearing that you like to know what you are doing before you do it and, if you knew what to do that would make a difference with Jason and Luke, you would do it. Did I get that right?

Paul: Yes. That's exactly right.

The therapist now asks both of the parents to talk a little bit about what Jason and Luke do that causes problems at home and in the community. She also wants to know what each of the parents hopes the other will do in relation to the various concerns. While they are talking, Ann gets up and quietly and effectively removes a plastic hanger from Luke who is about to use it to hit Jason. Then she returns to her seat. The therapist smiles at Ann and touches Ann's knee with her hand. She continues to talk to Jane and Paul. What becomes clear is that Jane often feels deserted by Paul and Amy. She is thankful for Ann's help, but she wants Paul to be more involved. Paul's reluctance has had more to do with the part of him that needs to feel competent than with wanting out of the family, as Jane feared.

Jane: [facing Paul] I guess I need to know that you don't blame me for our family being turned upside down.

Paul: Blame you? I feel totally guilty. I don't know how to be a parent to these boys. I don't know how to be a good husband to you either, and I haven't for almost a year. So I work. I keep hoping the girls can help you, because I sure don't know what to do.

Therapist: So I am hearing that both of you feel lost, but neither of you wants to lose the other. And it's never a consideration for either of you that maybe Jason and Luke shouldn't be with you. It's just that they have had a hard life and now everyone in the family is having a hard time.

While the therapist has been talking to Jane and Paul, Jason pulls a chair up next to Amy. Amy reaches out and runs her hand through his curly hair, touseling it a bit. Jason leans into Amy, his head under her arm.

Therapist: [to Amy] How do you know how to do that with Jason?

Amy: He doesn't let me do it often, but I actually love his hair. I love to play with it.

Therapist: It gives you pleasure. Do you think you could show your dad how to do that with Jason or perhaps could you show your dad how to find out what kind of touches Jason likes?

Amy:	Jason kind of lets you know by how he responds.
Therapist:	Jason, what would it be like for you if your dad played with your hair?
Jason:	Not dad. I want to wrestle with him like a bear.
Therapist:	Could you stand a bear hug from your dad?
Jason:	Yes. And I'll hug him hard too.
Therapist:	Jason, why don't you ask your dad if he will do that with you?
Jason:	Will you, dad?

Paul reaches out for his son, and takes him in his arms. He holds the boy close and firmly, rocking him back and forth, and simulating wrestling sounds. The therapist turns to Luke and asks him, "How do you like this mother here to touch you?" Luke puts his hands on his face and drops his face into his lap, laughing. The therapist asks Jane to move her chair closer to Luke and guides her in lifting Luke's head up with her hands. Jane smiles at Luke as she lifts his head up and holds it in her hand. The therapist then helps Luke hold Jane's face, something that Jason now starts to do with his father.

Therapist:	These children have had a lot of negative touch in their lives. They don't need anymore of that. This is the kind of touch that they need, as much and as often as they can get it. Earlier today, I watched Ann intervene with the boys. She was clear and firm when she removed the coat hanger, but she was not threatening. And they did not fight with her about it. This seems to me to be very effective. And I am wondering, Jane, what it would mean to you if you saw Paul touching the boys more with his gentleness and stepping in to prevent problems in the same way that Ann did today?
Jane:	I would feel so relieved and so much love for him.
Therapist:	Would you ask him if he thinks he could do that more with the boys?
Jane:	[to Paul] Do you? Could you do that?
Paul:	I sure think I can now.

Summary and Multicultural Evaluation

For many years, Satir was the only woman to have developed a complete model of family therapy. To be sure, much of her approach and emphasis on relationship will be welcomed by people who sense too much detachment or use of power in other systems of family therapy. Although feminists often have acknowledged Satir's courageous stand in favor of nurturance, connection, personal involvement, and even touch in therapy, they also have recognized that Satir was not primarily a feminist in her approach. Satir was concerned with **humanism**—the personhood of every man, woman, and child. She tended to play down the importance of political struggles and believed that change started from within, extended to relationships, and would eventually change the world (Satir & Baldwin, 1983).

Satir devoted a great deal of time to giving workshops and conducting training for family therapists. To her credit, she demonstrated her work with families before large audiences of mental health workers. It was in these public demonstrations that her concepts came alive and that her practice was validated. During her career, she worked with more than 5,000 families, representing a wide range of diversity.

Satir was an innovator, a creator, and an intuitive genius. Her dedication to a growth model—what she called a **seed model** (Satir et al., 1991)—provided an extremely positive lens through which to view human systems. Her belief in the self-esteem of every human being, the power of congruence, and her ability to touch the very hearts and souls of people brought a level of hope to family therapy that is often missed in models more dedicated to eradicating dysfunction or pathology. Her identification of communication stances provided therapists with an efficient way to access meaning in metacommunications. Further, these stances became the foundation for two of her most creative interventions: sculpting and family reconstruction. Most importantly, Satir taught people how to create useful learning experiences, even in very large groups.

Satir added a process lens to family therapy and counseling that helps clinicians view individuals, couples, and families in terms of human engagement, connection, and intention. Her work reminds us that process is often more important than content, but also that the two are linked: The message cannot be separated from the messenger or from the way in which the message is delivered and received. From her human validation process model, therapists can learn multiple ways to bring an awareness of process into the therapy session and to make what is present, but hidden, manifest so that every member may participate in needed change.

If you are interested in a more in-depth study of this approach, I recommend the following sources: McLendon (2000a, 2000b); McLendon and Davis (2002); Satir (1983, 1988); Satir and Baldwin (1983); Satir, Banmen, Gerber, and Gomori, (1991); and Satir and Bitter (2000).

Contributions to Multicultural Counseling and Gender Issues

Through her AVANTA Network (now called The Virginia Satir Global Network), Satir herself, as well as many of her trainers, made significant contributions in multicultural settings. Satir was the only major family therapist to offer human-relationships training on a regular basis to the Lakota Sioux in South Dakota. As in any culture that was new to her, she entered the first experience with an openness to learn about the culture, the people, the symbols, and the meanings inherent in the community. From this, she both adapted some of her therapeutic interventions and incorporated new possibilities unique to that culture. In her lifetime, Satir worked within many of the countries in Asia and the Pacific Islands, all of the countries comprising Europe, including many of the countries that used to comprise what was called the Eastern Bloc. Shortly before she died, Satir made a historic visit to Russia when it was still part of the U.S.S.R. She returned from that training experience convinced that significant change was well on its way.

In the tradition of Carl Rogers (1987a, 1987b, 1987c), members of Satir's Global Network have conducted human validation process groups with people from diverse cultures in an effort to increase mutual understanding. Satir trainers Margarita Suarez, Hugh Gratz, Selena Sermeno, Mona Mendoza, Sandy Ewell, Darlene de la Cruz, and Hilda Richards, to name a few, have offered these groups with Hispanic and African-American participants, as well as in various countries in Central and South America. John Banmen, Jane Gerber, and Maria Gomori brought Satir training to Hong Kong and later to other Asian communities and cultures. Laura Dodson brings Satir to many countries in Eastern Europe through her International Connections organization. In all of these instances, the power of congruence and the dedication to human connection has been extremely well received.

In addition, The Virginia Satir Global Network annual meeting regularly addresses multicultural issues and attempts to formulate humane responses to national and international concerns. Recent meetings have included programs on Central America, responses for a post-9/11 world, and dealing with trauma and grief in a multicultural world.

There are very few limitations related to this approach in multicultural settings, but the ones that do exist can be especially difficult in collectivist cultures. It shares some of the same conceptual difficulties that are associated with other humanistic models. There is a strong emphasis on personal responsibility and personal development. A model that considers placating, for example, to be a dysfunctional communication style may seem to be at odds with cultures that stress hierarchy, deference to authority, and putting the common good ahead of individual needs. In such cases, the culture may consider the loss of a personal identity to be less problematic than the loss of respect for the entire family.

Satir's model also stresses the importance of an **internal locus of control**. Again, in cultures and groups that value an external locus of evaluation, this can be problematic too. In many Asian cultures, for example, one is expected to look to tradition and the familial expectations of the extended family for guidance, rather than focus only on an internal sense of well-being, individual preferences, and self-esteem needs. This internal locus of control also gives some feminists and social constructionists concern, because it can too easily ignore the abuses of power inherent in patriarchal, dominant culture systems. Satir's personal stance and the model she developed took no political stance in relation to gender issues. Although Satir was an extremely strong proponent of women in families and larger systems, she never saw the human development of women as a counterpoint to male oppression. She did not see oppression as an outside force that required a different response than any other foreign element in life.

Satir referred to men and women as having **navel equality**; that is, we are all human, having emerged from our biological mothers as a result of the fertilization of a human egg by human sperm. Satir sought the rounded wholeness of all people. In this sense, Satir's facilitation of women was never at the expense of men.

Luepnitz (1988) reports a comment by Satir that speaks to her belief in one's personal power in the face of oppression:

> Years ago, I was on a panel with Murray Bowen, and at the end of my presentation Murray said in front of a large audience, "Isn't Virginia wonderful? She gets to all the right places by all the wrong means." And then he got up to kiss me. I could have used that as a downer. But I have something to do with how I respond to that. (p. 56)

It is also important to note Satir's openness and valuing of the gay, lesbian, and bisexual community. Satir saw all human beings as needing the freedom to be themselves. She saw all of us as part of a large, human continuum with differences that could be understood and appreciated, rather than placed at a distance, distorted, diminished, or denied. She once started a presentation at the Association for Humanistic Psychology conference by asking three women and three men to come up on stage. She then arranged them so that there were two men standing together, two women standing together, and a man and a woman standing together. She said: "You see, there are only two sexes, and there are only so many ways you can arrange them." Then she proceeded to teach the audience about communication and relationships regardless of which genders were involved.

Exercises for Personal and Professional Growth

Satir introduced the concept of the nurturing triad. In what ways do you remember your mother and father (or significant others in your life) working together for your welfare and that of your sisters and brothers, if you had any?

- If you can remember these experiences of cooperation, what did they feel like?
- What part of it do you (or would you like to) carry forward into the rest of your life?

When we are little, we often experience feelings of fear, frustration, and helplessness. What we don't realize is that our parents are often feeling the same things about their roles as our parents. In most cases, we manage to struggle along with each other; we become interdependent and learn to adjust and adapt. It is not uncommon in this process to develop family rules. Early in life, these rules come to us in a form that is absolute and even impossible. We already have discussed such rules in this chapter. Some of mine were: "I must never use an upset tone with the adults in my life." I think my parents words were: "Don't use that tone with me, young man!" Some others were: "I must always do things the right way—and the first time too." Also: "It is okay not to be the best, but I must always try to do my best."

- What are three of the rules you learned in your family?
- Were they received by you in the form of musts, oughts, or shoulds—and did they have to be followed always or never?
- Write them down below:

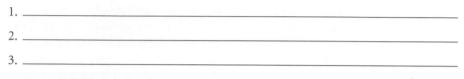

- To transform these rules as Satir would, find all the musts, oughts, and shoulds and change each of these words to *can*.
- Next, find all the always and nevers and change these words to sometimes.

So one of my early rules would now read: "I can sometimes do things the right way— and even on the first try . . . sometimes." How would your transformed rules read?

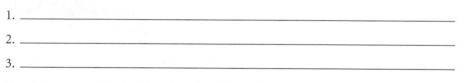

To really cement the **family rules transformation** into your life, think of three times when each of the transformed rules would be true and write those down.

1. _____
2. _____
3. _____

In practice, you will find that the rules are not as important as the impact that they have on the person and the family. When working with families, John Banmen (personal communication, January 9, 2006) suggests that you will want to change the impact, not just the rule. When rules fail to protect us and family distress increases, Satir noted that we often go into communication stances that are intended to help us cope. You will remember that she had stances for placating, blaming, being super-reasonable, and being irrelevant. Did you know that you can actually sculpt these stances? Let's try it.

- For placating, get down on one knee, put one hand over your heart, and lift the other hand up as if supplicating a superior being. Remember, you will be saying "yes" to everything that is asked of you. Where do you feel the stress in your body when you do this? What would it take for you to feel safe enough to stand on your own two feet—to stand for something?
- For blaming, stand with your right foot a little ahead of your left foot. Now stiffen your right arm and point at someone or something. Put your left hand on your left hip, tighten your jaw, and narrow your eyes. Now you are in a blaming stance.

Where do you feel the stress in your body now? Does it happen to be in your shoulders? Or do you feel it more in your legs? Is your head getting hot? Remember, you are in an aggressive stance because it is easier to attack than to go under.

- For being super-reasonable, stand stiffly at attention, like a military person might do. Okay, soldier, chest out, stomach in, chin down, eyes forward, arms at your side! In this stance, it is possible to turn off all feelings from the neck down. Remember, you are dealing only with information: as with a computer, information comes in and goes out. It does not matter how you feel about it. Principle is everything; just keep stating the right thing to do. Where do you feel the stress now? Is it in your lower back? Hmmm.

- For being irrelevant, change the position of your feet so that they are now turned inward—what we used to call "pigeon-toed" when I was young. Next, hang your body from your shoulders with your head lowered. Move your head from side to side so that you do not have the ability to focus on anything. Flop your arms back and forth too. This position is almost the exact opposite of the super-reasonable position. Initially, it may feel like a relief to be out of the super-reasonable position, but eventually you will become dizzy and disoriented.

- Okay, shake all of that off and reclaim your body. Stand with your feet comfortably balanced on the floor. Bend your legs a little, and stretch your arms out. Now relax and look straight ahead. Notice what you can see, hear, touch, feel, and handle. Imagine that, in this position of congruence, your experiences match your thoughts and feelings and you are capable of communicating with emotional honesty. This is the true antidote to the four positions you tried above. Can you feel more energy in your body when you stand like this?

Let's see what it is like to apply these communication stances. Pretend that you are a parent of a teenage daughter. Her name is Annie and she is 15. She comes home from cheerleading one night and she is visibly upset. She says, "Mom, Dad, I'm pregnant." What would be a placating, blaming, being super-reasonable, and being irrelevant response that you might make as Annie's parent? Write them down here:

Placating: _____

Blaming: _____

Super-reasonable: _____

Irrelevant: _____

Now write a congruent response. Take a moment. What are you really feeling? What response would take into account your best feelings, your daughter's needs, and the context?

Congruent: _____

As you do this, you may hear responses that are familiar. Maybe they came from other family members when you were younger. Maybe they still come from friends and relatives when stress is high. We are not limited to just one response. Sometimes we actually create a communication dance in an effort to cope. Do you know which ones you have used in the past? Practicing such responses will help you hear them when they come up in the families you see. Practicing congruence will make your life better.

If you have an extra class or two available in your course, you might also try either of the two Satir group processes described in this chapter. A family reconstruction is a bit more complicated than a *parts party*, but either one can increase personal awareness as well a bond group members to each other. For more information on family reconstruction, see Satir, Bitter, and Krestensen (1988) or Nerin (1986, 1993). For more information on conducting a parts party, see Satir, Banmen, Gerber, and Gomori (1991) or Bitter (1991).

Where to Go From Here

Satir developed a group known as the AVANTA Network for implementing her approach to family therapy. It is now called The Virginia Satir Global Network. The network is made up of mental health professionals from various disciplines, organizational consultants, and leaders in the not-for-profit and profit worlds. Many of these individuals worked and trained with Satir. There is an expanding third generation of practitioners who are using Satir's growth model as their core values and methods. The network also provides links to Satir training programs around the world on their Website. Information about the training programs that are offered through this group is available by contacting The Virginia Satir Global Network at:

The Virginia Satir Global Network®
4002 S. 184th Place
SeaTac, WA 98188-5014
Phone: 206-241-7566, fax: 206-241-7527
E-mail: **office@avanta.net**
Website at: **http://www.avanta.net**

For those on the east coast, Jean McLendon, the woman Virginia Satir handpicked to be her Director of Training, offers therapy, an intensive training program, and on-going supervision in the human validation process model at the Satir Institute of the Southeast in Chapel Hill, N.C. In my opinion, Jean's work, which can be seen on the outstanding Allyn and Bacon tape, *Satir Therapy with Jean McLendon: Family Therapy with the Experts* (McLendon, 2000b), is as close as one can get today to seeing what Satir was like with families. Jean can be reached at:

Satir Systems
87 S. Elliott Road, Suite 212
Chapel Hill, NC 27514
Phone: 919-967-2520, fax: 919-967-0515
E-mail: **jmclendon@satirsystems.com**
Website at: **http://www.satirsystems.com**

In California, Dr. Carl Sayles runs a Satir-based center called

The Healing Place
9849 Fair Oaks Blvd.
Fair Oaks, CA 95661, 916-961-2431

In Colorado, Sandy Novak and John Banmen teach at the

Satir Institute of the Rockies
1480 Lee Hill Road, #7
Boulder, CO 90304
Phone: 303-629-2960 or 303-931-4004

In Canada, there are at least two institutes that provide Satir training and programs. The first is in the Vancouver, British Columbia area where John Banmen, one of the best writers in the Satir model and a highly skilled trainer of therapists, is the director of training:

Satir Institute of the Pacific
#11213 Canyon Crescent
Delta, British Columbia, V4E 2R6
Canada
E-mail: **training@satirpacific.org**

In Manitoba, Maria Gomori, Gilles Beaudry, and their associates have a professional-development institute for counselors, therapists, social workers, and others from the helping professions:

Satir Professional Devleopment Institute of Manitoba
Maria Gomori
Phone/fax: 204-284-4104
E-mail: **gomori@mb.sympatico.ca**
Gilles Beaudry
Phone: 204-233-9393
E-mail: **beaudrygi@merlin.mb.ca** or
John or Sigrid Sawchuk
Phone: 204-831-7858

Recommended Readings

Banmen, J. (Ed.). (2003). *Meditations of Virginia Satir: Peace within, peace between, and peace among.* Burien, WA: AVANTA: The Virginia Satir Network. This is a book of the meditations for which Satir was well known. The book is nicely edited by John Banmen to feature Satir's spirituality.

Contemporary Family Therapy: An International Journal. (March, 2002, Vol. 24, Number 1). New York: Springer Science+Business Media B.V. This issue of the journal is completely devoted to the Satir model, with articles covering the most up-to-date advances in theory and practice.

Satir, V. M. (1976). *Making contact.* Millbrae, CA: Celestial Arts. This is Satir's communication model written for families and lay people.

Satir, V. M. (1978). *Your many faces.* Millbrae, CA: Celestial Arts. This is Satir's Mandala and routes to self-esteem written for families and lay people.

Satir, V. M. (1983). *Conjoint family therapy* (3rd ed.). Palo Alto: CA: Science and Behavior Books. This is the book that Satir called the Bible for her approach. In the third edition, she added two very important chapters for those who follow her work: (1) a chapter on how she meets people individually or in families and how she connects to them, and (2) a chapter on how she worked with large groups, a process she had to employ many times in the last 2 decades of her life.

Satir, V. M. (1988). *The new peoplemaking.* Palo Alto, CA: Science and Behavior Books. A complete updating of her classic work, this is the last book on which Satir herself worked. It is written for therapists and consumers alike, and it gives a real flavor of what Satir's real-life presentations were like. This book is published in 27 different languages.

Satir, V. M., & Baldwin, M. (1983). *Satir: Step-by-step.* Palo Alto, CA: Science and Behavior Books. Part I of this book is an actual typescript with commentary on one of Satir's family therapy sessions. Part II, largely written by Michelle Baldwin, is an excellent presentation of the human validation process model.

Satir, V. M., Banmen, J., & Gerber, J. (Eds.). (1985). *Meditations and inspirations.* Berkeley, CA: Celestial Arts. Satir used humanistic meditations to prepare herself and others for work—either as a family or a large group. Here are some of her favorite meditations.

Satir, V. M., Banmen, J., Gerber, J., & Gomori, M. (1991). *The Satir model: Family therapy and beyond.* Palo Alto, CA: Science and Behavior Books. This is the most comprehensive presentation of the human validation process model. Written after Satir's death and based on her level II, process community training, this one book covers everything that was ever central to her model.

DVD Reference

In the video that accompanies this theory, Jean McLendon, an internationally known Satir trainer, works with Dr. Bitter's actual family. He is joined by his wife Lynn Williams and their two children, Alison, age 15, and Nora, age 9. We join the video in progress: Jean has been getting to know the family, and then she wants to hear what family members want with the time they have together. Notice in this work how Jean pays very close attention to the *emotional life* of the family and to the feelings that must be involved in their interactions. Her careful listening makes it possible for the rest of the family to *listen compassionately* too.

References

Banmen, J. (Ed.). (2003). *Meditations of Virginia Satir: Peace within, peace between, and peace among.* Burien, WA: AVANTA: The Virginia Satir Network.

Bitter, J. R. (1987). Communication and meaning: Satir in Adlerian context. In R. Sherman & D. Dinkmeyer (Eds.), *Systems of family therapy: An Adlerian integration* (pp. 109–142). New York: Brunner/Mazel.

Bitter, J. R. (1991). Satir's parts party with couples. In T. Nelson & T. Trepper (Eds.), *101 interventions in family therapy* (pp. 132–136). New York: Haworth.

Buber, M. (1996). *I and thou* (W. Kaufmann, Trans.). New York: Touchstone. (Original work published 1937)

Golden Triad Films, Inc. (1968a). *Virginia Satir: Blended family with a troubled boy* [VT 101]. Kansas City, MO: Author.

Golden Triad Films, Inc. (1968b). *Study guide for teaching tapes featuring Virginia Satir.* Kansas City, MO: Author.

Kramer, S. Z. (1995). *Transforming the inner and outer family.* New York: Haworth.

Luepnitz, D. A. (1988). *The family interpreted: Feminist theory in clinical practice.* New York: Basic Books.

McLendon, J. A. (2000a). The Satir system: Brief therapy strategies. In J. Carlson & L. Sperry (Eds.), *Brief therapy with individuals and couples* (pp. 331–364). Phoenix., AZ: Zeig, Tucker & Theisen Publishers.

McLendon, J. A. (Speaker). (2000b). *Satir Therapy with Jean McLendon: Family Therapy with the Experts* (ISBN # 0-205-33207-2). Boston: Allyn & Bacon.

McLendon, J. A., & Davis, B. (2002). The Satir system. In J. Carlson & D. Kjos (Eds.), *Theories and strategies of family therapy* (pp. 170–189). Boston: Allyn & Bacon.

Nerin, W. F. (1986). *Family reconstruction: Long day's journey into light.* New York: Norton.

Nerin, W. F. (1993). *You can't grow up 'til you go back home: A safe journey to see your parents as human.* Gig Harbor, WA: Magic Mountain Publishing.

Pelonis, P. (2002). *Facing change in the journey of life.* Athens, Greece: Fytraki Publications.

Rogers, C. R. (1987a). Inside the world of the soviet professional. *Counseling and Values, 32*(1), 46–66.

Rogers, C. R. (1987b). Our international family. *Person-Centered Review, 2*(2), 139–149.

Rogers, C. R. (1987c). Steps toward world peace, 1948–1986: Tension reduction in theory and practice. *Counseling and Values, 32*(1), 12–16.

Satir, V. M. (1983). *Conjoint family therapy* (3rd ed.). Palo Alto: CA: Science and Behavior Books.

Satir, V. M. (1988). *The new peoplemaking.* Palo Alto, CA: Science and Behavior Books.

Satir, V. M., & Baldwin, M. (1983). *Satir: Step-by-step.* Palo Alto, CA: Science and Behavior Books.

Satir, V. M., Banmen, J., Gerber, J., & Gomori, M. (1991). *The Satir model: Family therapy and beyond.* Palo Alto, CA: Science and Behavior Books.

Satir, V. M., & Bitter, J. R. (2000). The therapist and family therapy: Satir's human validation process model. In A. Horne (Ed.), *Family counseling and therapy* (pp. 62–101). Itasca, IL: F. E. Peacock.

Satir, V. M., Bitter, J. R., & Krestensen, K. K. (1988). Family reconstruction: The family within—a group process. *The Journal for Specialists in Group Work, 13*(4), 200–208.

Selye, H. (1974). *Stress without distress.* New York: J. B. Lippincott.

CHAPTER 7

Symbolic-Experiential Family Therapy

Introduction

Key Concepts

Therapy Goals

The Therapist's Role and Function

Techniques

A Symbolic-Experiential Therapist With the Quest Family

Summary and Multicultural Evaluation

Recommended Readings

References

Introduction

Symbolic-experiential family therapy, sometimes known as experiential family therapy or the experiential/symbolic approach, has a strong relationship to other existential, humanistic, and phenomenological orientations. The experiential approach stresses choice, freedom, self-determination, growth, and actualization. It is an interactive process involving a family with a therapist who is willing to be real. The focus is on **here-and-now** interaction between the family and the therapist, rather than on exploring past experiences.

Carl Whitaker, who died in April 1995, was the best known exponent of this freewheeling, intuitive approach. For much of his career, he preferred to work with a co-therapist, and many of his associates from Thomas Malone and Gus Napier to David Keith became scholar-practitioners in this experiential model. In 1988, Whitaker published a book based on an earlier video that featured an intensive 3-day symbolic-experiential family session with "a farm family"; his co-therapist was William Bumberry (Whitaker & Bumberry, 1986; Whitaker & Bumberry, 1988). These sessions are excerpted below.

John and Marie, the parents, came to the sessions with their five adult children: Vanessa, age 30; Gail, age 28; Doris, age 27; Mike, age 23, and Marla, age 18. Mike and Gail were delayed in arriving and were able to be present only for the last day. It was Vanessa who had asked for the family consultation. She was "studying to become a therapist" (Whitaker & Bumberry, 1988, p. 5), and she wanted to address some of the struggles in her family that kept her tied up.

Whitaker: How did you decide to come? What would you like to get out of it? How can I help? (pause) Let me tell you how I deal. I'd like to hear about you to get a sense of the pain you are going through. So I can feel my way into the family. But I need to be clear with you, that I'm sort of the coach on this baseball team, I'm not playing on it. You have to make the final decision about what you do with your living. (pause) I should warn you that I get mean. (Whitaker & Bumberry, 1988, p. 7)

University of Wisconsin Madison Archives

Carl Whitaker

This opening is different from what most practitioners are taught in graduate training programs. What do you think of this beginning? What if everything you ever were taught about counseling and therapy was effective, but not much fun? Would it be okay with you to introduce fun, the unusual, even the outrageous into the session? Would you do it from the very beginning or wait until you had established a rapport? What role do you think a family counselor or therapist should play? Do you like Whitaker's idea of being a coach on a team? How would a coach act? Would it be different from what you think a professional counselor or therapist would normally be?

Family practitioners often start family sessions with some form of assessment that keeps the practitioner personally aloof and distant. Whitaker favored a more assertive, proactive introduction in which he claimed the I-position he was interested in taking in therapy. His boldness was always authentic, emanating from a desire to create a real interaction between the family and himself. By initiating his own stance, the family was free to react in whatever way seemed useful to them and he, in turn, would respond to their responses: An interactive, experiential dance was immediately underway. In this dance, the therapist may still lead, but she or he also pays attention to the efforts of the dance partners, adjusting the rhythm to movements offered by others.

In the early part of the first session, Whitaker asked about the father's family-of-origin. This was a topic initiated by the father that Whitaker followed, but he constantly looked for ways in which the historical data informed the current situation and relationships in the family. The first question was related to the father's dad.

Whitaker: Is he dead, too?

Dad: Yes.

Whitaker: When did he die?

Dad: In 1972.

Whitaker: What was wrong?

Dad: He was 89 years old. Infirmity and old age. He lived a pretty good life.

Whitaker: And Mom? . . . Was Dad a farmer too?

Dad: Yes.

Whitaker: What did Mother die of?

Dad: She died at 62 of pneumonia. We could have avoided it if we had realized it.

Whitaker: And what about Dad? Did he remarry?

Dad: No.

Whitaker: How many brothers and sisters?

Dad: None.

Whitaker: You're the only child? No wonder you're spoiled, huh?

Mom: That's it!

Whitaker: That's the real problem, huh?

Mom: Yes. If he had been brought up . . . he would have had a sister. Really! A sister wouldn't have been that different in age. Molly was walking in the milkhouse one day and slipped. She lost the baby at 8 months.

Doris: Older or younger?

Mom: She would have been younger. It would have been good because she would have told him, "Get out of here! Don't do that!" Brothers and sisters will tell each other. Friends are afraid.

Whitaker: Is that true of wives, too, or are you being a good sister to him?

Mom: Maybe I am. Maybe I'm too good to him.

Whitaker: Why don't you get over that?

Mom: I don't know. It's hard for me.

Whitaker: Just a sucker are you? . . . Just naturally?

Mom: What? What did you say?

Whitaker: Are you just a natural-born sucker?

Mom: Maybe I am! Oh, I get mad at him a lot of times, but he just walks away. He won't fight! He walks to the back 40 (acres) and I can't find him. I get mad because he won't fight it out. He just walks away!

Whitaker: Why don't you get a bow and arrow or something?

Doris: Take the tractor.

Whitaker: Or a shotgun full of rock salt? They used to talk about that when I was a kid. (Whitaker & Bumberry, 1988, pp. 15–19)

In this segment, Whitaker used his intuition to frame interactive positions for the two parents: Dad's "spoiled child" position was counterbalanced with Mom's "natural-born sucker" position. Whitaker's insinuation was that this man, who almost had a sister in real life, managed to marry one: She was a woman, the father knew, who would continue to sacrifice parts of herself (be a sucker) to care for him and keep him spoiled. This interactive mutuality flies in the face of the more linear conceptualization of father "as the problem," an unfeeling man who has failed to support the other members of the family. Because Mom has been willing to dedicate herself to a life of service, it has also served her children to support their relationship tacitly. They have gotten service too, but more important, none of them really wants to take care of Dad if Mom "resigns."

The unusual suggestion of using a bow and arrow or a shotgun on Dad suggested that Mom might start to consider the possibility of stepping out of a victim role and do something about her life in relation to this man. By suggesting an aggressive idea far beyond anything the mother would consider herself, she was free to entertain her less-threatening, but still suppressed, desires to be angry with—or even rage at—Dad. Whitaker's more-outrageous suggestions are examples of what he calls **seeding the unconscious** (Whitaker & Bumberry, 1986). Because he owned his own projections (his own spoken, over-the-top ideas, feelings, concepts, or metaphors), the family members did not have to feel blamed or guilty for having their own reactions and feelings.

In this first session with the family, Whitaker also explored Dad's escape into work, suggesting at one point that he loved his cows more than he did his family, an idea that the mother did not experience as crazy. At the same time, Whitaker also indicated that the mother started loving the kids more than the father. Naming these two movements as "affairs" once again established the mutuality of their distancing from each other. In following the mother's comments about her husband's "workaholic" ways, Whitaker also uncovered her concern about the father's attraction to other women and his interest in and ability to dance with other women.

Toward the end of the first session, Dad talked about feeling burnt out on farming and all that it demands of him. Whitaker sensed that this was the same as being burnt out on life, and he directly asked about the father feeling suicidal, a possibility that Mom indicated her husband hints at.

Whitaker: How much longer do you think you're going to live?

Dad: Well, that's a good question. As far as I'm concerned, I'm ready any day.

Whitaker: Oh really?

Dad: Sure.

Whitaker: Why?

Dad: I lived a good life. I did everything I ever wanted to do. If I lived again, I'd do it the same. . . . I have no regrets. It was hard work, but one thing with it, you always had the satisfaction of seeing your accomplishments. While with a lot of things, a good factory job for instance, you get good money, but you have nothing to show for it. But on the farm, if you're lucky and have a good crop, you can take care of your food and clothes. You have no debt and no credit.

Whitaker: I just had a funny feeling. Is he a softy? I thought he was going to cry.

Mom: He never cries at funerals, or anything. Even his Dad's funeral. I was sobbing away.

Doris: He did at the end.

Mom: Yes, I saw him at the end. A teeny bit.

Doris: Well, we all have our levels.

Whitaker: I thought he was going to cry just now. Did you feel like crying a minute ago?

Dad: Well, I feel . . . sometimes I get that way. You know, but . . . . Well, like with my Dad. If you had seen what he went through. I was glad he could go. (Whitaker & Bumberry, 1988, pp. 29–31)

In the closing moments of the first session, the father's humanness began to show, and even though the family engaged in a discussion of Dad's feelings at an earlier time, Whitaker stayed with the present and with the process he observed right in the session. Dad's humanness was emerging now. It was not a special, unique, past event.

At the beginning of the next session, it slipped out that Mom consulted with Marla about what to bring on the trip to therapy. Then she forgot to pack night clothes for either her husband or herself, a fact that led Whitaker to suggest the old folks were really in trouble now. Whitaker's presence almost seemed to intensify in this next session. He constantly probed the session's content for areas in which covert sexuality could have been made manifest; his interventions almost always exaggerated implied possibilities in the family, raising their anxiety enough to motivate more honest and direct interactions.

It became clearer as the session progressed that both Vanessa and Marla had difficulties in establishing and maintaining close relationships with significant men in their lives. Their approach-avoidance postures with men seemed to reflect the pain and distance that existed in their parents' relationship. As a more-open conversation related to the adult daughters' pain in relation to men emerged, both parents seemed to distance themselves with references to the past, outside distractions, or silence. At one point, Whitaker joined Dad in yet another discussion of tractors only to trigger raging anger in Vanessa: She was leading the way for the family to break the silence and address each other with emotional honesty.

In this family, multiple triangles began to show themselves, as well as many nonproductive role-reversals. Vanessa could not seem to decide whether she wanted a boyfriend or a guru in her life, and she tended to get them mixed up: The man on whom she would most like to lean, her father, seemed all but unavailable to her. Marla stood up to her father's demands, unlike her mother, but neither of them ever felt as though they had won with him. Mike was the only person left to whom the mother felt she could turn. "He's the only one who understands me! He understands the whole situation. He sees it all as clear as a bell. As clear as a picture!" (Whitaker & Bumberry, 1988, p. 143). At different points in the session, Whitaker accused Mike of being mother's "other man" or even a parent to his own mother. Whitaker wondered out loud if Mike might also be Marla's grandparent. Making the different transactions and adopted roles manifest was Whitaker's way of putting everything on the table and letting the family sort out what was needed, what was useful, and what was useless.

Toward the end of the session, the openness that had occurred between family members led Dad to wonder about the four miscarriages his wife had had, occurrences he associated with the spraying of herbicides. He talked about the guilt he had felt for years.

Whitaker: Why don't you tell people things? Just stupid?

Dad: Could be. Sometimes I don't think about it until it's too late.

Whitaker: I don't mean the facts. I mean you telling about your suffering. They tell you. Why shouldn't you tell them? (Whitaker & Bumberry, 1988, pp. 168–169)

As the third day begins, the therapy group was transformed by the addition of Mike and Gail to the session. Whitaker also sensed that he was running out of time, and his challenges to family members were more direct as he sought to release them from their defensive postures and let them live as real people with each other. Both Mike and Gail demonstrated the same reluctance to emerge that the other family members had in the first session. Although Mike was asked to reveal something of his own craziness in the family, it was Gail, Whitaker recognized, who had been scapegoated as the unhealthy or weak one in the family.

Whitaker: If you stayed in diapers I think Mom would be great. She wouldn't have to notice that she was getting older. But if you ever try to be a person, instead of a baby for her . . . .

Gail: I'm trying! I think it's an identity that has to come over the years.

Whitaker: That's one of the things that bothers me. Don't say you're trying! Trying doesn't help! It only helps if you make it. It's like saying you're trying to make money. It only matters if you make it. You have to be as mean as hell to make it. Have you ever learned to be mean?

Gail: Oh, that's another good one! I'm basically too good to be mean!

Whitaker: That's what I'm worried about. That's how Mother is. She's too good to even get in Heaven. I don't think they could stand her. God would be embarrassed.

Gail: She is a good woman. . . . She is a person.

Whitaker: I didn't see any evidence of it! All I saw was her pain and suffering and emptiness. I don't even believe her story about the old man. I think she did it to him. She made him push her around, so she could be a nobody and blame him for it. It sounds like you're doing the same thing.

Gail: No. I'm not exactly like her.

Whitaker: . . . Do you ever get mean inside? You know, like you'd like to kill the whole gang? . . . You've got to learn to be murderous! You've got to be able to feel like killing people inside of yourself in order to get to be a person. Otherwise, you will end up being a sucker. Mother has never had the courage to even want to kill anybody, unless it was me.[1] (Whitaker & Bumberry, 1988, pp. 179–182)

Just as Whitaker had seeded the unconscious with sexual innuendo, he now gave aggressive desires a full and open place within the family system. The expression of internal aggression was heightened further when Whitaker brought out a set of four batacas (soft bats that can be used to attack one another symbolically without causing any real hurt or harm). He handed one bat to Gail, one to Marla, and one each to Mom and Dad. "We'll give the old man this one. It's kind of broken, like old men's things are apt to be" (p. 185). Whitaker urged each of them to bat each other in the head, but they are reluctant to do so. Both Mom and Marla test them out on themselves. With some encouragement, Dad lightly hits Mom, and she retaliates. Harder and harder, she pounds away while Dad lowers his bataca and endures. The adult children are cheering her on. She is no longer slumped over in pain and constriction: no longer defeated. She is alive and forceful, almost transformed. Whitaker said, "He's no puppy dog. You've got to do better than that!" (p. 187).

After a while, Mom stopped and invited Dad to have a turn, which he declines. He removed his glasses, a symbolic gesture that Whitaker noted immediately. Eventually, Dad asked if there were a game associated with the batacas. Whitaker answered that it was a game played just the way that the two of them did it. The winner was the one who beat the hardest, and the loser was the one who gave up first. Doris and Mom encouraged Gail to try it. She was reluctant. But Vanessa volunteered to do it with her, and the two women faced off with Vanessa hitting normally while Gail barely touched her with the bataca.

Vanessa:	Gail is just tapping me.
Gail:	Don't hit too hard.
Vanessa:	You're not fragile.
Gail:	[with the other family members cheering them on] Do you have to sit there cheering? (Whitaker & Bumberry, 1988, p. 190)

Toward the end of the session, Whitaker challenged Gail's position as the family martyr and as the **scapegoat**. Although scapegoats often result in families in which parents suffer and cannot make good contact with each other, Whitaker noted that letting go of the scapegoated position is hard to do. "It's not easy to change presidents once they're in office" (p. 192).

Three years later, Vanessa called for a follow-up appointment. They were having a family reunion, and they all wanted Whitaker updated on their lives. Gail asked for two sessions: one day for another therapy session, and one day for some sense of catching up and closure. During the first session, Mom's loneliness (to the point of suicidal thoughts) emerged, along with her continuing reluctance to burden her children with it. It was in the interaction between Mom and her children that real change was noted in the family dynamics. The adult children were able to weep with their mother and insist that she keep the communication channels open with them. By way of summary, over the last 3 years Gail's use of medications had been reduced, and she was living independently. Mike had taken over the family farm, and Vanessa was invested in an intimate relationship about which she felt very good. Dad had initiated more closeness with Mom, finally having built a new home for her, small and cozy, and spent time together at night.

Whitaker's aim was always to unmask pretense and create new meaning while liberating family members to be themselves. As in the other existential approaches, techniques are secondary to the relationship that the therapist is able to establish with the family. Whitaker did not propose a set of methods; rather, it is the personal involvement of the therapist with a family that makes a difference. When techniques are employed, they arise from the therapist's intuitive and spontaneous reactions to the present situation and are designed to increase clients' awareness of their inner potential and to open up channels of family interaction.

Key Concepts

Subjective Focus

Symbolic experiential family therapists focus on the subjective needs of the individual in the family as they attempt to facilitate family interaction that will result in the individuality of each member (Hanna & Brown, 2004). They operate on the assumption that all family members have the right to be themselves but that the needs of the family may suppress this individuation and self-expression. In this sense, there is no right or wrong—or even preferred—way for a family to be: The goal is family-member authenticity.

An Almost Atheoretical Stance

Whitaker's approach to family therapy was pragmatic and atheoretical, to the point of being antitheoretical. He believed that theory can be a hindrance to clinical practice (Whitaker, 1976). He maintained that clinicians may use their theory to create distance in the name of being objective or that unseasoned practitioners may use theory as a way of controlling their anxiety about dealing with a family (Guerin & Chabot, 1992). This does not mean that he was without beliefs or values: He simply hadn't projected these beliefs and values into an organized presentation on the nature of human beings and the systems in which they live. Still, his highly intuitive form of therapy was aimed at intensifying present experiencing. Indeed, his personal style was unconventional and provocative, and he valued his capacity for "craziness," which was the ability to reach into his own, almost child-like unconscious to understand what was going on in the family. Through his own spontaneous reactions, he was able to tap material that a family kept secret. Although the family members may view secret material as crazy, it is the process of keeping secrets that actually drives family members crazy.

Being Is Becoming

Whitaker, like Paul Tillich (1959, 2000), believed that being is becoming. The way in which people avoid growth and becoming is by doing and escaping either into the past or the future: They engage in what Whitaker (1989) called "metaliving" (p. 52). To really live is to be present, to narrow all of one's energies into serving the present moment and the people and challenges in that moment. It is in the present that one can learn to listen to oneself and to experience and start to actualize one's potential. Whitaker advocated the development of a child-like capacity for play as an antidote to metaliving. Being a child-like adult, using role-reversals, and discovering the humanness in one another: All of these support both fully living and becoming. Whitaker (1989) noted: "The child who discovers maleness in his mother and femaleness in his father has made a profoundly valuable discovery about [self]" (p. 57).

Intimacy: The Desired Outcome

Whitaker suggested that what we all want is intimacy. We start life intimately. We are in the wombs of our mothers and, while we are there, the mother is also remembering the intimacy of having "been one" with her mother. Birth starts the first and foremost dialectic in our lives, the struggle between I-ness and we-ness. The baby is propelled into separation, but immediately seeks the comfort and safety of the mother's breast, the familiar heartbeat, the nurturance of being held and cuddled. As the child gets older, she or he ventures out from the mother and significant others, only to return: There is then another dialectic between individuation and belonging. Because all of this becomes distorted as we grow, Whitaker (1989) identified three kinds of intimacy: the delusion of intimacy, the illusion of intimacy, and the fact of intimacy.

The delusion of intimacy often is experienced when one falls in love with another. The other is invested with desired attributes and capacities far beyond what any given person could possibly have. "It's a kind of psychological hallucination that frequently precipitates a two-person psychosis" (p. 59). In spite of a lack of evidence to support this kind of intimacy, it is unshakable and admits no contradiction from self or others. The illusion of intimacy is the desire for one-ness. It bypasses the dialectic of individuation and belonging by creating an illusory third position: I and we are the same and there is no need to deal with the individual and the couple as separate realities. This experience misrepresents the fact of intimacy, but it is also what Whitaker calls "an excellent example of the symbolic experience" (p. 60). It is an illusion that cannot stand up to scrutiny but, in its symbolic nature, it nonetheless leads to a change in the individual's way of living and interpersonal relationships.

The fact of intimacy requires individuals to break through the illusion of intimacy and to wrestle fully with the dialectic of individuation and belonging. It first requires that we develop a real intimacy with ourselves: That is, we must embrace what Whitaker called "the intimacy of isolation" (p. 61) and find a way really to listen to ourselves outside of the social structures in which we live. In real intimacy, there is a sense of cross-identification.

> The exposure of one individual to the physical, visual presence of the other automatically sets up a sense of difference: "He's taller, he's fatter, he's older, he's smarter." But it also activates in a much more powerful way the identification that "he's human like me, he's suffered, he feels badly, or he feels happy, as I do." (p. 63)

The Dialectics of a Healthy Family

I have already mentioned that the first family dialectic is between individuation and **belonging**. Simply stated, the freer people are to individuate, the freer they are to connect and find a real sense of belonging without resorting to what Minuchin, Rosman, and Baker (1978) call **enmeshment**. Within families, there is also the dialectic between the roles we assume and our personhood. Roles are part of our jobs, our relationships with families and friends, and the duties and places we hold in the larger social groups to which we belong. In spite of all these roles, each of us is also an integrated whole—a complete person with feelings, values, hopes, and desires. Parallel dialectics, therefore, exist in all individuals: dialectics that seek a balance between intuition and cognition, impulse and control, love and hate, public and personal relations, craziness and trickiness, and stability and change. Again, letting one aspect of the mind augment the other is preferable to addressing any two capacities as opposing forces.

For example, most of us accept a certain amount of outside control in our lives, whether it comes from the family or the larger communities in which we live. Taken to an extreme, we enter into a deadened pattern of living, presenting only a public self, playing expected roles, and doing what is expected, rather than fully living. Impulse is our demand for freedom and space: the right to be our own person and follow our own path. Whitaker believed that these dialectics never can be resolved, only balanced in a kind of dialectic dance. In this sense, the balance between love and hate is always in play. One cannot love someone fully unless one is willing to also hate—and to be hurt. The healthy family does not attempt to resolve these dialectics in a rigid adherence to given roles, a set of rules, or resorts to trickiness when individuals and systems no longer can control the demands and challenges of life. Growth come from each individual's increased freedom to express her or his opposite-ness within the family system.

Therapy Goals

In Whitaker's view, the goal of family therapy is to promote the feeling dimension: spontaneity, creativity, the ability to play, and the willingness to be "crazy." Keith (2000) writes: "We seek to increase the creativity (what we call craziness or right-brained living) of the family and of the individual members" (p. 113). The central goal is to facilitate individual autonomy *and* a sense of belonging in the family. Experiential family therapists operate on the assumption that if individual family members increase their awareness and capacity for experiencing, more-genuine intimacy will result within the family circle. According to Keith and Whitaker, it is experience, not education, that changes families. Keith assumes that most of human experience occurs on the unconscious level, which can best be reached symbolically. For him, "symbolic" refers to finding multiple meanings for the same process.

A central tenet of Whitaker's approach is that therapists need to be aware of their own responses to families in order to be therapeutic. The therapist functions best as an instigator of family openness, realness, and spontaneity. Experiential therapists place value on their own responses as a measure of healthy interaction. Furthermore, their personal experience determines their work in family therapy. Whitaker sees experiential therapy as a way for therapists to be actively engaged in their own personal development. Thus, therapy is a process that helps the therapist as much as the family.[2]

The Therapist's Role and Function

Experiential therapists tend to create family turmoil and then coach the members through the experience. They primarily are interested in the interaction between themselves and the family. The therapist's role requires immediacy, a willingness to be oneself, vitality, a degree of transparency, and willingness to use personal reactions during the family sessions. Although experiential therapists are willing to act as temporary experts and issue directives to the family, they are just as likely to maintain long periods of silence to augment the family members' anxiety. Whitaker liked to think of himself as a coach or a surrogate grandparent. His enactment of these roles required structure, discipline, creativity, and presence (Keith, 2000). The relationship between the active and vital therapist and the family is the catalyst for growth and movement.

Therapeutic interventions are aimed at intensifying what is going on in the here and now of the family session. The focus of therapy is on the process of what is unfolding during the session, a time when the seeds of change are planted. Instead of giving interpretations, the therapist provides an opportunity for the family members to be themselves by freely expressing what they are thinking and feeling. Whitaker did not treat families. Instead, he saw his role as creating, with the family, a context in which change can occur through a process of reorganization and reintegration (Becvar & Becvar, 2003).

As a therapist, Whitaker strove to grasp the complex world of a family by focusing on impulses and symbols. He was interested in going beyond the surface level of interactions by dealing with symbolic meanings of what evolved between the family and himself. In his sometimes outrageous style, he gave voice to his own impulses and fantasies, and in doing so he encouraged family members to become more accepting of their moment-by-moment experiencing (Goldenberg & Goldenberg, 2004).

Whitaker talked about the process of family therapy in anywhere from three phases (engagement, involvement, and disentanglement) to eight (pre-therapy, the blind date, the early mid-phase, the central work phase, the full alliance, the impasse, the augmented impasse, and the ending). According to Keith (2000), the counselor's role changes throughout therapy. During the early phases, the therapist assumes an all-powerful position from deciding who will be in therapy and why to setting the logistics and boundaries of the sessions, and the therapist's relationship to the family. Initially, the therapist increases the anxiety a family is experiencing so that family members are challenged to recognize interpersonal patterns. In this context, families are almost forced to come up with alternative ways of operating.[3] At various times in therapy, the counselor shifts from being a dominant and parental figure to being an advisor and a resource person. The more authentic the expression of the family members becomes, the less overt the interventions of the therapist. Eventually, family members are expected to assume responsibility for their own living and changing. As the family assumes more independence, the co-therapists generally become more personal and less involved in the family system. The therapy team respects the family's initiative as it moves toward termination or ending.

Because this approach emphasizes the counselor's personal characteristics over the use of techniques, therapy for the therapist is viewed as being essential. This therapy may include marital and family counseling, as well as personal counseling to increase the therapist's access to his or her own creativity. The reason behind recommending family therapy for therapists—coupled with the study of their own family—is not only to assist them in the process of individuation from their families but also to help them establish a greater sense of belongingness to their families (Keith 2000). Therapists, like families, must learn to hold the tension between opposite positions in their own dialectics.

Techniques

In Whitaker's model, change must be experienced rather than understood or designed. Families will tend to stay the same unless the therapist can disturb or frustrate the family process. Keith (2000) put this notion as follows: "Whether they change or not has to do with their level of desperation, which must outweigh the pressure for homeostasis, or remaining the same" (p. 118). Within the symbolic experiential therapy session, the focus of techniques is on expressing blocked affect.

Whitaker believed that the person of the therapist is the main therapeutic factor that facilitates change within a family. He did not use planned techniques or structured exercises but placed emphasis on being with a family. His interventions were aimed at challenging the symbolic meaning that people gave to events. In his view, the ability to be caring, vital, firm, and unpredictable is a more effective therapeutic instrument than any technical strategies (Whitaker & Bumberry, 1998).

Still, there are some interventions that seem to reoccur regularly in Whitaker's work (see Whitaker, 1989; Whitaker & Bumberry, 1988). These include:

- **Play:** In Whitaker's work, play is a dialectic. The more you can play, the greater your capacity for seriousness. Play is at the heart of what he considers "craziness." If one is free to be crazy, one also is free to adapt, to be sane. Among the many kinds of play that Whitaker integrated into his work, many were physical encounters of the kind we see young children enacting. He was especially fond of wrestling, piling on, and even hitting, although he often padded the aggression of hitting with large boxing gloves or the use of batacas. Symbolically acting out one's fears and negative emotions reduces the toxic nature of one's impulses and transforms them into less-threatening forms of play.

  Whitaker also played with ideas and possibilities. Often in an effort to seed the unconscious, he would suggest notions and options that many people would never consider—and which seldom are suggested as part of therapy. In another part of the interview with the family I featured at the beginning of the chapter, Whitaker suggested to one of the adult daughters that if she was having trouble with men, maybe she should be a lesbian. When the daughter admitted that she had thought of that, he took it even further and suggested that maybe the safest relationship would be incest with her sister, a notion that led him to play with the idea of what constitutes a practical taboo. Although many family practitioners might consider these therapeutic musings inappropriate, playing with ideas not only seeds the unconscious, but it clearly opens up further communication about serious concerns within the family.

- **Therapeutic sharing:** If the therapist can manage to share parts of his or her life without becoming the client, then the picture of the therapist's own realness can provide a model for greater expression and experiencing in the family. Whitaker often did this by expressing what he was thinking and feeling in reaction to family members or family processes. He clearly did not share everything, and even he would admit that there is a large amount of experienced and educated intuition in choosing what to bring out and what to leave alone. As a general guide, he tended to share parts of himself to normalize family experiences, increase existential anxiety in the service of movement, or to seed the unconscious.
- **Paradox and double messages (double binds):** The concepts of **paradox** and **double binds** are more highly associated with strategic family therapy, and they will be more fully developed in a later chapter. Paradox often is used to direct clients to continue what they are doing rather than to try to give something up. Double binds are contradictory messages from which an individual cannot escape and that often lead to confusion or even desperation in the individual. Whitaker differentiated his use of paradox and double binds from simple mechanical exercises by noting that their use was in the service of real intimacy—indeed, an integration of even greater intimacy.

In the therapy session at the beginning of the chapter, Whitaker engaged the youngest daughter of the family in a discussion about meanness and even murder that exemplifies his use of paradox and double messages. He said to Gail:

Whitaker:	You have to be as mean as hell to make it. Have you ever learned to be mean?
Gail:	Oh, that's another good one! I'm basically too good to be mean!
Whitaker:	That's what I'm worried about. That's how Mother is. She's too good to even get in Heaven. I don't think they could stand her. God would be embarrassed.
Gail:	She is a good woman. . . . She is a person.
Whitaker:	I didn't see any evidence of it! All I saw was her pain and suffering and emptiness. I don't even believe her story about the old man. I think she did it to him. She made him push her around, so she could be a nobody and blame him for it. It sounds like you're doing the same thing.
Gail:	No. I'm not exactly like her.
Whitaker:	. . . Do you ever get mean inside? You know, like you'd like to kill the whole gang? . . . You've got to learn to be murderous! You've got to be able to feel like killing people inside of yourself in order to get to be a person. Otherwise, you will end up being a sucker. Mother has never had the courage to even want to kill anybody, unless it was me.

- **Evolving a crisis:** If a kind of "meta-event" with the power of a psychological orgasm occurs within the therapy session, then stimulating it—to evolve into a full-blown crisis—is one way to release the family into a greater sense of becoming. This is what happens in Whitaker's session when he starts to have yet another conversation with the father about tractors, and Vanessa bursts into a raging anger. When these events happen, Whitaker believes it is probably best to let them just hang in the air, rather than trying to resolve them in some artificial attempt at meaning.[4]
- **Seeding the unconscious:** This refers to Whitaker's process of taking a family member's inference far beyond anything the family member normally would consider. These psychological seeds suggest the forbidden, the taboo, the anxiety-provoking, and the hidden. These seeds are symbolic and emanate from the therapist's fantasy. They are owned by the therapist so that the family is free to disregard them or attach

> meaning as each family member sees fit. At one point in Whitaker's sessions with the family, Vanessa asked what she could do about her "boyfriend problem."

Whitaker: That's a great fantasy! I tell you what . . . I just thought of a solution. Become a lesbian!

Vanessa: I've thought of that.

Whitaker: You see? Why are you asking me? You already have the answer. Then you won't have to worry about boyfriends at all.

Vanessa: But that didn't work.

Whitaker: That didn't work? Well maybe it's because you didn't find the right woman.

Vanessa: I thought of that.

Whitaker: Do you know . . . I never thought of that . . . do you think that incest between sisters would be taboo? (*laughter*) Between brothers it is, but I don't see how it could be between sisters. (Whitaker & Bumberry, 1988, p. 150)

- **Silence:** Whitaker used silence to let therapy be, to let it percolate. "Silence is its own communication" (Whitaker, 1989, p. 192). In symbolic experiential therapy, silence is associated with the freedom to transcend social demands, the need for progress, and even the family as a whole. It is what Whitaker called vegetating, and it happens in the solitude of quiet where there is freedom to think and feel. Whitaker may have had other purposes in mind when, in the early part of his career, he would appear to doze off in therapy sessions, but he worked with an ever-present co-therapist and his retreats into silence or even sleep gave him time to reflect on his experiences with the family and the feelings he had in response to them.

  Out of silence often came some of Whitaker's more intuitive suggestions. He might talk about a dream he was just having or even share a sexual fantasy, two types of interventions that he did much less as he got older. Still, relaxing into silence often led to some surprising and intuitive leaps. Once, while a couple continued their argument about money and finances, Whitaker emerged out of silence to say, "What she really wants to know is when you are going to stop f#%king your secretary." And even though nothing like that had been part of the conversation, the look on the man's face almost immediately confirmed that he was so extra-maritally engaged.

Whitaker liked to be part of a co-therapy team. He felt that having a co-therapist freed him to act in whatever manner seemed to fit the situation; he knew that his co-therapists would be available to help the family deal with what had happened. Over the years, Whitaker teamed with some of the most sensitive and innovative family therapists in the field, including Thomas Malone, Gus Napier, and David Keith, to name a few. This co-therapy arrangement allows for a sharing of the emotional involvement of the therapeutic process. Furthermore, the practice affords both therapists opportunities to have fun together, to disagree, to embellish on each other's interventions, and to model creative and productive interaction (Goldenberg & Goldenberg, 2004).

Keith (2000) maintains that practicing family therapy stirs up emotional reactions in the therapist. Because countertransference tends to be unconscious, the use of a co-therapist lessens the danger of acting out such feelings with a family. Each therapist can use his or her subjectivity more freely when the colleague can function as a counterbalancing force. For example, Napier and Whitaker (1978) would express their thoughts and consult about the family during the therapy session.

A Symbolic-Experiential Therapist With the Quest Family

Jane made the initial contact, stating that she needed help with her boys, and she wondered if the therapist would see her with them? The symbolic-experiential therapist asked if Jane were a single parent and who else might be in the family.

Jane noted that she was married to Paul and had two older children, both girls, but insisted that the problem was really between her and the two boys.

Therapist: Well, why don't you round everyone up: Dad, your four children, and you, and then we can meet.

Jane: Well, I don't know if I can do that. Paul is a doctor, and he is very busy. I don't think he really believes in counseling or therapy.

Therapist: I see. Well, we have a problem then, because I don't work with individuals, just families.

Jane: Well, the boys and I are a family together. Couldn't you see us just one time to get a sense of what is going on.

Therapist: No, I'm sorry, but that wouldn't work.

Jane: But Paul and the girls don't even know I am calling you.

Therapist: I think it might be important to tell them—and to mention that I would need to see all of you.

Jane: I just can't involve them right now.

Therapist: Okay. You certainly have a right to make that choice.

Jane: So you will see just me and the boys?

Therapist: No. I didn't say that.

Jane: Okay. Okay. I will try to get everyone together.

Therapist: Great. Call me when you have that arranged.

The symbolic-experiential practitioner begins the session by reviewing with the family how he was first contacted, and that it was important to him to have everyone present. Paul, Jane, and the four children are all present for the first meeting. The therapist notes that he was aware that Jane felt she had some difficulties with the two boys, who were newly adopted, and wondered if Jane was raising the boys all by herself or if other members were involved too. "The way Mom talks, I get the feeling that she is the only one who wants the boys, and even she has her doubts: The rest of you just want them gone. They're not really part of this family anyway, are they?" Paul and Amy are the first to react.

Paul: That's not true. I'm just very busy at work, always have been.

Therapist: I don't buy that for a moment. I don't think Jane would have felt the need to limit the meeting in the first place if you were both on board with parenting these new kids.

Amy: If anyone is out of the family, it's me—and Ann, really. Mom has been so tied up with these two boys that I hardly see her. Ann tries to help out: I don't think Mom could get along without her, but Mom doesn't really know what's going on in Ann's life.

Therapist: Or yours?

Amy: Or mine! Definitely not mine. I feel like I am old enough, and I am mostly on my own.

Amy's response seems to trigger Jane's tears, but she says nothing. Both Amy and Ann note that they are okay with their parents' decision to add the boys to the family, but they don't really feel connected to them yet. "The boys can be difficult," Amy says. During all of this, Jason and Luke are very talkative, interrupting often, and in constant motion. Jane tries to corral the boys once or twice and to make them sit down. Sometimes, they sit briefly, but then they are on the move again. Paul leans forward to give the boys a stern look, but says nothing.

Therapist: Paul, are you interested at all in how Jane is doing with all of this right now?

Paul: I already know it's not going well.

Therapist:	Would you ask her what she's experiencing?
Paul:	(turning to Jane) It doesn't seem to be going well.
Therapist:	Are you interested in what she's experiencing or not really?
Paul:	What are you experiencing?
Jane:	I'm exhausted. They exhaust me. This goes on morning to night, and if it were not for Ann, I would be lost. I know you are busy and gone, but I wish you would help out more. I wish you were home more, and that you made time for the boys the way you used to do for Amy and Ann. (turning to the therapist) Both of the boys were terribly hurt in their young lives, and they often seem intent on hurting each other even more.
Therapist:	Are you done talking to Paul now? Are you interested in his response, or do you just want to avoid it?
Jane:	(continuing) Jason likes to be the boss of Luke, and Luke sometimes goes along with it and sometimes not. Jason is very loud. Luke is quieter.
Therapist:	Are you catching Dad up on the boys or just ignoring me?
Jane:	I don't know what I'm doing.

> Just as the therapist is about to respond, a small fight breaks out between the two boys. Luke pushes his brother and Jason turns around and gives Luke a swift kick to the chin. Luke starts to yell/cry, and Jason retreats behind Amy.

Paul:	(standing, to Jason, sternly) Sit down, and don't move!
Therapist:	(to the parents) Maybe Jason and Luke fight to show the two of you how it's done. Maybe if the two of you had it out, they wouldn't have to.
Jane:	I am trying to set a good model for them about not fighting.
Therapist:	Yes. You are being very good and suffering, and they are being very bad and getting on with their lives. Hell, they even seem to enjoy it!
Jane:	So you want Paul and me to kick and hit each other.
Therapist:	Is that how you fight?
Ann:	No. We don't fight. When we can, we talk it out.
Therapist:	But mostly, you suffer, and Paul stays at work, and Amy goes to school, and Ann tries to rescue her mother, and the boys are the only ones living life the way they want to. Do you think it is even remotely possible that Paul could handle your suffering, or have you given up on him?

> Jane begins to talk to Paul about how lonely she feels, raising the two boys. She wishes he were more available to her and to Jason and Luke. She believes that the two boys need him in their lives. Paul responds that he feels supervised by Jane when he is around the boys. It's not like when they were raising Amy and Ann. Then he felt like the girls belonged to both of them, and they were "on the same page" when it came to raising them. Now he feels like the boys really belong to Jane, and she watches him as if he were going to hurt them or something.
>
> While they are talking, Ann gets up and quietly and effectively removes a plastic hanger from Luke who is about to use it to hit Jason. Then she returns to her seat.

Therapist:	(to Ann) Nice going. I feel very partial to that hanger, and I hate to see blood on it. (turning to the parents) Look, if what you are both saying is anywhere close to real, then both of you are lost. Jane is alone, lonely, deserted, and she uses the excuse of "protection" to supervise Dad and keep control of a situation that is actually out of control. And Paul watches for any sign from Jane that he is not doing something right or isn't

needed, so that he can escape into work—where he feels competent. In the meantime, Ann goes about quietly taking care of whatever needs to be handled.

Ann: That sounds right to me.

Jane: So you're saying that if I leave Paul and the boys alone that Paul will do more with them.

Therapist: I doubt it. He's as afraid of them as you are.

Jane: I don't remember saying anything about being afraid of the boys.

Therapist: Of course you are. You stay on top of the boys all the time, because you are afraid of what they will do. So is Paul. He just arranges not to have to see it. If you are not afraid of them, you do different things with them than you are doing.

Jane: Like what?

Therapist: What did you do with Amy and Ann when they were Jason and Luke's ages?

Jane: I played with them.

Paul: That's the problem. We don't really know how to play with them. I don't know how to play with them at all.

In the second session, the therapist brings a two-inch foam mat to the center of the room. The boys immediately run and jump on it while the rest of the family watch, looking at the therapist and hoping to get some direction. The therapist suggests that maybe the boys should drag the old man onto the mat and teach him how to wrestle. As the boys pull at Paul, Amy and Ann almost instinctively push their father who grabs at Amy. They all fall to the mat. Ann joins them and the whole group is soon rolling around and piling on Dad.

Jane: Be careful now.

Ann reaches up for her mother and pulls Jane in with the rest of them. In just moments, all of them are rolling around, taking turns piling on each other. No one is getting hurt. There is laughter and screaming and jumping and lots and lots of contact. While Luke rides Paul's back, Paul is also arm wrestling with Jason, letting him win, but putting on a great show of it. Amy and Ann are tickling Luke and their mother. For the first time since therapy began, they all look like they are having fun, like they are alive.

Therapist: (sitting on the edge of the mat) I'm beginning to think that there may be some hope for all of you. Jane, you still seem like a reluctant participant in all of this. What's going on for you?

Jane: First I was afraid that the boys would get hurt, that everyone would be too rough with them. They've been so abused in their lives. Then I was afraid the boys would hurt Paul, because they can be so rough too.

Therapist: You can't fully love someone if you aren't willing to hurt them occasionally or be hurt by them.

Jane: I guess I worry too much.

Therapist: I guess you'll have to decide whether you are ready to live life or want to sit on the sidelines watching it go by.

In a short while, Amy and Ann each pick up one of the boys and seem to leave Paul and Jane in the middle of the mat. The parents are talking about what they are feeling in the middle of this playground: What it was like to have the boys crawling on them and to have Amy and Ann all piled in together. But mostly they talk about missing each other and missing the ease of their lives together. This time, however, they are not blaming Jason or Luke, but seem to be searching for each other in terms of their shared hopes and desires. The therapist remains quiet, listening but removed. As Paul and Jane seem to wind down, having said what was on their minds, Paul reaches out for Luke and takes him in his arms. He holds the boy close and firmly, rocking him back and forth, and simulating wrestling sounds.

Therapist: That's the nice thing about having more than one child. There is always another one to hold. (getting up to leave the room) I'll see all of you next week.

Summary and Multicultural Evaluation

In some ways, Whitaker's symbolic-experiential approach to family therapy is not unlike other approaches that focus on the therapist/client relationship. Like Satir's human validation process model, and individual approaches such as existential therapy, person-centered therapy, and Gestalt therapy, symbolic-experiential therapy assigns a central role to the importance of the therapist as a person and views the quality of the therapeutic relationship as significantly affecting the process and outcomes of therapy. Symbolic-experiential family therapy applies many of the processes of these relationship-oriented therapies to working with families. Relying on empathy, intuition, joining, spontaneous interactions, enactments, and experiments, the experiential therapist attempts to understand the family's dynamics and to create experiences that will lead to family vitality, growth, and change. It is clear that this approach places primary value on therapist self-awareness and the full use of the therapist's self in encountering a family.

Whitaker's insistence on "nontheory" foreshadows the efforts of social constructionists to confront the dominant culture and change standardized and fixed approaches to functionality. Indeed, feminists see in Whitaker someone willing to "play with patriarchy" (Luepnitz, 1988, p. 88), to change role patterns and role definitions so completely that meanings are turned upside down and inside out. Whitaker confronted men in therapy more than almost any other therapist, and he also was able to get to their vulnerability better than most. He had been known to tell men that they were hopeless, that they could not stand their own envy of women who give birth, and that women were constantly struggling to bring them alive. In a film from the Philadelphia Child Guidance Clinic, he told a client who had said that he could never accept his mother's nurturance, "I know; that's what makes your wife's job so gruesome."

Symbolic-experiential family therapists add an organic-growth lens to therapy that asks family practitioners to consider what seeds they are planting and whether the ground is fertile, prepared, or disturbed enough to facilitate growth and change. Like a great gardener, Whitaker often spent more time removing weeds than providing structure. Symbolic-experiential therapists remind us that individuals and systems have all the resources within themselves if they are challenged and freed to evolve.

If you are interested in a more in-depth study of this approach, I recommend the following sources: Keith (2000); Kempler (1981); Napier (1988); Napier and Whitaker (1978); Whitaker (1989); Whitaker and Bumberry (1986, 1988); and Whitaker and Malone (1953, 1981).

Contributions to Multicultural Counseling and Gender Issues

Although there is nothing in the almost atheoretical symbolic-experiential approach that either supports or denies a multicultural perspective, it is hard to understand how this model, as it is most commonly demonstrated, could be positively received by those cultures for which respect and saving face are central to the culture's worldview. For example, the self-disclosures and confrontational nature of symbolic-experiential therapy would almost certainly have to be significantly modified for people from many of the Asian cultures. Still, Whitaker always focused on the relationship between himself and the family: He believed that effectiveness in therapy involved being able to join with families and family members. He, as well as some of his colleagues who integrated a structural orientation with experiential therapy (for example, Gus Napier), would find ways to adapt their approach and address cultural differences.

Sherry Cormier (personal communication, March 23, 2005) suggests that this approach may be inherently multicultural because of the unique adaptation the therapists make to each individual family system—and because of the realness and authenticity of the therapist.

In the area of gender issues and sexual/affectional orientation, Whitaker and his colleagues have been much more vocal than they are in relation to cultural diversity. As I have already mentioned, Whitaker held women in high regard, as well as appreciating those qualities most associated with women's development (such as nurturance, intuition, expressiveness, caring, and vulnerability, to name a few). Although he did not write directly about these qualities, it is evident from his work that he valued them. Napier and Whitaker (1978) actually noted the contributions made by the women's movement to family life, calling the wife-and-mother "the pioneer [who helps everyone in the family to] achieve both a sense of individual autonomy *and* a sense of closeness and unity" (p. 234). Napier (1988) carries this sense of autonomy and closeness into the arena of coupling and marriage in one of the most important books related to couples counseling. He and his partner, Margaret, help couples in their Atlanta-based practice to maintain both a sense of self and connection to the other.

What made Whitaker so unusual in the field of family therapy was his willingness to confront, challenge, and even chide men during therapy sessions. More than almost any other family therapist, Whitaker seemed to believe that humanizing males was central to his work, and he regularly worked at opening up males to much more intimacy than most ever dreamed was possible. His belief that a multiplicity of roles is possible in families at a symbolic "as if" level has provided many opportunities for humanizing men and creating more intimacy. Whitaker and Keith (1981) suggested that, if a young son asked his father if he could serve part of the dinner that the father often served, the father should respond: "Sure, you sit over in this chair and serve the meat and potatoes, and I'll sit in your place and complain" (p. 190).

Whitaker and his associates also demonstrate an enormous appreciation for diversity of sexual/affectional orientations in their work—although taken out of context, Whitaker's recommendation of same-sex partnerships for heterosexuals, who find dealing with the other sex frustrating, can seem demeaning to some members of the LGBT community. And although Whitaker's writings occasionally approached marriage as important and even therapeutic (although it is legally denied to lesbian and gay individuals in most states), his actual practice was always open to couples involving any two people of either gender who sought real intimacy in their lives.

The limitation related to this approach with multicultural clients and even with regard to gender and sexual/affectional orientation is that a disregard for theory and political realities leaves many important issues unexamined or, worse, inconsistently addressed. Although feminists might appreciate many of the attributes that Whitaker brought to the therapeutic process (Luepnitz, 1988), Whitaker was not a feminist therapist. His model does an extremely good job of addressing relationships between individuals, family members, and either of these with the therapist, but it provides little or no perspective on social activism.

Exercises for Personal and Professional Growth

The directive to "be spontaneous" is practically impossible to achieve, and yet, authentic spontaneity is often the part of the great masters that we remember and admire the most. Whitaker's spontaneity was at the center of everything he did in therapy. He preferred real encounters to calculated approaches. It was not that his model lacked structure, but structure always was intended to be in the background and to support the authentic sharing that Whitaker believed would free up the potential in individuals and families. In this sense, Whitaker and the other symbolic-experiential therapists are not so much into **self-disclosure** (or disclosures intended to make a point) as they are into self-revelation (or a revealing of authentic responses within the therapeutic context).

So how do we learn to be more spontaneous and authentic? I suggest some graduated exercises, designed to increase self-awareness and experiment with self-revelation. My first recommendation is to videotape your counseling sessions often, at least once a week. Then watch the tape a number of times, not with a critical eye regarding your work, but with a series of self-reflective questions in mind:

- At critical moments in the process, what was I sensing (feeling, thinking, considering)? What was present in my mind and heart, but not said?
- If I could have been immediately in touch with those unspoken responses, what would it have been like to say them out loud?
- How would I have phrased them? (Write these down for later reference.)
- How do I think they would have been received by the various family members and the family as a whole?
- Am I okay with the anxiety it might have raised in the family or in certain family members?
- Would the presence of a co-therapist help in making sure that I was not merely imposing my own countertransference on the family?

Although these questions initially will seem contrived and artificial (because they are), they are really just part of training a habit of the heart. You cannot let out what is inside until you develop the capacity to know what you are feeling and what your responses might be. Immediacy can be learned, but it takes practice and experience; it also requires time to learn to trust that what you feel and think can be useful to others. Considering what effect your responses might have is not intended to limit what you say, but rather, through such consideration, to learn to trust whatever might come out of you.

Doing this first exercise in role-played situations is also a good idea. If you are part of a class studying this symbolic-experiential approach, have a small group of people become a family and, as they present themselves to you, see if you can push yourself beyond safe responses: Use the first three questions listed above to bring your most authentic responding forward—into the counseling or therapy session.

When you have had some time to practice authentic responses in simulated family-practice sessions, you also might try responses designed either to seed the unconscious or to use paradox and double binds to augment real intimacy. Using the descriptions above and the examples in Whitaker's therapy session at the beginning of the chapter, practice with a role-played family responding from your fantasies; if you allow yourself to be outrageous, what would you say? If you could extend the family members' fantasies, worries, or concerns even farther than they are willing to take them, what would that be like? What would your version of asking someone to be mean in order to be real sound like? When practicing, it is important for the family role-players to stay in role and to respond as ordinary families might: This will give you some sense of what happens when you push the limits. Such practice sessions should put you in a state that Erv and Miriam Polster (1999) call a safe emergency: It may seem risky, but it is for growth, and it will not harm you.

There are other excellent models for immediacy and authentic responding. Some are gentler than many of Whitaker's interventions, such as those we might hear from Virginia Satir. Some are similar to Whitaker's work, but used with individuals, such as many of the Gestalt therapists, especially Erv and Miriam Polster (1974, 1999) whose work I highly recommend to you. Watching these great masters at work and asking yourself how it would feel for you to respond the way they do is a good place to start.

Authenticity in therapy, being as real as possible, is not an automatic skill for most of us. Indeed, much of our therapeutic training focuses on appropriate responses and interventions, and almost requires us to give up our natural, immediate, and intuitive skills. To reclaim them takes time and practice. Co-therapy supports and protects both families and practitioners in such reclamations but, in the end, it is often time and experience that helps us to find the pace and rhythms of our work and to express the real and the authentic that is part of us as human beings.

Where to Go From Here

There is no specific society or organization of symbolic-experiential therapists. Many of the most prominent leaders in this mode from Carl Whitaker, Gus Napier, and Thomas Malone to Thomas Leland, John Warkentin, and Richard Felder were associated from the early 1960s with the Atlanta Psychiatric Clinic, and most still live in the Atlanta area. Before Whitaker's death, he was a prominent member of the faculty at the Evolution of Psychotherapy conferences, sponsored by the Milton Erickson Foundation. Whitaker and Salvador Minuchin, the most prominent developer of structural family therapy, co-presented many times in multiple arenas: Both men seemed to feed well off each other, both influencing and being influenced by the other. Today, Gus Napier, David Keith, and William Bumberry are the most prolific scholars and contributors to the development of this model.

Recommended Readings

Connell, G. M., Bumberry, W. M., & Mitten, T. J. (1999). *Reshaping family relationships: The symbolic therapy of Carl Whitaker.* New York: Brunner/Mazel. Two of the people who wrote this book worked extensively with Carl Whitaker. Symbolic-experiential therapy is presented in six stages, together with essential interventions for each stage. This book provides a great deal of structure to the process without taking away the fluid dynamics with which experiential therapists are most associated.

Napier, A. Y. (1988). *The fragile bond: In search of an equal, intimate, and enduring marriage.* New York: Harper & Row. This is Napier at his most powerful and persuasive, and this book provides what many consider to be the essence of great systemic work with couples. Although focused on partners, the ideas and information contained in this text are easily integrated and used in family therapy sessions.

Napier, A. Y., & Whitaker, C. A. (1978). *The family crucible.* New York: Harper & Row. A case presentation of the Brice family in therapy with Napier and Whitaker, this is the book that put symbolic-experiential family therapy on the map, taking the reader from the beginning structuring of therapy through the creative twists and turns of two brilliant co-therapists with a fascinating family.

Neill, J. R., & Kniskern, D. P. (Eds.). (1982). *From psyche to system: The evolving therapy of Carl Whitaker.* New York: Guilford Press. A retrospective of Carl Whitaker's early work as it evolved from the 1950s to the 1970s, from a focus on individuals to a focus on families.

Whitaker, C. A. (1989). *Midnight musings of a family therapist* (M. Ryan, Ed.). New York: Norton. This is the last book that Whitaker wrote before he died. It includes a brief autobiographical sketch, as well as his positions on the purpose of living and life, marriage and the family, the process of therapy, and becoming a symbolic-experiential therapist.

Whitaker, C. A., & Bumberry, W. M. (1988). *Dancing with the family: A symbolic-experiential approach.* New York: Brunner/Mazel. Whitaker and Bumberry use intensive family therapy sessions with a family from rural America to demonstrate symbolic-experiential family therapy in action. The sessions cover topics related to sex, depression, death, marriage, and children. In this book, both a typescript of the sessions and commentary are provided.

Whitaker, C. A., & Malone, T. P. (1981). *The roots of psychotherapy.* New York: Brunner/Mazel. (Original work published in 1953) This 1981 edition is a reissue of their classic book, the first to develop an experiential model in psychotherapy.

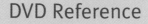

DVD Reference

As you will see in the symbolic-experiential video segment, there is always anxiety in a family experiencing distress, but unlike some other models, symbolic-experiential therapists seek to increase the anxiety rather than alleviate it. Whitaker compared his work to surgery, suggesting that in order to remove pathology, the surgeon had to be able to tolerate what is sometimes a significant loss of blood.

Graham Disque is Professor of Counseling at East Tennessee State University. He has a long history of working within an experiential model—even though his own approach has evolved recently into the practice of acceptance therapy and other postmodern approaches. In this video, he uses two interventions that are highly associated with symbolic-experiential therapy: He asks almost all of his questions in relational form; that is, he frames questions in terms of the relationships that the family members have with each other. He also prods and pokes at family members, especially the mother and father, in an effort to augment the feeling levels of the family and get to more honest, direct interactions.

References

Becvar, D. S., & Becvar, R. J. (2003). *Family therapy: A systemic integration* (3rd ed.). Boston: Allyn and Bacon.

Connell, G. M., Bumberry, W. M., & Mitten, T. J. (1999). *Reshaping family relationships: The symbolic therapy of Carl Whitaker*. New York: Brunner/Mazel.

Goldenberg, I., & Goldenberg, H. (2004). *Family therapy: An overview* (6th ed.). Pacific Grove, CA: Brooks/Cole.

Guerin, P. J., & Chabot, D. R. (1992). Development of family systems therapy. In D. K. Freedheim (Ed.), *History of psychotherapy: A century of change* (pp. 225–260). Washington, DC: American Psychological Association.

Hanna, S. M., & Brown, J. H. (2004). *The practice of family therapy: Key elements across models* (3rd ed.). Belmont, CA: Brooks/Cole.

Keith, D. (2000). Symbolic experiential family therapy. In A. M. Horne (Ed.), *Family counseling and therapy* (3rd ed., pp. 102–139). Itasca, IL: F. E. Peacock.

Kempler, W. (1981). *Experiential psychotherapy with families*. New York: Brunner/Mazel.

Luepnitz, D. A. (1988). *The family interpreted: Feminist theory in clinical practice*. New York: Basic Books.

Minuchin, S., Rosman, B. L., & Baker, L. (1978). *Psychosomatic families: Anorexia nervosa in context*. Cambridge, MA: Harvard University Press.

Napier, A. Y. (1988). *The fragile bond: In search of an equal, intimate, and enduring marriage*. New York: Harper & Row.

Napier, A. Y., & Whitaker, C. A. (1978). *The family crucible*. New York: Harper & Row.

Neill, J. R., & Kniskern, D. P. (Eds.). (1982). *From psyche to system: The evolving therapy of Carl Whitaker*. New York: Guilford Press.

Polster, E., & Polster, M. (1974). *Gestalt therapy integrated: Contours of theory and practice*. New York: Vintage.

Polster, E., & Polster, M. (1999). *From the radical center: The heart of Gestalt therapy: Selected writings of Erving and Miriam Polster*. Cleveland, OH: Gestalt Institute of Cleveland.

Tillich, P. (2000). *The courage to be* (2nd ed.). New Haven, CT: Yale University Press. (Original work published 1959)

Whitaker, C. A. (1976). The hindrance of theory in clinical work. In P. J. Guerin, Jr. (Ed.), *Family therapy: Theory and practice* (pp. 154–164). New York: Gardner.

Whitaker, C. A. (1989). *Midnight musings of a family therapist* (M. Ryan, Ed.). New York: Norton.

Whitaker, C. A., & Bumberry, W. M. (speakers). (1986). *A different kind of caring: Family therapy with Carl Whitaker* [Videotape #5001] (Producers, W. M. Bumberry & S. Tenenbaum). New York: Brunner/Mazel.

Whitaker, C. A., & Bumberry, W. M. (1988). *Dancing with the family: A symbolic-experiential approach*. New York: Brunner/Mazel.

Whitaker, C. A., & Keith, D. (1981). Symbolic-experiential family therapy. In A. Gurman & D. Kniskern (Eds.), *Handbook of family therapy* (pp. 187–225). New York: Brunner/Mazel.

Whitaker, C. A., & Malone, T. P. (1981). *The roots of psychotherapy*. New York: Brunner/Mazel. (Original work published in 1953)

Endnotes

[1] It is important to note that Carl Whitaker was bringing 50 years of experience and the protection of having a co-therapist with him when he made an intervention like this. Family practitioners who are new to the field would run into both legal and ethical difficulties if they modeled this intervention indiscriminately. What made the suggestion of killing "the whole gang" safe in this family was that (a) Gail had no history or capacity for such aggression in her present life; (b) she looked to her mother for any example of how to be aggressive, and her mother was not ready to be aggressive either; and (c) the statement came in the context of the whole family being present and was easily recognized by the group as symbolic. One of the great difficulties of watching the great masters of therapy work is that it is easier to copy what they do than to recognize the process and create our own authentic responses. This case example asks practitioners to consider what their authentic responses would be to Gail who lacks enough aggression (assertiveness) even to claim a place for herself in the family.

[2] The idea that "therapy is a process that helps the therapist as much as the family" does not change the ethical requirement to, first and foremost, protect the well-being of the family and each of its members. It suggests only that both the client(s) and the therapist(s) can grow and develop within these therapy sessions.

[3] During the early phases of therapy, when the therapist is more prominent in instigating change, the probability that **transference** issues will arise is very high. This is one reason that Whitaker worked with a co-therapist, and it speaks to the importance of both therapists having worked through their own personal and family issues. A therapist who is not comfortable with his or her own growth and development will find this approach to be very challenging.

[4] Both evolving a crisis and seeding the unconscious are therapeutic interventions that are designed to escalate emotional experience. There is an ethical responsibility not to engage in these activities in a haphazard way—or simply because the family practitioner has the opportunity. Therapist availability—her or his engaged connection to both self and clients—is essential to the positive use of these interventions.

CHAPTER 8

Structural Family Therapy*

Introduction

Key Concepts

Therapy Goals

The Therapist's Role and Function

Techniques

A Structural Family Therapist With the Quest Family

Summary and Multicultural Evaluation

Recommended Readings

References

Introduction

The origins of structural family therapy can be traced back to the early 1960s when Salvador Minuchin was conducting therapy, training, and research with delinquent boys from poor families at the Wiltwyck School in New York. This approach to family therapy flourished in the 1970s when Minuchin and his colleagues at the Philadelphia Child Guidance Clinic developed the theory and practice of structural therapy more fully. In his book *Families and Family Therapy,* Minuchin (1974) focuses on the interactions of family members as a way of understanding the structure, or organization, of a family. Structural family therapists concentrate on how, when, and to whom family members relate. Through this information, the structure of a family and the problems that bring the family into therapy can be assessed.

Structural family therapy views the individual as part of a social context, and has both its roots and current practice firmly lodged in an appreciation and dedication to cultural diversity and working with the poor. The distinctive features of this approach are its emphasis on structural change as the primary goal of therapy and the therapist's active role as the agent in the process of restructuring the family (Colapinto, 2000). Minuchin (1974) writes:

---

*I want to acknowledge the diligent efforts and contributions of Dr. Harry Aponte in developing this chapter and in making sure it was up to date.

The Minuchen Center for the Family

Salvador Minuchin

Therapy based on this framework is directed toward changing the organization of the family. When the structure of the family group is transformed, the positions of members in that group are altered accordingly. As a result, each individual's experiences change. (p. 2)

Harry Aponte is one of structural family therapy's most eloquent scholar-practitioners. More than anyone else, he has continued Minuchin's early family therapy work with the poor, and he has developed an **ecostructural model** uniquely designed to challenge oppression based on race, culture, and poverty.

In his book *Bread and Spirit: Therapy with the New Poor*, Aponte (1994) reports on his work as a therapist-consultant with the Gonzaga family: "a blue-collar family of Mexican ethnic background" (p. 40). The parents, both in their early 40s, have 5 children: "Fred, 16, Aida, 14, Esteban, 13, Aldo, 11, and Elena, who is 4." The original purpose for seeking therapy centered on Aldo, who was having trouble in school and acting immaturely at home. The parents also reported considerable conflict between themselves, even though the father was quiet during most therapy sessions and seemed to remain on the periphery of the family. When the session begins, Aldo is sitting between Aponte and Mr. Gonzaga.

Aponte:	[to Mr. Gonzaga] Why don't you switch chairs so you will be next to me. (Aldo and Mr. Gonzaga switch chairs.) Okay. Introduce your family to me.
Mr. Gonzaga:	(pointing to the boy next to him) Aldo.
Aponte:	Aldo. How old is Aldo?
Aldo:	Eleven.
Aponte:	And him? (pointing to the next boy)
Mr. Gonzaga:	Esteban. (skipping over his wife) Elena.
Mrs. Gonzaga:	(interjecting spontaneously) Elena is four.
Mr. Gonzaga:	(continuing) Aida, Fred.
Aponte:	(to Mr. Gonzaga) You've been coming for a couple of months, right?
Mr. Gonzaga:	Six, seven months.
Mrs. Gonzaga:	Three months. (p. 42)

In the initial part of this session, we see Aponte joining with the father, a process that also serves to unbalance the power relationship between the two parents, strengthening the father's position and bringing him in from the periphery of the family. In part, this therapeutic intervention was chosen as part of an hypothesis generated from the pre-interview data on the family. The Gonzaga family had been seen for several months by two female therapists who described the father as "uncommitted to the therapy" (p. 41). The father is Latino, and it is not uncommon for fathers in these cultures to remain on the periphery of the family. Still, he was coming to every session. Perhaps he was just quiet or resentful, leaving the impression he didn't care. Perhaps the co-therapists were unsure of how to involve him and projected that uncertainty onto the father. Aponte posed some additional questions to himself before even meeting the family: "What was [Aldo's] relationship with his father in this triangle with his parents? It was likely that he had his mother's attention since she was so active. Was he looking for his father?" (p. 41).

What effect do you think a difference in the gender of the therapist might have on this family; that is, if the therapist is male, especially a male from another Hispanic culture, do you think Mr. Gonzaga might respond

Dr. Harry J. Aponte

Harry Aponte

differently than when he is working with the female co-therapists? Do you think that sometimes a boy needs more input from his father than his mother? Would you feel the same about a young girl: that she needed more input from her mother than her father? From your point of view, does the approach in the case reinforce the patriarchy in any way? What ideas from society and culture influence your feelings about these questions?

Returning to the therapy session, we see Aponte join with the father and identify with his confusion in an effort to seek out a focus for their work:

Aponte:	(to Mr. Gonzaga) I listened to [the co-therapists] describe a little bit about what's been going on. It was so complicated that I couldn't keep up with it.
Mr. Gonzaga:	That's right. (laughing)
Aponte:	. . . but there seemed to be so many things that you fight about and so many things that you are worried about. You two have got problems, and Aldo has problems. Anyway, it just seemed like so many things, that I already got confused. . . . So, if you could pick just one thing, just one problem, that we could concentrate on during this hour out of all the things that you have talked about, then we could try to do something about it . . . .
Mr. Gonzaga:	What would you like to talk about?
Aponte:	This is your family. . . . You just pick out one thing, and we'll work on that.
Mrs. Gonzaga:	Well, we came here for Aldo. That's why we came. Everything was discussed along with Aldo, but we still haven't solved Aldo's problem, why he behaves the way he does at times, why he gets behind schedule in his work, why he hasn't been keeping up, why he acts babyish. . . .
Aponte:	Among all these other problems that you have, you would rather talk about Aldo?
Mrs. Gonzaga:	Well, the other children are fine, and . . . we just keep going round and round, my husband and I. He thinks one way, and I think another way, but we are getting to understand each other better now because we know it will never change. You know, it will be that way all the time. (laughs)
Aponte:	That's one way to solve a problem (laughs) all right.
Mrs. Gonzaga:	He thinks one way, and I think another way. We can't change that. . . . We work to understand each other, but we respect each other. Like he thinks he's the boss, and I let him think he is the boss. (laughing)
Aponte:	(to Mr. Gonzaga) Which means you're not [the boss]? (laughs) But . . . of all these things, which one do you want to talk about during this hour. . . .
Mr. Gonzaga:	Well, whatever you want to talk about. I don't have too much of a big problem. I know what I am supposed to do. Her problem or Aldo's I guess. We worried about Aldo because he was behind too much in school.
Aponte:	Aldo. So you've both decided that it's Aldo? Okay, and you [Mrs. Gonzaga] have already described what you've thought was going on with Aldo. I think you said that he was acting immature, like a baby, and he wasn't keeping up in class. . . . (to Mr. Gonzaga) Do you see it exactly the way your wife's describing it . . . ?
Mr. Gonzaga:	No, I see it the same way. It's just like she says. [But] he acts up more when she's there. When I'm around, he doesn't act like that. . . . I think it is probably like I told her. You let him slide too much or something. . . . All she does is holler and holler, but she don't do nothing.
Aponte:	So that's easy. . . . If she were a little tougher with him then you wouldn't have a problem.
Mrs. Gonzaga:	That's his view, not mine. . . . He's been very strict with him all the time. So, strict is okay, but not when you scare him.

Aponte:	You think he's too strict with Aldo?
Mrs. Gonzaga:	He's strict with all of them.
Aponte:	Okay. (to Mr. Gonzaga) Find out from Aldo if he's scared of you. (pp. 42–45)

This last intervention takes the counseling process out of the realm of trading accusations and creates a boundary around the father and son in which a new dimension to their relationship can be enacted. Regardless of how Aldo feels about his father, the enactment directs the father and son to interact, to talk.

Mr. Gonzaga:	Are you scared of me?
Aldo:	No.
Mr. Gonzaga:	Are you afraid of me? (in a threatening sounding tone)
Aldo:	No.
Aponte:	(joking to Aldo) You'd better give the right answer or he'll punch you in the mouth. (Mr. Gonzaga and Aponte both laugh.)
Mr. Gonzaga:	. . . Is there anything that you're supposed to be afraid of?
Aldo:	Of hitting.
Mr. Gonzaga:	That's your problem, and your mother—she don't hit you. That's what I think it is.
Mrs. Gonzaga:	They never get . . .
Aponte:	(to Mrs. Gonzaga) Wait. Wait. This is between them.
Mr. Gonzaga:	She keeps on telling him, "Don't do this." . . . and he keeps on going and going. . . . He just keeps on doing it.
Aponte:	You believe him though, when he said he wasn't scared of you?
Mr. Gonzaga:	In a way I do and in a way—he's not really scared of me. It's just a problem that he has, respect in a way if he don't do things the way he's supposed—if I tell him more than three or four time, I going to. . . .
Aponte:	He's going to get it.
Mr. Gonzaga:	That's right.
Aponte:	But do you think that he's said enough now [so] you believe what he said to you just now that he doesn't live in fear of you all the time?
Mr. Gonzaga:	He plays with me, you know. We joke with each other and I don't see that makes him afraid of me, because if he can joke with me, then he, he shouldn't be afraid of me. . . .
Aponte:	Check it out with him.
Mr. Gonzaga:	Do you agree with me or don't you—what I just got through saying?
Aldo:	Yes.
Aponte:	Did he understand you?
Mr. Gonzaga:	What did I say?
Aldo:	You said that if I don't do the thing right and you tell me about five times, then you'll hit me.
Mr. Gonzaga:	What else?
Aldo:	That I ain't afraid of you, because I always joke with you. . . .
Aponte:	You know what the real test is of whether a kid is afraid of you or not?
Mr. Gonzaga:	What is it?
Aponte:	Whether he can disagree with you.
Mr. Gonzaga:	On his own?

Aponte:	That's the test.
Mr. Gonzaga:	. . . (to Aldo) Is there anything that you can disagree with me—you think I am wrong?
Aldo:	No.
Mr. Gonzaga:	That you don't agree with me. Then anything I say is right. . . .
Aldo:	Not anything.
Mr. Gonzaga:	Okay. What is it you don't like or. . . .
Aldo:	When you force me.
Mr. Gonzaga:	Oh, how do I force you?
Aldo:	Like you say, "go, go read" even after I did it.
Mr. Gonzaga:	Then what?
Aldo:	Then I just go do it.
Mr. Gonzaga:	Oh, you don't want to go read. Is that it, or what is it?
Aldo:	No, cause I already did it.
Mr. Gonzaga:	Oh, it's when I send you again to go read—you read when I am not home, right? Then I tell you to go read again.
Aldo:	Sometimes.
Mr. Gonzaga:	That's when you don't agree with me. How come you didn't say anything? You just proved to me (silence)—I guess because you are afraid of me. . . . Is that right?
Aldo:	I'd. . . . (pause)
Mr. Gonzaga:	(to Aponte) And then you were right about me. He goes along with me whether he likes it or not.
Aponte:	They have to learn how to be able to say—like, you know—I'm sure—what kind of work do you do?
Mr. Gonzaga:	I'm a packer.
Aponte:	I'm sure you have somebody over you, a foreman or somebody. . . . You disagree with the person . . . you know how to say, "Hey, that's not the way to do it," or "This isn't the time," without it becoming a big problem. . . . If he doesn't learn to do that, he won't grow up.

At this point in the session, the mother asserts that she has tried to teach the boys to stand up for themselves, to fight back when they feel they are being mistreated. Aponte, however, returns to the father, noting that the mother cannot teach the boys how to be men: The father has to do that. He has to teach them "how to disagree with [him] in a respectful way" (p. 48). He directs Mr. Gonzaga to do that with Aldo. The father starts haltingly. He is not sure how to do it. He asks another son, Esteban, for help. Together, they identify that Aldo tends to make faces, but not talk. "So Aldo's problem isn't that he fights with you. His problem is that he doesn't fight with you" (p. 49).

Removed from the power struggle with his wife, [the father] takes responsibility for the problem, and [Aponte] holds him to it. [Aponte] is sensitive to the cultural expectations of manhood and respect. He calls on the father to teach his son to disagree in order to help him be a man in his own image. That the therapist is also male and of a similar age allows him to approach the father with a feeling of comradery. A therapist with a different personality, gender, or background would, of course, have to find avenues toward the same goals that were congruent with his or her circumstances.

Mr. Gonzaga:	I thought it was his problem, but it's my problem. (laughs)
Aponte:	It's your problem, absolutely.

| Mr. Gonzaga: | Okay, Aldo. It's my problem. I guess you're right about that. I have to start someplace. It better be me, I guess. . . . Yeah. Right. It's my turn. (pats Aldo on the shoulder) We'll work it out. (p. 50) |

> In the next part of the session, a similar issue with Freddie surfaces. In this discussion, it becomes evident that the mother often tries to step into the middle of difficulties between the father and his sons. She tries to mediate and protect.

Aponte:	(to Mr. Gonzaga) . . . I don't want them to talk this way about you, because you wouldn't be talking to them the way you talk to them if you didn't care about them, right?
Mr. Gonzaga:	Yeah, I think you're right.
Aponte:	. . . I want them to respect you, you know, but I also want them to be close to you. This means they have to learn from you, not from me, and not from their mom. . . . Am I coming down too hard on you?
Mr. Gonzaga:	No, no. You're coming on pretty good.
Aponte:	Okay. (p. 54)

> Freddie and his father engage in some very straight talk about how Freddie feels when his father gets upset and puts him down.

Aponte:	. . . He needs to improve himself, but he needs to feel that you have respect for him too, and that you care. He has to think that, "In my father's eyes I'm somebody, somebody who's worth listening to, somebody who's worth caring for," because if he doesn't feel that you respect him, then what does he know—does anybody respect him if his own father can't respect him?
Mr. Gonzaga:	Yeah, you're right. I got a father too.
Aponte:	. . . You're the most important man in the world to these kids. (long silence)
Mr. Gonzaga:	. . . What he's really saying is . . . that it is the important thing to communicate between him and me, talk it out and get it out. (p. 55)

Key Concepts

Structural family therapy is an approach to understanding the nature of the family, the **presenting problem**, and **the process of change**. In this perspective the key concepts are family structure, family subsystems, and boundaries, each of which is briefly described below.

Family Structure

According to Minuchin (1974), a family's structure is the invisible set of functional demands or rules that organize the way family members relate to one another. The structure that governs a family's transactions can be understood by observing the family in action or by seeing interactions unfold among family members in the therapy sessions. To understand a family's structure, it is useful to pay attention to who says what to whom and in what way and with what result. By noting family process, rather than listening for mere content, the therapist can detect problematic transactions. Repeated sequences that emerge in a therapy session reveal rigid structural patterns of a family. Of particular interest is the appropriateness of hierarchical structure in the family.

For example, if every time a woman complains about her husband, he hangs his head and says nothing, the theme of the process is the avoidance of conflict. If a father's expression of anger leads almost inevitably to an asthma attack in his daughter, the sequence is complementary (an exchange of opposite kinds of behaviors) and reveals problems in the power structure between parent and child. In violent families, therapists often find a symmetrical sequence (an exchange of similar behaviors) in which each person assumes an absolute position in an argument from which neither can withdraw. Each part of the symmetrical sequence happens at once, leading to an almost automatic escalation of the fight (Fishman, 1993). An example of such an argument is:

Husband:	Where are you going?
Wife:	Out.
Husband:	Did I say you could go out?!
Wife:	You don't tell me what to do!
Husband [shouting]:	The hell I don't!
Wife [shouting back]:	The hell you *do!*

Aponte (1994) speaks of three structural aspects that families use to organize themselves. They are **alignment**, force (or power), and boundaries, which we now shall consider in more depth.

> . . . *alignment* refers to the joining or opposition of one family member to another as the family carries out an operation. *Force* (or power) defines the relative influence of each member on the outcome of an activity. *Boundary* tells who is included and excluded from the activity in question, and what each person's role is in the operation. (p. 18)

Underorganized families have patterns and sequential interactions that describe their processes with each other, but they are harder to diagnose and often appear chaotic. They lack the consistency needed for dependability; coherency for internal compatibility; and flexible structure for coping:

> These are the fundamental mechanics of an organized family structure. Yet, one cannot say a family is well functioning just because it has a workable structure. These are only mechanics. The spirit of the family is what breathes meaning into that structure. (p. 19)

Family Subsystems

The family is considered a basic human system, which is composed of a variety of subsystems. The term subsystems encompasses various categories and roles: spousal (wife and husband), parental (mother and father), sibling (children), and extended (grandparents, other relatives, and even the church, school, and community). [No one has done more to articulate an integration of family and community therapy than Harry Aponte (1994).] Members of subsystems who join together do so to perform tasks that are essential for the functioning of that subsystem, as well as to the overall family system. Determining that the parental subsystem is appropriately separate from the child subsystem is central to structural therapy. It is important to note that each family member plays roles in different subgroups. For example, Tom is a father in the parental subsystem, a husband in the spousal subsystem, and the third brother in the sibling subsystem of his own family-of-origin. Ann is the daughter of Tom, but she is also the sister of Julie in her sibling subsystem, the wife of Hank in her spousal subsystem, and a member of her church choir in her extended community subsystem. Subsystems are typically determined by factors such as gender, age, common interests, and role function. These subsystems are also defined by rules and boundaries.

In structural family therapy, subsystems have appropriate tasks and functions. When family members of another subsystem take over or intrude on one in which they do not belong, the result is usually some form of structural difficulty. For example, the sex life of the adults in the family belongs to the spousal subsystem; when children are allowed to witness, comment on, or investigate their parent's sexual activity, they are inappropriately involved in the spousal subsystem. This extreme example may be easier to understand than noting that parents ought to allow their children to form their own relationships, including settling their own disagreements or fights. This second example is just as important as the first: Working out brother and sister relationships is a task for the sibling subsystem, not the parental subsystem. Parents have their own activities and functions to address.

Boundaries

The emotional barriers that protect and enhance the integrity of individuals, subsystems, and families are referred to as boundaries. The demarcation of boundaries governs the amount of contact with others. These interpersonal boundaries can best be conceptualized on a continuum ranging from rigid boundaries (disengagement) to diffuse boundaries (enmeshment).

Rigid boundaries lead to impermeable barriers between subsystems and with subsystems outside the family. In some cases, because of a generational gap, parent and child may be unable to understand or relate to each other. In this process of disengagement, individuals or subsystems become isolated, and relationships suffer or even deteriorate. Family members become isolated not only from one another but also from other systems in the community. In a case in which a teacher notified the police that a student in her sixth-grade class had been missing for several days and that she had been unable to contact his parents in spite of repeated tries, police officers went to the house to investigate. Finding the father at home and engaged in personal projects, they asked about his son. They discovered that both parents were unaware that the boy also had been missing from home for 3 days. Again, this is an extreme form of disengagement that illustrates a physical as well as emotional cutoff.

At the other end of the spectrum are diffuse interpersonal boundaries, which are blurred to the extent that others can intrude into them. A diffuse boundary leads to enmeshment, which is characterized by family members' over-involvement in one another's lives. This can be experienced as an extreme form of giving support or as too much **accommodation**. In some collectivist cultures, enmeshment can be both normal and functional, an accepted way of life (Sue & Sue, 2003). In most Euro-American cultures, however, enmeshment tends to be a problem. Although overly concerned parents invest a great deal of interest in their children, they often tend to foster dependency and make it difficult for the children to form relationships with people outside of the family. This results in a loss of independence for both the children and the parents.

Minuchin, in working with a **psychosomatic family**, once demonstrated enmeshment in the therapy session by pinching a 12-year-old diabetic daughter and asking the father if he felt the pain of the pinch. The father responded that he did. When Minuchin asked the same question of the mother, she said that she did not feel the pain but that she had "poor circulation" (Fishman, 1993, p. 43).

In the middle of the continuum between rigid and diffuse boundaries are clear or healthy boundaries, which consist of an appropriate blending of rigid and diffuse characteristics. Healthy boundaries help an individual attain a sense of her or his own identity yet allow for a sense of belongingness within the overall family system. In healthy families, there is an ability to cope effectively with the various stresses of living by maintaining a sense of family unity and, at the same time, there is the flexibility that allows for restructuring of the family and meeting the individual developmental needs of its members. Accommodation is essential to functional coping. Spouses must accommodate the differences and needs of the other, and parents must learn to accommodate the needs of their children as the family goes through developmental stages in the family life cycle (Carter & McGoldrick, 2005). Structural family therapists warn us not to pathologize families engaged in normal transitions and the stresses involved in personal change and growth.

Structural family therapists also make the point that the community services established to help families and individual members within families often engage in a peculiar form of both diffuse and rigid boundaries (Aponte, 1994; Elizur & Minuchin, 1989; Fishman, 1993). In some instances, school counselors are engaged with the children, as well as community mental health counselors with the children and family members at the same time that the social welfare agencies are involved in case management. To some of these arrangements, we also can add correctional facilities and interventions or residential treatment centers and psychiatric services for some family members. Although all of these community systems may exchange a great deal of information about the family (diffuse boundaries), some of which may even violate the confidentiality requirements of counseling and therapy, they seldom share or organize the goals, purposes, and processes of the various intervening agencies (maintaining, instead, rigid boundaries). Under such conditions, the multiple forms of help offered families and family members regularly functions at cross-purposes with each other.

Therapy Goals

The goal of structural family therapy is to transform the system by bringing about structural change within the system, modifying the family's transactional rules, and developing more appropriate boundaries. Colapinto (2000) points out that by releasing family members from their stereotyped roles and functions, the system is able to mobilize its resources and to improve its ability to cope with stress and conflict. When the system is transformed, the symptoms of dysfunction remit. Aponte (1994) and Fishman (1993) both note the importance of working with other community systems in an effort to coordinate services and therapeutic interventions with families.

In general, the goal for families is the creation of an effective hierarchical structure. Parents are in charge of their children and give them increasing independence and freedom as they mature. The structural family therapist attempts to change the rules governing interactional patterns so that individual family members (and family subsystems) have clear boundaries. A healthy family is characterized by a system that supports the growth of the individual members and, at the same time, encourages the growth of the family unit. In working with enmeshed families, the aim is to assist individuals in achieving greater individuation. In the case of disengaged families, the goal is to increase interactions among members.

Structural therapists do not limit their interventions to families alone; they are interested in the role that the community has in relation to the family. In their book *Institutionalizing Madness: Families, Therapy, and Society*, Elizur and Minuchin (1989) develop the idea that, because the larger social structure affects the organization of a family, it is essential that the influence of the community on the family be considered.

Fishman (1993) reports a case that demonstrates the impact of the family and community systems working together:

> A mildly retarded 19-year-old woman was living in a system that was organized to provide for her every need. The society provided an abundance of helping services, and between the family and the outside helpers the young woman was prevented from becoming more independent. After a cautious suicide attempt, she confided to a therapist that she desperately wanted to try to get a job in a horticultural nursery, make a life away from home, and manage her own money. (p. 44)

The daughter's desires were both attainable and useful, but the societal services that had been set up to help her were actually holding her back. Further investigation revealed that these same community resources supported the parents' over-protectiveness, so that two major subsystems seemed to create a structural system from which it was practically impossible to escape. The daughter's "cautious suicide attempt" made it possible for her to enlist the support of the therapist in a needed change. Aponte (1991) makes it clear that integrating structural family therapy with social work requires community organization skills and specialized training for the therapist.

The Therapist's Role and Function

Minuchin (1974) identifies three interactive functions of the therapist: (1) joining the family in a position of leadership, (2) mapping its underlying structure, and (3) intervening in ways designed to transform an ineffective structure. Structural therapists assume that individual change will result from modifying a family's organization and from changing its transactional patterns. The therapist's basic task is to actively engage the family as a unit for the purpose of initiating a restructuring process.

Structural therapists are active in challenging rigid transactional patterns that characterize certain families as they attempt to organize themselves to cope with stressful situations. The therapeutic endeavor involves pushing for clearer boundaries, increasing the degree of flexibility in family interactions, and modifying a dysfunctional family structure (Goldenberg & Goldenberg, 2004). It is the job of structural therapists to join with the family, to block stereotyped interactional patterns, and to facilitate the development of more-flexible transactions. This is what Harry Aponte did in the example at the beginning of this chapter when he suggested that Mr. Gonzaga ask his son, Aldo, if the boy was afraid of his father. You'll remember that when the mother tried to interfere, the therapist blocked her participation in the conversation.

Colapinto (2000) writes that structural therapists play a number of different roles with families, depending on the phase of therapy. From the initial session, therapists are engaged in a dance with the family. Soon after this dance begins, they become stage directors who create scenarios in which problems are played out according to various scripts. Therapists lay the groundwork for a particular situation, create a scenario, assign roles and tasks to a family, and issue directives to family members. Then they sit back as a spectator and observe the family in action. Therapists must offer a combination of support and challenge. They need to sustain certain patterns and undermine other patterns. They must learn the appropriate balance between accommodating and negotiating with a family.

Techniques

It should be mentioned that, more than being a set of techniques, structural family therapy provides a context for viewing a family, offering a clear description of how a family should operate. Minuchin's approach is a therapy of action, rather than insight, although recent developments in his approach suggest that he is at least interested in connecting current patterns to learned experiences during childhood (Minuchin, 2004; Minuchin, Nichols, & Lee, 2007). Initially, however, he believed that action changed behavior without the need for insight. Enactments also provided opportunities that led to new experiences and to transformed family organizations.

Structural family therapy aims to modify the present organization of the family with minimal exploration and interpretation of the past. Therapists join the family system they are helping, and they make interventions designed to transform the organization of that family. *Joining* is the process of building and maintaining a therapeutic alliance. As the family accepts the leadership of the therapist, it becomes possible for him or her to intervene actively. The therapist joins the family for the purpose of modifying its functioning, not to solve the family's problem. In order for the therapist to become a part of the family system, it is critical that he or she establishes rapport by being sensitive to each of the family members. Through the process of joining, the family learns that the therapist understands the members and is working with and for each of them. The family and the therapist form a therapeutic partnership to achieve a common goal: "to free the family symptom bearer of symptoms, to reduce conflict and stress for the whole family, and to learn new ways of coping" (Minuchin & Fishman, 1981, p. 29). By joining the family and accommodating to its style, the therapist gains a picture of how members cope with problems and with one another. The aim is to change dysfunctional patterns while they occur in the session; there is a focus on realigning faulty hierarchies and correcting family structure.

Aponte (1994) integrates a spiritual element in his ecostructural model and notes that therapists cannot join with families from a valueless position.

> My contention here is that value biases are pervasive in all aspects of therapy. The question is not one of *whether* the therapist's values will come face to face with the family's values in the crucible of therapy, but *how*. How can therapists work with their professional and personal values to benefit the families they treat? Negotiating the values that form the basis of problem definition, assessment, therapeutic interventions, and goal-setting becomes central to the therapeutic process. (p. 175)

In their book *Family Therapy Techniques*, Minuchin and Fishman (1981) emphasize the importance of the therapist's use of self. They believe that therapists need to be comfortable with different levels of involvement. A wide range of techniques may be employed, depending on what fits the situation, the family, and the therapist. At times, therapists may want to disengage from a family by prescribing a course of action. At other times, they may engage and operate as a coach. And yet at other times, they may align with one member of the family, a process called **unbalancing**, which involves the therapist lending his or her authority and weight to break a stalemate maintained by the family system.

Minuchin's professional approach is active, directive, and well thought out. His style is typically assertive and has even been blunt at times. It is not uncommon for him to ask, say, the children in the family to solve a sibling problem by discussing it without the parents interfering. He then will block any attempt by the parents to interfere. At other times, he will ask the children to consult with the parents regarding possibilities for change (Minuchin, 2004). A therapist can use whatever strategy is appropriate for meeting a therapeutic goal. These therapeutic techniques need to be suited to the personal characteristics of the family. Minuchin draws from many other approaches and combines strategies. Although his basic theory has remained relatively constant, he has moved toward eclecticism in techniques (Nichols & Schwartz, 2006). Techniques include joining, accommodation, working with family interactions, tracking sequences, enactments, **intensifying**, boundary making, restructuring (strengthening diffuse boundaries and softening rigid one), reframing, issuing directives, and family mapping. Three of these now will be outlined briefly: Family mapping, enactments, and reframing in Figures 8.1–8.3.

Family Mapping.   Minuchin (1974) developed a method for mapping the structure of the family. In drawing a family map, the therapist identifies boundaries as rigid, diffuse, or clear; transactional styles are identified as enmeshed or disengaged. Certain symbols have been employed to indicate these structures:

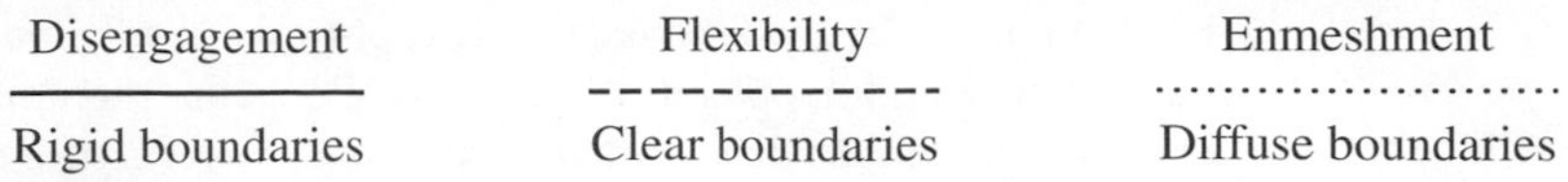

Disengagement	Flexibility	Enmeshment
————————	– – – – – – – –	····················
Rigid boundaries	Clear boundaries	Diffuse boundaries

Figure 8.1

Diagrams of rigid, clear, and diffuse boundaries in structural family therapy.

A variety of maps can highlight the functioning and nature of interpersonal relationships within the family and can be used fruitfully in the therapy sessions. For example:

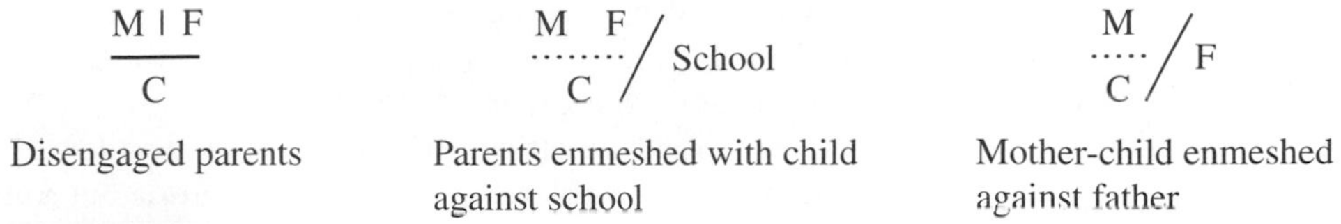

$\dfrac{\text{M | F}}{\text{C}}$	$\dfrac{\text{M} \cdots \text{F}}{\text{C}} \Big/ \text{School}$	$\dfrac{\text{M}}{\text{C}} \cdots \Big/ \text{F}$
Disengaged parents	Parents enmeshed with child against school	Mother-child enmeshed against father

Figure 8.2

Examples of maps used in structural family therapy to depict different family relationships.

In addition, the following symbols are used to indicate emotional responses and consistent patterns of interpersonal contact.

Coalitions are indicated by the symbol: }

Conflict is identified with the symbol: ———| |———

Detouring is represented by the symbol: ————————▶

Involvement is indicated by two parallel lines: ═══════

Over-involvement is represented by three parallel lines: ≡≡≡≡≡

Scapegoating of a child by two parents who are in conflict with one another might be drawn like this:

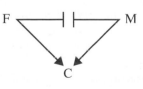

Figure 8.3

Symbols used in structural family therapy for emotional responses and consistent patterns of interpersonal contact.

Most of Minuchin's mapping processes are incorporated in McGoldrick, Gerson, and Shellenberger's (1999) book on genograms.

Enactments.   In enactments, the therapist asks family members to act out a conflict situation that would happen at home. This allows the therapist to observe how family members interact and to draw conclusions about the structure of the family. The therapist also blocks existing patterns, determines the family's ability to accommodate to different rules, and encourages family members to experiment with more-functional rules. Change occurs as a result of enacting and dealing with problems, rather than merely talking about these problems (Colapinto, 2000).

Reframing.   When the therapist reframes, he or she casts a new light on and provides a different interpretation of a problem situation in a family. The presenting problem can be explored in ways that allow the family to understand an original complaint from many angles. Through reframing, it becomes possible to grasp the underlying family structure that is contributing to an individual's problem. In this way, one family member does not bear the full burden of blame for a problem or the entire responsibility for solving it.

In a session at the Boston Family Institute, Minuchin (1979) demonstrated reframing, enactment, and boundary setting with a family that included an anorexic 12-year-old girl. After suggesting that the girl's problem was not anorexia but stubbornness and a desire to be the youngest, the baby of the family (a reframe), Minuchin asked the siblings to discuss how they would handle the girl's temper tantrums and stubbornness. He watched this *enactment* very carefully in an effort to discern the hierarchy that existed among the children. Occasionally, he used his hands in a gesture designed to stop the mother from interfering with the children's discussion, setting an appropriate boundary for the directed task. Through reframing and boundary setting, Minuchin was able to shift both the burdens and patterns in the family so that the members had more flexibility in addressing the presenting issues.

A Structural Family Therapist With the Quest Family

Paul and Jane Quest bring all four of their children to the first meeting with a structural family therapist. The structural family therapist has some sense of the family from a brief phone interview and knows that this is a family that is evolving and seeking help with blending into a more harmonious unit. The therapist is aware that Paul is absenting himself from family struggles through his work, and she has heard the desperation that seems to be in Jane's voice when she talks about "the boys."

We will now look at parts of conversations that the structural family therapist had with the family over several counseling sessions. Movement from personal and organizational assessments to tracking sequences to exploring childhood experiences of the parents to enacting a new process through dialogue are all part of the therapy.

Starting with Paul, she asks the parents what they hope to achieve through the family sessions they will have together. Paul indicates that he has been very busy both with work and community projects, but says that he always has been busy. He feels he relies on Jane to handle matters at home, but he also wants to be involved. When the possibility first arose, he was excited about having the boys join the family, but the changes required have been hard on everyone, especially Jane, and he wants whatever help the family can get. Jane notes that she is relieved to be there. She doesn't feel she can cope without help, and the family seems to be "falling apart." Both Amy and Ann have tried to help with the boys, but they have their own lives, and Jane doesn't feel that the girls really connect with Luke and Jason. It is like "I have two separate families."

Amy and Ann sit together next to their father and across from the two empty chairs placed close to Jane for the boys. Jason and Luke are up and moving around. Addressing Paul first, the therapist begins the session.

Therapist: You know, Paul, I think that Jane was used to raising little girls, and she probably knows a lot about that, but she seems almost lost when it comes to little boys.

Paul: With these two boys, I think we all are lost. [therapist nods] Amy and Ann were pretty easy to raise.

Therapist: Yes, but at least you know what it is like to be a boy, and you have some idea about how a father raises boys. Or do you? How was it for your father and you?

Paul: Well, he was a surgeon with a large practice. My mother largely raised me. I admired my father when I was growing up, and I wanted to be like him, but I didn't really know a lot about him until I went to medical school.

Therapist: So you are away from the house just like your father was. You know, Paul, I don't think that is going to work so well with these two boys. They seem to need a lot more attention— really, some direct care and input from you.

Paul: You mean spend more time with them?

Therapist: Yes, but also to teach them things and to help them learn how to handle life and difficulties in a new way. How was it for Jason and Luke before they came to live with you?

Paul: Both of the boys were hurt a lot in some really awful ways. Some of what they do to each other and even to pets and other people, they had done to them. Jason likes to be the boss of Luke, and Luke sometimes goes along with it and sometimes not. Jason is very loud, and he will enforce his desires. Luke is quieter, and I often see him becoming a victim in relation to Jason. Jason doesn't like to be held or tucked in—not even a story or a song at bedtime. These are things I used to always do with Amy and Ann. And yet, as much as Jason can sometimes push you away, he cannot stand to be alone. He always needs someone engaged with him.

Just as the therapist is about to ask another question, a small fight breaks out between the boys. Jane immediately gets up with the intention of making both of the boys sit down in the circle.

Therapist: Jane, I wonder if you would let Paul handle this. I would like to see how it goes. (Jane slowly sits back down.)

Paul asks Amy and Ann if they would mind sitting by their mother? Without speaking, both of the young women move. Paul gets up and takes each boy by the arm and directs them to chairs next to him. In a voice that seems calm, but controlled and quite firm, Paul says "Sit there and don't move." The boys quiet down almost immediately and sit there, looking at each other, then their Dad, and then back at each other.

Therapist: How did that go?

Jane: It won't last.

Therapist: Nothing lasts. But, Paul, how was that for you? (Paul stays silent.) Did you notice that they seemed to listen to you and do as you asked?

Paul: Jane's right. It won't last.

Therapist: Maybe not. But something needed to happen, and you got it to happen. . . . I am wondering if you and Jane could have a talk about what things Jason and Luke need to learn, what they need to handle, and which of you might be best able to get these essential messages across to them.

Paul and Jane identify a number of concerns from the boys' use of violence to resolve conflict to the special needs they will have related to education. Paul mentions sports, fishing, and camping. Jane wants music lessons for the boys—perhaps the violin. Paul suggests taking them to work with him occasionally. Jane is interested in developing a love of the arts (museums, galleries, etc.). Both parents think Jason and Luke should take part in the work of the household, but Paul means working out in the yard and Jane means cleaning their rooms and the bathroom.

The sequences of their conversation seem to follow a fixed pattern: Paul suggests something he feels is important for the boys' growth and development or to bring them into the family more fully. Jane acknowledges what he says, but then immediately advances an idea of her own—almost as a substitute for what Paul is suggesting. Paul starts to speak, and then Jane makes reference to what they always did with the girls. "And it worked." Paul then falls silent for a while before bringing up another possibility or responding to Jane's ideas.

Therapist:	I think the way this conversation is going, Jane, that there must be a right way to help Jason and Luke, and Paul does not seem to know what it is unless you guide him?
Jane:	I just want him to be more involved with the boys.
Therapist:	Probably won't happen if none of the things he wants to do with them is considered acceptable. Why don't you like his ideas?
Jane:	There's just so much to be done, and what he wants seems more like . . . well, play.
Therapist:	I don't know if that's true. It's like I was saying before: I think you know a lot about raising Ann and Amy. You did a nice job with them, but boys are harder. They need something different, maybe something that only Paul can give them, like how to be a gentle, caring man in the company of both women and other men.
Jane:	So you're saying that taking them to baseball games or fishing or to work with him is enough?
Therapist:	It may not be enough, but it's a good start. (turning to Paul) Tell me again what it was like for you with your father. Did you go to baseball games or fishing?
Paul:	Not much. My father was very busy. But I always wanted to go. And when he said that we could go, I would get very excited—even though most of the time, he would have to cancel. I would be very disappointed, but I tried to understand. He did important work.
Therapist:	So do I understand that you would not want to disappoint Jason or Luke?
Paul:	That's right. If I say I am going to do something with them, I would make sure I showed up for it.
Therapist:	I don't know, but that sounds pretty important to me too. (turning to Jane) What was it like for you, Jane, with your mother and father?
Jane:	My mother ran everything. My father was a beat cop. He was a good one, well respected, but when he came home, he was always tired. He wanted to read the paper or watch TV. It was Mom who made sure that we had music lessons, were exposed to the arts, and took part in after-school activities. She signed us up, and she got us there.
Therapist:	How was your father with your brother?
Jane:	They didn't have much of a relationship. Dad would help Joey whenever he could, but Joey was clearly Mom's favorite, and she let him get away with everything. He's really pampered—even to this day.
Therapist:	So you're not exactly sure what it looks like when a man gets involved in raising his sons.

Jane: No. I guess not.

Therapist: Amy, I am wondering what it was like when you were younger? Did your mother make space for you and Ann to have time with your Dad or did you, too, have to raise a ruckus to get him to spend time with you?

Amy: I think we had time with Dad—not as much time as we had with Mom, of course—but we had time. Ann would often fix him breakfast in bed, and they would sit and talk. And he would always read to us before bed at night. He took us fishing once and to a ball game or two, but we really weren't into that.

Ann: What I remember most is the vacations we would take. Sometimes, we would camp out, but a lot of the times it was these long car trips to see national monuments or historic sites. Dad knew a lot about different places and history. And Mom would have us all singing in the car or playing car games.

The therapist asks Amy and Ann if they would have a conversation with Jason and Luke about what their childhood was like, to sort of catch the boys up and let them know ways in which they could all be happier together. The therapist asks Amy and Ann: "What, for example, do the two of you know that might help a 6- and a 4-year-old boy find places in the family?" For some time, Amy and Ann talk with Jason while Luke listens. Occasionally, Jane wants to interject something, but the therapist holds up her hand and keeps the conversation among the four children. Amy and Ann talk about very concrete things they used to do when they were young children—each individually with different parents and in pairs or as a family. As they talk, they start to sound both nostalgic and excited. Ann often asks, "Is that something you would like to do too?" Jason almost always responds in the affirmative with Luke nodding. A different kind of connection is forming. After a break in the session . . .

Therapist: Amy and Ann, what do you think could happen between your mother and father that would help things here? Could you talk to them about that?

Ann: I think they . . .

Therapist: Talk directly to them. They're right here.

Ann: I have to say, Mom, that I think the idea of letting Dad do more with Jason and Luke is a good idea—even if it does seem like play. The boys are only 6 and 4: Play is what they should be doing.

Jane: And what do we do when one of them hits a neighbor or the dog—and your father is at work?

Ann: I don't know. Maybe we say, "Wait until your father gets home!"

Amy: Dad just has to work it out to be at home more, maybe not do so many extra things for the town until Jason and Luke feel more like they are part of us.

Paul: So you, too, think I should do more with Jason and Luke?

Amy: I think you have to, Dad. We can't anymore. Ann and I have our own lives. I will be going to college soon. When Mom panics or worries, I think you just have to tell her that you know she's scared, but you will handle it and it will work out. Not on everything, but on the important things.

Paul: Like fishing.

Ann: Like fishing and baseball and ice cream and cleaning up their rooms too.

Through all of this discussion, Paul nods. He seems to understand what is being proposed and, when asked for his reaction, he says, "I think I just needed a plan, and to know what to do." The therapist indicates that Paul always knew what to do. He just needed some family space in which he could do it. The therapist asks Jane if she is in agreement with her daughters that maybe she (Jane) can step back a little from assuming all of the responsibility for how life with the boys goes and allow her husband to take more of a hand in both disciplining the boys and helping them to grow up. Jane agrees to do this, and the session ends.

Summary and Multicultural Evaluation

The basic processes of structural family therapy have been delineated by Becvar and Becvar (2003). The focus is on the structure or organization within a family. Therapists observe transactions and patterns, and are involved in joining, accepting, and respecting the family in its efforts to reorganize and to achieve its goals. This assessment process explores the symptoms and the organization of the family before, during, and after symptomatic enactments. A structural map is formed, which provides the therapist with a basis for intervening firmly and directly so that the family will move toward health. To these initial assessments, Minuchin (2004; also Minuchin, Nichols, & Lee, 2007) adds an exploration of the childhood family-of-origin sequences of each parent to see where the original patterns and cycles were formed and what meaning was attached to them. He also asks the children and parents to enter into conversations that explore possibilities for change rather than leaving the family plan solely to the parents. Family members are both supported and challenged as they try new behaviors in the session.

Contributions to Multicultural Counseling and Gender Issues

No modern approach to systemic family therapy has done more to advance the plight of the disadvantaged, poor, and the working poor than structural family therapy. The work that started with families in the slums (Minuchin, Montalvo, Guerney, Rosman, & Schumer, 1967) has been maintained through four decades of dedicated service, interest, and care (see Aponte, 1994; Elizer & Minuchin, 1989; and Minuchin, Colapinto, & Minuchin, 1998). The impact of poverty on families across cultures (from poor and working class Caucasian families to those from **marginalized cultures**) has been carefully delineated by Hart and Risley (1995). It has been structural family therapists, however, who have transformed an understanding of this impact into pragmatic and even spiritual interventions. Since those who are poor in the United States include a large number of oppressed individuals and discriminated cultures, many of the leaders of structural family therapy have developed a special sensitivity to the issues of racism and the overt marginalization of Spanish-speaking, African-American, and Asian cultures. Indeed, an appreciation of cultural diversity seems to be integrated into every part of their therapeutic process. McGoldrick (1998) and McGoldrick, Giordano, and Garcia-Preto (2005) discussed at length the issues and processes related to ethnicity and family therapy. Again, it seems to be structural family therapists who use this information to frame the manner in which therapists join with families, assess transactions and interactional sequences, and plan enactments.

Minuchin's extension of systemic process into larger systems is to be applauded. He and his colleagues have addressed (a) the disconnection and break-up of families enforced by the mental health systems in several countries (Elizur & Minuchin, 1989), (b) the development of ecostructural models (Aponte, 1994; Minuchin et al., 1998), and (c) the application of this approach to oppressed individuals and systems, including gay and lesbian couples, where structural family therapy finds no difference in the systemic processes observed. Because of Minuchin's own Argentine background, as well as the Hispanic cultures of many of his colleagues, the ability to join fathers successfully in family therapy has been a particular strength, and it makes this model particularly well suited to cultures that place a high value on the authority of the father. Jose Szapocznik and colleagues have applied structural family therapy to Hispanic boys, Cuban families, adolescent refugees, drug abuse, and, most recently, HIV/AIDS (Pequegnat & Szapocznik, 2000; Szapocznik, 1985, 1989; Szapocznik et al., 1989; Szapocznik & Herrera, 1978).

There are very few limitations related to this approach in multicultural settings. A sensitive interest in and valuing of the extended family and culture have become part of the structural family therapy model. While the idea of enmeshment as dysfunctional, establishing clear boundaries, and becoming more individualized will not fit well with some collectivist cultures (Berg & Jaya, 1993; Itai & McRae 1994; Sue & Sue, 2003), Aponte and other structural family therapists understand this and adapt the model accordingly. Their focus on parents as partners dealing with issues both internal and external to the system fit well with both individualistic and collectivist cultures.

Boyd-Franklin (2003) is very supportive of the use of structural family therapy with African-American families. She notes that assessing power in African-American families is complicated, because the decision-making power in a family may be another relative or even someone outside of the extended family system:

> This person might be a grandmother, grandfather, aunt, uncle, mother, father, minister, boyfriend, or girlfriend. From a therapeutic perspective, this creates a complex situation because these individuals often do not appear early in the treatment process and are frequently not even mentioned by those who attend the sessions. (p. 207)

Boyd-Franklin (2003) suggests the following questions to explore who the true decision makers might be in African-American families:

- To whom did you speak before you made that decision?
- Did anyone disagree with you on that issue?
- Who has the final word on that issue in your family?
- To whom do you listen when you need advice? (p. 207)

Empowerment of families in the face of oppression caused by those who are designated as helpers has been an essential focus of this model. Minuchin et al. (1998) characterize their work with the poor as a fight for those "hurtling headlong downstream" (p. 4). Their emphasis is both on rescue and prevention. Their work with agencies and helpers to bring needed services to the poor has been one of the greater contributions to the family therapy movement.

Aponte (1992, 1994) especially has integrated a focus on diversity into the training of structural family therapists. He notes that the polarities of identification and differentiation exist within us as dialectic, emerging often as a new sense of self. In this same sense, diversity and the universal (what is the same about all of us) are also dialectic: You can't have one without the other.

> Sameness becomes stale without diversity. Diversity is chaotic without sameness. Oneness implodes without separateness. Separateness scatters without oneness. People need a core of family tradition together with cultural and racial identity. They also need the uniqueness of their existential selves. . . . The tension of diversity is partner to the harmony of unity. These complex dialectics of diversity are the axes of therapists' perspectives on peoples' personal and social identities. (Aponte, 1994, p. 149)

Although feminists would join Minuchin in his consideration of larger systems affecting the family, he has not been favorably disposed to feminist interventions designed to save the woman at the expense of the family unit. Feminists noted and criticized the early and middle stages of Minuchin's development when he would join with the father in the family structure, reinforcing the patriarchy and male authority in the system (Luepnitz, 1988). Indeed, the process of unbalancing developed in this model (and also used by Bowen therapists and strategic practitioners) has all too often been used in favor of men and at the expense of women, even in potentially abusive and dangerous situations. Although this is not a criticism that one tends to hear of the masters of this approach today, it is still a caution that is important to acknowledge for those studying the complete range of structural therapeutic interventions.

Structural family therapists add organizational and sequence lenses that help family practitioners discover and understand the patterns, process, and interactions within the organization or structure of the family. The sequencing lens is also highly supported in strategic family therapy (Haley, 1984; Madanes, 1981). Tracking sequences or patterns is at the heart of what differentiates family systems therapy from other approaches. Sequences exist in the here-and-now, face-to-face engagement of couples and family members, as well as in the enactment of rules and routines within the family structure. Much longer sequences also occur in the patterns experienced during the ebb and flow of both individual and family development, in transgenerational interactions, and in the interactions of family members with churches, schools, and other community functions and agencies (Breunlin, Schwartz, & MacKune-Karrer, 1992). When therapists become proficient at tracking sequences, everything from joining to assessment to enactments and interventions for change is affected.

If you are interested in more in-depth study of this approach, we recommend the following sources: Aponte (1994); Aponte and DiCesare (2002); Colapinto (2000); Fishman (1993); Minuchin (1974, 1984); and Minuchin and Fishman (1981).

Exercises for Personal and Professional Growth

Let's start by taking another look at your genogram:

- Although much of structural mapping is already incorporated in genogram development, you may want to look for areas in your own family where there may have been, for example, disengagement, enmeshment, conflict, coalitions, or even scapegoating. When you find these elements in your genogram, try to identify the family rules and the transactional sequences that characterized these problems.
- Also, find the areas in your family where there were clear and appropriate boundaries: Places where individuals had their own space, but could still belong to and contribute to the system as a whole; places where members of subsystems could work out their own relationships without outside interference; and places where individuals who were part of more than one subsystem could move freely between them without confusion or dysfunction. Again, what were the family rules and transactional sequences that supported well-functioning parts of your family life?

Four of the more important tasks in structural family therapy are joining, mapping, setting boundaries, and enactments. Here's a chance to try out these interventions.

Guy and Patsy have a little boy named Steve. Steve's birth was quite difficult, and early on he had several serious childhood illnesses, one of which could have been fatal. When he began to speak, he developed a speech hesitation that never has been addressed effectively. Consequently, the mother, Patsy, became overly protective and even pampering. Guy is a hard worker, but he distances himself from his son, secretly feeling that his wife is spoiling the child. Guy keeps his thoughts to himself, however, and works even harder. Patsy creates a life built around her son and actually doesn't mind that Guy is gone all the time.

We might structurally diagram this family in the following way:

$$\underset{\text{C}}{\overset{\text{M}}{\cdots\cdots}}\Big/\text{F}$$

- Using the figures presented in this chapter, what does this diagram suggest?
- With whom would you initially join in an effort to transform this family system?

Imagine that Steve has gotten in trouble with the law for drug use. Patsy says that it was just a boy experimenting: "No big deal!" Guy thinks it is a sign of worse things to come. He hesitatingly suggests that Steve's mother "keeps Steve too close to her and keeps him from growing up." Think of what you might say to join with this family: Write your interventions below:

_____

_____

_____

_____

Okay, let's see what you can do with another family. In this family, Helen, the mother, and Tim, the father, waited 10 long years for the birth of their child, Alex. The couple went through hormone therapy, *in vitro* fertilization processes, and artificial insemination. Helen endured almost 7 months of bed rest after she became pregnant to make sure that Alex arrived healthy and well. Alex was born prematurely, and he had to spend a month in the hospital before going home. Alex started out sleeping in what Helen and Tim called "the family bed." He is now school age, and he is still in bed with them, between his mother and father. For several weeks when Alex started first grade, both of his parents (Tim worked the night shift) would go to school with him and spend the whole day there. When the school suggested that Alex should come to school alone, the parents balked and have been in a fight with the school ever since.

We might structurally diagram this set of relationships in this way:

- Pretend that you have been asked to consult with the family and the school. What do you think this mother and father would say at the meeting? What would the school officials say?
- How would each side pull Alex into the process?
- What boundaries, if any, would you want to set between the home and the school?
- What boundaries, if any, would you want to set at home?
- Can you think of an enactment that you might suggest that would help to establish reasonable subsystem boundaries?
- Can you think of an enactment that you might use to transform the family system and its relationship to the school?

Where to Go From Here

Minuchin has moved several times since he left the Philadelphia Child Guidance Center. He has trained a wide range of clinicians and teachers from every branch of the helping professions. Training in structural family therapy is most easily found in New York at the Minuchin Center for Family Therapy and in Philadelphia at the Philadelphia Child and Family Therapy Training Center where structural family therapy continues to be taught and developed. Information about the workshops and training programs offered by faculty from these two centers is available at:

The Minuchin Center for the Family
114 East 32nd Street, Suite 406
New York, New York 10016
Phone: 212-481-3144, fax: 212-481-5395
E-mail: **MinuchinCenter@minuchincenter.org**

and

Philadelphia Child and Family Therapy Training Center, Inc.
Marion Lindblad-Goldberg, Ph.D., Director
P.O. Box 4092
Philadelphia, Pa. 19118-8092
Phone: 215-242-0949, fax: 215-831-2639
E-mail: **marionlg@philafamily.com**

Recommended Readings

Aponte, H. J. (1994). *Bread and spirit: Therapy with the new poor*. New York: Norton. This book is Harry Aponte's delineation of ecostructural family therapy and a real contribution to the development of the person of the therapist and spirituality in structural family therapy.

Aponte, H. J., & Van Deusen, J. M. (1981). Structural family therapy. In A. S. Gurman & D. P. Kniskern (Eds.), *Handbook of family therapy* (pp. 310–360). New York: Brunner Mazel. At the height of structural family therapy's popularity, Aponte and Van Deusen contributed one of the clearest presentations of the model ever written.

Colapinto, J. (1991). Structural family therapy. In A. S. Gurman & D. P. Kniskern (Eds.), *Handbook of family therapy* (Vol. II: pp. 417–443). New York: Brunner Mazel. In the second handbook on family therapy, Colapinto provides a valuable 10-year follow-up to the original chapter by Aponte and Van Deusen (1981).

Fishman, H. C. (1993). *Intensive structural therapy: Treating families in their social context*. New York: Basic Books. With wonderfully illustrated case pre-

sentations, Fishman presents a great book on family therapy techniques that argues for including a wider network in family therapy sessions.

Minuchin, S. (1974). *Families and family therapy*. Cambridge, MA: Harvard University Press. This is the book in which Minuchin lays the foundation for structural family therapy and, even now as a classic, it is the basis on which all further developments of the model have evolved.

Minuchin, S., & Fishman, H. C. (1981). *Family therapy techniques*. Cambridge, MA: Harvard University Press. In this book, Minuchin and Fishman delineate the interventions that changed the focus of family therapy and provided practitioners with a guide to assessment and interventions.

Minuchin, S., Lee, W-Y., & Simon, G. M. (1996). *Mastering family therapy: Journeys of growth and transformation*. New York: Wiley. A book of personal journeys and development in the lives and work of family therapists.

Minuchin, S., Montalvo, B., Guerney, B., Rosman, B., & Schumer, F. (1967). *Families of the slums*. New York: Basic Books. This is the original work Minuchin and his colleagues conducted with poor families. The foundations of structural family therapy are presented in the context of the initial cases from which the model developed.

Minuchin, S., Rosman, B., & Baker, L. (1978). *Psychosomatic families: Anorexia nervosa in context.* Cambridge, MA: Harvard University Press. Minuchin and colleagues present their application of structural family therapy to the problems related to anorexia and, in the process, change the way *pathologies* are conceptualized within family systems.

DVD Reference

Salvador Minuchin and his associates made organization, power, and function in the family a central focus for both assessment and intervention. In this model, much of the language that has defined family systems therapy was initially developed and used. In this model, we are introduced to the concepts of hierarchy, macro-systems and subsystems, boundaries, disengagement, and enmeshment as well as the therapeutic processes of joining and accommodating, structural mapping, unbalancing, enactments, and setting boundaries.

This structural family therapy video segment is based on an early therapy session conducted by Salvador Minuchin. The presenting problem is slightly different and, of course, the people involved are different, but both this session and the original addressed issues related to an eating disorder in a large, enmeshed family, headed by a mother who had to be involved in every aspect of her children's lives. This video focuses on boundary setting in therapy, using both verbal and physical interventions to establish and maintain an appropriate subsystem boundary in the family.

References

Aponte, H. J. (1991). Training on the person of the therapist for work with the poor and minorities. In K. G. Lewis (Ed.), *Family systems application to social work: Training and clinical practice* (pp. 23–40). New York: Haworth.

Aponte, H. J. (1992). Training the person of the therapist in structural family therapy. *Journal of Marital and Family Therapy, 18*(3), 269–281.

Aponte, H. J. (1994). *Bread and spirit: Therapy with the new poor—Diversity of race, culture, and values.* New York: Norton.

Aponte, H. J., & DiCesare, E. J. (2002). Structural family therapy. In J. Carlson & D. Kjos (Eds.), *Theories and strategies of family therapy* (pp. 1–18). Boston: Allyn & Bacon.

Aponte, H. J., & Van Deusen, J. M. (1981). Structural family therapy. In A. S. Gurman & D. P. Kniskern (Eds.), *Handbook of family therapy* (pp. 310–360). New York: Brunner Mazel.

Becvar, D. S., & Becvar, R. J. (2003). *Family therapy: A systemic integration* (5th ed.). Boston: Allyn & Bacon.

Berg, I., & Jaya, A. (1993). Different and same: Family therapy with Asian-American families. *Journal of Marital and Family Therapy, 19*, 31–38.

Boyd-Franklin, N. (2003). *Black families in therapy: Understanding the African American experience* (2nd ed.). New York: Guilford.

Breunlin, D. C., Schwartz, R. C., & MacKune-Karrer, B. (1992). *Metaframeworks: Transcending the models of family therapy.* San Francisco: Jossey Bass.

Carter, B., & McGoldrick, M. (Eds.). (2005). *The expanded family life cycle: Individual, family, and social perspectives* (3rd ed.). Boston: Allyn & Bacon.

Colapinto, J. (1991). Structural family therapy. In A. S. Gurman & D. P. Kniskern (Eds.), *Handbook of family therapy* (Vol. II, pp. 417–443). New York: Brunner/Mazel.

Colapinto, J. (2000). Structural family therapy. In A. H. Horne (Ed.), *Family counseling and therapy* (3rd ed., pp. 140–169). Itasca, IL: F. E. Peacock.

Elizur, J., & Minuchin, S. (1989). *Institutionalizing madness: Family, therapy, and society.* New York: Basic Books.

Fishman, H. C. (1993). *Intensive structural therapy: Treating families in their social context*. New York: Basic Books.

Goldenberg, I., & Goldenberg, H. (2004). *Family therapy: An overview* (6th ed.). Pacific Grove, CA: Brooks/Cole.

Haley, J. (1984). *Ordeal therapy: Unusual ways to change behavior*. San Francisco: Jossey Bass.

Hart, B., & Risley, T. R. (1995). *Meaningful differences in the everyday experiences of young American children*. Baltimore, MD: Paul H. Brookes.

Itai, G., & McRae, G. (1994). Counseling older Japanese American clients: An overview and observation. *Journal of Counseling and Development, 72*, 373–377.

Luepnitz, D. A. (1988). *The family interpreted: Feminist theory in clinical practice*. New York: Basic Books.

Madanes, C. (1981). *Strategic family therapy*. San Francisco: Jossey Bass.

McGoldrick, M. (1998). *Re-visioning family therapy: Race, culture, and gender in clinical practice*. New York: Guilford.

McGoldrick, M., Gerson, R., and Shellenberger, S. (1999). *Genograms: Assessment and interventions* (2nd ed.). New York: Norton.

McGoldrick, M., Giordano, J., & Garcia-Preto, N. (2005). *Ethnicity and family therapy* (3rd ed.). New York: Guilford.

Minuchin, S. (1974). *Families and family therapy*. Cambridge, MA: Harvard University Press.

Minuchin, S. (1979). Anorexia: That's a Greek word. Boston: Boston Family Institute.

Minuchin, S. (1984). *Family kaleidoscope*. Cambridge, MA: Harvard University Press.

Minuchin, S. (Speaker). (2004, June). *New developments: 40 years later*. Presentation at the annual meeting of the South Carolina Association for Marriage and Family Therapy, Mount Pleasant, SC.

Minuchin, P., Colapinto, J., & Minuchin, S. (1998). *Working with families of the poor*. New York: Guilford.

Minuchin, S., & Fishman, H. C. (1981). *Family therapy techniques*. Cambridge, MA: Harvard University Press.

Minuchin, S., Montalvo, B., Guerney, B., Rosman, B., & Schumer, F. (1967). *Families of the slums*. New York: Basic Books.

Minuchin, S., Nichols, M. P., & Lee, W-Y. (2007). *Assessing families and couples: From symptom to system*. Boston: Allyn & Bacon.

Minuchin, S., Rosman, B. L., & Baker, L. (1978). *Psychosomatic families: Anorexia nervosa in context*. Cambridge, MA: Harvard University Press.

Nichols, M. P., & Schwartz, R. C. (2006). *Family therapy: Concepts and methods* (7th ed.). Boston: Allyn & Bacon.

Pequegnat, W., & Szapocznik, J. (2000). *Working with families in the era of HIV/AIDS*. Thousand Oaks, CA: Sage.

Sue, D. W., & Sue, D. (2003). *Counseling the culturally diverse*. New York: Wiley.

Szapocznik, J. (1985). *Coping with adolescent refugees: The Mariel boatlift*. Westport, CT: Praeger.

Szapocznik, J. (1989). *Breakthroughs in family therapy with drug abusing and problem youth*. New York: Springer.

Szapocznik, J., & Herrera, M. C. (1978). *Cuban Americans: Acculturation, adjustment, and the family*. Miami, FL: Ediciones Universal.

Szapocznik, J., Rio, A., Murray, E., Cohen, R., Scopetta, M., Rivas-Vazquez, A., Hervis, O., Posada, V., & Kurtines, W. (1989). Structural family versus psychodynamic child therapy for problematic Hispanic boys. *Journal of Consulting and Clinical Psychology, 57*, 571–578.

CHAPTER 9

Strategic Family Therapy

Introduction

Key Concepts

Therapy Goals

The Therapist's Role and Function

Techniques

A Strategic Family Therapist With the Quest Family

Summary and Multicultural Evaluation

Recommended Readings

References

Introduction

Strategic family therapy, so-called because the therapist designs interventions for change, has its foundation in **communications theory**. The key contributors to the communication model included **Gregory Bateson, Jay Haley, Don Jackson**, and **Paul Watzlawick**, all of whom were associated with the development of the **Mental Research Institute** (MRI) in Palo Alto, California. Satir was also part of MRI in its early years, but she left the center to develop her own, more humanistic approach when strategies became the MRI focus.

In the 1960s, Bateson first proposed a blending of general systems theory with metaphor. He introduced his group to Milton Erickson, who was carving out a professional reputation for his skill at dealing with resistance through unconventional techniques, including hypnosis, metaphor, and paradoxical directives. Strategic family therapy received its impetus from his therapy (Haley, 1973). Haley, a key strategic therapist, was affiliated during his development with the MRI communications group, with Erickson, and with Minuchin's structural therapy. He was influenced by all of these approaches and, because he was a prolific writer, he was able to have a significant impact on the development of strategic family therapy. Jay Haley died on February 13, 2007. Both Haley and his partner/wife, Madeleine Richeport-Haley, considered strategic therapy to be a natural extension of Erickson's work in systemic contexts.

While Watzlawick (1978), Segal (1991), and others stayed with the MRI and developed a similar strategic approach called **brief family therapy**, Haley left to work with Minuchin

Jay Haley

at the Philadelphia Child Guidance Clinic. In the 1970s, he and Cloe Madanes (who was his wife at the time) established their own Family Institute in Washington, D.C. They focused on working with **family hierarchy**, power, and strategic interventions; they contributed to the development of this approach through their therapy practice, writings, and training of family therapists. At that time, structural family therapy enjoyed the status of being the most popular therapeutic approach; during the 1980s, the strategic approach (or a blend of strategic and structural) was clearly receiving top billing in the field of family therapy (Haley, 1984; Madanes, 1981).

One of Haley's gifts was his ability to consult with other therapists on difficult cases and to develop individualized and powerful strategic interventions from directives aimed at correcting family hierarchy to ordeals to paradoxical interventions that prescribe the symptom and even restrain improvement in families (Grove & Haley, 1993; Keim, 2000). In a consultation case in child psychiatry, Haley (1976, 1984) demonstrated the effectiveness of both creating an ordeal for the family greater than the one they were experiencing and the paradoxical process of restraining improvement in the family.

Two college-educated parents from middle-class backgrounds came to see the therapist about the older of their two boys: His name was Timmy, age 5, and his younger brother was Billy, age 3.[1]

The problem was Timmy, the 5-year-old. He had never been toilet-trained. In fact, he had never had a bowel movement in the toilet, but only elsewhere. His brother had been routinely toilet-trained. Timmy simply did not use the toilet. As he put it, "I poopy in my pants, and when I go to bed, sometimes I lay down and poopy in my pajamas. (Haley, 1984, p. 175)

In the initial interview with the parents, it is clear that they have received conflicting directives from family doctors that range from ignoring Timmy's problem to getting very firm with him. They have been directed to sit him on the toilet until he goes, and they even have provided him with books and a television in the bathroom. Nothing works. Timmy actually constipates himself in an effort to poop only where he wants to and when he wants to. The mother has the primary responsibility for childcare during the day, and the father helps in the evenings. They have held different positions on Timmy's problem until recently, with the father being more lenient. But as Timmy gets closer to school-age, his parents are concerned that he will not be allowed to enroll.

Therapist:	This has gone on for a couple of years, and it seems to have become the center of your life.
Father:	That's true.
Mother:	We've tried everything.
Therapist:	Well, one of the things that concerns me is this: It has been going on such a long time, what would be some consequences of getting over it?

The therapist in this session is about to propose what Haley calls an **ordeal**. It is a task or problem that is harder to solve or more complicated than the presenting problem. Ordeals are paradoxical interventions, especially when their intent is to help the family by restraining improvement and focusing on other issues. Other forms of paradox include **prescribing the symptom** (for example, telling a family member that she or he needs to get more depressed not less) and **positioning** (for example, when the client indicates that things are really bad, the therapist suggests that they are probably hopeless).

What do you think of the use of paradoxes and ordeals in therapy? Do you think they could raise any ethical issues for therapists? In your opinion, what systemic perspectives would support their use? When would they be inappropriate, perhaps even dangerous? In the larger consideration of strategies in therapy, what would guide the development of an intervention: Effectiveness? Intent? Change? Are values involved? Does the relationship with the therapist matter? What if an intervention makes things worse for a while—or forever? What if the therapist makes a mistake, and the interventions are simply not working? How do you know when to stay the course and when to change tactics? What issues of power are involved in therapist imposed strategies? Would they have any place at all with more collaborative approaches? These are all issues that have been inherent in the evolution of strategic family therapy and they persist, as we shall see, even in the more-current practices associated with **solution-focused** and **solution-oriented therapies**.

Returning to the case of Timmy and his family:

Therapist: What would happen if you didn't have this problem anymore?

Mother: I'd have a lot more freedom, because I wouldn't have all the extra wash and extra work. I wouldn't worry so much about whether we can go here or there, and what we'll do if he has one in his pants while we're there. Going out with less changes of clothes would be great. We could go places we hesitate to go now. . . . Instead of going through three or four pairs of underpants and long pants a day, as we do now, he would be able to stay in one outfit from morning until evening. My attitude about him would change a lot.

Therapist: Well, it's something to think about. We'll meet again in two weeks, since I will be on vacation next week, and we'll examine the consequences of getting over this for your family. This has been going on a long time, and when it goes away, it will make some differences. You'll relate to each other differently. You need to think about all those sides of it—the dark side, too. Let me leave you thinking about those consequences instead of going right ahead with the cure.

In this ordeal, the therapist has indicated that the family may not be able to handle being "normal" and that they should neither work toward a *cure* nor even be concerned about improving their lives with one another. When the family returns 2 weeks later, he repeats the basic question with which they were left. At first, the parents reported only being able to think about positive outcomes.

Therapist: (appearing disappointed) I see. You must have thought about some of the obvious things that you might have to deal with if all of a sudden you were *normal* and everything was going well.

Father: We could only think of good things that would happen.

Therapist: Fine. Let's hear about those.

Father: Well, we could go for rides together more often, things like that. (smiling) Of course, I might also be tempted to stay away from home more. But I am not sure I would, because I'm really a 40-hour-a-week man.

Therapist: Well, it's been 40 hours a week plus school in the evening. That means you have more drive than other people, and now that you're graduated, you don't have the school excuse for being away from home at night. If you didn't have to help your wife at home with the boy's problem, would that make a difference? (turning to the wife) Do you think your husband might work nights more then?

Mother: I don't think he would. He doesn't put in overtime unless it is necessary. (smiling) But you know, now that the school excuse is gone, he's talking about going on and getting a master's degree.

Father: (laughing) It crosses my mind occasionally. . . . I think we'd go out together more as a couple if we were over this problem. Now we tend to find things too hectic, and we say we're too tired to do this or too tired to go out tonight, and so on. I think without this problem weighing us down, we'd go out and do things together more.

Therapist: . . . I see. Then without this problem you'd have to face the problem of choosing where to go out together, and all that, as normal couples do. You haven't had to face that.

Mother: I think we could do that. In fact, we like to do things with the kids on the spur of the moment. But right now we have to pack so many clothes for Timmy. That can turn you off before you get started. Too much trouble, so forget it. I think that would change.

Therapist: What problems would that bring? We're talking about what would happen in your family if you did not have this symptom. You'd have to go out more; you'd have to decide when to go, where to go, and who to see.

Father: We both like to do that. If it is a nice day, we say, "Let's go down to the shore." Without the problem, we'd go earlier in the day and stay longer. That wouldn't be a negative thing if we were over the problem.

Therapist: Well, you don't know that, because you haven't had that situation.

Father: Well, that's true.

Therapist: One other consequence is that if a mother succeeds in getting over a problem like this with her child, she can be showing *her* mother that she's a better mother than *she* is. I don't know if that would be a difficulty you would have. . . . Sometimes a mother doesn't like her daughter to be competent and surpass her, and so daughters protect their mothers by not being very competent as mothers themselves. I wonder if you could tolerate being a better mother than your mother.

Father: This is a different way of thinking. You have to put yourself in someone else's shoes and look at the situation more objectively.

Therapist: I want you to look at it more objectively and consider all the consequences of getting over this.

Mother: I can tolerate being a good mother. I think what you brought up might be a problem, but only if I was closer to my mother. Actually, we're not very close. In fact, she doesn't like to visit and take care of my kids because of the messy pants.

Therapist: That would be a consequence, then. There wouldn't be an excuse for her not visiting, and she might come and see you more often, perhaps even get closer.

Mother: . . . I wouldn't mind being closer. Actually, if we were closer, we probably would discuss *her* problems, not my problems, since she prefers that.

Therapist: What sort of problems would your mother tell you about?

Mother: Oh, she drinks a bit, and my father has quite a drinking problem.

> The more that the mother talked about her family-of-origin, the more it became apparent that a closer relationship with them is not what she really wanted. This provided the therapist with the opportunity to reframe the boy's problem as an excuse, a service really, that allowed the mother some distance from her family. Throughout these strategic interventions, it was essential for the therapist to remain "deadpan," but benevolent when continuing to note how hard it would be on the family for all of them to be normal. As the negatives were developed more prominently, the parents started to become annoyed, but they remained polite.

Therapist: At the dinner table at home, you'll have to find something other than this problem to talk about. As you describe it, that seems to be what you talk about from when father comes home right through dinner.

Father: I think we would be able to find something else to talk about.

Mother: Yes, really. Pooping in the pants isn't our only subject of conversation.

Therapist: There are just quite a few changes that would come about in your lives if you didn't have this problem. These changes are the ones that couples indeed face when they get over such a problem during successful therapy. I am just warning you about these changes. As a mother, what will you do with yourself if you didn't have that laundry to do? What would you think about if you didn't have this problem? And what about the father/son relationship? Wouldn't you have to do more with the boy if the boy didn't have messy pants? But the main thing is: Could you tolerate being normal parents and a normal husband and wife going out together and enjoying yourselves? (Haley, 1984, pp. 176–182)

The following week the parents were supposed to come back, but the mother called and said she would rather not come that day. Timmy had had a bowel movement in the toilet the night before, and she didn't want to "rock the boat" by coming in and talking about it. She asked for another week before an interview. The therapist agreed and when they came in the next week, he found they had solved the problem. (Haley, 1984, pp. 182–183)

Mother: That Friday, for the first time, he did it in the toilet. He also did it Saturday and Sunday. Monday, he didn't have a bowel movement at all. On Tuesday, he had one in the toilet again. I just thought it was such a success that if we stayed away from therapy, it would give it a chance to settle into a routine . . . . The last two times, instead of us asking him, he came and told us he had to do it. Would we please put the seat on the toilet for him? That was the last two times.

Therapist: He hasn't soiled his pants in two weeks?

Mother: Not at all.

Therapist: This is really great! . . . It's kind of a sudden change. What do you think might have caused this change?

Father: We put some pressure on him. I spent about half an hour in the bathroom with him on Thursday trying to persuade him to go. By that time he was quite constipated. It had been more than a week since he had gone, and we were afraid of the physical consequences. So we were at a point where we were going to have to do something to clean him out. It would have to be an enema, I told him.

Timmy: (playing with toys in the corner) I do my bowel movements in my toilet now.

Father: Yes, you do. (turning back to the therapist) The threat of an enema was there when I talked to him Thursday. I let him try again Friday, before we were supposed to come here for our interview, but I went so far as to get the enema ready. At that point he obviously seemed to be weighing the choice between—well, I think between hurting himself by going, and getting the enema. I guess he decided that he was going to risk hurting himself. Once he did it, he was elated, and he did it again the following night. Then three nights in a row.

Therapist: That's great. My only reservation is that this is too sudden and too much of a change. Is it possible you might need to have a relapse because it happened so fast?

Father: That's possible, I suppose, but I believe he really has been afraid to do it for fear of hurting himself. I remember he once passed a big one in bed, and he actually cried out because it hurt. I think this was on his mind. Once he did it without hurting, he didn't seem to be afraid to do it anymore. He seems to like the idea of going every day. Now he even tells us when he has to go.

Therapist: You feel you can handle him like a normal child now? You don't need to go back the way he was? (mother laughs)

Father: Well, I'll tell you something. In just the last two weeks a lot of other things he was a problem about have changed. He's eating much better. The dinner table is more relaxed.

I come home from work and my wife is more relaxed. There's less friction between her and Timmy. And we can talk about *other* things when I get home.

Therapist: So there have been a lot of changes.

Father: I think so. We're more relaxed about the whole thing.

Therapist: . . . You really don't think you need to relapse on this problem?

Mother: I don't think so.

Father: No.

Therapist: . . . All right. Any other problems that concern you that you want to talk about?

Father: No, I can't think of any. But we still don't know why the boy had this fear. What do you think is inside him that would lead to this?

Therapist: Well, he's normal now, and I don't think that we need to explain normality. I think we can move on to other things. I was really wondering if there are any other family problems or marital problems.

Mother: I don't think we have any. I think we've got a very good marriage.

Father: I don't think there is a problem.

> Follow-up with this family confirmed that the boy was continuing to use the toilet in the manner for which it was designed. The whole family was tolerating "being normal" just fine. (Haley, 1984, pp. 183–185)

On Tuesday, February 13, 2007, Jay Haley died. He was married to Madeleine Richeport-Haley, who continues his work today.

Although the **Washington School of Strategic Family Therapy**, founded by Jay Haley and Cloe Madanes, gained a great deal of recognition in the United States, two other strategic training programs contributed to the development of this model: These training programs were located in the Center for Family Studies in Milan, Italy, and, as I have already mentioned, at the MRI in Palo Alto, California, the latter of which is really the birthplace of the strategic approach.

Each of these approaches to strategic process tends to be enacted in a slightly different form. An example of each of these models in action follows.

The MRI Model

MRI therapists believe that problems in families are simply solutions that are ineffective, given the circumstances. Nichols & Schwartz (2006) note that there are really three classes of problem-maintaining solutions, and each implies a different therapeutic strategy. In the first class, the client needs to act, but fails to; in the second class, the client needs to stop acting, but doesn't; and in the third class, the client tries to solve a problem at a level that is ineffective. For example, a family may deny that a problem exists when it does: Doing something is required, but no one is willing to do it. A teenager who drives recklessly and crashes the car three times, but is given the keys again and again might be a example of this position. Sometimes families try to solve a problem that really isn't a problem: Two children bicker over what television show to watch, and the parents step-in, announcing that they need to help the kids get along better before their fighting turns violent. And sometimes a family engages in solving a problem at one level when only working at another level will really solve the problem. For example, a son waits to be picked up by his divorced father so that they can go fishing together. At the last minute, the father has a business deal come up and sends the boy a check for $100 with a promise to go fishing later, a promise that is never fulfilled.

Another example of the MRI approach involves an incorrigible teenage girl and her family who came to therapy because nothing was working. She had already been

Paul Watzlawick

in trouble with the law and had been sent to live with relatives with no change in her behavior. Her parents, although at the end of their rope, were constantly trying to reason with her and restrict her behavior. This is an example of trying to solve a problem at one level when a different level is required: You can't reason with an unreasonable person. The MRI therapist ended the first sessions with the family by telling the girl that she had a lot of power over her parents: Her use of persistent nagging to wear her parents down was so effective that it was worth being in a constant state of rage, being banned from the family for short periods, or going to jail overnight. She would get used to these small prices paid for enormous power. She was asked to sit in the waiting room while the therapist worked with the parents to help them get used to this arrangement.

This communication (a) directed the teen to keep doing what she was already doing, a strong likelihood anyway; (b) suggested that the therapist was in **coalition** with her and there to help the parents, thereby increasing the likelihood of their compliance in therapy; and (c) set the stage for interrupting a pattern in which the parents tried to reason with their daughter's unreasonableness. Toward this end, the parents were asked to act unreasonably in the face of their daughter's nagging, since reasoning clearly wasn't working. The parents were asked to teach the child the meaning *quid pro quo*. They were directed to say to their daughter something like: "I would like you to do something for me. Of course, I can't make you do it, but I am hoping that you will." This was to be said once, and if nothing happened, then the parents were to become reasonably unreasonable. Maybe the parents would be late in picking the daughter up for an important appointment or wreck a favorite piece of clothing in the wash. If the daughter complained, the parents were to respond that they didn't know what was wrong with them. They might be sorry, but that would be it, unless, of course, the mother also wanted to claim that she was depressed, which might explain her behavior (Segal, 1991).

This process, over time, interrupted the interactive patterns of the parents arguing with their daughter. Although she initially increased her efforts to draw them into a fight, she eventually reduced her fighting and even engaged in what the family considered more considerate behavior.

On Saturday, March 31, 2007, in the evening, one the MRI models most prolific writers and theorists, Paul Watzlawick (pronounced Vats-la-vick) died peacefully in his home. He was 85 years old.

The Milan Model

The original Milan group included Maria Selvini Palazzoli, Luigi Boscolo, Gianfranco Cecchin, and Guiliana Prata (1978). Their approach was founded on the belief that families operated paradoxically, wanting change in a problem or problem person, but demanding that everything stay the same. Using counterparadox, reframing, positive connotations to problems, and circular questioning, developed from studying both the MRI and Washington School models of strategic therapy, they were able to help families successfully, seeing them as a team at one month intervals. In 1980, Boscolo and Cecchin split from Selvini Palazzoli and Prata, preferring to develop new training methods. Before Selvini Palazzoli and Prata went their separate ways in 1982, they focused on an **invariant intervention** with families who were seeking help for anorexic or psychotic children (Becvar & Becvar, 2003).

This intervention required the parents to leave the home before dinner on at least two occasions, giving the children a note that indicated they would be back later. They were not to give the children any information about these absences either before they left or after they returned. The purpose of this intervention was to break up coalitions between one or both of the parents and the problem child, and to strengthen the spousal/parental subsystem. This prescription became part of the following case.

A middle-aged couple with three daughters came to therapy. The oldest was Carla, aged 20 and suffering with anorexia, Olga was 15, and the youngest child, Alice, was 6 years old. There had been a fourth pregnancy a couple of years earlier, which the parents decided together to end by abortion. This was supposedly a family secret, kept from the children. However, an early call from the father indicated that Carla knew, but her mother did not know that Carla knew—nor did he want the issue coming up in therapy in front of the children. The Milan therapists brought this secret out in the open by consulting by phone with the father and mother.

During the first session, everyone, especially the father, kept in hiding. Still, it became clear that Carla was an intelligent young woman who had done very well in school in spite of the fact that her parents never supported her. Her sister, Olga, was favored by both parents for no apparent reason. Alice stayed quiet and seemed rather dull to the therapists. The family went on vacation to Egypt between the first and second session, and Carla and her parents came back upset, because Olga had joined up there with some other young people and showed up only for meals, ignoring her family the rest of the time.

Therapist:	Who do you think was most offended by Olga's making herself scarce?
Carla:	Dad.
Therapist:	When did you first notice that Dad considered you nothing but a fine, sensible girl, whereas it was Olga he was really enthralled with, even to the point of having jealous feelings about her?
Carla:	(while Dad remains poker-faced) I never noticed any such thing.
Therapist:	But it is written all over your face—how little you relish having to drink tea with a bunch of old [fogies] while your Dad sits fuming at Olga's gallivanting about with a crowd of young people. I suspect that Olga has discovered one of the oldest of womanly wiles: She who plays hard-to-get will get chased.
Mother:	(with Olga laughing sardonically) Olga has been playing the femme fatale for 2 years, even during our vacations at our lake home: She goes off with a whole lot of boys no one knows anything about. And yes, my husband resents this very much.
Therapist:	(to Carla) How come you haven't caught on yet to the fact that your being around all the time, and so easily available, has caused the glamour to wear thin? Familiarity breeds contempt, you know.
Carla:	(angry) Well, I *have* to stay around because of Alice, see? And Alice needs me more than ever right now.
Therapist:	. . . Alice needs you more than ever right now. Who made you feel you should be the one to have to take care of Alice, seeing that Mom is not up to doing a proper job of it.
Carla:	(under her breath) Dad . . . but not because Mom isn't up to it, it's just that she's so nervous, she makes a lot of mistakes . . . .
Dad:	(emphatically, stressing every word) I never said anything of the kind to Carla.
Carla:	(jumping to her feet, standing straight in front of her father, and shouting) Oh yes you did, and for years and years too. Do you want me to repeat your exact words, here, in front of all of them? Do you? You started this when I was 8 years old and Mom got

sick. When I was a little girl, the two of you would squabble constantly, and I'd always take your part because you were my idol, you were God, and she was the neurotic one, and I'd always side with Dad because I'd think, "Dad's the one who's right," and I went on thinking Dad was right all the time, until I found out it's he who is to blame, really, more than anyone else, and that I had this idea of my mother lodged in my head because he put it there.

Dad: (raising his hand in a request to speak, and then speaking formally) Kindly allow me, doctor, to say that I consider it my duty now to shed proper light on the matter. My wife has always been neurotic. She is a sick woman. Her dear, departed mother knew this all too well, and she spoke to my parents about it, and her sisters know about it, too.

Therapist: Well, I must say that if I were in your wife's shoes, with everyone in the know about my predicament—my mother, my husband, my in-laws, my daughters—all of them considering me a neurotic, and my firstborn daughter enlisted by her father to patch up all the mistakes I made in Alice's bringing up—well, I wouldn't feel very comfortable, to say the least. (Selvini Palazzoli, Cirillo, Selvini, & Sorrentino, 1989, pp. 73–77)

Throughout these interchanges, including the comments of the therapist, the mother showed no reaction, sitting quietly with her head down. During the next several months, the Milan therapists saw only the parents, prescribed the invariant intervention with increasingly longer disappearances, and eventually removing Carla from responsibility for her mother and sister. As Carla assumed responsibility only for herself, her anorexia became less useful in her life.

Key Concepts

It was at MRI that Gregory Bateson, who was married to Margaret Mead, brought his anthropological interest in family process to a group of practitioner-scholars who would eventually develop a communications model for understanding schizophrenia (Bateson, Jackson, Haley, & Weakland, 1956). They introduced theorists and practitioners to the concept of the double bind. A double bind is a situation in which (a) two or more people in a significant relationship have repeated experiences in which a negative injunction ("Don't do . . . something") is paired with a second, equally powerful, contradictory injunction, and (b) both injunctions are enforced by the threat of punishment, demand a response, and allow no perceived possibility of escape. As you can see, double binds are more than simple, contradictory messages. If the victim does not fear punishment and does not feel trapped by the requirement to respond to both messages, there is no sense of being bound. A parent sees his daughter holding hands with another young woman at school. They are talking and laughing together. When she comes home, her father calls her into his den, and the double bind begins: "I saw you with Ann Harper this afternoon. I need to know if the two of you are . . . (pause) . . . well, lesbians. I don't know if I will ever be able to love you again if you are. I don't even know how I will stand having you in the house, but I need to know. So, are you? Are you a homosexual?" This is exactly the kind of double bind that "closets" millions of teenagers in America.

This concentration on communication and the conflicts that exist between overt messages and metacommunications (messages about messages) would influence numerous family therapists outside of the strategic world: Virginia Satir, Murray Bowen, and Salvador Minuchin, to name a few. MRI therapists believe that every message contains both information (content) and a directive (or command). A woman says to her partner: "There is a dead mouse in the garage." Immediately, the partner gets up and goes to remove the dead mouse, placing it in a plastic bag in the garbage. In this interchange, information is provided (a dead mouse has been located), a directive has been implied and understood (the partner should pick it up and clear it out), and there is a metacommunication that is more covert (the woman is in charge and therefore the partner should act immediately).

To be human, therefore, is to communicate and strategic therapists believe no one can *not* communicate. All behavior communicates both information and directives and, again, one cannot *not* behave. The directive (or command) part of any message always includes the person's definition of power in the relationship in which the communication takes place. When a child says, "I had a bad dream (information), the tears in her eyes command that the parent make it better. There is a sense of helplessness expressed by the child even though, paradoxically, the child is powerful enough to direct a specific action from the parent.

Over time, families elevate certain command messages to family rules. Family rules are not laws as much as they are regular and routine ways of interacting. Such rules are revealed when therapists track repetitive sequences in family process. The purpose of family rules is to maintain homeostasis: Families, like all systems, resist change and want to stay in the routines that have become known and familiar. In the strategic models, there is really no underlying individual or group motivation for family behavior. Rather, causality is viewed as circular with every part of the family affecting every other part. Families, therefore, develop and follow rules; they function within patterned interactions designed to keep things just the way they are. These patterns involve communications and responses called feedback loops. When family process functions in rule-oriented routines, allowing little or no change, the family is said to be operating within a negative feedback loop. On the other hand, when a family member's behavior becomes a problem and the response of the rest of the family only makes the problem worse, the family is now engaged in a positive feedback loop.

When a child's behavior gets worse no matter what the parents do, it is likely that they are responding to the child in a rigid manner governed by family rules about everything from family roles and authority to expectations and acceptable behavior. Since the response is only making the problem worse (a positive feedback loop), the wise thing would be for the parent to do the opposite of what he or she is doing—or at least do something different. But the parent does not perceive a different approach as an option, because it is against the rules. Strategic therapists, therefore, are not oriented toward behavior change (or first-order change), but rather seek a change in the family rules (second-order change). Toward this end, one of the most common strategic interventions is reframing, which is defined below.

In all models of strategic family therapy, the problem is not addressed as a symptom of some other systemic dysfunction (as in Bowenian or structural family therapy). Rather, the problem brought by the family is treated as real and is to be solved. This is a pragmatic approach based on the notion that change occurs through a family carrying out a therapist's directives and changing its transactions. Understanding and insight are neither required nor sought. No value is placed on the therapist's interpretation. Nor is the focus of therapy on growth or resolving issues from the past; rather, it is on solving problems in the present. Therapy in these models tends to be brief, pragmatic, behavioral, and focused on process rather than content. The process orientation deals with who is doing what to whom under what conditions. The presenting problem is seen as both the real problem and a metaphor for the family system's functioning.

In the Washington School of Strategic Family Therapy, considerable emphasis is given to power, control, and hierarchies in families right in the therapy sessions. Haley

Cloe Madanes

(1976) developed a belief in problem hierarchies while he was working with Minuchin and the structural family therapists. Dysfunctional hierarchies were often characterized as rigid, resistant to change, disordered in their use of power, and almost obsessive about control. For Haley, every family problem involved a dysfunctional hierarchy, and his use of *ordeals*, was designed to reorganize the family into a more functional hierarchy, complete with clear boundaries and an appropriate use of power. Cloe Madanes (1981, 1984) also sought to confront problems directly. She was particularly interested in the ways that children used problems to engage and/or rescue a parent. In her work, helping children to engage their parents more openly clearly tended to make symptomatic behavior unnecessary. Madanes shares with the Milan group the belief that the child often develops symptoms to protect others caught in a network of family coalitions.

Therapy Goals

The MRI Model

This model is so behavioral in approach that it can be described in a two-step process: Define the problem and then resolve the problem. When the problem is resolved, therapy has reached its first and only goal and the counseling sessions are over. Indeed, part of defining the problem also is defining clear, achievable, measurable goals. This process is so concrete that the client tendency to talk in abstractions or seek nirvana is all but negated. Although reframing and paradoxical interventions often can be seen as cognitive interventions, they are simply means to an end—and that end is always behavior change.

MRI therapists would argue that people are not pathological; they simply live in systems that get stuck in problem-maintaining patterns. It is not their job, therefore, to be concerned about problems or issues that might seem obvious to others, but are not identified by the clients. Improvement in the form of movement forward is a more than acceptable end. When people take their car to a garage for repairs, they want to know what to do to get the car moving again. They do not seek a complete re-modeling of the car, nor do they want a master's degree in auto mechanics. Similarly, there are no perfect families. When a family is moving again, the job is done.

The Washington School

The goal of Haley's strategic therapy is to resolve a presenting problem by focusing on behavioral sequences. Haley is even more behavioral in his approach than the MRI people. He has little use for insight as a goal of therapy. He is concerned about getting people to behave differently, and he is unconcerned with helping people figure out why they act as they do. It is his view that behavior change is the main goal of therapy, because if there is a change in behavior, feelings will change as a result. He hopes to prevent repetition of maladaptive sequences and attempts to introduce a greater number of alternatives. The intent of strategic interventions is to shift the family organization so that a presenting problem is no longer functional. Washington School strategic therapists have short-range goals that guide their interventions.

Strategic family therapists assume that people often develop problems during transitions from one developmental stage to the next; therapy moves the family forward to the appropriate stage of family life. Haley (1973) identifies these phases of family life as (1) the courtship period, (2) the early years of marriage, (3) childbirth and rearing of children, (4) the middle years of marriage, (5) weaning parents from children, and (6) retirement and old age.

In the last ten years or so, Madanes (1990) has adopted a more humanistic approach to strategic therapy, and she currently believes that harmony and balance should be goals directly sought in family therapy. Similar to William Glasser's (1998) beliefs about individual needs, Madanes thinks family members need to love and be loved, find fulfillment in work, play, and seek joy. This is facilitated when clients come into balance individually and with each other, such that reason and emotion are connected and complementary, doing good for others is balanced with self-care, and love foreshadows hurt but also helps one through it.

Echoing the sentiments of Virginia Satir, Madanes (1990) states:

> Kindness and compassion, empathy and forgiveness are not qualities of an individual but interactions that develop and are sustained in the context of the family. To encourage kindness in ourselves and in others is consistent with every model of therapy. The practice of altruism is at the basis of all therapy, since therapy itself is a calling that requires an interest in doing good for others. (p. 13)

The Milan Model

Consistent with the MRI and Haley models they had studied, the early Milan therapists were also behaviorally oriented. But since they viewed dysfunctional family patterns as **family games** and sought to disrupt these processes, they began to rely more and more on game exposure and reframing motivation. These were clearly more-cognitive interventions, but no less strategic in nature. The power in family games was in maintaining the *status quo*, and it was still the therapist's job to take a stand that would redirect family interaction into more useful channels.

Maria Selvini Palazzoli

Selvini Palazzoli and Prata split and experimented for some time with what they called the *invariant prescription*. This directive to the family had the clear goal of strengthening the bond between the parents and breaking up the parent–child coalitions that were responsible for maintaining the family's games. Since family games in this model always refer to painful and disturbing interactions, one of the goals of this model is to develop more-flexible and open communication patterns in the family. In the last 10 years, Selvini Palazzoli has left the strategic model altogether and has begun to engage in insight-oriented, long-term therapy.

Boscolo and Cecchin left the strategic model even earlier, preferring to focus on a more collaborative model that features circular questioning and joint goal setting with families. What they bring to therapy is a curiosity and interest that is enacted from a de-centered or not-knowing position. Indeed, their work shares with the social constructionists the goal of making clients experts in their own lives. It is from this model that **reflecting teams** (Andersen, 1991) developed in Norway. This model also has strong ties to **linguistic therapy** (Anderson, 1997) and **narrative therapy** (White & Epston, 1990): All three postmodern approaches to individual and family practice are discussed in a later chapter.

The Therapist's Role and Function

In the early stages of strategic family therapy, the therapist's role was that of a consultant, an expert, and a stage director. Clearly, the therapist was in charge of the session. There was very little focus on the client/therapist relationship; instead, the therapist was directive and an authority figure. This was true in both the MRI model and in the work of Jay Haley.

Because Haley (1976) believed that direct educational methods were of little value, he tended to be unwilling to explain himself to his clients; instead, he operated covertly. In this model, the therapist is primarily interested in the control of power within the therapeutic relationship. Haley believed that the responsibility for initiating change rested with the therapist, not with the client. Because he viewed his task as assuming the responsibility for changing the organization of a family and resolving the problems that it brings to therapy, he operated directively, giving the members specific directives on what they were to do, both inside and outside of the therapy sessions. These instructions were aimed at changing the manner in which clients behaved with other family members, as well as with the therapist; they also guided the development of both the overt and covert interventions that may follow.

A basic feature of Haley's approach is that it is the therapist's responsibility to plan a strategy for solving the client's problems (Haley, 1973). At the initial phase of therapy, clear goals are established, a plan is developed, and specific therapeutic strategies are carefully designed to address problems. Because therapy focuses on the social context of human dilemmas, the therapist's task is to design interventions aimed at the client's social situation (Madanes, 1981). In the last decade, Madanes (1990), introduced relational, humanistic dimensions to strategic therapy. For her, the role of the therapist includes the development and modeling of **altruism**, and altruism includes capacities for caring and empathy, understanding and forgiveness, compassion and connection, and balance and harmony.

The more-postmodern models developed in Milan and the United States during the 1990s call on the therapist to function as an investigator. These models are very collaborative. Where the original function of the MRI "one-down" position had a manipulative intent even when it was genuinely applied, Boscolo and Cecchin, as well as the solution-focused/solution-oriented therapists we shall consider in the next chapter, seem completely dedicated to a client-empowering inquiry process. Optimism, persistence, and anticipatory inquiries about new possibilities are all parts of the role and function of the therapist.

Techniques

Like structural family therapists, strategic therapists tend to track sequences, use reframing techniques, and issue directives. Key techniques shared by strategic family therapists are joining, reframing, directives, and paradoxical interventions.

Joining.   This process has a similar meaning to that used by structural family therapists. It is used to help clients feel comfortable and to help the therapist, at least initially, stay neutral in the counseling process. Haley (1976) refers to this initial process with families as the social stage of counseling. Early models of strategic joining included the goal of going with the resistance of the family in order to more effectively redirect the family or its members. As the strategic models have evolved into more-collaborative approaches, the process of joining as a partnership is often central to the work.

Reframing.   This process can mean different things at different times. At times, problematic behavior patterns become entrenched and rigid. Reframing provides a means of reinterpreting the behavior and its context. In general, it aims at changing perceptions or interpretations used by family members in maintaining either family homeostasis or family problems. It can be used, as with the Milan group, to assign positive connotations to problems and family interactions. It also is used to highlight positive intentions behind otherwise problematic behaviors. For example, a father's workaholic approach to life can be reframed as his way of demonstrating care and concern for his family. The ultimate objective of a reframing technique is to help family members view problematic behaviors from a different vantage point. From a new vantage point, an intractable problem may become solvable.

Directives.   In strategic models, there are really only three modes of communication a therapist can use. The therapist can ask a question, seeking information or perhaps suggesting a different perspective. The therapist can use a declarative sentence as in paraphrasing, reflecting, or noting a process or change in process that seems important to the family. The third mode, **directives**, is used to create experiments with new behaviors or processes, to undermine or reverse dysfunctional patterns or sequences, or, as in the Washington School, to provide suggestions that address the specific needs of the case.

For example, when Haley (1976) discovered that a father was siding indirectly with his daughter (who was wetting her bed) against his wife, he directed the father "to wash the sheets when the daughter wets the bed. The task will tend to disengage daughter and father or cure the bedwetting" (p. 60). This is a simple, straightforward directive designed to change the system and end the problem. Straightforward directives include giving advice, making suggestions, coaching, and giving ordeal-therapy assignments (Haley, 1984).

In the MRI model, directives are used to encourage clients to act when inaction has failed to address the problem or to stop acting when there is really no problem to solve. Most often, however, families in this model are directed to act in a different way, because the current way involves trying to solve problems at the wrong level for change.

Recently, Selvini Palazzoli and her associates in Milan have started using an invariant prescription. This, too, is a directive aimed at breaking up dysfunctional coalitions between parents and children.

Paradoxical Interventions.   Paradoxical interventions are directives that either counter the families own paradoxical living or change the positive feedback loops that maintain or escalate the presenting problems. The most common paradoxical directives include **prescribing the symptom, restraining family change**, or even **amplifying family difficulties**. Haley (1976) assumes that families both seek his help and resist it at the same time, often resulting in a power play between family members and the therapist. By using the indirect procedures first formulated by Milton Erickson, the counselor can deal with an individual's resistance to change creatively and therapeutically. Haley believes that paradoxical strategies force the family to change.

The most useful paradoxical interventions are designed so that the clients win whether they follow the directive or not; that is, change should occur regardless of the stance the family takes in relation to the therapeutic paradox. For example, a client who complains that he or she cannot sleep may be directed to stay awake—and perhaps use the time to develop a list of things that can be done for the person's partner later in the day. This is called prescribing the symptom, and it is designed so that if the directive is followed, the client has complied with therapy and changed the perception and process of it. If the directive is resisted, the client sleeps and the problem is over.

Similarly, a client who is depressed may be told: "Maybe you should not give up this symptom too quickly. It gets you the attention that you say you want. If you got rid of your depression, your family might not notice you. And further, your depression is providing something needed in your family—even if we don't know what that is yet. Change that is too quick may be too hard for your family to handle. So your family needs to go slowly into any possible changes." This paradoxical intervention is called a restraining technique, perfected at MRI, especially by John Weakland. Again, if the client maintains the symptom, the client demonstrates control over it and is no longer helpless to change it. If the client chooses to resist the directive and let go of the depression, the problem is not merely controlled but eliminated.

Process and Techniques at MRI

At least initially in the development of this strategic therapy model, the MRI therapists considered their work to be brief therapy and would limit the sessions with a family to no more than 10 (Segal, 1991). The MRI process involves introducing the family members to their treatment process and its limitations. This usually occurs after the family and the therapist have met and some attempt has been made to put the family at ease. Most often, everyone in the interview is encouraged to use first names. The therapist seeks to assume a **one-down position** with the family, diminishing any idea of the therapist as expert. During assessments, therapists use the one-down position to clarify what they are hearing: "Could you repeat that for me? I didn't quite get it." Later, when directives are issued, the therapist again might suggest that "there is no real significance to these suggestions: just something that might help a little, if at all."

After an introduction of the process, the therapist inquires about the nature of the problem that brought people into therapy. It is not uncommon for couples or families to frame the problem as a negative they want to avoid: "We want the fighting to stop." MRI therapists seek to reframe this description by asking, "If this problem were coming to an end, what would you notice as a difference?" The therapist might also ask: What is the problem making the client(s) do—perhaps even unwillingly.

Next, problem-maintaining behaviors are assessed. What have the person and other family members done to try to solve the problem? How have these solution trials worked out? Generally, many of the attempted solutions have a single process in common. Reversing that process will be key to ending the problem. For example, solutions related to anxiety about public speaking all may share the common goal of perfect delivery. Therefore, any directive or **homework** assignment that makes perfection impossible also will release the person from the anxiety.

MRI therapists believe that change does not happen in counseling sessions: It happens between sessions. Setting goals for treatment that engage the family members in real action is essential to this model. When a change in perspective is sought, the most common approach is to use reframing. When changes in patterns, interactions, or behaviors are sought, homework, directives, and paradoxical interventions characterize the most common **behavioral interventions**. Each new behavior is presented as a possibility, but it is laid out step-by-step in very specific, concrete terms.

Termination is based on effectively reaching a state in which problems have improved or have been eliminated. That is, there is no need to keep clients in therapy once they have reached the desired goals. Segal (1991) lists three criteria for termination:

(a) a small but significant change has been made in the problem,

(b) the change appears durable, and

(c) the patient implies or states that she or he can handle things on her or his own. (p. 199)

Process and Techniques at the Washington School

Haley and Madanes developed ordeal therapy, which is a clinical method for working strategically with marital or family dysfunction (Haley, 1984). Strategic ordeals provide ritual challenges that are designed to be more difficult than the family problem, and they facilitate a bonding among family members who go through the ordeal together. Madanes (1990) applied this approach to families in which an older child had sexually molested a younger one; she required the family to insist that the perpetrator kneel down in front of the molested child, confess the crime, and beg for forgiveness. The ordeal was not complete unless the confession and begging were sincerely enacted, and the parents were put in charge of rating the level of sincerity expressed.

Strategic therapy as taught and practiced by Haley and Madanes starts with common, everyday, friendly social greetings. The purpose of this social phase of therapy is to help everyone relax and feel as comfortable as possible. These strategic therapists often start with the father to augment his participation in the session, but the next phase is not complete until each person present has given his or her perspective on the presenting problem. Haley views symptoms as a form of communication aimed at gaining control over other family members. For instance, a child's acting-out behavior may symbolize a way to communicate his or her fear of an impending divorce. It is not unusual for Haley, like Minuchin, to ask the family to discuss the various perspectives shared among themselves and to bring the process into an interactional phase in which patterns actually are demonstrated. Embedded in this process is an inquiry into family hierarchy and power, which is revealed as family members describe and enact the problems they face. Madanes and Haley generally end their first session with some form of goal-setting. In subsequent sessions, they use indirect methods of provoking the parents and the children to interact and communicate in a way that would make the symptoms unnecessary.

In writing about the elements of strategic family therapy, Madanes (1981) describes the use of strategic interventions. Each problem is defined as involving at least two people. It is the therapist's job to figure out who is involved in the problem and in what way. The therapist then decides on which interventions will reorganize the family most effectively so that the presenting problem will no longer serve the same function. Interventions are designed to involve certain family members with one another or to disengage other members of a family.

Strategic therapists monitor the outcomes of their directives. If a strategy is not working after a short time, they will design a new one. In working with a family, they freely borrow any technique from one another's approaches if it proves to be useful in dealing with a presenting problem.

Haley maintained that his methods, including the use of paradoxical interventions, are not overly manipulative, because all forms of therapy utilize interpersonal influence and depend on the therapist's expertise in solving a family problem. It should be pointed out that all forms of paradoxical intervention do not have to rely so heavily on the power base, authority, and confrontational style of the therapist. For example, Madanes (1981, 1984) has designed techniques for working with a family that are less confrontational than Haley's. Her approach tends to be gentler: She uses humor, fantasy, and playfulness, all of which are a part of her **pretend techniques**. She might ask a child to pretend to have symptoms and the family to pretend to help the child. Madanes views the problem from a metaphorical standpoint. Her goal is to open up possibilities for creating more-adaptive behavioral patterns and for the families to abandon dysfunctional or symptomatic patterns of behaving.

Process and Techniques in Milan

The Milan therapists essentially engaged in longer-term, brief therapy. Similar to the MRI therapists, the Milan group would see a family for 10 sessions, but they would schedule appointments a month apart, taking almost a year to complete therapy in some cases. They always worked as a team, with one of them interviewing the family and the others working behind a one-way mirror. During the first stage of therapy, the team would meet to formulate an initial hypothesis or guess about the presenting problem: This was called the presession. At the actual meeting (the session), the initial hypothesis would be tested through observation and revised as necessary. About 40 minutes into the session, the entire team would meet without the family to devise an intervention. The interviewer would then return to the family to implement the intervention. In the early years, the intervention was usually either a **positive connotation** in which the problem, as well as every family member's behavior, was construed as effective in preserving family harmony, or as a ritual designed to help the whole family act in a new way that challenged rigid family rules or undermined dysfunctional coalitions. And some rituals were designed to highlight the positive connotations associated with the family: "Each night, we would like all of you to go to every other person and verbally express your understanding of how their behavior serves the family harmony." Whatever the prescription and no matter how the family reacted, the therapy team would meet after the family left for a postsession discussion. In the postsession, the reactions of family members were analyzed, and preparations for the next meeting, a month later, were made (Boscolo, Cecchin, Hoffman, & Penn, 1987). During subsequent sessions, the team often would see only the parents.

Because strategic interventions almost always led to some resistance from the family, Milan therapists adopted a stance of neutrality. They based this posture on the belief that all problems were systemic and causation was circular, not linear, so the therapist should be careful not to align or take sides with any member of the family: They should be neutral, and support the whole system. Nichols and Schwartz (2006) note: "This neutrality was often manifest as distance, so that the therapists delivered these dramatic interventions while acting aloof; not surprisingly, families often became angry and didn't return" (p. 163).

During the 1980s, Selvini Palazzoli and Prata, having split from the rest of the original Milan team, gave up paradoxical interventions and experimented with what they called the invariant prescription. Working with families suffering from member psychosis or anorexia, this prescription was used to break-up the triangles and dysfunctional coalitions that often seemed to be present. The prescription was designed to strengthen the parental/spousal subsystem while disengaging the child from patterns that maintained the problem. The prescription to the parents reads:

> Keep everything that has been said during this session absolutely secret from everyone. Should your daughters ask questions about it, say that the therapist has ordered everything to be kept only between her and the two of you. On at least two occasions between now and your next scheduled appointment, you are to "disappear" from home before dinner without any forewarning. Leave a note worded as follows: "We shall not be in tonight." Each time you go out, pick some place to meet where you are reasonably sure no one will recognize you. If, when you get back home, your daughters ask you where on earth you've been, simply smile and say: "That concerns only the two of us." Each of you is also to keep a sheet of paper, well out of everyone's sight, on which to jot down personal observations of how each of your daughters has reacted to her parents' unusual behavior. At our next meeting, which will again be with only the two of you, each of you will read your notes out loud. (Selvini Palazzoli et al., 1989, p. 16)

In the 1990s, Selvini Palazzoli retreated from strategic therapy and her work with the invariant prescription to return to long-term therapy with individuals and families. Similarly, Boscolo and Cecchin, after their split from the original team, became enamored with the more-collaborative approaches that would become characteristic of postmodern, social constructionism. They began to emphasize the centerpiece of their interview process, called circular questioning. Circular questioning is essentially relational questioning. It asks family members to respond to probes designed to elicit descriptions of relational processes. Rather than asking a client how he or she experiences personal depression, these Milan therapists asked: "Who is most upset when Maria is depressed?" If the answer is "Dad," the next question follows from that answer: "What does Dad do to try and help?" or even "How does your mother react when your father tries to help Maria?" Circular questions have the effect of revealing family patterns and getting the family to think beyond linear causation in relation to their problems. Similar to the inquiry processes of solution-focused/solution-oriented and narrative therapies, the effectiveness of these questions is ensured when they flow from an authentic curiosity on the part of the therapist.

A Strategic Family Therapist With the Quest Family

Paul and Jane Quest bring all four of their children to the first meeting with a strategic family therapist. After meeting each of the members of the Quest family, the strategic therapist starts by asking, "So what's the problem? What brought all of you here today?" Jane notes that she is really concerned about Jason and Luke and their level of aggressive and violent behavior. She doesn't feel she can cope without help, and the family seems to be "falling apart." Paul feels a great part of the problem is that he is away from home at critical times during each day.

Amy and Ann sit together next to their father and across from the two empty chairs placed close to the mother for the boys. Jason and Luke are up and moving around. Addressing Paul first, the therapist begins.

Paul: Well, the reality is that these boys were horribly treated when they were very young. They were hurt and abused in ways that are too horrible for most people to imagine. I don't even like to think about it. Whatever they do, they have had much worse happen to them: Cigarette burns on their bodies, beatings, and punishments that adults could not withstand.

Therapist: And now they're doing the same thing to others?

Paul: Yes, that's right. It's always something. And I am very tied up in my work, which makes it hard for me to provide the kinds of things that the boys might need.

Jane: I don't disagree with anything that Paul said. The boys have had more tragedy in their young lives than I could stand. They were hurt, and they lost their mother. Their father is court-ordered to stay away from them and, if they ever find him, he will probably be implicated in their mother's death. How do young children comprehend any of that? I have always felt so sorry for them. I wanted to erase all the bad when they first came to us. I wanted them to have a childhood like Ann and Amy had, but it is just too much to do by myself. It's too hard. I am exhausted all the time.

Therapist: Tell me, Paul, is it likely that you will be able to spend more time at home and with the boys, or is the effort to raise these two mainly going to stay with Jane.

Paul: I don't foresee the demands on my time at work being less. I try to come home in emergencies, but I really want the emergencies to come to an end. We're a big family now; we need the money I make.

Ann begins to express her concern that, unless her dad is home more, nothing will get better. She believes her mother won't ask for his help, but it is her opinion that only her father can handle Jason and Luke. A phone next to the therapist rings, and the therapist stops to talk to a therapy team that is observing behind a one-way mirror. After listening to the team, the therapist speaks for the team.

Therapist: The team believes that money is important: It is a way in which families acknowledge who is in the family and who is out. The team feels that it should be part of the parents' way of handling matters with the children. We are willing to pay each of the four children a dollar if all of them can get through a week without hitting anyone, hurting anyone or anything. If all of them make it, they all get the money. If even one of them fails, they all fail. So if Amy gets upset with Ann and hits her, the money is gone. (turning to the boys) Jason and Luke, would you like to be part of this game?

Jason: Not hit for a dollar?

Therapist: Yep. No one can hit anyone else, or break anything on purpose, or hurt animals or each other. No violence of any kind. If you all do it, I will give your mother the money, and she can give it to each of you. I am wondering, Paul, if you would be willing to match any amount that I might give out in this deal.

Paul:	Paying the kids for good behavior? Do you really think this is a good idea?
Therapist:	Don't they pay you for your good work at the hospital and in your clinic?
Paul:	Yes, they do, but . . .
Therapist:	Isn't that in part how you know you belong there and are of worth?
Paul:	So you want me to pay the boys.
Therapist:	No, that would be Jane's job. She's the parent at home. You and I are just responsible for getting the money to her.
Jane:	Is this just for the boys, because Amy and Ann don't hit.
Therapist:	No. They are all your children, and they are all in this together. I'm as concerned and hopeful for Amy and Ann in all of this as I am for Jason and Luke. The point is that they either all make it, or none of them do. Jane, you are in charge of observing it all and deciding whether they get the money or not.

The phone rings again.

Therapist:	The team believes that we need to define violence more clearly. In this family, it is using any form of body contact, head, body, hand, foot, to hurt others or do damage to other people or animals or things. And there has to be the intention of hurting: You have to want to hurt or make someone cry. Now, what if some hitting went on and you weren't in the room, Mom, and somebody comes and says, "Mom, Mom, they hit me, but you didn't see it." Would it count? (Haley & Richeport-Haley, 2003, p. 82)
Jason and Luke:	No.
Jason:	It wouldn't count.
Therapist:	So, do you all agree that your mother has to see the violence for it to count?
Jason:	Yes.
Therapist:	Amy and Ann, do you agree?
Amy and Ann:	Yes. Yes.

At the beginning of the second interview, the therapist announces that she would like to know about how the no-violence week went and whether money should be given out, but she will need to save that for the end of the session. First, she wants to get something very clear.

Therapist:	I think it is important for everyone here to know where the family stands in relation to their new arrangement. I am specifically concerned about whether there is any idea in anyone's mind about Jason and Luke being returned to foster care. Are they in the family or not?
Paul:	Well, I think it obviously starts with me. You are thinking that I really don't want the boys, don't you? Well, that's not true. I admit that I was unsure about it when Jane brought it up, and maybe I don't do all that I should with them, but they are ours now. That's not going to change.
Therapist:	Actually, Paul, I wasn't thinking it was you who had doubts.
Jane:	I admit that I have wondered about whether I have put too much on our family with this. Maybe we can't . . . maybe I can't raise Jason and Luke. But I have never heard Paul say that the boys were staying no matter what.
Therapist:	So what does that mean to you?
Jane:	I don't know if we are a family yet, but we have to become one.
Therapist:	No. You are already a family. You just have to decide whether you like being one or not.
Jane:	And do Amy and Ann believe that we are a family?

Therapist: That doesn't really matter. Siblings seldom get along—not very often. Someone is always secretly wishing that one of the other children would disappear or go away. But then someone outside of the family does something to hurt or threaten one of them, and they are all for one and one for all. You can't judge anything by what brothers and sisters feel at any moment in time.

Paul: We are keeping Jason and Luke. That's not in question.

Jane: I'm with him.

> The therapist turns the conversation to what real effects the conviction of being a family will have for Jane and Paul—and what effects they think it might have on the four children. Part of what they discuss is the experience that Paul had on the weekend when he took Jason and Luke fishing without Jane or his daughters. It had been a great day. Jane had used the time to take Amy and Ann to a movie.

Therapist: We are getting close to the end of our time today. So do we give out the money or not.

Amy: I guess we don't, because actually Luke hit Jason yesterday when he was mad at him.

Jane: Yes, but it was the only time all week. And later, Luke came to try to be good by helping me with the dishes. They have to be rewarded for their effort. They really tried.

Therapist: I don't know. Paul, what do you think?

Paul: I think Jane is right. Maybe we could compromise and give 50 cents each for the effort. And we could give everyone another chance for this next week.

Therapist: Okay, that works for me.

> Paul and the therapist each give Jane the money, and Jane gives it out to each of the four children. Amy and Ann take the dollar politely and quietly while Jason and Luke jump up and down in excitement.
>
> It was 2 weeks before the next meeting could be arranged. There was no contact between the family and the therapist, so any differences in the family would be the focus of the first part of the next session.

Therapist: So how are things better?

Jane: The boys did not hit or hurt anyone or anything for the last 2 weeks . . . since we were last here. But Jason still does things that he is not supposed to do. He took mashed potatoes to his room and fed them to the cat. He drank half of a large bottle of mouthwash. I thought he was going to get sick or drunk or something.

Therapist: You know, Jason, I believe this is too big a burden for you to carry all alone. I appreciate what you are doing to be the family's designated problem child, but you really shouldn't have to carry this burden all by yourself. I have a magic wand. Did you know that? (The therapist reaches in a bag she keeps by her chair.) I can wave this wand and, for 5 minutes, we can let Ann be the problem and you can be her: You can be the good kid. Want to play this game? Want to try out the wand?

Jason: Yeah. I get to be the good kid?

Therapist: Yep. And Amy can help you, because she has watched Ann for a long time, and she knows what Ann does to be a good kid. And Luke, maybe you could help Ann be the problem.

Paul: Do you have an evil voice, Ann?

Ann: Yes, it's the one I use when you and Mom are gone. (Everyone laughs.)

> Ann says she is going to glue Jason's clothes drawer shut so he won't be able to change his clothes ever again. Jason responds in his sweetest voice that Ann would get in trouble, and he would not want to see that happen. He notes that she has gotten in

a lot of trouble recently and it worries Mom. Amy tells Jason to tell Ann that he just wants to save her from getting punished. Ann responds that she likes getting punished, because she doesn't care and at least she gets to have some fun along the way. She looks at Jason and says, "You're too good." Jason responds: "I am the good boy."

After 5 minutes, the family seems almost playful and relaxed. The therapist is ready to end the session.

Therapist: I am wondering if you would think about something for the next 2 weeks when we can meet again. What would still concern you if this was our last session together? I am not saying that this week or even next time will be our last session together. I just want to get some clarity about what is still on each of your minds.

Two weeks later, the family comes to another session. Although there were still some incidents that required parental intervention, there was no violence and increasingly the problems were the kind that every family had. Both Paul and Amy were spending more time at home, and the interactions between the family members ebbed and flowed in the ways that families always do when they have been together for many years. Early in the first part of the session:

Jane: And much to all of our surprise, even Amy is finding more time to be at home and join in on family events. I don't know if we told you, but Ann had a birthday last week, and Amy planned a party at the house. She, Jason, and Luke actually put on a funny skit for her.

Therapist: Well, Ann, let me add my best wishes to you for your birthday. It sounds like it was a wonderful time.

Ann: Thanks, it was nice.

Therapist: I am wondering: If this were our last session, what things would still be of concern to you?

Paul: Really, I can't think of anything. I think we are all on the right track at the moment.

Amy: I have enjoyed being around home again. It is nice to see Dad there more too.

Therapist: So no real concerns left?

Amy: Not really. I worry that Dad might get absorbed in work again, and I just hope he waits until after I go to college.

Therapist: Ann.

Ann: No, nothing bothering me. I actually like being a problem. I even tried it out a bit this week—staying out later than I was supposed to.

Jane: I didn't know that!

Ann: (smiling) Jason covered for me.

Summary and Multicultural Evaluation

Strategic family therapy gained much of its popularity from focusing on problems and solutions. By accepting that the presenting problem really was the problem, it avoided the appearance of ignoring the problem in favor of system correction. And by concentrating on solutions, strategic therapists were able to use the same planning and measurement of effectiveness that are inherent in behavioral models. It is, however, the refusal of most strategic therapists to address insight or even an understanding of family processes that generates the most criticism.

It is interesting to note that practitioners and students of strategic therapy often have more insight into the cases that are presented than the people or families involved. If discovering the use and purpose of a symptom or a problematic organizational problem helps the therapist make a difference, why would this information not be useful for the family members too? Would such information not reduce confusion? Is a mother who was directed paradoxically to "hover over her daughter" going to use this technique with all of her other children? Or does the family have to return to the therapist for a new prescription each time a problem develops? It is difficult to see how even a focus on brief therapy would be harmed by a session devoted to debriefing the therapeutic process and an understanding of what processes made a real difference.

Strategic family therapists contribute to the development of a sequence lens, an organizational lens, and a developmental lens in family therapy and counseling. This is especially true of Jay Haley's work, which was heavily influenced by and oriented toward the structural model. What Haley (1980) made clear is that family developmental tasks, like launching children into adulthood and preparing them to leave home, are also enacted in sequences and are heavily influenced by the organization and leadership of the family. Strategic therapists also teach us that even if the end does not justify any means, there are always at least several means to any end. More than most approaches to family therapy, strategic therapists are **perspectivists** whose very work—especially when therapy is conducted in teams—implies that multiple lenses make a difference in therapeutic outcome.

Contributions to Multicultural Counseling and Gender Issues

For a model of family therapy that has spread all over the world, much of the approach has offered little or nothing with respect to addressing the unique needs of different cultures. The Milan group started in Italy and has had tremendous influence throughout Europe, but nothing from even Europe's different cultures has been incorporated in the model. Rather than incorporating culturally diverse perspectives into their work, MRI therapists have preferred to rely on what they call common sense. But this is all too often an American style of common sense. "Common sense is always somebody's common sense, and each somebody has a worldview inscribed with beliefs about sex, class, race, and other distinctions that are fundamental to social existence" (Luepnitz, 1988, p. 80). The determination of strategic family therapists in America to see every problem in its social context almost demanded a consideration of the political climate and atmosphere in which social contexts exist. Among all of the strategic models, those associated with Haley have been the most culturally integrative. Haley, himself, "is very aware of [clients' cultures] and often asks them how they would handle a particular problem in their culture (Madeleine Richeport-Haley, personal communication, April 15, 2005). But, as Haley (1976) has suggested, although all problems could be framed in political, cultural, and economic terms, the therapist then would be forced into the role of revolutionary. Such a role, for him, is simply not pragmatic, since there is no guarantee that a better society can be created and, in any case, such change is far too long in coming.

> Courtesy and respect are minimum requirements for therapy. Haley (1996) also believes that therapists must adapt to certain basic premises of a culture. If a husband will not sit down with his wife and treat her as an equal, the couple can be seen separately and their problems worked out. The goal is not to make members of the client family behave like members of the ethnic group of the therapist but to respect the clients' culture and still resolve their problems. One can ask the family how a particular issue would be dealt with in the country-of-origin. (Haley & Richeport-Haley, 2003, p. 19)

When the symptom is expressed in religious terms, Haley and Richeport-Haley (2003) tend to approach incidents of cultural difference as behavioral manifestations of alternate belief systems. They propose one of four approaches to such incidents: (1) to minimize the alternate belief and treat the family structurally and strategically; (2) to use parts of the alternate belief to reach therapeutic goals; (3) to refer the client to a cultural healer in the local community; or (4) to collaborate with a cultural healer in the local community.

In the early 1990s, Haley moved to San Diego and began to teach at the California School of Professional Psychology. He and Madeleine Richeport-Haley concentrated on making training materials for therapists, an interest of Haley's that extended back to his work on the Bateson project. He had made a series of films associated with *Learning and Teaching Therapy* (Haley, 1996) and *The Art of Strategic Therapy* (Haley & Richeport-Haley, 2003). Three films were made on Bali. He also consulted with healers in Puerto Rico and Brazil.

Boyd-Franklin (2003) generally appreciates the problem-solving focus of strategic family therapy. Especially in multiproblem families, sorting through issues and developing a focus for therapy can be extremely useful. While she has some concerns about the use of paradoxical interventions too early in therapy, she is very supportive of the use of reframing when redefining symptoms within the family.

Without insight and understanding, strategic interventions fall easily into the-ends-justify-the-means approaches to therapy. There are plenty of examples in the strategic reports of the 1970s and early 1980s of interventions that maintained sexism within families. A depressed man was congratulated for getting his wife to have sex with him the way he desired "by demanding what you have coming to you" (Madanes, 1981, p. 192). In this chapter, we used examples that were blatantly sexist, such as when the therapist suggested that Olga had learned how to use the "feminine wile" of playing "hard to get." Even the Haley/Richeport-Haley proposal, above—that a man and a woman can be seen separately if their culture does not recognize women's equality—perpetuates sexism while trying to be culturally sensitive. To be fair, other strategic interventions involve empowerment of women and broadening men's useful participation in the family, but until Madanes' (1990) infusion of values in therapy, there was nothing in strategic therapy that required or sought the integration of an ethical, social, or political value system. There is very little chance that the writings, training, or therapy of the strategic family approach will address the problems inherent in family life and society for women. Indeed, in an interview for *The Family Therapy Networker*, Selvini Palazzoli actually suggests that, in spite of recognized patriarchy, some women get a lot out of playing the victim (Simon, 1987).

If you are interested in a more in-depth study of this approach, we recommend the following sources: Haley (1963, 1973, 1976, 1980, 1984); Haley and Richeport-Haley (2003); Madanes (1981, 1984, 1990); Segal (1991); and Watzlawick (1978), Watzlawick, Beavin, and Jackson (1967), or Watzlawick, Weakland, and Fisch (1974). In the next chapter, we shall consider the evolution of strategic family therapy in its postmodern forms, solution-focused (Berg & Miller, 1992; de Shazer, 1982, 1985, 1991; de Shazer & Berg, 1993) and solution-oriented (O'Hanlon & O'Hanlon, 2002; O'Hanlon & Weiner-Davis, 1989) family therapies.

Exercises for Personal and Professional Growth

Did it ever occur to you that problems in a family just might be the way the family has of keeping everything the same—or maintaining homeostasis? When you think back to your own family, were there problems that surfaced that had the effect of pulling some members of the family together? Maybe a sickness or difficulties at school? Did you have a relative, maybe a grandparent, come to live with you when you were still at home? What effect did that have on the family system?

Haley (1980) suggested that the main task of adolescence was to leave home, and it involved both the person leaving and those who would launch her or him. Too often, however, this task is thwarted: Young people stay home to keep their parents together or to reduce the conflict that everyone thinks will occur when the nest is empty. Have you left home yet? If so, what happened when you left? Were you prepared to leave? Were your parents ready to launch you? Did conflict between your parents go up, down, or stay about the same? If you haven't left home yet, what do you think will happen if you do?

These questions ask you to look at one type of developmental sequence that is common to most families sometime during the family life cycle. In systems theory, there is no use in assigning cause-and-effect markers to any part of the sequence, because the whole process is interactive and recursive: Each part is affecting every other part. What we can do instead is track the sequences that occur in family patterns. Starting with the patterns in our own lives helps us to get accustomed to tracking similar sequences in the families we will serve.

Human sequences generally involve behavior or action, communication, and meaning. Breunlin, Schwartz, and MacKune-Karrer (1992) identified four types of sequences: face-to-face interactions, routines, ebb-and-flow processes, and transgenerational sequences.

Face-to-face sequences are interactions that tend to occur in a short period of time for a specific purpose. They can come in many forms, but sometimes are easier to see when in the form of an argument or a fight between family members.

- How did your parents fight when you were young? How do they fight now? What is a common sequence that seems to repeat itself over time?
- How do you fight with significant others? How do they get started? Are you the starter or the responder or both?
- Describe the pattern. What actions are taking place while communication is occurring?
- How do fights in your family end?
- What is missing from the sequence that would help to change the outcome?

Most families develop sequences that extend over time and space, and are enacted in no less than 24-hour patterns: We call these sequences family *routines*. Routines are important, because they help family life run efficiently—often wordlessly—with everyone knowing what typically will happen. Routines make life predictable, and we come to depend on them—almost as if enacting them is a family rule.

- What were the routines in your home when you were growing up? What are your routines now? Are they related?
- How did a typical day go at in your family-of-origin? What is a typical day like in your home now?
- Who has to do what in order for others to do what they need or want to do?
- What happened when the normal routines were interrupted or became impossible to complete? If a family member is missing, does someone else pick up that person's part of the routine? How does that go?

Some sequences are developmental and appear intermittently over the course of a family's life. You probably have noticed already that behavior problems ebb and flow and so do affective disorders: No one behaves badly all the time and no one is anxious or depressed all the time. Symptoms, like family life itself, have a tendency to ebb and flow.

- Think about your family life cycle. Do you have any sense of what your parents were like when they were single and on their own? How did they conduct their lives then?
- What sequences and transactions occurred in order for them to get together?
- How did their life patterns change with your birth and the birth of each of your siblings?
- As you got older, became a teen, did the patterns in your family life alter? In what ways?
- Was there a divorce in your family? How did divorce change the ebb and flow of your life and the lives of other family members?

- Are there elderly members of your family? What are the sequences involved in their lives and in caring for them in old age?

Transgenerational sequences extend across generations. Sometime, we even see families in which the sequences skip a generation only to re-emerge later. For example, a family may have two parents who suffer from alcohol abuse, and their children become determined that they will not fall victim to liquor. They grow up, have children, raise them in an alcohol-free environment, but later discover that their children have trouble with alcohol anyway when they reach adulthood. Indeed, many of the same sequences that maintained the problem for the grandparents are also present in the grandchildren.

Transgenerational sequences do not have to be manifest in problems and symptoms. What aspects of your life have been continued from one generation to the next? You might say something like, "This is the way my mother did it and her mother did it, and so it is just the way I do it." Take cooking on the holidays, for example: Is there any pattern that you learned from previous generations that you still do?

- Are there any cultural or religious rituals that always have been a part of your family? How are they enacted?
- Are there any family rituals around birth, coming of age, leaving home, starting your own family, retirement, or death that have been part of the family history for generations?

When you start to track these sequences in client-families, you will notice that the most powerful sequences engage people in communication (both verbal and nonverbal); they involve specific actions that are loaded with meaning. When sequences constrain members of the family, the patterns need to be identified and reconsidered. When sequences facilitate well-functioning systems, they can be allowed to operate imperceptibly—just below conscious awareness.

Where to Go From Here

MRI therapists still offer training programs at the Mental Research Institute in Palo Alto, California. They offer introductory and intensive, advanced courses, as well as training in Spanish and programs integrating strategic practice in the schools. For more information, you can contact them at:

The Mental Research Institute
A Research and Training Institute for the Interactional Study of Individuals, Families and
 their Communities
555 Middlefield Rd.
Palo Alto, CA 94301
Phone: 650-321-3055, fax: 650-321-3785

Jay Haley's 25 training films in the field can be accessed at **haley-therapies.com**. Although Haley and Cloe Madanes were no longer partnered in either marriage or professional activities at the end of Haley's life, Cloe was and is living and working in La Jolla. Her training programs can be accessed at:

Cloe Madanes
The Robbins-Madanes Center for Strategic Intervention
2223 Avenida de la Playa, Suite 105
La Jolla, CA 92037
Phone: (858) 454-1540
E-mail: **CloeM@aol.com**

Recommended Readings

Grove, D. R., & Haley, J. (1993). *Conversations on therapy: Popular problems and uncommon solutions.* New York: Norton. This is a series of cases that were presented to Haley for consultation. It allows the reader to sit in on strategy sessions with one of the best strategists in the field.

Haley, J. (1976). *Problem solving therapy.* San Francisco: Jossey Bass. This is the book that fully presents Haley's model of strategic family therapy and it is the book with which most people interested in this model start.

Haley, J. (1984). *Ordeal therapy: Unusual ways to change behavior.* San Francisco: Jossey Bass. In this book, Haley describes the use of ordeal in his therapeutic work: how to design them, how to prescribe them, and what is needed for effectiveness.

Haley, J. (1996). *Learning and teaching therapy.* New York: Guilford. This is the book that the Washington School uses as a main text for training.

Madanes, C. (1981). *Strategic family therapy.* San Francisco: Jossey Bass. Madanes has complained from time to time that her work gets blended with Haley's and even ascribed to him. For those who want to know what she uniquely brings to the process and development of the model, this is the book.

Madanes, C. (1990). *Sex, love, and violence: Strategies for transformation.* New York: Norton. This is the book in which a consideration of values is added to the process of strategic family therapy. In it Madanes moves her work into the realm of strategic humanism.

Selvini Palazzoli, M., Boscolo, L., Cecchin, G., & Prata, G. (1978). *Paradox and counterparadox: A new model in the therapy of the family in schizophrenic transition.* Northvale, NJ: Jason Aronson. This is the original Milan team presenting their strategic approach to work with difficult families in Italy.

Selvini Palazzoli, M., Cirillo, S., Selvini, M., & Sorrentino, A. M. (1989). *Family games: General models of psychotic processes in the family.* New York: Norton. In this book, Selvini Palazzoli has formed a new Milan group and is reporting on her work with Prata, using the invariant prescription.

Watzlawick, P., Beavin, J. H., & Jackson, D. D. (1967). *Pragmatics of human communication.* New York: Norton. This is one of the early MRI books and still is considered a classic in strategic therapy. It highlights much of the genius of three great systemic thinkers.

Watzlawick, P., Weakland, J. H., & Fisch, R. (1974). *Change: Principles of problem formation and problem resolution.* New York: Norton. This is the book that put MRI on the map and demonstrated the translation of systemic and strategic thinking into practice. The work of John Weakland is very important to this volume.

DVD Reference

There are several forms of strategic family therapy addressed in the textbook. The first model of this approach was developed at the Mental Research Institute (or MRI) in Palo Alto, California. There, the ideas of Gregory Bateson and later those of Milton Erickson were tested out with families, many of whom had a member diagnosed with schizophrenia. Jay Haley was part of this initial group, but he eventually left for the east coast where he worked with Salvador Minuchin at the Philadelphia Child Guidance Center before starting his own institute in Washington, D.C. Both the MRI and the Washington models influenced the development of a third approach in Milan, Italy, at a center under the direction of Maria Selvini Palazzoli.

In this video, we focus on the strategic intervention model developed by Jay Haley and Cloe Madanes in Washington, D.C. It involves the use of a co-therapist team behind a one-way mirror who occasionally phone in directives to the family through the consulting therapist. You will notice that Dr. Bitter stops periodically to answer the phone and then passes the directive on to the family. For demonstration purposes, these interventions happen more than they normally might, and each of them involves a paradoxical directive, usually prescribing the symptom. Think about how comfortable or uncomfortable you might be in this process. You also might want to think about the context in which the paradox is given and what ethical issues also might be involved.

References

Andersen, T. (1991). *The reflecting team: Dialogues and dialogues about the dialogues.* New York: Norton.

Anderson, H. (1997). *Conversation, language, and possibilities.* New York: Basic Books.

Bateson, G., Jackson, D., Haley, J., & Weakland, J. (1956). Toward a theory of schizophrenia. *Behavioral Science, 1,* 251–264.

Becvar, D. S., & Becvar, R. J. (2003). *Family therapy: A systemic integration* (5th ed.). Boston: Allyn & Bacon.

Berg, I. K., & Miller, S. D. (1992). *Working with the problem drinker: A solution-focused approach.* New York: Norton.

Boscolo, L., Cecchin, G., Hoffman, L., & Penn, P. (1987). *Milan systemic family therapy.* New York: Basic Books.

Boyd-Franklin, N. (2003). *Black families in therapy: Understanding the African American experience* (2nd ed.). New York: Guilford.

Breunlin, D. C., Schwartz, R. C., & MacKune-Karrer, B. (1992). *Metaframeworks: Transcending the models of family therapy.* San Francisco: Jossey-Bass.

de Shazer, S. (1982). *Patterns of brief family therapy: An ecosystemic approach.* New York: Guilford.

de Shazer, S. (1985). *Keys to solutions in brief therapy.* New York: Norton.

de Shazer, S. (1991). *Putting difference to work.* New York: Norton.

de Shazer, S., & Berg, I. K. (1993). Constructing solutions. *Family Therapy Networker, 17*(3), 42–43.

Glasser, W. (1998). *Choice theory.* New York: HarperCollins.

Grove, D. R., & Haley, J. (1993). *Conversations of therapy: Popular problems and uncommon solutions.* New York: Norton.

Haley, J. (1963). *Strategies of psychotherapy.* New York: Grune and Stratton.

Haley, J. (1973). *Uncommon therapy: The psychiatric techniques of Milton H. Erickson, M.D.* New York: Norton.

Haley, J. (1976). *Problem-solving therapy: New strategies for effective family therapy.* San Francisco: Jossey Bass.

Haley, J. (1980). *Leaving home.* New York: McGraw-Hill.

Haley, J. (1984). *Ordeal therapy: Unusual ways to change behavior.* San Francisco: Jossey Bass.

Haley, J. (1996). *Learning and teaching therapy.* New York: Guilford.

Haley, J., & Richeport-Haley, M. (2003). *The art of strategic therapy.* New York: Brunner Routledge.

Keim, J. (2000). Strategic family therapy: The Washington School. In A. M. Horne (Ed.), *Family counseling and therapy* (3rd ed., pp. 170–207). Itasca, IL: F. E. Peacock.

Luepnitz, D. A. (1988). *The family interpreted: Feminist theory in clinical practice.* New York: Basic Books.

Madanes, C. (1981). *Strategic family therapy.* San Francisco: Jossey Bass.

Madanes, C. (1984). *Behind the one-way mirror.* San Francisco: Jossey Bass.

Madanes, C. (1990). *Sex, love, and violence: Strategies for transformation.* New York: Norton.

Nichols, M. P., & Schwartz, R. C. (2006). *Family therapy: Concepts and methods* (7th ed.). Boston: Allyn & Bacon.

O'Hanlon, S., & O'Hanlon, B. (2002). Solution-oriented therapy with families. In J. Carlson & D. Kjos (Eds.), *Theories and strategies of family therapy* (pp. 190–215). Boston: Allyn & Bacon.

O'Hanlon, W. H., & Weiner-Davis, M. (1989). *In search of solutions: A new direction in psychotherapy.* New York: Norton.

Segal, L. (1991). Brief family therapy. In A. Horne & L. Passmore (Eds.), *Family counseling and therapy* (2nd ed., pp. 179–205). Itasca, IL: F. E. Peacock.

Selvini Palazzoli, M., Boscolo, L., Cecchin, G., & Prata, G. (1978). *Paradox and counterparadox.* Northvale, NJ: Jason Aronson.

Selvini Palazzoli, M., Cirillo, S., Selvini, M., & Sorrentino, A. M. (1989). *Family games: General models of psychotic processes in the family.* New York: Norton.

Simon, R. (1987). Good-bye paradox, hello invariant prescription: An interview with Maria Selvini Palazzoli. *The Family Therapy Networker, 11*(5), 16–33.

Watzlawick, P. (1978). *The language of change.* New York Basic Books.

Watzlawick, P., Beavin, J. H., & Jackson, D. D. (1967). *Pragmatics of human communication.* New York: Norton.

Watzlawick, P., Weakland, J. H., & Fisch, R. (1974). *Change: Principles of problem formation and problem resolution.* New York: Norton.

White, M., & Epston, D. (1990). *Narrative means to therapeutic ends.* New York: Norton.

Endnote

[1]This excerpt was adapted from a lengthy report of the case presented by Haley (1984) in his book *Ordeal Therapy*.

Solution-Focused and Solution-Oriented Therapy

Introduction

Key Concepts

Therapy Goals

The Therapist's Role and Function

Techniques

A Solution-Oriented Therapist With the Quest Family

Summary and Multicultural Evaluation

Recommended Readings

References

Introduction

The many strategic family therapy models and their historical antecedents brought new perspectives both to the ways in which families functioned and the ways in which therapists could effectively intervene. Milton Erickson taught the strategic therapists the power of embedded and indirect messages. Milan therapists added both collaboration and circular questioning to the process. Haley's strategic approach and the Mental Research Institute (MRI) model framed family problems as ineffective solutions; problems resulted when families and individuals used solutions that mistakenly reinforced unwanted patterns. MRI therapists, especially, saw families as stuck and sought to reduce the family's insistence on doing more of the same. Throughout the 1980s and 1990s, Steve de Shazer, his partner Insoo Kim Berg, and Eve Lipchik began to turn the MRI model around by focusing more on what did work in families and by uncovering effective solutions that were present but often hidden in families (see Berg & de Shazer, 1993; de Shazer, 1988; de Shazer & Berg, 1993).

Their solution-focused model began in Milwaukee, Wisconsin, in 1979, with the founding of the Brief Family Therapy Center (BFTC), an alternative center to the community agency services with which the founders had been associated. The original working group at BFTC included therapist/trainers and students who are now the leaders of this approach, including Eve Lipchik, Scott Miller, John Walter and Jane Peller, and Michele Weiner-Davis. Steve de Shazer died in a hospital in Vienna, Austria, on September 11, 2005. Insoo Kim

Steve de Shazer

Insoo Berg

Berg was by his side. On January 10, 2007, Insoo Kim Berg died suddenly in Milwaukee, Wisconsin. She was 72 years old. Because of their deaths, BFTC closed its operations on October 15, 2007. Until her passing, Insoo Kim Berg was the model's foremost clinician, applying solution-focused therapy to couples and families, as well as addressing some of the more serious of life concerns, such as substance abuse.

Michele Weiner-Davis eventually left BFTC and developed a solution-oriented collaborative approach to therapy with Bill O'Hanlon, who now calls his approach **possibility therapy**. O'Hanlon quickly became one of the leading writers and spokesmen for solution-oriented therapy. Although O'Hanlon had never worked at BFTC, he had many of the same background experiences that de Shazer had: Both had studied at MRI; both incorporated the work of Milton Erickson in their therapy; and both were fascinated by the possibilities for brief therapy that existed in an optimistic search for solutions O'Hanlon and Weiner-Davis (2003) saw what they originally called solution-oriented therapy as an expansion of the solution-focused model. I will note some of the differences between solution-oriented therapy and solution-focused therapy later in this chapter.

John Walter and Jane Peller are solution-focused therapists who worked and studied at BFTC, and they have co-authored two important books in this model (Walter & Peller, 1992, 2000). They now work in Evanston, Illinois, as therapeutic consultants and trainers. The techniques that most people associate with the solution-focused approach are **exception questions**, **scaling questions** and the **miracle question**, which are defined later in this chapter. Walter and Peller understand these questions to be examples of **questions of difference**. Questions of difference open up space in relationships for thinking about and understanding self and others in a new way. They often ask people in therapy for signs that life and relationships would be better: It is from these signs that real solutions are fashioned and designed.

Sometimes questions of difference are facilitated by asking troubled family members to listen to each other from a bit of a distance—and to reflect on what differences they notice. Walter and Peller (2000) presented a case that involved a 15-year-old daughter, her mother, and her stepfather. The mother and stepfather brought their daughter for a consultation after the daughter had been evaluated at a hospital for drug abuse. The parents were concerned that their formerly happy child was now a "sullen adolescent. According to [the stepfather], she would stay out for days on end, she would come home smelling of alcohol, and her grades (which used to be Bs and As) were now Cs and below" (p. 141). What bothered the stepfather the most was the yelling and fighting that occurred among the three of them. Complicating this matter was the fact that the mother's mother was close to death and in a hospital.

What would your inclinations be with this family? Do any flags go up for you just because this is a blended family with a stepfather? Does your own experience as an adolescent—or perhaps with adolescents of your own—make you anxious, especially when you hear that alcohol is involved? Like the stepfather, would you worry about grades dropping from Bs and As to Cs and below? The problems seem so prominent in the presenting data, can you still imagine staying focused on a search for solutions and the resources that are already available to the family members? Indeed, do you think you could find a way to talk to this family without being concerned about their presenting problem at all? What questions would you ask? Would you ask about a time in which the parents and their child were not at odds with one another (called an exception question)?

Throughout this conversation, our part, as consultants,[1] was to listen to their ideas and ask questions of difference. Examples of the questions were: "How are your ideas about your daughter different than before?" "What effect do you think these ideas about your daughter have had on her?" "What difference do your ideas make to her perception of you and herself?" Mother did not know the answers to these questions but she hoped her daughter missed the closeness that she and her daughter had before all this turned sour. Stepdad thought that their ideas about their daughter had no effect on her at all. In fact, he thought that his stepdaughter thought of no one but herself. (p. 141)

The answers given by the parents only served to deflate the daughter, causing her to withdraw more and more in disbelief.

Consultant:	I would now like to hear from your daughter and get her ideas about the situation. I would like the two of you to listen to her and my conversation—and pay particular attention to how each of you might change by listening to it.
Mother:	Okay.
Consultant:	(turning to the daughter) So what ideas and thoughts did you have as you listened to your parents' conversation with me?
Daughter:	(defensively) Well, I am not as bad as they think I am. I am not a bad person—and I am not a bad kid. I don't think they understand that my life is not easy. School just keeps getting harder and harder with no real help. I want to do well, but I am really far behind. I don't like my teachers, and for the most part, they don't like me. I also don't get homework. I wish they wouldn't give us any, because I don't know what to do, and I just keep doing worse and worse.
Consultant:	School is hard enough: Homework is just like piling it on.
Daughter:	Yes. It seems to me that the only kids who benefit from homework are the ones who don't need it—who get it done before they even leave school or on the bus going home. The rest us—especially me—try to avoid it as long as possible, and then when I do try, it doesn't work out.
Consultant:	Is that an area in which you would like some help or is there something else?
Daughter:	No, I would like some help. I would like to get caught up. I would like to get A's and B's again. Giving me more homework isn't going to do it if I don't get it. I would love it if my mom or someone else would help me understand it, so I could do better.
Consultant:	Tell me what it is like for you with your parents.
Daughter:	They're my parents. I love them, but they want to control everything I do. I over-react to being controlled. I actually think they should trust me. Other people my age have a lot more freedom than I do. The older I get, the more worried they get. I really don't want them to worry. I don't want them to worry, because it is hard on them—and it is hard on me; the more worried they are, the more they want to make me stay home, not see or talk to my friends, not go out, or do anything fun. Then, I start to feel that everything is just so unfair, and all I want to do is get out. So I take off. I don't really do anything bad. I just have fun. And when I come home, I know I am going to be in trouble, and they are going to clamp down even harder. I would probably do the same thing if I were my parent, but that doesn't mean I like it.
Consultant:	So there really is a lot weighing on you.
Daughter:	Yeah, but that's just the way it goes. I just wish they believed I wasn't a bad person and that they didn't have to worry about me so much.
Consultant:	Well, I want to thank you for sharing all this information with me in front of your parents, especially since you did not want to come to the meeting in the first place. I want to turn back to your parents now, and I am wondering if, like them, you would be willing to listen to the conversation that I will have with them and maybe take some notes about what differences you notice in yourself.
Daughter:	Yeah. I can do that.[2]

Consultant: (turning to the parents) So what thoughts did you have as you listened to this conversation? How did it make a difference to you to hear our conversation?

Mother: That is the most I have heard her talk and share since she was 12 years old!

Consultant: How did what she and I talked about make a difference for you?

Mother: I could see that she is the same daughter I once knew. (Her breathing relaxes a bit.) I thought I had lost her. She has just been so angry and she wouldn't talk about anything.

Consultant: So this was really different. Now that you think she is still the daughter you knew before, what difference does or will that make for you?

Mother: Well . . . then, I guess I don't have to worry as much as I do. I can relax a little bit.

Stepfather: Well, I'm not so sure about that. I was an adolescent once, into drugs and drinking. I think I have a pretty good idea about what she is into.

Consultant: So as you listened to your daughter and me talk what difference did the conversation make for you?

Stepfather: Well, I guess what I am saying is that I don't trust what she is saying. I think she is trying to snow-job us, particularly her mother, who is easier to fool.

Consultant: So, how is what you are describing different from before?

Stepfather: It isn't.

[Consultant's comments] I then turned to the daughter and asked her to reflect on her experience of my conversation with her parents. She said she knew that her stepdad did not trust her, but again, she said that she is not as bad as he thinks she is. I asked how that made a difference to her, to think that he did not trust her or that he thinks that she is worse than she is. She said that it made no difference to her—she didn't care. Even though she said she didn't care, I could not help but see in her eyes that she felt hurt by his words about her. She went on to describe her experience of trust between her and her friends, and between her and her parents. She spoke in detail about how her friends make decisions and what criteria they use to make "wise choices."

I then turned to parents to have them reflect on this conversation.

Consultant: First, I want to say how honored I feel that your daughter allowed me to have this very meaningful conversation with her, and to take the risk to have this conversation in front of the two of you. What thoughts did you have as you witnessed this privileged conversation?

Stepfather: You know, I am beginning to realize that maybe she is unhappy, not because of her mother or me, or because of drugs or boys. But maybe she is unhappy because she is 15. When you are 15, you are unhappy.

Consultant: Okay, that is an idea. How does thinking about her that way make a difference to you?

Stepfather: Well, maybe I don't have to do anything about it. Maybe I could just listen instead.

[Consultant's comments] These conversations and reflections are examples of inviting members of the family to reflect on what newness may have developed in the conversation with the other family members. In this example, the mother seemed to be quite touched by hearing her daughter talk with the consultant. What she heard her daughter say seemed to reassure her that her daughter was in many ways still the daughter she knew earlier. She seemed to take this as sign that she could relax a bit.

The daughter reflected on how untrue her stepfather's opinion was. She went on partly to defend herself but also to help the consultant understand that she was not a bad daughter. She trusted her friends and made good choices.

The stepfather's reflections the second time are different. Rather than hearing only the same old thing, he hears how she is unhappy and perhaps how that is not anybody's fault. His further inference is that if it is not his or her mother's fault, but just part of being a teenager, then perhaps he too can relax a bit. He seems less judgmental and more sympathetic with her unhappiness. (pp. 142–143)

Although the relationship of solution-focused and solution-oriented (or possibility) therapy to strategic family therapy is practically impossible to miss, it would be incorrect to think of these models as mere extensions of the strategic approach. Both models are more appropriately grounded in the postmodern, social constructionist approaches that we shall consider in the next chapter. Briefly, postmodern thinking differs from a *modernist* approach in that the latter posits an objective reality in which there is an essence to almost everything. In a modern worldview, people have problems, and psychopathology is a set of disorders that are real and affect real people in ways that can be accurately described. Postmodernists reject the idea of essences and believe that reality depends on the relationships between observers and what they observe: There are, therefore, multiple realities, and these realities are socially constructed, often in the form of narratives or stories. In this sense, each narrative or story depends on who is telling it to whom and for what purpose. Problem narratives or **problem-saturated stories** may involve a person or family as part of the story, but they need not be the only stories that count. Indeed, problem-saturated stories and solution-oriented stories can often co-exist in the narratives of a single family—even though the solution stories temporarily may be ignored, deflected, or discarded when problem stories seem paramount and overwhelming.

Adopting this postmodern perspective, both solution-focused and solution-oriented (or possibility) therapies spend minimal amounts of time listening to clients articulate their problems. Both approaches share the belief that the development of a preferred solution is more important than clarifying and directly addressing the problem, which has already gained a dominant position in the life of the family. Indeed, solution-focused therapists would be content to work on solutions without knowing what the problem is at all (de Shazer, 1991). This is not to indicate that solution-focused therapists do not acknowledge, validate, and make space for honoring a client's problems and suffering; rather, it is a matter of emphasis and focus on what the client wants or prefers (de Shazer & Dolan, 2007). One of their primary tools in therapy is the miracle question, in which clients are asked to envision life without symptoms or problems, as well as the means they would use to create a preferred life.

Even the most difficult and therapy-resistant clients can be redirected as soon as a focus on solutions becomes central to everything the clinical practitioner does. In the case below, Insoo Kim Berg joins with a man's delusions in an effort to eliminate resistance and then reframes the man's quest in a manner that envisions a good relationship and better marriage with his spouse.

Berg (2002) described a case in which a man and a woman came to therapy, because the husband was convinced—in spite of having no evidence—that his wife was having an affair. In the initial part of the session, he would accuse and she would deny, a process that was ruining their marriage and their relationship. His suspicions (the story he told himself) were so strong that he could not dismiss them. Toward the end of the session, the therapist asked the woman if she would mind waiting outside while she talked to the husband. When the woman left, the therapist said to the husband that his wife probably was having an affair.[3] "Finally," he said, "Someone who understands."

> "The problem," continued the therapist, "is that your wife is really good at hiding it. No amount of detective work by you has revealed a single thing that could be used to catch her in an affair."

Therapist: As long as she knows that you are watching her, she will continue to be on guard, and we will never catch her. Our only hope is for you to act as if you do not suspect anything at all. In fact, you may have to act as if you have a wonderful marriage and a wonderful relationship. In this way, she will eventually let down her guard, and you might have a chance at catching her. Mind you, though, she is very good. This could take some time.

Husband: I can do that though. It might work. I think it will work.

Therapist: So what would you be doing with your wife if you wanted her to have full confidence in your devotion to her and to the marriage? How would you behave with her, and what would you do?

> The therapist and the husband discussed everything from compliments to gifts to spending time with his wife and engaging in real affection. Demonstrations of trust were identified and planned for a 2-week period.

Therapist: I think you've got it. It will take some time, but if she comes to really believe in your trust and affection, it is inevitable that she will let down her guard and reveal her affair. Do you think you can last? Do you think you can keep it up even as she becomes happy with you and your relationship?

Husband: Yes, I think I can.

> Two weeks later, the wife reported that her husband's behavior was completely different with her. Indeed, the last 2 weeks had been the best in their marriage. She felt they were closer than they had ever been before.

Key Concepts

Both solution-focused and solution-oriented approaches are centered in storied conversations. Similar to other social constructionists, these practitioners believe that problems are "problems," because they are described as problems. Language is an interactive process and, if therapists choose to engage in complaint-centered discussions, then problems are maintained and even developed. Indeed, O'Hanlon and Wilk (1987) suggest that problems do not exist outside of the therapy session; they are present because they are talked-about. Solution-focused and solution-oriented therapists, therefore, prefer to engage in conversations about what goes well, what is possible, and what will help clients to feel accomplished and better. The more people talk about the solutions they want to create for their lives, the more "they come to believe in the truth or reality of what they are talking about. This is the way language works, naturally" (Berg & de Shazer, 1993, p. 9).

One of the few differences that seem to exist between solution-focused therapy and solution-oriented therapy is the extent to which the past and presenting problems are addressed. Solution-focused therapy differs from both strategic models and traditional therapies by minimizing the past—and even the present—in favor of the future. It is so focused on what is possible that it has little or no interest in understanding the presenting problem. de Shazer (1991), who was often the most radical of the group, suggested that therapists do not need to know a problem in order to solve it and that there is no necessary relationship between problems and their solutions. Solution-oriented therapists, on the other hand, believe that solutions work best when the solution is directly related to the "doing of the problem" (O'Hanlon & O'Hanlon, 2002)—at least in the present and perhaps for some time in the past.

If understanding problems is less important or, in the case of solution-focused therapists, even unimportant, so is searching for the *right* solutions. O'Hanlon and Weiner-Davis (2003) believe that there are multiple solutions that any person or family might consider and that what is right for one person or family may not be for others. Families are not stuck because they want to be or need to be or have some underlying purpose in maintaining a problem, as is often suggested in the strategic models. Individuals and families come to therapy because they want to change. And each family has within it the resources necessary for effective living and change. Clients, therefore, are the best people to choose the goals they want to achieve in therapy.

Individuals and families bring narratives to therapy. Some are used to justify their belief that life can't be changed or, worse, that life is moving them further and further away from their goals. de Shazer (1991) preferred to engage clients in conversations that led to progressive narratives whereby people create situations in which they can make steady gains toward their goals (for example, "Tell me about times when you feel good, when things are going your way, and when you enjoy your family and friends.") It is in these stories of life-worth-living that the power-of-problems is deconstructed and new solutions are made manifest and possible. These therapists seek only to guide the changer and the changed—they are one and the same—in a self-chosen direction.

O'Hanlon and Weiner-Davis (2003) suggest that there are three ways in which change can be negotiated: (1) changing the doing of the problem; (2) changing the perception of the problem-situation; and (3) engaging in a discussion of resources, strengths, and solutions.

Therapy Goals

The movement to a more-collaborative model of therapy is mirrored in the goals of solution-focused and solution-oriented therapies. Like the MRI model, these therapists still want to move people from problem to solution, but they believe that the solutions already exist within the family and within the family members. Their goal is to engage clients in an optimistic conversation about the present and future. They wonder out loud about what might be possible if the clients used skills they have used before, rediscovered internal and external resources, or made use of exceptions as options to develop. In this sense, the goal of therapy is to unstick people from their current patterns and perceptions and help them discover new, concrete possibilities for their immediate futures.

Setting goals is an important part of solution conversations in therapy. de Shazer (1991) took an almost behavioral approach to describing effective goals, a process that also fits well with many of the requirements of managed care agencies. He believed that effective goals are: small rather than large; meaningful to the clients; described concretely; fit the actual lives of the participants; require in them a sense that they are working hard; and start something new rather than end a problem (that is, they are based on new behaviors rather than the elimination of old ones).

The Therapist's Role and Function

The more postmodern models developed in Milan and the United States during the 1990s call upon the therapist to function as an investigator. These models are very collaborative. Where the original function of the MRI one-down position had a manipulative intent even when it was genuinely applied, Boscolo and Cecchin as well as the solution-focused/solution-oriented therapists became completely dedicated to a client-empowering inquiry process. Optimism, persistence, and anticipatory inquiries about new possibilities are all parts of the role and function of the therapist.

Just as there is no single or even right way to perceive reality, there is also no correct way for a family and its members to be. Solution therapists believe that each family has within it the resources and possibilities for change that can lead to more functional and fulfilling lives. It is only problem-saturated and complaint-oriented stories reinforced by constant retelling that keep families stuck. It is a much different perspective to think of a family as stuck than to think of it as resistant to help. The latter requires the therapist to outmaneuver the client. The former allows the therapist to cooperate with the client in an effort merely to get moving again. Solution-focused/solution-oriented therapists do this by looking for exceptions to complaint-oriented stories, reminding families of past successes, considering what was previously ignored, focusing on client strengths, and generating hope through new possibilities. It is in the development of such therapeutic conversations that families create new stories that act as self-fulfilling prophesies.

Techniques

Because clients often come to therapy in a problem-oriented state, even the few solutions they have considered are wrapped in the power of the problem orientation. Solution-focused/solution-oriented therapists counter this client presentation with optimistic dialogues that highlight their belief in achievable, usable goals that are just around the corner. Such conversations involve reframing "the problem in a more positive, functional light and [complimenting] clients on the perseverance and resourcefulness; [clarifying] the logical bind clients have created for themselves; and [linking] a hypnotic-like directive to an inevitable sign of progress" (Nichols & Schwartz, 2006, p. 326). Within this general process, the following kinds of interventions are common to solution-focused and solution-oriented (possibility) therapists:

The Miracle Question.   The miracle question (de Shazer, 1985, 1988) is almost perfectly designed to feed our universal human desire for a miracle when we are faced with a serious problem. Essentially, the question posed to clients is: "If a miracle happened and the problem you have were solved overnight, how would you know it was solved, and what would be the signs that something is different?"[4] Clients then are encouraged to enact "what would be different" in spite of perceived problems.

Exception Questions.   Similar to White and Epston's (1990) process of eliciting "**unique events**," which we shall consider in the next chapter, solution-oriented therapists ask exception questions that direct clients to times in their lives when the problem didn't exist. "Was there a time when you didn't have this problem?" "Have you had any of those times recently?" "How are those times different?" "What has changed?" "What do you do to make them different?" "What do you notice about yourself and others when things are different?" This exploration reminds clients that problems are not all-powerful and have not existed forever; it also provides a field of opportunity for evoking resources, engaging strengths, and positing possible solutions. Solution-focused/solution-oriented therapists focus on small, achievable changes that may lead to additional positive outcomes. Their language joins with the client's, using similar words, pacing, and tone, a foundation for what social workers call a **strengths perspective**.

Scaling Questions.   Solution-focused/solution-oriented therapists also use scaling questions when changes that are required in human experiences are not easily observed, such as with feelings, moods, or communication. For example, a woman reporting feelings of panic or anxiety might be asked: "On a scale of 0 to 10, with 0 being how you felt when you first came to therapy and 10 being how you feel the day after your miracle occurs and your problem is gone, how would you rate your anxiety right now?" Even if the client has moved only from 0 to 1, she has improved. How did she do that? What does she need to do to move another number up the scale? Scaling questions can also be used to regulate reality: "On a scale of 0 to a 100, with 0 being never and 100 being always, how often do you actually experience this problem?" "What lower level would have to be achieved in order for you to feel better?" "What would you be doing to get it there?" "What would others be doing?" Scaling questions also can be used to encourage a commitment to change: "On a scale of 1 to 10, how sure are you that you will be able to stick to the changes you've chosen for this week?" "What will you have to do to accomplish your goals?"

Signs and Questions of Difference.   As I noted in the presentation of the case above, questions of difference are intended to open up space in relationships for thinking about and understanding self and others in a new way. Walter and Peller (2000) used this method when they asked the daughter to listen to the counselor's conversation with her parents and vice versa. The directive given to the listener was to see what differences each party noticed in her or himself when they listened to the other. Solution-focused practitioners often ask people in therapy for signs that life and relationships would be better: It is from these signs that real solutions are fashioned and designed. de Shazer's (1985, 1988) **formula first-session tasks** were also ways to get at clues to solutions within family process. He would ask couples or families to observe things that happened during the week that they would like to keep going. Those aspects of the family's life that they would like to continue served as signs of difference in what was otherwise a negative, problem-focused family orientation. Another **formula task** is called a **prediction task**: "Today, let's predict whether your problem will be better or the same tomorrow. Tomorrow, rate the way your day went and compare it to your prediction. What do you think made a difference in a right or wrong prediction? Do this each day until we meet again."

Compliments.   For **compliments** to be effective, they must come from a genuine appreciation of what the clients have done or achieved. Questions of surprise and delight are often used to convey a compliment: "Wow! You really did that well. How did you do that?" Such compliments focus on strengths and direct family members toward successful interactions and interventions: solutions that already work.

Embedded Messages.   Reflecting the influence of both Milton Erickson and the MRI model, de Shazer (1982) began to work with **embedded messages** in paradoxical interventions. In essence his directives joined with what the family was already doing, but used pauses to emphasize doing something different.

> We've thought a lot about your situation, and I'm going to read you our ideas.
> We know that you'd like to (pause) *Mrs. Jones stop being bitchy* [3] and (pause) *stop hollering at Bob* (pause) but we don't think that would be a wise idea right now because you need to continue trying to teach Bob to be responsible for himself (pause) and that's the best way you've found. If you were to (pause) *Mrs. Jones stop hollering* right now, that might upset the balance in your family in some way. (p. 139)

Although this example of indirect communication included similar directives for the father and son—and it is more clearly representative of a pre-solution-focused, MRI approach used at BFTC, such embedded messages still are used to join with clients and suggest a different course of action. We saw some of this in the example of Insoo Kim Berg working with the man who believed his wife was having an affair. de Shazer also embedded expectations for success in his dialogues with clients simply by using the word *when*: "When you get up tomorrow and things are different, what will you notice first?", or "When you notice a positive difference this week in your relationship, write it down so that we can see how it came about."

Summary Messages.   **Summary messages** usually come at the end of a session—especially the first session. If a team approach has been used, then the summary often comes from the team. The summary lets the client know what the therapist(s) has heard and understands about the family's problem, and seeks to clarify anything that the interviewer might have missed. Such a summary is followed by a compassionate expression of the emotional impact the problem has had on the couple or family, coupled with compliments for how they have endured or what strengths have been mobilized to face the problem. The solution-focused practitioner then makes a suggestion for building on success or creating a new solution. Some of the most common solutions include the formula tasks, do more of what is already working, do something different (like an experiment to see what will happen), go slowly (taken from the MRI model and designed to reduce resistance and fear), do the opposite (a solution that is especially useful when two people seem locked in a repetitive pattern), or assigning the prediction task (Nichols & Schwartz, 2006). Solution-oriented practitioners often design summaries to turn problem-oriented conversations toward solutions.

Solution-oriented therapy has a number of interventions that are often parallel to, but that also differentiates it from, solution-focused therapy by working directly with the family's stated problem(s) (see Gale, 1991). None of these techniques is intended to be applied in a rigid manner. They are simply options to consider in the process of (a) validating the experiences of the client; (b) identifying actions that are at least potentially under the client's control; and (c) developing solution-oriented actions and stories for preferred outcomes. All of these interventions start with the solution-oriented practitioner making a conscious effort to join with the client's language (use of words and phrases) and to use the interview process to presuppose change: The counselor wants to know what will be happening *when*, not if, change occurs.

Introducing Doubt.

Introducing doubt uses questions about the assumptions involved in problem-oriented stories or presentations that challenge such notions as real, permanent, or inevitable. Such doubt has the effect of making space for additional possibilities.

Normalization.

Similar to a process used by Adlerians, the solution-oriented practitioner often will reframe problems as normal, everyday occurrences when the family or family members have been pathologized or have begun to self-pathologize their situation. **Normalizing a problem** implies that because it is not so extreme, it can be addressed and solved.

Changing the Doing of the Problem.

O'Hanlon and Weiner-Davis (2003) believed that changing the doing and viewing of the perceived problem changes the problem; that is, effective solutions have some relation to processes that counter problematic patterns. "There are two main ways to change the 'doing' of the problem:

1. Identify and alter repetitive patterns of action and interaction involved in the problem; and
2. Identify and encourage the use of solution patterns of action and interaction" (O'Hanlon & O'Hanlon, 2002, p. 207).

Changing the doing of the problem can happen in multiple ways. O'Hanlon and O'Hanlon (2002) suggest possible changes in frequency/rate, duration, timing, intensity, invariant quality, or sequence and order of the problem; they also suggest interrupting or preventing the problem altogether, adding a new element to the problem, breaking up the problem into smaller units, performing the problem differently, doing the problem when the family is not having the problem, reversing the directionality of the problem, linking the problem to an ordeal, or changing the actual behavior and performance of the problem. It is easy to see the influence of the MRI model on the O'Hanlons—and even their continuing connection to it. Although changing the doing of the problem may be effective as an initial change, the real focus of this therapy is on the generation and encouragement of solutions.

Working With the Future.

As preferred solutions are developed, they are transformed into specific, concrete goals. In anticipation of implementing these goals, possible obstructions to success are considered and ways around those obstructions are developed. **Working with the future** is not dissimilar to the kind of work that William Glasser (2000) does in implementing reality therapy.

Multiple-Choice Questions.   Using **multiple-choice questions** is a rather simple intervention that makes use of the kinds of questions that we all experienced in school. They are questions about the family's problem(s) with a twist: The suggested A-B-C answers have embedded within them solutions or directions that are new possibilities for the clients.

A Solution-Oriented Therapist With the Quest Family

Paul and Jane Quest bring all four of their children to the first meeting with a solution-oriented family therapist. This solution-oriented family therapist includes specific time in the assessment session to clarify and get at the right problem for the family to solve. While solution-focused therapists tend to downplay the importance of problem identification, one difference for solution-oriented therapists seems to be in the connection they see between problem identification and generating solutions. The assessment session is, in fact, divided into roughly two halves, so that the connection between problem and solution is central to the investigation.

After meeting each of the members of the Quest family, the solution-oriented therapist starts by asking, "How can we work together to help you change your situation?" Jane ignores the solution-oriented question and notes that she is really concerned about Jason and Luke, their level of aggressive, violent behavior, and her energy in trying to handle everyone and everything. She doesn't feel she can cope without help, and the family seems to be "falling apart." Paul feels a great deal of sympathy for his wife, says he had hoped that both Amy and Ann would be more help for her with the boys, but they have their own lives, and he realizes that part of the problem is that he is away from home at critical times during each day.

Amy and Ann sit together next to their father and across from the two empty chairs placed close to the mother for the boys. Jason and Luke are up and moving around. Addressing Paul first, the therapist begins.

Therapist:	Paul, what do you think would make a difference with Luke and Jason?
Paul:	Well, the reality is that these boys were horribly treated when they were very young. They were hurt and abused in ways that are too horrible for most people to imagine. I don't even like to think about it. Whatever they do, they have had much worse happen to them: cigarette burns on their bodies, beatings, and punishments that adults could not withstand.
Therapist:	So you have some sympathy for these boys. You must feel that they need a lot of positive experiences to make up for all that has happened to them. Is that right?
Paul:	Yes, that's right, but I also recognize that it is hard for Jane to provide those positive experiences when she is putting out fires all the time. Not literally putting out fires . . . well, sometimes, maybe, but she has to stay on top of everything, and there is always something. And I am very tied up in my work, which makes it hard for me to provide the kinds of things that the boys might need.
Therapist:	So time and energy are big parts of this problem that really make it difficult to find workable solutions. Jane, what do you think would make a difference in the lives of Jason and Luke?
Jane:	I don't disagree with anything that Paul said. The boys have had more tragedy in their young lives than I could stand. They were hurt, and they lost their mother. Their father is court-ordered to stay away from them and, if they ever find him, he will probably be

implicated in their mother's death. How do young children comprehend any of that? I have always felt so sorry for them. I wanted to erase all the bad when they first came to us. I wanted them to have a childhood like Ann and Amy had, but it is just too much to do by myself. It's too hard. I am exhausted all the time.

Therapist: So for you, too, it is a matter of what kind of time you spend with them and the energy level that it takes.

Jane: Yes, and it is about what we do together as a family. I wanted us to all be part of raising these boys. I often feel very much alone.

Therapist: I don't hear what you are saying as a sense of helplessness in you, more just a statement of fact: There is a lot you have to do with Jason and Luke, and you are alone when you have to do it. Like, Paul, did you, too, hope that Ann and Amy would be of greater assistance to you? Or do you feel you need Paul more available—or both?

Jane: Ann does try to help with the boys—a lot. Amy is in her last year of high school and is very involved in lots of different activities. I think that's appropriate. I feel guilty about needing so much of Ann's time. I think I am robbing her of time with her friends . . . and really a carefree life that I want for all of my children. I could use more help from Paul, but he is a doctor and his work has always been important to him and to all of us, really.

Therapist: Amy and Ann, what's your theory about why this problem with Jason and Luke exists?

Ann: Well, for one thing, they are boys. They're rougher. Actually, you talk about energy, well, they're the ones who have it. If they're awake, they're going full bore.

Just as the therapist is about to ask another question, a small fight breaks out between the boys. Jane immediately gets up and makes both of the boys sit down in the circle.

Therapist: Jason, I don't know if you know this, but I have an imaginary magic wand. (The therapist waves her hand in the air as if to demonstrate holding the wand and using it for magic.) Would you like to try my magic wand?

Jason: Yeah, I like magic wands.

Therapist: (passing the wand to Jason, smiling) Be careful: Don't drop it. I am wondering if you could wave the magic wand and zap your family here with it, what would be happening? What would be different first?

Jason: They would be happy . . . .

Therapist: What would make everyone happy?

Jason: We will play together a lot. . . . Dad will come home more . . . .

Therapist: What will you play together?

Jason: Baseball. I like to throw baseballs with him . . . but he's at work.

Luke: No, wrestle. I want to play wrestling. Daddy, I want to play tickling and wrestling. . . . Can we?

Jane: It's like everyone needs more time with you, Paul. I think they miss you. I miss you.

Therapist: It's back to that time thing again. I don't know, Paul. What do you think?

Paul: We, Jason and I, have played catch sometimes. And I often wrestle with the boys when I come home. I didn't know it meant so much to them. I actually like it too.

Therapist: It's about some of those positive experiences you were hoping to provide for the boys. And when you do these things, do you notice any difference in how your life with them goes?

Paul: Yeah. Actually, things often go well for a number of hours. I think Jane relaxes some. Amy and Ann go off to do other things, and both Jason and Luke, well, they seem to laugh a lot.

Therapist: Yes, laughter is wonderfully healing, isn't it? What else would you like for the boys?

> Paul and Jane's number one hope is to give the boys a good education. Paul mentions sports, fishing, and camping. Jane wants music lessons for the boys—perhaps the violin. Paul suggests taking them to work with him occasionally. Jane is interested in developing a love of the arts (museums, galleries, etc.). Both parents want Jason and Luke to feel fully part of the family, to share in the family benefits, and to do their part in the work of the household. Paul says it won't be long before Jason can mow the lawn, and Jane laughs, indicating that she would really be happier if they were cleaning their rooms and the bathroom. They paint a picture of normalcy that breaks down the divisions among them and has everyone engaged with each other.

Therapist: What should we do as parents to get this to happen?

Paul: Well, I think it obviously starts with me. I can free up more time to be at home and to really do some things with the boys. I think that would be fun anyway. Maybe this will also give Jane more of a break.

Jane: Maybe we could set aside some time to talk about how we are going to do this together. If I felt that we were really in this together, I think we could manage anything.

Therapist: So what will you do first?

Paul: Sit down with Jane, look at my schedule, and plan some changes in it, so I can be home more.

Jane: That would be wonderful.

> At the end of the session, the therapist summarized the conversation they all had had together, noting that the introduction of two new people to the family had a real impact on the system emotionally, but emphasizing that they had developed some possibilities that seemed very likely to succeed. The therapist asked the parents to notice any differences that occurred between sessions and especially to note things in their daily lives they would like to see continue. It was 2 weeks before the next meeting could be arranged. There was no contact between the family and the therapist, so any differences in the family would be the focus of the first part of the next session.

Therapist: So how are things better?

Jane: There's been some real improvement thanks to Paul, but the boys are still hitting, and . . . .

Therapist: There's been some real improvements? Like what would those be?

Jane: Well, I think Paul and I are on the same page. It really helped when we sat down to talk about what we wanted for all of our children, not just Jason and Luke, but Amy and Ann too.

Paul: And what we wanted for us . . . what time we wanted to have with each other.

Therapist: So on a scale of 1 to 10, with 1 being extremely poor and 10 being great, where would you rate your family 4 weeks ago.

Paul: We were at a 2.

Jane: Definitely a 1.

Therapist: And what rating would you give your family today?

Paul: I would say we are at a 6.

Jane: Maybe a 5.

Therapist: Wow! So any way you look at it, that's a jump of about 4 points in 2 weeks. That seems great to me. There are many families that would not have made such a jump. What did you do that accounts for such an increase?

Jane:	I really think it is all due to Paul spending more time with Jason and Luke, playing with them, but also giving them their baths and reading them stories at night before bed.
Paul:	Oh, no. It's not just me. You have been fixing them special foods, we, not I, took them to a movie—and it was your idea. And the other day, when Luke hit Jason, you got down next to him and quietly reminded him that we don't hit people and asked him if there was another way he could let people know he was upset.
Therapist:	So let me see if I am getting this: You are both spending more time with the boys, doing family things, and you are finding that you have more energy and the boys are responding better. Are there other things that you are doing that seem to work for you?
Jane:	Well, I have been insisting that Ann go out more with her friends and take some time for herself. She, too, seems happier, which is a relief to me. And when she is home, eating with us say, she laughs more and is really good at getting the boys to talk to all of us.
Therapist:	So freeing Ann from being your helper has actually increased her effectiveness with Jason and Luke. What an amazing turn of events. It's almost paradoxical.
Jane:	And much to all of our surprise, even Amy is finding more time to be at home and join in on family events. I don't know if we told you, but Ann had a birthday last week, and Amy planned a party at the house. She, Jason, and Luke actually put on a funny skit for her.
Therapist:	Well, Ann, let me add my best wishes to you for your birthday. It sounds like it was a wonderful time.
Ann:	Thanks, it was nice.
Therapist:	What things have you noticed that make things better at home.
Ann:	Mainly that Mom is in a better mood, Dad is home more, and the boys will do things for him that I could never get them to do. I guess they just needed more time with him. I remember that being important to me when I was their ages.
Amy:	I agree with Ann. There is a different mood in the house, and it makes it easier for all of us.
Therapist:	So on that scale of 1 to 10, where would you rate your family's life right now?
Amy:	(looking at Ann for agreement) I agree with Dad: It's at least a 6, maybe a 7.
Therapist:	I would really like to lock that 7 into place. What steps would have to be taken so that you could all feel like you had reached a 7 by our next meeting?
Ann:	I think just keep doing what we are doing.
Jane:	I would need to see that the boys were participating more in taking care of their things and helping around the house. If we were at a 7, they would put the dinner dishes on the counter after eating without being told. They would put their clothes in the hamper. They would remember to brush their teeth. And instead of hitting, they would come to me when they are upset and talk it out.
Therapist:	Wow!! You have some pretty high standards for a 7. What are the chances that Jason and Luke will do all of that in the next 7 days?
Paul:	Not much. But I do think it works to tell them once what needs to be done and then, if necessary, take them to do it. Reminding doesn't really help with them. Like, I think we should only wash the clothes that they put in the hamper, and if I have to pick their other clothes up, then I put them in my closet until they run out of clothes and learn to put them away or in the hamper. That's what we used to do with Amy and Ann, and they have turned out okay.
Therapist:	So you join Jane in wanting to help the boys learn to be responsible, and you have some ideas about how you might teach that to them. And if you did this next week, what improvements would you be looking for?

Paul:	I think that they might remove their own dishes every night and only need to be asked to do it maybe three or four times.
Therapist:	So about half the time, they might just do it on their own. And would that be good enough for a 7, or would there have to be more?
Jane:	That would be good enough. That would really be a lot of improvement—especially from a month ago.
Therapist:	How would you rate your confidence level that you and Paul working together can help this happen?
Jane:	My confidence level? It's already at a 7.
Therapist:	What do you boys think?
Luke:	Jason can take my plate for me.
Jason:	No I can't, but I can remember to take my own.
Therapist:	Every night?
Jason:	Almost.
Therapist:	Well, almost every night will certainly get this family a 7. So great!
Luke:	Me, too. I can do almost.

Summary and Multicultural Evaluation

For some time now, the solution-focused and solution-oriented models have been dominated by the scholarship and clinical practice of its founders. More than any other approaches, these solution models are the bridge from the systemic therapies of the last 50 years to the current emphasis on postmodern social constructionism. Toward the end of her life, Berg still used one-way mirrors and team consultations in her work, but she clearly had adopted the more collaborative nature of social constructionist approaches. She believed clients should choose their own goals, but she also had never lost the emphasis of the MRI model on measurable outcomes. To be sure, it is this latter emphasis that appeals most to the managed care industry. It is the second generation of solution-focused therapists, however, who are moving the model away from a focus on techniques toward a focus on therapeutic relationships (Lipchik, 2002; Walter & Peller, 2000).

Like other postmodern approaches, solution-focused/solution-oriented practitioners rely on questions both to structure therapy and to develop preferred outcomes with clients. Although the miracle question, exception questions, and scaling questions have all become well-known and integrated parts of these models, they represent variations on the effort to acknowledge differences in families that can make a difference. They all lead to clues, signs, and options that are the foundation for co-creating desired outcomes. Many of the same criticisms that initially have been leveled at other models, such as the Adlerian model, also have been visited on the solution models. It is said that these approaches are simplistic; they are too brief and have no evidence of lasting change; and they force family members to acquiesce to a new language without really changing the system. To be sure, research on clinical effectiveness is sorely needed. In the meantime, solution-focused and solution-oriented therapies are two of the fastest-growing approaches to individual, group, couples, and family therapies.

Solution-focused therapy and solution-oriented (possibility) therapy contribute greatly to a teleological lens in therapy. The emphasis on the present and future presupposes a goal-orientation in families as well as therapy. These models elevate human desires and make the implementation of hope both concrete and pragmatic. In rendering the practice of psychopathology useless, these models blend the encouragement and strengths-focus of the

Adlerians with Satir's valuing of the change process and the collaborative efforts of social constructionists.

Dolan (2005) summarizes the major tenets of solution-focused brief therapy as follows:

- If it ain't broke, don't fix it. If it works, do more of it;
- If it is not working, do something different;
- Small steps can lead to large changes;
- The solution is not directly related to the problem;
- The language requirements for solution development are different from those needed to describe a problem;
- No problem happens all the time. There are always exceptions which can be utilized; and
- The future is both created and negotiable.

If you are interested in a more in-depth study of this approach, I recommend the following sources: Berg & Miller (1992); de Shazer (1982, 1988, 1991); Gale (1991); Lipchik (2002); O'Hanlon & Weiner-Davis (2003); O'Hanlon & Wilk (1987); and Walter & Peller (1992, 2000).

Contributions to Multicultural Counseling and Gender Issues

Steve de Shazer spent a great deal of time in Europe. Insoo Kim Berg has taken solution-focused therapy to various parts of Asia. O'Hanlon and other solution-oriented therapists also work around the world. With the exception of Berg's references to gender and culture, however, there has been very little focus on gender and culture—and the impact these perspectives have on family life and family problems. Both solution models miss a real opportunity to explore culture and gender in terms of the unique solutions that such multicultural perspectives might provide.

Selekman (1997) devotes only two pages to these issues in which he acknowledges the critique of family therapy that feminist have brought to the table (for example, Avis, 1986; Bograd, 1990; Goodrich, 1991; Luepnitz, 1988; and Whipple, 1996). He even offers a small case in which the **complaint-oriented story** of a woman and her child includes concerns that her husband is too busy to come to therapy, that she seldom gets to see her own friends, and that she is very tired. The solution that is co-constructed addresses the traditional values and expectations associated with patriarchy and leads to the woman confronting her husband and taking time for herself. Although valuable as an introduction of gender issues in solution models, nothing further is offered as a positive use of gender in the development of solutions. For example, any of the following questions might fit these approaches quite well, but they are missing-in-action.

- What do you think your partner (spouse) can teach you that would be effective in helping you reach your goals?
- If you were your spouse or children, what changes in you would signify that your relationship or family life was getting better?
- What aspects of being female would you like to see valued and continued in your life?
- What activities would you be doing with your partner and family that would tell you that you were a true friend and teammate?

Selekman does offer a set of questions that solution therapists should ask themselves before working with families. These include:

[if you are a white therapist] "Have I examined my own white identity in terms of what it means to be white in our society?"

"How do I feel about being white and my own ethnic and/or cultural background?"

"How does being white and/or being from a different ethnic or cultural background affect what I can see, hear, and think about this family?"

"In what way does being white in our society grant me . . . privileged status?"

"How does this privileged status and power imbalance affect my relationships with the African American families I am working with?"

"If you were African American, Asian, Latino, how comfortable would you feel working with a white therapist?"

"What would your concerns be with a white therapist?" (pp. 48–49)

Again, this is a good start: Those who support a multicultural perspective will especially like that these questions start with a focus on therapist competence. What is lacking, however, is any guidance on how to implement a multicultural perspective into solution-focused or solution-oriented therapy. Imagine solution-oriented questions like the following:

- What were the times in your life like when you felt empowered?
- When there is improvement in society and the community in which you live with regard to racism, sexism, or other forms of discrimination, what differences will you notice?
- If a miracle were to happen tonight, and you woke up tomorrow in a world in which you were no longer oppressed or marginalized, what would be the difference? What would you be able to do differently with your life?
- [to a person struggling with acculturation to a new country] What have you noticed about those who have been here for some time and seem to you to have some skills in negotiating a life between your culture and the host culture?
- [if you are a member of the dominant culture] If I decided that racism, sexism, heterosexism, etc., were really my responsibility to change, what would I be doing differently in my daily activities?
- [again, if you are a member of the dominant culture] What skills would I need to feel competent in confronting people from within my dominant culture who are actively engaged in discriminatory or oppressive acts?

Can you think of other solution-focused or solution-oriented questions that might incorporate a multicultural and/or gender perspective in therapy? How would you introduce these questions into the process? Would you wait for gender and cultural issues to surface in the counseling sessions, or do you think that such inquiries should be part of all therapeutic interviews?

Exercises for Personal and Professional Growth

Let's see what will happen if we apply solution-focused/solution-oriented therapy to our own lives. Are there any miracles you would like to create? If you woke up tomorrow morning and your miracle had happened, what would be different? What would you notice first? What would be other clues or signs that the miracle had really happened and life was different? What would you be doing differently? Too often, people wait for certain conditions or opportunities to materialize—or they wait for a particular feeling—before they engage in change. Similar to the Adlerian model we have already studied and the cognitive-behavioral models we will consider later, solution therapists know that the miracle of change requires us to **act as if** such conditions were already present. If we can act as if the miracle has happened, we create the conditions for its enactment, and the feelings we need to support the change arrive shortly thereafter.

So what miracles do you envision for yourself as a person and a professional? What will it be like to begin acting on that vision immediately? How would the doing of this new miracle be different from what you are doing with your life and professional development now? Take some time to write your desired miracles down on the following page (or on a separate piece of paper). As a hint, it may be useful to remember that the really important differences often are related to the kinds of relationships we have with others.

Miracle desired:

_____

_____

_____

_____

What would you be doing differently? _____

_____

_____

_____

How will you know when your miracle is accomplished? _____

_____

_____

_____

Now let's turn to a case and get a little practice with forming solution questions. I am thinking of a woman who came to see a therapist for depression; she feels that she lacks energy or enthusiasm for any part of life, but she especially feels that returning to work—where she anticipates that she will be criticized for her efforts—is a source of great worry. She currently avoids any relationships unless she is absolutely sure that she will be supported and nurtured. Anyone with expectations of her only fuels her self-depreciation and her sense of hopelessness. The woman's culture is African American. She grew up in a family that believed in preparing their young for life's harsh realities by being perfectionistic in their expectations and punishing children for poor performance.

Using some of the techniques associated with solution-focused therapy, can you think of questions you might ask (a) within the solution-focused or solution-oriented models; (b) from a cultural perspective; and (c) from a gender perspective? Try filling in the chart below.

There are, of course, no right questions to ask. Or, more accurately, there are many different questions that can be asked in an effort to create solutions or movement toward solutions.

Solution-Focused Techniques	Your Ideas
Scaling Questions	a. b. c.
Exception Questions	a. b. c.
Signs or Questions of Difference	a. b. c.

So do each of the questions that you listed have an intent? Have you thought about what the intent of each question might be? Choosing some questions over others shapes the kind of discussions that you will have in therapy. If you would like to compare the questions you wrote to another set of possibilities (and they are only possibilities, not the right answers), see the set available in the Endnotes.[6]

Where to Go From Here

Steve de Shazer and Insoo Kim Berg founded the Brief Family Therapy Center (BFTC) in Milwaukee, Wisconsin, in 1982, where they developed and promoted solution-focused therapy. When the center closed, the videos, books, and other programs at BFTC were transferred to the Solution Focused Brief Therapy Association. You can reach this association at **http://www.sfbta.org**.

Bill and Stephanie O'Hanlon offer training and programs in solution-oriented or possibility therapy from their center in Santa Fe, New Mexico. You can reach them at:

Bill O'Hanlon and Possibilities
551 Cordova Rd., #715
Santa Fe, NM 87501
Phone: 800-381-2374
E-mail: **possiBill@aol.com**
Website: **www.brieftherapy.com**

Michele Weiner-Davis has devoted her most recent work to the popular book market with books and programs on divorce-busting and learning to live a more fully engaged life. She still lives and works in Illinois:

Michele Weiner-Davis
P.O. Box 197
Woodstock, IL 60098
Phone: 815-337-8000

Two of the best books on solution focused therapy are written by John Walter and Jane Peller (1992, 2000). They also provide training and consultation through their center in Chicago.

John L. Walter and Jane E. Peller
1620 W. Thome
Chicago, Illinois 60660
Phone: 847-475-2691
E-mail: **j-peller@neiu.edu** or **walterpeller@aol.com**

Recommended Readings

Berg, I. K., & Miller, S. D. (1992). *Working with the problem drinker: A solution-focused approach.* New York: Norton. Insoo Kim Berg and Scott Miller applied solution-focused therapy to the problem of substance in a fresh and useful approach that should be adopted by most people working with addictions.

de Shazer, S. (1985). *Keys to solutions in brief therapy.* New York: Norton. This book is a starter kit for doing solution-focused therapy.

de Shazer, S., & Dolan, Y. (2007). *More than miracles: The state of the art of solution-focused brief therapy* (with H. Korman, E. McCollum, T. Trepper, & I. K. Berg). Binghamton, NY: Haworth. This is the last book in which de Shazer was a co-author; it was completed just weeks before his death. In this volume, the authors present the most-current practices in solution-focused brief therapy and answer questions and issues raised about their approach.

Lipchik, E. (2002). *Beyond technique in solution-focused therapy: Working with emotions and the therapeutic relationship*. New York: Guilford. One of the original staff at the BFTC, Eve Lipchik's book brings a real sense of heart and soul to solution-focused work. For those who consider emotion an essential part of therapeutic work, this book is a significant manual.

O'Hanlon, W. H., & Weiner-Davis, M. (2003). *In search of solutions: A new direction in psychotherapy* (rev. ed.). New York: Norton. This is the book that both delineates solution-oriented therapy and starts to differentiate it from the solution-focused model used by de Shazer and Berg.

Walter, J. L., & Peller, J. E. (1992). *Becoming solution-focused in brief therapy*. New York: Brunner Routledge. This is the most concrete, clear, and useful presentation of solution-focused therapy on the market. This is a book that is meant to be used and referenced when deciding how to approach specific cases: It is enormously practical and will serve managed-care practitioners extremely well.

Walter, J. L., & Peller, J. E. (2000). *Recreating brief therapy: Preferences and possibilities*. New York: Norton. This is a follow-up to the authors' 1992 book. It presents solution-focused therapy from a decidedly social-constructionist perspective and offers up questions that lead to signs of solutions and to noticing differences that can change perspectives and actions.

DVD Reference

The solution-focused and solution-oriented models of family therapy grew out of the founders' initial training in strategic family therapy, but their aim was to turn strategic family therapy on its head. Both Steve de Shazer and Insoo Kim Berg moved away from the problem-focused, therapist-as-expert interventions of the strategic models to develop methods of focusing on solutions. Indeed, de Shazer often said that he didn't even need to know the problem a family was having—only what they wanted for their lives instead.

Solution-oriented therapy was developed by Bill O'Hanlon and Michele Weiner-Davis. They used a method of inquiry that was situated within the postmodern perspective of the client-as-expert. Both the solution-focused and solution-oriented models are joined in the work of John Walter and Jane Peller. In this video, we use their focus on questions of difference to develop the multiple stories about the son in this family. The segment ends with a demonstration of scaling questions as they might be used in a solution-focused model.

References

Avis, J. M. (1986). Feminist issues in family therapy. In F. P. Piercy, D. H. Sprenkle, & Associates (Eds.), *Family therapy sourcebook* (pp. 213–243). New York: Guilford.

Berg, I. K. (Speaker). (2002, December 12). Case presentations (J. Carlson, Moderator). *Brief Therapy Conference*. Orlando, FL: Milton H. Erickson Foundation.

Berg, I. K., & de Shazer, S. (1993). Making numbers talk: Language in therapy. In S. Friedman (Ed.), *The new language of change* (pp. 5–24). New York: Guilford.

Berg, I. K., & Miller, S. D. (1992). *Working with the problem drinker: A solution-focused approach*. New York: Norton.

Bograd, M. (1990). Scapegoating mothers: Conceptual errors in systemic formulations. In M. P. Mirkin (Ed.), *The social and political contexts of family therapy* (pp. 69–89). Needham Heights, MA: Allyn & Bacon.

de Shazer, S. (1982). *Patterns of brief family therapy: An ecosystemic approach*. New York: Guilford.

de Shazer, S. (1985). *Keys to solutions in brief therapy*. New York: Norton.

de Shazer, S. (1988). *Clues: Investigating solutions in brief therapy*. New York: Norton.

de Shazer, S. (1991). *Putting difference to work*. New York: Norton.

de Shazer, S., & Berg, I. K. (1993). Constructing solutions. *Family Therapy Networker, 17*(3), 42–43.

de Shazer, S., & Dolan, Y. (2007). *More than miracles: The state of the art of solution-focused brief therapy* (with H. Korman, E. McCollum, T. Trepper, & I. K. Berg). Binghamton, NY: Haworth.

Dolan, Y. (2005). A brief overview of solution-focused brief therapy. In Milton H. Erickson Foundation, *Evolution of Psychotherapy Handout CD*. Phoenix, AZ: Author.

Dreikurs, R. (1997). Holistic medicine. *Individual Psychology, 53*(2), 127–205.

Gale, J. E. (1991). *Conversation analysis of therapeutic discourse: The pursuit of a therapeutic agenda*. Norwood, NJ: Ablex.

Glasser, W. (2000). *Counseling with choice theory: The new reality therapy*. New York: HarperCollins.

Goodrich, T. J. (1991). Women, power, and family therapy: What's wrong with this picture? *Journal of Feminist Family Therapy, 3*(1/2), 5–38.

Lipchik, E. (2002). *Beyond technique in solution-focused therapy: Working with emotions and the therapeutic relationship*. New York: Guilford.

Luepnitz, D. A. (1988). *The family interpreted: Feminist theory in clinical practice*. New York: Basic Books.

Nichols, M. P., & Schwartz, R. C. (2006). *Family therapy: Concepts and methods* (7th ed.). Boston: Allyn and Bacon.

O'Hanlon, S., & O'Hanlon, B. (2002). Solution-oriented therapy with families. In J. Carlson & D. Kjos (Eds.), *Theories and strategies of family therapy* (pp. 190–215). Boston: Allyn & Bacon.

O'Hanlon, W. H., & Weiner-Davis, M. (2003). *In search of solutions: A new direction in psychotherapy* (rev. ed.). New York: Norton.

O'Hanlon, W. H., & Wilk, J. (1987). *Shifting contexts: The generation of effective psychotherapy*. New York: Guilford.

Selekman, M. D. (1997). *Solution-focused therapy with children: Harnessing family strengths for systemic change*. New York: Guilford.

Walter, J. L., & Peller, J. E. (1992). *Becoming solution-focused in brief therapy*. New York: Brunner Routledge.

Walter, J. L., & Peller, J. E. (2000). *Recreating brief therapy: Preferences and possibilities*. New York: Norton.

Whipple, V. (1996). Developing an identity as a feminist family therapist: Implications for training. *Journal of Marital and Family Therapy, 22*(3), 381–396.

White, M., & Epston, D. (1990). *Narrative means to therapeutic ends*. New York: Norton.

Endnotes

[1] Walter and Peller (2000) use the word consultant because it allows them to move away from the pathology/deficit model implied by *therapist/client* or even *counselor/client* relationships and explicitly involved in the relationship of doctor/patient.

[2] The preceding dialogue was constructed based on the case materials presented by Walter and Peller (2000). The following conversation is quoted directly from this source.

[3] This use of a joining through paradox is an example of an intervention that requires skill and experience. The same intervention used in other situations might have very negative effects.

[4] The phrasing of the miracle question is not essentially different from what Adlerians call **"The Question"** (Dreikurs, 1997), although Adlerians used the information differently than solution-focused/solution-oriented therapists. Adlerians believe that the client's

symptom or problem actually protects them from what they say they would be doing differently, while solution-focused/solution-oriented therapists use the answer to co-construct with the family the goals of therapy.

[5]The use of the word "bitchy" would be highly offensive in most cases, but de Shazer used it because it fit with the language and experience of the family.

[6]Any number of different solution-focused/solution-oriented questions might be used in an effort to help this woman. One set of possible questions might be in the table below:

Solution-Focused Techniques	Your Ideas
Scaling Questions	a. When you came here today, you said you were at about an 8 on a 10-point depression scale. Where do you feel you are now on that scale and what did you do to create movement?
	b. You have had a number of strong African American role models in your life. Where would you place yourself on a scale of 1 to 10 in terms of how you measure up to the models you want to be like?
	c. Women often are told that they can't compete with men in the world of work, that they can't do as well or achieve as much. Where would you place yourself on a scale from 1 to 10 in terms of how well you feel you can challenge that position?
Exception Questions	a. What have you noticed about the days you are not depressed or are less depressed? What things are you doing on those days that are different from other days?
	b. You seem to admire Maya Angelou. Are there days in which you experience aspects of Maya Angelou in you? What are you doing on those days?
	c. Who are the people who really support you as a woman—and especially as a woman in the workforce? What is it like to anticipate their positive evaluation of you? How do you prepare yourself to receive their compliments? What do you do differently with their support?
Signs or Questions of Difference	a. What would be some **signs** that you are making progress and can let go of the depression?
	b. What would be some **signs** that you were being respected as a strong African-American woman who was respected and appreciated for what she had to offer in the workplace?
	c. What would be some **signs** that you had become the woman you most want to be? What would you notice as you moved toward your goal?

CHAPTER 11

Postmodernism, Social Construction, and Narratives in Family Therapy

Introduction

Key Concepts

Therapy Goals

The Therapist's Role and Function

Techniques

A Narrative Therapist With the Quest Family

Summary and Multicultural Evaluation

Recommended Readings

References

Introduction

What most of the family therapy approaches we have studied so far have in common is a belief in some essential function(s) of family systems. Each has a claim to its own version of reality. Adlerians want to unlock negative interactions dominated by mistaken goals and to help families adopt more-functional approaches based on social equality and democratic living. Similarly, as we shall see, cognitive-behavioral therapists seek to uncover the irrational beliefs that interfere with effective behavioral patterns and reinforce more-desirable behaviors. Bowen emphasizes the need for differentiation of self, the power of families to transmit problems over generations, and the difficulties caused by triangulation. Satir stresses congruent communication, nurturance, connection, and support through the process of change. Even Whitaker's more atheoretical approach consistently aims at enlarging a family's ability to experience by creating interpersonal stress and coaching members in alternate ways of relating. Both Minuchin and Haley believe, to varying degrees, in the foundational nature of family structure and the use of problems within family systems to maintain structure, as well as more or less fixed family patterns.

Each of these approaches to family therapy rests on the assumption that there is something essential about a system (expressed in processes, structures, or rules) that can be discovered and that, when discovered, will reveal the universal principles that explain all human behavior within the system. In this sense, most of American family therapy shares with medicine, economics, the sciences, and even religion the search for universal truth that we associate with a modernist perspective. The simultaneous existence of multiple and often antithetic truths has led, however, to increasing skepticism in the possibility that a singular, universal truth will one day explain human beings and the systems in which they live.

This skepticism is growing in many fields as paradigm shifts create entirely new ways of looking at the world: Einstein's theory of relativity shook the foundations of Newtonian physics, and tomorrow it is possible that the work of people like Stephen Hawkings (1988, 2001) will challenge even Einstein's beliefs. The global village is a reality, with television exposing us more and more to multiple cultures, multiple political systems, and multiple ways of understanding human life and the world in which we all live. We have entered into a postmodern world in which truth and reality are understood as conceptualizations, points of view bound by history and context.

To differentiate a modern from a postmodern perspective, it is helpful to look at their differing views of reality. Modernists believe in objective reality that can be observed and systematically—even scientifically—known. They further believe that reality exists independently of any attempt to observe it. Another modernist idea is that people seek therapy when they have deviated too far from some objective norm (that is, toward psychopathology). Clients are depressed, for example, when the range of their moods is below that of what we would consider normal, everyday blues. Postmodernists, in contrast, believe in subjective realities that cannot exist independently of the observational processes used. To postmodern constructionists, reality is based on the use of language and is largely a function of the situations in which people live and the stories people construct around those situations.

Let's say that thunder booms and lightning cracks near your home: If the language you associate with this event includes words like "danger," "frightening," and "too close for comfort," then your response to this event will be much different than if the language includes "exciting," "awesome," and "beautiful." One set of word constructions puts you in retreat from the event while the other set brings you closer to it.

So far, my description of postmodern approaches may seem similar to cognitive therapies, but there is a major difference. Social constructionists, especially narrative therapists, approach self-language and self-talk much more holistically: People live *storied* lives, and their stories have contexts or backgrounds of interpreted experience, but they also intend and move toward anticipated outcomes in the future. Michael White (2005) would note that our storied lives are made up of events within certain circumstances (or contexts) sequenced across time indicating a theme or plot. People live as if they are in the middle of a novel about themselves that is headed toward a probable outcome. So where cognitive therapists seek to change faulty or irrational beliefs, social constructionists understand that such beliefs are only part of a larger story and, if new beliefs or ideas are not congruent with the larger story, they will probably not be accepted.

In this sense, a problem exists when people agree there is a problem that needs to be addressed: A person is depressed when he or she has internalized a definition or story of self as depressed. Once a definition of self is internalized, it is hard to recognize behaviors that are counter to the definition; that is, it is hard for someone who is suffering from depression to differentiate a good mood from a bad mood, even when he or she is in it. Similarly, it is hard for a family to recognize when "the bad kid" is being good or when the critical parent is trying to be kind.

In all fields of study, some approaches, or knowledge-positions, gain more power than others. For a given period in history, these positions are presented as the truth and people who support that truth develop processes and proofs that are designed to maintain the knowledge-position against all others. The French philosopher and political scientist Michel Foucault (1970) investigated knowledge positions in many fields, seeing them not as different truths but as stories about life. He noted that currently popular and widely accepted stories become or act as a dominant culture; these stories are designed for self-perpetuation and the minimization of alternate stories.

In postmodern thinking, language and the use of language in stories create meaning. There may be as many stories of meaning as there are people to tell the stories, and each of these stories is true for the person telling it. Further, every person involved in a situation has a unique perspective on the reality of that situation. Assuming that each perspective has validity, if only subjective validity, the concept of universe (single reality) evolves to that of a multiverse (multiple realities). When Kenneth Gergen (1985, 1991), among others, began to emphasize the ways in which people make meaning in social relationships, the field of social constructionism was born.

Gergen's (1999) social constructionism became the foundation for activating a postmodern view in therapy. Four of his main points are essential to understanding the therapies we shall consider in this chapter. They are:

- There is nothing in the world "reality" that demands the explanations we give: This forms the basis for the consideration of multiple realities (a postmodern perspective);
- Our modes of explanation are derived from social relationships (with more popular explanations enjoying what might be called consensual validation and with other explanations relegated to lesser positions of agreement and popularity). All explanations, however, are social: To make sense is to make sense to somebody in some way that invites a shared view—even if that view is shared just enough to invite disagreement;
- Since explanations are also descriptions, our descriptions of self and the world create our future. We live storied lives with earlier stories flowing into and being the foundation for present and future stories;
- Because our use of language creates our future, it is vital that we reflect upon it for our own well-being. (pp. 47–50)

Postmodern, social constructionism signaled a paradigm shift in both individual and family therapies. Reacting perhaps to a perceived abuses of power in some mainstream individual and systemic therapies, social constructionists tend to disavow the role of expert in therapy, preferring a more collaborative or consultative stance. In social constructionism, empathy and therapeutic process are more important than assessment or technique. Narratives and language processes (linguistics) have become the focus for both understanding families and helping them construct desired change.

Steve Madigan is a narrative therapist and Director of Training at Yaletown Family Therapy in Vancouver, British Columbia. He "works as a consultant with corporations, hospitals, drug and alcohol centers, and other professional groups. He presents workshops throughout North America. One of his areas of interest is eating disorders, and he is currently working on a book about disordered eating" (Carlson & Kjos, 1999, p. 4). Building on the foundational works of Michael White and David Epston (1990), Madigan has become one of the leading narrative therapists in the northern hemisphere.

In a consultation session he conducted in 1998 for a video series of master therapists, Madigan worked with an African-American boy and his mother (Madigan, 1999). Ollie, the young adolescent, recently had gotten in trouble at school for using his belt to hit a white child who had annoyed him, an incident that was taken all the way to court, under a charge of battery, and resulted in court-ordered counseling. After greeting the mother and son, Madigan learns that the mother thinks that taking her son to court went too far and that the parents of the other boy made too big of a deal out of it. Ollie relates that he was in the bathroom when the other boy came in. The other boy said, "Hi, Ollie," and hit Ollie on the arm; the boy's hit surprised and hurt Ollie. When the boy left and then came back, Ollie returned the greeting by hitting the boy with his belt: "I was just playing around with him" (Carlson & Kjos, 1999, p. 10).

Before the session even begins, a whole host of often complicated questions arise that relate to how we might think about this case. Do you believe Ollie *is* a problem child or is he a boy facing a problem? Does he have a problem or does the problem have him? If the person and the problem are fused and Ollie has come to see himself as synonymous with the problems he faces, how might the counselor separate the client and the problem (through what will be defined later as externalizing the problem) so that the client is able to separate them on his own behalf and not be subjugated by the impact of the problem on his life? What are the effects of race and prejudice in this case? Should the counselor focus on empowerment of the client or address the negative impact of the power systems of the school, the courts, or even white society? Should both be addressed in this counseling session? How would the counselor become an advocate for this young man? Is that a proper role for the counselor?

What are the real differences in therapy when the therapist-as-expert is replaced by the client-as-expert? Because of what they consider a misuse of power in therapy, social constructionists prefer to take a decentered (or consultative) stance characterized by what is sometimes called a not-knowing approach or an approach infused with interest and curiosity that seeks to investigate and develop client stories by asking the next most interesting question.

Madigan: (to Ollie) I see, I see. Now, have you ever been to court before?

Ollie: No.

Madigan: No, and is this a new kind of trouble that you'd be involved with or an old kind of trouble?

Ollie: New.

Madigan: A new kind of trouble, I see, and when your mom was saying that you're troubled with school, is school troubling at all for you or . . . ?

Ollie: Sometimes.

Madigan: Yeah, how would school be troubling for you?

Ollie: 'Cause there's just some people that, ah, that do certain things.

Madigan: How do you mean? I kind of know what the trouble is like up in Canada, but I'm not sure it's the kind of trouble that might go on down here.

Ollie: Like, ah, some people in my class have bad attitudes, and stuff like that. They, ah, one time I asked the teacher (we were reading something in the book): I asked the teacher what page we were on, ah, that person say "You should know, Ollie. Why don't you, why don't you ask somebody else?" Or something like that.

Madigan: . . . that's what somebody in your class said, yeah?

Ollie: And then I sorta told him, "Be quiet," and then the substitute sent me to the office.

Madigan: . . . so would you have a reputation as someone who has a troubled reputation or a not-troubled reputation?

Ollie: Not troubled.

Madigan: . . . Yeah, so do you think that people aggravating you will eventually get you . . . to have a troubled reputation? Do you think that that's possible and that you'd have to give up your good boy reputation?

Ollie: Ah, no, I don't think so, not all the time. Like if somebody aggravated me, sometimes I won't do anything; sometimes, I'll just tell the teacher.

Madigan: I see. I see. Which would you prefer to have: A troubled boy reputation or a good boy reputation?

Ollie: A good boy reputation.

Madigan: How come?

Ollie: 'Cause, I don't, I don't want to be bad. I don't like to be bad or do anything.

Madigan: Why not? Why don't you want to be bad?

Ollie: 'Cause then you'll get suspended from school or something . . . or something like that.

Madigan: Yeah, and is that a bad thing, if you were to get suspended?

Ollie: Yeah. . . . 'Cause, then, you'd, if you're out, then you then don't learn that much.

Madigan: Okay, so if you're out of school, then you just won't be able to learn much. And, why is that a problem if you don't learn much?

Ollie: 'Cause, if you're not in school, then you just won't be able to learn then. The teacher won't be able to teach you anything.

Madigan: Yeah, so what's your sense of what happens to people who don't have teachers teaching them and aren't learning? What happens to people like that?

Ollie: When they grow up, they don't have a good job or something like that.

Madigan: Yeah. Why would it be important for you to have a good job?

Ollie: So I can have a good living when I get older. . . . Ah, so I can have like a good house and stuff like that.

Madigan: Good house?

Ollie: Yeah, and then I wouldn't be like, whatcha call it, ah, I wouldn't be in trouble or anything when I get older like going to jail or anything.

Madigan: Be in trouble. You said, "Not going to jail." Jail, okay. So part of the reason, if I can just recap for you, that you would want to be or to have a good boy reputation is that it would allow you to finish school and have people teaching you. You would make a good living. You could buy a good house and . . . it would help you not to get in trouble, and it would help you stay away from jail. Would there be any other reasons why you might want to, ah, you know, stay away from a troubled reputation?

Ollie: 'Cause if you have a troubled reputation, you won't have any friends. . . . If you have a good boy reputation, you'll have friends . . . .

Madigan: You'll have friends. Okay. Now, it seems like a lot is riding on [this]. You get a lot for having a good boy reputation, and would I be right in saying, you don't get much from having a troubled reputation?

Ollie: Mmm. (Carlson & Kjos, 1999, p. 10–15)

Madigan goes on to explore with Ollie's mother the negative effects of a troubled reputation. With both Ollie and his mother, Madigan has succeeded in externalizing "trouble" so that it can no longer be fused to a primary, internalized description of Ollie, but is addressed as an external force that operates on him, makes his life miserable, and causes even more trouble to follow. In this way, the subject or client is separated from the problem, and the therapist can join with family members in re-authoring a preferred story with preferred outcomes. Ollie's mother wants him to realize that getting into more trouble will only hurt him. She does not trust the school or the legal system, both of which, she believes, went too far with her son.

Mother:	Okay, I had experience with schools . . . another district school that I didn't have, never had this type of problem. This school district out here, ah, it just seems like the least little thing, anything, things could be straightened out, they, the district, make a big thing out of it. . . . And that, and if the kids get to high school, and he doesn't watch what he's doing, I mean real careful, be real careful, they're out.
Madigan:	I see. Do you have a sense as to why the school district here is structured this way and the one you used to be in is not?
Mother:	Ah, yes, I know why.
Madigan:	Why is that?
Mother:	Ah, I was told that they hadn't got used to the, ah, black kids goin' to his school.
Madigan:	As a mother, what is it like to have that told to you: That the school is operating in certain ways, because black kids are now in the school?
Mother:	Well, I don't like it. I've never had anyone to bother me. I mean, no matter what color they were: I never had no one to bother me. But it seems like once the boys get in that school district, they really have to be careful. The girls can get out pretty good if they . . . don't get to be bad girls, but the boys have to really watch their selves real careful in everything they do.
Madigan:	So do you think race had something to do with the way Ollie was treated?
Mother:	I think so, because if it hadda been . . . two white boys, I don't think they woulda, they wouldn't have went to court.
Madigan:	. . . As a mother, how does it feel to have Ollie exposed to this system that maybe he might get treated differently because of the color of his skin?
Mother:	Well, I don't like it.
Madigan:	. . . So do you think that trouble might find the African-American children in the school quicker then . . . and they'll develop reputations of trouble more than other children in the school: That they're more likely to take that on?
Mother:	I think so. (Carlson & Kjos, 1999, pp. 20–24)

What follows is a conversation, mainly between Madigan and Ollie's mother, about the pain and hardship that is involved in racism at Ollie's school. Mother notes that the principal at Ollie's new school does not make it clear that fighting of any kind will not be tolerated: He does not want to take sides. She says that life was different when she went to school: Kids would just take what was handed out, and today's children and adolescents won't do that. Even black mothers are treated differently than white mothers at the school, with white mothers given much more leeway in disputes than black mothers. Madigan now returns to a conversation with Ollie to see what his experience is of the racism his mother has described.

Madigan:	(to Ollie) Do you have a hunch as to why that is? No? It just happens that way, or is it something that you've known before?
Ollie:	It just happens that way.
Madigan:	. . . Do you have a hunch as to why it might just happen that way? No? Do you ever have talks with your mom about why things happen that way sometimes?
Ollie:	Not really.
Madigan:	No. Do you think that [it] might be important to talk with your mom or your dad or your brothers about this?
Ollie:	Mmmhm. (Carlson & Kjos, 1999, p. 30)

Madigan now returns to re-author and *re-member* those aspects of Ollie's story that support his good boy reputation. He asks what friends of Ollie might think of him or say about him. Ollie suggests that he doesn't start stuff, that he doesn't disrespect people. He also notes that he is a good friend, a good student, and good at sports.

Madigan: (turning to the mother) . . . Are there things that you could tell me about Ollie that would lead me to believe that he is a really good boy and that he has a good reputation?

Mother: Okay, he does his homework; he doesn't talk back to you; [and he] doesn't say bad words. . . . He doesn't run away.

Madigan: Would I be right in thinking that you're proud of Ollie?

Mother: Yes.

Madigan: As having him as a son?

Mother: Yes.

Madigan: Did you know that your mom was proud of you and who you were as her son and who you were as a growing man? Yeah? What's it like to hear that she believes that you're a good boy and do your homework, and you don't talk back, don't use bad words, and that you don't run away—and that she recognizes that as qualities in you?

Ollie: I feel good.

Madigan: . . . Yeah, yeah. I'm just wondering, given what's happening, you know that there's a bit of a story out there of you getting into trouble, how is it that you might circulate the story more about you being a good boy and to gain that good boy reputation back. And I'm wondering if it might help if I, if I was to write a letter to the principal and say [that] I met you and had a really nice talk with you and really stand behind . . . your good boy reputation? Would that, do you think that might fill it out a bit more?

Ollie: I don't know. I really don't know.

Madigan: I'm just wondering if other people might, might need to stand up on your behalf, Ollie, and say, you know, "Yes, he did get into trouble and he's sorry for it. Now, we need to struggle hard to get his reputation back as a good boy, because we fear that he might just become a troubled, or viewed as a troubled boy." Can you think of ways that we might circulate and make this good boy reputation grow a bit more?

Mother: I think like when something happen at school, they should stop making a big issue out of it, and then it won't go this far.

Madigan: . . . Yeah. (speaking to Ollie) . . . well, I'm wondering if, if yourself and the people that are close to you and think that you're a good boy might be able to find time and begin thinking of ways to circulate these rumors about yourself being a . . . good person, . . . wanting to finish school and wanting to have a good living and wanting to own a house and wanting to not be in trouble or go to jail and knowing . . . you're not disrespectful, and that you're a good friend, that you're a good student, you're good at sports, and that you don't get into a whole lot of trouble. I mean, how is it that you can make that story bigger about yourself? We know exactly what you can do to make the "trouble" story bigger, don't we? So I'm just wondering if you have any ideas about how you can make . . . the good boy reputation stronger about yourself. Like if you brought some of this respectful and friendly and not getting [into] trouble ways to school: Do you think that might help?

Mother: I think so. So the district needs to change their attitude [so they] . . . won't point the finger at someone like they're a bad person.

Madigan: . . . Are there ways in which these views can be brought to the district? I mean, I'd certainly be willing to write a letter to the district on behalf of Ollie and yourself. . . . Okay, do you mind if I keep in contact with Ollie a little bit? To see how he's, things are going . . .

Mother: Yes, yes.

Madigan:	And maybe be one of the people on his side to continue to put forward this idea. Would you mind if I dropped you a line from Canada?
Ollie:	No.
Mother:	That's good.
Madigan:	And, maybe if there's other kids that I'm working with, maybe I can send you stories about them. You know, what they've found whether it would be troubled reputations or racism.
Mother:	. . . I'd like to say I didn't know we would get to tell this story, but it's a true story.
Madigan:	Yeah. And I just want to tell you that I really believe your story. And I'd like to stand behind your story in any way that I can. And, I'm very sad that this story is going on for you.
Mother:	Yeah, mmmhm, okay.
Madigan:	I'm saying that as a person here with you, and I'm also saying that as a white person. So thank you so much for coming and sharing this story with us.
Mother:	Okay. Thank you.

Madigan and others wrote letters[1] supporting Ollie's good boy reputation and communicated with the counselor who worked with Ollie and his mother. A school psychologist in Ollie's district supported his good boy reputation and shared that message with others in the school. The counselor, who worked with Ollie and his mother, monitored these activities and helped Ollie and his mother tell their story to others. (Carlson & Kjos, 1999, pp. 32–38)

Therapy often requires a balance that is difficult to achieve—a balance between strengthening the individual in the face of a difficult life and recognizing and addressing the crushing impact that bigotry, prejudice, and oppression have on the lives of children and their families. Leaning too much toward empowerment in therapy can seem to ignore the real effects that racist systems inflict on individuals and families; on the other hand, merely blaming the system, no matter how justified that blame may be, often leaves clients with a rationale for failure, but little else. Social constructionists, like narrative therapist Stephen Madigan, take the social advocacy position that individual/family stories need to be re-authored at the same time that social systems need to be changed. Similar to Madigan's approach with Ollie and his mother, narrative therapists, especially, have sought to help victims of school bullying, for example, by listening to those who have been hurt, but also by seeking to meet with the perpetrators of peer violence in groups at the school. It is in paying attention to both individuals and the systems in which they live that narrative therapists make a real claim to re-constructing systemic therapy.

Key Concepts

At a time when strategic and structural therapists, with their emphasis on brief, therapist-directed change, were the dominant culture in family therapy, Milan therapists, introduced in the chapter on strategic family therapy, began to design multiple-therapist interventions based on the work of Bateson and Haley, but with a twist. Their process of circular, or relational, questioning was embedded in long interviews involving both hypothesizing and neutrality that explored the family history and the meaning attached to events and problems (Selvini Palazzoli, Boscolo, Cecchin, & Prata, 1980). The Milan therapists asked questions that allowed the family members to verify or modify a hypothesis about the nature of the clients' problems. The stance of the therapists had to be experienced by family members as both neutral and non-blaming. Milan therapists brought to their process a determination that family members could decide what to change if enough questions and discovery led to new or clearer meanings in their lives. They greatly softened the rather aggressive stance that North American strategic therapists took in relation to families and change. They activated an appreciation for the belief systems that supported observed behaviors in families. In this sense, the Milan group became a bridge between modern and postmodern approaches to family therapy (Tomm, 1998).

In this chapter, we shall look at three models that have come to symbolize the application of postmodern, social constructionist therapy with families. The most prominent of these models is now called **narrative therapy**, and it was developed by two friends and colleagues from Down Under: Michael White in Australia and David Epston in New Zealand. Their model is clearly the most used social constructionist approach to therapy today. Before we consider narrative therapy, however, we shall look at the **not-knowing position** developed by two colleagues in Houston, Texas, Harold Goolishian and Harlene Anderson. Their collaborative stance is similar to what narrative therapists will call a **decentered position**, and it serves as a foundation for **linguistic therapy**. We shall also consider Norway's Tom Andersen and his associates: Their use of **reflecting teams** represents the most direct link to the strategic model used in Milan, but from a postmodern perspective. It incorporates Gergen's (1999) emphasis on multiple viewpoints, multiple realities, and relational (or social) explanations. Reflecting teams open up therapy so profoundly that they have been incorporated into the other two models (sometimes under slightly different names).

The Linguistic Approach: Harlene Anderson and Harold Goolishian

The linguistic approach is a collaborative dialogue or conversational style developed by Harlene Anderson and the late Harold Goolishian (1992) of the Houston Galveston Institute. Rejecting the more therapist-controlled and theory-based interventions of North American family therapy, Anderson and Goolishian developed a therapy of caring and being with the client. Informed by and contributing to the field of social constructionism, they came to believe that human life is constructed in personal and family narratives that maintain both process and meaning in people's lives. These narratives are constructed in social interactions over time, and the sociocultural systems in which people live are a product of social interaction, not the other way around. In this sense, therapy is also a system process created in the therapeutic conversations of the client and the listener/facilitator.

When people or families come for therapy, they are often stuck in a dialogic system that has a unique language, meaning, and process related to the problem. Therapy is another conversational system that becomes therapeutic through its "problem-organizing, problem-dis-solving" nature (Anderson & Goolishian, 1992, p. 27). It is the therapist's willingness to enter the therapeutic conversation from a *not-knowing position* that facilitates this caring relationship with client. In the not-knowing position, therapists still retain all of the knowledge and personal, experiential capacities they have gained over years of living, but they allow themselves to enter the conversation with *curiosity* and with intense *interest* in discovery. From this position, clients become the experts who are informing and sharing with the therapist the significant narratives of their lives. The not-knowing position is empathic and is most often characterized by questions that "come from an honest, continuous therapeutic posture of not understanding too quickly" (Anderson, 1993, p. 331).

In this model, the questions the therapist asks always are informed by the answers the client/expert has provided. The therapist enters the session with some sense, from referral or intake, of what the client or family wishes to address. Their answers provide information that stimulates the interest of the therapist, still in a posture of inquiry, and another question proceeds from each answer given. The process is similar to the Socratic method without any preconceived idea about how or in which direction the development of the stories should go. The intent of the conversation is not to confront or challenge the narrative of the client but to facilitate the telling and retelling of the story until opportunities for new meaning and new stories develop: "Telling one's story is a representation of experience; it is constructing history in the present" (Anderson & Goolishian, 1992, p. 37). By staying with the story, the therapist–client conversation evolves into a dialogue of new meaning, constructing new narrative possibilities.

Similar to White and Epston's (1990) narrative therapy, linguistic therapy seeks to turn thin descriptions into thicker ones and transform problem-saturated stories into preferred stories. Anderson (1996) believes the telling of one's story is the foundation for its retelling and, ultimately, a retelling of the retelling. With each new telling, the story thickens, nuances are noted, new possibilities emerge, and emergent solutions are co-constructed.

The Reflecting Team: Tom Andersen

In northern Norway, there are 2 months each winter in which the 24-hour day is mostly dark and 2 months each summer in which the day is mostly light. Most Norwegians live in the southern part of the country, which is more closely related to the rest of Europe. In the north, however, the communities are fewer and farther apart. It is in the north that Tom Andersen (1987, 1991) practices family therapy.

Andersen is a psychiatrist who has pioneered community-based mental health programs and has initiated a reflecting team approach to family therapy in Norway. Norwegian health programs have been nationalized, and everyone has equal access to both physical and mental health services. When Andersen started to visit the smaller communities in the north, he immediately recognized that help would often include work with extended families. Starting in the mid-1970s, he and his colleagues began to study the structural and strategic approaches used in the United States, incorporating some of the behind-the-mirror processes that Haley had popularized. This process involved a therapist who interviewed a family in one room while a team of consulting therapists watched through a one-way mirror in another room. Occasionally, strategic interventions were sent into the therapy session from the observing team. In the early 1980s, the Milan use of circular questions and longer interviews replaced many of the strategic interventions the team had used for some time. Still, the therapy team remained detached from the family, continuing to work behind the observation mirrors as they had for many years.

In a curious way, their therapy process paralleled the Norwegian environment: The family spent long periods in the light of the therapy room while being kept in equally extended darkness about what the therapy team was thinking and doing. Andersen (1991) reports that it was a family mired in misery that pulled the therapy team out of the darkness and into the light. One day when the team was getting nowhere with its interventions, a therapist knocked on the door of the interview room and asked the family members if they would like to watch and listen to the team's conversation about the family. When the family agreed, the lights in the observation room were turned on, and the family and their interviewer listened to the team process their session. This was the birth of the reflecting team, an approach that has quickly gained wide acceptance in family therapy.

Over time, an interviewing process that Andersen (1991) calls "dialogues and dialogues about the dialogues" has been developed to facilitate the use of a reflecting team. An initial interview with a family involves the development of an extensive picture of the clients, the therapist, and "the history of the idea of coming for therapy" (pp. 131–133). A second level of dialogue is about the family's stories of how their family picture and history came to be; each person in the family may have a different story. A third level of dialogue is about the future, about how the family members would like the picture of themselves to change and what alternate stories about their lives might be developed. Each of these levels involves careful listening to the language that the clients use to construct their current realities, as well as the ones they would prefer.

When the reflecting team responds to the family, the team members are expected to let their imaginations flow, subject only to a respect for the system and a sensitivity about what the family can handle. Reflections most often are offered as tentative ideas directly connected to the verbal and nonverbal information in the preceding dialogue. Reflections that start with phrases such as, "I am wondering . . . ," "It seems to me that . . . ," and "Perhaps a possibility would be . . ." all activate the kind of tentativeness that is useful in this process. The team remains positive in reflecting, reframing stories and parts of stories, looking for alternate stories, and wondering out loud about the possibility and impact of implementing these alternate stories. The family and the initial interviewer listen and the interviewer notes family reactions, looking for ways in which the reflecting team may be expanding the family's ideas. The session ends with the initial interviewer seeking the family members' reactions to what they have experienced (Becvar & Becvar, 2003).

Andersen (1992) clearly places his reflecting-team approach in the environment of social construction:

> The open conversations that constitute "the Reflecting Process" have brought clients and professionals toward more egalitarian relationships. . . . The listener is not only a receiver of a story but also, by being present, an encouragement to the act of making the story. And that act is the act of constituting one's self. (p. 66)

The Narrative Approach: Michael White and David Epston

Of all the social constructionists, Michael White and David Epston (1990) most reflect the influence of Michel Foucault (1979, 1980) in their use of narrative in therapy. Foucault asserts that those perspectives that become dominant-culture narratives have to be challenged at every level and every opportunity, because their function is, in part, to minimize or eliminate alternate knowledge-positions and alternate narratives. Because of the power of dominant-culture narratives, individuals and families tend to integrate these positions as if they are the only possible ones to take—even if those positions are not useful to the individual or the family. In the United States, for instance, dominant-culture narratives favor those who are male, white, Anglo-Saxon, rich, Protestant, heterosexual, physically able and healthy, and between the ages of 18 and 35. Like those who identify themselves with feminist therapy, White (1992) believes that a dominant culture is designed to perpetuate viewpoints, processes, and stories that serve those who benefit from that culture but that may work against the freedom and desires of the individual and the family.

Dulwich Centre, Adelaide, South Australia

Michael White

I have just noted that societal narratives in the United States—and actually in most countries—perpetuate a strong preference for men, often discriminate against diversity, and are designed to exclude gay men and lesbians from being full members of a given community. These narratives are so strong that even the people who suffer within these stories believe them. Hence, many women accept their inequality with men; members of minority cultures discriminate against one another and against other cultures; and gay men and lesbians, like the heterosexual community, may also be homophobic, if to a lesser extent.

Families, too, incorporate the dominant-culture narratives about what a family should be and, to the extent that problems can be met and handled within these narrative structures, life seems to go smoothly. When the dominant story loses its power to meet the needs and demands of family life, the family has a problem. Within the family, narratives are maintained that allow each individual, as well as the system, to construct meaning in the lives and relationships of the family members. These stories become dominant culture for a given family unit and are given the same power over individuals that a societal narrative often has. Beneath every dominant story, however, there are always subordinate stories that can be developed and lived (White, 2007).

According to White (1998), individuals construct the meaning of life in interpretive stories, which are then treated as truth. The construction of meaning can happen monologically (by oneself) or dialogically (with others), with the latter having the greater power in our lives because we are social beings. In this sense, an individual is most often a socially constructed narrative system. The process of living our story is not simply metaphorical; it is very real, with real effects and real consequences in family and societal systems. Families are micro-systems, small social systems, with communal narratives that express their values and meanings; they are embedded in larger macro-systems, such as culture and society. Because individual people are systems within systems within still other systems, they can lose freedom easily. Therapy is, in part, a reestablishment of individual and family freedom from the oppression of external problems and the dominant stories of larger systems.

Like Anderson and Goolishian (1992) and Andersen (1992), White and Epston (1990) developed a therapeutic process based on questions. Their questions, however, are purposeful and politically organized to deconstruct oppressive narratives. Their therapy starts with an exploration of the family in relation to the presenting problem. It is not uncommon for clients to present initial stories in which they and the problem are fused, as if one and the same. When a young adolescent woman, for example, presents herself by saying, "I'm anorexic," she is starting from a rather **thin description** of herself. In this description, she and the problem are one; they are fused. White uses externalizing questions to separate the problem from the people affected by the problem. These questions, sometimes called **"relative influence questioning"** (p. 42), assist the clients in charting the influence of the problem in their life, as well as charting their own influence in the life of the problem. This shift in language already begins the **deconstruction** of the original narrative in which the people have become problem saturated; in narrative therapy, the problem is objectified as external to the person.

Jim starts by saying that he gets angry far too much, especially when he feels that his wife is criticizing him unjustly: "I just flare! I pop off, get upset, fight back. Later, I wish I hadn't, but it's too late. I've messed up again." Although questions about how his anger occurs, complete with specific examples and events, will help chart the influence of the problem, it is really the following kinds of questions that externalize the problem and counteract any fusion the person might have with the symptom: "What is the mission of the anger, and how does it recruit you into this mission?" "How does the anger get you, and what are you doing when it becomes so powerful?" "What does the anger require of you, and what happens to you when you meet its requirements?"

In this narrative approach, externalizing questions are followed by questions that search for a point of entry into a re-authoring conversation; such conversations often start with an inquiry into unique outcomes: "Was there ever a time in which anger wanted to take you over, and you resisted? What was that like for you? How did you do it?" Unique outcomes often can be found in the past or present, but they also can be hypothesized for the future: "What form would standing up against your anger take?" It is within the account of unique events that alternate narratives can often be facilitated and developed.

Descriptions of actual events, like unique outcomes, in the lives of individuals or families are generally facilitated by landscape of action questions (White, 1992). Following a description of a unique event, White would regularly use landscape of identity questions to support the development of new identity conclusions:

- What do you think this tells me about what you have wanted for your life, and about what you have been trying for in your life?[2]
- How do you think that knowing this has affected my view of you as a person?
- Of all those people who have known you, who would be least surprised that you have been able to take this step in challenging the problem's influence in your life? (p. 133)

The development of unique outcome stories into solution stories is facilitated by what Epston and White (1992) call circulation questions:

- Now that you have reached this point in life, who else should know about it?
- I guess there are a number of people who have an outdated view of who you are as a person. What ideas do you have about updating these views?
- If other people seek therapy for the same reasons that you did, can I share with them any of the important discoveries that you have made? (p. 23)

One of the most prominent of solution-oriented therapists, William O'Hanlon (1994), in a review of White and Epston's work, describes their narrative therapeutic process in the following steps:

- The collaboration with the person or the family begins with coming up with a mutually acceptable name for the problem;
- Personifying the problem and attributing oppressive intentions and tactics to it;
- Investigating how the problem has been disrupting, dominating, or discouraging the person and the family;
- Discovering moments when the clients haven't been dominated or discouraged by the problem or their lives have not been disrupted by the problem;
- Finding historical evidence to bolster a new view of the person as competent enough to have stood up to, defeated, or escaped from the dominance or oppression of the problem;
- Evoking speculation from the person and the family about what kind of future is to be expected from the strong, competent person that has emerged from the interview so far;[3]
- Finding or creating an audience for perceiving the new story (pp. 25–26)

Epston has developed a special facility for carrying on therapeutic dialogues between sessions through the use of letters (White & Epston, 1990). His letters may be long—chronicling the process of the interview and the agreements reached—or short, highlighting a meaning or understanding reached in the session or asking a question that has occurred to him since the end of the previous therapy visit. These letters also are used to encourage clients, by noting their strengths and accomplishments in relation to handling problems, or to note the meaning of accomplishments for others in their community:

> [This] re-authoring therapy intends to assist persons to resolve problems by: (1) enabling them to separate their lives and relationships from knowledges/stories that are impoverishing; (2) assisting them to challenge practices of self and relationship that are subjugating; and (3) encouraging persons to re-author their lives according to alternative knowledge/stories and practices of self and relationship that have preferred outcomes. (Epston, White, & Murray, 1992, p. 108)

Each of the three models described above, although developed in unique settings, have certain attributes in common that are based on a postmodern, social constructionist perspective. The therapy process is collaborative, empowering, and seeks to develop in clients preferred stories to the ones that are problem saturated or oppressive to the person or the system. Social constructionists believe that there is no essence, no absolute truths, but rather multiple perspectives and interactions from which meaning is relationally co-constructed. The language that is used in therapy and in life has real effects in terms of therapeutic outcome.

Therapy Goals

Social constructionists believe that real people live in families and that each person is living the story of his or her life; each person contributes to the story of family life, and all of the stories are in constant co-construction. Human beings make meaning that is expressed in language and narratives; in this sense, families are meaning-making and meaningful systems. When the narratives of meaning become saturated with problems and overwhelming to those who live with and through them, social constructionists enter the personal and familial searches for alternate possibilities, unique outcomes, and preferred stories.

Although somewhat different from therapist to therapist, social constructionists share an interest in the generation of new meaning and preferred realities (in the form of stories) for the lives of the people and families they serve. They seek to enlarge perspective and focus, facilitate the discovery or creation of new options, and co-develop solutions that are unique to the people and families they see. Social constructionism almost always includes an awareness of the impact of various aspects of dominant culture on human life, and therapists in this model seek to challenge dominant culture and develop alternate stories about self, others, and ways of acting, knowing, and living.

The Therapist's Role and Function

In social-constructionist theory, the *therapist-as-expert* is replaced by the **client-as-expert**.[4] The therapist enters into dialogues in an effort to elicit the perspectives, resources, and the unique experiences of the client(s). A heavy emphasis is placed on the use of questions, often relational in nature, that empower the people in families to speak, to give voice to their diverse positions, and to own their capabilities in the presence of others. The past is history and sometimes provides a foundation for understanding and discovering differences that will make a difference. But it is the present and the future in which life will be lived. The therapist supplies the optimism and sometimes a process, but the clients generate what is possible and contribute the movement that ultimately actualizes their preferred outcomes.

Therapists in the social-constructionist model are active facilitators. The concepts of care, interest, curiosity, empathy, contact, and even fascination that are essential to the person-centered therapists, the **existentialists**, the Gestalt therapists, and other humanists re-emerge here as a relational necessity. The not-knowing position, which allows therapists to follow, and be guided by the stories of their client(s), creates participant–observer and process–facilitator roles for the therapist and integrates therapy with a postmodern science of human inquiry. Collaboration, compassion, reflection, and discovery characterize the interactions of therapist and client in a social-constructionist model.

Techniques

In these postmodern models, therapists do not think of themselves as applying techniques so much as adopting a decentered, not-knowing approach or position in therapy. Therapeutic process is more about a way of being than the use of specific interventions. Among the most important aspects of these models are the following:

Listening With Curiosity.   Whether the therapist is part of a reflecting team or is a single interviewer, all social-constructionist theories place a strong emphasis on listening to clients without judgment, blame, or criticism. This is true at even the most fundamental level of assessment: To diagnose is to bring judgment, usually a negative judgment, and it already blames and/or oppresses the client. Social constructionists, in favoring the idea of stories or narratives, bring to their work a focused and demonstrable interest, curiosity, and fascination with following the development of a story closely and intensely. This process has been called a decentered position or decentered practice (White, 1997), and it starts with the therapist taking a not-knowing approach to therapy. Anderson and Goolishian (1992) use a form of inquiry that is very close to Socratic questioning: In consulting with a 44-year-old male client, they note:

> The intent was not to challenge the man's reality or the man's story, but rather to learn about it, and to let it be re-told in a way that allowed the opportunity for new meaning and new narrative to emerge. (p. 35)

In this sense, therapist knowledge is transferred away from professional dogma about normal and abnormal toward a discovery discourse about the yet unsaid. Social constructionists want to create meaning and new possibilities out of the stories they share, rather than out of a preconceived and ultimately imposed theory of importance and value.

Questions that Make a Difference.   Depending on the approach, the questions therapists ask may aim to create a unique conversation, be part of a dialogue about earlier dialogues, uncover unique events, or explore dominant-culture processes and the effects that culture has on individuals and families. As the individual and family stories begin, the therapist is looking for the next most interesting question, a question that will facilitate the development of the story, fill it out, thicken it, or reveal new meaning and new possibilities. Questions that are circular, or relational, often facilitate story development better than content-embedded questions, but both are used.

White (1992) developed his approach to questions based in part on his understanding of Jerome Bruner. Bruner (1986, 1991) had noted that narratives allowed people to organize their life experiences and memories in such a way that they created coherent stories about themselves in the world: Life events were connected meaningfully across time. West and Bubenzer (2002) note that "White used Bruner's ideas about the time, action, and conscious-ness components of narrative as a scaffolding on which to build his views of the process of narrative construction" (p. 359). Using Bruner's language, Epston and White (1992) call questions about personal or family stories landscape of action questions; these are similar to the *who, what, where,* and *why* questions so often associated with journalism. Questions about meaning and values are referred to as landscape of consciousness or landscape of identity questions. "What might have happened recently that demonstrates how you stood up for yourself?" is an example of a landscape of action question; "What does it say about you that you were able stand up for yourself?" is an example of a landscape of identity ques-tion. Landscape of action and landscape of identity questions are used to build scaffolding in both externalization and re-authoring conversations that can support the development of subordinate, but preferred stories (White, 2007).

Deconstruction and Externalization.   Human beings and families come to therapy when their lives are overwhelmed by the problems they face. Both people and systems of people express their concerns in problem-saturated stories to which they are fused. Social construc-tionists differ from many early family therapists in believing that it is neither the person nor the family that is the problem. Living life means coping with problems, not being fused with them. Problems and problem-saturated stories have real impacts on real people and domi-nate living in extremely negative ways. Externalization is one process for deconstructing[5] the power of a difficult or painful narrative and separating the person or family from identifying with the problem. This separation facilitates hope by allowing clients to respond in a pre-ferred way to that which is not useful in their storied lives.

Narrative therapists take a stance that is similar to that of feminist family therapists, whom we shall consider in the next chapter: They deconstruct the power of the dominant culture's knowledge/positions by holding commonly held views up to the light of history, as well as to alternate, often personal data that refute what the dominant culture proposes as axiomatic. Both deconstructions seek to empower the person and the family as competent to address the problems faced.

Because people and problems are separate and not the same, there is a reciprocity of influence that almost always is present. Part of therapy involves mapping the influence that a person or family has had on the development of the problem, but externalization also requires a mapping of the influence the problem has had on the individual, the family, friends, and associates. This inquiry separates the problem from the people and declares it to be an *It*: Whatever *It* turns out to be, it has real power and real influence, but it has also been handled, challenged, or addressed—or it can be. Only when people are separate from their problems can they re-discover the power to cope and to take a stand against that which oppresses them. Zimmerman and Dickerson (1996) provide an exhilarating account in which problems are personified and actually speak about their destructive aims and purposes in lives of individuals and families.

Some questions that work toward externalization might be:

- What shall we call this problem? What name do you give it?
- How did this problem come into your life?
- What does it require of you?
- What influence does this problem have on your life? What influence do you have on the life of the problem?
- What conclusions have you drawn about your life because of this problem? What does it intend for your life? Is that the same thing that you intend for your life?
- Have there ever been times when the problem was threatening to take control of you, but didn't? What was different about how you met the challenge of this problem at those times?

Alternate Stories and Re-Authoring.   Whether involved in a free-flowing conversation or engaged in a series of questions in a relatively consistent process, social constructionists seek to elicit new possibilities and privilege them in the life narratives and processes of the people they serve. White and Epston's (1990) inquiry into unique events is similar to the exception questions of solution-focused/solution-oriented therapists. Both seek to build on the competence already present in the person or the family. The development of alternate stories, unique events, preferred realities, and thickened narratives are the enactment of ultimate hope: Your life story always has been more than the problem let you think it was, and now you know what that more is.

White and Epston (1990) note that problems are dependent on their effects in human life in order to maintain themselves. In this sense, problems need people to cooperate with them. When people or families decide not to cooperate with their problems, the capacity to debilitate is reduced or eliminated. Still, problems are very powerful, often supported by outside structures, and never give up easily. Those unique times when people refuse to cooperate with a problem are often overlooked, dismissed, or rendered useless when seen as an exception. It is these very exceptions, however, these unique events that provide the material for developing preferred outcomes and alternate stories. Inquiries that seek to develop the significance of unique events may involve the following kinds of questions:

- When the problem asked you to participate in it, were you ever able to decline the invitation? How did you do that?
- Are there times when you simply don't fall for the tricks of the problem and are able to take a stand against it?
- What facts or events are in your life that contradict the problem's effects on you and your relationships?
- Was there ever a time when you refused to submit to the demands of the problem?

Unique events almost always are present in the lives of individuals and families. They may be present in the history of the person or family; they may occur between therapy sessions; they even may occur within a therapy session. When unique events emerge within the therapy session, there is an immediacy to this development that is quite powerful and that allows re-authoring to be more compelling. On those rare occasions when unique outcomes are not readily available, they always can be anticipated or even imagined.

> The existence of these intentions and hopes can be considered a present act of defiance in the "face" of the problem and can also lead to an investigation of those historical experiences that have informed persons that things might be different in the future—perhaps what they might have "glimpsed" that has kept their hope alive. (White & Epston, 1990, p. 61)

Involving Outside Communities in Therapy.   People live in groups—in the family, in communities, in cultures, and even in society as a whole. They are supported and maintained by these relationships. Indeed, we all are co-constructed within these relationships. It is for this very reason that psychotherapy in the 1970s turned so fully toward family interventions. To imagine that a single session or set of sessions can overcome the power of a dominant-community explanation of life or relational expectations requires a certain hubris that does not often deliver meaningful change. Narrative therapy seeks to join and engage the individual and family in communities that can support multiple perspectives and hope for a better future. This process takes many different forms, some of which have challenged the most fundamental aspects of current psychotherapeutic practice.

One form is to involve as many people associated with the problem as possible to challenge the right of the problem to exist. For example, a young girl was once referred by a school system in Australia to Michael White, because she was being bullied at school. Now, traditional therapy might have worked with her in an attempt to help her cope with this experience, either by standing up to it or by protecting herself from it. In both cases, the burden, and therefore the responsibility, are clearly left on the shoulders of the victim. White's approach was to contact the school and request a consultation with the boys who were engaged in peer violence.

White and Epston both keep lists of people who have successfully challenged different kinds of problems in their lives and who have re-authored preferred realities. They often invite former clients to be outside witnesses for current clients and to serve as reflective voices in the session. A narrative interview of outside witnesses is structured to elicit aspects of the client's story that the witnesses were drawn to and that resonated with aspects of the witnesses' own lives; they are also asked what their reflections tell them about what the client values or intends for her or his life. Though carefully structured, the interview of outside witnesses is similar to Tom Andersen's reflecting teams.

Another form of therapeutic community is embedded in White's (1995, 1997, 2000) use of **definitional ceremonies**. Based on the work of Barbara Meyerhoff (1982, 1986), White realized that community members could become a reflecting team for individuals and families who were in need of a particular audience for the performance of new identities. This work sometimes involved bringing other family members into the reflecting process, but it was not limited to family. It also could include people from the community or representatives of one's culture—even representatives from multiple cultures. Sometimes people who were feeling subjugated by similar problem-saturated stories could both support the performance of a new story they witnessed and use it as a means for developing alternate stories in their own lives.

Bitter et al. (2004) provide a transcript of a cultural definitional ceremony in action. In this ceremony, a young Hispanic woman and her mother tell their life stories, speak of the value they place in their relationship, and essentially affirm who they are before a witness audience. That audience, in turn, acts as a reflecting team and speaks of the meaning they experienced in the stories of these two women. In the final movement of the ceremony, the mother and daughter thicken the meaning of their lives by incorporating the comments from the reflecting team.

Letters and Documents.   David Epston pioneered the use of documents and letters in narrative therapy (White & Epston, 1990). In essence, he replaced the traditional professional notion of a private file under lock and key kept for each client with the idea of an archive of materials left on loan to the therapist for specific purposes and for a limited amount of time. Archives contain much different materials than traditional medical—or even psychological—files: They tend to include letters, documents, memorabilia, and other important markers in the storied lives of individuals and families. Seldom do they include diagnostic materials or case notes.

In adopting this archival approach, White and Epston (1990) discovered that they could replace case notes with letters that were sometimes brief (perhaps noting a question that occurred to the therapist after the client left). Some letters were longer, with details that might include (a) what had happened in the therapy session; (b) the influence the problem had on the client and vice versa; (c) a discussion of unique events, exceptions to the problem, or preferred outcomes and what use these might be to the client now; (d) the impact of the client on the therapist; and/or (e) circulation questions that encourage a larger distribution of a new story about the person or family. These letters might be written shortly after the therapy session ends, but they are mailed through regular postage, often arriving days later. The effect is to encourage the development of new and preferred stories between sessions. The value of these letters has been estimated to be the equivalent of 3 to 5 therapy sessions (McKenzie & Monk, 1997; Nyland & Thomas, 1994).

Within Epston's practice, there are many different uses for letters. The therapist and/or family members sometimes issue *letters of invitation* when a person who is important to the therapeutic process is missing or unwilling to come. Such letters have been effective in coaxing everyone from absent fathers to abuse victims into the family therapy. Epston also uses *redundancy letters* to separate, retire, or fire people who have been absorbed into ineffective roles: a child who parents the parent, a brother who acts as father, or a spouse who is counselor to a partner. There are also *letters of prediction*:

> Often, at the end of therapy, I ask permission to make my predictions for a person's, relationship's or family's future. I regularly use the period of six months as my time-frame. I often refer to this time-frame as "your immediate future." I post these predictions in "letters," folded and stapled, with "private and confidential" prominently displayed on them, along with "Not to be viewed until _____ (date in six months' time)." (White and Epston, p. 94)

A prediction letter speaks to the development of a new story. It suggests a 6-month follow-up, either in the form of a client/family reflection process or an actual therapy session. And because most people don't wait for the 6 months to pass, reading the prediction(s) establishes a self-fulfilling prophecy.

The variety of letters used by narrative therapists is almost endless. Therapists in this model often write letters of reference (both within families and between families and other people or groups); letters of counter-referral that apprise referring people or agencies of new developments in the client's life; letters for special occasions; and brief letters validating human existence or offering post-session thoughts, to name a few types (White & Epston, 1990).

Over time, accumulated letters become the substance of a documented life. As client stories unfold, and twist and turn, and gain depth or movement, the written record grows and marks the turning points and accomplishments of a lifetime. Some turning points also are cause for celebrations, and narrative therapists use certificates, similar to diplomas, to mark declarations of independence from problems that have previously controlled living, or to provide declarations of self-certification performed in definitional ceremonies.

When Ollie, Stephen Madigan's client in the interview at the beginning of this chapter, adopted a good-boy reputation for himself, Madigan sent a counter-referral letter to Ollie's school, announcing the development of a good-boy reputation as a significant event in Ollie's life. This led the school psychologist to take an interest in Ollie and to help distribute the good news. If the therapist–client relationship had continued, it might have served Ollie quite well to hold a definitional ceremony in which Ollie would have had the opportunity to perform aspects of this reputation before witnesses and perhaps to be honored for the effort with a certificate of recognition.

A Narrative Therapist With the Quest Family

Paul and Jane Quest bring all four of their children to the first meeting with a narrative therapist. Jane initially had consulted the community-based clinic for help related to her two sons. When she told her family that she was taking the boys for counseling, the two daughters said that they would come too, and they talked their father into coming. The narrative therapist began the session by welcoming everyone and asking about the history of the idea that led all of them to be there. Jane gave a brief summary of the family history and concluded by saying how much she appreciated that her daughters had been willing to come and bring their father along.

Paul noted that he was very busy at work and always had been. He felt he relied on Jane to handle matters at home, but he also indicated a somewhat hesitant interest in being more involved. Amy and Ann both indicated that they were there as a support for their mother, but each had serious doubts about how the family might help the boys. They were okay with their parents' initial decision to add the boys to the family, but they didn't really feel connected to them yet. "The boys can be difficult," Amy noted. The boys were very talkative, interrupting often, and in constant motion.

Therapist: There's a lot going on in your life. A lot of issues and a lot of feelings about those issues. I'm wondering what's most important to you? What problem is taking the most unfair advantage in your life?

Jane: I feel like I am living in two families: I am part of the family with Paul, Ann, and Amy, and I am almost a single parent with Jason and Luke. (with tears in her eyes) I can't seem to get everyone together.

Therapist: It's hard to be in two different families: Sometimes, two is less than one. [Jane: Yes.] What is it that keeps your two families apart?

Jane: I don't know. The boys need so much, and I feel pulled apart, like I can't do everything.

Therapist: Everything requires a lot of you. [Jane: Yes.]

Therapist: Paul, do you share Jane's feeling that there are two separate families that all of you are in?

Paul: I hadn't thought of it that way, but yes, I think that's true—especially for Jane. (pause) I have my work, and then there is our home: I guess that's my version of two separate worlds.

Therapist: What do two separate worlds require of you, Paul?

Paul: Well, both of them have their stressors, but I know how to handle work. I don't seem to know what to do anymore at home.

Therapist: Is there a sense in you that you used to know what to do at home?

Paul: Yes. When Amy and Ann were little, I felt like I knew what they needed, what Jane needed, and what to do from the moment I walked in the door. Work was hard then, too, but there was a balance to the two worlds. Now, I spend more time at work, because that is what I know how to do.

Therapist: Amy and Ann, is that what you remember too? Do you remember that your father knew what to do with you? Did he know how to be part of your life?

Amy: I think he still does know that: I can't imagine a better father. He has always been there for us. He comes to our school activities, takes us on vacations, and even lets us travel with him.

Ann: Dad is always the one who helped me with my homework. He's actually the one I talked to about boys.

Jane: You see, this is what I mean. The three of them manage quite well together. I just can't find a way to put the boys and me into that world.

Therapist: Would it be correct to say, Jane, that for you there are two worlds with you as the bridge and that Paul is really facing three worlds: one is work, then one with you and Amy and Ann, and one with you and Jason and Luke?

Jane: I'm not sure that I am really part of the family with Paul and Amy and Ann anymore.

Therapist: So one of the effects of these separate worlds is that you don't really know if you belong in one of them?

Jane: Yes, I mean no. I don't know what I mean. I just feel a lot that the boys and I are not part of all of them.

Paul: It works both ways, Jane. I don't know how to be part of your life either. I don't know what to do with Jason and Luke.

Therapist: So would it be safe to say that the two of you are losing your belonging with each other (pause) . . . and your sons are losing their chance to belong before their chance even begins?

> A small fight breaks out between Jason and Luke. Jane immediately gets up and makes both of the boys sit down in the circle. Amy and Ann move in to occupy the boys, while the therapist explores the effects of separate worlds on the belonging of the parents to each other and to their four children. The therapist notes that she can see the effects of the separate worlds on the family, but she wonders out loud about the family's influence on these separate worlds.

Paul: I think we introduce fear into these worlds. We didn't used to feel fearful—at least, I didn't. I would look forward to coming home. I would know what to do. Now, I am afraid of what will have happened while I have been at work—what the boys have done this time. I am often afraid of letting Jane down. Even when I try, I seem to mess up.

Therapist: So you feel like fear gets infused in the world at home?

Paul: (picking up Luke who has been crawling around and placing him in his lap) Yes, and I feel it before I even get home, so I know I am adding it. It is really nothing the boys have done.

Jane: I feel that fear too. From the moment I get up until well into the day.

Therapist: (to Paul) I am just wondering. . . . Is holding Luke right now something that emerges out of fear or something that emerges from your capacity to create belonging?

Paul: Well, I don't feel fearful at the moment.

Therapist: So is this something you do when you are making a space for the boys to belong in the family?

Paul: Yes, I guess it is.

Therapist: Would this be what it looks like when you are standing up to fear and keeping it at bay? [Paul: Yes.] I am wondering if you, Jane, and perhaps Amy and Ann, too, if you have noticed other instances in which Paul or any of you have taken a stand against fear and created a sense of belonging instead?

The conversation now turns to other events in their lives when Paul or Jane have done things to create a sense of belonging. Amy and Ann talk about things that they all used to do when the two of them were young and what it would be like to do similar things with Jason and Luke. Amy and Ann also talk about the power they see in their parents when they are working together on a project or to help one of them: "Nothing can really stop them."

Therapist: Paul and Jane, can you officially help Jason and Luke belong to this family or is it too late? Have there been too many difficulties coming from your separate worlds to make "bridging" and "belonging" impossible?

Paul: No, it is not too late. We can do this. We really do know how to do this.

Therapist: Luke, you have been sitting so nicely in your father's lap. I am wondering if you like it there? Do you like to sit in your dad's lap? (Luke nods.)

Jason: I like to sit in laps too.

Jane: Come and sit in my lap.

Therapist: Jason, is it possible for you to ask to sit in a lap when you want to rest or just feel like you belong? I am wondering if you are a good "asker"?

Jason: I'm a good asker. I'm a good runner too, but I like sitting now.

Therapist: I have a request. I would like all of you to think about this effort to belong and how it might fit for all of you—and I will think about it too. Do you think we could all reflect on this before any decisions about the boys are made? And maybe then we could meet again in about a month. (People nod.) I am wondering what we might call this time we spent together today?

Amy: Hope.

Summary and Multicultural Evaluation

A mere hundred years ago, Freud, Adler, and Jung were part of a major paradigm shift that transformed psychology, as well as philosophy, science, medicine, and even the arts. Now we are engaged in another dramatic turning point at the beginning of the 21st century. Postmodern constructions of alternate knowledge sources seem to be one of the paradigm shifts most likely to affect family counseling and psychotherapy in the immediate future. The creation of the self, which so dominated the modernist search for human essence and truth, is being replaced with the concept of storied lives. Diversity, multiple frameworks, and an integration/collaboration of the knower with the known are all part of this new social movement to enlarge perspectives and options. For some social constructionists, the process of "knowing" includes a distrust of the dominant-culture positions that permeate families and society today. For these people, change starts with deconstructing the power of cultural narratives and then proceeds to the co-construction of a new life of meaning.

Just as Rogers (1980) elevated the person in individual therapy to the level of expert in his or her own life, social constructionists invite us into a client-as-expert lens that makes listening, interest, discovery, and curiosity primary skills in the therapy process. Like the Adlerian model, a great deal of emphasis is placed on **hermeneutics**, the many diverse ways in which people interpret life through stories and bring meaning to lived experience. At the heart of this model is a valuing of multiple perspectives that eventually find full development in metaframeworks (Breunlin, Schwartz, & MacKune-Karrer, 1992).

Perhaps our biggest challenge is learning how to live in meaningful and peaceful ways. Social constructionist approaches to counseling allow us the opportunity to choose our stances toward the past and the future in ways that offer hope, in ways that accentuate difference rather than pathology, strength rather than weakness, possibility rather than limitation. (D. L. Bubenzer, personal communication, May 16, 2004)

If you are interested in more in-depth study of the newer approaches to family therapy, I recommend the following sources: Andersen (1991); Anderson (1993, 1996); Anderson and Goolishian (1992); Epston and White (1992); Freedman and Combs (1996); McNamee and Gergen (1992); O'Hanlon (1994); West, Bubenzer, and Bitter, (1998); White (1992, 1995, 1997, 1998, 2007); White and Epston (1990); and Zimmerman and Dickerson (1996).

Contributions to Multicultural Counseling and Gender Issues

Postmodern, social constructionist approaches to therapy have almost a perfect fit with the basic philosophy and tenets of multiculturalism. The constructs of multiple realities and a diversity of truths is at the heart of both a postmodern worldview and multicultural perspectives. Narrative therapy, especially, is well situated to challenge the oppressive values and beliefs of the dominant culture. When clients bring individual or family concerns to a narrative therapist, there is a clear inclination within the therapeutic process to address patriarchy and **sexism, racism, ageism, heterosexism**, and other forms of discrimination and oppression that have real effects on people and systems. As we saw in the opening case example provided in the work of Stephen Madigan, it is possible to address the development of the individual, the family, and society all at the same time within narrative therapy.

Because of this incorporation of multiple perspectives within the therapeutic process, clients experiencing different levels of acculturation within a family system can each claim validity for personal stories in development while at the same time co-constructing the larger stories of family, culture, and society. Individuals both affect and are affected by the larger interactive systems in which they live. In this sense, postmodern, social constructionist approaches are dedicated to a diversity of perspectives in the co-construction of preferred outcomes. Nowhere is this more evident than in White's (1995, 2007) work with *definitional ceremonies* (also see Bitter, Robertson, Roig, & Disque, 2004) and Andersen's (1991) *reflecting teams*.

Because the world is made up of different cultures, in the widest sense of that term, no real assumptions about people based on **stereotypes** of any kind can be useful in counseling. The decentered and not-knowing positions of narrative and linguistic therapists offer the best hope for developing and understanding the multiple stories that are present in families. Indeed, the kind of curious interest that permeates closely followed stories not only brings respect and value to difference, but also provides a foundation for thickening cultural as well as individual stories. This is most evident in the work that narrative therapists do in de-constructing the dominant-cultural perspective inherent in psychopathology. Rather than seeing problems as resident within the individual or system, narrative therapists believe that problems are external forces embedded in social (or relational), cultural, and political contexts. Given the nature of the dominant culture, individual and family problems are commonly related to issues of gender, ethnicity, race, class, and sexual orientation. Under the co-leadership of Cheryl White and David Denborough, the Dulwich Centre in Australia has constantly addressed the oppression of women and members of the LGBT community (Denborough, 2002; Dulwich Centre Publications, 2001).

Because the therapeutic process is oriented toward exploration and specifically addresses the real effects of dominant and oppressive stories and practices, there is a real deconstruction of imposed power through the process of externalization (Boyd-Franklin, 2003). It is in the effort to identify and co-construct preferred realities, unique outcomes, and alternate knowledge stories that individuals escape from dominance and oppression. And because these preferred realities and unique outcomes are already embedded within the individual's or the family's culture, the process supports the development of the person, the system, and the culture—all at the same time.

It is important to remember that there is no such thing as a community or a culture without a diversity of voices. There are feminist voices, for example, even in the most repressive of patriarchal regimes. There is no such thing as a culture without both strengths and weaknesses, demonstrations of competence and demonstrations of ineffectiveness, and experiences of freedom and growth, as well as those of restraint and control. When social constructionists ask the following kinds of questions, they are exploring the real effects of culture on the person while also developing avenues for re-authoring lives:

- What influence has your culture had in your life?
- What challenges have you faced growing up in your culture and how have you handled them?
- What is significant in your life and the lives of your family and community that I must know if I really want to understand you?
- What has been difficult for you or restrained you as you have grown up?
- What resources exist within your cultural community that support you and from which you draw strength in times of need?

A postmodern, social constructionist perspective is so interwoven with positive multicultural aspects that it is hard to find a problem from this perspective. Corey (2005) has suggested that some cultures that value the therapist-as-expert (for example, some Asian cultures) may feel a lack of trust for a counselor who insists that the client is expert. In practice, however, a decentered, not-knowing position is merely a manner of inquiry, not a philosophical position imposed on the family. The questions and language that follow from a not-knowing position signify a position of respect that is valued by almost all cultures. Further, social constructionism transforms the neutrality of some family systems models into advocacy, as the opening case with Stephen Madigan demonstrates. Indeed, social constructionists are some of the most powerful voices in therapy for the oppressed.

 ## Exercises for Personal and Professional Growth

I have some questions I would like to ask you. Would you be willing to see what comes up for you as you consider some ideas about your life and profession? What is the history of the idea of your becoming a family practitioner? Was there a time when the idea was not with you? How did you recognize it as a part of your thinking? What kind of effect does the idea have on your personal and professional development? What influence has the field had on you so far? What do you expect the influence will continue to be? What influence have you had on the field? What influence do you want to have? Were there people who influenced the development of the idea you have about becoming a family practitioner? What was that influence? What influence have you had on them? Do they know that they influenced you? What would it be like for you to catch them up on your decision to become a family counselor, psychologist, social worker, or therapist? How is being a family practitioner different from anything you have done before? What changes have been brought about in you as you grow into the work? Who will be the first to notice these positive changes in you? What does it say about you that you are able to pursue this career objective and profession? What do you predict for the coming year—both personally and professionally?

I probably could have asked better questions if you and I were sitting face-to-face and having a full conversation. When I am listening to someone, the questions that come to mind often follow from my interest and curiosity in them—and do not sound quite so contrived. As you are reading this, I am wondering what questions would you ask yourself. What questions would open you up to hope and meaning and an unfolding of the importance of family practice in your life? Would you take a moment to think about what those questions might be and what answers might follow?

Questions and some possible answers for consideration:

1. _____

_____

_____

_____

2. _____

_____

_____

_____

3. _____

_____

_____

_____

Probably one of the more difficult skills to develop in narrative therapy is externalization. In part, this is because we have to learn to disconnect from the dominant stances in psychology and psychiatry that have long contended the person is the problem. If we are not separated from this notion, then externalizations tend to sound contrived and artificial. Effective externalization questions start with a real belief that problems are always separate from people and have real effects on the lives of people to whom they attach. Can you believe that people do not have or do problems, but rather are simply affected by the problems they must face? If you can come to that belief, then developing externalization questions will be easier and will feel more natural.

I am thinking about a case that David Epston once had. A young woman, who had recently been discharged from a hospital with little hope of recovery, came with her sister and brother-in-law for a consultation about anorexia. Her self-description was as thin as her body, and her identity was almost completely fused with the problem of anorexia. She was very thin, wearing a sweater that she was able to pull over her legs in an effort, I suspect, to hide how she looked from herself, as well as from others. David Epston patiently asked her externalizing questions for a long time (45 minutes, I believe) with little or no response from the young woman. His patience and curiosity allowed him to search for a question or set of questions to which the client could attach meaning. When you think about this case, what questions might you ask her in an effort to externalize the anorexia from the person? Write some possible questions out below. If you would like to know the question David asked that eventually got a response from the woman in this case, see the Endnotes.[6] But first, you might want to write out the questions you would ask.

Questions you might ask this client in an effort to externalize the anorexia:

1. _____

_____

2. _____

_____

3. _____

_____

White (1989) provides two papers that are very helpful in learning to form externalizing and re-authoring questions. These essays are called "The externalizing of the problem and the re-authoring of lives and relationships" and "The process of questioning: A therapy of literary merit." I recommend both of these essays to you. Together, they will give you a map for asking questions of action and meaning that develop stories across time, that is, from the past to the future (D. L. Bubenzer, personal communication, May 16, 2004).

Where to Go From Here

One of the best places to go for an overview of postmodern, social constructionist models and work is on the Internet at **http://www.narrativeapproach.com**. There you will find links to various training centers around the world, books and other information on narrative therapy and its applications, and papers and ideas still in development. The most well-known training and publication center for narrative therapy is in Australia. Michael White is a therapist and the most prolific writer of the group at the Dulwich Centre:

Dulwich Centre
345 Carrington Street, Adelaide, South Australia 5000
http://www.dulwichcentre.com.au/

Dulwich Centre Publications has a wide range of books, including the complete works of Michael White and David Epston. Their publications and training programs can be accessed through:

Dulwich Centre Publications Pty Ltd.
ACN: 087 569 579
Hutt Street, P. O. Box 7192, Adelaide, South Australia 5000
Phone: (61-8) 8223 3966, fax: (61-8) 8232 4441
E-mail: **dulwich@senet**

Some other postmodern, social constructionist, and narrative therapy training centers in the United States and around the world include:

Evanston Family Therapy Institute
Jill Freedman and Gene Combs
636 Church Street, #901, Evanston, IL 60201

The Family Therapy Centre
David Epston
6 Goring Road, Sandringham, Auckland 4 New Zealand
Counsellor Education Programme
University of Waikato, Private Bag 3105, Hamilton, New Zealand
http://www.soe.waikato.ac.nz/counselling

and

Bay Area Family Therapy Training Associates
Jeffrey L. Zimmerman and Victoria C. Dickerson
21760 Stevens Creek Boulevard, Suite 102, Cupertino, CA 95015
Phone: 408-257-6881, fax: 408-257-0689
E-mail: **baftta@aol.com**, website: **http://www.baftta.com**

Those who are seeking masters or doctoral degrees in Counselor Education can focus on postmodern, social constructionism at Kent State University, working with John West and Don Bubenzer. They can be reached at:

Department of Counseling, Health and Career Technical Teacher Education
Counseling and Human Development Services Program
P. O. Box 5190, Kent, Ohio 44242-0001
Phone: 330-672-2662
Websites: **http://chdsw.educ.kent.edu** or **http://www.kent.edu**

Recommended Readings

Andersen, T. (1991). *The reflecting team. Dialogues and dialogues about the dialogues.* New York: Norton. The most complete presentation of the reflecting team process developed by Andersen and associates in Norway and now incorporated in most social constructionist models.

Anderson, H. (1996). *Conversation language and possibilities: A postmodern approach to therapy.* New York: Basic Books. Harlene Anderson provides a full account of the linguistic model she developed with the late Harold Goolishian, and brings it to life with cases and examples.

Epston, D., & White, M. (Eds.). (1992). *Experience, contradiction, narrative & imagination: Selected writings of David Epston and Michael White, 1989–1991.* Adelaide, South Australia: Dulwich Centre Publications. This book presents cases and Michael White's comprehensive article on deconstruction and therapy.

Freedman, J., & Combs, G. (1996). *Narrative therapy: The social construction of preferred realities.* New York: Norton. Freedman and Combs conduct one of the best training programs on narrative therapy in the United States. It is very comprehensive while still managing to keep most of the poetry and politics of the model intact.

Friedman, S. (Ed.). (1993). *The new language of change: Constructive collaboration in psychotherapy.* New York: Guilford. This book is a compilation of articles with contributions from Tom Andersen, Harlene Anderson, Insoo Kim Berg, Steve de Shazer, Jennifer Dickerson, Lynn Hoffman, Bill O'Hanlon, and Jeffrey Zimmerman, to name a few.

Gergen, K. J. (1991). *The saturated self: Dilemmas of identity in contemporary life.* New York: Basic Books. Covering subjects from anthropology to psychoanalysis, as well as film, fiction, and literary theory, Gergen explores the impact of communication and technology on the development of identity stories and lays the foundation for social constructionism in therapy.

McNamee, S., & Gergen, K. J. (Eds.). (1992). *Therapy as social construction.* Newbury Park, CA: Sage. Another compilation of articles covering theory, practice, and applications of social construction in therapy process. The chapter by Anderson and Goolishian is one of the best presentations of the not-knowing position.

Payne, M. (2000). *Narrative therapy: An introduction for counsellors.* Thousand Oaks, CA: Sage. This is one of the clearest and most complete presentations of narrative therapy available in print; it is designed for the beginning counseling student in Human Services or masters in Counseling programs.

West, J. D., Bubenzer, D. L., & Bitter, J. R. (Eds.). (1998). *Social construction in couple and family counseling.* Alexandria, VA: American Counseling Association. This ACA publication provides couples and family counselors with a great introduction to social constructionism, covers everything from narrative therapy to solution-focused therapy, and ends with a great summary written by Karl Tomm.

White, M. (1995). *Re-authoring lives: Interviews and essays.* Adelaide, South Australia: Dulwich Centre Publications. A set of essays and interviews that explicate narrative therapy and its relationship to therapeutic practice and systems theory. The chapter on reflecting teamwork as definitional ceremony is especially good.

White, M. (1997). *Narratives of therapists' lives.* Adelaide, South Australia: Dulwich Centre Publications. Essays on therapeutic practice, supervision, definitional ceremonies, and decentered positions in counseling make this one of White's most important contributions.

White, M. (2007). *Maps of narrative practice.* New York: Norton. This book provides therapeutic maps for a whole range of narrative conversations, including externalization, re-authoring, re-membering, and scaffolding. There are also excellent chapters on definitional ceremonies and unique outcome conversations.

White, M., & Epston, D. (1990). *Narrative means to therapeutic ends.* New York: Norton. This is the foundational book in narrative therapy. The co-constructors of the model provide the philosophical, anthropological, and therapeutic underpinnings of their work, including complete presentations on externalization, re-authoring, and the use of documents (letters, certificates, etc.) in therapy.

Zimmerman, J. L., & Dickerson, V. C. (1996). *If problems talked: Narrative therapy in action.* New York: Guilford. An adventure in reading about narrative therapy, this book is written in much the same way that narrative practice is conducted, complete with problems talking, and authors and clients talking back to them.

DVD Reference

Narrative therapy is a postmodern, social constructionist approach, grounded in decentered questions that reflect curiosity about the client and the problem at multiple levels. Naming the problem is the first step in exploring the effects of the problem in the client's life. This exploration is often facilitated by externalizing questions that make it possible for the client to stand back from the problem, or separate from it. Unique events in the client's life then are used to re-author new meaning, new possibilities, and new stories.

In this narrative therapy video segment, Dr. Graham Disque, Professor of Counseling at East Tennessee State University, demonstrates the careful unfolding of multiple stories and the development of a named external force, in this case fear, that operates on the family and affects the members' sense of safety with the world and each other.

References

Andersen, T. (1987). The reflecting team: Dialogue and meta-dialogue in clinical work. *Family Process, 26,* 415–428.

Andersen, T. (1991). *The reflecting team. Dialogues and dialogues about the dialogues.* New York: Norton.

Andersen, T. (1992). Reflections on reflecting with families. In S. McNamee & K. J. Gergen (Eds.), *Therapy and social construction* (pp. 54–68). Newbury Park: Sage.

Anderson, H. (1993). On a roller coaster: A collaborative language systems approach to therapy. In S. Friedman (Ed.), *The new language of change* (pp. 323–344). New York: Guilford.

Anderson, H. (1996). *Conversation language and possibilities: A postmodern approach to therapy.* New York: Basic Books.

Anderson, H., & Goolishian, H. (1992). The client is the expert: A not-knowing approach to therapy. In S. McNamee & K. J. Gergen (Eds.) *Therapy as social construction* (pp. 25–39). Newbury Park, CA: Sage.

Becvar, D. S., & Becvar, R. J. (2003). *Family therapy: A systemic integration* (5th ed.). Boston: Allyn & Bacon.

Bitter, J. R., Robertson, P. E., Roig, G., & Disque, J. G. (2004). Definitional ceremonies: Integrating community into multicultural counseling sessions. *Journal of Multicultural Counseling and Development, 32,* 272–282.

Boyd-Franklin, N. (2003). *Black families in therapy: Understanding the African American experience* (2nd ed.). New York: Guilford.

Breunlin, D. C., Schwartz, R. C., & MacKune-Karrer, B. (1992). *Metaframeworks: Transcending the models of family therapy.* San Francisco: Jossey Bass.

Bruner, J. S. (1986). *Actual minds, possible worlds.* Cambridge, MA: Harvard University Press.

Bruner, J. S. (1991). The narrative construction of reality. *Critical Inquiry, 18,* 1–21.

Carlson, J., & Kjos, D. (Eds.). (1999). *Narrative therapy with Dr. Steve Madigan: Study guide and interview transcripts for family therapy with the experts.* Boston: Allyn & Bacon.

Corey, G. (2005). *Theory and practice of counseling and psychotherapy* (7th ed). Belmont, CA: Brooks/Cole.

Denborough, D. (2002). *Queer counseling and narrative therapy.* Adelaide, South Australia: Dulwich Centre Publications.

Derrida, J. (1992). *Derrida: A critical reader* (D. Wood, Ed.). Oxford: Blackwell.

Dulwich Centre Publications. (2001). *Working with stories of women's lives.* Adelaide, South Australia: Author.

Epston, D., & White, M. (Eds.). (1992). *Experience, contradiction, narrative, and imagination: Selected papers of David Epston and Michael White, 1989–1991.* Adelaide, South Australia: Dulwich Centre Publications.

Epston, D., White, M., & Murray, K. (1992). A proposal for reauthoring therapy: Rose's revisioning of her life and a commentary. In S. McNamee & K. J. Gergen (Eds.). *Therapy as social construction* (pp. 96–115). Newbury Park, CA: Sage.

Foucault, M. (1970). *The order of things: An archeology of the human sciences*. New York: Random House.

Foucault, M. (1979). *Discipline and punishment: The birth of the prison*. New York: Pantheon.

Foucault, M. (1980). *Power/knowledge: Selected interviews and other writings*. New York: Pantheon Books.

Freedman, J., & Combs, G. (1996). *Narrative therapy: The social construction of preferred realities*. New York: Norton.

Friedman, S. (Ed.). (1993). *The new language of change: Constructive collaboration in psychotherapy*. New York: Guilford.

Gergen, K. J. (1985). The social constructionist movement in modern psychology. *American Psychologist, 40,* 260–275.

Gergen, K. J. (1991). *The saturated self*. New York: Basic Books.

Gergen, K. J. (1999). *An invitation to social construction*. Thousand Oaks, CA: Sage.

Hawkings, S. (1988). *A brief history of time: From big bang to black holes*. New York: Bantam Books.

Hawkings, S. (2001). *The universe in a nutshell*. New York: Bantam Books.

Madigan, S. (Speaker). (1999). *Narrative therapy: Family therapy with the experts* (Moderators: J. Carlson & D. Kjos). Boston: Allyn & Bacon.

McKenzie, W., & Monk, G. (1997). Learning and teaching narrative ideas. In G. Monk, J. Winslade, K. Crockett, & D. Epston (Eds.), *Narrative therapy in practice: The archeology of hope* (pp. 82–117). San Francisco: Jossey-Bass.

McNamee, S., & Gergen, K. J. (1992). *Therapy as social construction*. Newbury Park, CA: Sage.

Meyerhoff, B. (1982). Life history among the elderly: Performance, visibility, and remembering. In J. Ruby (Ed.). *A crack in the mirror: Reflexive perspectives in anthropology* (pp. 99–117). Philadelphia: University of Pennsylvania Press.

Meyerhoff, B. (1986). Life not death in Venice: Its second life. In V. Turner & E. Bruener (Eds.). *The anthropology of experience* (pp. 261–286). Chicago: University of Illinois Press.

Nichols, M. P., & Schwartz, R. C. (2006). *Family therapy: Concepts and methods* (7th ed.). Boston: Allyn & Bacon.

Nyland, D., & Thomas, J. (1994). The economics of narratives. *The Family Therapy Networker, 16*(6), 38–39.

O'Hanlon, W. H. (1994). The third wave: The promise of narrative. *The Family Therapy Networker, 18*(6), 18–29.

Payne, M. (2000). *Narrative therapy: An introduction for counsellors*. Thousand Oaks, CA: Sage.

Rogers, C. (1980). *A way of being*. Boston: Houghton Mifflin.

Selvini Palazzoli, M., Boscolo, L., Cecchin, F. G., & Prata, G. (1980). Hypothsizing-circularity-neutrality: Three guidelines for the conductor of the session. *Family Process, 19*(1), 3–12.

Tomm, K. (1998). Social constructionism in the evolution of family therapy. In J. D. West, D. L. Bubenzer, & J. R. Bitter (Eds.). *Social construction in couple and family counseling* (pp. 173–187). Alexandria, VA: American Counseling Association.

West, J. D., & Bubenzer, D. L. (2002). Narrative family therapy. In J. Carlson & D. Kjos (Eds.). *Theories and strategies of family therapy* (pp. 353–381). Boston: Allyn & Bacon.

West, J. D., Bubenzer, D. L., & Bitter, J. R. (Eds.). (1998). *Social construction in couple and family counseling*. Alexandria, VA: American Counseling Association.

White, M. (1989). *Selected papers*. Adelaide, South Australia: Dulwich Centre.

White, M. (1992). Deconstruction and therapy. In D. Epston & M. White (Eds.). *Experience, contradiction, narrative, and imagination. Selected papers of David Epston and Michael White, 1989–1991* (pp. 109–151). Adelaide, South Australia: Dulwich Centre Publications.

White, M. (1995). *Re-authoring lives: Interviews and essays*. Adelaide, South Australia: Dulwich Centre Publications.

White, M. (1997). *Narratives of therapists' lives*. Adelaide, South Australia: Dulwich Centre Publications.

White, M. (1998). Liberating conversations: New dimensions in narrative therapy. Washington, DC: Workshop at the *Family Therapy Networker's* Annual Symposium.

White, M. (2000). *Reflections on narrative practice: Interviews and essays*. Adelaide, South Australia: Dulwich Centre Publications.

White, M. (2005). Workshop Notes. Adelaide, South Australia: Internet:http://www.dulwichcentre.com.au/articles.html.

White, M. (2007). *Maps of narrative practice*. New York: Norton.

White, M., & Epston, D. (1990). *Narrative means to therapeutic ends*. New York: Norton.

Zimmerman, J. L., & Dickerson, V. C. (1996). *If problems talked: Narrative therapy in action*. New York: Guilford.

Endnotes

[1]Steve Madigan is from Canada; David Epston is from New Zealand; and Michael White is from Australia. As such, the HIPAA regulations in the United States do not apply to them. For those who work in the U.S., the writing of letters to and for clients could raise some legal problems with regard to the new HIPAA regulations. Such letters under HIPAA most likely would constitute a disclosure that would require the client's—or in this case, because the client is a minor, the guardian's—written authorization. Indeed, the letter to the school district is so broad that it may even involve people who cannot be named in a HIPAA authorization. Even when letters are sent only to the client, the client would need to provide the clinician with an authorized address designated for its privacy. Clients also would retain the right to say that they did not want anything mailed to them from the clinical practitioner. If there are letters sent to non-clients, such as absent parents or other family members, the client would need to grant a written authorization first. It is likely that these letters would be part of the client's protected health information (PHI) under HIPAA.

These same regulations in the U.S. would affect therapists who want to engage others in the community as a part of therapy. If a therapist in the U.S., for example, contacts a school on behalf of a peer-abuse victim, again HIPAA authorization would be needed and would, perhaps, be extremely difficult to get. HIPAA is another example of a well-intentioned safeguard that eventually becomes a trap and limits effective therapy.

[2]When a series of unique events has evolved into an alternate story about a person, a similar question to this one can be used to **thicken** the alternate story and bring it even more fully to life.

[3]Such speculation often is enhanced by naming the alternate story. If the new narrative is about a strong, competent person, then these words also can serve as the name for the story in the same way that Steve Madigan referred to Ollie's alternate story as a "good boy story" in the example used earlier in this chapter.

[4]When social constructionists refer to the client-as-expert, it is sometimes asked: "Well, then, what is the therapist's expertise?" The answer is that the therapist becomes an expert at creating conversations in which the client's expert knowledge about self can take center stage—and in which options and alternate stories can be developed from the client's personal experiences (see Anderson, 1996; Anderson & Goolishian, 1992).

[5]Jacques Derrida (1992) applied the concept of *deconstruction* to literature: By taking apart narrative texts, he was able to demonstrate that stories did not add up to only one true meaning. Narrative therapists also use deconstruction in this way, but they also add the political intent of dismantling dominant discourses (Nichols & Schwartz, 2006).

[6]After trying many different externalizing questions in multiple forms, David said to the woman: "You know, most people tend to know when they are dying. How does anorexia trick you into believing that you are not dying?"

The young woman responded: "It lies to me."

"How do you know that?" David asked.

"Because," the woman answered, "My sister says I am dying and she would not lie to me."

When the client calls anorexia "it," the externalization is already in process and there is now just enough space between the client and the problem to find room for an alternate story.

CHAPTER 12

Feminist Family Therapy*

Introduction

Key Concepts

Therapy Goals

The Therapist's Role and Function

Techniques

A Feminist Therapist With the Quest Family

Summary and Multicultural Evaluation

Recommended Readings

References

Introduction

Feminist therapists integrate many theoretical orientations into their work with families. Some use object-relations theory (reconsidered and reconstituted to empower women) as a therapeutic model, and others employ Adlerian, existential, Gestalt, person-centered, or cognitive principles. Still others have adopted the systemic approaches of Bowen, Satir, Whitaker, Minuchin, and even the strategic therapists. The professions that most affect families are being transformed by women.[1] Feminists come from all cultures and may be "liberal, Marxist, Zionist, Christian, radical, and lesbian separatist" (Luepnitz, 1988, p. 14)—even conservative. In short, they interact with and incorporate psychological, social, cultural, and political positions that span the spectrum of human life.

Feminism has a long, significant, and often harrowing past. Recording this story will require a longer introduction than I have used in other chapters. Philosophically, feminism is at least as old as the publication of Mary Wollstonecraft's (1792/1989) *A Vindication of the Rights of Women*. In the United States, the first wave of the women's rights movement starts with a gathering of women at Seneca Falls, New York, in 1848 where, among other reforms, Elizabeth Cady Stanton declared that the right of women to vote was essential. In 1878, Susan B. Anthony's amendment was introduced in Congress. It would take 42 years for often harassed and jailed supporters to get the right to vote ratified in 1920.

Almost every right afforded women today has come through the efforts of feminists. In addition to the right to vote, I include here the rights to have access to contraceptives, work

---

*I want to acknowledge the diligent efforts and contributions of Dr. Roberta Nutt in developing this chapter and making sure it was up to date.

outside the home, receive equal pay for equal work, refuse sex—even with women's own husbands, receive a higher education, have access to safe and legal abortions, participate in sports, hold political office, choose a career that interests them, be free from sexual harassment in the workplace, and enter into legal and financial transactions, to name a few. And still, there is a long way to go. According to Goodrich (2003),

- Women receive about 73 cents to every dollar earned by a man for the same work;
- Women hold less than 12% of the board seats on *Fortune* 1000 companies;
- Women make up 46.5% of the work force in America, hold almost 50% of the managerial and specialty positions, and yet are less than 13% of the corporate officers and less than 5% of the *Fortune 500* top money makers;
- More than 60% of the poor and the working poor are women; and
- Women make up less than 15% of the Congress in both houses.

Some attempts have been made to describe the continuum of feminist theory (Enns, 1993, 2004; Enns & Sinacore, 2001). Four of the most enduring points on the continuum were originally developed to describe the "second wave" of feminism in the 1970s. **Liberal feminists** saw therapy as a means of empowering the individual woman and helping her to overcome the limits and constraints of patriarchal socialization. Personal fulfillment, dignity, and equality were sought as a means of negating male privilege in both social and work environments. **Cultural feminists** believed therapy could be an avenue for infusing society with women's values, including altruism, cooperation, and connectedness. They noted that oppression included the devaluing of women's strengths and that all people need a world that is more nurturing and relationally based. **Radical feminists** were more likely to focus on patriarchy and the social activism that is required to eliminate it. Within family therapy, their goals included the transformation of gender relationships; sexual, procreative, and reproductive rights; and the equalization of household chores, partnerships, parenting, and access to employment outside the home. **Socialist feminists** were the first to broaden the perspective to include the multiple discriminations based on race, socioeconomic status, national origin, and other historical biases. In therapy, their goals included an assessment of how education, work, and family roles impact the individual, and a determination to transform relationships that are socially burdened and externally imposed. There is a lot of overlap in just these four descriptions: They are neither discrete nor comprehensive.

To these four ongoing descriptions of feminism, Enns, Sinacore, Ancis, and Phillips (2004) add four descriptions of diversity feminisms, each engaged in the process of integrating feminism with multicultural perspectives. **Postmodern feminists** address patriarchy as one form of dominant-knowledge position, and "use deconstruction and discourse analysis to examine how reality is socially constructed and influenced by power and hierarchical relationships" (pp. 414–415). **Women-of-color feminists** note that racism, classism, sexism, and heterosexism are all interlocked and cannot be considered separately when they are all experienced together. These oppressions affect all people and within the context of therapy, **womanists**, an often preferred term by feminists of color, actualize an appreciation of women's culture, its strengths and emotional value, and seek to develop wholeness in both genders and all cultures. **Lesbian feminists** believe that heterosexism is at the core of women's oppression with its insistence on male–female relationships and sexuality, its sexualized and romanticized images of women, and its almost total marginalization of strong women in same-sex relationships. **Transnational feminists** seek to link women's individual experiences to those of women throughout the world and across national boundaries. Sexual violence, prostitution, and other international processes that hurt and demean women are the focus of these global feminists.

Given the variety of feminist stances, it is impossible to point to a single, unified **feminist family therapy**. What feminists do share in common is (1) a belief that patriarchy is

Louise Silverstein

Thelma Goodrich

alive and sick in sociopolitical life and the life of families; (2) a realization that "the normal family" has too often been defined as one with heterosexual parents and has not been so normal or wonderful for mothers, reflecting the discrimination against women evident in world systems beyond the family; (3) a willingness to analyze power and challenge power differentials in relationships, therapy, and society; (4) a commitment to reforming families and society in ways that fully empower and enfranchise women economically, socially, and politically; and (5) therapeutic processes that include a positive attitude toward women, social analysis, explicit consideration of gender issues for both genders, and treating the **personal as political** (Avis, 1986; May, 2001; Silverstein & Goodrich, 2003).

Many researchers have noted the ways in which heterosexual family life is configured in favor of men and to the detriment of women (Bernard, 1972; Degler, 1980; Durkheim, 1951; Luepnitz, 1988). Perhaps the most significant early study of normal families has been the Timberlawn research (Gurman & Kniskern, 1981; Lewis, Beaver, Gossett, & Phillips, 1976; Walsh, 1993). Luepnitz (1988) summarizes the findings as follows:

> Women in the "adequate" (also called normal) families were "overwhelmed with responsibility," "obese," "psychosomatically ill," and "sexually dissatisfied." The men in these same families were "functioning well" and were not sexually dissatisfied. Thus . . . an adequate family consists of a husband and children who are functioning adequately and a wife who is not. (pp. 10–11)

Although there is some evidence that normal families are evolving and broadening in definition (Walsh, 2003) and some changes have been noted in family roles as women have moved into the workforce and balanced a larger number of roles, feminist family therapists still take stands against societies or cultures that define the pathologizing and subservience of women as normal. Just as social constructionists see dominant positions asserted and maintained in narratives, feminists know that patriarchy also is expressed in narratives. Like Foucault (1980), many feminists use a careful examination of history to generate alternate stories, to contextualize current human experience, and to deconstruct the power and mythology maintained in a patriarchal system.

Early family systems therapies avoided gender issues and contributed to gender oppression both in theory and practice. In part, this is because the major players in the movement were men (Ackerman, Bateson, Bowen, Haley, and Minuchin) and the only female pioneer, Virginia Satir, preferred to think of herself as a humanist rather than a feminist—even though much of her work challenged stereotypic roles and centered therapy in relational nurturance. Luepnitz (1988) believes that these early family therapists were so caught up in their struggle with American psychiatry and its orientation to the individual that they simply didn't have the energy or focus to challenge the normal family too. It was a generous speculation on her part. As Silverstein (2003) points out, it is next to impossible for people in privileged positions to identify on their own the ways in which that privilege oppresses others.

Rachel Hare-Mustin (1978) became the first feminist family therapist to critique and challenge in print family therapy's assumptions and practice, and later she would call for a total revision of family therapy that made gender issues central to assessment and practice. In 1984, Monica McGoldrick, **Carol Anderson**, and Froma Walsh would organize a meeting called the Stonehenge Conference, that included 50 prominent women in family therapy. (For some of the results of that meeting, see McGoldrick, Anderson, & Walsh, 1989.) Out of that meeting, four women, Marianne Walters, Betty Carter, Peggy Papp, and Olga Silverstein (1988) would start The Women's Project.

Silverstein (2003) points out that The Women's Project was important not only for the critique it produced but also for the way in which the four women worked. Each of these leading female practitioners in family therapy found a way to come to common ground without losing either individuality or respect for each other. In addition, they identified the common patterns found in family assessment, such as the enmeshed, overinvolved mother and the peripheral, disengaged father, as political constructions of a patriarchal society and its gender socialization processes. They challenged the value of neutrality in family therapy and proposed a feminist stance in which gender roles, distribution of power and finance, and other constraints inherent in normal family life would be challenged.

Although recent developments in feminist family therapy are many and diverse (Silverstein & Goodrich, 2003), the background I have provided here sets the context for the family counseling session that follows. Patricia E. Robertson is a feminist therapist who works with individuals, couples, and families from feminist/multicultural/person-centered/social constructionist perspectives. She is the Chair of the Department of Human Development and Learning at East Tennessee State University where she teaches in the counseling program and also conducts a private practice. In the following session with an African-American woman named Leola and her two adult daughters, Stacy, age 24, and Jessica, age 22, Robertson demonstrates what a feminist orientation brings to both personal development and family process.

Robertson has some notes from a phone call with Stacy about the situation, and she knows a little of Leola's family history. She also knows that Stacy and Jessica are worried about their mother as they start the process of leaving home.

As this session is about to start, what kind of relationships do you believe are enhancing and rewarding between mothers and daughters and between sisters? How would these relationships develop and change across the family's life cycle? To what will Robertson have to stay attuned as a Caucasian woman working with a single-parent family of African-American women? Do you think a Caucasian woman should even be seeing an African-American woman and her daughters? What do you think about white, male privilege—or the idea that men in society have assigned certain unearned advantages to being white males and conferred dominance on themselves through law, custom, and tradition (McIntosh, 1986, 1995, 1998)? How do you think white privilege and patriarchy might influence the therapist, the women in this family, and the therapy relationship itself?

Some feminists would argue that women should be seen only by female therapists, just as some women-of-color feminists might argue for a similar equality of experience in therapists. Women of color, financially impoverished women, and lesbian women may look on white feminist therapists as having many of the same unearned advantages as white males. How would this affect the counseling relationship? What do you think it would mean for three women of color to address issues of race with Robertson, a white woman? Similarly, what would it mean for a lesbian, **bisexual**, or **transgender** woman to address issues of sexual orientation with a straight practitioner—or for a financially impoverished client to address issues of money with a financially advantaged therapist? Do you think men can be feminists, too? If men can adopt pro-feminist positions, and heterosexuals can adopt pro-LGBT positions effectively, and therapists of financial advantage can work to understand impoverished women and families, under what conditions can these therapists from advantaged positions be effective in counseling people who have experienced oppression, discrimination, and marginalization? What should the interplay of feminism and multiculturalism be in family counseling and therapy? How do you think sexism, racism, and classism, among other oppressions, have influenced your own life, and what part do you think an awareness of them should have in family therapy?

The session now begins:

Robertson: I would like to get to know the three of you and what you hope to have happen here. I want to see if I can feel my way into your family's lives and maybe discover what possibilities there are for all of you. One of you called to make the appointment: Which of you made that first call?

Stacy: I did. I guess I wanted to get some help for my mother.

Robertson: Can you tell me a little bit about what hopes you had for your mother—and maybe for you too?

Stacy: Well, my mother had ended a relationship with this man who was like her partner for over 4 years. I really thought they might get married for a while. When she ended it, she was really sad . . . for a long time . . . over a month. And it kind of scared me how sad she was. It took us a while to get in here, and I don't think she's that sad any more, but she was.

Robertson: So you were worried about her, and you wanted her to have someone besides you to talk to.

Stacy: I wanted her to be happy again.

Robertson: Okay, a month feels like a long time to you for your mother to be sad. I am wondering what it was like for you—and Jessica, too—to lose this man in your mother's life, because maybe he was part of your lives too.

Stacy: I liked him okay.

Jessica: I didn't really. He just seemed to need a lot from Mom, and I kind of felt like I lost her when he was around.

Stacy: Yes, but she was happy with him for a long time. And he was kind most of the time and stuck around more than most of them do. I don't really think that my mother is very good at picking men.

Robertson: (turning to the mother) I don't know, but that might be hard to hear from your daughter. What is it like to hear her idea about you and men?

Leola: It's nothing new. She has said that before. I'm always choosing men who are wrong for me. They're all what I would call wounded dogs in some way or another. I can't seem to let them be. My daughters are concerned about me—and about what it is, I guess, that attracts me to them.

Robertson: So your daughters seem to believe that you have a "flawed picking mechanism": that you choose men you know are not going to be nurturing to you. Is that what you believe, too? Somehow, you know that these men are going to be bad for you ahead of time, and you choose them anyway: Would that be how you see it?

Leola: I wouldn't call what I have a "flawed picking mechanism" exactly. It is more like an unfulfilled need. I find these wounded dogs, or they find me, and after they're healed, then the trouble starts. You know, the relationship starts out good—with mutual respect and giving. But it ends up with me doing all of the giving and nurturing.

Jessica: Is that how you feel about Ralph?

Leola: Yes. Yes, it is. We did well together for quite a while, but he was not really there at the end.

Robertson: Tell me about meeting this last man you were with: Tell me about Ralph. What drew you to him? When you met him, what did you see in him that was attractive?

Leola: Oh, he had many strengths that I had not seen in a man for many years. He was quiet, gentle-natured, caring, and he had a great body for a man of his age. He was a little what I would call distant quiet. The more involved we became, the more we learned how much we had in common, but he was still distant in many ways. And after about 5 years, I am wondering if I really knew him at all. Maybe (pause) . . . maybe, I was just seeing what I wanted to see.

Robertson: So you fell in love with this man, and you used the words *caring*, *gentle*, and *was he sensitive*? . . . at least at the beginning. (Leola nods.) As far as you could tell, he was different in ways from your former partners.

Leola: He *was* different. Especially in the sense that he was not insecure about me being well educated and, well, out-spoken. He listened intently to what I was saying, to my ideas and even to my ambitions. (pause) But he turned out to be like all of the others. He began to take me for granted. And I think that was the worst part: I was always giving in or making the effort. I get angry when I think about it now, although I should be used to it, but for quite a while, I did feel sad.

Robertson: It's heartbreaking, really. I can feel the hope with which you entered into the relationship, and I know what it is like to put your heart fully into it. All you want is for it to be accepted and returned in kind.

Leola: (pause) Another counselor once told me that my problem with picking men is the result of my father dying when I was very young. She said that I had never gotten over it and that I have this fear of losing men: So I cling to them.

Robertson: So you've been told that losing your father early in childhood has "made" you choose men that are unhealthy for you—that you are almost hopelessly desperate for them.

Leola: Yes. That is exactly what I was told. And sometimes, I worry about that happening for my daughters, because they have seen it in me, and they lost their father at a young age too.

Stacy: Don't worry about us, Mom. We just want you to be happy.

Robertson: Having your mother be happy is very important to you, isn't it, Stacy?

Stacy: Yes, it is!

Robertson: Well, one of the things that I've heard clearly from you, Leola, is that you have, at least once, fallen in love with the health you saw in the man, not with his lack of health: He was caring, accepting, appreciative, gentle, and sensitive. He had a career: He was ambitious, just as you have been. Perhaps, some of the things you saw initially turned out to be a front, or maybe he just couldn't sustain them over a longer period of time. He wouldn't be the first man to make a woman his focus—his work—until she has been "won," and then to retreat from the efforts of everyday life and love. But Leola, at least initially, you saw a healthy, loving man, and you loved him back.

Leola: Yes, that's right. There was real love between us in the beginning.

Robertson: (pause) I also heard you say—and I think this is just a very important piece of your life—that you have been very courageous in leaving relationships with men who treated you poorly. You've had, let's see (looking at her notes), four long-term relationships, and at some point in time in each of them, you realized that the relationship was not going where you wanted it to go or that it was not healthy and good for you. You truly knew what you wanted—and that you weren't getting it: So, you left.

Leola: I've never had anyone note that before. I was courageous when I left. In the past, the focus has always been on my problem in getting into these relationships from the beginning. But you know, you're right. In the beginning, these men were offering me something very different from what I was getting when I left. And I do seem to know when it is time to go, time to move on.

Robertson: Tell me about the feeling you have at this moment, right now when you think about being affirmed for the courage to leave.

Leola:	I feel good. I feel confident.
Robertson:	Yes. Where do you feel it? Where do you feel that strength in your body?
Leola:	I feel it all over. (standing for a moment in her strongest pose) I feel kind of like Wonder Woman!
Robertson:	(smiling, almost laughing with Leola) Yeah. That's just great! I love the show of strength in you. And you seem to feel such delight in it. As I look at Jessica and Stacy, I see their pride in you too.
Leola:	(sitting again) It feels a little funny to do that, but that's just what comes out of me.
Robertson:	Tell me about other times in your life where you've looked closely at your choices, and you might have felt like Wonder Woman—you might have felt this strength pulsing through you.
Leola:	Hmmm.
Jessica:	I know I can think of a great example: When you were applying for the position of Vice-President at the bank.
Leola:	Yes, that's right. I thought I was the most qualified of the internal candidates. Actually, I was the most qualified. I was very assertive about being considered seriously for the position, and I was the only candidate who was a person of color. I was talking to a couple of colleagues one day, and they said that they felt my assertiveness was "playing the race card." It really pissed me off. I've been told that so much in my career. Even if they don't mention it, it is assumed that everything I do is because of my race. Even my promotions are because of my race. I was angered by their comments and responses, and I found myself tempted to just be quiet. I want to have a good, working condition with my colleagues—and have a positive working environment in general. But then, I decided that I still would be clear with the committee regarding my feelings about my competence and qualifications.
Robertson:	So, in some ways, you bought into their message about the race card in that you questioned whether you should be quiet.
Leola:	I didn't exactly buy into the race card position or question my abilities. I kept quiet to save their feelings.
Robertson:	So at times, you chose to silence some of your inner feelings to keep your colleagues from getting upset, but even with that, you have continued to move forward. You have continued to seek promotions, and you have continued to believe in and communicate your competence. Is that the strength that Jessica felt was part of this example, this story?
Jessica:	Yes. She was so strong.
Leola:	Yes, I am. What others say can hurt. And after all, I have to work with these . . . a . . . well, anyway. But I never forget what is said to me. I just find a way to let the important people know what I can do.
Robertson:	I know, Leola, and you know this too, because you have experienced it: Often times what happens in this society we live in is that people, who are not part of the dominant culture, are sent messages from their birth—from the very beginning of their lives— that they are "less than." And often womyn and people of color find their behaviors pathologized. Even though they must endure all sorts of pain and hardship, the focus gets put on them and some created pathology that they are carrying. I think this is a way to keep us from the really important discussions. For example, in your work environment: When you have colleagues who say, "Oh, you're playing the race card," then the focus is on you and what you're doing instead of focusing on a broader discussion, like why there are not womyn of color in positions of power. It also eliminates the

conversation about who is truly more competent. So regardless of your color and your true worth, there's no discussion about how womyn of color enhance the workplace, because the discussion has moved to talking about "you playing the race card."

Jessica: Mom, that's really what has happened to you. It happens to all of us.

Robertson: Yes. Jessica, say more about that. How does it happen with you?

Jessica: I am just starting my career, but I constantly feel that I am not just me where I work. I have to represent all Black women. Everyone is watching, waiting for me to make a mistake. It was that way in college too. There were so few Black students and virtually no Black professors. If I was absent from class—even in large classes—everyone knew the Black girl was missing. If I did poorly on a test, it was evidence that I didn't belong there, not that I just played around too much. And if I did well on a test, it was because of all the extra help I supposedly got.

Robertson: So you know about this kind of racism and sexism. You can validate your mother's experience. You have lived it.

Jessica: Yes.

Robertson: Do you also see that the discussion about your mother choosing unhealthy, neglectful, or abusive men is the same thing? There have been four men out there who have been in a relationship with your Mom, and they don't know how to be with a womyn and maintain a caring, nurturing relationship. When we talk about something being wrong with your mother's choices—her actual process of choosing or those difficult life experiences that are supposed to have incapacitated her for the rest of her life—we get away from the discussion of why these men are the way they are. Why are they seemingly incapable of initiating or maintaining nurturing relationships?

Jessica: Men are hopeless.

Robertson: That's your experience of them: Men are hard for you too.

Jessica: Yes.

Robertson: And where are you, Stacy, in all of this?

Stacy: I like men. I like boyfriends, but I don't want anything serious. I have a couple of them around.

Leola: You do? A couple?

Stacy: Yes, Mother. Three, actually.

Robertson: So you have men in your life, but you like to keep them at a bit of a distance. Not let any of them get too close.

For a while, the conversation turns to what kinds of relational experiences the daughters have had in their young lives. As the conversation develops, Leola starts to express a fear that her own lack of a quality relationship with a man is having a negative influence on her daughters. Robertson asks them if they think that is true. Do they worry about not being able to form a quality intimate relationship when they want to?

Stacy: I feel really strong in the relationships I have. I know what I want and what I don't want, and right now, I don't want any real attachments. I like having my own place, making my own decisions, spending my time and money the way I like to. I don't want you worrying about me, Mom.

Robertson: Would you be willing to give your mother the same gift, Stacy, and not worry about her? Do you think she can handle herself and choose what is best for her?

Stacy: (pause) I didn't before I came, but I think I can now. My mother is a pretty strong woman when she wants to be.

Jessica: I like what you said to her earlier. I think our mother is strong. And part of her strength is that when she decides to love someone, she does it all the way. She puts her whole self into it. Then, she gets hurt sometimes. But that goes with it, you know. You can't fully love someone without being hurt now and then. I think it takes real strength and courage to love fully, knowing that it is possible to get hurt.

Robertson: Yes. And knowing when it is time to move on even if moving on does hurt. Grieving a loss is not a sign of weakness: It is a sign of authenticity. Your mother will have to determine her own timeline for her sadness. Leola, I hope it is okay for me to say this, but I really don't think you have much to worry about with these two. They seem like pretty articulate, strong young womyn to me. (pause) Where do we go from here?

Jessica: I would like to be part of that discussion about what is wrong with men who can't seem to commit themselves to a relationship or about people at work who can't seem to get past the color of my skin. I am wondering if we could have some time to talk about that. I really feel like my mother could help me with some of this.

Robertson: I would love to be a witness to that conversation, myself. I think I would learn so much from all of you.

Key Concepts

Feminists see patriarchy as the oldest and most universal dominant-culture position in the world, extending across cultures, religions, nations, and history. Like all dominant-culture positions, patriarchy is designed to maintain itself and to advance views that benefit the powerful and the privileged: It also disenfranchises all other views, perspectives, values, and ways of being—in this case, disenfranchising everything associated with women's ways of knowing and being in the world. For many years, major schools of family therapy ignored patriarchy or treated it as unimportant or even nonexistent, noting that fathers in hetero-sexual families were often absent, physically and emotionally. Indeed, some schools of family therapy suggested that mothers "ran" families and that, if anything, fathers needed to have more influence, not less. Both Ferguson (1983) and Luepnitz (1988) have noted, however, that the personal patriarchy of former centuries has been replaced by the "public patriarchy of the 20th century. While under earlier forms of patriarchy it was a male *person* who limited women's expenditures, freedom to work, and sexual activity, in the case of the public patri-archy, it is the state, the welfare agency, and the media that control these things" (Luepnitz, 1988, p. 16). Most of the founding masters of family therapy have developed models that have all too often joined the dominant culture in establishing heterosexual, dual-parent families as the norm and conveying to women what good mothering and femininity are. Indeed, the dominant culture of patriarchy functions even in the absence of fathers and is passed along in our descriptions of the normal family.

Honoring the Experiences and Perceptions of Women

From the advent of the second wave of the feminist movement, there always has been an emphasis on **consciousness-raising**, grassroots political action, and a consideration and reconsideration of the evolving needs of women. Central to these activities was a determination to value the experiences and perceptions of women (Brown, 1994; Worell & Remer, 2002).

In counseling, psychology, social work, and family therapy, the perspectives of women were almost completely absent. Of all the early therapy approaches, only Adler and his fol-lowers developed models that recognized and addressed discrimination against women and proposed individual and family interventions based on social equality. Freud, Erikson,

Piaget, and Kohlberg developed complete developmental theories and "normed" them on boys, each suggesting in one way or another that girls were probably the same or lesser. In developmental psychology, Gilligan (1982; Gilligan, Ward, & Taylor, 1988) was the first person to propose a developmental model based on young women. It is not until the late 1980s and 1990s that a consideration of women was proposed as central to family therapy (McGoldrick, 2005; McGoldrick, Anderson, & Walsh, 1989). Given the extensive negative effects that family life often has had on women, feminist family therapists start by listening to, acknowledging, and validating the experiences, needs, perspectives, hopes, and desires of women in family relationships and family life (Braverman, 1988; Goldner, 1985: Goodrich, 1991; Goodrich, Rampage, Ellman, & Halstead, 1988; Hare-Mustin, 1978).

The Personal Is Political

Because the individual, personal, and psychological lives of women are largely determined by and reflect the power of **gender-role socialization**, sexism, and oppression, women's experiences and stories are both about them and about the absorption and impact of these political realities (Brown, 1994). In individual and family therapy, this principle calls on psychologists, social workers, counselors, and therapists to reframe and affirm women's characteristics that have been previously devalued—emphasizing empathy, nurturance, cooperation, intuition, interdependence, and relationship focus. Feminists avoid pathologizing behaviors that represent an adherence to female gender-role norms—and often see psychopathology as a reasonable response to damaging social and interpersonal events in the woman's environment. Feminists point out that borderline, dependent, and histrionic personality disorders have been developed to pathologize women suffering from societal and familial oppression. In examining the effects of imposed gender-role socialization on both women and men, feminist therapists seek to transform society, as well as individuals and families.

Social Transformation and Advocacy

Patriarchy has such negative effects on human life that feminist counselors, psychologists, and social workers actively try to change society and to counter its influence on individuals and families. In spite of the advent of democracy, society has actually continued the development of hierarchical structure with both values and power controlled from the top. In this sense, the professions, including counseling, psychology, social work, and family therapy, are a rung in the ladder of a socio-political structure that seldom has accepted or appreciated women's contributions and experiences. "From a feminist perspective, personal liberation cannot occur without social transformation including altering the core assumptions and structures of the [psychological] profession[s]" (Reynolds & Constantine, 2004, p. 349).

Feminists in family therapy understand that there is an inherent power imbalance between therapeutic practitioners and clients. A tremendous emphasis, therefore, is placed on forming egalitarian, often decentered therapy relationships that seek to empower clients to take control of their own lives and free them from rigid expectations and structures. These collaborative relationships are meant not only to facilitate therapeutic practice, but also to serve as models for social relationships in general.

But feminist interventions do not stop at the end of a therapy session. More than almost any other model, this approach encourages therapists to be social advocates for change, to be politically aware and engaged, and to confront discrimination, oppression, and impediments to individual and family development where they are present in everyday community experiences. When a single woman, an impoverished mother, for example, must deal with a social service agency, a feminist therapist often will go with her for support. And further, that same therapist may organize a social action effort to improve the service of that agency and to advocate for the needs of women and children.

Therapy Goals

Feminist family therapists recognize that both individuals and families need help in developing egalitarian relationships, learning to value women's voices and perspectives, and making room for gender-unique identity development. Some of the goals of therapy include centralizing an analysis of sex-role socialization in the life of families; identifying internalized sex-role messages and beliefs, and challenging and replacing sex-role stereotypes and scripts with more self-enhancing belief and stories. The goals related to challenging sex-role stereotypes are important for both men and women, and boys and girls. The end goal of this kind of therapy is to promote and establish egalitarian relationships characterized by respect, caring, nurturing, the exercise of choice, and flexibility in addressing necessary functions and tasks (Worell & Remer, 2002).

Families cannot be separated from the larger contexts in which they exist. Feminists believe that evaluating the influence of social roles and norms on personal and familial experiences is essential. This is especially true in examining how sexism and patriarchy, and racism and classism oppress women and men alike. Feminists seek to model and encourage social activism by demonstrating the skills needed for enacting social change. They work to encourage a feminist identity development for women in conjunction with both cultural identity development—and, when appropriate, lesbian/gay identity development.

Downing and Rousch (1984) identified five stages in their **feminist identity development model**. These stages are: (1) **passive acceptance**, (2) **revelation**, (3) **embeddedness**, (4) **synthesis**, and (5) **active commitment**. Feminist family therapists often meet heterosexual family members stuck in and suffering from the effects of stage one: In this stage, they *live* a preference for dominant-culture values. Male protector roles are reinforced as are women's subservient roles. Female members of these families may be self-depreciating, and the entire family may devalue women in general; females are often in subordinate positions while the males (and male-values) are affirmed, even when these values are misogynistic. Stage two can be facilitated through political awareness, contact with alternate perspectives, and even through therapy. Revelation usually starts with a new understanding of women's personal deprivation of power. Women in stage two often feel conflicted as new information challenges old aspects of their self-concepts. Conflict also emerges in relationships as new roles and values are supported and challenge those in the dominant group. Beginning feelings of anger at oppression often are aimed at the nearest oppressor.

When women become embedded in a feminist identity (stage three), they endorse the value of women in general and seek women as friends and colleagues. They may reject men as representing the dominant group that has oppressed them. They are *female-focused*, and they begin to identify with a feminist culture. They are more able to identify oppression as it happens, and they experience anger toward it. In stage four, a synthesis emerges. Women are still female-centered and female-affirming, but they also may start to appreciate affirming men and effective parts of the dominant culture. Women begin to work closely with supportive members of the dominant culture, and they enlarge their understanding of oppression to see what it does to other groups, other cultures, and other people.

Some women reach what feminists call an active commitment (stage five). It is characterized by self-appreciation, personal freedom, pride in and appreciation of women in general, and even a selective appreciation for parts of the dominant culture. But, most importantly, this stage is characterized by an understanding that the personal is political and that real change requires political and social activism.

Feminist family therapists have the goals of (a) meeting families and their members in whatever form and at whatever stage they are in; (b) facilitating development; (c) allowing and contextualizing the expression of feelings from fear and anger to pride and celebration; (d) helping members of the dominant culture look at themselves, challenge their perspectives, and find ways to become supportive of their partners and children (see

Pittman, 1990, 1993); and (e) helping family members engage in political or social activism as needed and appropriate.

The Therapist's Role and Function

Because feminist therapists may incorporate any number of different psychological and therapeutic models into their work, the role and function of the therapeutic practitioner may change somewhat from person to person. What is constant for feminist therapists is a congruence, informed by feminist principles, between their personal and professional lives. Gender role and power analyses are regular parts of their work with families, as is their commitment to reflective practice and "monitoring their own biases and distortions, especially the social and cultural dimensions of women's experience" (Herlihy & Corey, 2005, p. 353).

Feminist family therapists place a high value on egalitarian relationships. They believe in making their values explicit, being emotionally and intellectually present, using self-disclosure appropriately "with purpose and discretion in the interests of the client" (Feminist Therapy Institute, 2000, p. 39), viewing clients as consumers, encouraging social equality in relationships, reflective practice, and social activism.

Feminist family therapists place a high value on listening to and acknowledging women's voices. Toward this end, they often reframe and affirm previously devalued characteristics, including empathy, nurturance, cooperation, intuition, interdependence, care-giving, assertiveness, and relational orientations. Feminist family therapists also value women-to-women relationships, such as those that exist between lesbian partners and/or parents, mothers and daughters, grandmothers and granddaughters, sisters, aunts and nieces, and women-to-women friendships.

Most feminist therapists work to **de-pathologize** behaviors and interactions that represent adherence to dominant-culture imposed female gender-role norms. In this regard, diagnostic labels can be extremely oppressive of women, focusing on symptoms rather than causes, reinforcing stereotypes rather than encouraging diversity, supporting the power of the therapist at the expense of the clients, negating social change as an option, and limiting the development of a therapeutic relationship with both negativity and disrespect. Feminists are especially critical of the diagnosis of borderline personality disorder as described in the *DSM-IV-TR* (American Psychiatric Association, 2000): It is excessively applied to women over men and reflects a critical devaluing of women in general. Brown (1994) notes that almost all women who actually have the symptoms described in this disorder were raped or sexually/physically abused at some time in their lives. If a diagnosis must be used, post traumatic stress disorder would be far more accurate and would elicit from the therapist the kind of empathy, sympathy, caring, and engagement that abused and hurt women deserve. In family therapy, feminists also work to eliminate the blaming of women for everything from over-involvement to father absence to triangulation that has too often characterized systemic approaches. Even the language of family therapy, until recently, has reflected a male-dominated profession, valuing differentiation over enmeshment (or even close connections), thinking over emotion, and joining over real contact and caring. In the early years of family therapy, only Satir placed nurturance at the center of her work. Part of the role of feminist family therapists today is to reclaim that which has been traditionally associated with women as essential to the therapeutic process.

Techniques

Although feminist family therapists may incorporate any number of different systemic approaches that they find congruent with feminist principles, there are certain skills and interventions that tend to be used across models (Worell & Remer, 2002). These interventions often are chosen in relation to the developmental stage of the family and its members. These skills and interventions include:

Egalitarian Relationships.   All feminist therapy is based on a collaboration between the therapist and the clients. The goal is to form a partnership that reduces the power differential in therapy, focuses on inclusion rather than exclusion, and consults the clients about both process and outcome at every step along the way. Most feminist therapists place a high value on informed consent [or what Brown (1994) calls empowered consent], laying out the values, beliefs, and convictions they have about people, life, and therapy for prospective clients. They invite clients into a discussion about what is desired in therapy. They clarify expectations, goals, and process. They even want clients to question the therapist when any part of therapy is unclear or when specific concerns emerge.

Consciousness-raising.   Consciousness-raising is done primarily in groups. For the most part, these groups are leaderless and allow the participants to speak to the truths of their own lives. Consciousness-raising was developed during the early part of the second wave of feminism as a means for women to (a) gain a validated voice, (b) share personal stories, and (c) raise awareness of the multiple ways in which women experience discrimination, oppression, and marginalization. Consciousness-raising stands in direct opposition to passive acceptance, self-depreciation, and the depreciation of women in general. Although it is useful at any stage of feminist identity development, it is almost essential in helping individuals and families move from stage one to stage two.

GlenMaye (1998) identifies both personal and political aspects to consciousness-raising. The personal starts at a subjective level in which personal feelings, perceptions, and needs are named and defined in one's own language—and leads to the telling of personal life stories.

> The political dimension of consciousness raising involves (1) linking one's personal experiences to one's position as a woman in a male-dominated society, (2) identifying oneself as a woman who shares a common fate with all women, and (3) taking action to change oneself and the social structures that oppress women. (p. 37)

Feminist social activism in therapy involves "seeing women as a strength and a source of new wisdom" (p. 45). Recognizing that women make up more than half of the population of the world and are often marginalized in other ways by racism, heterosexism, poverty, and disabilities, no single perspective can address all of the issues facing *all* women; bringing these diverse voices to the center of therapy is an act of empowerment. Finally, although "one woman cannot do everything, . . . one woman can do something" (p. 45)—and that something can make both a personal and a political difference.

Gender Role and Power Analyses.   At the heart of feminist therapy is an analysis of both gender roles and power—and how they contribute to the health or dysfunction experienced personally and by families. Families are the institutions that have most thoroughly absorbed the stereotyped roles and power imbalances imposed by dominant global cultures. Noting the ways in which gender roles affect all members of a family helps to bring about *revelations* (stage two) regarding imbalances in workload and divisions of labor; uses of money; sexual happiness and fulfillment; and parenting, to name a few areas. Gender roles and power distribution are also associated with self-esteem issues around weight or size; stress related to income, productivity, and multitasking; work inside and outside the home; the expression of emotion and the ability to solve problems; and performance and satisfaction concerns in sexuality. Feminist therapists seek to name the effects of gender roles and power on all family members, equalize the burdens family members experience, redistribute the power in families more equitably, and increase flexibility of roles so that all members of a family can begin to benefit from mutual support and respect.

In lesbian and gay partnerships and families, patriarchal gender roles, stereotypes, and power structures often are discarded in favor of alternate arrangements. But even then, different divisions of labor, uses of money and ownership, the procreation of children, and parenting, to name a few, all have to be newly created and invented with few, if any, role models for success—and generally large doses of discrimination to handle. In single-parent families, most often headed by women, the burdens of home and survival may land on an individual with minimal resources. In both cases, feminist family therapists seek to deconstruct patriarchal mandates and engage the larger community in support of more diverse family models.

Self-disclosure.   Appropriate self-disclosure always involves a judgment on the part of the therapist: that sharing some aspect of the therapist's life will directly benefit the client. One of the most-common reasons that feminists use early self-disclosure is to provide clients with informed consent and reduce the power differences between practitioners and clients. "Effective therapist self-disclosure is grounded in authenticity and a sense of mutuality. The therapist considers how the disclosures may affect the client by using what relational-cultural theorists refer to as 'anticipatory empathy'" (Herlihy & Corey, 2005, p. 359). Appropriate self-disclosures can connect an individual's or family's struggles to the collective experiences of women and families; they can normalize thoughts, feelings, and actions; and they can help clients to realize that they are not alone in their struggles.

Bibliotherapy.   Stage three is often facilitated by books related to feminist principles. Non-fiction, autobiographies, "her story," feminist psychology and counseling, self-help books, educational videos and films, and even novels: All can be used to help women and families become embedded in alternate stories, new information, and escape from dominant culture norms. Recent books that have had a real impact in terms of embedding a feminist identity include: Baumgardner and Richards (2000); Bornstein (1995); Boston Women's Collective (1998); Collins (2000); Crawford (1995); Ehrenreich (2002); Enloe (2004); Faludi (1992); Hernandez and Rehman (1998); hooks (2000); Hurston (1998); Tong (1998); and Wolf (2002, 2003), again to name a very few. Recently, a depressed woman who claimed Christianity as a central part of her life read Margaret Atwood's (1998) novel, *A Handmaid's Tale*. The novel begins in a future time when fundamentalist Christian conservatives have taken over the United States and women, by law, are divided into either subservient wives with privileges or handmaidens who provide totally disengaged sex for men: The book both scared the client and amazed her. She began to read parts of it to her husband, and this opened up a dialogue between them about how she was feeling and what she wanted to be different for her children. It did not end their marriage or their spiritual devotion: It did change the way they related to each other and the religion with which they chose to affiliate.

Assertiveness Training.   Assertiveness has everything to do with standing up for oneself: It is essential to self-esteem and to being strong, confident, and capable in the world. People in general—and women in particular—are robbed of natural assertiveness when their voices are silenced (Belenky, Clinchy, Goldberger, & Tarule, 1996; Gilligan, 1982). **Assertiveness training** helps women explore what they think and feel—and then translate their beliefs into clear non-aggressive communication, effective action, and the experience of personal power. Such training stands in direct opposition to denied rights, stereotyped gender roles, and imposed cultural or societal mandates. It also counters experiences of depression, anxiety, stress and distress, and other forms of psychological reactions. Assertiveness follows from positive self-evaluation. It implies that the individual has developed an "I" (or self) inside her or him, and that this "I" can be claimed in "I-messages" and "I-statements." Having a voice and being able to use it almost always facilitates movement from stage three (embeddedness) to stage four (synthesis). Still, for all its importance, assertiveness in women, especially women-of-color, is almost always characterized as aggression by people who are determined to "keep women in their place."

Nowhere is the lack of voice more damaging than in the development of an LGBT identity. Lesbians, who often are closeted because of societal discrimination, lose voice and assertiveness both for being women and for their sexual/affectional choices and identity. Cass (1979) delineated a lesbian/gay identity model very similar to the feminist identity model presented in this chapter. In it, she notes that coming out as a LGBT person is a process, one that feminist family therapists support with timing and patience. Even though there is strong evidence that coming out has numerous psychological, social, and experiential benefits, LGBT individuals have to be in charge of when and how and to whom they share their sexual/affectional identities.

Therapist: You are struggling with whether to tell your parents that you are in a lesbian relationship. Without wanting you to feel pressured about this decision any further than you already do, I am just wondering what you think the worst possible result will be.

Client: (pause) I am just thinking about my family: my grandparents on both sides that live within a mile of my parents—and my parents, oh my God, my parents (another pause) I guess I am afraid they won't love me anymore . . . .

Therapist: Yes, I really understand that fear. But, you know, they don't love you now—not the real you. They may love a picture they have of you, but they don't even know the real you. What does that feel like?

Reframing and Relabeling.   Reframing has been a part of family therapy since it's inception, but its most common use has been either to elevate positive intentions or to shift the focus from individual to systemic perspectives. In addition to these uses, feminist family therapists use reframing to shift the scapegoating of women and the blaming of victims to a consideration of how dominant knowledge (or cultural) positions have negatively affected individuals and families.

Husband: My wife seems to be depressed all the time, and I don't know what to say to her to help her.

Therapist: Perhaps becoming depressed is a normal reaction to all the expectations that seem to be on her from just living every day.

Husband: Like what? What do you mean?

Therapist: Your partner works 40 hours a week at a paid job, doesn't she? In this society, she is also expected to raise the children (you have two), feed the family, clean up the house, meet her husband's needs, and manage everything cheerfully. My guess is that you and the children expect that of her too. Would it be true that she does everything . . . except be cheerful?

Relabeling is another form of reframing that is used to deconstruct the power and negative effects of psychopathological labels and diagnosis, as well as the effects of societal norms and expectations. Relabeling focuses on the causes of life difficulties rather than the naming of them. Relabeling normalizes human development so that women do not, for example, lose attractiveness after the age of 30 or become inadequate or a failure just because the geometric progressions of women's lives leave them overburdened, distressed, and often burned out. Relabeling helps feminist therapists support people where they are at and open up new possibilities for change.

Therapist: What were you told in the hospital?

Woman: I am borderline.

Therapist: You were molested and raped in your childhood—let's see, starting when you were 6 years old. Your mother was in jail on drug charges when you were sent to live with your aunt and uncle. An older male cousin also molested you; your uncle abused you; and you have been in two marriages where men have verbally and physically abused you, but *you* are *borderline*!?!

Woman: (crying) I . . . I . . .

Therapist: You have been traumatized all your life. You are not *borderline*. You are to be congratulated for escaping the war zone in which you have had to live.

A Feminist Therapist With the Quest Family

Paul and Jane Quest bring all four of their children to the first meeting with a feminist therapist. The feminist therapist begins the session by welcoming everyone and by meeting and greeting each family member. She notes that she knows very little about the family, but that she has met Jane with Jason and Luke a few days earlier and that Jane has given her a brief idea of her concerns. She suggests that maybe Jane might want to express her concerns again with everyone present, and then see whether others share her concerns.

Jane: I guess my main concern is both for the two boys who are new to our family and for the whole family, really, in terms of how we all fit together. I guess I feel like we don't all fit together anymore, and it breaks my heart. I also feel tired most of the time, even with the help that everyone puts in.

Jane finishes her introduction and becomes very quiet. The rest of the family seems to enter into the quiet too; it seems to pervade the room.

Therapist: I think you mentioned the other day that Jason and Luke had a difficult and often painful start in life, and raising them has taken more effort and energy than you had originally thought. They are quite different from Amy and Ann when they were the boys' age. I can hear the tiredness in your voice as you speak. I also think I hear something like determination: Is it to persevere no matter what?

Jane: Yes. I will not let these boys *not* make it.

The therapist turns to Paul and asks him how he is feeling. Paul notes that he is very busy at work and always has been. He feels he relies on Jane to handle matters at home, but he also wants to be involved. He was excited about having the boys join the family, but the changes required have been hard on everyone. He wants whatever help the family can get.

Therapist: Do you share Jane's determination to make sure that the boys make it?

Paul: I am determined to do whatever Jane wants to do. To tell you the truth, I really don't know what to do most of the time. I try to help.

Therapist: Amy and Ann, what are your thoughts on all of this?

Amy and Ann both indicate that they are here because their parents want them to come. They were okay with their parents' decision to add the boys to the family, but they don't really feel connected to them yet. "The boys can be difficult," Amy notes. And indeed, the boys are very talkative, interrupting often, and in constant motion.

In the therapy room, Jane tries to corral the boys once or twice and make them sit down. Sometimes, they sit briefly, but then they are on the move again. The therapist asks her how she feels trying to get the boys to sit down. Jane says that they do this all the time. They exhaust her. She feels irritated at the moment with them, but she thinks she may be feeling angry quite soon. "What would happen for the time being if we just let them do what they want to do?" the therapist asks. "There is really nothing they can hurt in here or that will hurt them." Jane thinks that will be okay, if the therapist doesn't mind.

In her mind, the therapist is creating a holding place for the family, a place where they can relax a little in the session with some individual space for each of them while still being connected to each other. Her support of Jane with the boys is gentle and aims at relieving Jane of any burden she might feel to make the boys behave. The therapist is aware that Paul, Amy, and Ann use the word "help" in relation to Jane with Jason and Luke, which leaves the main responsibility for the boys in Jane's hands, but at this point she is still exploring the goals and needs of the whole family.

Therapist: Amy and Ann, I guess I don't hear the same determination your mother has and your father supports in bringing these two boys into your family. Could you share with me what you are feeling about this situation?

Amy: I feel like I am getting ready to leave for college. In a few months, I will be out of here. I have a busy year this year, too, and I like spending my free time with friends. I think I would like to spend more time with my Mom and Dad, because I am worried that I will miss them a lot next year, but Jason and Luke take up a lot of energy. I don't see how they could have much time for me.

Ann: Well, I am not leaving, not for quite a while. And I actually like Jason and Luke, even though they are a pain sometimes, but I miss having time with my friends. I have to help Mom, or I don't think we would make it.

Therapist: So, Ann, you feel that you are in a different place than your sister.

Ann: Yes. I don't blame her for anything. If it were my last year in high school, I would be hanging out too. I envy her sometimes though.

Therapist: I am interested in your thoughts about "not making it" if you didn't help. Who wouldn't make it?

Ann: Mom wouldn't, for sure. And I don't think Jason or Luke would turn out very well.

Therapist: Your mother, it seems to me, has tremendous strength.

Ann: Yes, but she can't do it all.

Therapist: You feel that she is overburdened, taking on too much, doing most of everything.

Amy: It's different than when we were young.

Therapist: In what way?

Amy: Well, for one thing, Dad was around more.

Jane: He's very busy these days—at the height of his career, really.

Therapist: Yes, I hear that he's quite busy, and I am wondering what that means for you, Jane?

Jane and the therapist enter into a discussion about how lonely she sometimes feels, raising the two boys. She is also exhausted, and she is not sure she would make it without Ann's help. Although she never says it directly, the therapist gets the feeling that Jane thinks of Paul's work as "real" and her work is "just what she is supposed to do." She takes the risk of suggesting this idea to Jane. Even though Jane hasn't used those words exactly, they sound right to her.

Therapist: If raising these children and caring for your family isn't real work, why are you the one who is tired and exhausted?

Jane: I don't know. I just am.

Therapist:	How do you feel at the end of the day, Paul? Are you generally exhausted?
Paul:	No. Not really. If work has gone well, I may even be excited . . . until I get home.
Therapist:	What is it like for you to hear Jane's feelings?
Paul:	Well, there is no doubt in my mind that taking care of all of us is real work. I couldn't do it. I mean I try to help and everything, but day-in and day-out: It would be too much.
Therapist:	So you understand her feelings?
Paul:	Yes.
Therapist:	Does that translate into wanting to do something about the way things are going?
Paul:	Yes. I don't want her feeling lonely. I don't want her feeling exhausted. And I don't want the boys lost in all of this.
Ann:	Dad, this isn't going to work the way it is going. I think you need to be home more.

> Ann's directness with her father comes from a strong place within her. It is clear that she has an opinion and wants to be heard. On the other hand, what Paul is saying also seems genuine and authentic to the counselor, and it seems to open the door to something that could make a difference for the family.

Therapist:	Paul and Jane, I am wondering what agreement the two of you had with regard to bringing Jason and Luke into the family? Did you talk about it at all?
Paul:	Yes, we talked about it. Maybe we didn't say everything we needed to say, but we didn't know what it would be like either. We talked about it. We both agreed to bring them into our home. Amy, Ann, and I: We all knew how much it meant to Jane, and we were proud of her for wanting to . . . well, really . . . save the boys' lives.
Therapist:	I can hear that. What I am not hearing is what the nature of the agreement was. Were all of you going to bring Jason and Luke into the family, or just Jane? Paul, were you part of the parenting plan, or was that just for Jane to do?
Jane:	I don't know how much Amy and Ann really had a say in it. I really wanted Jason and Luke to come to our home.
Paul:	But we all talked about it. I was ready to be the boys' father too—with you.
Therapist:	Do you feel, Paul, that you are doing that? Are you being a father to Jason and Luke?
Paul:	Not the way I would like to.
Therapist:	What keeps that from happening?
Paul:	I don't know. I guess that's it: Jane seems to know what to do, but it is killing her, and I haven't a clue.
Therapist:	We live in a world where it is extremely easy for a man—when he feels like he doesn't know what to do—to simply leave or escape into work or withdraw, because aren't women supposed to know how to take care of everything at home?
Jane:	You asked what the agreement was between us regarding Jason and Luke. I think I wanted the boys more than Paul, certainly more than Amy or Ann.
Therapist:	And what does that mean to you?
Jane:	It's not his fault that things aren't working out. (This response makes the therapist think that her comment on gender roles in society may have been heard as "blaming" by Jane. She notes this for later, but does not want to explain it further at this point.)
Therapist:	Was the agreement that you would take care of everything at home?
Jane:	No. Paul said he wanted to be the boys' father.
Therapist:	Did you believe him?

Jane: I did. I don't know. Things change.

Paul: I still want to be the boys' father.

Therapist: I think it might be important that you really look at Paul and see if you believe him. When you look at him, what do you think? Do you feel you can count on him to be a partner with you in raising Jason and Luke?

Many things follow in the discussions that extend over the next seven sessions. It becomes clear that both Paul and Jane have absorbed gender-role expectations and positions that have kept them locked in stereotypic patterns. Even when Paul has "tried to help," a phrase that carries powerful meanings in their relationship, he often has given up, because he feels that he is not doing things correctly in Jane's estimation. She acknowledges that she is very protective of Jason and Luke, more so than she ever thought necessary with Amy and Ann. Both of the parents have incorporated the societal mandate that women are in charge of child-rearing, and men are only breadwinners: It is a mandate that interferes with the family's flexibility in meeting the challenge of raising two hurt and formerly abused children.

The feminist family therapist wonders out loud whether the family might support Jane in taking some much needed time for herself. Paul is encouraged to cut back on his work outside the home and spend the kind of time with his sons that he chose to have: to be the father the boys need and to which he aspires.

In the third session, it becomes clear that Paul has substituted Ann's input for Jane's, and that Ann is now heavily involved with helping Dad with Jason and Luke. It is not that Paul is simply imposing on Ann. It is also that Ann is not sure how to reclaim her life as an adolescent; she is not sure even how to re-enter the lives of her friends or what activities at school to take up. Caring for her brothers at home has both limited her chances to engage her peers and given her an excuse for not challenging herself to see what she is capable of doing. The third session has much to do with exploring how Ann got seduced into the role of caretaker so easily and at such a young age: It ends in the family supporting Ann in taking steps toward important others outside of the home.

In the fourth session, Paul's worry about not knowing what to do with his sons is eased by a discussion with Amy and Ann about what he used to do with them when they were little and what it meant to them to have him in their lives. This discussion takes up most of the fourth session. It ends with a statement of faith from the therapist.

Therapist: You are going to find your own way of being with Jason and Luke. It probably will have some similarities to what you did with Amy and Ann, and it also will be different. I believe that if you are left on your own, without Jane or Ann helping, you and Jason and Luke can find ways to enrich each other that no one can even foresee right now.

As Jane and Ann took more time for themselves, and Paul became more engaged with his sons, Jason and Luke's behavior got worse for a while. Paul handled it much differently than Jane or Ann had. He had a tendency to distract them, change the plans for what he was doing with them, and sometimes he would just quietly ask them to "stop doing crazy things for about 5 minutes" so he could have a break. Amazingly, after a few weeks, the boys actually would give him these breaks—almost exactly to the time Paul had asked for. The best time for all of them was when Paul would take Jason and Luke outside to play or to the park for sports.

Jane and Paul continued to see the feminist therapist for months after family life began to feel more balanced. They worked on their communication, their relational needs, and their parenting partnership. They planned for Amy going off to college, and the changes that would bring. They supported Ann in bringing new friends into her life. And always, there was Jason and Luke with challenging behaviors and ever-increasing needs. Amy never did feel especially close to Jason or Luke, and she did not miss them much once she was gone. Ann had a brief period of difficulty after Amy left: She was caught bringing alcohol into her school. She did it to be part of the crowd with whom she had found a place. Jane and Paul considered bringing her to a session with them, but felt that Ann was "already embarrassed enough." They did not punish her or restrict her, and their faith in her seemed to make a real difference in how she saw herself. A year later, child-rearing was not magically easier, but Jane and Paul felt they were real partners: Neither one was alone anymore.

Summary and Multicultural Evaluation

Although the diversity of feminist therapy with families makes it impossible to delineate a singular process or a set of techniques employed by all, feminist practice does tend to have some commonalities. First, it is conducted with conscious purpose including (1) a positive attitude toward women, (2) valuing that which is considered feminine or nurturing in society and social interactions, (3) acknowledging a diversity of families, from single-parent families to LGBT families, as normal and valuable, (4) being conscious of a diversity of cultures in which women live and the relationship between multiculturalism and feminism, (5) a willingness to confront patriarchal process and reinvolve fathers in heterosexual families, and (6) empowering women while supporting egalitarian families. Helping women give voice to the meanings in their lives, demonstrating interest in and empathy for women's stories, and contextualizing as well as validating women's experiences are all processes associated with feminist therapy, and they developed in many ways from the early experiences that women had in consciousness-raising groups.

GlenMaye (1998) lists the following processes in defining empowerment practice with women:

- Working with women in ways that recognize and affirm them as fully human;
- Reflecting the often hidden but present power that permeates women's lives;
- Liberating the voices of women who have been silenced or suppressed, including the liberation of one's own voice;
- Making a commitment to listen to other women and affirm differences;
- Acknowledging and confronting the role of oppression in women's lives;
- Creating an environment of safety, trust, and support through which women, often together with other women, are encouraged to believe in themselves and speak their truths;
- Creating opportunities to experience strength, worth, capability, and competence in daily life;
- Helping individuals carry self-determination into social and political action for systemic change; and
- Embracing the roles of empowerment model, advocate, activist, educator, and facilitator in therapy.

Contributions to Multicultural Counseling and Gender Issues

Feminist consciousness of diverse perspectives has infused family therapy with some of its most significant issues. In addition to helping families address issues of power and to reconsider and change gender-based roles and rules, feminists have called on the profession of family therapy to stop ignoring the social problems of family violence, cultural discrimination, ageism, poverty, race, and class, as well as discrimination against gay men and lesbians (GlenMaye, 1998; Nichols & Schwartz, 2006; Nystrom, 2005; Walters, Longres, Han, & Icard, 2003). Feminist research and therapeutic practice continually work to enlarge the focus and consciousness of family therapists, calling on us to participate in the largest social reconstruction of all.

Feminist family therapists and feminist approaches in general, more than any other models, actually work to incorporate multiculturalism and an appreciation for diversity at every level. So you would think that the intersection of feminism and multiculturalism would be easy to find and a snap to implement. It turns out that this is not exactly the case. Feminism did not always include an appreciation of diversity, starting out in many ways as a movement for Caucasian middle-class women with the assumption that the experiences of all women were related and similar. Women of color (for example bell hooks) challenged feminism to incorporate a consideration of race; they noted that racism was often more visible and had greater impact on them than sexism, but that both occurred regularly in their lives. The challenge to merge the two perspectives continues even today.

In October, 1998, the Advancing Together Conference was held in Michigan. The Michigan Conference, as it came to be known, included 175 women and a handful of men who came together to explore the possibility of integrating feminism and multiculturalism. Ruth Fassinger (2004), one of the organizers/participants, notes:

> We learned that feminism and multiculturalism do not always fit together and "integrate" neatly. We learned that not all kinds of diversity are equally valued—by either feminists or multiculturalists. We learned that having expertise in one arena does not imply adequate knowledge in another. We learned that well-meaning colleagues often misunderstand one another because they come from different experiences, speak different scholarly languages, and have different agendas. . . . We learned that hierarchy is extraordinarily difficult to dismantle even under the best efforts. . . . In all of this bubbling stew of our own little "melting pot," we experienced a wide range of passions—anger and confusion, exhilaration and joy, ignorance and arrogance, comfort and bonding, anticipation and frustration, and profound respect for our colleagues and the enormity of the task we had laid out for ourselves in an impossibly brief weekend. (pp. 344–345)

Although these discussions are occurring rather late in the development of both models, it is important to note that these are the only models that are having the discussion at all. And indeed, the values they share in common are substantial enough to provide a strong foundation for an ultimate integration. Both feminism and multiculturalism seek to address and eliminate sexism, racism, ageism, classism, poverty, heterosexism, and other forms of oppression, discrimination, and privilege. Although one of the sticking points sometimes has been an insistence by multiculturalists that a respect for differences in culture includes leaving some formal aspects of patriarchy in place, feminists note that there is no country left in the world without feminist voices in it. This is true even in fundamentalist Islamic states, as well as some of the more traditional Hispanic and Asian cultures. Matsuyuki (1998), for example, notes that Japan has feminist counseling centers, established by and for Japanese women, that encourage the development of voice and self-determination but in a manner that is effective within the Japanese culture.

This kind of integration is really the model for the future. All oppression is negative and has real effects on individuals and families. It is always possible to support women as well as those aspects of culture that are most important to women—and especially to women of color: For just as it does no culture any good to maintain patriarchy, it also does no woman any good to actualize feminism in a manner that isolates or dissociates her from her family and culture. Within any given culture, there are indeed feminist cultural voices who can find solutions to the problems they must face. And more important, these same voices can inform an analysis of power, assess the interplay of external environment and personal reality, and open up avenues for integrating ethnic, gender, and racial components of identity (Kanuha, 2005; Lie & Lowery, 2003; Lorde, 1984).

It is easy to note that feminists bring a gender perspective or lens to family therapy. They also infuse developmental perspectives and the multicultural lens with issues significant to women around the world. No culture is perfect. All cultures have positive and negative aspects encoded in daily life by both tradition and law. Feminist therapists in all cultures are committed to challenging those parts of their cultures that continue to discriminate against oppressed and/or marginalized groups within the society.

The 1998 Michigan conference was sponsored by Division 17 of the American Psychological Association. Five years earlier, Division 35 met in Boston to clarify the future of feminist psychology (Worell & Johnson, 1997). For the past 6 years, there has been a Divisions 17 and 35 Interdivisional Task Force developing guidelines for psychological practice with girls and women. The document, at this writing, is currently going through the APA approval process.

Exercises for Personal and Professional Growth

Feminist therapy invites us to consider gender issues, gender-role stereotypes, and culture as a central part of our work with families. Unless we consciously address these aspects of our lives, the mandates of the dominant culture will float just below the surface of our work, reinforcing the *status quo*. Change starts with cataloguing the various aspects of privilege that make up the societies in which we live. The first exercise I would like to suggest can be done on your own or in a group with other colleagues. It involves listing the privileges that go with being white, male, and heterosexual.

Get at least three large pieces (poster size) of paper. Label the first one **white privilege**, the second one **male privilege**, and the third one **heterosexual privilege**. Now list all of the privileges you can imagine for each of these categories. In a group, it will be helpful to have a mix of men, women, and people of different cultures as you discuss what might go on the charts. Pay attention not only to what goes up on the charts but also the emotions that are elicited as people make contributions. Try to stay open to the perspectives of others; learn from their experiences; put yourself in their shoes. If you are doing this alone, list as many aspects of privilege for each chart as you can. When you finish, you can check the brief lists I have provided in the Appendix at the end of this chapter. You may have many more items than I have listed: The Appendix is not intended to be even close to complete.

Next, imagine you are someone other than yourself: Imagine you are the other gender, from a different culture, or have a different affectional/sexual orientation. If you have lived within the contexts of one or more privileged states, what would it be like to grow up with the world designed to marginalize or oppress you? What would it feel like if you were part of a group against which others discriminated? If you were raised as part of a group that experienced oppression, did you notice it? How did it affect you? Did you absorb any of the aspects of the dominant culture? Was it just because it was so strong, or did it produce some of the privileges associated with that normed position? What do you think it would be like to be a member of these privileged groups? Would you approach life differently? What would you do to protect and maintain the privilege?

The second exercise I would like to suggest begins with pulling out your genogram again. This time, go back through the genogram from the perspective of gender. For each man and woman in the diagram, write an adjective next to his or her name that seems to exemplify their approaches to being a woman or a man. Which people in your genogram most represent the way you want to be a woman or a man? Were any of them your parents?

Brother or sisters? Which people most represent the exact opposite of what you want to be as a woman or a man? What are the traits that draw you to people or repel you? If there are no people in your diagram you want to emulate, are there other role models in your life to whom you have turned? Who are they, and what are their relationships to you?

The third and final exercise I would like to suggest is that you start a journal that focuses on your experiences with gender, culture, and affectional/sexual orientation. You might start by talking about what and how you learned when you were little and then leave the journal open for current and new learnings that may come your way.

Start with what it was like for you to become a girl or a boy—and what you thought it would be like to become a woman or a man. How were you raised with regard to gender? Did your parents do anything different with you based on gender than they did with brothers and sisters? What were your experiences in school with regard to gender? Was one gender called on more often than the other? Were there certain subjects that were promoted or discouraged based on gender? What are your experiences now with regard to gender? Have you experienced either privilege or limitations based on gender in the workplace?

Did you grow up with other cultures? Did you have friends from other cultures? Did people from other cultures come to your house? Your neighborhood? Were they welcomed or treated badly? What was your first experience with someone from a different culture? What are your experiences now with different cultures? Have your perspectives changed? In what ways? Are there aspects of different cultures in your friends and acquaintances that you have really come to appreciate? What are those aspects?

When you came into puberty, was your affectional/sexual orientation immediately obvious to you? Did you experiment with both heterosexual and same-sex experiences or did you seem dedicated to just one type of experience? Did you hear comments, jokes, or presumptions leveled at people who were gay or lesbian . . . or even presumed to be? How did any of this make you feel? Do you still have gut reactions to those who enact a different affectional/sexual orientation? If so, what are those gut reactions? Where do you think you learned them? What meaning does all of this have for you?

The questions I have posed are by no means exhaustive. They are only intended to get a journal going that you might use to record new experiences as you grow into this profession. To be sure, gender and culture will be two of the primary lenses through which an understanding of family and our ability to work effectively with the diversity that makes up modern practice will be processed.

Where to Go From Here

In March, 2002, the American Counseling Association (ACA) approved a Women's Interest Network for members concerned with women's issues in all areas of counseling, including couples and family counseling. You can become part of this network by contacting:

Women's Interest Network
Dr. Elizabeth Kincade (Facilitator)
E-mail: **ekincade@iup.edu**

The American Psychological Association (APA) has three divisions (#17, #35, and #51) that address gender issues for women, men, and psychology. For further information about the benefits of belonging to these divisions, you can contact:

American Psychological Association
750 First Street, N.E.
Washington, DC 20002-4242
Phone: 202-336-5500 or 800-374-2721

Websites: **http://www.apa.org**
   http://www.apa.org/about/division/div17.html
   http://www.apa.org/about/division/div35.html
   http://www.apa.org/about/division/div51.html

The Association for Women in Psychology (AWP) welcomes counselors, social workers, psychologists, and other helping professionals. It holds an annual conference dedicated to feminist issues in therapy and the lives of women. They have a specific agenda related to reforming psychology and mental health research and practice. You can access AWP at:

Website: **http://www.theworks.baka/awp**

AWP, Division 35 of APA, and the Society for the Psychology of Women co-sponsor a resource list (POWR-L) that you can access at no cost at:

LISTSERV@URIACC (Binet) or **LISTSERV@URIACC.URI.EDU**

The National Association of Social Workers (NASW) also addresses a wide range of issues related to gender, race, ethnicity, sexual/affectional orientation, and culture. They have specific programs on diversity, feminism and women's issues, and gay/lesbian issues. They can be reached at:

National Association of Social Workers
750 First Street, N.E., Suite 700
Washington, DC 20002-4241
Website: **http://www.naswdc.org**

The American Association for Marriage and Family Therapy (AAMFT) has spent the last decade becoming more gender conscious and diversity centered. You can go to their website and find a wide range of articles, policies, and statements on women's issues and cultural appreciation in family therapy. Find them at:

American Association for Marriage and Family Therapy
112 South Alfred Street
Alexandria, VA 22314-3061
Phone: 703-838-9808
Website: **http://www.aamft.org**

Both the University of Kentucky and Texas Woman's University offer training programs in counseling women, feminist therapy, and family psychology. These programs can be reached through:

Dr. Pam Remer
University of Kentucky
Dept. of Educational and Counseling Psychology
251-C Dickey Hall
Lexington, KY 40506-0017
Phone: 859-257-4158
E-mail: **Premer@uky.edu**
Website: **www.uky.edu/Education/edphead.html**

and

Dr. Roberta Nutt
Texas Woman's University
Counseling Psychology Program
P. O. Box 425470
Denton, TX 76204
Phone: 940-898-2313

E-mail: **RNutt@mail.twu.edu**
Website: **www.twu.edu/as/psyphil/cppc**

Two other important contacts for feminist family practitioners are:

National Organization for Women (NOW)
1000 16th Street, N.W., Suite 700
Washington, DC 20036
Phone: 202-331-0066
Website: **www.now.org**

and

National Abortion and Reproductive Rights Action League (NARAL)
1156 15th Street, N.W., Suite 700
Washington, DC 20005
Phone: 202-973-3000
Website: **www.naral.org**

Haworth Press publishes two journals important to the feminist model: the *Journal of Feminist Family Therapy—An International Forum* and *Women and Therapy: A Feminist Quarterly*. These journals provide readers with international access to authors exploring the relationship between feminist theory and the practice of both individual and family therapy. They include articles that address theory as well as research and clinical applications and often have articles that relate to feminist multicultural approaches. You can order these journals at:

The Haworth Press Inc.
10 Alice St.
Binghamton, NY 13904
Website: **www.haworthpress.com/store**

Recommended Readings

Brown, L. (1994). *Subversive dialogues: Theory in feminist therapy*. New York: Basic Books. Widely considered the most important book on feminist therapy and practice, the author provides multiple case examples to illustrate the application of theory to practice.

Enns, C. Z. (2004). *Feminist theories and feminist psychotherapies: Origins, themes, and diversity* (2nd ed.). New York: Haworth. A complete textbook on feminist theory and psychotherapy, presenting chapters on liberal, cultural, radical, and socialist feminism as well as chapters addressing postmodern, women-of-color, lesbian, and global feminist perspectives. Self-assessment questionnaires help readers to find their places within different models.

Fassinger, R. E. (Ed.). (2004). Centralizing feminism and multiculturalism in counseling (special section with multiple articles.). *Journal of Multicultural Counseling and Development, 32,* 344–448. This

issue of the journal provides nine articles that are the result of and extend the learning from a meeting held in the state of Michigan, called the Advancing Together Conference, in October, 1998. These articles demonstrate the difficulties and power in integrating feminism and multicultural counseling.

GlenMaye, L. (1998). Empowerment of women. In L. M. Gutierrez, R. J. Parsons, & E. O. Cox (Eds.), *Empowerment in social work practice: A sourcebook* (pp. 29–51). Pacific Grove, CA: Brooks/Cole. Linnea GlenMaye is now the Director of Social Work at Wichita State University. When she was at the University of Nevada, Las Vegas, she wrote one of the best chapters available on empowering women. From the field of social work, this is must reading for all people in the helping professions.

Luepnitz, D. A. (1988). *The family interpreted: Feminist theory in clinical practice*. New York: Basic Books. This book reviews the major family therapy models up through the late 1980s, applying a feminist analysis to each one. It also has one of the best reviews of the history of families ever written, and it offers a feminist psychoanalytic (broadly defined) model for working with families. The case studies are excellent.

May, K. M. (Ed.). (2001). *Feminist family therapy*. Alexandria, VA: American Counseling Association. This edited book clearly and concisely defines feminist family therapy and offers some great application chapters in relation to working people of color, adolescents, heterosexual and gay/lesbian couples, and women and men as individuals. It also addresses issues of anger in relationships, sexuality, and caring for the elderly.

McGoldrick, M., Anderson, C. M., & Walsh, F. (1989). *Women in families: A framework for family therapy*. New York: Norton. One of the largest, most complete anthologies to consider the lives of women in families, this book contains a wide range of contributors at the heart of feminism and family therapy.

Silverstein, L. B., & Goodrich, T. J. (Eds.). (2003). *Feminist family therapy: Empowerment in context*. Washington, DC: American Psychological Association. This is both the newest and the most comprehensive volume written on feminist family therapy. It includes chapters that address feminist psychology, cultural diversity, working with men and women in family contexts, and covers the most current research in the field.

Worell, J., & Remer, P. (2002). *Feminist perspectives in therapy: Empowering diverse women* (2nd ed.). New York: Wiley. Many feminists consider this book essential for conducting therapy. Focusing on empowerment and diversity, Worell and Remer demonstrate how to integrate feminism and multiculturalism, delineate the changing roles of women, outline counseling from theory to practice, and provide a feminist model for diagnosis and assessment. All of this is applied to issues in therapy from mood disorders to sexual assault and abuse to choosing new careers and lives.

DVD Reference

Feminist family therapy grew out of the second wave of feminism that began in the 1960s and 1970s. So many people contributed to this model that it is impossible to identify one person as its founder. The main principles of the model focus on the personal as political, valuing the voice and perspectives of women as well as men, challenging sex-role stereotyping, and forming egalitarian relationships in both families and the therapeutic process.

In the feminist family therapy video segment, Dr. Patricia Robertson, a feminist therapist and Professor of Counseling at East Tennessee State University, works with an African-American family consisting of a single parent and her two adult children. This demonstration highlights therapeutic interventions in which the voices of women are valued; sex-roles are challenged both within relationships and at work; concerns are de-pathologized and reframed; and the personal experiences of the women are validated.

References

American Psychiatric Association. (2000). *Diagnostic and statistical manual of mental disorders* (4th ed., text rev.) (*DSM-IV-TR*). Washington, DC: Author.

Atwood, M. (1998). *A handmaid's tale*. New York: Anchor.

Avis, J. M. (1986). Feminist issues in family therapy. In F. P. Piercy, D. H. Sprenkle, & Associates (Eds.), *Family therapy sourcebook* (pp. 213–242). New York: Guilford.

Baumgardner, J., & Richards, A. (2000). *Manifesta: Young women, feminism, and the future*. New York: Farrar, Straus and Giroux.

Belenky, M. F., Clinchy, B. M., Goldberger, N. R., & Tarule, J. M. (1996). *Women's ways of knowing: The development of self, voice, and mind* (10th anniv. ed.). New York: Basic Books.

Bernard, J. (1972). *The future of marriage.* New York: Bantam Books.

Bornstein, K. (1995). *Gender outlaw: On men, women, and the rest of us.* New York: Vintage. Boston Women's Collective. (1998). *Our bodies, ourselves for the new century.* New York: Touchstone.

Braverman, L. (Ed.). (1988). *A guide to feminist family therapy.* New York: Harrington Park Press.

Brown, L. (1994). *Subversive dialogues: Theory in feminist therapy.* New York: Basic Books.

Cass, V. (1979). Homosexual identity formation: A theoretical model. *Journal of Homosexuality, 4,* 219–235.

Collins, P. H. (2000). *Black feminist thought: Knowledge, consciousness, and the politics of empowerment* (2nd ed.). New York: Routledge.

Crawford, M. (1995). *Talking difference: On gender and language.* Newbury Park, CA: Sage.

Degler, C. (1980). *At odds: Women and the family in America from the revolution to the present.* New York: Oxford University Press.

Downing, N. E., & Rousch, K. L. (1984). From passive acceptance to active commitment: A model of feminist identity development. *The Counseling Psychologist, 13,* 695–709.

Durkheim, E. (1951). *Suicide: A study in sociology* (J. A. Spaulding & G. Simpson, Trans.). Glencoe, IL: Free Press.

Ehrenreich, B. (2002). *Nickel and dimed: On (not) getting by in America.* New York: Owl Books.

Enloe, C. (2004). *The curious feminist: Searching for women in a new age of empire.* Berkeley, CA: University of California Press.

Enns, C. Z. (1993). Twenty years of feminist counseling and therapy: From naming biases to implementing multifaceted practice. *The Counseling Psychologist, 21*(1), 3–87.

Enns, C. Z. (2004). *Feminist theories and feminist psychotherapies: Origins, themes, and diversity* (2nd ed.). New York: Haworth.

Enns, C. Z., & Sinacore, A. L. (2001). Feminist theories. In J. Worell (Ed.), *Encyclopedia of gender* (Vol. 1, pp. 469–480). San Diego, CA: Academic Press.

Enns, C. Z., Sinacore, A. L., Ancis, J. R., & Phillips, J. (2004). Toward integrative feminist and multicultural pedagogies. *Journal of Multicultural Counseling and Development, 32,* 414–427.

Faludi, S. (1992). *Backlash: The undeclared war against American women.* New York: Anchor.

Fassinger, R. E. (Ed.). (2004). Centralizing feminism and multiculturalism in counseling (special section with multiple articles.). *Journal of Multicultural Counseling and Development, 32,* 344–448.

Feminist Therapy Institute. (2000). *Feminist therapy code of ethics* (revised, 1999). San Francisco: Author.

Ferguson, A. (1983). On conceiving motherhood and sexuality: A feminist materialist approach. In H. Trebilcot (Ed.), *Mothering: Essays in feminist theory* (pp. 153–184). Totowa, NJ: Rowman & Littlefield.

Foucault, M. (1980). *Power/knowledge: Selected interviews and other writings.* New York: Pantheon Books.

Gilligan, C. (1982). *In a different voice.* Cambridge, MA: Harvard University Press.

Gilligan, C., Ward, J. V., & Taylor, J. (Eds.). (1988). *Mapping the moral domain.* Cambridge, MA: Harvard University Press.

GlenMaye, L. (1998). Empowerment of women. In L. M. Gutierrez, R. J. Parsons, & E. O. Cox (Eds.), *Empowerment in social work practice: A sourcebook* (pp. 29–51). Pacific Grove, CA: Brooks/Cole.

Goodrich, T. J. (Ed.). (1991). *Women and power: Perspectives for family therapy.* New York: Norton.

Goodrich, T. J. (2003). A feminist family therapist's work is never done. In L. B. Silverstein & T. J. Goodrich (Eds.). *Feminist family therapy: Empowerment in social context* (pp. 3–15). Washington, DC: American Psychological Association.

Goodrich, T. J., Rampage, C., Ellman, B., & Halstead, K. (1988). *Feminist family therapy: A casebook.* New York: Norton.

Gurman, A. S., & Kniskern, D. P. (1981). *Handbook of family therapy.* New York: Brunner/Mazel.

Hare-Mustin, R. (1978). A feminist approach to family therapy. *Family Process, 17,* 181–194.

Herlihy, B., & Corey, G. (2005). Feminist therapy. In G. Corey, *Theory and practice of counseling and psychotherapy* (7th ed., pp. 338–381). Belmont, CA: Brooks/Cole.

Hernandez, D., & Rehman, B. (1998). *Colonize this!: Young women-of-color on today's feminism.* New York: Seal Press.

hooks, b. (2000). *Feminist theory: From margin to center* (2nd ed.). Cambridge, MA: South End Press.

Hurston, Z. N. (1998). *Their eyes were watching God.* New York: Perennial.

Kanuha, V. K. (2005). Social work practice with women-of-color. In D. Lum (Ed.). *Cultural competence, practice* stages, and client systems: A case study approach (pp. 173–203). Belmont, CA: Brooks/Cole.

Lewis, J. M., Beaver, W. R., Gossett, J. T., & Phillips, V. A. (1976). *No single thread: Psychological health in family systems.* New York: Brunner/Mazel.

Lie, G-Y, & Lowery, C. T. (2003). Cultural competence with women-of-color. In D. Lum (Ed.). *Culturally competent practice: A framework for understanding diverse groups and justice issues* (2nd ed., pp. 282–309). Pacific Grove, CA: Brooks/Cole.

Lorde, A. (1984). *Sister outsider.* Freedom, CA: The Crossing Press.

Luepnitz, D. A. (1988). *The family interpreted: Feminist theory in clinical practice.* New York: Basic Books.

Matsuyuki, M. (1998). Japanese feminist counseling as a political act. *Women and Therapy, 21*(2), 65–77.

May, K. M. (2001). *Feminist family therapy.* Alexandria, VA: American Counseling Association.

McGoldrick, M. (2005). Women and the family life cycle. In B. Carter & M. McGoldrick (Eds.). *The expanded family life cycle: Individual, family, and social perspectives* (3rd ed., pp. 106–123). Boston: Allyn and Bacon.

McGoldrick, M., Anderson, C. M., & Walsh, F. (1989). *Women in families: A framework for family therapy.* New York: Norton.

McIntosh, P. (1986). *White privilege: Unpacking the invisible knapsack.* (Available from the Wellesley College Center for Research on Women, Wellesley, MA, 02181).

McIntosh, P. (1995). White privilege and male privilege: A personal account of coming to see correspondence through work in women's studies. In M. L. Andersen & P. H. Collins (Eds.). *Race, class, and gender* (2nd ed., pp. 76–87). Belmont, CA: Wadsworth.

McIntosh, P. (1998). White privilege, color, and crime: A personal account. In C. R. Mann & M. S. Zatz (Eds.). *Images of color, images of crime* (pp. 207–216). Los Angeles, CA: Roxbury.

McIntosh, P. (2004). White privilege and male privilege. In S. M. Shaw & J. Lee (Eds.). *Women's voices, feminist visions: Classic and contemporary readings* (pp. 86–93). Boston: McGraw-Hill.

Nichols, M. P., & Schwartz, R. C. (2006). *Family therapy: Concepts and methods* (7th ed.). Boston: Allyn & Bacon.

Nystrom, N. M. (2005). Social work practice with lesbian, gay, bisexual, and transgender people. In D. Lum (Ed.). *Cultural competence, practice stages,*

and client systems: A case study approach (pp. 203–219). Belmont, CA: Brooks/Cole.

Pittman, F. (1990). The masculine mystique. *Family Therapy Networker, 14,* 40–52.

Pittman, F. (1993). *Man enough: Fathers, sons, and the search for masculinity.* New York: Perigee.

Reynolds, A. L., & Constantine, M. G. (2004). Feminism and multiculturalism: Parallels and intersections. *Journal of Multicultural Counseling and Development, 32,* 346–357.

Silverstein, L. B. (2003). Classic texts and early critiques. In L. B. Silverstein & T. J. Goodrich (Eds.). *Feminist family therapy: Empowerment in social context* (pp. 17–35). Washington, DC: American Psychological Association.

Silverstein, L. B., & Goodrich, T. J. (Eds.). (2003). *Feminist family therapy: Empowerment in social context.* Washington, DC: American Psychological Association.

Tong, R. P. (1998). *Feminist thought: A comprehensive introduction.* Boulder, CO: Westview Press.

Walsh, F. (1993). *Normal family processes* (2nd ed.). New York: Basic Books.

Walsh, F. (2003). *Normal family processes* (3rd ed.). New York: Guilford.

Walters, K. L., Longres, J. F., Han, C., & Icard, L. D. (2003). Cultural competence with gay and lesbian persons of color. In D. Lum (Ed.). *Culturally competent practice: A framework for understanding diverse groups and justice issues* (2nd ed., pp. 310–342). Pacific Grove, CA: Brooks/Cole.

Walters, M., Carter, B., Papp, P., & Silverstein, O. (1988). *The invisible web: Gender patterns in family relationships.* New York: Guilford.

Wolf, N. (2002). *The beauty myth: How images of beauty are used against women.* New York: Perennial. (Original work published 1991)

Wolf, N. (2003). *Misconceptions: Truth, lies, and the unexpected on the journey to motherhood.* New York: Anchor.

Wollstonecraft, M. (1989). *A vindication of the rights of women.* Amherst, NY: Prometheus Books. (Original work published 1792)

Worell, J., & Johnson, N. G. (Eds.). (1997). *Shaping the future of feminist psychology: Education, research, and practice.* Washington, DC: American Psychological Association.

Worell, J., & Remer, P. (2002). *Feminist perspectives in therapy: Empowering diverse women* (2nd ed.). New York: Wiley.

Endnote

[1]Some of the most prominent women in fields related to family therapy include: Betty Bardige, Mary Field Belenky, Blythe McVicker Clinchy, Carol Gilligan, Nancy Rule Goldberger, Jill Mattuck Tarule, Jill McLean Taylor, and Janie Victoria Ward, all of whom have made major contributions to human development. Michele Bograd, Laura Brown, Paula J. Caplan, Phyllis Chesler, Barbara Ehrenreich, bell hooks, Dell Martin, Jean Baker Miller, and Lenore Walker bring feminist voices to sociology and psychology. Carol M. Anderson, Marianne Ault-Riche, Judith Myers Avis, Pauline Boss, Lois Braverman, Annette M. Brodsky, Betty Carter, Nancy Chodorow, Dorothy Dinnerstein, Virginia Goldner, Thelma Jean Goodrich, Rachel T. Hare-Mustin, Molly Layton, Harriet Goldhor Lerner, Deborah Anna Luepnitz, Kathleen May, Monica McGoldrick, Peggy Papp, Cheryl Rampage, Sallyann Roth, Louise B. Silverstein, Olga Silverstein, J. Pamela Weiner, Dorothy Wheeler, Barre Thorne, Froma Walsh, and Marianne Walters, to name a few, have centralized gender and multi-culturalism in family systems therapy.

Chapter Appendix

In this chapter, I have used the word privilege to talk about those things that are granted automatically to those in power. McIntosh (2004) argues that the word privilege is too pleasant a term, and does not reflect the *unearned advantages* represented in the lists below. So although I continue here to use the word privilege, which is part of the wider literature in the field, these privileges should be understood to be *unearned entitlements* and *conferred dominance* that are assumed simply because of a given status.

White privilege: If I am white . . .

- Every President of the United States and most of the leaders of the Western world are the same race as I am.
- I can be in the company of people of my race most of the time.
- I can presume to be trustworthy.
- I can avoid spending time with people different from me, whom I mistrust and who mistrust me.
- I can rent or purchase a house in any area I can afford.
- I can expect my neighbors to be at least neutral if not pleasant to me.
- I can go shopping alone—almost anywhere—knowing that I won't be followed by detectives or store managers (even under the guise of it being for my own protection).
- I can turn on television, read books, look at magazines and newspapers, and see people of my race all over the place, most of whom are presented in a positive light.
- History is based on my people of my race: We are civilized, and I am told that all great advancements were accomplished by people of my race.
- I can be sure that my children will be exposed to the art, literature, history, music, mathematics/sciences, and other cultural materials of my race.
- I can be fairly sure of having my voice heard in different groups; I can find a publisher for my ideas and views; I have an almost constant feeling that I count in the society in which I live. I can speak strongly, if I so choose, without the fear of putting my race on trial.
- When I use checks, credit cards, debit cards, and other financial transaction materials, I can count on my skin color not to work against me: I am not automatically presumed to be financially unreliable.
- I can arrange to protect my children from people who might not like them.
- I do not have to train my children to be aware of racism for their physical survival.

- I can be fairly sure that my children will not be targeted and scrutinized in schools and the workplace because they are different.
- I can have idiosyncratic behaviors (talking with my mouth full), and not have people put this down to my color or associated with the "bad morals" of my race.
- I can do well in anything I pursue without being called a "credit to my race."
- I do not have to know the specifics of my own culture, and I can remain oblivious to the language and customs of people of color.
- I can criticize our government and its policies from within the power group; indeed, if some change is proposed I don't like (such as bilingual education or healthcare for immigrants), I can mobilize government action to block it with a fair hope of winning.
- If I ask to speak to "the person in charge," *he* will be the same race as I am.
- If I am stopped by police, audited by the IRS, or just walking in some neighborhood not my own, I can be sure that I am not singled out because of race.
- I can easily buy toys, games, and other products designed for my race.
- If I am pro-active with regard to racial equality, noting racial issues at hand, arguing for the promotion of a person of color, or developing policies that are more favorable to people of color, I can be sure that I will have more credibility than a person of color might receive for the same positions.
- I can worry about racism without being seen as self-serving.
- I can get into school or a job without being seen as the Affirmative-Action candidate who is only there because of skin color.
- I can think over my options, and I have many, be late for meetings, choose public accommodations, etc., all without having to consider the issue of race.
- I can be sure if I need medical or legal help, race will not work against me.
- If I am not a very credible leader, it is not because of my race.

Male privilege: If I am male . . .

- Every President of the United States and most of the world leaders are male.
- I was allowed to be more aggressive than girls when I was little.
- I was not limited to certain areas of opportunity when I was little . . . or now.
- I had a reasonable expectation of being called on in class when I raised my hand—even if I had nothing useful to say.
- I was presumed to have the potential to do math and science in school, regardless of how far I went.
- I fit all the developmental norms, because all of the developmental models were, in fact, normed on boys and men.
- There were more sports designed for me, with more role models and heroes, and when I participated in sports, people actually came to watch.
- It was not presumed when I learned to drive that I could not handle a stick shift or learn to provide maintenance to my own car.
- I was given greater freedom to move and act in the world than my sisters, my female cousins, or even my mother.
- When I reached puberty, I did not have to be responsible for sex: That was the "girl's responsibility," because I wasn't going to get pregnant.
- When I reached puberty, I could feel as though I had a place in the world and go out on dates, for instance, without fear of being raped, attacked, abused, or brutalized.
- I can aspire to *any* job without being blocked by a glass ceiling or prevented from any form of advancement based on my gender.
- When I do take a job in a traditionally female career (teaching, nursing, etc.), I stand out in a positive light, and I may even be in charge soon: If the salaries go up, it is actually because more men, like me, are going into the profession.

- I can walk out to my car late at night without having to look over my shoulder or check who might be in the car next to mine.
- I do not have to fear being attacked by men whom I have known and thought of as friends.
- I seldom experience spouse abuse.
- I can leave children, housework, care of the elderly in my family, and even my own care in the hands of my spouse without a second thought—even if she is working another forty-hour-a-week job.
- I can presume control of the finances of the house and expect that my decisions about money, activities, and other essential aspects of daily living will go my way.
- I can use my size, voice, and power to get what I want.
- I can presume that the television remote control is mine, as are all other gadgets in the house, and not give them up to anyone else.
- If I accept a task in relation to the family, it is often one associated with my gender (e.g., lawn mowing, barbequing, etc.) and, for these tasks, I should have the very best equipment that money can buy—even if we have to go into debt to get it.
- I can enter into financial transactions on my own without a co-signer when I am young or my spouse's approval when I am older.
- I can keep my own name when I marry. I presume that my spouse will take my name when I marry. My last name will be my children's last name—no matter how bad or absent a parent I become.
- I can do things to "help out" around the house without assuming responsibility for them or even presuming that I will do the same things again, because, after all, anything related to homemaking or child-rearing is not really my responsibility or area of expertise.
- I can demonstrate incompetence at handling housework or the children with reasonable certainty that the "woman of the house" will take over.
- When I do my fair share around the house or in the rearing of our children, I will be considered unusual, a great guy, a great catch, a gift and a miracle, just for doing more than other men do with their families.
- If I go to buy a car, fix a car, get another major appliance, negotiate a loan at the bank, or deal with a service provider, I am not presumed to be so incompetent that anything can be put over on me—and I can be sent away in tears.
- I am excused for only having and expressing two emotions: happiness and anger. I also presume that I have an absolute right to my anger.

Heterosexual privilege: If I am heterosexual . . .

- Every President of the United States and most of the world leaders profess to be heterosexual.
- I am able to enter into puberty feeling that I am not alone, different, or damaged goods. I do not need a developmental process for "coming out" or integrating a sexual identity.
- Most of the world does not hate me just because of my affectional/sexual orientation. My spouse and I, together and individually, are welcome into almost any community into which we may wander.
- I am welcomed in almost any religion of my choice. I am not presumed to be going to hell for "the great sin."
- I am not the butt of jokes, targeted by other people's homophobia, discriminated against because of my attractions and sexual differences, or hated as less than human.
- I can date openly. I can express affection openly. I easily integrate my sexuality into my identity. I do not have to be in the closet.

- I can go to public places and into private homes without fear of being attacked physically, verbally, emotionally, or spiritually.
- I can go to high school, college, camp, and other public places without fear that a homophobic mob will harass, hurt, or kill me.
- I do not have to presume that the police may be more dangerous to me than the people from whom they are supposed to protect me.
- I can openly join the military and proclaim my love for the other sex: People can ask and people can tell without the fear of being dishonorably discharged.
- I can co-habitat with a lover without fear of being thrown out of the apartment or rental in which we live.
- I can marry and have children with all the rights associated with the former and without fear of interference from government agencies with regard to the latter.
- I do not have to fear that other family relatives or even child protective services will have more say over what happens to my children than I do in a court of law.
- My children do not have to answer questions about why I live with my partner.
- I have no difficulty finding a neighborhood in which people approve of my household.
- Our children are given texts and classes that implicitly or explicitly support our kind of family and do not turn them against my choice of life partner.
- I can travel with my partner without expecting embarrassment, hostility, or discrimination in those we deal with.
- Most people I meet will see my marital status as a positive aspect to my life; they will assume I am likeable, competent, and have good mental health just because of being heterosexually engaged with a familial partner.
- I can talk about the social events of my weekend at work or with acquaintances without having to monitor my language or fear the reactions of others.
- I will feel welcomed and normal in the different arenas of public life, both institutional and social.
- If I am married in one state, I am married in them all.
- I do not have to go through multiple legal maneuvers just to achieve the same rights that are automatically given to me through marriage.
- I am allowed spousal benefits through my spouse's employment, including those that have to do with healthcare, savings plans, childcare, retirement benefits, etc.
- I can leave property, retirement funds, directions for my estate, etc., to my life partner automatically.
- I can visit my life partner in the hospital and be presumed to be the person most likely to be consulted about necessary surgeries, living wills, post-operative treatment, etc.
- Laws and constitutional amendments are not constantly being developed to limit my existence and my activities in the country and in the world.
- As a woman, I can be out with other women and not be presumed to be and hated for being a lesbian simply because I do not live chiefly with women or because I have a husband.
- As a man, my overt heterosexuality protects me from attacks for being "queer" when I am out with other men or engaged in men-only activities.

CHAPTER 13

Cognitive-Behavioral Family Therapy*

Introduction

Key Concepts

Therapy Goals

The Therapist's Role and Function

Techniques

A Cognitive-Behavioral Therapist With the Quest Family

Summary and Multicultural Evaluation

Recommended Readings

References

Introduction

Compared to other approaches to family practice, **cognitive-behavioral family therapy** (CBFT) is in its early adolescent period (Dattilio, Epstein, & Baucom, 1998). Still, it is the preferred model in most managed-care settings, because it continues to promise measurable results in a relatively short period of time, and it backs up its claims with copious amounts of empirical research and outcome studies. **Aaron Beck**, **Albert Ellis**, **B. F. Skinner**, and **Joseph Wolpe** are considered the epistemological grandfathers of the cognitive-behavioral model, but clearly it is an approach that has benefited from theoretical and clinical masters, such as **Albert Bandura**, Judith Beck, **Frank M. Dattilio**, Arthur Freeman, John Gottman, Neil Jacobson, John Krumboltz, Donald Meichenbaum, Gerald Patterson, Christine Pedesky, and Richard Stuart, to name a few.

Ellis (1962/1994, 1977, 1982) was the first to systematize a cognitive approach to therapy and apply it to both individuals and couples. His protégés later would apply the model to families (Huber & Baruth, 1989). His A-B-C model separated **activating events (A)** from distressing **consequential emotions (C)** by concentrating on the **irrational beliefs (B)** that actually cause disturbed feelings and behaviors. Marital and family dysfunction, according to Ellis, occur when couples or parents with children have illogical and unrealistic ideas about their relationships and introduce negative, often extreme, evaluations of self and others when problems

---

* I want to acknowledge the diligent efforts and contributions of Dr. Frank Dattilio in developing this chapter and making sure it was up to date.

arise. Ellis (1995) enlarged his cognitive model to include and acknowledge the important role that behavioral responses play in interpersonal problems and concerns. Still, his more-or-less linear approach to causation (beliefs are attached to events and therefore cause distressed emotions and behaviors) was not a good fit for the family therapy movement, and it has not been used as widely with couples and families as have other models we have studied.

B. F. Skinner (1953) transformed behavioral therapy from its classical Pavlovian roots with the introduction of **operant conditioning**. His model suggested that those behaviors that are reinforced tend to continue while those that are not reinforced tend to diminish and then become **extinct** altogether. Any behavioral response may have an environmental **stimulus** that cues it, but if the behavior is not reinforced, it will not be incorporated into individual or relational actions. We can diagram Skinner's operant conditioning model like this:

$$\text{Stimulus Cue } (S_c) \rightarrow \rightarrow \rightarrow \text{ Response } (R) \rightarrow \rightarrow \rightarrow \text{ Stimulus Reinforcer } (S_r)$$

Skinner was also the first behaviorist to note that **aversive controls** can sometimes suppress certain behaviors for a while, but they can also become a reinforcing agent. We see this all too often when the behavioral interactions in couples' conflicts actually escalate the distress and antagonism. Some children and many adolescents actually use their parents' controlling behaviors as reinforcers for additional negative behaviors and an excuse for rebellion. When patterns of negative behavioral interactions and the application of aversive controls in families occur, dysfunction in the form of school, work, and interpersonal problems is often the result (Biglan, Lewin, & Hops, 1990).

Both John Krumboltz (Krumboltz & Krumboltz, 1972) and Gerald Patterson (1980; Patterson & Forgatch, 1987) developed programs using Skinner's operant-conditioning approach to help parents live more effectively with children and adolescents. They emphasized preventative care in which the adults would act as stimulus models for desired behaviors and become **positive**, social **reinforcers** in the shaping of mature and competent young people. **Rewards** and consequences quickly replaced the dubious effectiveness of **punishment**. Careful assessments of **baseline** behaviors made it possible to define a beginning point and measure improvements and accomplishments along the way.

Dr. Frank M. Dattilio

Frank Dattilio

In recent years, Frank M. Dattilio (1989, 1993b, 1998, 2005a) has introduced CBFT into mainstream family therapy. Dattilio is a clinical associate professor of psychiatry at Harvard Medical School and the University of Pennsylvania School of Medicine. Using Aaron Beck's (1979, 1988) concept of **cognitive schemas** or underlying core beliefs that people maintain about themselves, others, and the world (and how everything functions), Dattilio has applied this work successfully with couples and families; he helps families to identify the individual and collective schemas that support **automatic thoughts**, distortions, and resulting useless interactions. This is all done against the backdrop of a systems approach, providing a foundation for integration with other modalities (Watts, 2001). In a case involving a couple, John and Ruth, with four children, Rob, age 17, Adam and Jennifer, age 15, and Susan, age 13, Dattilio demonstrates how early family-of-origin schemas combine to form parental schemas that, in turn, lead to family schemas that impact each member of the family system. The parents start by expressing a desire to work on the tension that seems to be present in the family.

Dattilio: OK. Well, in essence that's what these sessions are designed to do, but we can also explore some other issues as well, particularly discontents that family members have with one another. Does that sound fair to everyone?

Jennifer: It doesn't to me! I think this is bogus, and I really don't want to be here.

Dattilio: So why did you agree to come?

Jennifer: I didn't. I was forced.

Ruth: Oh, Jennifer, come on now!

John: You were not forced. We need to be here as a family.

Jennifer: I don't care. I don't want to be here. I don't even want to be part of this stupid family.

Dattilio: I hear you, Jennifer, and I want you to know that I never expect individuals to come here against their will. So if you feel that strongly, you can leave, provided that your parents are OK with you being absent from the group. (long pause)

Jennifer: Well, so what do I do, just leave now?

Dattilio: Yes, if you wish.

Jennifer: So where do I go?

Dattilio: Well, that's really up to you, Jennifer.

Jennifer: Well, that's dumb. I'm not going to just sit outside in the car, bored! This is so stupid!

Dattilio: OK, you are welcome to stay. But I'm interested in hearing why you don't want to be here. What turns you off about this whole idea?

Jennifer: Because this is all bull, and it's not my problem, it's Mom's. (She [glares] at her mother.)

Dattilio: Hmm. I wonder whether anyone else sees things the way Jennifer does? (brief pause)

John: I don't. I think we all have some issues here that need to be discussed, besides Mom. But Mom does have her problems, I'll agree with that.

Dattilio: OK. Anyone else have an opinion? (No one [says] anything. John [glances] at Ruth, while she [looks] around at the kids.) (Dattilio, 1998, pp. 64–65)

> What do you think about Jennifer's claim that she was forced to come to therapy? Do you think that there are some times that mandated family therapy can work and should be enforced? Do you think it was possible that Jennifer was forced to come—even though her parents deny it? The family said that they came to talk about the tension in the family, and Jennifer certainly is manifesting some tension right now. Do you think the tension is only or even primarily with her or do you think she is a manifestation of tension in other parts of the family system? Do you think John rescued Ruth from Jennifer's anger when he spoke? Do you think he will do it again? If you were going to begin to assess family tension, how would you operationalize or define it? Or would you simply listen further to see what issues and concerns may evolve? Who in the family do you think will speak next?

Rob: I'd like to say something—I think our family definitely has some major problems. Everyone is, like . . . all over the place, and there's no sense of, how would you say . . . ?

Dattilio: Family unity?

Rob: Yeah! Sort of. I mean, like, Dad is sort of off in his own world—no offense, Dad—and Mom is doing her thing and trying to do for everyone else . . . it's sort of nuts.

Dattilio: So I'm hearing you say that things at home are somewhat chaotic at times and you're bothered by this?

Rob: Yes, but not "at times" . . . a *lot* of the time.

Dattilio: OK, but I want to get back to Jennifer's statement about how Mom makes her problems everyone else's. Does that seem true? Do you all feel the same way Jennifer does?

John: No, I'm having a problem with Jennifer's statement. Ruth and Jennifer have really been locking horns lately, and Jennifer will often take advantage every chance she can to blame her mother, or anyone else for that mater, except of course herself.

Jennifer: I do not! Get real, Dad!

Dattilio: John, in addition to your concerns about Jennifer, you sound a bit protective of your wife.

John: Well, sure, but that's the way I really see it.

Dattilio: OK, but is there any agreement with any of what the kids are saying?

John: Maybe some—I mean, look, Ruth has some problems. She's had a really rough upbringing, so I sort of see our roles as being supportive to her and just not giving her a hard time. (p. 65)

This general statement was followed by comments from Adam, Susan, and Jennifer suggesting that, in an effort to keep her girls from hurt, Ruth really became overprotective and restrictive. Once again, John attempted to keep negative comments away from Ruth when his daughters spoke, but Dattilio intervened and asked Susan to be open and honest about what she thought and felt. It was mentioned that Ruth treated the boys, Adam and Rob, differently—that she was not as restrictive with them. John commented that protection was a family value in both his family and Ruth's. This led Dattilio to explore the family schemas in each parent's family-of-origin. In both families, but for very different reasons, the men in the family were designated as protectors, and the women were relatively passive in relation to the men.

All family members returned for the second session, which Dattilio began by asking:

Dattilio: During our last session, I identified what's called a "family schema"—that your family protects each other in different ways. So what do you think is the basic reason why you do this? In other words, what is the belief that exists with your family that causes you to be so protective, as opposed to the idea of everyone just taking care of themselves? Does anyone have any ideas? (John and Ruth [glance] at each other sardonically, while the children [appear] to be distracted by extraneous thoughts. It [is] as though no one [wants] to speak.)

Ruth: Is it bad to do this?

Dattilio: Well, not necessarily. But the pattern that evolved in the family has caused some conflict. What we need to do is begin to address this, and maybe even change or modify some behaviors so that you get along with one another a little better. But . . . let me get an answer to my question, because I think that this is a very important question. Again, where do you believe this basic belief of protectiveness comes from within your family?

(silence)

John: Well, I guess as the father, I feel to blame for some of it. While I support Ruth, I've also kind of dumped on her by not taking more of an active role with the kids. I said that my father wasn't around when I was growing up, so I've always felt somewhat lost in my role, and I have to kind of improvise at times. Therefore, I sort of duck out, so to speak, but then feel guilty when the kids jump all over Ruth. So then I kind of become protective. I don't know, it's weird.

Dattilio: It sounds as though, as a result of Ruth's upbringing, she's felt compelled to assume all the responsibility for the family, perhaps in part to compensate for you. So there may be several family beliefs that are distorted to some degree, as well as individual distortions regarding your roles in the family. Does that sound possible?

Adam: What do you mean, "distortions"?

Dattilio: Good question, Adam. Let me explain. (pp. 68–69)

Dattilio went on to show the family members a sheet of paper with the 10 most common **cognitive distortions** used in human interaction and personal reflection. They are: **arbitrary inference, selective abstraction, overgeneralization, magnification and minimization, personalization, dichotomous thinking, labeling and**

mislabeling, tunnel vision, biased explanations, and **mind reading**. I will define these later in this chapter. For each of the 10, Dattilio noted possible ways in which each distortion might be used within the family by various members. He also noted how these distortions related to the couples schema of protectiveness that emerged from the experiences John and Ruth had in their families-of-origin. At the end of his presentation, Dattilio asks the family to think about possible distortions that each member might use in this family.

Rob: Oh! I have one that Mom does big time.

Dattilio: All right, let's hear it.

Rob: I'm not sure which one this is, but, like, if we're out past curfew, she freaks out and starts accusing us of being up to no good—like we're guilty until proven innocent.

Dattilio: That's an arbitrary inference, and one that you may perceive Mom as doing. Do any of the other family members engage in the same distortion?

Adam: Yeah, Jen does!

Jennifer: I do not, dweeb!

Adam: Yes, you do.

Susan: You do, Jen. You're just like Mom.

Dattilio: OK, look, guys, we're just trying to identify cognitive distortions that we all engage in from time to time. This isn't meant to be a jousting match. Also, we want to identify those distortions that you engage in yourselves more than those you see in other family members.

John: All right! I have one about myself, as much as I hate to admit it. I sometimes get annoyed when my decisions are questioned. I guess I equate compliance from the kids with respect, yet I tend to dump a lot of responsibility onto Ruth.

> . . . In therapy with a family like this one, the next step after identifying these distortions is to teach the family members to begin to question and weigh the evidence that supports the internal statements they make to themselves, and (ideally) to challenge any erroneously based assumptions. . . . The trick here is to try to introduce the model in a creative way, so as to not bore the family with theories. . . . In fact, one of the techniques used is to assign spouses or family members a pad of paper and a pencil, so that they can capture their automatic thoughts on paper during the course of their interaction at home. (Dattilio, 2002).

Dattilio: All right, John, that's a good one—so some of your beliefs, and one that you are choosing to identify as being based on a distortion, is that "the boss should never be questioned." It's a matter of "Do as I say, not as I do."

John: Yeah, I guess. Boy, that sounds awful when someone else actually says it.

Dattilio: Well, let's address that. Let's just analyze it for a moment and see if we can challenge some of the basic tenets of the belief. Now, do you have any idea why you believe this way—that the man should be the boss and his decisions should go unquestioned?

John: Well, I don't know. I know I didn't get that from my father, so I guess, as I said before, I was left to sort of improvise as to what the father's role should be. I also think that Ruthie's father had something to do with it early on. When we were first married, he used to . . . sort of . . . drill me.

Dattilio: Drill you?

John: Yeah, you know, like take me aside and give me his advice about how I need to act as the man of the house. Also, well, this may sound odd, but I kind of got the impression that this was what Ruthie was more comfortable with. You know, like she kind of—oh, I forget the word that you guys use all of the time. It's a popular term.

Dattilio: Enabled it?

John: Yes, enabled, that's it! She enabled me to be that way, I guess. I mean, in other words, that she kind of leans on me more than I lean on her, because she knows that I am used to it from the way I grew up.

Dattilio: . . . Might this be tied to the schema of taking care of each other? How does this all relate?

Rob: Well, I was thinking about that for a while when you were talking to Dad, and I think that we're like a pack of wolves that sort of just look out for one another casually, and if one of us is in need, somebody will step in—but we never talk about it openly otherwise.

Dattilio: . . . OK, but how does this cause conflict?

Susan: . . . I think that maybe the conflict comes when one person has one expectation and the other has a different expectation, and it's never communicated. We just sort of . . .

Dattilio: Mind-read. (pp. 70–72)

In the third session, Dattilio returned to John's irrational belief that "The boss should never be questioned." After establishing that there was no "substantiating evidence" (p. 74) for John's belief—and that, indeed, enforcing it did not work on the kids, Dattilio went on to teach John how to get the thought out of his head and out of his life. Using a piece of paper, Dattilio outlined a process for generating alternate thoughts and responses that looks like this:

Situation or Event	Automatic Thought	Cognitive Distortion	Emotion	Challenging Self-Statement	Alternate Response

This pad-and-pencil tool is used initially for assessment and analysis, but it also can be turned into a self-monitoring intervention that various family members can use as homework between sessions (Dattilio, 2002). Dattilio used John as a prime example, but he really was teaching the rest of the family at the same time.

Dattilio: . . . each time a situation occurs where you have a negative automatic thought, write it down. Use the extreme left-hand column to record the situation in which you had the thought. In the next column, list exactly what the thought was. Next try to attempt to identify what type of distortion you were engaging in. You can refer to the sheet I gave you last session. After that, note the emotional response that accompanied it, and then try to challenge that thought or belief by weighing the evidence in favor of it. Finally, you might want to write down an alternative response, using any new information that you may have gathered. (pp. 75–76)

Dattilio then asked John to think of a recent example and try it. John remembered that Adam arrived home 5 minutes late. His automatic thought of "He's defying me" and "He doesn't respect my position" involved cognitive distortions identified as arbitrary inference, dichotomous thinking, and personalization. His self-statements led to feelings of anger and upset. He challenged the statement by reminding himself not to take it personally, and he replaced the notion of defying with testing the limits. His alternate response was to talk to Adam rather than punish him, and he believed that Adam would be more receptive to this approach.

In subsequent sessions, Dattilio introduced four assumptions germane to family life (see Schwebel & Fine, 1994). They are:

- *Assumption 1:* Individuals seek to maintain balance in their environment in order to fulfill their needs and wants. . . . This process lends itself to the development of each individual's personal theory (PT) of family life and family relationships.
- *Assumption 2:* Individual members' cognitions affect virtually every aspect of family life. These are determined by five categories of cognitive variables identified by Baucom, Epstein, Sayers, and Sher (1989):

  (a) Selective attention (what is noticed),
  (b) Attributions (how individuals explain why any given event occurs),
  (c) Expectancies (what individuals predict will occur in the short-, middle-, or long-term future),
  (d) Assumptions (individuals' perceptions about how the world works), and
  (e) Standards (how individuals think the world should be).

- *Assumption 3:* Certain obstacles block healthy family functioning. The roots of these obstacles lie within individual family members' PTs—specifically in the cognitions in the PTs.
- *Assumption 4:* Family members need to become more aware of their family-related cognitions—how these cognitions affect them in certain situations, when they cause distress, and how to replace unhealthy ones with healthy ones. (Dattilio, 1998, pp. 77–78)

Using these assumptions, Dattilio helped the family members to re-examine the various roles that each person had adopted in the family. When he opened up a conversation about the relationship between Ruth and Jennifer, it became obvious that Ruth was afraid she was losing her daughter: Ruth's automatic thought was that no one needed her in the family. "Like if I died, it wouldn't matter" (p. 79). This led to a re-examination of their respective roles with each other. The two of them were locked in a no-win behavioral interaction in which both wanted more contact, but their differing styles interfered. Jennifer wanted to be in charge of when she spent time with her mother, but her mother's aggressive insistence on closeness alienated Jennifer and pushed her away. After reframing the problem as one that involved distorted thinking and useless behaviors in both parties, Dattilio asks:

Dattilio: Now, Jennifer, is it possible that there might be some distortion in the way you view your mother's behavior, and more so her intentions in attempting to be close with you?

Jennifer: I don't think so. I pretty much see what I see.

Dattilio: . . . I'm asking you to just consider for a moment that your view, regardless of its basic accuracy, may be slightly distorted by certain things, like your anger and your need for privacy. Things like that. That perhaps Mom's intention isn't so much to rob you of your individuality or keep you a child, but to share in your life.

Jennifer: I don't know. Maybe . . .

Dattilio: . . . What evidence would you need to see as proof of that? That her intention is actually positive toward your genuine growth?

Jennifer: That she just back off a little.

Dattilio: So a change in her behavior would tell you that she really cared.

Jennifer: Well, yeah!

Dattilio: OK, so if her behavior would change, if she were to back off, how would that change how you think and feel about her and the situation?

Jennifer: Well, I wouldn't mind talking to her about some things, when I'm ready. At least I could breathe some. (p. 81–82)

Dattilio spent 20 sessions meeting with Ruth and her family. Automatic thoughts and distortions continued to be identified and challenged, and alternate responses and new behaviors employed. Ruth and Jennifer got along much better 6 months after treatment ended. Rob left for college and, even though Adam and Susan engaged in sibling bickering, in general, the family was a lot happier.

This is the report that Dattilio received in a casual meeting with John in their community. In most cases, however, at the end of therapy cognitive-behavioral family therapists would have returned to many of the same measures that were used to assess the family at the beginning. In clinical research settings, it would not be uncommon to do 6-month and 12-month follow-up assessments too. These assessments would seek to measure the effectiveness of the treatment plan in meeting the targeted goals for this particular family.

Key Concepts

The Russian neurologist/psychologist, **Ivan Pavlov** (1927/2003), was studying the relationship between saliva and digestion in dogs when he discovered that saliva could be produced artificially by pairing up a metronome tone and the application of meat powder to a dog's tongue. After a while, the tone alone would actually get the dog to salivate. Indeed, some of the dogs would start salivating the minute that Pavlov walked in the room. This model of learning is now called **classical conditioning**, and it can be diagrammed as follows:

Meat powder $\rightarrow \rightarrow \rightarrow \rightarrow \rightarrow \rightarrow \rightarrow \rightarrow$ **Salivation**

(an unconditioned stimulus or **US**)   (an unconditioned stimulus response or **UR**)

/

paired with

/

Metronome tone or bell $\rightarrow \rightarrow \rightarrow \rightarrow \rightarrow$ **Salivation**

(a conditioned stimulus or **CS**)   (a conditioned response or **CR**)

In classical conditioning, the US (or meat powder) automatically will produce a UR (or salivation). The CS (or tone) must be presented virtually simultaneously with the US, and this pairing must be repeated consistently over many, many trials before the CS alone produces the CR (salivation). Further, repeated use of the CS without the US eventually will lead to the extinction of the CR. Much of what is called **systematic desensitization** for phobias and other anxieties is built on this model (see Wolpe, 1990). This is also true for what used to be called implosion and is now called **exposure therapy** (Becker & Zayfert, 2001).

Skinner's (1953, 1974) operant-conditioning model shifted the focus of **behaviorism** from stimuli that **cued** a given behavior to stimuli that reinforced human behavior. **Reinforcement** in the operant conditioning model is the key to shaping new behaviors, keeping acceptable old ones, and getting rid of those that are useless. Reinforced behaviors—those that receive some reward or eliminate some aversive stimuli, as in **negative reinforcement**—tend to keep going or even increase. Further, large, complex behaviors can be *shaped* by breaking them down into smaller, more achievable actions. Behaviors that are not reinforced may keep going for a while, but eventually they stop or *extinguish*. Usually, **continuous primary reinforcement** is initially prescribed for the step-by-step shaping of new behaviors. It is **intermittent reinforcement**, however, that is the strongest behavioral motivator. Slot machines in Las Vegas, for example, have long used carefully modulated, variable ratio reinforcement to keep people betting money even when they are losing.

It was not lost on early behavioral counselors and consultants that the person in charge of administering reinforcements was another reinforcer: a **social reinforcer** who also would serve as a model for what was expected (Bandura, 1969; Krumboltz & Krumboltz, 1972). In therapy, social reinforcement helps the therapist influence and direct change.

Albert Bandura and Richard Walters (1963) developed a **social learning theory** that reintroduced the role of thinking, attitudes, convictions, beliefs, and values as mediators between stimulus and response. Bandura's (1977, 1997) conceptualization of the interaction between stimulus, personal positioning, and action became the foundation for cognitive-behavioral therapy, as it is practiced today. When the cognitive therapies of Beck (1979) and Ellis (1997), for example, were added to his behavioral approach, the quality of an individual's thinking became a central focus and was used to distinguish effective living from pathological behavior.

In these models, thinking that is rational, consensually validated, optimistic, and reality-based tends to produce happier people with more functional behaviors than people who are self-absorbed, given to extreme forms of thinking, or pessimistic. This is not a new discovery: Adler (1932) made this very distinction, calling the rational, consensually validated orientation "common sense" and the irrational, self-validating orientation a "private intelligence" or **private logic**. We know whether a person is using common sense or functioning from a private logic by the way she or he communicates.

What a person thinks is understood through talk: that is, through one person expressing thoughts and feelings to another. When our thoughts are rational and congruent with our feelings, the actions that follow tend to make human sense. Irrational or extreme thoughts tend to produce disturbing and extreme feelings that lead to ineffective and often pathological behaviors.

We can say that people first think and decide (cognitions); then they generate feelings (emotions) to support and enact those decisions; and lastly they act. The process is often so fast that it cannot be experienced in steps. As an example, most people are in touch with their emotions first. This is what usually brings them into treatment. It is not until further examination that they realize that their cognitive processes actually preceded their emotions. Cognitive-behavioral therapy most often uses interventions that make people aware of their ideas and corrects irrational beliefs and expands or alters emotional responses in an effort to influence positive changes in behavior—although in some cases therapy focuses only on behavioral change with the understanding that thinking and feeling will align. When therapists intervene, the work is usually remedial in nature, addressing both distorted cognitions and the behaviors that follow (Dattilio, 2005c; Dattilio & Padesky, 1990).

When this model is applied to families, the therapist's attention is directed initially to three areas of focus: (1) the nature and rate of patterns of upsetting behavioral interactions; (2) how family members express and hear the thoughts and feelings of others; and (3) the methods and skills families employ to solve problems (Dattilio, 2005a Dattilio, Epstein, & Baucom, 1998). An additional focus is placed on how all of this affects the family system. Thus, if an adolescent continually is missing a curfew set by the parents, what the parents think, how they express their thoughts and feelings, and what they do to solve the problem must all be part of an initial assessment, along with the impact that this has on the family as a whole. Parents who believe that their child is bad (disobedient, defying authority, rebellious, hanging out with the wrong crowd, using drugs, or delinquent) will almost certainly engage the child antagonistically. Parents who see their child as testing limits, experimenting with freedom, or even making normal adolescent mistakes are much more likely to engage the child in rational problem solving. Therapy, then, starts with an assessment of the automatic thoughts and cognitive distortions that lead to discordant interactions in families.

Based on the earlier work of Aaron Beck, Dattilio (1993b, 1998, 2005b) identifies eight common cognitive distortions that may occur with couples and families. They are:

1. **Arbitrary inference:** A conclusion generated about an event without substantiating evidence, such as deciding your children are engaged in delinquent behavior when they come home 5 minutes late.

2. **Selective abstraction:** Taking things out of context, paying attention to distortion-supporting details, but ignoring other important information, such as noticing your child's or spouse's mistakes, but never commenting on positive attributes or accomplishments.

3. **Overgeneralization:** Generalizing from one or two incidents to assigning someone a consistent, ongoing attribute; an example is when one family member is late picking up another family member, and the late individual is declared to be completely unreliable.

4. **Magnification and minimization:** Making more or less out of a situation or event than is warranted by the facts. An example is when an adolescent gets Bs on her report card, and her parents declare that she will never get into a good college: She might as well go to beauty school. Later, when the child's grades have improved, but are not straight As, the parents lament that the additional As didn't really help her much.

5. **Personalization:** A form of arbitrary inference that occurs when external events are attributed to oneself without sufficient evidence, such as when a comment about a movie star's weight is taken to mean "She thinks I'm fat."

6. **Dichotomous thinking:** Classifying experiences as all or nothing, always or never, complete success or failure, totally good or totally bad, absolutely right or absolutely wrong. This kind of polarization is evident when one spouse says, "I wish you would have picked up some ice cream when you went shopping," and the other spouse thinks, "Nothing I ever do is good enough."

7. **Labeling and mislabeling:** Attaching trait labels to self or others for what is essentially a single or small set of incidents, as in making a mistake and declaring oneself stupid or declaring that an adolescent's desire to watch TV rather than practice the violin is a sign of laziness or indolence.

8. **Mind reading:** Another arbitrary inference in which one individual believes that she or he knows what another is thinking or will do—even though nothing had been verbally communicated between the two people. Anytime spouses, parents, or children say they know what other people are going to say or do when they find out about a problem or misdeed, they are engaging in mind reading: It is a guess that is framed in the negative more often than not.

Most of our irrational, automatic thoughts can be characterized as one or more of these eight distortions. In turn, these distortions are supported by underlying core beliefs that people develop about the world and how it works; such core beliefs are called *schemas* (see Dattilio, Epstein, & Baucom, 1998; Fiske & Taylor, 1991; Young, 1999). Schemas about relationships and family life are developed from what we learned in our families-of-origin, our cultural backgrounds, societal norms, and early relationship experiences. They are seldom clearly articulated. Most often they exist as a vague sense of what "should be"—just below our awareness. Schemas turn into pre-set, personal positions that orient the individual's experience of self and others in narrow and prescribed ways: The use of selective attention, attributions to others, expectations, assumptions, and "standards" or personal and family rules related to how life should be both reflects these schemas and leads to distorted thinking.

A couple always involves two people, each raised in the schemas of their families-of-origin. As each person experiences life, he or she adapts and adjusts his or her core beliefs about relationships and family life. When they come together to form a family, they develop joint beliefs as a result of blending their life experiences and adaptive stances. Each new child enters into this joint family schema and, through further adaptation and experiences, each child also changes the family schema. When the players in a family are set, the family schema tend to be maintained through routines and relatively consistent and predictable interactions (Dattilio, 2005a; Dattilio & Epstein, 2003).

Therapy Goals

One of the first goals of cognitive-behavioral family therapy is to determine whether the focus can be on the family as a whole or must first address issues related to the couple (Dattilio & Epstein, 2005). A number of therapy indicators or markers must be considered in this assessment. Who seems to be leading or has power and control in the family? Are the parents still available to work together as a team or are they engaged in an emotional divorce, if not a legal one? Or is one of the parents overly enmeshed with the children while the other parent is absent or withdraws to the periphery? Do the parents have psychological needs or issues—either individually or together—that spill over into family life and limit their ability to parent effectively?

Assuming that the couple's relationship is strong enough potentially to provide leadership for the family, the second goal of cognitive-behavioral family therapy is to determine whether the parents merely need educational input or if the family, and especially one or more of the children, need immediate changes in order to regain functional status. For the former, a psychoeducational consultation, for example, can be used to teach parents effective ways to handle and correct everyday problems from getting up and eating properly to bed-wetting, temper-tantrums, and backtalk or whining. When the misbehaviors of the children are more disturbing, perhaps involving anger, aggression, dangerous activities, or, conversely, depression, anxiety, and suicidal ideation, then more direct behavioral interventions and management processes are required.

The overall goal of cognitive-behavioral family therapy is to address automatic thoughts, cognitive distortions, and schemas that lead to antagonistic interactions and to plan modifications of emotions and behaviors that will lead to more harmonious family lives. This goal is specified for each individual couple or family unit and is based on a variety of cognitive and behavioral assessments used to establish couple or family baselines and targeted goals (Dattilio, 2005a). It is these targeted goals that are the basis for developing treatment plans and the evidence-based interventions designed to bring about effective change.

The Therapist's Role and Function

The foundation for cognitive-behavioral therapy with individuals and families has always been related to a scientific inquiry into human behavior. It is important to note, however, that science, in and of itself, does not preclude warmth, caring, compassion, and an interest in the well-being of others. Indeed, some of the most humanistic of therapists have believed in and contributed to behavioral models of individual and family therapy. What tends to remain constant in this work is a dedication to an assessment of cognitive expression and measurement of observed behaviors. In this model, thinking leads to decision making; the generation of emotions supports the decisions and fuels the enactment of behavior. The role and function of the therapist is to identify and correct faulty or distorted thinking (called **cognitive restructuring**) while also taking a baseline measurement of dysfunctional behaviors and then developing interventions that will measurably improve functioning. Periodic assessments of the baseline thoughts, feelings, and behaviors are conducted throughout therapy as a measure of progress. One of the common misconceptions about cognitive-behavior therapy is that it places little or no emphasis on emotion. This is clearly not the case (Dattilio, 2001).

When the couple must be the focus of therapy before family issues can be resolved, cognitive-behavioral therapists have a long history of developing individual and relational interventions to strengthen individuals and couples. The function of these interventions is to confront the faulty or distorted thinking, beliefs, schemas, and convictions that are used to maintain disturbing and dysfunctional emotions and behaviors. Some of these faulty or distorted beliefs may be rooted in spousal families-of-origin, which may be addressed by the therapist during the course of treatment (Dattilio, 2006). Couples, too, often are asked to address the "shoulds" and "musts" that are inherent in their relationship and that may inhibit true satisfaction and eliminate the possibility of flexibly and creatively addressing the problems they face. Couples also have benefited from therapy that includes an assessment of behavioral patterns that reinforce problems in their relationships, followed by the creation of a mutual exchange of rewards between the partners (see Christensen & Jacobson, 2000; Gottman, 1999, 2000; Liberman, 1970; Stuart, 1969, 1980). The focus is on helping couples request what they want from each other in a specific, positive, immediately employable, non-conflictual manner. These mutual-request processes often are supported by training in communication, negotiation, and **problem solving**, usually ending in actual written contracts or agreements between the partners.

From a family perspective, the goal of behavioral couples therapy is, in addition to augmenting intimacy and satisfaction in the relationship, to create a parental team capable of working with and focusing on the needs of misbehaving and sometimes disturbing children. The process of cognitive-behavioral therapy might be described in stages: (a) an introduction; (b) an assessment of baseline thinking and behaving within parent–child dyads; (c) a cognitive reorientation of parental positions and involvement; (d) developing and implementing behavioral strategies for needed change; (e) behavioral practice and implementation at home, at school, and in society; and (f) evaluation, follow-up, and termination.

Since any constant behavior or pattern of interaction that occurs within a family is continually being reinforced, the first task of the therapist is to understand it. Cognitive-behavioral therapists tend to focus on dyadic interactions—spouse to spouse or parent to child—in order to understand how each person is reinforcing the other (Nichols & Schwartz, 2004). When a parent and a child are locked in a mutually reinforcing, negative interaction, it is usually because one or both of them feel that their position is being challenged, and this should not happen. A cognitive reorientation starts by helping the parent realize that the challenging behavior is happening, and the normal parental response is actually helping to maintain it. Choosing new, more effective behavioral responses to children's misbehavior generally requires, first, a new approach to *thinking* about the child, what she or he is doing, and what the parent does in response. When the parent can step back from automatic, repetitive, and patterned responding, any number of effective techniques can be employed to help the child behave well and have a happier, more productive life.

Techniques

Many of the same techniques used for assessment and interventions with individuals also are applied to cognitive-behavioral family practice. For an excellent overview, see Dattilio (2005c). When problems in the family and/or the behaviors of children become severe and extremely disturbing, cognitive-behavioral family therapists almost always rely on cognitive restructuring, as well as highly structured operant conditioning processes used in the behavioral management practices developed by Gerald Patterson (1985; Forgatch & Patterson, 1998) and his associates at the Oregon Social Learning Center. I will introduce you to this parenting model, among others, in the next chapter. Here, I want to focus on assessment procedures and cognitive-behavioral interventions often used with couples and families. First, let's look at assessments.

Self-Report Questionnaires.   Cognitive-behavioral family practitioners sometimes focus on **self-report questionnaires** that are designed to reveal unrealistic beliefs and expectations, irrational ideas and schemas, cognitive distortions, and repetitive patterns of discordant behavior or interactions. This is particularly the case when individual family members experience difficulty in coming forth with this information verbally. Among the most used are the Relationship Belief Inventory (RBI) (Eidelson & Epstein, 1982); the Inventory of Specific Relationship Standards (ISRS) (Baucom, Epstein, Rankin, & Burnett, 1996); and the Marital Attitude Survey (MAS) (Pretzer, Epstein, & Fleming, 1991), which assesses attributions for relationship problems to self and partner, as well as investigating expectations for change. Some cognitive-behavioral family therapists have adapted these scales for the parent–child relationship, but most rely on the many scales that have been developed outside of the CBFT model (see Corcoran & Fischer, 2000).

Assessment of Cognitions: Interviews. Beck (1995) used Socratic questioning in an effort to identify the chain of thoughts that are triggered by specific events and lead to the emotional and behavioral responses reported by the client. The use of the **downward arrow technique** is designed to develop a cognitive map that leads from automatic thoughts to cognitive distortions to underlying core beliefs in the individual's private schema. An example presented by Dattilio, Epstein, and Baucom (1998) is diagrammed in Figure 13.1.

Assessment of Interactions: Interviews. Cognitive-behavioral family practitioners also use interviews to assess the patterns, frequency, and settings associated with negative interactions. They are interested in the antecedents, conditions, and reinforcers involved in ongoing behavioral exchanges. Although negative interactions are often the focus of the initial

"I need to scream because Harry doesn't always listen to me."

⬇

"If I don't scream, I'll never be heard."

⬇

"If I am not heard, I am nobody."

⬇

"If I am nobody, I will be helpless."

⬇

"If I am helpless, people will run over me."

⬇

"Harry will run over me and this will give him complete control."

Figure 13.1

Example of the downward arrow technique.

Source: Dattilio, Epstein, & Baucom, 1998, p.14.

sessions of therapy, many CBF therapists also conduct a **functional analysis** of family patterns that are viewed as more positive and enhancing of family harmony. Such an analysis often opens the door to situational variations in family patterns that can be used to initiate change. In addition to these behavioral descriptions of interactions, the CBF practitioner inquires about the thoughts and emotions that have influenced both positive and negative interactions.

Behavioral Observation.   **Behavioral observation** starts from the moment the cognitive-behavioral practitioner meets the couple or family for the first time. The goal is to detail the actual behaviors and interactions that take place, as well as the consequences and reinforcements that can be observed. Both content and process are important in these assessments: The former is used to identify cognitive distortions and will become the focus of most interventions; the latter defines patterns that will need to be interrupted and redirected. Dattilio, Epstein, and Baucom (1998) note that observations of family interactions will "vary according to (1) the amount of structure the clinician imposes on the interaction and (2) the amount of structure in the clinician's observational criteria or coding system" (p. 16). And indeed, some formal coding systems require a large amount of structure. The advantage of less structure is that the counselor gets to see family communication and behavioral exchanges in as naturalistic a manner as possible. There are times, however, when the best information comes from directing the family to engage in actual problem solving. Similar to Minuchin's (1974) notion of enactment, these structured interventions become a form of action research for the CBF practitioner. The therapist may direct the family to work on solving a curfew problem, but as the process unfolds, the practitioner will intervene to adjust and modify interactions so that the outcome is more effective.

And now, let's look at the interventions.

Communication Training.   The more that some families and behaviors seem out of control, the more effective communication becomes necessary. Effective communication includes congruent expression of thoughts and feelings, listening to and acknowledging the messages of others, giving clear directives and polite requests, setting clear and reasonable limits and expectations, and using I-statements in relation to personal and family needs. In almost all cases, family members do better with each other when they send constructive messages rather than aversive ones. When appropriate, several sessions are used to help family members take turns listening to others, paraphrasing and acknowledging the messages sent, and developing rational and effective responses. Along the way, automatic thoughts and cognitive distortions are identified and challenged.

Problem-Solving Training.   Most families have difficulties directly related to their problem-solving processes. Taking time to teach effective problem solving is central to CBF therapy. The steps in effective problem solving are: (a) getting a clear definition of the problem that all family members can accept, including the behaviors present or missing that contribute to the problem; (b) brainstorming as many possible behavioral solutions as possible without evaluating them; (c) listing the advantages and disadvantages of each proposed solution, prioritizing them when appropriate, and selecting a solution that seems most useful to the family members involved; and (d) enacting the solution for a trial period and setting a time and process for evaluating its effectiveness.

Challenging Irrational Beliefs.   Albert Ellis (2000) was the first to carefully explicate how irrational ideas or beliefs would lead to dysfunctional emotions and disturbing behaviors. His ABC approach helped countless clients distinguish Activating events from irrational

Beliefs that actually cause the emotional consequences that are then presented as symptoms or presenting problems. Challenging irrational beliefs is at the heart of cognitive-behavioral therapy, and in family therapy it is almost always the adults who must address their belief systems first.

Identifying Automatic Thoughts and Cognitive Restructuring.   Irrational beliefs are almost always first identified in therapy sessions. They are so automatic that clients need training in how to spot them and submit them to analysis. Datillio (1998, 2002) encourages clients to use a notebook or pad of paper to catch automatic thoughts between sessions. Clients are asked to pay attention to when their moods are getting worse and to ask themselves, "What am I thinking right now?" The form used in the case at the beginning of the chapter is then employed in an analysis of the irrational beliefs. For example:

Situation or Event	Automatic Thought	Cognitive Distortion	Emotion	Challenging Self-Statement	Alternate Response
Dishes are not done when I get home	He's thoughtless and does not care about me at all.	Personalization	Angry/hurt	This is one incident, and maybe there is a good reason	Check what is going on with him first.

Central to the cognitive restructuring and the development of new self-statements and alternate responses are (a) weighing the evidence in the present situation, (b) developing hypotheses about other possible conclusions, (c) gathering more evidence, (d) rating your degree of belief in the revised cognition, and then (e) checking your emotional response to your alternate response. This process is an example of **self-monitoring**, which is essential to the process of teaching family members to be psychologically self-sufficient (Cormier & Nurius, 2003).

Contracting and Behavioral Change Agreements.   Designed to renegotiate severe levels of hostility in families, contracts spell out rewards for behaving in a certain manner. Contracts delineate specific behaviors required to gain specific rewards and are usually both written and signed by all parties. A form of contract called a **contingency contract** speaks to a mutual exchange of behaviors in which each party gets something they want from the other person if both agree to deliver it. For example, the parent agrees to fix specific foods the child likes if the child agrees to show up for dinner on time. For detailed guidelines on written contracts between parents and children, see Webster-Stratton and Herbert (1994). Many different forms of behavioral-change agreements are used as part of homework between family sessions. Homework is most effective when the desired behaviors are defined clearly and focus on the substitution of positive behaviors for negative ones.

Acting "as if."   New behaviors and even new orientations to family life are sometimes hard to come by, because individuals bring a lot of baggage from past events with them. Practicing new behaviors and new positions or roles in the family can start if people are willing to act "as if" they were the people they want to be—in some cases, "as if" they were the family they want to be.

Homework.   Homework, or out-of-session assignments, have been cited as an integral part of a number of theoretical and therapy formats, particularly when working with couples and families (Dattilio, 2002). Such assignments as bibliotherapy, self-monitoring, behavioral task assignments, and activity scheduling are all important as effective methods to support changes with families.

A Cognitive-Behavioral Family Therapist With the Quest Family

Jane Quest came alone to the first meeting with a cognitive-behavioral, systemic therapist (Atwood, 1992). Jane had been referred for therapy by her family pediatrician after she requested the name of a therapist for the boys. When she appeared in the counselor's office, she was visibly upset, reporting that she was at her wit's end. She had wanted so much for her "new" children, but they had such pain and difficulties in their young lives, and they did not know how to get along. Jane felt like she was losing her whole family. Her older daughters had, and needed, lives of their own. Paul was absorbed in his work. And she simply didn't know how to control Jason and Luke.

The Quest family as portrayed by Jane sounded like an all-too-typical family structure with exaggerated and stereotyped male and female social roles. For all practical purposes, the mother was in charge of the home: She and the children were engaged, over-involved, and ineffectively interacting on a daily basis. The father was operating outside of the family with as little involvement as possible—and possible feelings of abandonment. He had chosen to be the breadwinner in a family and otherwise withdrew. These exaggerated role models do not work very well today—especially when there is a major shift in the family structure, as the Quest family had experienced with the addition of the two boys. Jane really had two families: She was facing what would soon be the empty nest of her first family and the disordered and disrupted nest of her second family.

The cognitive-behavioral therapist asked Jane to bring the whole family to the second session and to keep careful records over the next week, charting what Jason and Luke did and who responded to them in what manner. She also wanted Jane to become an observer who could start to assess what was effective with the boys in terms of improvement or what led to a worsening of the situation.

Jane brought her whole family to the second session. Starting with Paul, the cognitive-behavioral therapist asked each family member how he or she felt about coming to the session.

Paul noted that he was very busy at work and always had been. He felt he relied on Jane to handle matters at home, but he tried to do what he could to help out. He had been excited about having the boys join the family initially, but the required changes had been hard on him and, he thought, everyone. Jane again stated that she was at her wits end, but noted that she had been able to chart Jason's and Luke's behaviors during the week. For some reason, the more she charted, the less they got into problems, so this had been somewhat of a better week, but she didn't expect it to last. Amy and Ann both indicated that they were there because their parents wanted them to come. They were okay with their parents' decision to add the boys to the family, but they didn't really feel connected to them yet. The boys, for their part, were very talkative, interrupting often, and in constant motion.

In the therapy room, Paul eventually asked if Jane wanted him to corral the boys and make them sit down. Jane responded, "in a minute," taking out her chart and noting what the boys were doing and how long it lasted.

Paul: She's become almost obsessive about that thing, that chart you gave her.

Therapist: Actually, I appreciate Jane's efforts with that chart a great deal. It is hard to know what might be changed if we don't first have a pretty good idea of what is currently happening. I am wondering, Jane, if you could share with your family and me what you have learned from your observations this week.

Jane: The boys fight a lot, but we all know that. They fight about anything and everything. They actually average about 14 serious, "hitting" fights a day, and they have another 8 to 12 what I would call "bickering" fights in between the real ones. They also break, hurt, or destroy something—on average about 3 times a day. Although this week that seems to have happened less as the week has gone on.

Therapist: What do you think accounts for this?

Jane: Both of the boys were terribly hurt in their young lives, and they often seem intent on hurting each other even more. Property—especially if it is important to someone—and pets are usual targets for them. I usually get very concerned about protecting them from each other and protecting others from them. I'm always shouting "no," and running after them. But this week, I reached for the chart, just like you told me to do, and often by the time I made notes the problem was over or it was too late to do anything. So I let it slide. (pause) And even though I would have thought that letting things slide would lead to disaster, the amount of destructiveness seemed less.

> Just as the therapist is about to ask another question, a fight breaks out between the boys with Luke hitting Jason as hard as he can. Jane starts to get up to make both of the boys sit down in the circle. Paul explodes.

Paul to Jason: STOP! Don't even think about hitting him back. Sit down before I hit you! And I mean now: Both of you. Jane, can't you do something with them?

Therapist: Is that your usual way of stopping a fight, Paul? Do you find yourself yelling at the boys a lot or wanting Jane to step in?

Paul: I'm not around Luke and Jason that much, but it does seem to me that the fighting goes up when I come home.

Jane: Not actually. (looking at her chart) The fighting level stays about the same whether you are home or not.

Therapist: And when they fight, Paul, do you find yourself exploding at them often?

Paul: More so when we are in public, I guess. But yes, the noise gets to me, and I get angry.

Therapist: Okay, so how would you say that approach is working for you?

Paul: It's not. I get so angry sometimes, though, I can't seem to stop myself.

Therapist: Are you aware of what you say to yourself when you hear the boys start to fight?

Paul: Well, they shouldn't be fighting.

Therapist: Maybe not, but they are. You're a doctor. You have a patient with a tumor. It *shouldn't* be there, but . . .

Paul: But it is. And I can remove a tumor.

Therapist: Yes, and do you yell at it first?

Paul: No.

Therapist: Because you can assess the situation and figure out what to do. But when Jason and Luke start fighting, you are not so sure what to do, and you want to overpower it.

Paul: So what should we do?

Therapist: Well, I have some ideas about that, but they all start with each of you staying calm and assessing the situation—just like in your medical practice. There are three words I like a lot: What is, is! It would be nice if some things were different or easier or less disruptive, but they aren't. It's unfortunate—perhaps even criminal—that the boys were abused and that you have to handle the fallout from those events, but that's just the way life is. What is, is: Your family simply is the way it is.

Paul: And yelling about it won't help.

Therapist:	That's right. It hasn't helped in the past, and it is unlikely to help in the future.
Paul:	But I get so embarrassed when they are like this in public. They make me so mad.
Therapist:	Embarrassment is a hard experience when you are known in the community and you have a professional reputation, but really, it's not Jason and Luke who make you angry so much as what you tell yourself about them.
Paul:	What do you mean?
Therapist:	What is, is. You have two boys who have been hurt and abused in their lives, and that is what they have learned to do in return. In order for you to get angry at them, don't you have to be saying things like: "They should be over this by now" or "This shouldn't be happening to me" or "Their behavior will reflect badly on all of us as a family, and people will know that we can't handle them."?
Paul:	It's more: "This is never going to end, and our lives are never going back to normal, back in control, again."
Therapist:	And that would be awful.
Paul:	Yes, it would be.
Therapist:	Jane, do you find yourself yelling and getting angry at Jason and Luke too?
Jane:	Yes, I do. When I see Paul get so mad, I cringe, because I know that is how I sound too. It can't be good. I want to be a better mother, but I just feel at the end of my rope all the time. I think the things I say to myself are something like what Paul said: "Will this ever end? I don't think I can stand it." But also, it is what you said: "They should be over this by now. This awful behavior should not be happening."
Therapist:	Amy and Ann, what is it like for you with Jason and Luke?
Amy:	(after a pause and looking to her sister for clearance to talk) I have to say that life with them can be pretty hard, especially on my mother, and I find myself staying away as much as possible. I have a lot going on, and I will be going to university in less than a year. Ann, though, she cannot get away as much—and recently she has given up some of her school activities and her grades are suffering a bit.
Therapist:	Ann, is that true? (Ann nods.) Well, I can only imagine that your parents need to thank you for that gesture, that service really. I am sure it gives them a welcome break to address something, like your grades, that they know they can handle. It's generous of you to let them feel competent again, but I really think that it is time for them to start acting in a competent way with Jason and Luke. What do you think?

Ann does not have a real response to the therapist's question, so the therapist turns her attention to Paul and Jane. After briefly exploring what parenting was like in each of their families-of-origin, the therapist suggests that each of them has a model in their backgrounds for parental teamwork. And, of course, they had been an effective parenting team when they were raising Amy and Ann, so they know how to be a team, even if they haven't been practicing it recently.

Therapist:	With Jason and Luke, the two of you need more teamwork, not less. What would you be doing differently if you functioned as a team with them?
Paul:	(pause) One thing that would be different is that we would face them together when we were both home.
Jane:	And we would talk about what we were going to do and be consistent: We would both know to take a stand at about the same time, early before things get out of hand, and we would be firm. Mostly, I guess, we would know what to do and do it.
Therapist:	And what blocks the two of you from doing that now?
Jane:	This feeling that nothing works; that it is endless.

Paul:	It's not fun.
Therapist:	So when you wake up thinking that nothing works, it will never get better, and the fun of parenting is gone, you start out feeling depressed or at least discouraged, and you have given away all of your energy before the day even starts.
Jane:	That's very true. I just think if I felt better about everything, about Jason and Luke, then I would do better.
Therapist:	Let's see if we can work at this from the other end. I think if we can work it out so that you act as if everything will work out, then the feelings you want will show up soon enough. I want the two of you to imagine waking up tomorrow and acting as if Jason and Luke were already fully integrated members of the family, they had learned appropriate ways to handle themselves, and everyone was looking forward to the day—and any misbehavior one or the other might do was an exception to what was expected, not the rule. What would you, as a parental team, be doing then?

> The therapist's discussion with the family led to the formulation of a contract between the parents. As strong as Paul sometimes appeared, he really felt that he needed Jane's backing when he was dealing with Jason and Luke. For her part, Jane felt that she needed Paul at home more, not just to help her out, but to be a real part of the family. Paul agreed to rearrange his schedule so he would have more time at home, and Jane agreed to stand next to Paul over the next few weeks whenever he had to discipline one or both of the boys. Each of them also asked the other to reinforce calmness before starting to talk or intervene.

Therapist:	Amy and Ann, if Jason and Luke were *real* brothers of yours, not visitors or intruders, not just extra people in the house, but full members of the family, how would you interact with them?
Ann:	I guess we would do more with them.
Amy:	I am sorry, but we cannot do that! They would be a disaster around our friends. I'm not ready for that.
Therapist:	Is there something short of taking them to meet your friends that would be approaching normal for your family?
Amy:	We could fight with them if you want us to.
Therapist:	Is that what you and Ann do?
Ann:	We don't fight so much, but we do get on one another some. She hates it when I get into her stuff, and I hate it when she doesn't tell me stuff.
Therapist:	I can imagine that there are things that you need to get on Jason and Luke about. Do you ever do that?
Amy:	Not really. We usually tell Mom or Dad and get out of the way. At least, that's what I do.
Therapist:	Yes, well, I think you and Ann need to have your own relationships with Jason and Luke. You know, get on them when you need to, help out when you can. But your Mom and Dad need to stay out of things that are among the four of you. Like, how do you handle it now if they are doing something irritating?
Amy:	I am always telling Luke that I don't want him in my room when I am getting dressed in the morning. He either leaves or I move him.
Therapist:	And does that handle it?
Amy:	Yes.
Therapist:	Then why bring your Mom or Dad in?
Amy:	I guess I just think they should know what the boys are doing.
Therapist:	I don't think so. You handled it. It's done. Just like you handle things with your sister and she with you. Give your parents a rest. Leave them out of it.

By the following session, things had improved somewhat at the Quest home. The parents had enacted their contract with each other, and a real sense of being a team seemed to be emerging again. The amount of misbehaviors had stayed about constant, but still less than before Jane started charting. And now the parents were able to talk about specific behaviors in Jason and Luke that they felt they needed to modify. Their first goal was to reduce and eventually eliminate hitting between the boys and any other being. Together with the therapist, the following plan was devised:

- Paul and Jane would focus their attention so that they could start to intervene when voices were getting louder and before the hitting actually occurred.
- Paul and Jane would calmly help the boys talk through a problem and choose a different behavior, if possible.
- If hitting occurred, the child would automatically be in time-out for at least 5 minutes before being allowed to go back. This would be enacted firmly and calmly with no excuses accepted.
- During the day, Jason and Luke would be given special treats for each hour that they were able to play well together or with others with no violence. The treats might include sweets and other desired foods, stickers, etc. Although the rewards would be given each hour initially, the goal was to move toward longer and longer periods of non-violent play.
- Paul and Jane would play games and have fun with the boys daily, like they used to do with Amy and Ann, in order to model cooperative fun.
- Paul and Jane would comment regularly on the positive things that the boys did with each other, ignoring as much of the negative as they could.

Writing this plan was easier than enacting it. It was put into effect in fits and starts. Adjusting to new behaviors takes time, and some of Jason and Luke's behaviors actually got a little worse before they started to get better. Paul and Jane, too, would make mistakes. They would get involved too late at first and arrive only in time to enforce a time-out. If too much piled up during the day, some interventions were not done so calmly. And yet, over the next few weeks, with support from the therapist, Paul and Jane got into a pretty good pattern with each other and with Jason and Luke. More important, Paul actually started to feel that "we are a family, and I am enjoying doing things with them." Six months later, both Jason and Luke had gone a complete month without hitting each other or any other being. Amy left for college, but both she and Ann had incorporated Jason and Luke as full family members, taking them with them to various activities and engaging them in normal sibling interactions.

Summary and Multicultural Evaluation

Cognitive-behavioral therapy is one of the most widely adopted models of therapy in the world. In fact, Frank Dattilio's works alone have been translated into 25 languages (personal communication, January 21, 2006). The approach particularly appeals to the American ideal of pragmatism: It can be very concrete, and it is designed to get things done. Yet, at the same time, more contemporary writings stress the notion that cognitive-behavioral therapy need not be practiced in such a wooden, rigid fashion and can be tempered with the flexibility found in other therapeutic modalities (Dattilio & Epstein, 2003). The focus on targeted goals and concrete interventions also has broad multicultural appeal with cognitive-behavioral international societies developed all over the world (Dattilio, 1990, 1992, 1993a, 1995, 2005b; Dattilio & Bahadur, 2005). When this model is paired with a systemic orientation, family problems actually are treated as real problems that can be assessed, measured, and described. Specific techniques then can be applied to change interactions, as well as the expressed thinking and concrete behaviors that have maintained the problem. Further, change is not left to clinical judgment: It is not merely about *feeling* better. It follows from setting measurable goals and specific calculations of behavioral difference. For these reasons, it is often the preferred model in managed-care facilities and with third-party reimbursement programs.

Unlike the early forms of behavioral therapy, cognitive-behavioral approaches recognize that there is an interpreting being that exists between stimulus and response. And it is the interpretations (thinking) that orients the client toward certain stimulus cues, impacts the choice of responses, and anticipates and seeks certain reinforcers. By merging the disputing or challenging functions of cognitive models with the effectiveness of scientifically based change procedures, the needs of the whole system and the individuals within it can be addressed directly. This model places an emphasis on doing things differently rather than merely talking about problems. As soon as possible, cognitive-behavioral family practitioners formulate a plan with families, work with them collaboratively to choose techniques and interventions that are empirically supported, and then facilitate them in enacting processes of change in their everyday environment. If things are not working, the therapist reanalyzes the people and situation and adjusts the treatment plan, but there is really never a reason to give up on a person or a family (Cormier & Nurius, 2003). This is about science in action. It is evidence-based, using procedures that are at least as effective as, and often more effective than, other models at changing problem behaviors (Kazdin, 2001).

In this chapter, I have presented the skills and interventions required for change within families experiencing everything from disharmony to severe behavioral problems. In all cases, the list of skills and interventions are among the most empirically tested and researched of any of the models in this book. Whether helping families through a psychoeducational approach or with cognitive-behavioral family therapy, the role of the therapist or counselor is that of an educator who assists families in employing methods that actually work.

Cognitive-behaviorists add a pragmatic lens to family therapy and counseling that helps clinicians apply concrete interventions to real problems and dysfunctional interactions. They remind us that individuals, couples, and families always are interacting in ways that maintain behaviors through reciprocal and mutual reinforcement. Further, cognitive-behavioral family therapists know that the environment and social context influence roles and functions within families in ways that often go unnoticed, but nevertheless have a powerful impact. Increasingly, these family therapists are calling into question the reinforced roles and functions based on gender (Atwood, 1992). Environmental patriarchy has a powerful influence on how individuals and families enact their lives. It becomes the standard, expected practice within many communities, and it reinforces expected roles and behaviors in everything from the models that are presented to community reactions to difference and change.

If you are interested in a more in-depth study of this approach, I recommend the following sources: Atwood (1992); Baucom, Shoham, Mueser, Davido, and Sickle, (1998); Beck (1995, 2005); Dattilio (1998); Dattilio and Padesky (1990); Ellis (2000); Falloon (1988); Horne and Sayger (2000); Krumboltz and Krumboltz (1972), if you can find it; Schwebel and Fine (1994); and Sexton and Alexander (2002).

Contributions to Multicultural Counseling and Gender Issues

Cognitive-behavioral therapists approach culture as a context—and a reinforcing context at that—in which thinking and behaving are enacted. For those cultures that place less emphasis on talking, expression of feeling, and intrapsychic expression, cognitive-behavioral methods seem like a welcome relief. However, at the same time, some Mediterranean and Middle Eastern cultures have strict rules with regard to religion, marriage, family, and child-rearing practices, and this may cause them to be hesitant to question their basic cultural values (Dattilio, 1995). Pedersen, Draguns, Lonner, and Trimble (2002) note that Native Americans, Hispanic Americans, and Asian Americans often prefer an active, directive therapist concerned with solving immediate problems and bringing quick, effective relief to the family. Clients from each of these cultures join African Americans in preferring an approach that is goal-directed and focused on thinking, problem solving, planning, and evaluating. The problems of everyday living are addressed as real and not as a symptom of some other family dysfunction that many cultures would not recognize or consider bringing to therapy. Cognitive therapists note that each culture has its own set of rules and role expectations, and families are the social units in which these rules and roles are most often enacted. In this sense, culture has a very strong reinforcing impact on families and family life (Dattilio & Bahadur, 2005). Similar to Adlerians, however, cognitive-behavioral therapists believe that the interpretation family members give to culture will be more important than the actual positions inherent in cultural mandates. It is not so much what is expected of us from culture and society as it is what we think about it.

Cognitive-behavioral family therapy places a special emphasis on environmental context (Dattilio, 2005b). It is the clients' cultures that form much of the conceptualizations about what constitutes a family problem. Effective family goals also must allow the individuals within the family to function within the communities in which the family resides. What individuals and families think and what they find reinforcing also is heavily influenced by the cultural norms of the community. In this sense, understanding and working with culture permeates every aspect of effective assessment, diagnosis, and treatment (Spiegler & Guevremont, 2003).

Cognitive-behaviorists have repeatedly pointed out that prejudice is a learned response. It is taught and reinforced in environmental units as small as an interaction and as large as the macro-systems of society and culture. As couples and family systems begin to break down under the weight of social injustice and inequality, cognitive-behavioral therapists bring a large repertoire of interventions that can challenge the norms and help to enact the mutual reinforcements required for cooperative living.

When cognitive-behavioral family counselors integrate cultural and gender perspectives into their work, there are really very few limitations to this model. Normal and abnormal then are approached with **cultural sensitivity**. Cognitions are understood as culturally based, and both rational and irrational ideas are addressed within a cultural context. The same is true for assessing problem behavior and choosing behavioral goals and reinforcements for change.

Exercises for Personal and Professional Growth

Becoming a family counselor, therapist, psychologist, social worker, or practitioner is no easy task. In reconsidering our own families-of-origin and working with other families, we constantly are confronted with people, events, and situations that seem to trigger in us old and often interfering ways of thinking, feeling, and behaving. Cognitive-behavioral therapy provides us with a model through which we can engage in self-reflection and challenge those parts of us that may otherwise interfere with therapeutic process. One way to approach the exercises I will propose here is to look at them as one road to a differentiated self, a way to bring reason into alignment with the emotional experiences of our lives. They also may be useful in handling countertransference experiences in your work with families or to manage the pressure that young practitioners often feel in relation to supervision.

Let's start with your family-of-origin. Take another look at your genogram and start with the people in your immediate family. Were there relationships that involved you that you would describe as conflictual, difficult, or hurtful? Which relationships were those? Think of two or three examples of conflicts or difficulties, and try to remember how you felt.

This will be a start for filling in the following table for these relational experiences. From memory, describe the situations or events that come to mind in column 1. Next, go over to column 4 and describe the emotion you were feeling. If you can get back into that feeling, see if you remember what automatic thoughts were associated with the event and led to the feelings you had. This is already a good start toward identifying those things from your own life that may serve as a foundation for emotionally reactive triggers in your work as a therapist.

But now take it even further. What kind of cognitive distortions may be present in your automatic thoughts? Refer back to the list presented earlier in this chapter. If you felt emotionally reactive in your past experience, you can be sure that some kind of cognitive distortion was present. You may not have known it then, but now that you are older and have some distance from these events, you may be able to identify the kinds of thinking that led to difficult feelings in the past. Are any of these ideas and feelings still part of your interactions today? What self-statements might you use to challenge these old distortions? What alternate behavioral responses might follow if you are successful at challenging old or current emotional reactivities? Use this chart to go through this process:

Situation or Event	Automatic Thought	Cognitive Distortion	Emotion	Challenging Self-Statement	Alternate Response

Now, let's see where you might have learned to be emotionally reactive. Can you remember times when your father, your mother, your older or younger siblings were engaged in difficult relationships? What got your father or mother to react? Who was best at eliciting difficult emotions from them? What were the events or situations in which these difficult emotions were elicited? Use the same chart to identify what may have been going on with significant others in your life? Do any of them have similar thinking and reactions to what you experience in yourself? What was it like for you when you were not directly involved but watched others in problematic interactions?

Okay, now take a look at the relationships between your parents and your grandparents. Did any of them ever get into difficulty with each other? Could any of your grandparents push the buttons of their children or their daughters/sons-in-law? Did your parents get their parents to be emotionally reactive? What were the circumstances? What were the feelings generated and what thoughts must have been present to get to those emotions? Bowen believed in a multigenerational transmission process in families: Did any reactive thoughts and feelings make it all the way to you over several generations of use? These will likely be the most difficult ones for you to challenge, but it is worth the effort.

If you have already been seeing families in your practice, either as a student or a professional, what ways of being in a family, events in your work, or therapy situations stirred negative feelings in you—even if you chose not to act on them? Were the emotions you generated familiar to you or new to you? Were they part of some of the old patterns in your family-of-origin or something completely unexpected? This will be the area in which it is most important to use the chart above. I would urge all current and future family practitioners to follow Dattilio's (2002) recommendation and carry a pad and pencil with them throughout the day. At the end of each session, note the times in which you felt emotions that interfered with your therapeutic presence or your ability to stay focused. What thoughts were associated with these times? How did you behave or react? What can you do to challenge such thoughts and feelings right in the session the next time they occur?

Finally, let's think about supervision. Over the years, I have watched a lot of students and young practitioners rob themselves of their best work by worrying about the supervision process. This is especially true when they know that supervisors are watching their work. We can start with the idea that you *are* being watched and observed. If you start to ask yourself a set of evaluative questions, you almost always will be lost. Interfering questions might include: "How am I doing?" "What does the watching person think of me?" "Will I figure out the right thing to do?" These questions have a strong tendency to end in a negative judgment: "I am not doing so well." "I don't even know how to start, and how much worse could that get?" "My supervisor is so important to me: He or she probably thinks I am an idiot." "I can't even fully grasp the problem the family is presenting: I will never figure out how to help them." It is not too hard to see the cognitive distortions involved in these statements, and the more "awful-izing" we do in relation to these distortions, the worse we feel in therapy and the worse we do with the family. How would you challenge these ideas? Maybe you wouldn't even start with the ideas, but rather with the questions. You might consider how different your work might go during supervision if you started with these questions:

- What is it like for me to meet this family?
- What interests me about the family and the people in it?
- What do I need to do first to engage them, make them feel safe, or find a focus to our work together?

These are questions about process, and they will take you out of self-evaluation and into contact with the family you want to serve almost immediately.

 ## Where to Go From Here

People interested in cognitive-behavior therapy as it is applied to individuals and families will find a great deal of help and support at:

The Association for Behavior and Cognitive Therapies (ABCT), formerly the
Association for Advancement of Behavior Therapy (AABT)
305 Seventh Avenue, 16th Floor
New York, NY 10001-6008
Phone: 212-647-1890 or 800-685-AABT
Website: **http://www.abct.org**

In Pennsylvania, the Beck Institute offers postdoctoral work and short courses at:

Beck Institute for Cognitive Therapy and Research
GSB Building, City Line and Belmont Avenues, Suite 700
Bala Cynwyd, PA 19004-1610
Phone: 610-664-3020
Website: **http://www.beckinstitute.org**

Recommended Readings

Atwood, J. D. (1992). *Family therapy: A systemic behavioral approach.* Chicago: Nelson Hall. Atwood does an excellent job of integrating systemic perspectives with cognitive-behavioral interventions. Her approach covers both marriage and family issues with special sections devoted to adolescents and families in transition.

Beck, A. T. (1988). *Love is never enough.* New York: Harper & Row. This is cognitive therapy applied to the coupled relationship, and it provides a good foundation for understanding how couples get in trouble with each other and what they can do to change.

Beck, J. S. (2005). *Cognitive therapy for challenging problems: What to do when the basics don't work.* New York: Guilford. In this book, Judith Beck follows up on her 1995 book on the basics of cognitive therapy, and focuses on ways to intervene with the most difficult of problems. Although not specifically directed to families, the book nonetheless offers interventions that can be adapted to any population.

Dattilio, F. M. (1998). *Case studies in couple and family therapy: Systemic and cognitive perspectives.* New York: Guilford Press. Dattilio is one of the most articulate and integrative of the cognitive-behavioral family therapists, and this book provides an excellent set of examples for experiencing this approach in action.

Ellis, A. (2000). Rational-emotive behavior marriage and family therapy. In A. M. Horne (Ed.), *Family counseling and therapy* (pp. 489–514). Itasca, IL: F. E. Peacock. Ellis is the father of **rational-emotive therapy**, and his approach has evolved into a cognitive-behavioral model that is fully explicated in this chapter.

Falloon, I. R. H. (1988). *Handbook of behavioral family therapy.* New York: Guilford Press. Falloon edits a broad text that covers multiple behavioral interventions as they are applied to families. Each intervention is tailored to specific problem areas within a family.

Gottman, J. (1997). *The heart of parenting: Raising an emotionally intelligent child.* New York: Simon and Schuster. This is the more popular version of the extensive research that Gottman and his colleagues did on *meta-emotions* at their Seattle institute and the University of Washington. The book supports both the relevance of Haim Ginott's (1965/1994, 1969/1971) communication model for parents and children and Goleman's (1995) work on emotional intelligence.

Gottman, J. (1999). *The marriage clinic—A scientifically based marital therapy.* New York: Norton. In terms of evidence-based work with couples, this is the most used book in the United States. Gottman's assessments and interventions are all measurable, and they all are designed to end interactions that research indicates will lead to divorce, and to adopt behaviors that enhance marriage, increase satisfaction, and reduce the probability of divorce.

Horne, A. M., & Sayger, T. V. (2000). Behavioral approaches to couple and family therapy. In A. M. Horne (Ed.), *Family counseling and therapy* (pp. 454–488). Itasca, IL: F. E. Peacock. A complete explication of behavioral techniques and interventions as they apply to the couple and the family.

Krumboltz, J. D., & Krumboltz, H. B. (1972). *Changing children's behavior.* Englewood Cliffs, NJ: Prentice Hall. This is a classic work that is rather hard to find, but it is an excellent guide for both parents and practitioners who want to use behavioral techniques in everyday life with their children. The book is loaded with examples that highlight the principles involved, and the focus is on good process as much as desired outcome.

Schwebel, A. I., & Fine, M. A. (1994). *Understanding and helping families: A cognitive-behavioral approach.* Hillsdale, NJ: Lawrence Erlbaum. This book is currently out of print, but it brings together both the process and steps involved in cognitive-behavioral family therapy and the application of the behavioral family life education model. Theory and concepts are applied to family health, addressing assessment through cognitive and behavioral processes in families.

DVD Reference

The cognitive-behavioral video is an adaptation of an actual case conducted by Dr. Frank Dattilio, a distinguished cognitive-behavioral family therapist. We join the video as Dr. Bitter conceptualizes the family systemically; throughout the demonstration, however, he also will focus on developing a clear understanding of the underlying cognitions and cognitive schemas that are at the foundation of the family's dysfunction. The fighting that occurs among the family members is a direct result of everyone believing that he or she should be in charge of the family all the time. The young woman also is fighting against herself, feeling that if she does not challenge her parents and fight every effort to interfere with her power, she will become weak and humiliated, similar to the way she used to be. Toward the end of the video, the therapist has identified the irrational ideas that are part of the young woman's process and, together, the therapist and the client are ready to challenge the truth of them.

References

Adler, A. (1932). *What life should mean to you*. London: George Allen & Unwin.

Atwood, J. D. (1992). *Family therapy: A systemic behavioral approach*. Chicago: Nelson Hall.

Bandura, A. (1969). *Principles of behavior modification*. New York: Holt, Rinehart, & Winston.

Bandura, A. (1977). *Social learning theory*. Englewood Cliffs, NJ: Prentice Hall.

Bandura, A. (1997). *Self-efficacy: The exercise of control*. New York: W. H. Freeman.

Bandura, A., & Walters, R. (1963). *Social learning and personality development*. New York: Holt, Rinehart, & Winston.

Baucom, D. H., Epstein, N., Rankin, L. A., & Burnett, C. K. (1996). Assessing relationship standards: The inventory of specific relationship standards. *Journal of Family Psychology, 10*, 72–88.

Baucom, D. H., Epstein, N., Sayers, S., & Sher, T. G. (1989). The role of cognitions in marital relationships: Definitional, methodological, and conceptual issues. *Journal of Consulting and Clinical Psychology, 57*, 31–38.

Baucom, D., Shoham, V., Mueser, K., Davido, A., & Sickle, T. (1998). Empirically supported couple and family interventions for marital distress and adult mental health problems. *Journal of Consulting and Clinical Psychology, 66*, 53–88.

Beck, A. T. (1979). *Cognitive therapy and the emotional disorders*. New York: International Universities Press.

Beck, A. T. (1988). *Love is never enough*. New York: Harper & Row.

Beck, J. S. (1995). *Cognitive therapy: Basics and beyond*. New York: Guilford Press.

Beck, J. S. (2005). *Cognitive therapy for challenging problems: What to do when the basics don't work*. New York: Guilford.

Becker, C. B., & Zayfert, C. (2001). Integrating DBT-based techniques and concepts to facilitate exposure treatment for PTSD. *Cognitive Behavioral Practice, 8*, 107.

Biglan, A., Lewin, L., & Hops, H. (1990). A contextual approach to the problem of aversive practices in families. In G. R. Patterson (Ed.), *Depression and aggression in family interaction* (pp. 103–129). Hillsdale, NJ: Erlbaum.

Christensen, A., & Jacobson, N. S. (2000). *Reconcilable differences*. New York: Guilford.

Corcoran, K., & Fischer, J. (2000). *Measures for clinical practice*. New York: Free Press

Cormier, S., & Nurius, P. S. (2003). *Interviewing and change strategies for helpers: Fundamental skills and cognitive behavioral interventions* (5th ed.). Pacific Grove, CA: Brooks/Cole.

Dattilio, F. M. (1989). A guide to cognitive marital therapy. In P. A. Keller & S. R. Heyman (Eds.), *Innovations in clinical practice: A source book*. (Vol. 8, pp. 27–42). Sarasota, FL: Professional Resource Exchange, Inc.

Dattilio, F. M. (1990). Una guida alla teràpia di coppià àd orientàsmento cognitivistà. *Terapia Familiare*, No. 33 (Luglio) 17–34.

Dattilio, F. M. (1992). Les thérapies cognitives de couple. *Journal De Thérapie Comportmentale et Cognitive*, Mai Vol. 2(2), 17–25.

Dattilio, F. M. (1993a). Un abordaje cognitivo en la terapia de parejas. *Clínica Psicologica*, 2(1), Abril, 44–57.

Dattilio, F. M. (1993b). Cognitive techniques with couples and families. *The Family Journal, 1*(1), 51–65.

Dattilio, F. M. (1995) Cognitive-behavior therapy in Egypt. *Journal of Cognitive Psychotherapy* Vol. 9(4) Winter, 285–286.

Dattilio, F. M. (1998). *Case studies in couple and family therapy: Systemic and cognitive perspectives.* New York: Guilford Press.

Dattilio, F. M. (2001). Cognitive-behavior family therapy: Contemporary myths and misconceptions. *Contemporary Family Therapy, 31*(1), 15–30.

Dattilio, F. M. (2002). Pad and pencil techniques. In R. E. Watts (Ed.), *Techniques in marriage and family counseling* (Vol. 2, pp. 45–47). Alexandria, VA: American Counseling Association.

Dattilio, F. M. (2005a). Restructuring family schemas: A cognitive-behavioral perspective. *Journal of Marital and Family Therapy, 31*(1), 15–30.

Dattilio, F. M. (2005b). The critical component of cognitive restructuring in couples therapy: A case study. *Australian and New Zealand Journal of Family Therapy, 26*(2), June, 73–81.

Dattilio, F. M. (2005c). Cognitive-behavior therapy with couples (pp. 77–85). In G. O. Gabbard, J. S. Beck, & J. Holmes (Eds.) *Oxford Textbook of Psychotherapy.* Oxford, UK: Oxford University Press.

Dattilio, F. M. (2006). Restructuring schemas from family-of-origin in couples therapy. *Journal of Cognitive Psychotherapy, 20*(4), 359–373.

Dattilio, F. M., & Bahadur, M. (2005). Cognitive-behavioral therapy with an East Indian family. *Contemporary Family Therapy, 27*(3), 367–382.

Dattilio, F. M., & Epstein, N. B. (2003). Cognitive-behavioral couple and family therapy. In T. L. Sexton, G. R. Weekes, and M. S. Robbins (Eds.), (147–175), *The family therapy handbook.* New York: Routledge.

Dattilio, F. M., & Epstein, N. B. (2005). The role of cognitive-behavioral interventions in couple and family therapy. *Journal of Marital and Family Therapy, 31*(1), 7–13.

Dattilio, F. M., Epstein, N. B., & Baucom, D. H. (1998). An introduction to cognitive-behavioral therapy with couples and families. In F. M. Dattilio (Ed.), *Case studies in couple and family therapy: Systemic and cognitive perspectives* (pp. 1–36). New York: Guilford Press.

Dattilio, F. M., & Padesky, C. A. (1990). *Cognitive therapy with couples.* Sarasota, FL: Professional Resource Press.

Eidelson, R. J., & Epstein, N. (1982). Cognition and relationship maladjustment: Development of a measure of dysfunctional relationship beliefs. *Journal of Consulting and Clinical Psychology, 50,* 715–720.

Ellis, A. (1977). The nature of disturbed marital interactions. In A. Ellis & R. Grieger (Eds.), *Handbook of rational-emotive therapy* (pp. 170–176). New York: Springer.

Ellis, A. (1982). Rational-emotive family therapy. In A. M. Horne & M. M. Ohlsen (Eds.), *Family counseling and therapy* (pp. 302–328). Itasca, IL: F. E. Peacock.

Ellis, A. (1994). *Reason and emotion in psychotherapy* (rev.). New York: Kensington. (Original work published 1962)

Ellis, A. (1995). Rational-emotive behavior therapy. In R. J. Corsini & D. Wedding (Eds.), *Current psychotherapies* (5th ed., pp. 162–196). Itasca, IL: F. E. Peacock.

Ellis, A. (1997). The evolution of Albert Ellis and rational emotive behavior therapy. In J. K. Zeig (Ed.), *The evolution of psychotherapy: The third conference* (pp. 69–82). New York: Brunner/Mazel.

Ellis, A. (2000). Rational-emotive behavior marriage and family therapy. In A. M. Horne (Ed.), *Family counseling and therapy* (pp. 489–514). Itasca, IL: F. E. Peacock.

Falloon, I. R. H. (1988). *Handbook of behavioral family therapy.* New York: Guilford Press.

Fiske, S. T., & Taylor, S. E. (1991). *Social cognition* (2th ed.). New York: McGraw Hill.

Forgatch, M. S., & Patterson, G. R. (1998). Behavioral family therapy. In F. M. Dattilio (Ed.), *Case studies in couple and family therapy: Systemic and cognitive perspectives.* New York: Guilford.

Ginott, H. G. (1971). *Between parent and teenager.* New York: Avon. (Original work published 1969)

Ginott, H. G. (1994). Between *parent and child.* New York: Avon. (Original work published 1965)

Goleman, D. (1995). *Emotional intelligence: Why it can matter more than IQ.* New York: Bantam.

Gottman, J. (1997). *The heart of parenting: Raising an emotionally intelligent child.* New York: Simon and Schuster.

Gottman, J. (1999). *The marriage clinic—A scientifically based marital therapy.* New York: Norton.

Gottman, J. M. (2000). *Marital therapy: A research-based approach—clinician's manual.* Seattle, WA: The Gottman Institute.

Horne, A. M., & Sayger, T. V. (2000). Behavioral approaches to couple and family therapy. In A. M. Horne (Ed.), *Family counseling and therapy* (pp. 454–488). Itasca, IL: F. E. Peacock.

Huber, C. H. & Baruth, L. G. (1989). *Rational-emotive family therapy: A systems perspective.* New York: Springer.

Kazdin, A. E. (2001). *Behavior modification in applied settings* (6th ed.). Pacific Grove, CA: Brooks/Cole.

Krumboltz, J. D., & Krumboltz, H. B. (1972). *Changing children's behavior.* Englewood Cliffs, NJ: Prentice Hall.

Liberman, R. P. (1970). Behavioral approaches to couple and family therapy. *American Journal of Orthopsychiatry, 40,* 106–118.

Minuchin, S. (1974). *Families and family therapy.* Cambridge, MA: Harvard University Press.

Nichols, M. P., & Schwartz, R. C. (2004). *Family therapy: Concepts and methods* (6th ed.). Boston: Allyn & Bacon.

Patterson, G. R. (1980). Mothers: The unacknowledged victims. *Monographs of the Society for Research in Child Development, 45*(5, serial no. 186).

Patterson, G. R. (1985). Beyond technology: The next stage in developing an empirical base for parent training. In L. L'Abate (Ed.), *Handbook of family psychology and therapy* (Vol. II). Homewood, IL: Dorsey Press.

Patterson, G. R., & Forgatch, M. S. (1987). *Parents and adolescents living together (Vol. 1): The basics.* Eugene, OR: Castalia.

Pavlov, I. P. (1927/2003). *Conditioned reflexes.* New York: Dover Publications. (Original work published 1927)

Pedersen, P. B., Draguns, J. G., Lonner, W. J., & Trimble (Eds.). (2002). *Counseling across cultures* (5th ed.). Thousand Oaks, CA: Sage.

Pretzer, J. L., Epstein, N., & Fleming, B. (1991). The marital attitude survey: A measure of dysfunctional attributions and expectancies. *Journal of Cognitive Psychotherapy, 5,* 13–148.

Schwebel, A. I., & Fine, M. A. (1994). *Understanding and helping families: A cognitive-behavioral approach.* Hillsdale, NJ: Lawrence Erlbaum.

Sexton, T. L., & Alexander, J. F. (2002). Family-based empirically supported interventions. *The Counseling Psychologist, 30,* 238–261.

Skinner, B. F. (1953). *Science and human behavior.* New York: MacMillan.

Skinner, B. F. (1974). *About behaviorism.* New York: Knopf.

Spiegler, M. D., & Guevremont, D. C. (2003). *Contemporary behavior therapy* (4th ed.). Pacific Grove, CA: Brooks/Cole.

Stuart, R. B. (1969). Operant-interpersonal treatment of marital discord. *Journal of Counseling and Clinical Psychology, 33,* 675–682.

Stuart, R. B. (1980). *Helping couples change: A social learning approach to marital therapy.* Champaign. IL: Research Press.

Watts, R. (2001). Integrating cognitive and systemic perspectives: An interview with Frank M. Dattilio. *The Family Journal 9*(4), 422–476.

Webster-Stratton, C., & Herbert, M. (1994). *Troubled families—problem children.* Chichester, England: Wiley.

Wolpe, J. (1990). *The practice of behavior therapy* (4th ed.). Elmsford, NY: Pergamon Press.

Young, J. E. (1999). *Cognitive therapy for personality disorders: A schema-focused approach* (3rd ed.). Sarasota, FL: Professional Resource Press.

CHAPTER 14

Parenting for the 21st Century

Introduction

A Short History of Parenting

Key Concepts

Techniques

Summary and Multicultural Evaluation

Recommended Reading

References

Introduction

Not all family therapists subscribe to the idea of teaching parents. Indeed, many of the most prominent of the systemic practitioners (Bowen, Whitaker, Minuchin, Haley, and the other strategic therapists) repeatedly have declined to specify what they believe would constitute adequate parenting—and the idea of actually teaching parents to function better would not fit within their models. Among those approaches that were willing to define good parenting, three models have provided the core of the most-used programs in the United States: These models are the Adlerian/Dreikursian model; the communications models (Ginott, Gordon, and Satir); and the behavioral models (Gottman, Krumboltz, Meichenbaum, Patterson, and Skinner). There are several reasons for including a chapter on effective parenting in this book: (1) Family practitioners working in schools, hospitals, community agencies, and clinics are expected to address parenting issues in one form or another with most of the families they see; (2) often, the most critical stress point in a marriage is when couples first become parents (Gottman, 1999, Gottman, Katz, & Hooven, 1997); and (3) family coaching, an intermediate step between parent education and family therapy or family counseling is fast becoming a growth industry in the United States, Canada, and Europe. In this chapter, I shall start with the development of parenting approaches over the last 100 years, and I will end with a presentation of the skills and techniques that more than 50 years of research have validated as useful (Allen, Thompson, & Drapeaux, 1997; Brooks, Spearn, Rice, Crocco, Hodgins, & Schaaf, 1988; Burnett, 1988; Campbell & Sutton, 1983; Collins, Maccoby, Steinberg, Hetherington, & Bornstein, 2000; Croake, 1983; Hammett, Omizo, & Loffredo, 1981; Krebs, 1986; Landerholm & Lowenthal, 1993; Mullis, 1999; Nystul, 1982; Pilgrim, Abbey, Hendrickson, & Lerenz, 1998; Sharpley & Poiner, 1980; Snow, Kern, & Penick, 1997; Williams, Omizo, & Abrams, 1984).

A Short History of Parenting

John Broadus Watson was an unlikely candidate to become America's Founding Father of Behaviorism and to make this model the basis for one of the first parenting manuals in the United States. Born in Greenville, South Carolina, to an alcoholic father and a fundamentalist, Baptist mother, John was actually named after a well-known evangelist in that part of the country (Hoffman, 1994). His mother wanted him to be a preacher, but John would have nothing of it. He did not do particularly well at school or in life until he was rescued by Professor Moore at Furman University, who got him interested in the psychological sciences and sent him on to the University of Chicago. Watson was heavily influenced in his early career by the classical conditioning theories advanced by the Russian neurologist/psychologist, Ivan Pavlov (1927/2003). Indeed, Watson conducted similar studies to those of Pavlov, using rats in mazes, and studying the capacity of rhesus monkeys to mimic what they saw. In 1913, Watson wrote what amounted to an academic manifesto, calling for behaviorism to become the basis for the psychological sciences (see Watson, 1925/1970).

Later, at Johns Hopkins University, Watson began to combine Pavlov's conditioning theories with Thorndike's Darwinism. He initiated a longitudinal study of mother–child bonding and child **development** that included a special observation chamber he built at a Washington, DC, hospital. He became convinced that Pavlov's model could be applied to children, and he envisioned a kind of utopian world in which parents would use his methods to raise perfectly happy and healthy children (Hoffman, 1994).

It was during this period that Watson conducted his famous experiment with Little Albert and the rat. By pairing a loud noise (clanging cymbals), an unconditioned stimulus or US, with a white rat (a conditioned stimulus or CS), Watson taught Little Albert to be afraid of white mice. In this experiment, fear became the unconditioned response (or UR) and later the conditioned response (or CR). This learning could also be *generalized* by using a white rabbit and even a white beard to stimulate the fear response. This experiment appeared to demonstrate that phobias, for example, were learned responses. It is not clear whether Watson or others invented the "cure," but eventually behaviorists demonstrated that reintroducing the white rat (or rabbit) at a distance while calming the youngster would end the fear. Again, reducing that distance in steps while continuing to calm the child was the key, and it had to progress over many, many trials before the child could hold the animal in his lap. This process is the basis for what we now call systematic desensitization (Wolpe, 1990).

Watson began to write articles on child rearing for popular magazines ranging from *Cosmopolitan* and *McCall's* to *The New Republic*. In 1922, Watson was invited to offer a series of lectures on behaviorism at the New School for Social Research. His courses were popular with students, and he remained there until he was fired in 1926 for sexual misconduct.

In 1928, Watson produced a very successful series of articles for *McCall's*, again on child rearing, that was published later that year as *Psychological Care of Infant and Child* (Watson, 1928). This was really the first widely read parenting manual available in the United States. His approach advocated treating children like little adults. He wanted parents to be objective and aloof. He was not in favor of mother–child bonding, cuddling children, or even kissing and hugging them, except in a perfunctory manner just before bed. Perhaps remembering his own mother–child experiences, he warned that too much closeness wrecked adolescents and as young adulthood approached, it could ruin a child's vocational future. Watson was not even sure that children should grow up in families: He suggested that there might be some other environment in which children could be raised more scientifically with better results. In the 1930s, Watson returned almost exclusively to advertising. His children would later note that he was, as he preached, a distant father, who became quite self-absorbed in his middle years (Hoffman, 1994).

Alfred Adler reached the height of his popularity at about the same time that John Watson was experiencing his. Adler's (1927) book, *Understanding Human Nature*, was the first popular psychology book to sell in the hundreds of thousands of copies. Adler's (1930) approach to children was decidedly more phenomenological in orientation, and he advocated a much more personally engaged form of parenting and teaching than would be characteristic of behaviorism for years to come. Adler rejected a psychology built on instincts and biology, as in Freud's model, or on reflexes and environmental controls, as in Watson's model. He was more impressed with the capacity of even young children to form goals and to make individual choices in the service of reaching those goals. Adler conceptualized his theory as a **psychology of use**. While heredity and environment played their parts, it was what the person made of these building blocks that really shaped his or her life.

Even though Adler never used the language of behaviorism, in essence his approach placed an interpreting organism (the person or child) in between perceived stimuli and human response. He believed that stimuli, experiences, and activities all were perceived by individual humans and given meaning (or interpreted) before each person decided on (and chose) a response. In this sense, his learning theory is very similar to the cognitive-behavioral model we considered in the last chapter.

Adler believed that all human behavior was goal-oriented. Sometimes the goals are immediate or short-term, but people also strive for the more long-term life-goals of actualization, completion, or even perfection. Such completion goals are not inherent in the environment: They are created by the very people who strive for them. Human beings anticipate the ends they choose, and accept or desire whatever consequences are associated with those ends. Indeed, it is those anticipated endpoints that frame the way in which human organisms interpret experiences and evaluate themselves in relation to all other stimuli to which they attend.

The fundamental goal for children—and indeed, for all of us—is to belong, to have a place, to feel that we have worth and count with the people in our lives. There are hundreds of ways for individuals to meet this goal through cooperation, contribution, connection, shared competence, caring, compassion, and courage. Those who lack some or all of these capacities will have a tendency to find ways of belonging that are not so useful: They will make mistakes in how they see self, others, and life, and they may even develop useless goals.

Rudolf Dreikurs (1940a, 1940b), a child psychologist and colleague of Adler's, addressed the child's mistaken attempts to belong when he developed a typology of mistaken goals for children's misbehavior. These goals (attention-getting, power-struggles, revenge, and demonstration of inadequacy) were immediate, short-term motivations that accounted for misbehavior in young children. They are used to help parents understand the purposes for their children's disruptive behaviors, as well as to give structure to family interviews (see Dreikurs, 1950). By 1948, Dreikurs had developed the first of many books on how to raise children effectively, basing his approach on the development of a democratic atmosphere and social equality between parent and child (Dreikurs, 1948/1992). His model stood in opposition to both **authoritarian** and **permissive** approaches to child-rearing. Today, we would call this approach authoritative-responsive parenting (Baumrind, 1968, 1995). Dreikurs and Soltz (1964/1991) would eventually team up to write one of the most-used parenting books of all time, *Children: The Challenge*; they taught us that disturbing behaviors in children were a sign of **discouragement**, and the antidote was the application of **encouragement** and the use of **natural** and **logical consequences** (Dreikurs & Grey, 1968/1989).

In the last chapter, I noted the importance of Skinner's (1953, 1974) operant-conditioning model: Similar to Adler's model, Skinner believed that it was the outcome, the endpoint, or the result that really controlled and determined behavior. Behaviors that were reinforced continued and developed while behaviors that were not reinforced diminished and eventually extinguished. Further, large, complex behaviors could be shaped by breaking them down into smaller, more achievable actions. Usually, **continuous**

Dr. Eva Dreikurs Ferguson

Rudolf Dreikurs

primary reinforcement is prescribed initially for the step-by-step shaping of new behaviors. Intermittent reinforcement, however, is the strongest behavioral motivator. Skinner shared with Adler a belief that authoritarian, aversive parenting was usually non-productive. The use of corporal punishment,[1] coupled with aversive interactions, seldom worked and often made family life worse rather than better.

Bandura (1969) and Krumboltz and Krumboltz (1972) both noted that when a parent effectively administered reinforcements, they became another reinforcer, a *social reinforcer* who also could serve as a model for what was expected. It is this kind of social reinforcement that makes effective parenting both possible and enjoyable.

We know whether parents and children are functioning well by the way they communicate. Effective communication is not only important to family life: It is central to every aspect of shared living. John Dewey (1916), the great American educator and philosopher, noted that there was more than a linguistic connection between the words common, community, and communication. We are a community by virtue of the things we share in common, and we come to understand what we have in common through communication. What a person thinks is understood through talk: that is, through one person expressing thoughts and feelings to another. When our thoughts are rational and congruent with our feelings, the actions that follow tend to make human sense. Irrational or extreme thoughts tend to produce disturbing and extreme feelings that lead to ineffective and often pathological behaviors.

As I noted in the chapter on the human validation process model, Satir (1983; Satir & Baldwin, 1983) introduced the notion of a nurturing triad as a foundation for parenting: She hoped that two adults could form a team that would work in favor of the growth and development of the child. She believed that children needed a core of self-esteem if they were to become all that they could be (if they were to actualize their potential), and parents could bolster that self-esteem with positive attributions, encouragement, and by tending to the emotional development of young people. For Satir, congruent communication involved expressive clarity coupled with emotional honesty.

How many of us, when we were little, walked in on a heated argument between our parents and asked if they were fighting. If our parents responded that they were not fighting, that they were simply having "a discussion," their communication told us that our eyes and ears were dysfunctional and could not be trusted. Clarity and emotional honesty would have been served much better if the parents had said, "Yes, we are having a fight, but it is not about you. We will be okay, and you will be okay, and Mom and Dad need some time alone to work this problem out."

Satir (1987) noted that when distress increased in the family, each family member tended to adopt a communication stance that either facilitated problem resolution or exacerbated it. The four stress positions of blaming, placating, super-reasonable, and irrelevant have already been described (see the Satir chapter). They represent four ways in which individuals attempt to protect their self-worth when faced with difficult challenges; in actuality, these communication modes only make things worse. An Adlerian psychologist from Israel, Nira Kfir (1981), noted similar stances in relation to stressful situations, calling her positions **significance, pleasing, control**, and **comfort** respectively. These parallel stances describe both the communication (Satir) and the goals sought (Kfir) in many parent–child interactions. Satir described congruent communications as ones in which the speaker took into account personal needs, the needs and positions of others, and the context in which communication would take place. Her use of congruent communication requires what Adler called social interest, paying attention to the welfare of others as well as self. Bitter (1987) linked these two models in terms of theory, and Main (1986) applied them to parenting styles.

Satir was not alone in her emphasis on communication in parenting. Both **Thomas Gordon** (1970), a student of Carl Rogers, and Haim Ginott (1965/1994, 1969/1971) built entire parenting programs around effective communication with children. Gordon's **parent effectiveness training** would later be integrated with Dreikurs' democratic approach and would serve as the basis for the two largest parent-training programs in the United States (Dinkmeyer, McKay, & Dinkmeyer, 1997; Popkin, 1993). Ginott's communication model is now largely considered to be the foundation for John Gottman's **emotion coaching** approach to parenting (Gottman & DeClaire, 1997).

In cases in which either parents or children exhibit extreme behavioral problems or children have special difficulties such as autism, effective parenting still requires carefully monitored programs based on operant conditioning. Gerald Patterson (1980; Patterson & Forgatch, 1987) was one of the first to develop modern behavioral parent training models, and we still refer to his approach when the severity of behavioral interactions warrants it.

We now shall consider how these merging models contribute to our understanding of parenting and child-rearing. We also shall consider the latest recommendations for effective parenting.

Key Concepts

Let's start with a few questions: Where did you learn to be a parent? If you are not a parent yet, what will be your sources for learning effective methods? Will you do what your parents did with you? Where do you think they learned to be parents? Will you read a book? Will you become part of a parent study group? What methods of discipline were used on you? Will you keep any of those methods? Discard any? Design a whole new approach? What constitutes an emotionally/cognitively healthy child today? What can parents do that will make a significant difference?

There was a tribe of Native Americans from the northwest part of the United States that used to train their children not to cry within 3 days of being born. The method they used involved the parent holding a hand over the baby's mouth and nose when it cried until the baby passed out. Although the process "worked," it also caused brain damage as well as other difficulties. At one time, there was a purpose to the procedure: Perhaps crying babies would scare away wild game needed for food or give away the location of a camp during periods of war. The problem was that this method was still used by some parents into the 1900s, long after its usefulness had disappeared.

European heritage includes methods of parenting that are even more antiquated. We have to go back to the 16th century to find the societies in which current practices made sense. Those European societies were organized in strict hierarchies with kings, princes, and other nobility at the top and laborers and serfs at the bottom. Let us say that a child in a serf's family awakened one day, no longer wanting to cut hay for the lord of the manor. Or perhaps the child wanted to run away or try to impersonate a nobleman. These ideas and positions could easily get the child killed, so parents had to teach that child to "know his place." Two methods from that autocratic period remain today: One is called reward, used as an incentive or bribe for good behavior, and the other is called punishment,[2] used to curtail bad behavior by imposing authoritarian control. Of the two, the latter was then and is now used more often by parents than the former. Both procedures, however, reflect a belief in the superiority of one person or set of people over others.

Again, these methods, though still in prominent use, are out of date by anywhere from 300 to 400 years. Most western cultures currently exist within democratic states where the principle of equality is prized, if not fully enacted. In these countries, there is increasing evidence that equal rights for all citizens will eventually be won. No single culture will be allowed to dominate all others. Women will be able to stand equal with men before the law. Age, creed, color, and even sexual/affectional orientation will no longer be barriers to full participation in community life and our legal systems of justice. As a set of western nations, we still are working on these developments, but change is coming. Perhaps the last group to gain equal rights will be children.

It is not lost on children, even today, that they have standing in a democratic society. Attempts at child-control and imposition of adult authority are met with rebellion, either overt or covert, from a very early age. It only takes a trip on Saturday mornings to a restaurant or shopping center to demonstrate quickly that authoritarian parents have been reduced to yelling, screaming, blaming, frustrated, and angry people who fluctuate between coaxing, pleading, or reminding at one moment and outbursts or even public spankings the next. To make matters worse, when things really get out of hand, these same parents then give in—in order to get a little peace and quiet. The myth of external control outside of laboratory conditions has long been known, but authoritarian models still permeate almost everything that parents do with children—and are even reinforced by some popular psychologists (see Dobson, 1996, 2004).

An authoritarian approach is what people in many different cultures have always done. It is what many of our parents did with us. It is "normal." There's only one problem: It doesn't work, and it's not effective.

So what does work? Actually, a whole range of ideas, once considered outrageous, works, including:

- Taking children in as partners;
- Providing guidance and leadership;
- Taking time for training;
- Treating children as growing, developing people with different needs at different times in their lives;
- Giving choices;
- Using natural and logical consequences;
- Providing encouragement, recognition, and positive attention;
- Listening and emotion coaching;
- Negotiations and compromise;
- Modeling respect, cooperation, kindness, caring, compassion, and courage; that is, becoming what Krumboltz and Krumboltz (1972) call *prestigious models*.

One way to characterize the range of current parenting styles is to think of them on a continuum from autocratic/authoritarian to permissive and neglectful. Somewhere in the middle of the continuum would be models that Adlerians call democratic and that Baumrind (1968, 1971, 1991, 1995) refers to as authoritative-responsive. We might draw the continuum like this:

Autocratic/Authoritarian ⟷ Democratic/Authoritative-Responsive ⟷ Permissive ⟷ Neglectful

The autocratic/authoritarian model proceeds from the idea that adults are in charge of children, and that they should control them and demand that they behave. This model presumes that parents know the proper way for children to be and that they should use bribes and arbitrary punishments to keep children in line. Those of us raised in homes that believed in traditional discipline will be very familiar with the autocratic/authoritarian approach. It is characterized by high demand or control and low responsiveness. Here responsiveness refers to the level of warmth, reciprocity, and attachment in the disciplinary relationship between the parent and child.

Toward the other end of the continuum is permissiveness. This approach had its heyday in the late 1940s and the early 1950s when John Dewey's more progressive approach to education was force-merged with Freud's concerns for the fragile ego of the child. Permissiveness assumes that it is either harmful or useless to say "no" to a child, and it is characteristic of parents who will do anything to avoid conflict—regularly giving in to whining and temper-tantrums throughout the day (see Crowder, 2002; Ricker & Crowder, 1998, 2000). Permissive parenting is characterized by high responsiveness and low demand.

Diana Baumrind (1991) notes that there are some parents who are both indifferent to and uninvolved with their children. She calls such parents **neglectful**. This parenting style ignores children and their needs as long as possible. When interacting with them, such a parent often will respond just enough to get the child to go away. They are the parents whom structural family therapists call *disengaged*, seeking a goal Adlerians call a demonstration of inadequacy so that the children will leave them alone. Neglectful parents are characterized by both low demand and low responsiveness.

The parents who have been most effective over the last half century are those who fall in the middle of the continuum, who prepare their children for living in a democracy by helping them to develop their own perspectives, develop their own voices and opinions, and learn from the natural and logical consequences of daily living. This model, most often called democratic parenting or authoritative-responsive parenting, asks parents to be true leaders and models in the family. It involves an active engagement of children based on (a) giving them choices, (b) listening to and acknowledging their thinking and feeling, and (c) guiding them in a non-threatening/non-punitive manner. This approach is characterized by reasonable demands and adequate responsiveness.

A story Oscar Christensen tells about breakfast will make this range of parenting styles clearer (Christensen, 2004). When he was little, his mother decided what he would have for breakfast each morning. She made oatmeal mush and she cooked it to the consistency of paste. Needless to say, he wouldn't eat it. He played with it: Sometimes, he swirled it in his bowl; sometimes, he would pack it in his spoon and shoot it at his sister. Then his mother would make the second decision about him that day: She would declare that he was a bad boy and send him from the table. When the phone would ring around 11:00 A.M., Christensen would run to the kitchen to get graham crackers. Worse, his mother let him get them, because she felt a bit guilty for sending him from the table earlier. So he ate the graham crackers, and then he wasn't hungry at lunchtime.

Now, if you contrast that with the treatment his cousins got at his aunt's house, it seems quite different—even though the end is the same. In that house, there were 20 different cereals, because the mother could never say "no" to what the children requested or wanted. And each child was allowed to sample as many different cereals each morning as she or he wished. When his cousins were very young, the sampling could last until almost 11:00 A.M., and these kids were not hungry at lunchtime either.

The parents who would be most effective in teaching their children how to handle life would offer the child a choice: "What's it going to be: Captain Crunch or scrambled eggs?" Notice that this is not an unlimited choice in which anything goes. Even so, a child might say, "I want Frosted Flakes." An authoritative-responsive parent could reply that he or she under-stands the child's desire for Frosted Flakes, ". . . and maybe we can have them next week, but this morning we have Captain Crunch or scrambled eggs: Which is it going to be?"

Some parents worry that the child will choose not to eat at all, but that is also an acceptable choice to make—even for a 3-year-old. The natural consequence of not eating is that the child will get hungry and, perhaps, make a better decision about breakfast the next morning. Okay, let's say the child chooses Captain Crunch. If this child plays with the cereal long enough, it will lose its crunch and taste worse than oatmeal mush ever hoped to taste. Once the milk is poured on, however, the decision is irreversible: There is no way to re-crunch a soggy Captain, so the child will play with it. Now the parent gives the child a second choice for the morning: "What do you want to do, eat properly or get down from the table?" If the child gets down from the table, as any kid with taste buds will do, then that's it until noon. The parent does not have to feel guilty: The child made the choice. It is a logical consequence and, again, the child has the opportunity to make a different choice the next morning.

The authoritative-responsive or democratic parent also takes time for training. In these models, adults try to anticipate what the child will need to know and provide both experience and guidance. How do we train a child, for instance, that a stove is hot? Our parents probably slapped our hands away from the stove. My aunt, who had a degree in child development, would slap her child's hand and say, "No, hot!" You can see what a difference an education can make. It's possible, however, to realize when a child is big enough to push a chair up to the stove and get close to the burners. Wouldn't that be a great time to, perhaps, try an experiment where she or he holds a hand over the burner as it gets hotter? In the end, the children still may burn themselves once or twice: Experience is a potent teacher. But when parents take time to train, some childhood pains can be avoided.

Perhaps the most important aspect of the child that parents need to train relates to the development and expression of emotions (Goleman, 1995; Gottman & DeClaire, 1997). When children are very young and just learning to talk, teaching them the actual words for different emotions is essential. Words link feelings to meaning. School counselors often use large charts with many faces attached to different emotions to help children identify emotions, but parents can do the same thing by drawing a feeling-face or set of feeling-faces on fingers and letting children choose what they feel inside. Noticing that children express different moods and experience different levels of emotions is the first step in attaching words to the emotional diversity within.

Emotion coaching (Gottman & DeClaire, 1997)—that is, when parents engage children and adolescents in teaching them to value emotional experience and language by actively listening for it and reflecting it back to them—has been demonstrated to have many positive effects. Children who are emotion-coached form better attachments with family and peers; they are better problem solvers and do better in both math and reading (even when adjusted for IQ); when faced with stressful circumstances, they stay calmer longer; and when they are at rest, their hearts actually function more efficiently (lower heart rates). Emotion coaching also seems to provide some protection from infectious illness. It also helps young people maintain better moods (with less swings), and it alleviates almost all of the negative effects of divorce, except sadness. And the good news is that parents who emotion coach tend to have more validating marriages and get divorced far less often than the rest of the population. Gottman and his colleagues have demonstrated all of this in longitudinal studies conducted in their laboratory settings in Seattle, Washington (see Gottman, Katz, & Hooven, 1997).

A study by Jackson, Henrickson, and Foshee (1998) produced similar results for authoritative-responsive parenting, including high levels of academic success among European-American and Mexican-American youths. They also noted that this approach to parenting lowers levels of substance use or violence—especially in relation to the children of neglectful parents. In contrast, children of authoritarian parents were more obedient and almost never questioned authority, but they also had low self-esteem and less social competence in school. These children often reported elevated levels of psychological distress.

Earlier in this chapter, I noted that Rudolf Dreikurs (1940a, 1940b, 1948/1992, 1950) identified four goals for children's misbehavior: attention-getting, power struggles, revenge, and demonstrating inadequacy. Each of these immediate goals for children's misbehavior is part of a larger goal: *to belong.* They are mistaken but common ways that children seek to count and be valued within the family and in their community. Parents without training tend to react to mistaken behaviors in ways that actually reinforce useless, negative patterns and lead to ineffective interactions. Indeed with some children, punishments (such as, spanking) can actually become a reinforcer of negative behavior (Krumboltz & Krumboltz, 1972). We see this happen when defiant children continue or increase misbehavior immediately after an aversive response has been applied.

With training and guidance, most parents can learn authoritative-responsive ways to raise their children effectively and actually prevent the emergence of more-difficult and destructive behaviors (and goals) as young people get older. Some of the most effective interventions include the use of *natural* and *logical consequences* (Dreikurs & Grey, 1968/1989), *encouragement* (Dinkmeyer & Dreikurs, 1963/2000), *active listening* and *reflection* (Ginott, 1965/1994, 1969/1971, 1975; Gordon, 1970), *giving choices* and guiding children through problem solving by asking questions. As I have mentioned already, all of these ideas and interventions are central to the most evidence-based parent-education programs in the United States: **STEP: Systematic Training for Effective Parenting** (Dinkmeyer, McKay, & Dinkmeyer, 1997) and **Active Parenting** (Popkin, 1993). Each of these video-based programs is also available in Spanish. For some of the most important research on these programs, see Abbey, Pilgrim, Hendrickson, and Buresh (2000); Abbey, Pilgrim, Hendrickson, and Lorenz (1998); Bernino and Rourke (2003); Ciurczak and Co. (2003); CLAS (Culturally and Linguistically Appropriate Services) Review (2001); Fashimpar (2000); and Mullis (1999).

Techniques

Let's look at two sets of interventions and techniques that have been proven effective in raising children. The first set is for families in which the parents are functional partners and need to understand psychoeducational approaches to child-rearing. The second set is for families in which one or more of the children exhibit extreme and/or disturbing behaviors that threaten the development of the child, as well as the overall functioning of the family.

Positive Parenting for Functional Families

Parenting styles that are common in more harmonious families generally include the effective interventions that follow. These family processes are also encouraged when counselors or therapists are engaged in what behaviorists call functional family counseling or consultation (see Alexander & Parsons, 1973, 1982; Barton & Alexander, 1981) or trained leaders are engaged in *family coaching*: that is, using a psychoeducational model to provide essential information that otherwise competent people might need to be effective parents. These interventions are dramatically different from coaxing, reminding, bribery, yelling at children, spankings, groundings, and other efforts at control. These democratic, authoritative-responsive interventions can be learned, and they act as a preventative approach to child rearing.

Encouragement.   One meaning of encouragement is to build courage, and this courage is needed as family members face life's problems and tasks. In one sense, encouragement is a reinforcement of strengths and capabilities. It is placing value on the child as she or he grows. Encouragement recognizes a job well done, but also acknowledges effort and improvement. Whether approached from a behavioral standpoint (Krumboltz & Krumboltz, 1972) or an Adlerian perspective (Dinkmeyer & Dreikurs, 1963/2000), this kind of reinforcement is directed more at the development of the child than the **shaping** and accomplishment of parent-desired behaviors. What encouragement is not is bribery, arbitrary praise, coaxing, reminding, or demanding. It is having faith that children can learn to handle life, thereby helping children have faith in themselves: Such faith, as the root to the word *encour*agement suggests, comes from the heart. It is expressed in phrases like, "Try it and see"; "You can handle this"; "I know you can work it out," or "I believe in you."

Accentuating the Positive.   In general, children—like the rest of us—tend to grow better in a positive environment. A positive environment is not the same as permissiveness; it is not the same as never saying "no" or saying positive things to children that even they know are not true. It does mean that children do better when they have at least one parent who enjoys having them around, values who they are, has faith in their abilities, and can communicate these to the child. This is what social workers often refer to as a strengths perspective. It is even measurable: If children receive approximately five positive attributions to every negative one, they simply have a better life and grow in more productive ways (see Gottman & DeClaire, 1997). Unfortunately, as Hart and Risley (1995) have noted, positive reinforcement of children tends to decrease as socioeconomic status goes down. That is, the children who most need positive reinforcement too often get it least. Accentuating the positive is (a) noticing what children and other family members do well; (b) appreciating unique talents and contributions; (c) paying attention to those things that families want to see continue; and (d) minimizing mistakes and frustrations.

Natural Consequence.   A natural consequence is what results when parents ask the question: "What would happen if I did nothing?" For instance, a child won't eat breakfast: The natural consequence is that the child will get hungry. If no other food is served or allowed until noon, the child will most likely make a different choice the next morning (Dreikurs & Soltz, 1964/1991). This idea can be used in many more circumstances than parents generally think. It can be employed when a child is about to go off to school in clothing that is less than adequate for the weather or the school rules. It can be used when children leave their lunches behind, forget their homework, or are late for dinner.

Logical Consequence.   A logical consequence is a parent-initiated consequence that is designed to help children learn the needs of a given situation when a natural consequence is either too dangerous or inadequate. If a family lives on a busy avenue, it may be necessary for children to learn to play only in the yard and not in the street. A natural consequence of playing in the street would be either that nothing would happen or the child might get hit by a car. Neither result will provide needed learning. So, in this case, the parent sets a limit (play only in the yard) and if the child goes into the street, the parent brings the child inside until she or he can remember to stay out of the street. Behaviorists like to specify a time that the child will stay in (say, 5–10 minutes), but it works just as well if the child says when he or she is ready to resume play. If a second movement to the street occurs, the parent brings the child in for twice as long, and keeps doubling the time for subsequent occurrences until the child either learns where to play or is inside until the age of 32. In either case, the child is safe, which was the real goal in the first place. This consequence follows directly from the needs of the situation and is therefore logical—as opposed to arbitrary. It is focused on what the child needs to learn, not simply on what the parent demands. It can be implemented with little or no talking, and requires no arguments, outbursts, or aversive interactions (Dreikurs & Grey, 1968/1989).

Active Listening and Reflection.   Thomas Gordon (1970, 2000) was Carl Rogers' student, and he was the first person to coin the term active listening. Active listening is choosing to engage the child from his or her perspective, to see through a child's eyes, experience life as the child does, and to mirror or reflect back the child's ideas and feelings by paraphrasing them. Active listening is designed to communicate understanding to one's child before helping the child with suggestions, advice, or problem solving. It is most important when it mirrors the child's feelings in such a way as to affirm and acknowledge significant emotions in the child (Ginott, 1965/1994, 1969/1971, 1975): This is also the foundation for much of what we now call *emotion coaching*.

Child: John hit me.

Father: You were playing outside with John and something happened that led to John hitting you.

Child: Yes, and I don't even know why.

Father: It surprised you when John hit you and hurt your feelings too.

Child: I don't want to play with John anymore!

Father: You're really angry at John right now.

When children have problems, active listening tells them we understand. It acknowledges their feelings and lets them evolve until some new possibilities emerge and problem solving is then possible.

I-statements.   An **I-statement** states how the parent is feeling or what the parent needs in response to a specific problem. Perhaps an adolescent is playing a CD extremely loudly when a parent is trying to talk on a phone, complete some work at home, or just resting. An I-statement might be something like: "I am feeling stressed, because I am trying to talk on the phone to my sister, and the music is so loud that I cannot hear. Is there a way you can still listen to your music and I can talk to my sister too?" An I-statement keeps the ownership of the problem with the speaker. It avoids blame, criticism, and power struggles, and asks the child to negotiate a win-win settlement to the problem.

Who Owns the Problem?   Gordon (1970) also provides a guide for determining who owns a family problem and what actions should be taken. If a child has some need that is not being met or that is actually thwarted, then the child owns the problem, and the parent is wise to engage in active listening. For example, a child does not like her teacher at school: This is unfortunate, but it does not stop the parents from meeting their needs. The problem belongs to the child, and active listening is the best response.

Let's say that a child dresses for school in shorts in the middle of the winter in Canada. The shorts apparently are not bothering the child, not yet anyway, and they certainly do not interfere with the parents' needs. In this case, there is no problem. The parents should stay out of it and allow natural consequences to teach the child whatever lesson is still to be learned.

There are times, however, when child or adolescent behavior seriously interferes with parental needs, as in the loud-music situation mentioned earlier. In these cases, Gordon suggests I-statements. I-statements invite and almost always are followed by negotiation.

Giving Choices and Negotiations.   When children are small, parents often have to decide what is best for them and let children have only limited choices. Sometimes, the choices are between or among a small number of options: Rather than "What do you want to do today?" a parent might say, "We can go to the park, go bike riding, or go swimming. Which would you like to do?" Even when a choice is so severely limited as to have no behavioral options, the parent can frame the situation as a choice of style or attitude. "It's time for bed. Would you like to go up to bed on your own or would you like me to carry you upside down over my shoulders?"

If it hasn't happened already, about the time a child leaves elementary school for middle school, it is time to start negotiating in good faith most of the issues that come up. The child will have certain needs and desires as will the parents, and sitting down to work out win-win situations is important for the well-being of the family. Negotiation is central to the development of good relations and positive decision making in young people, from pre-adolescence until the child leaves home. The same behavioral agreements and mutual contingency contracts that have been effective with couples also have a place between parents and older children.

Emotion Coaching.   No one is currently more well-known for applying science to couples and families than **John Gottman** (1994, 1996, 1999; Gottman & DeClaire, 1997; Gottman, Katz, & Hooven, 1997). At the heart of his approach to parenting is an emphasis on raising emotionally intelligent children. This starts when parents first engage their infants, try to feel what the child is feeling, and begin to use words both to name the emotions and validate them. Of all the different emotions a child might have, it is by far easier to acknowledge happiness, joy, excitement, delight, and other positive emotions than it is to reflect and validate frustration, anger, rage, hurt, fear, or other negative and sometimes frightening emotions. It is these latter emotions, however, for which coaching and validating are most important.

With very young children, parents can start by drawing different emotional faces on a piece of paper or on the fingers of their hands. Asking little children to find a picture for how they feel is a good way to start teaching them about emotions. There are also relatively inexpensive charts available that have 50 or more faces and feelings on them and that can be used for the same purpose. As young people become adolescents, it is especially important to help them identify what they are feeling, first within family relationships and then within peer relationships. Using active listening to acknowledge and validate these emotions is often needed before inviting youngsters into problem-solving discussions.

Functional families focus on individual as well as family development: Freedom to grow is encouraged by giving children opportunities to experiment, contribute, challenge, and try new behaviors. Parents guide rather than control. They use the techniques above to foster learning rather than compliance. The parents collaborate with each other, and they invite children into appropriate collaborations too.

A Word or Two about Blended Families and Stepfamilies

Everything that we have learned about family systems tells us that, like other systems, they are designed for self-maintenance (or **family homeostasis**), self-renewal, and creative evolvement. When a new person enters an existing system, there will be those parts of the system that try to get the family to return to its original form. We often see children of divorced parents who never quite give up the hope that their biological mothers and fathers will get back together. Still, there are also parts of the system that will engage in renewal and evolvement. Stepparents increase the possibilities of renewal and evolvement if they enter the system as an explorer. How does the system work? What are the rules and processes that help it work? A stepparent may be the new spouse of the children's parent, but not their father or mother.

A stepparent might have an opportunity to be a friend, but that will require patience, caring, active listening, encouragement, accentuating the positive, and natural more than logical consequences—at least initially. Brady-Bunch families never function as smoothly as they appeared to do on television. Accepting that there will be difficulties, a long transition period, and two-steps back, now and then, for every step forward is an important awareness to bring to the process. At least initially, if a serious intervention or discipline is required, the original parent in the system should handle it, and the stepparent should be released by the spouse from any expectation that she or he should take the place of a missing or divorced parent.

A Chart for Growing Children Up.   It is possible to take the techniques and interventions listed above and place them in relation to desired learning outcomes for children and adolescents. In Table 14.1, I have provided a list of desired behaviors along with training processes and consequences appropriate for the different age levels in children. This is a guide that counselors and therapists can employ easily when engaged in functional-family counseling or consultation.

Parenting Difficult Children

When problems in the family and/or the behaviors of children become severe and extremely disturbing, cognitive-behavioral family therapists almost always rely on highly structured operant-conditioning processes, as well as the behavioral management practices developed

Table 14.1	**Living in Harmony With Our Children:** Training and Growth Throughout the Day and Throughout Childhood	
Desired or Expected Behaviors in Children	**Age**	**Training Process and Consequences**
Can sleep through the night	1–2 yrs.	Gradual and natural process (pay attention to child's need for closeness or personal space.
Can sleep through the night	3+ yrs.	If a pattern of waking or getting up at night develops (not due to sickness or other physical problems), let the child cry it out for a minimum of 15 minutes to see if she or he goes back to sleep.
Gets up when awakened	1–4 yrs.	Call child once; have a morning routine.
Gets self up	4+ yrs.	Get the child an alarm clock and make her or him responsible for getting up.
Gets self dressed	4–6 yrs.	Choose clothes the night before *with* the child, and then leave the child to dress self in morning.
Gets self dressed	6+ yrs.	Put clothes where child can get them, and stay out of it.
Eats a good breakfast	1–2 yrs.	Breastfeed if at all possible and gradually introduce healthy solid foods.
Eats a good breakfast	2–4 yrs.	Breastfeed as desired and give child a choice of solid foods: Once the choice is made, stick to it.
Eats a good breakfast	4+ yrs.	Teach the child to make various breakfasts and then stay out of it.
Brushes and flosses teeth	1–2 yrs.	Do it with them; make it fun; do not turn the process into a serious operation.
Brushes and flosses teeth	2–4 yrs.	Make it a game; do it *with* them after meals; gradually increase the thoroughness of the cleaning.
Brushes and flosses teeth	4+ yrs.	Make it the child's responsibility; eliminate sweets and sugar from the house if the child fails to brush and floss regularly.
Cleans room	2–5 yrs.	Make it a game; do it *with* the child initially; model a clean room in the adults' bedroom.
Cleans room	5+ yrs.	Give the responsibility to the child; keep adults' rooms clean; close the door to the child's room if it stays dirty.
Keeps the house clean	2–4 yrs.	Ask the child for help; involve the child in daily chores; make it fun.
Keeps the house clean	4+ yrs.	Have a family meeting; have everyone choose a chore or chores they will do for 1 week; then switch the chores around.
Has a good memory	4+ yrs.	Never remind a child; let the child learn from the consequences of forgetting.
Is able to communicate well and effectively	0+ yrs.	Talk as often as possible to the child, from infancy to adult life, using as wide a range of language in everyday contexts as possible.

(Continued on next page)

Table 14.1 (Contd.)

Desired or Expected Behaviors in Children	Age	Training Process and Consequences
Is creative and inventive	1–4 yrs.	Involve child in daily play that gradually asks the child to think about what else a toy could be or another way to play a game.
Is creative and inventive	4+ yrs.	Encourage children to try different things; to think in new ways; to solve problems in their own way; to develop a personal style; to dream; to follow and develop their talents.
Leaves on time for school	5+ yrs.	Set a morning routine; don't remind the child of the time or anything they will need for school; get child on the way when it is time to go.
Respects parent when parent says, "no"	3+ yrs.	Say "no" once; don't debate the issue; then act to implement "no."
Does not talk back to parents	2+ yrs.	Stop talking immediately; enact an appropriate consequence if needed; disengage from all conversation and leave room.
Does not whine at home (including temper tantrums)	2+ yrs.	All whining results in an automatic "no"—even if the parent wants to say "yes"; *leave the child alone.*
Does not whine in public (including temper tantrums)	3+ yrs.	All whining results in an automatic "no"—even if the parent wants to say "yes"; *take the child home.*
Does not whine or misbehave in the car (including temper tantrums)	3+ yrs.	Pull over to the side of the road and stop until child is calm; get out of car if necessary.
Gets along well with other children	1+ yrs.	As early as possible, involve the child in daily *peer* play.
Does not fight with other children	0–2 yrs.	Remove the victim; say nothing else.
Does not fight with other children	2+ yrs.	Stay out of the child's fights; tell any complainers that they can handle it.
Does not tattle on other children	2+ yrs.	Don't listen to any tattling; do not respond; walk away.
Does not hit other people or animals	0+ yrs.	Never spank or hit a child for any reason; if the child hits, say "no" and remove the child for a time-out; if pets are abused, tell the child that the pet will have to go to a new home, and then follow through with the consequence, if necessary (*threats never work*).
Puts dirty clothes in the hamper	2–4 yrs.	Make a game of it; put dirty clothes in the hamper *with* the child; involve the child in washing the clothes.
Puts dirty clothes in the hamper	4+ yrs.	Wash only once a week if at all possible; only wash clothes that are actually in the hamper.
Handles homework	5–10 yrs.	Work with PTA or PTO and the principal and teachers at your child's school to eliminate homework, since it has not been shown in 50 years to serve any educational purpose in the primary grades.
Handles homework	5+ yrs.	*With* the child, agree on a time and place for homework; establish a no-noise zone during that time; help the child with homework only if you are asked to help; otherwise, don't ask about it (*it is the child's responsibility*).

(Continued on next page)

Table 14.1 (Contd.)

Desired or Expected Behaviors in Children	Age	Training Process and Consequences
Reads books and other written materials	0+ yrs.	Read to the child every day until the child can read to you; then share the reading.
Is able to do arithmetic and mathematics well	0–2 yrs.	Play recordings of Mozart's string concertos and other classical music on a daily basis.
Is able to do arithmetic and mathematics well (continue with music)	2+ yrs.	Never do for the child what the child can do for self; allow the child to solve problems and learn from consequences of behavior; allow the child to make and correct her/his own mistakes; if possible, teach the child to play a stringed instrument.
Enjoys history and geography	5+ yrs.	Tell the child stories; have the child interview the grandparents and listen to their stories; take a walk every day; travel as much as possible (start with the child's town, then the state, then places beyond the state; and in each place ask about the history and development of this location).
Comes home on time	6–12 yrs.	Negotiate a time to come home and then expect the child fairly close to that time; late arrival results in not going out the next time.
Comes home on time	12+ yrs.	Ask: "What time can I expect you in?" and then, once established, leave it up to the child.
Has good friends	3+ yrs.	Invite your children's friends into your home as often as possible; make your child's friends welcome; discuss the value of friendship with older children; have friends yourself and invite them into your life often.
Is emotionally well developed	0–3 yrs.	Name different emotions you see or experience with your child; vary your expression of emotion; talk about emotions; don't yell or scream at the child.
Is emotionally well developed	3+ yrs.	Listen to your child's expression of emotion and reflect (paraphrase) it back to her or him; ask the child to tell you as much as possible about what the feeling is; ask additional questions to help a child problem solve around feelings of sadness or anger (especially those aimed at the parent) *emotion coaching*.
Sets the table for dinner	1–3 yrs.	Make it a game; encourage the child.
Sets the table for dinner	3+ yrs.	When the child chooses this chore for a week, serve dinner only if and when the table is set.
Cooks dinner/supper	2–4 yrs.	Involve the child in the preparation of meals; have fun and be patient.
Cooks dinner/supper	4–8 yrs.	Have the child be responsible for parts of the dinner.
Cooks dinner/supper	8+ yrs.	Have the child take a night in which she or he cooks the dinner or supper.
Cleans up the dishes after eating	2–6 yrs.	Make clearing the table a game and win the child's help.

(Continued on next page)

Table 14.1 (Contd.)

Desired or Expected Behaviors in Children	Age	Training Process and Consequences
Cleans up the dishes after eating	6+ yrs.	When the child chooses this chore for a week, prepare food the next day only if the kitchen and the dishes are clean.
Does daily or weekly chores	0–3 yrs.	Involve the child in daily work; make it fun.
Does daily or weekly chores	3+ yrs.	Have a family meeting once a week; allow the child(ren) to choose the chores they want to do for 1 week.
Takes a bath	0–4 yrs.	Make it fun; take it slowly; gradually give the cleaning over to the child.
Takes a bath	4+ yrs.	Establish a bath-time routine; then stay out of it.
Goes to bed on time	0+ yrs.	Establish a bedtime routine, including a constant bed-time; if the bath is finished and pajamas are on, then read them a story.
Stays in bed at night	2+ yrs.	Once the parent has said "goodnight," that's it; no more talking until the next morning except in a parent-perceived emergency.
Stays in bed at night	3+ yrs.	If the child gets up at night *on a regular basis* and comes to be with the parent, the parents should lock their bed-room door and not respond.

Sources: © James Robert Bitter, 2004; Dreikurs & Soltz (1964/1991); Glasser (1969); Gottman & DeClaire (1997); Main (1986); Ricker & Crowder (1998, 2000).

by **Gerald Patterson** (1985; Forgatch & Patterson, 1998) and his associates at the Oregon Social Learning Center. Taken together, these techniques are central to cognitive-behavioral family therapy and include:

Primary Reinforcement.   Primary reinforcement involves the use of candy and other phys-ical rewards with young children to shape and condition desired behaviors. For example, if a child likes chocolate pudding, the parent can use this reward as an incentive for the child to act in a certain way or learn a new behavior.

Social Reinforcement.   Behaviorists quickly learned that the people providing primary reinforcement are, themselves, also reinforcing. The attention, praise, encouragement, and caring that the person provides are often more important than any physical reward. Pairing words like "good job" or "you were great" or "what a nice effort you made" with a child's actions not only reinforces the child, but also makes the parent a prestigious reinforcer and positive influence in the child's life.

Continuous Reinforcement.   In the early stages of shaping new behaviors or maintaining current ones, reinforcement has to be applied at the same time that the desired behavior occurs and, initially, the reinforcement should happen every time the desired behavior occurs. When a child is ready for bed on time every night, the parent plays a game with the child. As long as the child likes playing the game with the parent, getting ready for bed is reinforced. It also takes on the power of being a family routine: It is normal and expected.

Intermittent Reinforcement.   The strongest kind of reinforcement is intermittent; that is, the reinforcement is applied at intervals rather than every time. In child rearing, it is used to teach patience, persistence, and more complex behaviors. Children who are reinforced intermittently tend to produce the behavior more often in an effort to keep the reinforcement coming. Most intermittent reinforcement is related either to behavioral production (a fixed or varied ratio) or to a (fixed or varied) amount of time between reinforcements. If I would like my child to learn to play happily with others rather than to get upset and angry, I might start by using continuous reinforcement, noticing every time the child achieves this goal for 10 or 15 minutes. As the child starts to get the hang of give-and-take and happy engagement, I might recognize it only every so often or after a number of different play situations. At such times, an effective reinforcement might be giving the child a big hug and saying, "It was so neat to see you playing happily with John. The two of you were having such fun."

Shaping.   Shaping is the process of teaching a larger, more complex behavior by starting with small, gradual steps that lead in successive approximations (Bandura, 1969) to the desired endpoint. Shaping involves providing reinforcement for each approximation in the behavioral sequence that the child makes. Commonly used in potty-training children, it is also the basis for using allowances to help children learn to handle money. Young children might get a small allowance every week just to get used to having money. Later, parents might want children to have a plan (or budget) for their money and provide additional funds as the child is able to demonstrate planning and responsible money management. When dealing with complex school problems and educational requirements, shaping makes progress possible when the more complex learning seems overwhelming. Helping children break a complex school assignment into separate tasks and acknowledging their efforts and achievements at each step along the way is another example of shaping.

Behavioral Extinction.   Behaviors that are ignored and/or not reinforced tend to stop or extinguish rather quickly. This is especially true when continuous reinforcement is discontinued. When intermittent reinforcement is discontinued, the behavior is likely to increase for a short period of time before extinguishing altogether. I often recommend that parents leave the room when a child starts to whine. Whining is often the first step to a temper tantrum. Both whining and temper tantrums demand an audience to be effective. When we stay and engage a child with a temper, we reinforce the temper tantrum. When we walk away, we remove the audience, and even though the temper may get a little louder initially, it will eventually stop and extinguish if we do not reinforce it. It is important to remember that when parents remove themselves, they must stay removed: Re-engaging every so often is intermittent reinforcement, the strongest kind.

Punishment and Other Aversive Interventions.   Strictly speaking, behaviorists use the word punishment to mean any stimulus that suppresses or decreases undesirable behaviors. In this sense, a **time-out** is a behavioral form of punishment. Although effective in some cases, punishment is, however, an intervention to be used sparingly. The problem with punishment and other aversive interventions is that they actually can begin to reinforce destructive behaviors. We see this all the time in families in which spanking[3] is used. Generally, children perform the same negative behaviors over and over and get spanked for them regularly with no improvement expected by either the parent or the child. When this happens, spanking is an aversive stimuli, but it is not suppressing or decreasing unwanted actions; rather, it is actually reinforcing them. Some behaviorists use processes like dirty deeds (assigned difficult tasks) and withholding privileges (Horne & Sayger, 2000) as punishment for severe misbehaviors, but even these efforts at control often lead to further power struggles and even revenge. Focusing on **behavioral exchange agreements** or contracts, positive reinforcement, the **Premack principle**, and controlling the situation rather than the child is almost always better.

Modeling.   Based on the social-learning theories of Albert Bandura (1969, 1971a, 1971b), parents are encouraged to become prestigeous models for their children (Krumboltz & Krumboltz, 1972). **Modeling** provides children with cues for what is expected and augments the power of social reinforcement that comes from the model. Modeling is often paired with role playing so that new behaviors can be observed, tried, and practiced with support and feedback.

Self-Control and Self-Monitoring.   Before parents can be taught to be effective in helping children change, they must learn cognitive-behavioral methods of self-control and self-monitoring (Cormier & Nurius, 2003). Disturbing behaviors in children tend to invite disturbing behaviors and feelings in adults, and vice versa. Cognitive-behavioral therapists ask parents: "What are you doing and how are you feeling?" If the answer is: "I am about to blow up," then the therapist will ask: "And will it actually help if you blow up and get into an argument with your child? Has that worked before?" When parents want to know what else they can do, the answer is that first they must calm themselves down. Reframing their position as "I don't like what my child has done, but exploding has not helped in the past and probably won't now" is the first step to self-control. In the chapter on cognitive-behavioral family therapy, Dattilio (1998) used his pad-and-pencil method to analyze irrational, negative thoughts and taught this method to parents so that they could learn to self-monitor and calm themselves. Helping parents gain a sense of self-control and communicate effectively almost always entails a certain amount of coaching by the counselor or therapist.

Communication.   The more that some families and behaviors seem out of control, the more effective communication becomes necessary. Effective communication includes turning toward the person with whom you are speaking, listening, acknowledging, and validating, tapping into emotional language, giving clear directives and polite requests, setting clear and reasonable limits and expectations, and using I-statements in relation to personal and family needs (Christensen & Jacobson, 2000; Gottman, 1999; Gottman & Silver, 2000).

Contracting.   Designed to renegotiate severe levels of hostility in families, contracts spell out rewards for behaving in a certain manner. Contracts delineate specific behaviors required to gain specific rewards and usually are written and signed by all parties. A form of contracting called contingency contracting speaks to a mutual exchange of behaviors in which each party gets something they want from the other person if both agree to deliver it (Stuart, 1969). For example, the parent agrees to fix specific foods the child likes if the child agrees to show up for dinner on time.

The Premack Principle.   When children fail to comply with required expectations, the Premack principle (Premack, 1965) is designed to reinstate the importance of necessary behaviors. The child is told that she or he must complete less-enjoyable activities before being allowed to do desired ones. "You will need to complete your homework before you watch TV." The use of a positive reinforcement to achieve an outcome the child may not be ready or want to do is central to Premack principle. I mentioned earlier the game that a parent might play with a child or a book that might be read if and when the child is ready for bed on time. It also follows that the child forfeits the pleasurable reinforcement if the desired behavior does not occur.

Time-out.   Time-out is the removal of a child, adolescent, or adult from a setting in which negative or undesirable behaviors are occurring and are perhaps even reinforced. The time away must be sufficient to break the behavioral pattern, stop any reinforcement of it in the environment, and provide the person with a fresh start. We often think of time-out in relation to children, but it is also useful when one parent relieves the other in the middle of stressful or ineffective adult–child interactions. Parents now and then need time-outs from the stress and difficulties associated with raising a family.

Summary and Multicultural Evaluation

The early history of parenting is tied closely to the need for survival. It is highly probable that the long period of development needed by human children led in some way to the emergence of agrarian life, a beginning of farms and farmland—homes and homeland. Well into the 20th century, children were needed to keep family farms going. As late as the 1920s, 66% of the population in the United States still lived in rural areas. Sixty years later, 80% percent of the population would live in urban and suburban areas (Rockefeller Commission Report, n.d.). In the late 19th and early 20th centuries, infant mortality for both white and black families was still relatively high (Bideau, Desjardins, & Perez-Brignoli, 1997). Although parents grieved the loss of their children, losing a child in childbirth or shortly after was neither unusual nor unexpected.

Watson's early admonitions to parents were not the imposition of one man's thoughts on the rest of the country. Rather, his distant, somewhat aloof stance and program for parents reflected the common sense of his culture at that point in history. It was in line with the rather autocratic family systems that had emerged in many different cultures. Even the advent of democracy in the Americas had done little to establish the *social equality* for all that it had promised. Women continue to struggle for equal rights even today. So do those people who have been relegated to marginalized cultures through discrimination and oppression. So does labor with management. The promise of social equality is not lost on children and adolescents either. Because they are often less educated, less experienced, and always younger, children carry no illusion that social equality means *being the same*. They do believe, however, that they have the same right to be valued and respected as everyone else: This is what social equality means to them, and they seek to enact it every day.

It was not until the middle of the 20th century that psychology began to adopt a developmental view of children. It was during this time that Erikson (1950), Kohlberg (1981), Piaget (1971), and others would demonstrate that children were growing and developing human beings who gained skills and capacities for thinking and living over time. This was a radically new conceptualization of childhood and adolescence. Even this new **perspective** was limited, however, since almost all of the developmental theories were normed on boys—with a wishful aside that suggested "girls were probably the same." It was 30 years later that Carol Gilligan (1982) showed us that girls do not develop at least morally in the same ways that boys do: She set in motion an entire set of studies related to young women (for example, Belenky, Clinchy, Goldberger, & Tarule (1986/1997) on *Women's Ways of Knowing*) that is still going on. In the last decade, we also have added brain research to our understanding of how children grow and develop (Ratey, 2001; Strauch, 2003).

The modern world in which we live has a decidedly postmodern bent. There are multiple perspectives and multiple approaches to almost everything, including parenting. Our models are no longer singular and provided within closed, often cloistered, communities: Rather they come to us through television, travel, books, newspapers, magazines, religion, schools, and cultures. There is much more diversity than could even have been imagined 100 years ago, but there is also a lot more confusion. Being an effective parent is no longer automatic, if it ever was, and it almost always requires some training and coaching if evidence-based approaches are to be used.

Parent study groups that started in the 1950s child guidance movements have now been systematized and programmed into kits, complete with videos, parent manuals, leadership guides, and posters (see Dinkmeyer, McKay, & Dinkmeyer, 1997; Popkin, 1993). These programs now come in Spanish as well as English; with manuals adapting them to Christian life; with differing programs for early childhood, late childhood, and adolescence; and with programs for schools, as well as the home. These psychoeducational programs are among the most researched products in use, and they continually are updated to incorporate new findings in effective parenting methods.

In this chapter, I have presented the skills and interventions associated with effective parent education in Western cultures, as well as the more structured and precise techniques required for change within families experiencing severe behavioral problems. In both cases, the list of skills and interventions are among the most empirically tested and researched of any of the models in this book. Whether helping families through a psychoeducational approach or with cognitive-behavioral, systemic family therapy, the role of the counselor is that of an educator who assists families in employing methods that actually work.

If you are interested in a more in-depth study of parenting, I recommend the following sources: Abner, Villarosa, and Beal (1992); Cormer and Poussaint (1992); Crowder (2002); Dinkmeyer and Dreikurs (1963/2000); Dinkmeyer, McKay, and Dinkmeyer (1997); Dreikurs (1948/1992); Dreikurs and Soltz (1964/1991); Gilligan (1982); Ginott (1969/1971, 1965/1994); Gordon (1970); Gottman and DeClaire (1997); Krumboltz and Krumboltz (1972), if you can find it; Main (1986); Martin (1993); Mathias and French (1996); Popkin (1993); Ricker and Crowder (1998, 2000); Rodriquez (1999); Satir (1987); Schwebel and Fine (1994); and Strauch (2003).

Contributions to Multicultural Counseling and Gender Issues

Many of the skills and interventions associated with effective parenting and functional families were developed originally within the cultures of European Americans: They now have been extensively tested and used in different cultures, including African-American, Hispanic-American, some Asian-American cultures, and families with disabled children (Gillette, 1989; Hammett, Omizo, & Loffredo, 1981; Krieg, 1985; Larrivee, 1982; Levenson, 1994; Lifur-Bennett, 1982; Maez, 1987; Mullis, 1999; Villegas, 1977). In North America, almost all effective parenting programs are available in Spanish as well as English, with special supplements that also address some religious orientations. Since the early 1990s, some excellent parenting books addressing specific populations also have begun to surface (Abner, Villarosa, & Beal, 1992; Cormer & Poussaint, 1992; Martin, 1993, Mathias & French, 1996, Rodriquez, 1999).

Effective family goals also must allow the individuals within the family to function within the communities in which the family resides. What individuals and families think and what they find reinforcing is influenced heavily by the cultural norms of the community. In this sense, understanding and working with culture should permeate every aspect of our efforts to train parents. I long have hoped that various ethnic communities might identify the parents in their communities who are recognized by their peers as models for effective parenting within the culture. Through the use of long interviews and other qualitative assessments, perhaps coupled with indirect observation, guidelines for effective parenting could be developed that are specific to various ethnic communities. The differences that we might discover could lead to a greater appreciation of diverse family life, as well as to an enhanced set of skills applicable across cultures.

We still have a long way to go in learning to parent and educate little girls and young women effectively in a patriarchal society. Faber and Mazlish (1974) were one of the first set of authors to see the advantage of applying Haim Ginott's communication model in a non-sexist way: Their book, *Liberated Parents, Liberated Children*, focused on relationships and feelings. It is still extremely useful 30 years later. Still, parenting young women requires a focus on realities we would rather not have to consider. Girls and young women are molested and raped more than boys or young men: We need to keep them safe while still providing opportunities for freedom and exploration. Young women still hear that they won't be able to compete in mathematics and the sciences at the same level as young men, a belief that is disputed easily when young women are given a **context** in which these skills can be developed. We also have a long way to go in terms of fulfilling the promise that little girls can grow up to be anything they want to be. In education, business, government, and religion, there are still glass ceilings imposed on women and areas of access they are denied.

Perhaps the prejudice of greatest focus today is against the lesbian, gay, bisexual, and transgendered community. The war raged against them by religious conservatives strikes at the very nature of what constitutes a family. And even though children raised by lesbian or gay parents often have to experience unwarranted prejudice and oppression, the evidence over many years is that children of lesbian or gay parents are raised as well or better than those raised in comparable heterosexual families (Ainslie & Feltey, 1991; Bailey, Bobrow, Wolfe, & Mikach, 1995; Baptiste, 1987; Bigner & Jacobson, 1989).

Last, I should note that Hart and Risley (1995) demonstrated in their studies that families in poverty often engage in parenting processes that (a) reflect the almost constant stress and pressure experienced by the adults; (b) lack the language development and emotion coaching necessary for growth; (c) engage children in negative communications that often reinforce low self-esteem; (d) use higher amounts of aversive and arbitrary interventions with children than occur in working-class and professional families. To say the least, such children start life with multiple deficits. Bringing positive parenting models and skills to low-income families is one way to begin to break these negative cycles.

Where to Go From Here

People interested in parenting will find a great deal of help and support at:

CMTI Press
Box 51722, Bowling Green, KY 42102-6722
Web site: **http://www.cmtipress.com/index.htm**

or

Active Parenting Today
1955 Vaughn Rd. NW, Suite 108
Kennesaw GA 30144-7808
Phone: 800-825-0060
Website: **http://www.activeparenting.com**

For Parent Effectiveness or Family Effectiveness Training, see:

Gordon Training International
531 Stevens Avenue West
Solana Beach, CA 92075-2093

Phone: 800-628-1197 or 858-481-8121

E-mail: **info@gordontraining.com** or **workplace@gordontraining.com** or **family@ gordontraining.com** or **schools@gordontraining.com**.

Some additional websites are dedicated to special interests. Parents looking for support and help with children while going through a divorce might find the following website helpful: **http://positiveparentingthroughdivorce.com**. And an excellent multicultural parenting web page can be found at: **http://www.csun.edu/~vcpsy00h/parenthood/ culture.htm**. Feminist parents might find the web page **http://www.feminist.com/resources/ links/links_fam.html** useful, as well as Feminist Mom's Center of the Universe. The APA has a website in which they summarize and list research related to gay and lesbian parenting. You can find this web page at: **http://www.apa.org/pi/lgbc/publications/lgsummary.html**.

One of the older parent education programs in the country is located in Kensington, Maryland. The Parent Encouragement Program (PEP) has developed a complete curriculum that integrates play, learning styles, early childhood education, and effective discipline through a variety of workshop-type courses. PEP can be franchised to various parts of the country by contacting:

PEP: Parent Encouragement Program
10100 Connecticut Avenue
Kensington, MD 20895
Phone: 301-929-8824
E-mail: **PEPoffice@aol.com**

Recommended Readings

Dinkmeyer, D., Sr., McKay, G., & Dinkmeyer, D., Jr. (1997). *STEP: The parent's handbook*. Circle Pines, MN: American Guidance Service. The STEP programs come in kits complete with parent handbook, videos, leader's manuals, and other support materials. There are separate programs for early childhood, late childhood, teens, and advanced parenting programs.

Dreikurs, R., & Soltz, V. (1991). *Children: The challenge*. New York: Plume. (Original work published 1964) After forty years, this is still one of the most practical and used parent education books in the United States. It is also available in multiple languages and used throughout the world.

Gottman, J., & DeClaire, J. (1997). *The heart of parenting: Raising an emotionally intelligent child*. New York: Simon & Schuster. This is Gottman's most readable presentation of emotion coaching and scientifically-based parenting in which he emphasizes the importance of feelings, emotion and problem-solving coaching, and authoritative-responsive parenting.

Krumboltz, J. D., & Krumboltz, H. B. (1972). *Changing children's behavior*. Englewood Cliffs, NJ: Prentice Hall. This is a classic work that is rather hard to find, but it is an excellent guide for both parents and practitioners who want to use behavioral techniques in

everyday life with children. The book is loaded with examples that highlight the principles involved, and the focus is on good process as much as desired outcome.

Main, F. (1986). *Perfect parenting and other myths*. Vermillion, SD: The Main Press. A delightful book to read, filled with funny stories, as well as wisdom about the imperfect art of parenting. This is also the only parenting book that actually applies Kfir's (1981) personality priorities to understanding parenting styles.

Popkin, M. (1993). *Active parenting today*. Atlanta, GA: Active Parenting. Active Parenting is one of the fastest growing parent training programs in the country. It, too, comes with a parents' manual, videos, and guidelines for leadership and parent programs for various developmental levels and teacher training programs too.

Ricker, A., & Crowder, C. Z. (1998). *Backtalk: 4 steps to ending rude behavior in your kids*. New York: Fireside. A short, to-the-point, best-selling book that presents the Adlerian/Dreikursian approach to working with difficult children. Carolyn Crowder has appeared on countless television shows, including *20/20* and *The Today Show*.

Satir, V. M. (1987). *The new peoplemaking*. Palo Alto, CA: Science and Behavior Books. This is Virginia Satir at her best. Her book provides parents with a sense of what it was like to listen to her in person, highlights the importance of self-esteem and how to create it in children, and delineates her communication stances so that parents can assess their own communication and consider the power of congruence.

DVD Reference

Most of the interventions you will see in the parenting video can be found in the works of Rudolf Dreikurs, Thomas Gordon, Haim Ginott, and John Gottman. The interventions are based on the use of natural and logical consequences; clear, emotionally honest communication; and encouragement. In this particular session, Dr. Bitter focuses on helping Joel control himself rather than trying to control his children. He teaches Joel how to act rather than talk, because the latter only feeds one child's need for negative attention and the other child's desire for power. This video also demonstrates a mutually respectful process by which therapist knowledge can be shared while a collaborative relationship is still maintained.

References

Abbey, A., Pilgrim, C., Hendrickson, P, & Buresh, S. (2000). Evaluation of a family-based substance abuse prevention program targeted for the middle school years. *Journal of Drug Education*, Vol. 30, No. 2, 2000.

Abbey, A., Pilgrim, C., Hendrickson, P., & Lorenz, S. (1998). Implementation and impact of a family-based substance abuse prevention program in rural communities. *The Journal of Primary Prevention*, Vol. 18, No. 3, 1998.

Abner, A., Villarosa, L., & Beal, A. C. (1992). *The black parenting book*. New York: Broadway.

Adler, A. (1927). *Understanding human nature* (W. B. Wolfe, Trans.). New York: Greenberg.

Adler, A. (1930). *The education of children* (E. Jensen & F. Jensen, Trans.). New York: Greenberg.

Ainslie, J., & Feltey, K. M. (1991). Definitions and dynamics of motherhood and family in lesbian communities. *Marriage and Family Review, 17*(1/2), 63–85.

Alexander, J., & Parsons, B. V. (1973). Short-term behavioral interventions with delinquent families: Impact on family process and recidivism. *Journal of Abnormal Psychology, 81*, 219–225.

Alexander, J., & Parsons, B. V. (1982). *Functional family therapy*. Pacific Grove, CA: Brooks/Cole.

Allen, S. M., Thompson, R. H., & Drapeaux, J. (1997, May). *Successful methods for increasing and improving parent and child interactions*. Paper presented at the National Head Start Association Annual Training Conference, Boston, MA.

Bailey, J. M., Bobrow, D., Wolfe, M., & Mikach, S. (1995). Sexual orientation of adult sons of gay fathers. *Developmental Psychology, 31*, 124–129.

Bandura, A. (1969). *Principles of behavior modification*. New York: Holt, Rinehart, & Winston.

Bandura, A. (1971a). *Psychological modeling: Conflicting theories*. Chicago: Aldine-Atherton.

Bandura, A. (1971b). Psychotherapy based upon modeling principles. In A. E. Bergin & S. L. Garfield (Eds.), *Handbook of psychotherapy and behavior change* (pp. 653–708). New York: Wiley.

Baptiste, D. A. (1987). The gay and lesbian stepparent family. In F. W. Bozett (Ed.), *Gay and lesbian parents* (pp. 112–137). New York: Praeger.

Barton, C., & Alexander, J. (1981). Functional family therapy. In A. Gurman & D. Kniskern (Eds.), *Handbook of family therapy* (pp. 403–443). New York: Brunner/Mazel.

Baumrind, D. (1968). Authoritarian versus authoritative parental control. *Adolescence, 3*(11), 255–272.

Baumrind, D. (1971). Current patterns of parental authority. *Developmental Psychology Monograph 4*(1), Part 2, 1–103.

Baumrind, D. (1991). The influence of parenting style on adolescent competence and substance use. *Journal of Early Adolescence, 11*(1), 56–95.

Baumrind, D. (1995). *Child maltreatment and optimal caregiving in social contexts.* New York: Garland.

Belenky, M. F., Clinchy, B. M., Goldberger, N. R., & Tarule, J. M. (1997). *Women's ways of knowing: The development of self, voice and mind* (10th anniv. ed.). New York: Basic Books. (Original work published 1986)

Bernino, J., & Rourke, J. (May, 2003). Obesity prevention in pre-school Native-American children: A pilot study using home visiting. *Obesity Research, 11,* 606–611.

Bideau, A., Desjardins, B., & Perez-Brignoli, H. (1997). *Infant and child mortality in the past.* New York: Oxford University Press.

Bigner, J. J., & Jacobsen, R. B. (1989). The value of children to gay and heterosexual fathers. *Journal of Homosexuality, 18*(1/2), 163–172.

Bitter, J. R. (1987). Communication and meaning: Satir in Adlerian context. In R. Sherman & D. Dinkmeyer (Eds.), *Systems of family therapy: An Adlerian integration* (pp. 109–142). New York: Brunner/Mazel.

Brooks, L. D., Spearn, R. C., Rice, M., Crocco, D., Hodgins, C., & Schaaf, V. (1988). Systematic training for effective parenting (STEP): An evaluation study with a Canadian population. *Canada's Mental Health, 36,* 2–5.

Burnett, P. C. (1988). Evaluation of Adlerian parenting programs. *Individual Psychology, 44,* 63–76.

Campbell, N. A., & Sutton, J. M., Jr. (1983). Impact of parent education groups on family environment. *Journal for Specialists in Group Work, 8,* 126–132.

Christensen, A., & Jacobson, N. S. (2000). *Reconcilable differences.* New York: Guilford.

Christensen, O. C. (Ed.). (2004). *Adlerian family counseling* (3rd ed.). Minneapolis, MN: Educational Media Corp.

Ciurczak & Co. (2003). The Business Training Institute, Inc. *Active Parenting.* Final program evaluation report.

CLAS (Culturally and Linguistically Appropriate Services) Review. (2001). Padres Activos de Hoy. University of Illinois at Urbana-Champaign. CLAS # CL03985.

Collins, W. A., Maccoby, E. E., Steinberg, L., Hetherington, E. M., & Bornstein, M. (2000). Contemporary research on parenting: The case for nature and nurture. *American Psychologist, 55*(2), 218–232.

Cormer, J. P., & Poussaint, A. F. (1992). *Raising black children.* New York: Plume.

Cormier, S., & Nurius, P. S. (2003). *Interviewing and change strategies for helpers: Fundamental skills and cognitive behavioral interventions* (5th ed.). Pacific Grove, CA: Brooks/Cole.

Croake, J. W. (1983). Adlerian parent education. *Counseling Psychologist, 11,* 65–71.

Crowder, C. Z. (2002). *Eating, sleeping, and getting up: How to stop the daily battles with your child.* New York: Broadway.

Dattilio, F. M. (1998). *Case studies in couple and family therapy: Systemic and cognitive perspectives.* New York: Guilford Press.

Dewey, J. (1916). *Democracy and education: An introduction to a philosophy of education.* New York: MacMillan.

Dinkmeyer, D., & Dreikurs, R. (2000). *Encouraging children to learn.* New York: Taylor and Francis. (Original work published 1963)

Dinkmeyer, D., Sr., McKay, G., & Dinkmeyer, D., Jr. (1997). *STEP: The parent's handbook.* Circle Pines, MN: American Guidance Service.

Dobson, J. (1996). *The new dare to discipline.* Carol Stream, IL: Tyndale House Publishers.

Dobson, J. (2004). *The new strong-willed child: Birth to adolescence.* Carol Stream, IL: Tyndale House Publishers.

Dreikurs, R. (1940a, November). The importance of group life. *Camping Magazine, 3–4,* 27.

Dreikurs, R. (1940b, December). The child in the group. *Camping Magazine,* 7–9.

Dreikurs, R. (1950). The immediate purpose of children's misbehavior, its recognition and correction. *Internationale Zeitschrift fur Individual-psychologie, 19,* 70–87.

Dreikurs, R. (1992). *The challenge of parenthood.* New York: Plume. (Original work published 1948)

Dreikurs, R., & Grey, L. (1989). *Logical consequences: A new approach to child discipline.* New York: Plume. (Original work published 1968)

Dreikurs, R., & Soltz, V. (1991). *Children: The challenge.* New York: Plume. (Original work published 1964)

Erikson, E. (1950). *Childhood and society* (2nd ed.). New York: Norton.

Faber, A., & Mazlish, E. (1974). *Liberated parents, liberated children.* New York: Avon.

Fashimpar, G. (2000). Problems of parenting: Solutions of science. *Journal of Family Social Work, 5*(2), 2000.

Forgatch, M. S., & Patterson, G. R. (1998). Behavioral family therapy. In. F. M. Dattilio (Ed.), *Case studies in couple and family therapy: Systemic and cognitive perspectives.* New York: Guilford.

Gillette, N. Y. (1989). Evaluation of the use of a systematic training for effective parenting program modified for low-income Puerto Rican parents of preschoolers (Doctoral dissertation, University of Massachusetts, 1989). *Dissertation Abstracts International, 51/03A,* 737.

Gilligan, C. (1982). *In a different voice: Psychological theory and women's development.* Cambridge, MA: Harvard University Press.

Ginott, H. G. (1971). *Between parent and teenager.* New York: Avon. (Original work published 1969)

Ginott, H. G. (1975). *Teacher and child.* New York: Avon.

Ginott, H. G. (1994). Between *parent and child.* New York: Avon. (Original work published 1965)

Glasser, W. (1969). *Schools without failure.* New York: Simon & Schuster.

Goleman, D. (1995). *Emotional intelligence.* New York: Bantam.

Gordon, T. (1970). *P.E.T.: Parent effectiveness training: The tested new way to raise responsible children.* New York: Peter H. Wyden.

Gottman, J. (1994). *What predicts divorce?* Hillsdale, NJ: Lawrence Erlbaum Associates.

Gottman, J. (1996). *What predicts divorce?: The measures.* Mahwah, NJ: Lawrence Erlbaum Associates.

Gottman, J. M. (1999). *The marriage clinic: A scientifically-based marital therapy.* New York: Norton.

Gottman, J., & DeClaire, J. (1997). *The heart of parenting: Raising an emotionally intelligent child.* New York: Simon & Schuster.

Gottman, J., Katz, L. F., & Hooven, C. (1997). *Meta-emotion: How families communicate emotionally.* Mahwah, NJ: Lawrence Erlbaum Associates.

Gottman, J., & Silver, N. (2000). *Seven principles for making marriage work: A practical guide from the country's foremost relationship expert.* New York: Three Rivers Press.

Hammett, V. L., Omizo, M. M., & Loffredo, D. A. (1981). The effects of participation in a STEP program on parents' child-rearing attitudes and the self-concepts of their learning disabled children. *Exceptional Child, 28,* 183–190.

Hart, B., & Risley, T. R. (1995). *Meaningful differences in the everyday experiences of young American children.* Baltimore, MD: Paul H. Brookes.

Hoffman, E. (1994). *The drive for self: Alfred Adler and the founding of individual psychology.* Reading, MA: Addison Wesley.

Horne, A. M., & Sayger, T. V. (2000). Behavioral approaches to couple and family therapy. In A. M. Horne (Ed.), *Family counseling and therapy* (pp. 454–488). Itasca, IL: F. E. Peacock.

Jackson, C., Henrickson, L., & Foshee, V. A. (1998). The authoritative parenting index: Predicting health risk behaviors among children and adolescents. *Health Education & Behavior, 25*(3), 319–337.

Kfir, N. (1981). Impasse/priority therapy. In R. J. Corsini (Ed.), *Handbook of innovative psychotherapies* (pp. 401–415). New York: Wiley.

Kohlberg, L. (1981). *The philosophy of moral development: Moral stages and the idea of justice.* San Francisco: Harper and Row.

Krebs, L. L. (1986). Current research on theoretically based parenting programs. *Individual Psychology, 42,* 375–387.

Krieg, P. E. (1985). Effects of systematic training for effective parenting (STEP) on perception and attitude of parents of learning disabled children (Doctoral dissertation, University of New Orleans, 1985). *Dissertation Abstracts International, 46/07A,* 1902.

Krumboltz, J. D., & Krumboltz, H. B. (1972). *Changing children's behavior.* Englewood Cliffs, NJ: Prentice Hall.

Landerholm, E., & Lowenthal, B. (1993). Adding variety to parent involvement activities. *Early Childhood Development and Care, 91,* 1–16.

Larrivee, R. C. (1982). A comparison of the effects of three parent education programs, STEP, PAT, and EP, on the perceptions and interactions of low income Head Start mothers and their preschool children (Doctoral dissertation, University of Massachusetts, 1982). *Dissertation Abstracts International, 42/12A,* 5068.

Levenson, C. A. (1994). Developing a parent education course for parents of children with disabilities and/or chronic illness (Doctoral dissertation, University of Nevada, Reno, 1994). *Dissertation Abstracts International, 56/01A,* 95.

Lifur-Bennett, L. (1982). The effects of an Adlerian and a behavioral parent education program on learning disabled children and their parents (Doctoral dissertation, California School of Professional Psychology, 1982). *Dissertation Abstracts International, 43/06B,* 1959.

Maez, A. (1987). The effects of two parent training programs on parental attitudes and self-concepts of Mexican-American mothers (Doctoral dissertation, University of California at Los Angeles, 1987). *Dissertation Abstracts International, 48/10A,* 2583.

Main, F. (1986). *Perfect parenting and other myths.* Vermillion, SD: The Main Press.

Martin, A. (1993). *The lesbian and gay parenting handbook.* New York: HarperCollins.

Mathias, B., & French, M. A. (1996). *40 ways to raise a non-racist child.* New York: HarperCollins.

Mullis, F. (1999). Active parenting: An evaluation of two Adlerian parent education programs. *Journal of Individual Psychology, 55*(2), 225 232.

Nystul, M. S. (1982). The effects of systematic training for effective parenting on parental attitudes. *The Journal of Psychology, 112,* 63–66.

Patterson, G. R. (1980). Mothers: The unacknowledged victims. *Monographs of the Society for Research in Child Development, 45*(5, Serial No. 186). Ann Arbor, MI: Society for Research in Child Development.

Patterson, G. R. (1985). Beyond technology: The next stage in developing an empirical base for parent training. In L. L'Abate (Ed.), *Handbook of family psychology and therapy* (Vol. II). Homewood, IL: Dorsey Press.

Patterson, G. R., & Forgatch, M. S. (1987). *Parents and adolescents living together: Vol. 1: The basics.* Eugene, OR: Castalia.

Pavlov, I. P. (2003). *Conditioned reflexes.* New York: Dover Publications. (Original work published 1927)

Piaget, J. (1971). *The language and thought of the child* (3rd ed.). New York: Humanities Press.

Pilgrim, C., Abbey, A., Hendrickson, P., & Lorenz, S. (1998). Implementation and impact of a family-based substance abuse prevention program in rural communities. *Journal of Primary Prevention, 18*(3), 341–361.

Popkin, M. (1993). *Active parenting today.* Atlanta, GA: Active Parenting.

Premack, D. (1965). Reinforcement theory. In D. Levine (Ed.), *Nebraska symposium on motivation.* Lincoln, NB: University of Nebraska Press.

Ratey, J. J. (2001). *A user's guide to the brain: Perception, attention and the four theaters of the brain.* New York: Pantheon Books.

Ricker, A., & Crowder, C. Z. (1998). *Backtalk: 4 steps to ending rude behavior in your kids.* New York: Fireside.

Ricker, A., & Crowder, C. Z. (2000). *Whining: 3 steps to stop it before the tears and tantrums start.* New York: Fireside.

Rockefeller Commission Report. (n.d.). Population and the American future: The report of the commission on population growth and the American future. Retrieved May 31, 2005, from http://www .population-security.org/rockefeller/003_population_ distribution.htm.

Rodriquez, G. G. (1999). *Raising nuestros ninos: Bringing up Latino children in a bicultural world.* New York: Fireside.

Satir, V. M. (1983). *Conjoint family therapy* (3rd ed.). Palo Alto, CA: Science and Behavior Books.

Satir, V. M. (1987). *The new peoplemaking.* Palo Alto, CA: Science and Behavior Books.

Satir, V. M., & Baldwin, M. (1983). *Satir: Step-by-step.* Palo Alto, CA: Science and Behavior Books.

Schwebel, A. I., & Fine, M. A. (1994). *Understanding and helping families: A cognitive-behavioral approach.* Hillsdale, NJ: Lawrence Erlbaum.

Sharpley, C. F., & Poiner, A. M. (1980). An exploratory evaluation of the systematic training for effective parenting (STEP) programme. *Australian Psychologist, 15,* 103–109.

Skinner, B. F. (1953). *Science and human behavior.* New York: MacMillan.

Skinner, B. F. (1974). *About behaviorism.* New York: Knopf.

Snow, J. N., Kern, R. M., & Penick, J. (1997). The effects of STEP on patient progress in an adolescent day hospital. *Individual Psychology, 53*(4), 388–395.

Strauch, B. (2003). *The primal teen: What the new discoveries about the teenage brain tell us about our kids.* New York: Random House.

Stuart, R. B. (1969). Operant-interpersonal treatment of marital discord. *Journal of Counseling and Clinical Psychology, 33,* 675–682.

Villegas, A. V. (1977). The efficacy of systematic training for effective parenting with Chicana mothers (Doctoral dissertation, Arizona State University, 1977). *Dissertation Abstracts International, 38/03A,* 1236.

Watson, J. B. (1928). *Psychological care of infant and child.* New York: Norton.

Watson, J. B. (1970). *Behaviorism.* New York: Norton. (Original work published 1925)

Williams, R. E., Omizo, M. M., & Abrams, B. C. (1984). Effects of STEP on parental attitudes and locus of control of their learning disabled children. *The School Counselor, 32,* 126–133.

Wolpe, J. (1990). *The practice of behavior therapy* (4th ed.). Elmsford, NY: Pergamon Press.

Endnotes

[1]It is important to note that behaviorists have a special definition of punishment that does not quite coincide with the everyday use of the term. The lay person understands punishment to be any negative action taken by one individual (usually the parent) against another (usually the child) that is intended to "teach the person to behave." Behaviorists agree that punishment is aversive, but it is the outcome that defines it: To behaviorists, a punishment is any action that suppresses or decreases an unwanted behavior—at least temporarily. Corporal punishment may do this initially, but some children get used to the pain, and they then see, for example, a spanking as a badge of courage: It actually becomes a *reinforcement*, increasing negative, undesirable behaviors.

[2]My use of the terms reward and punishment do not sit all that well with caring and conscientious behaviorists who have given a special, technical meaning to these terms. Behaviorists think of rewards as a form of positive reinforcement applied immediately after desired or target behaviors for the purpose of maintaining or increasing those behaviors. Similarly, behaviorists describe punishment as any action that suppresses or decreases an unwanted behavior (as in the use of time-out). Most parents—and, I would guess, most readers—do not give such technical meaning to these terms. In their common, everyday meanings, rewards are given often haphazardly and capriciously "because the child has been good," and punishment is applied to "teach the child a lesson," generally about who is in charge, who is in control (see Dobson, 2004).

[3]The negative effects of constant and/or severe spanking have been well-documented and include an increase in disturbing or anti-social behavior (even violence); lowered IQ, mood disorders, and anxiety in children, as well as later in their lives; and substance abuse. Although spanking young children has been shown to get immediate compliance in them, it is also strongly associated with parental abuse of children. Given that there are so many better ways to discipline children, it is hard to understand what benefit there might be to continuing this practice at all. The recommendation that a parent learn to spank young children dispassionately, just enough to make them cry (see Dobson, 1996), seems lost on parents who tend to use spanking when they are angry and frustrated. For more on this, see the web page created by the APA at **http://www.apa .org/releases/spanking.html**

PART 3

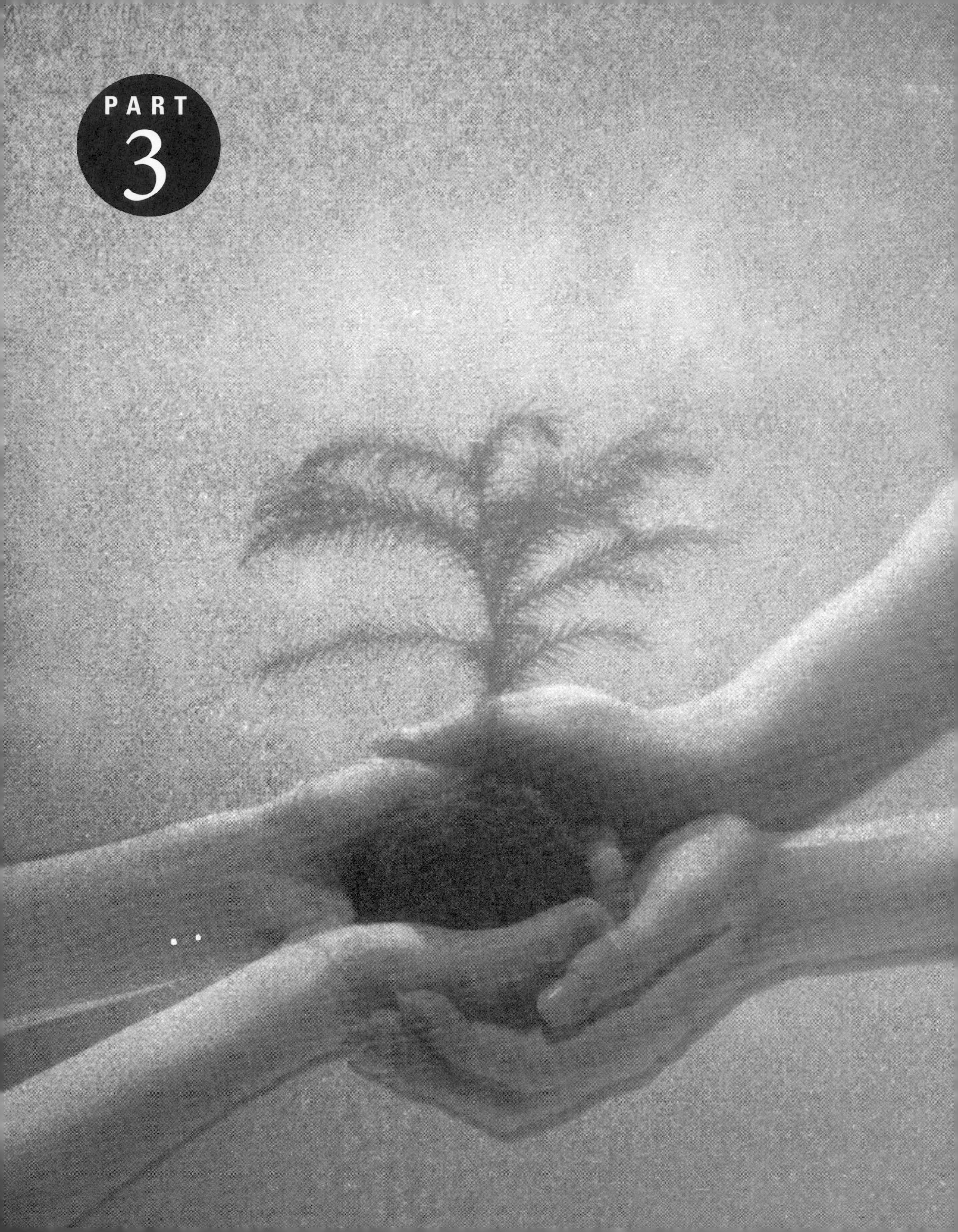

Integration and Application

Chapter 15 Integration I: From
Self-Discovery to Family
Practice—Forming a
Relationship and Family
Assessment

Chapter 16 Integration II: Shared Meaning,
Facilitating Change, and
Tailoring Interventions

Integration I:
From Self-Discovery to Family Practice—Forming a Relationship and Family Assessment

Discovering a Model or Set of Models for Professional Use

Videotaping Your Work and Taking Time for Reflection

A Process for Family Therapy Across Models

Summary

References

Discovering a Model or Set of Models for Professional Use

This chapter will begin with some ideas and questions that might be useful in helping you to discover the values, beliefs, and procedures that are a natural part of you and that might also feel essential to your work. I am hopeful that each of you will find a model or set of models that can act as your starting point, as a foundation for practice and integration. I also will start to propose a process for *integrating* the therapeutic systems in this book. I think of this process as happening in four stages or steps: **Forming a relationship, family assessment, hypothesizing** and sharing meaning, and **facilitating change**. The focus in this chapter will be on forming a relationship and conducting an assessment based on multiple perspectives.

There have been some excellent models of integration already developed in the field of family therapy (see Breunlin, Schwartz, & MacKune-Karrer, 1992/1997; Carlson, Sperry, & Lewis, 2005; Gehart & Tuttle, 2003; Hanna, 2007; Miksell, Lusterman, & McDaniel, 1995; Olsen, 1999; Walsh, 1998; Worden, 2003, to sample just a few). It is tempting, of course, to want to integrate the best parts of all models. This is fairly easy is some cases, such as blending structural family therapy and strategic family therapy. In other instances, the philosophies and therapeutic stances of these models are so different that there is really no way to merge one with the other. It is hard, for example, to see how Jay Haley's directive therapeutic stance with its ordeals and challenges could find common ground with the social constructionists' decentered, "not knowing" approach.

As I have emphasized elsewhere in this book, the key to professional happiness is finding a foundational approach that fits your personal values and the way you like to be with others. Such a foundation may be found in one model or a small set of models, but it won't come from an eclectic sampling of all models.

As you review the 10 theories presented in this book, which approach seems to jump out at you? Perhaps parts of several models stand out for you. Is there a model that seems to fit what you have always believed about yourself, your family, your friends, your culture, your community, and even life in general? Do several models speak to your beliefs? Are there any theoretical orientations that seem to explain your own development, that make sense out of the patterns of interactions and rules you have known in your family-of-origin, or that suggest ways to address current or past issues in your family relationships? There actually may have been something in every chapter to which you responded in a positive way, but what can you see yourself using with a family when you start your actual practice? Answers to these questions may serve as arrows, pointing you toward the model or set of models you will choose to call your own.

Videotaping Your Work and Taking Time for Reflection

When you start to develop foundational approaches for your work, be willing to experiment. Try different things out. See what works for you and what may not. Videotape your first family sessions as often as possible. Indeed, I urge all new practitioners—and even seasoned older ones—to videotape their own work at least once a week. Sit down to watch your tape at least twice. It is very difficult—some would say impossible—both to be in an experience and observe it at the same time.

When you watch yourself on tape, try to get past how you look and sound as quickly as possible: We all look and sound differently on tape than we think we do while we are in the session. Start with initial process questions: Focus more on what kind of relationship you form with each of the family members and with the group as a whole. What things increase your presence with each of them? Is there anything that seems to be distracting you from being present? When you listen to what the family has to say, are you just listening to the words or are you starting to see and experience the processes that are occurring too? What patterns or sequences emerge in the family process? What rules seem to be governing how the individual members behave and interact? What roles seem to be part of the family process? Are these roles helping or interfering with the kind of family life that the members desire? Do the people enacting these roles trigger any reactions or distractions in you? What problems are affecting this family? How is each person or the system as a whole coping? What relationships are family members forming with the problem that has entered or even taken over their lives? This is by no means an exhaustive list of process and assessment questions. It is just a way to begin addressing the ways in which you think, conceptualize, and assess the families you will meet in your practice.

When you watch yourself on tape, you will have a chance to *reflect* and *connect*. Reflection is largely an internal assessment: Ask yourself what thoughts, feelings, and reactions were triggered when you worked with the family. Were there things you did well and that made you feel competent and professional? Were there things you wished you had done differently? Did you feel triangulated into any parts of the family relationships? Asking these questions also will help you start to connect to patterns in your work. You will start to discover that you have comfort patterns, interventions you rely on to form relationships, do assessment, create meaning, and/or promote change. You also will begin to see that you can connect your personal and professional patterns to one or more of the models you have already studied. You won't so much adopt a model as you will arrive at it. When it is right, it will have the feeling of being a good fit.

This will be your foundational model or set of models. They will ground you, and add a sense of consistency and structure to your therapeutic process and interventions. Knowing your foundation also will allow you to pick and choose aspects from other approaches that will also fit well and can be consistently (even easily) integrated into your work.

Such an approach to integration always has been part of us. When we were little, we let our parents be our foundation, our anchor, our stability. We would venture out from them for a while, but we always would come back to what was known and safe. It was not long before we began to recognize that certain parts of us were central to our being, to our existence, and to our essence. The foundation moved from what was outside of us to what was in us. Sometimes, through experience, learning, and experimentation, we would bring new parts of life back to what felt like home. After a while, those new parts to our lives (or ourselves) became natural, normal, and useable. We integrated them as if they had always been part of our foundation. All of this took time, of course, but are there not some parts of us that are very different now from what we were like when we were 5 years old? And surprisingly, are not some parts of us still the same after all these years?

It will take time to grow into your professional stance. For the impatient, that's the bad news. The good news is that you are entering a profession in which lifelong learning and integration are both possible and necessary. One of my teachers, Virginia Satir (1983) would remind us: "It behooves all of us to continue being students. My recommendation is that we free ourselves to look anywhere and to use what seems to fit. This makes each of us a continually growing entity" (p. ix).

A Process for Family Therapy Across Models

Several forms and structures have been proposed as integrative models for family practice (for example, Breunlin, Schwartz, & MacKune-Karrer, 1992/1997; Carlson et al., 2005; Hanna, 2007; Nichols, 1995; Worden, 2003). Each of these approaches has the authors' own special blueprints for counseling and therapy. I like to think of family therapy in the same way that I experience classical music: The process of family therapy, it seems to me, has movements, and each of these movements has unique rhythms, tempos, notes, and functions but, taken together, they make up a larger whole. For me, there are four general movements to the overall flow of family practice, counseling, and therapy: (1) forming a relationship, (2) conducting an assessment, (3) hypothesizing and sharing meaning, and (4) facilitating change. Once in a long while, these four movements actually may happen within a single session. In most cases, however, each movement takes multiple sessions, and the flow of family practice seldom proceeds neatly from one movement to the next. Indeed, tending to the relational and assessment aspects of family therapy may have to happen many times throughout the process.

Forming a Relationship

Next to client characteristics (such as inner strengths, faith, and goal-directedness) and the clients' outside resources (such as education, social support, financial stability, and good fortune), the relationship between the family practitioner and the client accounts for the greatest amount of change in therapy. Specifically, client attributes and resources account for about 40% of change; relationship accounts for about 30% of change; therapeutic model or approach accounts for about 15% of change; and another 15% of change occurs just because the client comes to therapy (Blow & Sprenkle, 2001; Carlson et al., 2005; Lambert & Ogles, 2004). Even the act of coming to therapy is highly influenced by relational factors: Do the clients believe the counselor or therapist can help? Is the family practitioner motivationally oriented? Does the counselor or therapist effectively engage the client(s) in the process of family counseling or therapy?

Therapeutic relationships start with the first contact that practitioners have with clients. Even though it may be impractical in some cases, I recommend that therapists either make their own appointments or personally call clients after appointments have been made to answer initial questions and give clients a sense of what to expect when they come. Even on the phone, clients will communicate a lot through tone of voice, the language they use to describe their situations, and the types of concerns expressed. In addition to setting a time and place for the first meeting, family practitioners also should let clients know their position on who should be involved in therapy. Some therapists, like Whitaker, will insist that every member of the immediate and perhaps extended family be present; others will work with whoever is willing to come.

Effective therapeutic relationships, I believe, are highly related to a quality I will call *presence.* It is the ability to let all other matters in the therapist's life and work go—and to bring one's focus to the here and now. It is opening one's five senses to all of the information that they can take in, and to bring a focused interest in each person and to what they have to say as well as the way they say it. Satir called this quality of relationship making contact (Satir & Bitter, 2000). Others would call it joining, engagement, friendliness, or simple care and concern. Welcoming family members with openness and warmth reduces the initial anxiety that families may be feeling and increases the probability that each person will participate in the session.

Process and structure in the therapy sessions are the responsibility of the family practitioner. From the beginning, it is important to focus on interaction. Who sits where? Who talks to whom and what effects do other parties have on dyadic communications? Does the therapist want to start the session by hearing from each person, or would family process be seen more easily if the family members had a normal conversation about the issues that brought them to therapy? In either case, understanding family process often is realized more through *how* questions ("How is this discussion going for all of you?" or "How do you get yourself heard in the middle of a fight?") than with *what, why, where,* or *when* questions that tend to emphasize content (Gladding, 2007).

Conducting an Assessment

Conducting an assessment from an integrative perspective allows family practitioners to develop a holistic conceptualization based on many different assessment tools. The original systemic theories we studied make use of a wide range of assessment interventions, including teleological assessments; birth order; genograms; triangulation, emotional reactivity, communication stances; evolving a crisis; structural assessments and organizational process; enactments; tracking sequences; ordeals, or circular questioning. Cognitive-behavioral family therapists assess automatic thinking, emotional response, and behavioral patterns using self-reports as well as formal tests and rating scales. With the advent of postmodern, social constructionism, new assessment orientations have been proposed, including investigations of difference, exceptions, unique events, and new possibilities or solutions. This movement away from assessments of internalized pathology and systemic dysfunction is shared by feminist family therapists, who look at gender roles, power distribution, and the effects of patriarchy on the family.

Eight Lenses

One way to conduct an assessment of families across models is to think of each model as contributing one or more perspectives from which a family can be understood. Which perspectives might come to your mind? In 1992/1997, Breunlin, Schwartz, and MacKune-Karrer introduced the concept of metaframeworks as a means for transcending the various approaches to family therapy. Their integrative approach began by identifying "six core metaframeworks" (p. 55):

Internal family systems (or the individual as system); sequences (or patterns of interaction); organization (of the system); development; multicultural (or diversity); and gender. Gerald Corey and I added two additional perspectives through which families might be understood. We called these perspectives the teleological (or goal oriented) and process metaframeworks (Bitter & Corey, 2005).

We can think of each of these metaframework perspectives as lenses, such as one might have in a pair of glasses. Depending on which pair of glasses we wear and which lenses we look through, we will see, assess, and understand the family differently. Using multiple lenses allows family practitioners to *know* the family more intimately.

To me, initially hearing about a family's problem is like looking at a new puppy through a window in a pet store. I can generate quite a bit of excitement just looking, but I need to know more before I can buy it. I can enrich my knowledge of the puppy by going into the store and getting closer to it: I can observe how it moves, how it handles people and change, and how it seeks to meet its needs; I can pick it up, feel its fur, and play with it; and I can learn about its health, breed, gender, and likely development. In short, the more ways I can come to know the puppy, the greater my experiencing of that puppy will be. It also helps me form a better relationship with the puppy and keeps me from doing things that inadvertently may harm it.

The value of lenses is that they allow family practitioners to consider multiple perspectives, rather than being locked into a single viewpoint. When I meet a family, it may not be appropriate to use all eight of the lenses I am about to describe, but often several of the lenses will deserve special emphasis. They will be the ones associated with the areas of life in which the family feels most constricted.

The eight lenses tend to be recursive, each one influencing and being influenced by the others; you will recall that recursiveness is a common quality of systemic approaches. Although the primary use of lenses is in *assessment*, they also can guide counselors and therapists in *tailoring* therapeutic interventions to the specific needs of each family (see Carlson et al., 2005; Goldenberg & Goldenberg, 2002). A description of each of the eight lenses is presented next. I should warn you that some of this material is complex and will require careful reading and even some re-reading. I will provide examples where I can to make these ideas as clear as possible.

Internal Family Systems. Richard Schwartz (1995) developed and named this systemic model for working with individuals. He is not the only family practitioner, however, to have conceptualized individuals as a family of parts or a collection of selves. Virginia Satir accessed various parts of individuals through her phenomenological approach to family mapping, the wheel of influence, a self-mandala, and most directly through a parts party (Satir, Banmen, Gerber, & Gomori, 1991). Her parts party was a psychodramatic process for integrating extreme parts in individuals, and it was especially effective when working with couples when their parts were in conflict (Bitter, 1993b). Perhaps the most complete explication of the individual as a population of selves was offered by the master Gestalt therapist, Erv Polster (1995).

Each person is an organismic whole or system, complete with **structure**, organization, and subsystems. The many parts that constitute what I call *me* may be self-enhancing or self-destructive. Some are physical parts; some are cognitive, emotional, social, or spiritual. We each have developed our own particular configuration of parts through our social interactions and developmental experiences. We tend to use some parts more than others, and the parts we use the most tend to be personally chosen evaluations that say something about who we are and what is meaningful to us. Breunlin et al. (1992/1997) note that "all parts, in their non-extreme, natural state want something positive for the person and desire to play a valuable role in the internal system" (p. 66). Individuals experience conflict when internal parts become polarized or extreme—or when needed parts seem inaccessible.

Every theorist/practitioner who works with internal parts posits a super-entity that integrates, governs, organizes, and selects essential parts. Sometimes that entity is called the self; sometimes, it is called the person. Whatever the name, it is the whole of the system, that which is greater than the sum of the parts. It is to this self-person that proper leadership of our parts is assigned: "the Self is generally in the lead and the parts are there to advise, lend feelings or talents, or otherwise assist" (Breunlin et al., 1992/1997, p. 68).

External conflicts and interactions often stimulate polarized or extreme parts in individuals—and also serve to minimize the chance that more useful parts may be activated. Bowen (1978) noted that a differentiated self was the hallmark of functionality. In Bowen's model, differentiation had an internal and external function. In general, internal differentiation was achieved when rationality is given primacy over emotional reactivity: the person selects a calmer, more considered response than one that is automatic. External differentiation allows the person to disengage from patterned interactions and routines and to choose new responses that fit a person in charge of her or his own life. Both differentiation processes elevate certain internal parts over others and suggest that re-connecting to these parts is required for growth and development as a person—and as a therapist.

Some of the questions related to this lens include:

- Which parts do each of you rely on to describe who you really are?
- Sometimes we find the best parts of ourselves almost at war (or polarized) with other internal parts: Which parts cause internal conflict in you?
- Are there parts of you that are seldom used or that you feel that you used to have but now have lost or ignored?
- In difficult interactions, which parts of you do others seem to be able to consistently call forth?

The Teleological Lens.   Teleology is the study of final causes, endpoints, goals, and purposes. Teleological assessments are future-oriented. It is more important to know where a person or system is heading, what it intends, than to know where it has been. A teleological lens helps us to understand what motivates individuals, the systemic purpose of symptoms, the goals of triangulation, and the uses of patterned or sequenced interactions and routines.

Bowen, Satir, Minuchin, and the strategic therapists all use a teleological lens from time to time. No approach, however, uses this lens more than the Adlerians.

Purposive action and life goals are the basis for understanding the individual's movement through life that Adlerians call lifestyle (see Powers & Griffith, 1987). Adlerians also use the **personality priorities** (Kfir, 1981, 1989) of significance, pleasing, control, and comfort to understand impasses and goals in couples counseling. Personality priorities are similar to Satir's communication stances of blaming, placating, super-reasonable, and irrelevant, respectively. Indeed, one way of conceptualizing personality priorities is to see them as the goals of dysfunctional communication (Bitter, 1987).

In Adlerian family therapy, goal orientation and recognition allow the therapist to understand which goals motivate the mistaken interactions between parents and children (Bitter, Roberts, & Sonstegard, 2002; Christensen, 2004). Adlerians believe that the goals of children and adults interact in mistaken ways that often become patterns, sequences, or routines that seem automatic and unavoidable. Unlocking these mistaken goals often involves slowing down the sequences and making different choices based on preferred goals. It is easy to see how this same teleological lens is also part of the solution-focused/solution-oriented approach to family therapy.

A teleological perspective also is involved in interventions such as reframing. When family practitioners reframe difficult behaviors or interactions by noting the often good intentions or motivations behind individual actions, they are using a teleological lens.

Some of the questions that get at goals and purposes, and serve as a foundation for reframing, include:

- What purpose does the symptom, interaction, or process serve?
- How does the individual's behavior protect the self or the system?
- What are the social consequences of the action or interaction?
- How are the goals of family members at cross-purposes with each other?

Sequences: Tracking Patterns of Interaction.   At the heart of the early systemic approaches to family therapy was the conviction that family life is ordered and that family members interact in sequences that tend to be repeated in multiple forms over time. Breunlin et al. (1992/1997) refer to such patterns as embedded sequences, and suggest that they occur at four levels.

Level one sequences are face-to-face sequences that occur between two or more family members. Triangulation is often a level one sequence: Perhaps a mother is upset with her daughter; the daughter turns to her father; the father intervenes on the child's behalf with the mother, leading to a fight between the parents.

Let's consider a more specific example. Paul is watching a football game on television. Jane comes into the room and says, "There's a dead mouse in the garage." Paul feels interrupted and grumbles a bit, continuing to watch his game. Jane feels ignored, and she yells to their daughter Ann: "Will you please get that mouse out of the garage. . . . (sarcastically) Apparently, your father is too busy or just doesn't care!!"

Ann heads to the garage. Paul is now upset. He gets up, responding, "Everything always has to be done on your schedule. You can never just wait a few minutes." And he stomps out to the garage, giving directions to Ann as the door shuts.

This is a face-to-face sequence characterized by differing needs, reciprocal demands, blaming, hurt, and yes, triangulation. It ends with Paul giving in behaviorally, but having the last word. This sequence may be an idiosyncratic fight, triggered by conflicting needs, but the quality of the reciprocal attacks suggests that it is probably a recurrent pattern of fighting in which only the content of the fight has changed.

> The acts that are missing from [a level 1] interaction are often as important as the ones that are there: if a couple argues and neither party listens to the other, then the absence of listening is an important dimension of the sequence. (Breunlin et al., 1992/1997, p. 105)

Level two sequences are routines that family members use to support the daily activities and general functioning of the family. The Adlerian assessment of a typical day provides family practitioners with a picture of how level two sequences support individuals, as well as a smooth process for the whole system. Routines allow people and systems to accomplish more than one thing at a time. If routines stop or start to break down, then the whole system must readjust. Most of the time, however, routines are seamless and go unnoticed.

If Paul's "sports part" were not totally engaged, it is possible that the sequence in the example above could have had a different ending. Let's say that Paul is engaged in nothing in particular—or certainly nothing important. Jane comes into the room and says, "There's a dead mouse in the garage." Paul gets up to handle the problem because, after years of marriage, he knows that Jane hates mice, wants it removed without a fuss, and expects that Paul will handle such matters. It is a sequence that supports the functioning of the family. It is their routine. Neither questions it.

Level three sequences refer to those processes that occur during the ebbs and flows of life. These are much longer sequences that occur when the family must adjust to what Satir and Baldwin (1983) call a foreign element (or an outside force) or when developmental changes are required. Haley (1980) describes such developmental sequences when he talks about the processes involved in a young person leaving home.

When Amy, the youngest child, is about to finish high school and leave for a distant city to go to college, change in the family system is imminent. Most of the energy in the parental subsystem has been directed toward this young woman and her older sister for years, with accommodations that have distanced Paul and Jane. The prospect of Amy leaving has left Paul more self-absorbed. Jane, too, is feeling lost and unsure of what they will do as a couple when they are alone. Their fight is a message to Amy: "Don't leave. We are not ready for you to leave." Amy may, in fact, leave, but if her parents start to fall apart, she may also have to get "sick" and return home.

Such an ebb and flow sequence does not occur out of the blue. It has developed over time through numerous face-to-face sequences as well as the creation of and adjustments made to family routines. Effective resolution of level one and two sequences greatly facilitates a similar resolution of level three sequences.

Level four sequences are transgenerational. Bowen's (1978) intergenerational approach was designed to assess and address level four sequences—as was the intergenerational attachment work of Boszormenyi-Nagy and Spark (1973). These larger sequences are intended to provide a sense of continuity to life, and they may pass on values and rules about culture and gender that define the system from one generation to the next. Using Satir's *life-fact chronology* is a useful way to discover transgenerational sequences.

> In traditional societies, [transgenerational] sequences may pass from one generation to the next with little change. In rapidly evolving societies such as our own, however, sequences that were adaptive in one generation may create stress if they are replicated in a subsequent generation. (Breunlin et al., 1992/1997, p. 113)

Adaptive sequences require leadership that is balanced, fair, and cooperative. Satir (1983) believed that parents could form a nurturing, primary triad with each of their children: When needed, two would work for the developmental good of the third person. A foundation of self-esteem would allow for flexibility and would greet change as an inevitable part of life. Maladaptive sequences occur when rules are rigid and inflexible, when parts are polarized, and when change is resisted: Family members feel constrained.

Family therapy is often about developing more useful sequences at any or all of the four levels. Some useful sequence questions are:

- Who does what with whom when decisions are made, conflicts occur, or problems need to be handled? Give me an example: When was the last time such a sequence occurred?
- What routines support your daily living? How does a typical day go?
- The last time you had a crisis at home, how did it go? Who did what with whom?
- Are there processes, patterns, or sequences that characterize current or past transitions for this family?

The Organization Lens.   Perhaps no models addressed the organization in families more thoroughly than the structural-strategic models. Terms like macro-system, subsystem, enmeshment, disengagement, power, and hierarchy were all early systemic conceptualizations of organization. In these models, the living structure of the family was revealed in the rules, routines, rituals, and expected roles that held the system together. Interventions were designed to establish a more functional hierarchy and to redistribute the power in the system toward more productive goals and ends—ends that were by-and-large determined by the therapist or a team of therapists.

With the exception of the Adlerians and Satir, very little attention was given to what constituted a functional family. Today, we have a large body of research available to describe normal family processes (Walsh, 2003), as well as rich descriptions of family life in diverse cultures (see McGoldrick, Giordano, & Garcia-Preto, 2005). With the advent of feminist and postmodern, social constructionist approaches in family therapy, the concept of hierarchy gradually gave way to the requirements for effective leadership (Breunlin et al., 1992/1997). Effective family leadership involves the kind of collaboration that is possible in egalitarian relationships. Satir's notion of parents as two sides of a nurturing triad comes into play, and the role of family leaders is to organize the system in clear and useful ways. Collaborative leadership makes room for each of the members to grow and develop individually while still contributing to the family as a whole; family members who have a stake in any given outcome also are involved in the decision making that leads to that outcome; every part of the system has reasonable access to family resources; and family members are able to take appropriate responsibility for self, as well as for the system as a whole.

The key to effective organization is balance. In general, family leadership works best when the adults have enough maturity and life experience to start a family out of choice and a desire to raise the next generation. Balanced adult leadership is firm, but friendly; understands developmental processes and needs; and sets limits while remaining fair, flexible, and encouraging. Both individuality and connection have an important place in balanced family life, and both must fit with generational, cultural, and developmental needs. As children get older, they are invited in as partners in family decisions; leadership becomes more collaborative, egalitarian, and democratic; and family processes focus on cooperation, consistency, and caring. Children and adolescents benefit from emotion coaching: They have a sense of safety as well as the belief that they are valued. They have room to grow, to explore, and to experiment without losing the support system a family can provide. Children experience freedom within order (Dreikurs & Soltz, 1964). Some useful organization questions are:

- Are the parents effective leaders of the family? How do the children respond to parental leadership?
- Are any family members interfering in the tasks and activities of a subsystem to which they do not belong?
- Is the process of leadership balanced or unbalanced? Does it lead to harmony or conflict?
- Are there any internal parts of individuals that constrain effective leadership or do the parents simply need further education in this area?

The Developmental Lens.   In the 1940s, the concept of development took hold in psychology and affected everything we knew about individual cognitive, emotional, and behavioral growth. Outside of social work, developmental frameworks tended to be avoided in family practice until the late 1970s. For the last 35 years, family therapists have been developing a systemic developmental model called the family life cycle (Carter & McGoldrick, 2005). Unlike individual development models that tend to map the stages of life from birth to death, the family life cycle focuses on the development of family life through six transition periods.

1. A single, young adult leaves home to start an independent life;
2. Individuals marry or couple and begin to build a life together;
3. The couple has children and starts a family;
4. The children reach adolescence; it is a time when young people experiment with both autonomy and a freer sense of connection, but it is also a time when parental fears, concerns, and efforts at control typically increase. This also may be when the parents are dealing with mid-life marital and career issues: if divorce happens, it may constitute "an unscheduled family transition." (Ahrons, 2005, p. 381);
5. Parents launch their children into the world and prepare for a life without children; this stage may include multiple exits and re-entries, but it almost always requires a renegotiation within the couple relationship; and

6. The family enters into later years when the parents prepare for the end of their lives, often needing the care of their children who, at the same time, are caring for their own youngsters.

Because it was systemic in nature, the family life cycle provided a framework for understanding and anticipating many of the *ebb and flow* and *transgenerational* sequences common to family life. It also de-pathologized many of the family life experiences that brought couples and families into therapy. The original family life cycle focused almost entirely on the two-parent, Caucasian, **nuclear family**: Today, there are developmental models for:

- single-parent families;
- remarried, blended, or stepfamilies;
- cross-generational, extended families;
- lesbian, gay, and bisexual families (including developmental models for coming out that address both the needs of individuals and their families); and
- families from diverse cultures.

Carter and McGoldrick's (2005) comprehensive work also addresses the effects of poverty on the family and delineates the gender issues and roles that permeate a detailed assessment of the family life cycle.

Breunlin and colleagues (1992/1997) proposed an integration of individual and systemic developmental models, suggesting five levels of assessment: "biological, individual, subsystemic (relational), familial, and societal" (p. 159). Again, these levels are recursive with no particular order of development implied. Rather than looking at these levels as stages of development, family practitioners can assess individuals and families to see if they are achieving necessary *levels of competence* in each area to facilitate growth and development.

In the levels of biological, individual, and family development, transitions make it possible to assess the ways in which people and families are either less than competent or greater than competent (Breunlin et al., 1992/1997). Just as the body can have appropriately developed, underdeveloped, or overdeveloped functions, individuals can have parts that are competent, less than competent, or even overly competent. Again, balance and harmony are attributes of competence and functionality. In families, transitions are greatly affected by the competence of subsystems (relations within the family) and by the requirements imposed by larger systems in which the families are embedded.

Change is inevitable; change *is* life (Satir et al., 1991). In family practice, growth and development are both ideals and desired processes. A belief in development and evolution is optimistic and hopeful. Family practitioners who learn to move among and between levels within a developmental lens are able to bring a more holistic and de-pathologized viewpoint to assessment and treatment. The developmental lens is multidimensional and requires flexibility and fluidity in therapeutic application. In assessing various levels, we look for constraints and seek to remove them so that natural growth and transitions become possible once again. Some useful developmental questions are:

- Where is each person in the family in relation to personal biological, cognitive, emotional, and social development?
- Where is the family in the family life cycle, and how are they handling transitions?
- What relational processes have developed over time, and how have they changed or developed through transitional periods?
- What developments in the larger system (especially society or the world) are affecting the family?

The Multicultural Lens.   Discrimination and oppression have, unfortunately, been part of the human experience for a long time. The oldest and most pervasive forms of discrimination are related to gender, race, social class, and ethnicity, making multicultural and gender lenses in family therapy essential. If all cultures and both genders had equal access to resources, equal influence within all levels of systems, equal responsibility for the growth, development, and decision making of society in which personal systems are embedded, and an equal sense of belonging and value, then diversity would be a given, and an appreciation of difference would be natural. In reality, dominant cultures (Foucault, 1970, 1980) arise in every society. They organize around two immediate goals: (a) to reinforce themselves and (b) to minimize the power and influence of alternate positions. It is from the power base of dominant cultures that all discrimination and oppression flow.

In the United States, the dominant culture is male, heterosexual, Caucasian, English-speaking, Eurocentric, Christian, 35–50 years of age, rich, healthy, able, and educated. People who more closely match this description have greater access to money, power, laws, and politics. Knowledge and its creation also are controlled by those in power (Foucault, 1970). Historical narratives are filled with phrases such as "the divine right of kings," "manifest destiny," or "in the name of progress," but it all has to do with *privilege*. If you are not part of the dominant culture, it is likely you will experience discrimination and be *marginalized*, oppressed, or left out.

A multicultural lens challenges the idea of a dominant culture and introduces diversity and complexity into our understanding of the human condition. From this perspective, a dominant culture is simply one of many. From this perspective, family practitioners are invited to consider that their natural way of being is only one of many ways of being. As feminists have noted, family therapy, itself, includes an imbalance in the power relationship between the counselor and the client: The counselor is always the one offering help, and the client is always the one in need. This power imbalance is exacerbated when the therapist embodies most or many of the positions of power and privilege, and the client does not—especially if the client is, say, lesbian or gay, African Caribbean or African American, a recent immigrant, atheist, disabled, over 40 years of age, poor, and/or not well-educated.

McGoldrick et al. (2005) have developed the most comprehensive text on culture and family therapy. One of the many benefits of their book is a delineation of the multiple cultures that comprise Europe and have "melted" into the dominant culture we call America. This multiplicity challenges the notion that there is a single Western norm to which all people should aspire. It is, perhaps, ironic that those who gain some membership in a dominant culture often know the least about the specific cultures from which their families emerged. Just as there is no single American or Western culture, there are also no single African, Asian, Caribbean, Hispanic, Latino, Native American, or Pacific Island/Pacific Rim cultures. Therapy training programs now require courses in which therapists can reclaim an awareness of their heritage(s) and use this knowledge to assess a therapeutic "goodness of fit" (Breunlin et al., 1992/1997, p. 230).

When assessing goodness of fit, Breunlin and associates start with three levels of human cultural experience: (a) the intracultural experiences that happen within a cultural system and give definition and a sense of continuity to community life; (b) the intercultural experiences that happen between (or even among) cultural systems and serve to hold people together in a common bond (being Canadian, for example), and (c) the human universal experiences that ". . . provide a sense of commonality among all the nations of the world" (p. 194).

The multicultural perspective considers 12 areas of assessment:

- Membership as an immigrant or part of a host society;
- Level of economic privilege or poverty;
- Level of education and process of learning;
- Ethnicity;
- Religion;

- Gender;
- Sexual/affectional orientation;
- Age;
- Health and ability;
- Race, discrimination, and oppression;
- Minority versus majority status; and
- Regional background.

Each assessment area should produce a phenomenological meaning that may be different for each member of a family, as well as for the therapist. Acknowledging areas of *fit* and areas of *difference* is at the heart of the multicultural lens.

Families experience cultural change in at least two forms: one is the more gradual changes that happen within a culture over time and that are connected to "historical/ generational sequences" (p. 203). The other is the more abrupt change that results from immigration and acculturation within a host society. Although the former often allows families to absorb change without high levels of stress, the latter literally can implode family life. Many families not only immigrate, but also migrate, necessitating multiple accommodations and acculturations. Further, grandparents, parents, and children can be at different levels of acculturation, each with legitimate goals and hopes for their new lives together. A synergistic acculturation—in which both the culture of origin and the host culture are allowed to have a recursive effect on each other—seems to produce the most functional balance for individuals and families (Atkinson, Morten, & Sue, 2004; Miranda, Estrada, & Firpo-Jimenez, 2000). Acculturation, however, is a process of change, and respect for the needs of individuals at differing levels of acculturation is essential to a multicultural lens.

Some useful multicultural questions are:

- What cultures are in the family background of each of the family members?
- In what culture or region is the family currently living?
- Is immigration or migration a recent family experience?
- How do economics, education, ethnicity, religion, race, regional affiliation, gender, and age affect family processes?
- How is the fit between the therapist and the family with regard to economics, education, ethnicity, religion, gender, age, race, majority/minority status, and regional background?

The Gender Lens. With few exceptions, patriarchy has affected all people across the human lifespan. Feminists have challenged not only the fundamental precepts of family therapy (Luepnitz, 1988; Silverstein & Goodrich, 2003), but also the idea that the heterosexual family itself is good for women (Hare-Mustin, 1978). Women who work outside the home already have dual careers: Even in two-parent, heterosexual homes, women still bear the largest responsibility for and most of the work relating to child rearing, kin keeping, homemaking, and community care-giving. Financially, men still earn more than twice what women will make in comparable positions. When women earn significant wages, they often have far less than equal say in how heterosexual family finances are spent. Even in so-called normal families, married men are happier than married women, with the latter reporting both more dissatisfaction and more symptomatic experiences than other family members (Lewis, Beaver, Gossett, & Phillips, 1976). Between a man and a woman, there is almost no question about who will sacrifice for the good of the whole.

Traditional family therapies and the studies that supported them presumed that the dominant-culture norm was the correct one—even though this norm was patriarchal [male-centered, overly generalized, gender insensitive, and loaded with double standards (see Eichler, 1988)]. Feminists challenged the idea that the family was more important than and could be allowed to stand in opposition to the welfare of its female members. Feminists challenged the notion that interdependent male-female relationships meant that both parties had equal influence and options in a relationship. Interdependence certainly was not equal power to enact change (Taggart, 1985).

The feminist impact on family therapy has led to a reconsideration of many central tenets. Family therapy increasingly is accepted as a political process in which therapists no longer can ignore their personal influence and their responsibility to challenge unequal status and treatment of women. Power positions, like hierarchy, enmeshment, and unbalancing, are slowly being replaced with ideas about leadership, connection, and collaboration.

Gottman (2006) is completing a 12-year study of gay and lesbian couples. In looking at their relational processes, he notes that gay and lesbian couples use more humor and affection in their disagreements and disagreement generally is received more positively than in heterosexual couples. Further, gay and lesbian partners are more likely than heterosexual couples to remain positive after the disagreement is over. According to Gottman, "When it comes to emotions, we think [gay and lesbian] couples may operate with very different principles than straight couples. Straight couples may have a lot to learn from gay and lesbian relationships" (web page). When we compare gay and lesbian couples as parents to heterosexual couples as parents, there are no substantive differences in how the children are raised or how they turn out, but the positive emotional climate is noted (Flaks, Ficher, Masterpasqua, & Joseph, 1995).

Breunlin et al. (1992/1997) note that heterosexual families enter therapy at different levels in the "gender evolution" from traditional organizations and experiences to gender-aware, polarized, transitional, and eventually balanced. Each level has a characteristic organization and resulting internal experiences. Traditional organizations maintain complementary roles in which women are often oppressed and may feel angry. Gender-aware families may have begun to rethink the value of complementary roles; women's anger may be acknowledged, but men will often fear a "loss of nurturance" (p. 250). In polarized families, the expectations associated with gender roles breaks down, and there is often open conflict between male–female spouses; anger, worry, and fear interplay with intermittent feelings of guilt. Transitional families are those moving "toward mutuality and supporting flexible family roles and expectations" (pp. 250–251). Anger and fear are less extreme, and when gender differences come into conflict, they are treated more as temporary setbacks. Balanced families become democratic, cooperative organizations based on mutual needs and equal participation in family decision-making processes.

Although these levels seem linear in description, families often move between and even among levels, depending on the challenges they face and the distress they experience. Still, development toward a balanced gender organization and participation is in the best interest of every family and all of its members.

Some useful gender questions are:

- What gender role is each member of the family assuming?
- What effect has patriarchy had on this family and its members?
- Where are family members in terms of gender development?
- What ideas in relation to gender need to be affirmed or challenged?
- What effect would role reversals have on the personal parts and relational processes of the family members?
- What impact will my gender have on the family and the process of change?

The Process Lens. Since the advent of humanistic psychotherapy, counselors-in-training have been told that process is more important than content (Gladding, 2007): In actual practice, they are linked and both have significance. This idea is seminal in communications and experiential models of family therapy. The meaning of any communication always is contained within the metacommunication: how we communicate contextualizes what we have to say. Satir et al. (1991) contrast the power of congruent, emotionally honest communication in families with four dysfunctional communication stances: blaming, placating, super-reasonable, and irrelevant. Although congruent communication makes it possible for content to be heard, in dysfunctional communications, only the stress is registered—both in the sender and the receiver (Bitter, 1993a). Patterned communication processes have long been associated with family dysfunction. For example, a male batterer may go through an extended period of super-reasonable (controlling) communications designed to restrict the victim. Blaming characterizes the explosive violence that follows, and then almost immediately the cycle resolves itself in a placating remorse.

There is more to life, however, than repeated dysfunctional sequences: I have already noted the developmental processes in every family related to biological, individual, relational, family, cultural, and societal growth; as we have seen, there are also awareness processes related to **gender sensitivity**, multiculturalism, and integrating affectional/sexual orientation. Process is about our movement through life and also through significant events in life. Clarity of process tells us where we are and delineates where we are likely to go. It allows the therapist and family to examine where they are in the flow of life, the process of change, and the experience of therapy.

Biological, individual, and family developmental cycles are all givens. Process asks us to look at how people and families face these growth processes and cope with life's demands: In general, people and systems do better when they reflect a social interest in the welfare of others, cooperation, social equality, and courage (Adler, 1931, 1938). Families need flexible and adaptive roles that describe what people do rather than who they are. And although, in general, we value open systems, families also must be free to become periodically closed in the service of individual and family needs. There is a rhythm to the flow of life, and those who move with *purpose*, awareness, and human contact into a continuity of experience tend to have better coping skills and enriched lives. A process lens seeks to highlight these components of enriched living within the context of the family.

One of the most fundamental processes of life is the process of change. Satir and Bitter (2000) have described the process in experiential movements from a *status quo* to *new possibilities* (see the chapter on the human validation process model). Most of the time, the process of change is ongoing, and much of it can be assimilated with little disturbance or stress. When family disturbances are extreme, however, such as an affair in a relationship, a divorce, or a death, therapists often greet family members in chaos. They immediately become one of the family's external resources with a primary responsibility to help individuals re-connect with perhaps ignored, but much needed internal parts. Therapeutic movement through chaos is often delicate, embedded in the immediate experiences of the family. Somewhat paradoxically, change often is facilitated by staying present and not trying to change anything at all.

The process of therapy is connected intimately to the process of change. Carl Whitaker (1976, 1989) used to play with both family process and the process of therapy. He did so with a co-therapist present and many years of therapy experience. Like most family therapists, he recognized that systems were more powerful than individuals, and that the family practitioner can easily become triangulated or incorporated into the systemic processes of the family. In a sense, Whitaker often chose to become one of many foreign elements that could nudge the family into a new change process. In one session, he suggested that if the woman was depressed, there must be someone in the family who wanted her dead (Whitaker & Bumberry, 1988). This systems intervention goes beyond what the family initially is willing to consider and invites them into a shared responsibility for the welfare of the woman. At the heart of Whitaker's therapy were some very important process questions.

- What is the family doing with its time in therapy?
- What are they experiencing and what am I experiencing with them?

- What place does my informed and educated intuition have in this therapeutic process?
- What is my best use of self with this family?
- Where are we all heading together?
- What is happening right now?

In a more general sense, some useful process questions are:

- Where is the family in the process of change?
- Are there family members who lack a clear sense of purpose, function out of awareness, have poor contact with others, or lack experiences to support a productive life?
- What resources (internal and external) need to be accessed?
- Which communication patterns do family members use under stress?

These eight lenses for assessment are multidimensional. They were developed initially across several models of family therapy, and they serve as a basic structure for coming to know families more thoroughly. Families are multilayered systems that both affect and are affected by the larger systems in which they are embedded. Each of the eight lenses contributes something to a holistic understanding of family systems: From the internal parts of individuals to the systems and subsystems of the family to the family's relational processes with the larger systems that make up their lives, a multidimensional assessment becomes a foundation for effective case conceptualizations.

Formal Assessments

Although almost all family counseling and therapy approaches do some form of assessment, most rely on self report, direct observation, and clinical judgment more than formal investigations (see Thomlison, 2007). Feminists and social constructionists may choose to avoid formal assessment altogether—with the former concerned about diagnostic abuse of women and families and the latter asserting that such investigations are incompatible with a postmodern worldview (Sperry, 2004a). And to be sure, some of the most-used tests and scales, such as the Beavers Interactional Scales (BIS) and the Self-Report Family Inventory (SFI), mainly are associated with modernist systems theories such as structural and strategic family therapies.

Bray (2004) reports that the two most-common forms of family assessment are self-reports and direct observations: The data from these two approaches do not always match. Self-reports from multiple family members, as well as multiple direct observations, will increase the likelihood of an accurate assessment. Even when different assessments lack agreement, they can be used to identify areas of overlap and to cross-check information with the family members involved.

Most of the self-report questionnaires and scales have been developed for use with couples. With some common-sense adjustments, however, some of these scales also can be useful in assessing relationships between adults and older children. Current self-rating scales include: the Locke-Wallace Marital Adjustment Scale (LWMAS), the Dyadic Adjustment Scale (DAS), the Marital Satisfaction Inventory-Revised (MSI-R), PREPARE, ENRICH, the Areas of Change Questionnaire (ACQ), the Intimacy Needs Survey (INS), the Marital Disaffection Scale (MDS), SIDCARB, the Conflict Tactics Scale (CTS2), and the Sexual Desire Inventory (SDI) (Bagarozzi & Sperry, 2004).

The most-common family observational rating scales are: The Beavers Interactional Competence and Style (BICS), the Self-Report Family Inventory (SFI), the McMaster Clinical Rating Scale (MCRS), the Circumplex Clinical Rating Scale (CCRS), and the Global Assessment of Relational Functioning (GARF) found in the *DSM-IV-TR*. For a review of these observational scales, see Hampson and Beavers (2004).

Whether family practitioners choose to use formal tests and assessments depends largely on two criteria: congruence with the practitioner's chosen model and the need for quantitative data for research. Sperry (2004c) provides a useful protocol for those who choose to incorporate formal assessments in clinical practice. His six steps are: (1) initially interview the family; (2) choose and administer specific inventories; (3) collect additional data from records, outside sources, or other interviews; (4) review assessment data and plan treatment; (5) monitor ongoing clinical outcomes and modify treatment accordingly; and (6) evaluate outcomes (p. 125). These same steps are both facilitated by and required for the integration of effective case conceptualizations.

Case Conceptualization

Sperry (2004b) has proposed a process for case conceptualization as a means of linking theory to practice in couples and family counseling. Three components make up the process he proposes: a *diagnostic* formulation, a clinical formulation, and a treatment formulation.

A diagnostic formulation answers the question: "What happened?" It includes assessments of (a) what brought the family to therapy at this time; (b) how severe the difficulties are both within the family system and facing it; (c) how the individuals within the family are coping, including any presentations that may lead to a psychiatric diagnosis (American Psychiatric Association, 2000); and (d) what organic and medical concerns may be present. Two uniform systems of relational diagnosis are currently in use: the Classification of Relational Disorders (CORD) and the *DSM-IV-TR*'s Global Assessment of Relational Functioning (GARF).

A clinical formulation attempts to answer the question: "Why did it happen?" This formulation attempts to offer an explanation for the difficulties presented in the diagnostic formulation: It seeks a wider and more diverse perspective in understanding clients. It is during this phase of case conceptualization that an assessment based on the eight lenses described earlier comes into play. It is also during this part of the process that family practitioners seek to link their theories to a conceptualization of the family's individual, interpersonal, and systemic dynamics, as well as suggest what it is that may be causing the family problems. Such a clinical formulation is the bridge between diagnosis and treatment.

The treatment formulation answers the question: "Now that we have some understanding of what is happening and why, what can be done about it and what is the most effective way to do it?" A treatment formulation addresses goals for counseling and therapy, both those of the family and those co-constructed with the family. When possible, a treatment plan should include a consideration of interventions designed to reach desired goals, prediction about the length and course of treatment, and how outcomes will be evaluated.

The most useful case conceptualizations focus on the unique contexts, needs, and resources of the individual family members and the system as a whole. Assessment and diagnosis tend to require a deductive reasoning process that considers data in relation to established criteria: Does the family and its individual members meet criteria that would indicate functional or dysfunctional processes; medical health or disease; mental health or disorders; or social/relational support or isolation and/or oppression? Clinical formulations, on the other hand, tend to rely on inductive reasoning: How does all of the information collected fit into a unified whole? Given the multiple lenses that may be part of family assessment, is there a concept or theme, informed perhaps by one's theoretical perspectives, that can act as a meaningful explanation for what's going on? In the next chapter, we shall see how the eight lenses we have considered can be incorporated into a blueprint for therapy and how a focus on resources within individuals and families can promote family resiliency, ensure treatment efficacy, and prevent problem relapse.

Summary

We have already covered a lot of ground, and we still haven't addressed the multiple ways in which to facilitate change in families. Everything up to this point has been directed at forming a relationship and considering a multiple-lenses process in family assessment.

Devoting this much attention to relationships and assessments parallels what I believe should happen in actual family practice. If I had only an hour in which to see a family, I would want to spend at least 40–45 minutes of it tending to relational aspects and getting to know the family. That would leave only 15–20 minutes to propose and facilitate change, and I would think that might be about the right balance for me. In actual practice, of course, family therapy does not occur in discrete units and it is seldom accomplished in 1 hour. The facilitation of change often goes hand-in-hand with forming relationships and assessment, and each of the steps in this integrative process may last many sessions.

In the next chapter, we will consider ways to bring the information from different assessments together and how to hypothesize about and share the meanings we discover in working with families. We also will look at ways to tailor therapeutic interventions to facilitate change and ensure effective treatment. And, finally, I will apply this integrative model to the Quest family—one last time.

References

Adler, A. (1931). *What life should mean to you.* Boston: Little, Brown.

Adler, A. (1938). *Social interest: A challenge to mankind.* London: Faber & Faber.

Ahrons, C. R. (2005). Divorce: An unscheduled family transition. In B. Carter & M. McGoldrick (Eds.), *The extended family life cycle: Individual, family, and social perspectives* (3rd ed.) (pp. 381–398). Needham Heights, MA: Allyn & Bacon.

American Psychiatric Association (2000). *Diagnostic and statistical manual of mental disorders* (4th ed.). Washington DC: Author.

Atkinson, D. R., Morten, G., & Sue, D. W. (2004). *Counseling American minorities.* (6th ed.). New York: McGraw-Hill.

Bagarozzi, D. A., & Sperry, L. (2004). Couples assessment: Strategies and inventories. In L. Sperry (Ed.), *Assessment of couples and families: Contemporary and cutting-edge strategies* (pp. 135–158). New York: Brunner-Routledge.

Bitter, J. R. (1987). Communication and meaning: Satir in Adlerian context. In R. Sherman & D. Dinkmeyer (Eds.), *Systems of family therapy: An Adlerian integration* (pp. 109–142). New York: Brunner/Mazel.

Bitter, J. (1993a). Communication styles, personality priorities, and social interest: Strategies for helping couples build a life together. *Individual Psychology, 49*(3–4), 330–350.

Bitter, J. R. (1993b). Satir's parts party with couples. In T. S. Nelson & T. S. Trepper (Eds.), *101 interventions in family therapy* (pp. 132–136). New York: Haworth Press.

Bitter, J. R., & Corey, G. (2005). Family systems therapy. In G. Corey, *Theory and practice of counseling and psychotherapy* (7th ed., pp. 420–459). Belmont, CA: Brooks/Cole.

Bitter, J. R., Roberts, A., & Sonstegard, M. A. (2002). Adlerian family therapy. In J. Carlson & D. Kjos (Eds.), *Theories and strategies of family therapy* (pp. 41–79). Boston: Allyn & Bacon.

Blow, A. J., & Sprenkle D. H. (2001). Common factors across theories of marriage and family therapy: A modified Delphi study. *Journal of Marital and Family Therapy, 27*(3), 385–401.

Boszormenyi-Nagy, I., & Spark, G. (1973). *Invisible loyalties: Reciprocity in intergenerational family therapy.* New York: HarperCollins.

Bowen, M. (1978). *Family therapy in clinical practice.* Northvale, NJ: Aronson.

Bray, J. H. (2004). Models and issues in couple and family assessment. In L. Sperry (Ed.), *Assessment of couples and families: Contemporary and cutting-edge strategies* (pp. 13–29). New York: Brunner-Routledge.

Breunlin, D. C., Schwartz, R. C., & MacKune-Karrer, B. (1997). *Metaframeworks: Transcending the models of family therapy.* San Francisco: Jossey-Bass. (Original work published 1992)

Carlson, J., Sperry, L., & Lewis, J. A. (2005). *Family therapy techniques: Integrating and tailoring treatment.* New York: Routledge.

Carter, B., & McGoldrick, M. (Eds.). (2005). *The expanded family life cycle: Individual, family, and social perspectives* (3rd ed.). Needham Heights, MA: Allyn & Bacon.

Christensen, O. C. (Ed.). (2004). *Adlerian family counseling* (3rd ed.). Minneapolis, MN: Educational Media Corp.

Dreikurs, R., & Soltz, V. (1964). *Children: The challenge.* New York: Hawthorn.

Eichler, M. (1988). *Nonsexist research methods.* London: Allen and Unwin.

Flaks, D. K., Ficher, I., Masterpasqua, F., & Joseph, G. (1995). Lesbians choosing motherhood: A comparative study of lesbian and heterosexual parents and their children. *Developmental Psychology, 31,* 105–114.

Foucault, M. (1970). *The order of things: An archaeology of the human sciences.* New York: Random House.

Foucault, M. (1980). *Power/knowledge: Selected interviews and other writings.* New York: Pantheon Books.

Gehart, D. R., & Tuttle, A. R. (2003). *Theory-based treatment planning for marriage and family therapists.* Pacific Grove, CA: Brooks/Cole.

Gladding, S. T. (2007). *Family therapy: History, theory, and practice* (4th ed.). Upper Saddle River, NJ: Merrill/Prentice Hall.

Goldenberg, H., & Goldenberg, I. (2002). *Counseling today's families* (4th ed.). Pacific Grove, CA: Brooks/Cole.

Gottman, J. (2006). 12-year study of gay and lesbian couples: Gay and lesbian couples research: A case of similarities of same-sex and cross-sex couples, differences between gay and lesbian couples. Retrieved January 12, 2006, from http://www.gottman.com/research/projects/gaylesbian.

Haley, J. (1980). *Leaving home.* New York: McGraw-Hill.

Hampson, R. B., & Beavers, R. (2004). Observational assessment of couples and families. In L. Sperry (Ed.), *Assessment of couples and families: Contemporary and cutting-edge strategies* (pp. 91–115). New York: Brunner-Routledge.

Hanna, S. M. (2007). *The practice of family therapy: Key elements across models* (4th ed.). Belmont, CA: Brooks/Cole.

Hare-Mustin, R. T. (1978). A feminist approach to family therapy. *Family Process, 17*(2), 181–194.

Kfir, N. (1981). Impasse/priority therapy. In R. J. Corsini (Ed.), *Handbook of innovative psychotherapies* (pp. 401–415). New York: Wiley.

Kfir, N. (1989). *Crisis intervention verbatim.* New York: Hemisphere Publishing Corp.

Lambert M. J., & Ogles, B. M. (2004). The efficacy and effectiveness of psychotherapy. In M. J. Lambert (Ed.), *Bergin and Garfield's handbook of psychotherapy and behavior change* (5th ed., pp. 139–193). New York: Wiley.

Lewis, J. M., Beaver, W. R., Gossett, J. T., & Phillips, V. A. (1976). *No single thread: Psychological health in family systems.* New York: Brunner/Mazel.

Luepnitz, D. A. (1988). *The family interpreted: Feminist theory in clinical practice.* New York: Basic Books.

McGoldrick, M., Giordano, J., & Garcia-Preto, N. (Eds.). (2005). *Ethnicity and family therapy.* New York: Guilford.

Miksell, R. H., Lusterman, D., & McDaniel, S. H. (Eds.). (1995). *Integrating family therapy: Handbook of family pathology and systems theory.* Washington, DC: American Psychological Association.

Miranda, A. O., Estrada, D., & Firpo-Jimenez, M. (2000). Differences in family cohesion, adaptability, and environment among Latino families in dissimilar stages of acculturation. *The Family Journal, 8,* 341–350.

Nichols, W. C. (1995). *Treating people in families: An integrative framework.* New York: Guilford.

Olsen, D. C. (1999). *Integrative family therapy: Creative pastoral care and counseling.* Minneapolis: Fortress Press.

Polster, E. (1995). *A population of selves: A therapeutic exploration of personal diversity.* San Francisco: Jossey-Bass.

Powers, R. L., & Griffith, J. (1987). *Understanding lifestyle: The psycho-clarity process.* Chicago: AIAS.

Satir, V. M. (1983). *Conjoint family therapy* (3rd ed.). Palo Alto, CA: Science and Behavior Books.

Satir, V. M., & Baldwin, M. (1983). *Satir: Step-by-step.* Palo Alto, CA: Science and Behavior Books.

Satir, V. M., Banman, J., Gerber, J., & Gomori, M. (1991). *The Satir model: Family therapy and beyond.* Palo Alto, CA: Science and Behavior Books.

Satir, V. M., & Bitter, J. R. (2000). The therapist and the family therapy: Satir's human validation process model. In A. M. Horne (Ed.), *Family counseling and therapy* (3rd ed.) (pp. 62–101). Itasca, IL: F. E. Peacock.

Schwartz, R. (1995). *Internal family systems therapy.* New York: Guilford.

Silverstein, L. B., & Goodrich, T. J. (Eds.). (2003). *Feminist family therapy: Empowerment in social context.* Washington, DC: American Psychological Association.

Sperry, L. (2004a). Assessment of couples and families: An introduction and overview. In L. Sperry (Ed.), *Assessment of couples and families: Contemporary and cutting-edge strategies* (pp. 3–12). New York: Brunner-Routledge.

Sperry, L. (2004b). Case conceptualizations: The missing link between theory and practice. *The Family*

Journal: Counseling and Therapy for Couples and Families, 20(10), 1–6.

Sperry, L. (2004c). Clinical outcomes assessment of couples and families. In L. Sperry (Ed.), *Assessment of couples and families: Contemporary and cuttingedge strategies* (pp. 117–132). New York: Brunner-Routledge.

Taggart, M. (1985). The feminist critique in epistemological perspective: Questions of context in family therapy. *Journal of Marital and Family Therapy, 11*(2), 113–126.

Thomlison, B. (2007). *Family assessment handbook: An introductory practice guide to family assessment* (2nd ed.). Belmont, CA: Brooks/Cole.

Walsh, F. (1998). *Strengthening family resilience.* New York: Guilford.

Walsh, F. (2003). *Normal family processes* (3rd ed.). New York: Guilford.

Whitaker, C. A. (1976). The hindrance of theory in clinical work. In P. J. Guerin, Jr. (Ed.), *Family therapy: Theory and practice.* New York: Gardner Press.

Whitaker, C. A. (1989). *Midnight musings of a family therapist* (M. O. Ryan, Ed.). New York: Norton.

Whitaker, C. A., & Bumberry, W. M. (1988). *Dancing with the family: A symbolic-experiential approach.* New York: Brunner/Mazel.

Worden, M. (2003). *Family therapy basics* (3rd ed.). Pacific Grove, CA: Brooks/Cole.

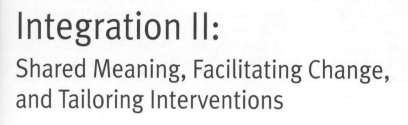

CHAPTER 16

Integration II:
Shared Meaning, Facilitating Change, and Tailoring Interventions

Hypothesizing and Shared Meaning

Facilitating Change

Tailoring Treatment

Ensuring Therapeutic Efficacy: Treatment Adherence and Relapse
    Prevention

An Integrative Therapist With the Quest Family

Some Final Thoughts

For me, there are four general movements to the overall flow of family practice, counseling, and therapy: Forming a relationship, conducting an *assessment*, *hypothesizing* and sharing meaning, and facilitating *change*. Once in a long while, these four movements may actually happen within a single session. In most cases, however, each movement takes multiple sessions, and the flow of family practice seldom proceeds neatly from one movement to the next. Indeed, tending to the relational and assessment aspects of family therapy may have to happen many times throughout the process.

Hypothesizing and Shared Meaning

Not all family counselors and therapists subscribe to offering hypotheses about the family and its problems—or even to sharing their conceptualizations of what seems to be going on. Whitaker, for example, sees no value in integrating an educative process into his symbolic-experiential approach. Those who do offer hypotheses and shared meanings range from the more-thorough descriptions (Adlerians, Bowen, Satir) to implied descriptions (structural, strategic, and cognitive-behavioral therapies) to those that do not necessarily require a systemic perspective at all to implement therapeutic change (solution-focused/solution-oriented, feminist, social constructionist, narrative therapies).

    Hypothesizing is bringing together a set of ideas about people, relationships, systems, and situations that focus meaning in a useful manner. In the integrative model I am proposing here, hypothesizing allows the family practitioner to bring together the understandings gathered through a multi-lensed assessment. In forming a hypothesis, Bitter and Corey

(2005) suggest two questions that need to be considered: "(1) How much faith do the therapist and family have in the ideas they generate? (2) How much of an influence is the therapist willing to be in the lives of people and families?" (p. 446)

The models we have considered in this book differ widely on answers to the question of therapist influence. Virginia Satir believed that family practitioners could not be in charge of people, but needed to be in charge of the family therapy process: to take responsibility for how counseling and therapy are conducted (Satir & Bitter, 2000). Some of the more-prominent leaders of family systems therapy were very assertive—and even directive—in their use of self in therapy: I include here Whitaker, Minuchin, Haley, Madanes, the MRI therapists, and Maria Selvini Palazzoli. Perhaps in reaction to these approaches, feminists and social constructionists have become quite vocal in expressing their concerns about the misuse (abuse) of power in family therapy. The more-collaborative, not knowing, decentered positions advocated by feminists, multiculturalists, and postmodern, social constructionists currently are finding favor at all levels of therapeutic work. Like the person-centered counselors and therapists that emerged in the 1940s, collaborative therapists want to engage families and family members as experts in their own lives.

Sharing hypotheses fits well with collaborative models. Various perspectives from the people involved and the eight lenses considered can be heard and a shared meaning can be co-constructed. Sharing ideas also gives family members a window into the heart and mind of the therapist, as well as each other. It is respectful and invites feedback, feedback that can support trust and cement a working relationship.

For more than 50 years, Adlerians have used a tentative approach to sharing ideas that works well with children and adults alike (Dreikurs, 1950, 1997). Starting with a passionate interest and curiosity in families and the perspectives of each member, Adlerians seek to reflect and clarify what they hear; when they have a guess or hypothesis to share, they often will seek permission for the disclosure: "I have an idea. Would you like to hear it?" A positive response from family members leads to a tentative framing of the idea: "Could it be that . . . ." This kind of approach allows family members to consider ideas without giving up their right to disagree. When a suggested idea does not fit, Adlerians expect their family practitioners to let it go and to search for more useful conceptualizations.

Describing the System

There are many different ways in which families and family systems can be described. Adlerians prefer a phenomenological explanation of the family constellation that focuses on the goals and purposeful behaviors of family members. Satir used an equally phenomenological approach to family mapping that focused on communication in dyads and triads. By far, however, the most common way of describing the family system is through the many uses of genogram work (McGoldrick, Gerson, & Shellenberger, 1999). Genograms bring together the work of Bowen with the structural and strategic family therapists; they provide the family with a map over several generations that incorporates family stories, relationships, convictions, beliefs, and emotional responses. In this sense, genograms are excellent repositories for the shared meanings that are developed in family counseling and therapy sessions. With the possible exception of the postmodern, social constructionist approaches, genograms can be adapted and used by every other model in this book.

Integrative Models

Carlson and associates (2005) review several integrative approaches to couples and family therapy that work across models and provide some guidance in developing integrated family treatment. Integrative approaches started to develop in the 1990s and, in the last decade, they have gained the kind of prominence that suggests they will be the models of choice in the future. From functional family therapy (Alexander & Parsons, 1982; Sexton & Alexander, 2003) to Olsen's (1999) integrative family therapy to the multisystemic approach (Sheidow, Henggeler, & Schoenwald, 2003), integrative models offer more-comprehensive descriptions and explanations, greater flexibility in application, address the needs of a broader population base, and lay the foundation for tailoring treatment and interventions to the specific needs of families.

Breunlin and associates (1992/1997) have proposed a blueprint for therapy to be used with their metaframeworks model. By extension, this blueprint also will work well with the eight lenses that I proposed in the previous chapter. As an approach that seeks to transcend models, it rests on the following presuppositions:

- A holistic view of human systems as multilevel entities . . .
- Change [occurs] through a collaborative effort between the therapist and the family to remove constraints . . .
- [The model] is inclusive of whatever has proved valuable in the field of family therapy, seeking both/and rather than either/or positions . . .
- The metaframeworks [lenses] are a recursive set of ideas that interact with and complement one another . . .
- The metaframeworks [lenses] tell us where to look for and identify the constraints that limit functioning and maintain problems . . .
- The goal of therapy is always to remove constraints. (pp. 281–283)

Based on these presuppositions, the metaframeworks blueprint for therapy suggests forming a collaborative relationship based on peer conversations; *co*-hypothesizing based on each of the lenses or perspectives that reveal the multileveled functioning of the system; planning ways of relating to the family, monitoring the process of the session(s), and creating events that may draw on any number of techniques from multiple models that have demonstrated effectiveness with families. Each of these movements within the blueprint result in and should be informed by feedback from the family and its members. When constraints are removed at one or more levels of functioning, the family will engage almost automatically in more productive behaviors and ways of relating.

Facilitating Change

The ideas of facilitation and collaboration are closely related, and each supports the other. Facilitation is associated with Satir's notion of process and the enabling of family members to access the resources inherent in the family. Collaboration is about taking clients in as partners in the exploration of difficulties and possibilities that will make up therapy. In this book, I have used the word techniques to suggest common interventions that are made within the various models. I should note, however, that the concept of *techniques* fits better with those approaches, such as structural and strategic family therapies, that present the therapist-as-expert in charge of making change happen. Collaborative approaches, such as Adlerian, feminist, and social constructionist therapies, rely on joint *planning* or co-construction. "Planning can still include what family therapy has called techniques or interventions, but with the family's participation" (Breunlin et al., 1992/1997, p. 292). Two of the most common ways to facilitate change are enactments and assignment of tasks, both of which are more effective when the family co-constructs them with the counselor or therapist.

Given the range of possible techniques, interventions, and processes designed to facilitate change in families, it is reasonable to ask what should guide the family practitioner in the selection of interventions. When you look at a family through each of the eight lenses I have suggested, it is helpful to consider the areas in which the family or its members feel constrained. It is from these areas that interventions can be developed to release the family into more productive ways of being. In general, internal parts function best when they are balanced (not polarized) and when each person experiences her or his parts as resources. Being able to think, and to think rationally, is generally more useful than emotional reactivity. Being able to feel is better than not feeling. Good contact and congruent communication with others is more rewarding than isolation or self-absorption. And taking reasonable risks in the service of individual and family growth or development is more beneficial than stagnation or a retreat into fear.

> Further, knowing the goals and purposes for our behaviors, feelings, and interactions tends to give us choices about their use. Similarly, understanding the patterns we enact in face-to-face relationships, the ebbs and flows of life, or across generations provides multiple avenues for challenging patterns and the enactment of new possibilities. (Bitter & Corey, 2005, p. 447)

Resilience

In recent years, a strong focus of family interventions has been in the area of **family resiliency** or the ability of the families and their members to bounce back from adversity and reorganize to get the most out of their internal and external resources. Further, the research on resiliency in at-risk youth is closely related to resiliency in families in general (Bernard, 2004).

Bernard (2004) summarizes some of what we have learned:

* Resilient children seek love by attracting the attention of available adults;
* When children receive empathy and caring, they develop a capacity for it, and it is a differentiating characteristic in resilient adolescent males;
* Compassion, altruism, and forgiveness are returned to the giver and act as a buffer against difficult times;
* Insight allows children and families living in great adversity to figure out that not all adults abuse others; that bizarre behavior is not normal; and that many children do have and all children deserve enough food to eat and a safe place to sleep;
* The development of autonomy and self-esteem, when linked to competence in any skill or task, will enhance intrinsic motivation;
* Refusing to accept negative messages about one's self, gender, or culture/race serves as a powerful protector of autonomy;
* Strong positive ethnic/gender identities are associated with high self-esteem, a strong commitment to doing well in school, a strong sense of purpose in life, greater confidence in one's own efficacy, and high academic achievement;
* An internal locus of control is associated with better health habits and fewer illnesses, and believing that events in one's life are determined largely by one's own efforts is associated with self-efficacy and mastery;
* A sense of humor is one of the most critical adaptive/mature defenses used by resilient individuals across the lifespan;
* A positive and strong future focus is consistently identified with task success, positive self-identity, and fewer health-risk behaviors;
* Creativity and imagination are critical to surviving and transcending trauma and risk;
* Optimism in addressing causes of bad events is related to the generation of hope, and hope is critical to positive outcomes, such as social competence, problem solving, and self-efficacy;
* Whether people draw strength from faith or spirituality or meaningful philosophies, stability and coherence are enhanced by having a sense of purpose, self-worth, and center of value; and
* Human organisms and systems seek stability in the face of change, and it is meaning that helps to create that stability.

Walsh (1998) says that the keys to family resilience require practitioners to address three areas: belief systems, organizational patterns, and communication processes. Resiliency belief systems make meaning out of adversity, incorporate a positive outlook, and tap into transcendence and spirituality. Resiliency is supported by organizational patterns that are flexible, connected internally and externally, and have social and economic resources. Communication processes that support resiliency are based on clarity, open emotional expression, and collaborative problem solving.

Resiliency is relationally based. It normalizes life and contextualizes adversity and distress. A focus on meaning attempts to make crises comprehensible and manageable. Taking initiative, persevering, having courage and encouragement, focusing on strengths and potential, and mastering what we can (and accepting what cannot be changed) all lead to hope, optimism, and increased confidence in being able to overcome adversity. Such hope and optimism also are strengthened when individuals and families feel connected to larger values and a sense of purpose, have faith, and learn from the challenges they face.

When families are organized flexibly, they have the capacity for change by reorganizing and adapting while maintaining enough continuity and dependability to provide stability. Such flexibility is aided by mutual respect and support, collaboration, and commitment to meeting individual needs, appreciating differences, and resetting boundaries to preserve the whole. Resilient parents engage in leadership that is nurturing, protecting, and guiding. There is an equality of partnership and, where possible, cooperative parenting and caregiving teams are formed. Almost all resilient families are able to tap into extended family, community resources, or family support networks and centers.

Bernard (2004) notes that:

> The Family Support Network (**http://www.familysupport.org**), for example, lists the following principles for Family Support Centers:
>
> - The relationship between the program and family is one of equality and respect.
> - Participants are a vital resource.
> - Programs are community-based and culturally and socially relevant to the families they serve.
> - Parent education, information about human development, and skill building for parents are essential elements of every program.
> - Programs are voluntary—seeking support and information is viewed as a sign of family strength. (pp. 62–63)

Both within families and between families and programs, resilience is facilitated by clear, consistent, and congruent communication in which words match actions and clarity is sought for ambiguous situations. Families and family members are invited to share the full range of feelings they experience; difference is tolerated—even appreciated; empathy is sought and provided; and people are urged to take responsibility for their own feelings and behaviors and to avoid blaming. The frosting on the cake is being able to access humor and engage in pleasurable interactions (Walsh, 1998).

Resilient families and the programs that support them focus on collaborative problem solving. Such problem solving invites all affected people to engage in identifying resources and brainstorming possible solutions. Shared decision making is fostered through negotiation, fairness, and reciprocity. Change is goal-oriented and involves taking concrete steps toward success. Resilient families are proactive. They do not wait to be fixed from the outside, but take charge of what they can, try to prevent further difficulties, and prepare for the future.

So many of the models we have studied have something to contribute to the development of resilient families. The Adlerian focus on goals, encouragement, and social connectedness also is supported in Satir's emphasis on nurturance and congruent communication. Bowen's emphasis on differentiated selves and a multigenerational focus makes it possible to consider alternatives rationally and tap into the resources inherent in a family system. The structural and strategic conceptualizations of family organization, leadership, and engagement also come into play. Simon, Murphy, and Smith (2005) recommend the use of resilience-seeking questions and statements with embedded compliments in family practice. Such questions are reflective of the approach advocated by solution-focused/solution-oriented therapists: "How have you kept things from getting worse?"; "How have you managed to hang in there when others would have given up?"; or "You are the experts on your family: What is one small idea or action that you would be willing to try to make things better?" An emphasis on solutions directly supports an optimistic outlook in seeking to overcome adversity. Cognitive-behavioral family therapy contributes greatly to our understanding of effective problem solving, and feminists and social constructionists remind us that much of what happens within a family is absorbed from outside forces and needs to be both humanized and contextualized.

Each of the eight lenses lends itself to both an assessment of constraints and an assessment of resources. Of the two, resiliency work suggests that the latter is, in the end, far more important than the former. Indeed, constraints tell the family practitioner only where to start. Resources are the basis for tailoring treatment. They provide a roadmap for the way out of crisis and adversity.

Tailoring Treatment

Tailoring treatment is about matching or fitting interventions to the needs and functioning of the family. Carlson et al. (2005) consider the following areas in the tailoring process:

- What is the situation and how severe is it?
- What are the capabilities of the system?
- What skills are available in the family and its members?
- What are the styles and status of the individuals involved?
- What is the families readiness for treatment?

In general, the more severe the situation, the more focused and immediate the initial interventions must be. As Satir used to suggest in times of chaos, families ought to implement no change that cannot be accomplished in a few seconds. Severity also is related to the level of the family's functioning. When some members of the family seem to be less severely affected, they can be enlisted as support for those in more difficulty. The most severely affected need to know that their needs are being addressed, that relief is possible, and that it can be planned.

The eight lenses are avenues for tailoring help to the family as a system. Somewhere within these eight areas, the family will be experiencing one or more constraints that keep them from being able to move forward and resolve their concerns. It is often in the very areas in which the family feels constraints that the resources also are found. Even when this is not true, bringing eight lenses to the process creates the possibility of searching for strengths in parts of the system that otherwise may have been overlooked. This is especially true when assessing the family from developmental, multicultural, and gender lenses.

When families and their therapeutic practitioners ask questions, such as "What skills do we need to make things better?" and "Who has the skills, and how can we access them?", they are engaged in tailoring with a focus on resiliency. Knowing and understanding the personalities and communication styles of the family members also can serve as a basis for tailoring (see Bitter, 1993a). Tailoring is essentially collaborative: It differs fundamentally from therapist prescriptions in its effort to involve families in decisions about what interventions constitute a good fit for family members.

Case conceptualization, as I have already noted, is the foundation for effective tailoring. Tailoring, however, is also important in relation to culture and gender; stress levels in families; and work, careers, and their relationship to family life (Carlson et al., 2005). And tailoring is an important part of engaging and keeping families in therapy (**treatment adherence**) and in the prevention of lapses and relapses.

Ensuring Therapeutic Efficacy: Treatment Adherence and Relapse Prevention

Families are most motivated to change when they are in distress. This is usually when the family first comes to seek help. It is not uncommon for the most change to take place in the first few sessions, but the staying power of the changes enacted does not seem to be very strong. Carlson and colleagues (2005) note that both lapses (temporary returns to former behaviors) and relapses (more-permanent returns to former patterns) will happen. Family practitioners increase the chance of facilitating more-enduring change when they plan for such relapses (Marlatt & Gordon, 1985; Steen, 2001). What are the family members' expectations for treatment? If it is successful, how will the family know? What are the goals the family members have for counseling or therapy? Are there beliefs or misconceptions about the process that need to be clarified? What is the family's commitment to change: On a scale from 1 to 10, how important is it to each member that changes occur? How discouraged or optimistic is the family? What resources do the family members have in terms of skills, education, or external supports? What are some things that might get in the way of successful change? Is there anything that can be done to prevent further constraints?

Taken together, the answers to such questions will give the family practitioner a sense of how much change the family can handle and how long it is likely to last. Predicting that there will be lapses or even relapses is not in and of itself discouraging: With proper timing, it can be used to normalize the process of change and help families prepare for when it happens. Some useful questions in this regard include: How will you notice when you have returned to old patterns and ways of doing things? What can you do after you have noticed a lapse? What resources will be available to you to help regain your momentum and to help integrate new patterns? What automatic thoughts might occur that would need to be challenged to support a return to more-productive behaviors? It is easy to see the influence of the cognitive-behavioral therapies in these questions and, indeed, most of the treatment adherence/**relapse prevention** models in the last 20 years have been based on this approach.

Questions related to treatment-plan development and relapse prevention require collaboration and negotiation with the family. As Carlson et al. (2005) note: "An acceptable treatment plan that is carried out appropriately is much better than an ideal one that is ignored" (p. 199). In the end, treatment approaches that are concrete, tailored directly to problem-relief and solutions, clear and simple to follow, and matched to the family's styles and processes are the most likely plans to be completed.

■ An Integrative Therapist With the Quest Family

Paul and Jane Quest bring all four of their children to the first meeting with an integrative family therapist. The integrative family therapist greets each family member personally and offers each adult and child her hand. As they proceed to the counseling room, the therapist already is sorting through eight lenses that she might use to begin an assessment, but her main interest is in activating a fully human curiosity about the family and their concerns. She will be looking for areas in their lives in which they are effective and dynamic and areas in which the family members may be unduly constrained. Jane had called a few days earlier, and had given her a brief idea of the family history. Starting with Paul, the therapist asked each family member what the history of the idea of coming to therapy was within the family.

Paul starts by indicating that their lives seemed to be turned upside down when the boys came to live with them. They were not as easy to handle as the girls had been and, although he relied on Jane to handle matters at home, he also felt that she might be collapsing under the strain. He was excited about having the boys join the family, but the changes required had been hard on everyone, and he wanted whatever help the family could get. Jane said she was relieved to be there. She did not think she could handle everything alone and, even with Ann's help, she often felt alone. Amy and Ann both indicated that they were there because their parents wanted them to come. They were okay with their parents' decision to add the boys to the family, but they didn't really feel connected to them yet. "The boys can be difficult," Amy noted. The boys were very talkative, interrupting often, and in constant motion.

Therapist: Paul, I am interested in your ideas about being a parent, again, with Jason and Luke. Your older children are young women, really: A year or two, and they will both be adults. So what do you want for yourself with the boys, and in what ways do Jane's efforts either help or hinder your desires?

Paul: Well, I don't really know the boys. I see them every day, but I am working a lot, and I know they are in our home, but . . . well, I really just don't know the boys very well.

Therapist: And is that something that you would like? Would you like to know the boys better?

Paul: Yes. Yes, I would.

Therapist: What would you call the part of you that would like to know the boys better? (using Internal Family Systems (IFS) language)

Paul: What do you mean?

Therapist: What would you call . . . (pause)? What part of you wants to know your boys better?

Paul: I guess I am just curious about who these boys are and what they might be in our lives.

Therapist: Ah, I see. So it is your *curious* part that gets interested in the boys.

Paul: Yes.

Therapist: And would I be right in saying that your curious part gets put on hold or constrained in some way so that you never fully get to know the boys?

Paul: Yes. That's true.

Therapist: Do you feel the constraint coming from within yourself or within the family process or both . . . maybe neither?

Jane: Paul does work very hard, so it is up to me to take care of the boys most of the time. (Here the sequence between the therapist and Paul seems to have triggered in Jane a need to intervene—possibly to rescue her husband.)

> Just as the therapist is about to ask another question, a small fight breaks out between the boys. Jane immediately gets up and makes both of the boys sit down in the circle.

Therapist: I noticed, Jane, that you handled that situation with the boys. You handled it quite well, but you were the only one who took action—and the rest of the family let you. Is this what you meant earlier about "feeling all alone" in relation to handling the boys?

Jane: Yes, I guess so. Well, they are *my* boys. (Jane's response speaks to the responsibility she feels for the boys, but it also says something about roles and leadership in the family.)

> The therapist might explore with any of a number of lenses in this case, but at this point in time, she chooses to stay with a gender lens.

Therapist: Paul, do you think of your wife and partner as modern or traditional?

Paul: Well, I've always thought of Jane as a modern woman with her own interests, but I would have to say that we are a lot like our parents—you know, I earn the money in the family, and Jane takes care of things at home.

Therapist: So that part of life is pretty traditional?

Paul: Yes.

Therapist: And does anything in that arrangement make it difficult for you to activate your curiosity and get to know the boys?

Paul: (long pause) . . . I think the boys have had a very difficult life before we got them. It is understandable that Jane wants to protect them (another pause) . . . . They were hurt very badly.

Therapist: Yes, it is understandable that Jane would want to protect the boys, but protect them from whom: You?

Paul: No, not me really; just everyone and everything. I know she sometimes feels overwhelmed by it all, and I think she actually feels better about it all when she is in charge.

Therapist: That seems to me to be something important to know for sure. Would you ask Jane if she agrees with you about feeling better when she is in charge?

Paul: Am I right? Is it easier for you when you feel in charge?

Jane: I guess so. I mean I do want help, but I want to make sure the boys are okay at all times. They could be hurt again, or they could hurt each other.

> The therapist now asks Paul and each of the girls if anyone can remember the boys doing serious damage to each other, and no one can. They have done damage to the neighbor's dog; Luke has taken things from each of the girls; and both boys have taken food and money from neighbors and family members. But no one can remember a time when they did serious damage to each other.

Ann: They are just very loud when they fight. You can hear them all over the house.

Therapist: From the tone of your voice, it sounds like the boys' fighting bothers you.

Ann: Of course. They are at it all the time, and if they are not fighting with each other, they are being a menace in other ways.

Therapist: Who else is worried about the boys' fighting and the other things that they do? Who else do they irritate?

Ann: Mom mainly. Dad is not there, or he is busy with other things, and Amy is gone a lot too. So mainly, it gets to Mom and me.

Therapist: Now, earlier your Dad and Mom seemed to agree that she wanted to be in charge in relation to the boys. Is that your experience too?

Ann: Oh, absolutely. Even when I am correcting the boys or stopping them from hurting the cat, I can feel my mother watching me. And afterward, she will say, "Remember that they have had a hard life. Don't be so angry with them."

Therapist: So your mother has a protective part, a rescuing part, and a vigilant part . . . and taken together, they often leave her feeling exhausted and perhaps anxious.

Ann: Yes, that's true. But it leaves me feeling exhausted too: I have to pay attention to both the boys and to whatever Mom is wanting. Most of the time, these days, I just want to escape.

Therapist: Paul, is that something you feel too—the desire to escape? Is that what is happening when you work a lot and are really busy?

Paul: I would have to say that's at least partly true. It's not that I don't do anything with the boys, but I do catch myself wondering if Jane is watching or wanting me to handle them differently. I don't really know what to do, and I don't want to do anything that Jane would disapprove of.

> The therapist now turns her attention back to the whole family. She acknowledges that bringing two new people into the family has been difficult—for the boys as well as everyone else. Blending a family with large age differences, different genders, different histories, and different developmental needs is never easy, and she commends everyone for being willing to create a better home for these young boys.

Therapist: There is a sequence that seems to be emerging here. One or both of the boys need attention or care or some kind of intervention, and either Jane handles it, wishing she had more help, or Ann or Paul—and perhaps Amy—step in, but each may feel constrained in their relationship with the boys because they are aware of Jane's protective and vigilant parts. Does that sound right?

Jane: I think it probably is right, although I did not think of it that way before. I worry about Jason and Luke all the time.

Therapist: If you were to give that worried part a name, what would you call it?

Jane: Wart! (Everyone laughs.)

Paul: I sometimes call Jane a worry wart—affectionately.

Therapist: So what does Wart say to you?

Jane: Be careful! Don't let anything bad happen to the boys. Don't let them get hurt or hurt each other.

Therapist: So the language that part uses is very intense and comes from a place of feeling impending danger.

Jane: Always.

Therapist: Now, is there a part of you that calms Wart?

Jane: I guess watching does it.

Therapist: Your vigilant part calms you.

Jane: Yes.

Therapist: I am wondering: Do you also have a faith part, some part of you that has observed long enough to know that things will work out alright? Is there a part of you that really knows Jason and Luke will be okay in the care of Ann or Amy?

Jane: Yes, they will. I do have faith in them.

Therapist: And how about Paul? How about the boys' father?

Jane: You see that is where my faith starts to waiver. Paul is so busy all the time, and I don't know if he will pay attention.

Therapist: What do you think, Paul? Do you have a sense that you could be available to Jason and Luke if you were not being watched closely?

Paul: I would like that. I think I need to be more present with the boys anyway. Like I said, I want to get to know them better. I am curious about who they are and what we could do together.

Jane: But will you watch them carefully?

Therapist: Jane, I am wondering if you could ask your worried part not to interfere for a moment. Could you ask your faith part to speak to Paul?

Jane: (a long pause) I remember when the girls were young, and you played with them every day, and you cleaned them up, and you fed them, and you read to them . . .

Paul: But . . .

Jane: No "but"; I just remember all of that, and I know you can do it again. I want you to do it again with me.

Therapist: You are remembering a time when you and Paul were not in traditional gender roles with the children, and when you were real partners in raising the children. It seems to make you really happy to remember that.

Jane: Yes. Yes, it does.

> The therapist comments that Jane and Paul seem to have a new perspective on what is possible. She wonders if the family might want to see how this perspective works out for a week or so, an idea that is welcomed by both the parents and the daughters. The therapist turns to Jason and Luke.

Therapist: Your father tells me that he is curious about the two of you and would like to get to know you better, to spend a little more time with you, maybe to play games you would like to play. How does that sound to you?

Jason: Dad wants to play with me, not Luke.

Paul: Sometimes I will want to play with just you, and sometimes, I will want to play with both of you, and even some other times, I will want to play with just Luke when you are busy.

Jason: I'm not busy.

Paul: I will keep that in mind.

> The session ends with the therapist and the family finding a time to meet the following week. In this session, the therapist made use of internal family systems, the gender lens, the sequence lens, and leadership lens. She looked for ways in which both the individuals and the family as a whole felt constrained. By noting the constraints as well as strengths, she was able to open the family process to new perspectives and new possibilities.

Some Final Thoughts

Lebow (1995) has noted that there is greater likelihood of family success when therapists are seen to be an ongoing part of the family's life: Open-ended, brief, intermittent therapy says to the family that the family practitioner is there to see them through initial changes and will be available to handle lapses, relapses, or additional needs that occur during the family's life cycle. Such open-endedness and intermittent, lifelong therapy relationships are facilitated when:

- collaborative tracking of progress indicates that treatment goals have been reached;
- when a review of treatment emphasizes the gains made and the client's successes;

- when what has been learned is related to how it can be consistently applied;
- when family members seem to carry the counselor or therapist within them; and
- when ending therapy is seen as appropriate; the accomplishments acknowledged and celebrated; and the conditions for returning to therapy are clear.

In my own 35-year career, I have had the privilege of being a family counselor with several families who sought help in three different generations. Indeed, in the last year, I entered into a therapeutic conversation with a mother of two young children. I had first seen this woman when she was 4 years old and her parents brought her in because the family was about to have a new baby, and their soon-to-be oldest child was not so happy about the prospect of a new arrival. Three decades later, I had the joy of seeing this young woman as an adult with different issues but with the same foundation of trust, caring, and love that we had earned with each other over the years.

I have suggested a format for how the many aspects of family practice models might be integrated and effectively applied to a wide range of families. This integration favors collaborative relationships, multi-leveled assessments, hypothesizing and shared meanings, and the facilitation of change through an application of resiliency-focused work and tailoring interventions for treatment adherence and relapse prevention. The real question, however, is what integration will work best for you. The answer to that question will unfold over time and be informed by the many clinical experiences in which you engage. I wish you the best in both your personal and professional journeys.

References

Alexander, J. F., & Parsons, B. V. (1982). *Functional family therapy*. Monterey, CA: Brooks/Cole.

Bernard, B. (2004). *Resiliency: What we have learned*. San Francisco: WestEd.

Bitter, J. (1993a). Communication styles, personality priorities, and social interest: Strategies for helping couples build a life together. *Individual Psychology, 49*(3–4), 330–350.

Bitter, J. R., & Corey, G. (2005). Family systems therapy. In G. Corey, *Theory and practice of counseling and psychotherapy* (7th ed., pp. 420–459). Belmont, CA: Brooks/Cole.

Breunlin, D. C., Schwartz, R. C., & MacKune-Karrer, B. (1997). *Metaframeworks: Transcending the models of family therapy*. San Francisco: Jossey-Bass. (Original work published 1992)

Carlson, J., Sperry, L., & Lewis, J. A. (2005). *Family therapy techniques: Integrating and tailoring treatment*. New York: Routledge.

Dreikurs, R. (1950). The immediate purpose of children's misbehavior, its recognition and correction. *Internationale Zeitschrift fur Individual-psychologie, 19*, 70–87.

Dreikurs, R. (1997). Holistic medicine. *Individual Psychology, 53*(2), 127–205.

Lebow, J. (1995). Open-ended therapy: Termination in marital and family therapy. In R. H. Miksell, D. Lusterman, & S. H. McDaniel (Eds.), *Integrating family therapy: Handbook of family pathology and systems theory* (pp. 73–86). Washington, DC: American Psychological Association.

Marlatt, G. A., & Gordon, J. R. (Eds.). (1985). *Relapse prevention*. New York: Guilford Press.

McGoldrick, M., Gerson, R., & Shellenberger, S. (1999). *Genograms: Assessment and intervention* (2nd ed.). New York: Norton.

Olsen, D. C. (1999). *Integrative family therapy: Creative pastoral care and counseling*. Minneapolis: Fortress Press.

Satir, V. M., & Bitter, J. R. (2000). The therapist and the family therapy: Satir's human validation process model. In A. M. Horne (Ed.), *Family counseling and therapy* (3rd ed.) (pp. 62–101). Itasca, IL: F. E. Peacock.

Sexton, T. L., & Alexander, J. F. (2003). Functional family therapy: A mature clinical model for working with at-risk adolescents and their families. In T. L. Sexton, G. R. Weeks, & M. S. Robbins (Eds.), *Handbook of family therapy: The science and practice of working with families and couples* (pp. 323–350). New York: Brunner-Routledge.

Sheidow, A. J., Henggeler, S. W., & Schoenwald, S. K. (2003). Multisystemic therapy. In T. L. Sexton, G. R. Weeks, & M. S. Robbins (Eds.), *Handbook of family therapy: The science and practice of working with families and couples* (pp. 303–322). New York: Brunner-Routledge.

Simon, J. B., Murphy, J. J., & Smith, S. M. (2005). Understanding and fostering family resilience. *The Family Journal, 13,* 427–436.

Steen, C. (2001). *The adult relapse prevention workbook.* New York: Guilford Press.

Walsh, F. (1998). *Strengthening family resilience.* New York: Guilford.

Appendix

Summary and Review of Family Models

I now will provide several tables that are designed to help you review the main points of the 10 theories of family therapy and counseling presented in this book. I am hopeful that these summaries will allow you to compare ideas and concepts across the various models of family systems therapies and family practice. Let's start with the founders of and main contributors to the approaches we have studied.

You may have noticed already that many of the 10 models in this book tend to reflect the personalities of the people who developed them. The personal, family, and professional life experiences of the great masters (as well as those who became key contributors to the models) informed the theory and early practice of each approach—and shaped the key concepts, goals, roles, functions, and skills that became associated with various forms of family practice. Table A.1 is a reminder of the key people who are associated with each model.

When you begin to develop your own approach to family therapy—whether you adopt one model or integrate and synthesize aspects of various models in a way that fits for you—you will become a new contributor to an existing approach or an actual pioneer and explorer in search of effective practice. It will be next to impossible for you to engage in family practice without bringing yourself and your values into play. So thinking about those who have blazed the trail before us and what influenced their journeys is also a way to think about our own values and journeys. Who the pioneers were as people and professionals had a direct influence on the key concepts that were a foundation for their work.

The key concepts of each of the 10 approaches address important perspectives related to understanding self and families. They also say something about the nature of human interactions and human systems. When you review the key concepts of these models, what do they tell you about the beliefs, values, and intentions of each theory's founders and contributors? What kind of world did they envision? What do they want for the families they serve? Table A.2 is how the various models we have studied have articulated the key concepts of each theory.

The key concepts of each model include goals that family practitioners have for individuals, couples, and families, as well as what they intend for their work. What goals would you envision in family practice? Are there goals you have for the therapy process? Are there goals you would develop for each family—perhaps each family member too? How should the goals of family practice be developed, stated, and used? Do you envision a collaborative process in the establishment of therapeutic goals? Would it be with a team of therapists? Would it be with the family? Would it be with both? Would you use your goals as general guides or would you want them to be specific, concrete, and measurable? How often would you review your goals? What measures would you use? Table A.3 is how the models we have studied have framed the goals of family therapy.

The various models we have studied have a rather wide range of roles and functions assigned to the therapist. Some of the earliest models supported more egalitarian relationships characterized by mutual respect, empathy, caring, and a genuine interest in others (for example, Adlerian family therapy and Satir's human validation process model). Starting with Bowen's coaching model, however, family practice entered a period of increasingly directive interventions, including Whitaker's symbolic play activities and the structural/strategic changes advocated by Minuchin, Haley, Madanes, and the practitioners at MRI. With the emergence of the feminist, solution-focused/solution-oriented, and social constructionist models of therapy in the last decade and a half, there has been a return to collaborative, cooperative, co-constructing relationships in therapy. Table A.4 is a review of the roles and functions of the therapist as proposed by each of the models we have studied.

Bitter and Corey (2005) suggest:

> The debate Carl Rogers (1980) first introduced to individual therapy in the 1940s has reemerged with family therapy in the form of these questions:
> • What expertise does the therapist have in relation to the family, and how should that expertise be used?
> • How directive should therapists be in relation to families, and what does that say about the use of power in therapy? (p. 442)

Over the last 30 years, family systems therapists have assumed many different positions with regard to multiculturalism, contributing in various ways to the development of this perspective in family therapy. Clearly, this is a perspective that was greatly enhanced by the work of Monica McGoldrick and her associates (2005), a work that is now becoming more integrated and enriched with considerations of gender, race, sexual/affectional orientation, age, economic class, ability and health, and cultural rituals (see McGoldrick, 2005). Table A.5 is a review of the multicultural perspectives of various family systems models and approaches.

For a long time, the field of family therapy and family practice paid little or no attention to gender issues in family systems. The work of Hare-Mustin (1978), Taggart (1985), and Luepnitz (1988), among others, documented both the need for and the uses of a gender perspective in family assessment and practice. Although there is still wide-spread resistance to egalitarian family relationships, the development of a balanced gender organization and participation has proven to be in the best interest of every family and all of its members. A gendered perspective seeks to develop non-sexist roles and egalitarian relationships in families. It challenges the patriarchy embedded in individual, relational, familial, cultural, community, national, and international systems. Table A.6 is a review of the gender perspectives of various family systems models and approaches.

I have used the word "techniques" in this book to suggest common interventions that are made within the various models. I should note, however, that the concept of techniques fits better with those approaches, such as structural and strategic family therapies, that present the therapist-as-expert in charge of making change happen. Collaborative approaches, such as Adlerian, feminist, and social constructionist therapies, rely on joint planning or co-construction. "Planning can still include what family therapy has called techniques or interventions, but with the family's participation" (Breunlin, Schwartz, & MacKune-Karrer, 1992/1997, p. 292).

Table A.7 shows how the models we have studied have presented the techniques of family therapy.

I hope the tables presented in this appendix are useful to you in reviewing the various aspects of the theories of family counseling, family therapy, family practice, and parenting. As I complete this work, I cannot help but wonder what you might add when your section is added to each table. Will you be the only practitioner of your model? Will you have joined a model already in progress? Will you have invited others into your work? What will the key concepts of your approach be? What goals will you have for yourself, for the families you serve, and for the therapeutic process? What will be your various roles and functions in counseling and therapy? What will you add to the eight lenses—especially to the multicultural and gender perspectives? What skills will you bring to working with families? How will you attempt to tailor interventions and facilitate change? You have a professional lifetime to discover the creativity that will blossom as you work. When you discover what works for you, it wouldn't hurt to write it down and share it with others.

Table A.1	Key Figures (For a structural diagram of key figures, see the Family Therapy Genogram on the inside covers)
Family Therapy Model	Key Figures
Multigenerational Family Therapy	Murray Bowen initiated the first systemic, theory-based treatment program for families at the National Institutes of Mental Health, hospitalizing whole families at one point. His focus on triangulation and differentiation of self set the stage for young therapists both to examine their own relationships in their families-of-origin and to make sense out of the dysfunctional family patterns with which they would be working. Other key figures include: Betty Carter, Thomas Fogarty, Phillip Guerin, Michael Kerr, and Monica McGoldrick.
Adlerian Family Therapy	Alfred Adler was the first psychologist ever to interview families in open forums, a practice he initiated in the 1920s. Considered a systemic thinker before we had the term, Adler believed that individuals and families must be understood within the social contexts of their lives. Other key figures include: James Bitter, Jon Carlson, Oscar Christensen, Don Dinkmeyer, Rudolf Dreikurs, Clair Hawes, Ray Lowe, Bill Nicoll, Manford Sonstegard, Len Sperry, and Richard Watts.
Human Validation Process Model	Virginia Satir, considered one of the great pioneers of family therapy, originally called her approach conjoint family therapy, emphasizing the importance of connecting with the self-worth of people who happened to live in families. Later, she would call her approach a process model; in 1983, she formally called her work the human validation process model, emphasizing the need that humans have to be validated, addressed from a position of congruence, and supported in nurturing family processes and environments. Other key figures include: John Banmen and Jean McLendon.
Experiential-Symbolic Family Therapy	Carl Whitaker was one of the most unique family therapists ever to have graced the field. He found a way to integrate systemic process with elements of psychoanalytic thinking, existentialism, and experimentations in authenticity that included, among other things, dozing-off in sessions, seeding the unconscious with his own fantasies, and engaging families in physical challenges and wrestling. Other key figures include: William Bumberry, David Keith, Thomas Malone, and Gus Napier.
Structural Family Therapy	Salvador Minuchin began his work with delinquent boys from poor families at the Wiltwyck School in New York City. In the 1970s, he moved to the Philadelphia Child Guidance Clinic and, together with colleagues, began more than 3 decades of developing his structural family therapy approach. Other key figures include: Harry Aponte and Charles Fishman.
Strategic Family Therapy	Jay Haley was one of the original group in Palo Alto, CA, to join Gregory Bateson, Don Jackson, and John Weakland in forming the Mental Research Institute (MRI). After writing a seminal paper on communication and schizophrenic families in 1956, these men would go on to study families in multiple forms and settings. Other key figures at MRI include: Richard Fisch, Lynn Hoffman, Lynn Segal, and Paul Watzlawick. Haley later would join with Cloe Madanes to form the Washington School for strategic family therapy. Before his death, Haley and his partner/spouse, Madeleine Richeport-Haley, lived and worked in Southern California. In Milan, Italy, Maria Selvini Palazzoli led a team of strategic therapists focused on the use of paradox and counterparadox in family therapy. Other key Milan figures include: Luigi Boscolo, Gianfranco Cecchin, and Giuliana Prata. Two North Americans, Peggy Penn and Karl Tomm, contributed to the development of the process of circular questioning that started in Milan.
Solution-Focused/ Solution-Oriented Family Therapy	Steve de Shazer and Insoo Kim Berg, both a marital and professional team, founded the Brief Family Therapy Center (BFTC) in Milwaukee, Wisconsin. Focusing only on the future and what people desired for their lives, they put strategic interventions in the service of solutions and preferred outcomes. Other key figures include:

(Continued on next page)

Table A.1 (Contd.)	
	Eve Lipchik, Scott Miller, Bill O'Hanlon, Jane Peller, John Walter, and Michelle Weiner-Davis.
Social Constructionism and Narrative Family Therapy	Heavily influenced by the philosophies of Gregory Bateson, Jerome Bruner, Kenneth Gergen, and Michel Foucault, postmodern, social constructionism seemed to burst on the scene in the 1990s. Michael White from Adelaide, South Australia, teamed up with David Epston from Auckland, New Zealand, to develop the basic writings of what we now call narrative therapy. Other key figures in narrative therapy include: Gene Combs, David Denborough, Vicki Dickerson, Jill Freedman, Stephen Madigan, Cheryl White, and Jeffrey Zimmerman. The narrative therapy approach had a companion model in the work of Harlene Anderson and the late Harold Goolishian, in Houston, Texas, who focused on a linguistic approach that emphasized a collaboration with clients. This same emphasis became central to the work of Lynn Hoffman and Karl Tomm. The reflecting teams used by Tom Andersen and his colleagues in Norway also has the effect of removing a single therapist from the position of imposing power on families. In recent years, Michael White has adopted the use of reflecting teams in his work and has widened their use in the development of *definitional ceremonies.*
Feminist Family Therapy	The list of women who have contributed to feminist theory in general and feminist family therapy specifically is practically endless. Starting with the efforts of women in the late 19th and early 20th centuries, women's rights and gender issues became a political force in Western cultures: voting, reproductive health, property rights, educational opportunities, and the right to work were the focus of the first feminist wave. The formation of the Women's Project in Family Therapy was a pivotal moment in the development of feminist family therapy. Key figures include: Carol M. Anderson, Marianne Ault-Riche, Judith Myers Avis, Betty Bardige, Mary Field Belenky, Bograd, Pauline Boss, Lois Braverman, Annette M. Brodsky, Laura Brown, Michele Paula J. Caplan, Betty Carter, Phyllis Chesler, Nancy Chodorow, Blythe McVicker Clinchy, Dorothy Dinnerstein, Barbara Ehrenreich, Carol Gilligan, Nancy Rule Goldberger, Virginia Goldner, Thelma Jean Goodrich, Rachel T. Hare-Mustin, bell hooks, Molly Layton, Harriet Goldhor Lerner, Deborah Anna Luepnitz, Dell Martin, Kathleen May, Monica McGoldrick, Jean Baker Miller, Roberta Nutt, Peggy Papp, Cheryl Rampage, Pamela Remer, Sallyann Roth, Olga Silverstein, Jill Mattuck Tarule, Jill McLean Taylor, Barre Thorne, Lenore Walker, Froma Walsh, Marianne Walters, Janie Victoria Ward, J. Pamela Weiner, Dorothy Wheeler, and Judith Worell.
Cognitive-Behavioral Family Therapy	The cognitive focus of this model really began with the work of Albert Ellis and was expanded and developed further through the work of Aaron Beck. The behavioral focus extended from classical conditioning (Ivan Pavlov) and operant conditioning (B. F. Skinner). Cognitive-behavioral family therapy rests mainly on the work of Frank Dattilio. Other key figures include: Albert Bandura, Donald Baucom, Judith Beck, Ian Falloon, Marion Forgatch, John Gottman, Neil Jacobson, Arnold Lazarus, Donald Meichenbaum, Christine Padesky, Gerald Patterson, Richard Stuart, and Joseph Wolpe.
Parenting	The first behavioral approaches to parenting were popularized by John Watson. Watson used classical conditioning to promote a scientific approach to child rearing. At about the same time, Alfred Adler advanced the first systemic approach to understanding adult-child interactions and taught parents, teachers, and mental-health providers in his child guidance clinics that all behavior was purposeful. Other key figures include: Don Dinkmeyer, Don Dinkmeyer, Jr., Rudolf Dreikurs, Marion Forgatch, Haim Ginott, Thomas Gordon, John Gottman, John Krumboltz, Gary McKay, Gerald Patterson, and Michel Popkin.

Table A.2	Key Concepts
Family Therapy Model	**Key Concepts**
Multigenerational Family Therapy	Bowen emphasized the role of theory as a guide in practicing family therapy. For him, a well-articulated theory is essential in remaining emotionally detached as a family therapist. Bowen's theory and practice of family therapy grew out of his work with schizophrenic individuals in families. He was much more interested in developing a theory of family systems therapy than in designing techniques for working with families. Key concepts include: differentiation of the self and emotional cutoff; triangulation and the nuclear family emotional system; the family projection process and the multigenerational transmission process; sibling position; and societal regression.
Adlerian Family Therapy	Adlerians believe that human beings are essentially social, purposeful, subjective, and interpretive in their approaches to life. Within the family, parents and children quickly become involved in repetitive, mistaken interactions that lead to unhappiness and disharmony: Adlerian family therapy seeks to unlock these patterns and support more-effective leadership and relationships. Key concepts include: democratic parenting; family atmosphere and family values; family constellation and birth order; and an interactional view of mistaken goals.
Human Validation Process Model	Satir's human validation process stresses enhancement and validation of self-esteem, family rules, congruence versus defensive communication patterns, sculpting, nurturing triads and family mapping, and family life-fact chronologies. It emphasizes factors such as making contact, metaphor, reframing, emotional honesty, congruent communication, creating new possibilities, drama, humor, and personal touch in the therapy process. Key concepts include: family life and family rules; family roles and family triads; functional and dysfunctional communication stances; and the process of change.
Experiential-Symbolic Family Therapy	Experiential-symbolic family therapists focus on the subjective needs of the individual in the family as they attempt to facilitate family interaction that will result in the individuality of each family member. They operate on the assumption that all family members have the right to be themselves but that the needs of the family may suppress this individuation and self-expression. In this sense, there is no right or wrong—or even preferred—way for a family to be: The goal is member authenticity. Key concepts include: an almost atheoretical stance; being is becoming; and the dialectics of a healthy family and intimacy.
Structural Family Therapy	Structural family therapy is an approach to understanding the nature and structure of the family system, the presenting problem, and the process of change. Key concepts include: accommodation, alignments, boundaries, disengagement, enmeshment, family structure; family systems and subsystems, force (power), and underorganized families.
Strategic Family Therapy	Strategic family therapy is an approach that focuses on solving problems presented and maintained by various family members. This model has at least three different orientations, represented by separate schools of thought. The first is the Mental Research Institute (or MRI); the second was developed by Jay Haley and Cloe Madanes and was originally housed in Washington, DC; the third was developed in Milan, Italy. Each approach contributed key concepts to this model, including: circular causality and feedback loops; double-bind theory; family rules, sequences, and homeostasis; messages and meta-messages; and power, control, and hierarchies.
Solution-Focused/Solution-Oriented Family Therapy	Both solution-focused and solution-oriented approaches are centered in storied conversations that seek to enable preferred outcomes by focusing on solutions rather than on problems. Key concepts include: multiple solutions rather than *right* solutions;

(Continued on next page)

Table A.2 (Contd.)	
	solution-focus rather than problem-focus; therapeutic conversations and progressive narratives; and negotiating change.
Social Constructionism and Narrative Family Therapy	Postmodern, social constructionism is a broad concept that really constitutes the next wave in family therapy, as well as in psychotherapy in general. Although many different models are emerging within this paradigm, we concentrated on three of them: The linguistic approach; reflecting teams; and narrative therapy. Each of these models shares the common beliefs that there are *multiple realities,* not just one; that we live *storied lives* created through *language* and *social discourse*; and that *therapy must reflect these beliefs* in its core processes. The key concepts for each of the three models are: linguistic therapy—client-as-expert; the not-knowing position; problem-dissolving and telling and retelling. Reflecting teams: dialogues and dialogues about dialogues; preferred realities; reflecting and tentative wondering. Narrative therapy: deconstruction and externalization; dominant-culture narratives; narratives as interpretive stories; unique outcomes and re-authoring; and letters, certificates, and narrative celebrations.
Feminist Family Therapy	Feminist family therapy developed as a means of empowering women in family relationships and addressing oppression in general and its effects on the family. Of particular interest to feminists has been the development of both genders within the family from childhood to adult life. Key concepts include: honoring the experiences and perceptions of women; patriarchy; the personal is political; and social transformation and advocacy.
Cognitive-Behavioral Family Therapy	Cognitive-behavioral family therapy is a blend of Pavlov's classical conditioning and B. F. Skinner's operant conditioning, coupled with the social learning theory of Bandura and the cognitive therapies of Albert Ellis and Aaron Beck. Key concepts include: baselines; behavior modification; behavioral self-monitoring; cognitive distortions and schemas; how family members express and hear the thoughts and feelings of others; the nature and rate of patterns of upsetting behavioral interactions; rational problem solving; rational thinking; and the skills families employ to solve problems.
Parenting	Effective parenting did not become a focus of psychology or family therapy until the last half of the 20th century. With the advent of child development theories in the 1930s and 1940s coupled with increasing urbanization, the need for new and more-effective approaches to parenting has been on the rise. Key concepts related to effective parenting include: appropriate use of reinforcement, time-outs, and incentives for positive behavior; democratic or authoritative-responsive parenting vs. authoritarian or permissive child-rearing; giving choices; listening and emotion coaching; modeling respect, cooperation, kindness, caring, compassion, and courage; negotiations and compromise; providing encouragement, recognition, and positive attention; providing guidance and leadership; taking children in as partners; taking time for training; treating children as growing, developing people with different needs at different times in their lives; understanding the mistaken goals of children's misbehavior; and using natural and logical consequences.

Table A.3	Therapy Goals
Family Therapy Model	**Therapy Goals**
Multigenerational Family Therapy	The practice of Bowen family therapy is governed by two goals: (1) lessening of anxiety and symptom relief and (2) an increase in each family member's level of differentiation of the self. To bring about significant change in a family system, it is necessary to open closed family ties and to engage actively in a detriangulation process. Although problems are seen as residing in the system rather than in the individual, the route to changing oneself is through changing in relation to others in the family-of-origin.
Adlerian Family Therapy	Adlerian family therapists want to engage parents in a learning experience and a collaborative assessment. Part of this assessment will include an investigation of the multiple ways in which parents function as family leaders—or lose the ability to do so. Under most conditions, a goal of therapy is to establish and support parents as effective leaders of the family. Goal disclosure also is used to facilitate an understanding of the motivations involved. These interventions serve another goal of therapy: to replace automatic, often nonconscious, negative interactions with a conscious understanding of family process. Based on an understanding of the family's specific motivational patterns, parents often leave the therapy session with suggestions designed to initiate a reorientation of the family.
Human Validation Process Model	The key goals of Satir's approach to family therapy are clear communication, expanding awareness, enhancing potentials for growth, especially in self-esteem, and coping with the demands and process of change. The human validation process model is concerned with the growth of individuals and the family, rather than merely stabilizing the family. The aim is for individual members of the family to become more sensitive to one another, to share their experiences, and to interact in new and genuine ways. The specific goals related to this change process are: generating hope and courage in family members to develop new options; accessing, strengthening, enhancing, or generating coping skills in family members; and encouraging members to exercise options that will result in health as opposed to the mere elimination of symptoms.
Experiential-Symbolic Family Therapy	In Whitaker's view, the goal of family therapy is to promote the feeling dimension: spontaneity, creativity, the ability to play, and the willingness to be "crazy." The central goal is to facilitate individual autonomy *and* a sense of belonging in the family. Experiential family therapists operate on the assumption that if individual members increase their awareness and capacity for experiencing, more genuine intimacy will result within the family circle. A central tenet of Whitaker's approach is that therapists need to be aware of their own responses to families in order to be therapeutic. The therapist functions best as an instigator of family openness, realness, and spontaneity. Experiential therapists place value on their own responses as a measure of healthy interaction. Whitaker sees experiential therapy as a way for therapists to be actively engaged in their own personal development. Thus, therapy is a process that helps the therapist as much as the family.
Structural Family Therapy	The goal of structural family therapy is to transform the system by bringing about structural change within the system, modifying the family's transactional rules, and developing more appropriate boundaries. When the system is transformed, the symptoms of dysfunction remit. Aponte and Fishman both note the importance of working with other community systems in an effort to coordinate services and therapeutic interventions with families. In general, the goal for families is the creation of an effective hierarchical structure. The structural family therapist attempts to change the rules governing interactional patterns so that individual members (and family subsystems) have clear boundaries. A healthy family is characterized by a system that supports the growth of the individual family members and, at the same time, encourages the growth of the family unit.

(Continued on next page)

Table A.3 (Contd.)

Strategic Family Therapy	The MRI model is a behavioral approach that can be described as a two-step process: Define the problem and then resolve the problem. When the problem is resolved, therapy has reached its first and only goal, and the counseling sessions are over. Part of defining the problem also is defining clear, achievable, measurable goals. This process is concrete. Although reframing and paradoxical interventions often can be seen as cognitive interventions, they are simply a means to an end—and that end is always behavior change. The goal of Haley's strategic therapy is to resolve a presenting problem by changing behavioral sequences. Haley is even more behavioral in his approach than the MRI people. He has little use for insight as a goal of therapy. He is concerned about getting people to behave differently. The intent of strategic interventions is to shift the family organization so that a presenting problem is no longer functional. Madanes adopted a more humanistic approach to strategic therapy; she currently believes that *harmony* and *balance* should be goals directly sought in family therapy. Madanes thinks family members need to love and be loved, find fulfillment in work, play, and seek joy. This is facilitated when clients come into balance individually and with each other, such that reason and emotion are connected and complementary, doing for others is balanced with self-care, and love foreshadows hurt but also helps one through it. The early Milan therapists were also behaviorally oriented. But since they viewed dysfunctional family patterns as *family games* and sought to disrupt these processes, they began to rely more and more on game exposure and reframing motivation. The power in family games was in maintaining the *status quo*, and it was still the therapist's job to take a stand that would redirect family interaction into more-useful channels. Selvini Palazzoli and Prata used the *invariant prescription* with the clear goal of strengthening the bond between the parents and breaking up the parent–child coalitions that were responsible for maintaining the family's games. Since *family games* in this model always refers to painful and disturbing interactions, one of the goals of this model is to develop more flexible and open communication patterns in the family.
Solution-Focused/Solution Oriented Family Therapy	The movement to a more collaborative model of therapy is mirrored in the goals of solution-focused/solution-oriented therapies. Like the MRI therapists, these therapists still want to move people from problem to solution, but they believe that the solutions already exist within the family and within the family members. Their goal is to engage clients in an optimistic conversation about the present and future. They wonder out loud about what might be possible if the clients used skills they have used before, rediscovered internal and external resources, or made use of exceptions as options to develop desired outcomes. In this sense, the goal of therapy is to un-stick people from their current patterns and perceptions and help them discover new, concrete possibilities for their immediate futures. Setting goals is an important part of "solution" conversations in therapy. deShazer takes an almost behavioral approach to describing effective goals, a process that also fits well with many of the requirements of managed-care agencies. He believes that effective goals are: small rather than large; meaningful to the clients; described concretely; fit the actual lives of the participants; require in them a sense that they are working hard; and start something new rather than end a problem (that is, are based on new behaviors rather than the elimination of old ones).
Social Constructionism and Narrative Family Therapy	Social constructionists believe that real people live in families and that each person is living the story of his or her life; each person contributes to the story of family life and all of the stories are in constant co-construction. Human beings make meaning expressed in language and narratives; in this sense, families are meaning-making and meaningful systems. When the narratives of meaning become saturated with problems, social constructionists enter into the personal and familial searches for alternate possibilities, unique outcomes, and preferred stories. Although somewhat different from therapist to therapist, social constructionists share an interest in the generation of new meaning and preferred realities (in the form of

(Continued on next page)

Table A.3 (Contd.)	
	stories) for the lives of the people and families they serve. They seek to enlarge perspective and focus, facilitate the discovery or creation of new options, and co-develop solutions that are unique to the people and families they see. Social constructionism almost always includes an awareness of the impact of various aspects of dominant culture on human life, and therapists in this model seek to challenge the dominant culture and develop alternate stories about self and others, and ways of acting, knowing, and living.
Feminist Family Therapy	Feminist family therapists recognize that both individuals and families need help in developing egalitarian relationships, learning to value women's voices and perspectives, and making room for gender-unique identity development. Some of the goals of therapy include centralizing an analysis of sex-role socialization in the life of families; identifying internalized sex-role messages and beliefs, and challenging and replacing sex-role stereotypes and scripts with more self-enhancing beliefs and stories.
	Families cannot be separated from the larger contexts in which they exist. Feminists believe that evaluating the influence of social roles and norms on personal and familial experiences is essential. This is especially true in examining how sexism and patriarchy, racism and classism, oppress women and men alike.
	Feminist family therapists have the goals of (a) meeting families and their members in whatever form and at whatever stage they are living; (b) facilitating development; (c) allowing and contextualizing the expression of feelings from fear and anger to pride and celebration; (d) helping members of the dominant culture look at themselves, challenge their perspectives, and find ways to become supportive of their partners and children; and (e) helping family members engage in political or social activism as needed and appropriate.
Cognitive-Behavioral Family Therapy	One of the first goals of cognitive-behavioral family therapy is to determine whether the focus can be on the family as a whole or must first address issues related to the couple. Assuming that the couple's relationship is strong enough potentially to provide leadership for the family, the second goal of cognitive-behavioral family therapy is to determine whether the parents merely need educational input or the family and especially one or more of the children need immediate changes in order to regain functional status. For the former, a psychoeducational consultation, for example, can be used to teach parents effective ways to handle and correct everyday problems from getting up and eating properly to bed-wetting, temper tantrums, and backtalk or whining. When the misbehaviors of the children are more disturbing, perhaps involving anger, aggression, dangerous activities, or conversely depression, anxiety, and suicidal ideation, then more-direct behavioral interventions and management processes are required.
	The overall goal of cognitive-behavioral family therapy is to address automatic thoughts, cognitive distortions, and schemas that lead to antagonistic interactions and to plan modifications of behavior that will lead to more-harmonious family lives. This goal is specified for each individual couple or family unit and is based on a variety of cognitive and behavioral assessments used to establish couple or family baselines and targeted goals. It is these targeted goals that are the basis for developing treatment plans and the evidence-based interventions designed to bring about effective change.
Parenting	The goals of effective parenting include the development of children as psychological, cognitive, emotional, and behavioral beings; the creation of a nurturing and harmonious family atmosphere; and the preparation of children for effective living as adults. Parenting is a task and it involves skills that can be taught and learned. Psychoeducational programs have the goal of providing information to parents that support them as leaders and provide them with both an understanding of childhood behaviors and their motivations and ways of redirecting children toward positive growth and development.

Table A.4	Therapist's Role and Function
Family Therapy Model	Therapist's Role and Function
Multigenerational Family Therapy	Bowen viewed himself as an objective researcher who aimed to help individuals in the family assess and understand their relational styles within the family system. Bowen therapists function as teachers, coaches, and neutral observers who are responsible for establishing the tone of family therapy. Bowen taught individuals or couples about triangulation and then expected them to go back to their families-of-origin to extricate themselves emotionally from these triangular patterns. The purpose of going home again is not to confront family members, or even to establish peace and harmony, but to encourage clients to come to know others in their families as they are. Bowen helped individuals or couples gather information, and he coached or guided them into new behaviors by demonstrating ways in which individuals can change their relationships with their parents, siblings, and extended family members. He instructed them in how to be better observers and also taught them how to move from emotional reactivity to increased objectivity. He did not tell clients what to do, but rather asked a series of questions that were designed to help them figure out their own roles in their families' emotional processes. Bowen therapists maintain that therapy sessions can be viewed as rehearsals for becoming differentiated; the main therapeutic work of relating to members of their families in new ways happens outside the therapy session. As a prerequisite to practicing effectively with families, therapists must be aware of how they have been influenced by their own families-of-origin. The premise underlying the significance of understanding our families-of-origin is that the patterns of interpersonal behavior we learned in our families-of-origin will be repeated with clients unless the practitioner has achieved differentiation.
Adlerian Family Therapy	Adlerian family therapists function as collaborators who seek to join the family from a position of mutual respect. Within this collaborative role, Adlerians stress the functions of systemic investigation and education. The systemic investigation focuses on (a) the family constellation or system, (b) the motivations behind problematic interactions, and (c) the family process throughout a typical day. The results of this investigation are used to disclose and discuss the mistaken goals or ideas that may be involved in problematic parent–child interactions. In raising mistaken goals to a conscious consideration, the therapist is able to develop family interventions and recommendations designed to correct mistaken goals and provide parents with an understanding of parenting skills associated with more-effective and harmonious living. Adlerian family therapists often use a public therapy process they call *open-forum* family counseling. Similar to the process first used by Adler in Vienna, the therapist counsels a family in front of a group of parents, teachers, and other community members. The counselor in these sessions has two clients: the family-in-focus and the audience. By working with the commonalities between the family and the audience, the therapist educates many families through one.
Human Validation Process Model	The Satir therapist's role and function is to guide family members through the change process. Who the therapist is as a person is far more important than specific intervention techniques. Therapists are best conceived of as facilitators in charge of the therapeutic process; they do not have the task of making change happen or curing individuals. The therapist's faith in the ability of family members to move toward growth and actualization is central to this approach. This attitude infuses the therapy experience with nurturance, support, safety, and human validation. Satir views the therapist as a resource person who has a special advantage in being able to observe the family situation. She uses the analogy of a camera with a wide-angle lens, which allows the counselor to see things from each person's vantage point. As an official observer, the therapist is able to report on what the family cannot see. Satir described many roles and techniques that family therapists employ in helping a family achieve its goals. The therapist creates a setting in which people can risk looking clearly and objectively at themselves and their actions; assists family members in building self-esteem; helps clients identify their assets; takes the family's history

(Continued on next page)

Table A.4 (Contd.)

	and notes past achievements; decreases threats by setting boundaries and reducing the need for defenses; shows that pain and the forbidden are acceptable to explore; uses certain techniques for restoring the client's feeling of accountability; helps family members see how past models influence their expectations and behavior, and looks for change in these expectations; delineates roles and functions; completes gaps in communication and interprets messages; points out significant discrepancies in communication; and identifies nonverbal communication.
Experiential-Symbolic Family Therapy	Experiential symbolic therapists tend to create family turmoil and then coach the members through the experience. They primarily are interested in the interaction between themselves and the family. The therapist's role requires immediacy, a willingness to be oneself, vitality, a degree of transparency, and willingness to use personal reactions during the family sessions. Although experiential therapists are willing to act as temporary experts and issue directives to the family, they are just as likely to maintain long periods of silence to augment the member's anxiety. Whitaker likes to think of himself as a coach or a surrogate grandparent. His enactment of these roles requires structure, discipline, creativity, and presence. The relationship between the active and vital therapist and the family is the catalyst for growth and movement.

Therapeutic interventions are aimed at intensifying what is going on in the here and now of the family session. The focus of therapy is on the process of what is unfolding during the session, a time when the seeds of change are planted. Instead of giving interpretations, the therapist provides an opportunity for the family members to be themselves by freely expressing what they are thinking and feeling. As a therapist, Whitaker strives to grasp the complex world of a family by focusing on impulses and symbols. He is interested in going beyond the surface level of interactions by dealing with symbolic meanings of what evolves between the family and himself. In his sometimes outrageous style, he gives voice to his own impulses and fantasies and, in doing so, he encourages family members to become more accepting of their moment-by-moment experiencing. |
| **Structural Family Therapy** | Minuchin identifies three interactive functions of the therapist: (1) joining the family in a position of leadership, (2) mapping its underlying structure, and (3) intervening in ways designed to transform an ineffective structure. Structural therapists assume that individual change will result from modifying a family's organization and from changing its transactional patterns. The therapist's basic task is to engage the family actively as a unit for the purpose of initiating a restructuring process.

Structural therapists play a number of roles with families, depending on the phase of therapy. From the initial session, therapists are engaged in a dance with the family. Soon after this dance begins, they become stage directors who create scenarios in which problems are played out according to different scripts. Therapists lay the groundwork for a particular situation, create a scenario, assign roles and tasks to a family, and issue directives to members. Then they sit back as spectators and observe the family in action. Therapists must offer a combination of support and challenge. They need to sustain certain patterns and undermine other patterns. They must learn the appropriate balance between accommodating and negotiating with a family. |
| **Strategic Family Therapy** | In the early stages of strategic family therapy, the therapist's role was that of a consultant, an expert, and a stage director. Clearly, the therapist is in charge of the session. There is very little focus on the client/therapist relationship; instead, the therapist is directive and an authority figure. This is true in both the MRI model and in the work of Jay Haley.

Because Haley believes that direct educational methods are of little value, he tends to be unwilling to explain himself to his clients; instead, he operates covertly. In this model, the therapist is interested primarily in the control of power within the therapeutic relationship. Because he views his task as assuming the responsibility for changing the organization of a family and resolving the problems that it brings to therapy, he operates directively, giving the family members specific directives on what they are |

(Continued on next page)

Table A.4 (Contd.)	
	to do, both inside and outside of the therapy sessions. Because therapy focuses on the social context of human dilemmas, the therapist's task is to design interventions aimed at the client's social situation. In the last decade, Madanes introduced relational, humanistic dimensions to strategic therapy. For her, the role of the therapist includes the development and modeling of altruism. Altruism includes capacities for caring and empathy, understanding and forgiveness, compassion and connection, and balance and harmony. The more-postmodern models developed in Milan call on the therapist to function as an investigator. These models are very collaborative. Optimism, persistence, and anticipatory inquiries about new possibilities are all parts of the role and function of the therapist.
Solution-Focused/ Solution-Oriented Family Therapy	The solution-focused/solution-oriented therapists became dedicated completely to a client-empowering inquiry process. Just as there is no single or even right way to perceive reality, there is also no correct way for a family and its members to be. Solution therapists believe that each family has within it the resources and possibilities for change that can lead to more functional and fulfilling lives. Solution-focused/solution-oriented therapists do this by looking for exceptions to complaint-oriented stories, reminding families of past successes, considering what was previously ignored, focusing on client strengths, and generating hope through new possibilities. It is in the development of such therapeutic conversations that families create new stories that act as self-fulfilling prophesies.
Social Constructionism and Narrative Family Therapy	In social constructionist theory, the therapist-as-expert is replaced by the client-as-expert. The therapist enters into dialogues in an effort to elicit the perspectives, resources, and the unique experiences of the client(s). A heavy emphasis is placed on the use of questions, often relational in nature, that empower the people in families to speak, to give voice to their diverse positions, and to own their capabilities in the presence of others. The therapist supplies the optimism and sometimes a process, but the clients generate what is possible and contribute the movement that ultimately actualizes their preferred outcomes. Therapists in social constructionist models are active facilitators. The concepts of care, interest, curiosity, empathy, contact, and even fascination are essential. The not-knowing position, which allows therapists to follow, affirm, and be guided by the stories of their client(s), creates participant/observer and process-facilitator roles for the therapist and integrates therapy with a postmodern science of human inquiry. Collaboration, compassion, reflection, and discovery characterize the interactions of therapist and client in a social-constructionist model.
Feminist Family Therapy	Because feminist therapists may incorporate any number of psychological and therapeutic models into their work, the role and function of the practitioner may change somewhat from person to person. What is constant for feminist therapists is congruence, informed by feminist principles, between their personal and professional lives. Gender-role and power analyses are regular parts of their work with families as is their commitment to reflective practice and monitoring their own biases and distortions, especially the social and cultural dimensions of women's experience. Feminist family therapists place a high value on egalitarian relationships. They believe in making their values explicit, being emotionally and intellectually present, using self-disclosure appropriately with purpose and discretion in the interests of the client, viewing clients as consumers, encouraging social equality in relationships, reflective practice, and social activism. Joining with multiculturalists, feminists seek to promote social justice for women and men of color and other oppressed or marginalized groups, such as the LGBT communities. Feminist family therapists place a strong value on listening to and acknowledging women's voices. Toward this end, they often reframe and affirm previously devalued characteristics. Most feminist therapists work to de-pathologize behaviors and interactions that represent adherence to dominant-culture imposed female gender-role norms.

(Continued on next page)

Table A.4 (Contd.)	
	Feminists are especially critical of the diagnosis of Borderline Personality Disorder. In family therapy, feminist also work to eliminate the blame of women for everything from over-involvement to father absence to triangulation that too often has characterized systemic approaches. Part of the role of feminist family therapists today is to reclaim that which traditionally has been associated with women as essential in the therapeutic process.
Cognitive-Behavioral Family Therapy	The foundation for cognitive-behavioral therapy with individuals and families always has been related to a scientific inquiry into human behavior. What tends to remain constant in this work is a dedication to an assessment of cognitive expression and measurement of observed behaviors. In this model, thinking leads to decision making; the generation of emotions supports the decisions and fuels the enactment of behavior. The role and function of the therapist is to identify and correct faulty or distorted thinking (called cognitive restructuring) while also taking a baseline measurement of dysfunctional behaviors and then developing interventions that will measurably improve functioning. Periodic assessments of the baseline thoughts, feelings, and behaviors are conducted throughout therapy as a measure of progress.
	Since any constant behavior or pattern of interaction that occurs within a family is continually being reinforced, the first task of the therapist is to understand it. Cognitive-behavioral therapists tend to focus on dyadic interactions—spouse to spouse or parent to child—in order to understand how each person is reinforcing the other. When a parent and a child are locked in a mutually reinforcing, negative interaction, it is usually because one or both of them feel that their positions are being challenged, and this should not happen. A cognitive reorientation starts by helping the parent realize that the challenging behavior is happening, and the normal parental response is actually helping to maintain it.
Parenting	The role of parent educators and those who work with parenting in family practice is to train effective parent leaders who guide the development of children; create a safe and nurturing environment; and prepare the children to leave home eventually and engage in independent living. Effective parents teach, set limits and boundaries, give choices, negotiate, consult, emotion coach, validate, model effective living, and guide problem solving, to name a few of many skills. They are encouraging, engage in active listening, and use natural and logical consequences to teach, instead of aversive punishments intended to control the immature.

Table A.5	Multicultural Perspectives
Family Therapy Model	**Multicultural Perspectives**
Multigenerational Family Therapy	Starting in 1982 with the original publication, McGoldrick, Giordano, and Garcia-Preto (2005) set about the task of delineating family characteristics in a wide range of cultures from Africa, the Americas, Asia, Europe, and the Middle East. Their original belief that culture was transmitted almost biologically from one generation to the next has become more fluid and dynamic over the years, and there simply would not be a multicultural perspective (or lens) in family therapy without their work. That culture is becoming a central metaphor in Bowen therapy and is viewed both developmentally and dynamically is a testimonial to how far the theory and, indeed, the field has advanced.
Adlerian Family Therapy	Adlerian family practitioners approach culture phenomenologically. Similar to birth order, culture becomes a vantage point from which individuals and families view life.

(Continued on next page)

Table A.5 (Contd.)

	It is not the vantage point that determines the individual's position, but rather the interpretation the individual gives it. Adlerians believe that the interpretation each family member gives to the culture will be a very strong factor in how the person sees self and life, and interacts with other people. Sometimes, the most effective initial intervention is to listen carefully to each family member and to help him or her sort out the various positions that person has adopted.
Human Validation Process Model	Satir was the only major family therapist to offer human relationships training on a regular basis to the Lakota Sioux in South Dakota. As with any unfamiliar culture, she entered the first experience with an openness to learn about the culture, the people, and the symbols and meanings inherent in the community. From this, she both adapted some of her therapeutic interventions and incorporated new possibilities unique to that culture. In her lifetime, Satir worked within many of the countries in Asia, the Pacific Islands, and all of the countries comprising Europe, including many of the countries that used to comprise what was called "the Eastern Bloc."
Experiential-Symbolic Family Therapy	Although there is nothing in the almost atheoretical symbolic-experiential approach that either supports or denies a multicultural perspective, it is hard to understand how this model, as it is most commonly demonstrated, could be received positively by those cultures for which respect and saving face are central to the culture's worldview. For example, the self-disclosures and confrontational nature of symbolic-experiential therapy would almost certainly have to be significantly modified for people from many of the Asian cultures. On the other hand, this approach may be inherently multicultural because of the unique adaptation the therapists make to each individual family system—and because of the realness and authenticity of the therapist.
Structural Family Therapy	No systemic family therapy has done more to advance the plight of the disadvantaged, poor, and the working poor than structural family therapy. Structural family therapists have transformed cultural understandings into pragmatic and even spiritual interventions. Since those who are poor in the United States include a large number of oppressed individuals and discriminated cultures, many of the leaders of structural family therapy have developed a special sensitivity to the issues of racism and the overt marginalization of Spanish-speaking, African-American, and Asian cultures. Indeed, an appreciation of cultural diversity seems to be integrated into every part of their therapeutic process.
Strategic Family Therapy	Haley and Richeport-Haley (2003) tend to approach incidents of cultural difference as behavioral manifestations of alternate belief systems. They propose one of four approaches to such incidents: (1) to minimize the alternate belief and treat the family structurally and strategically; (2) to use parts of the alternate belief to reach therapeutic goals; (3) to refer the client to a cultural healer in the local community; or (4) to collaborate with a cultural healer in the local community. The Milan group started in Italy and has had tremendous influence throughout Europe, but nothing even from Europe's different cultures has been incorporated in the model. Rather than incorporating culturally diverse perspectives into their work, MRI therapists have preferred to rely on what they call *common sense*. But this is all too often an American common sense. Common sense is always *somebody's* common sense, and each somebody has a worldview inscribed with beliefs about sex, class, race, and other distinctions that are fundamental to social existence.
Solution-Focused/ Solution-Oriented Family Therapy	Very little has been written in these models that addresses the importance of cultural issues or orientations at all. Selekman does offer a set of questions that solution therapists should ask themselves before working with families. These include: "Have I examined my own white identity in terms of what it means to be white in our society?" "How does being white and/or being from a different ethnic or cultural background affect what I can see, hear, and think about this family?" "In what way does being white in our society grant me . . . privileged status?" "If you were African American, Asian, or Latino, how comfortable would

(Continued on next page)

Table A.5 (Contd.)

	you feel working with a white therapist?" "What would your concerns be with a white therapist?"
Social Constructionism and Narrative Family Therapy	Postmodern, social constructionist approaches to therapy have almost a perfect fit with the basic philosophy and tenets of multiculturalism. The constructs of multiple realities and a diversity of truths is at the heart of both a postmodern worldview and multicultural perspectives. Narrative therapy, especially, is well situated to challenge the oppressive values and beliefs of the dominant culture. When clients bring individual or family concerns to a narrative therapist, there is a clear inclination within the therapeutic process to address patriarchy and sexism, racism, ageism, and other forms of discrimination and oppression that have real effects on people and systems.
Feminist Family Therapy	Both feminism and multiculturalism seek to address and eliminate sexism, racism, ageism, classism, poverty, heterosexism, and other forms of oppression, discrimination, and privilege. Although one of the sticking points has sometimes been an insistence by multiculturalists that a respect for differences in culture includes leaving some formal aspects of patriarchy in place, feminists note that there is no country left in the world without feminist voices in it. This is true even in fundamentalist Islamic states, as well as some of the more-traditional Hispanic and Asian cultures. An integration of feminism and multiculturalism is really the model for the future. For just as it does no culture any good to maintain patriarchy, it also does no woman any good to actualize feminism in a manner that isolates or dissociates her from her family and culture.
Cognitive-Behavioral Family Therapy	Cognitive-behavioral therapists approach culture as a context—and a reinforcing context at that—in which thinking and behaving are enacted. Native Americans, Hispanic Americans, African Americans, and Asian Americans often prefer an active, directive therapist concerned with solving immediate problems and bringing quick, effective relief to the family. Cognitive therapists note that each culture has its own set of rules and role expectations, and families are the social unit in which these rules and roles are most often enacted. What individuals and families think and what they find reinforcing is also heavily influenced by the cultural norms of the community. Cognitive-behaviorists have repeatedly pointed out that prejudice is a learned response. It is taught and reinforced in environmental units as small as an interaction and as large as the macro-systems of society and culture.
Parenting	Although the main parent-education programs were developed in Western cultures based on American-European models, for more than a decade they have incorporated a wide range of cultures and diverse family arrangements. Both *STEP* and *Active Parenting* programs are available in Spanish. Although there are numerous books that have been written specifically to the needs of parents and children in different cultures, none of have been translated into active training programs yet.

Table A.6 — Gender Perspectives

Family Therapy Model	Gender Perspectives
Multigenerational Family Therapy	Monica McGoldrick and her colleagues and associates are probably the most prolific and dependable sources addressing gender issues in family therapy. Her work with Carol Anderson, Betty Carter, Peggy Papp, and Froma Walsh, to name a few, literally forced the field of family therapy (and especially AAMFT) to integrate gender as significant perspectives in therapeutic work. Their gender work, along with the work of Rachel Hare-Mustin and the members of the Women's Project, has integrated the perspectives of women and a consideration of gender issues in family therapy.
Adlerian Family Therapy	Although most feminist commentaries ignore the Adlerian model, they would find strong support for valuing the voice and perspectives of women and children in the writings of Adler, Bitter, Carlson, Christensen, Dreikurs, Hawes, Nicoll, Sperry, and

(Continued on next page)

Table A.6 (Contd.)	
	others. Adler's early pro-feminist positions, including his belief in the right of women to choose whether or not to have children and his call for equality between the sexes are foundational elements in both feminist and Adlerian theory. Dreikurs, especially, recognized the sociological impact of the subordination of women on the lives of both women and men. In his major text on marriage, he documented societies in which women were noted to have had a superior position, suggesting that superiority by either gender eliminated the true value of social equality.
Human Validation Process Model	Satir's focus on an internal locus of control gives some feminists and social constructionists concern, because it can too easily ignore the abuses of power inherent in patriarchal, dominant-culture systems. Satir's personal stance and the model she developed took no political stance in relation to gender issues. Although Satir was an extremely strong proponent of women in families and larger systems, she never saw the human development of women as a counterpoint to male oppression. She did not see oppression as an outside force that required a different response than any other foreign element in life. Satir referred to men and women as having navel equality; that is, we are all human, having emerged from our biological mothers as a result of the fertilization of a human egg by human sperm. Satir sought the rounded wholeness of all people. In this sense, Satir's facilitation of women was never at the expense of men.
Experiential-Symbolic Family Therapy	In the area of gender issues and sexual/affectional orientation, Whitaker and colleagues have been much more vocal than they are in relation to cultural diversity. Whitaker held women in high regard, appreciating those qualities most associated with women's development (nurturance, intuition, expressiveness, caring, and vulnerability, to name a few). Although he does not write directly about these qualities, it is evident from his work that he values them. What makes Whitaker so unusual in the field of family therapy was his willingness to confront, challenge, and even chide men during therapy sessions. More than almost any other family therapist, Whitaker seemed to believe that humanizing men was central to his work, and he regularly worked at opening up men to much more intimacy than most ever dreamed was possible. Napier focuses on an equality of autonomy and closeness in coupling and marriage that parallels much of Whitaker's work with families. Whitaker and his associates also demonstrate an enormous appreciation for diversity of sexual/affectional orientations in their work.
Structural Family Therapy	Although feminists would join Minuchin in his consideration of larger systems affecting the family, he has not been favorably disposed to feminist interventions designed to save the woman at the expense of the family unit. Feminists noted and criticized the early and middle stages of Minuchin's development when he would join with the father in the family structure, reinforcing the patriarchy and male authority in the system. Indeed, the process of unbalancing developed in this model has all too often been used in favor of men and at the expense of women, even in potentially abusive and dangerous situations. Although this is not a criticism that one tends to hear of the masters of this approach today (Aponte and Fishman), it is still a caution that is important to acknowledge for those studying the complete range of structural therapeutic interventions.
Strategic Family Therapy	Without insight and understanding, strategic interventions fall easily into "the ends justify the means" approaches to therapy. There are plenty of examples in the strategic reports of the 1970s and early 1980s of interventions that maintained sexism within families. A depressed man was once congratulated for getting his wife to have sex with him the way he desired by demanding what he had coming to him. Another blatantly sexist example in strategic interventions was when a therapist suggested that a woman had learned how to use the feminine wile of playing hard to get. Even the Haley/Richeport-Haley proposal for working with cultural diversity (that a man and a woman can be seen separately if their culture does not recognize women's equality) perpetuates sexism in an effort to be culturally sensitive. To be fair, other strategic interventions involve empowerment of women and broadening men's useful participation in the family, but until Madanes' infusion of values in therapy, there was nothing in strategic therapy that required or sought the integration of an ethical, social, or political value system. There is very little chance that the writings, training, or therapy

(Continued on next page)

Table A.6 (Contd.)

	of the strategic family approach will address the problems inherent in family life and society for women. Selvini Palazzoli actually has suggested that in spite of recognized patriarchy, some women get a lot out of playing victim.
Solution-Focused/ Solution-Oriented Family Therapy	Selekman devotes only 2 pages to issues in which he acknowledges the critique of family therapy that feminists have brought to the table. He even offers a small case in which the complaint-oriented story of a woman and her child includes concerns that her husband is too busy to come to therapy, that she seldom gets to see her own friends, and that she is very tired. The solution that is co-constructed addresses the traditional values and expectations associated with patriarchy and leads to the woman confronting her husband and taking time for herself. Although valuable as an introduction of gender issues in solution models, nothing further is offered as a positive use of gender in the development of solutions. For example, any of the following questions might fit these approaches quite well, but they are missing-in-action: "What do you think your partner (spouse) can teach you that would be effective in helping you reach your goals?" "If you were your spouse or children, what changes in you would signify that your relationship or family life was getting better?" "What aspects of being female would you like to see valued and continued in your life?" "What activities would you be doing with your partner and family that would tell you that you were a true friend and teammate?"
Social Constructionism and Narrative Family Therapy	The decentered, not-knowing positions of narrative and linguistic therapists offer the best hope for developing and understanding the multiple stories that are present in families. Indeed, the kind of curious interest that permeates closely followed stories not only brings respect and value to difference, but also provides a foundation for thickening gender and cultural stories, as well as individual ones. This is most evident in the work that narrative therapists do in de-constructing the dominant-cultural perspective inherent in psychopathology. Rather than seeing problems as resident within the individual or system, narrative therapists believe that problems are external forces embedded in social (or relational), cultural, and political contexts. Given the nature of the dominant culture, individual and family problems commonly are related to issues of gender, ethnicity, race, class, and sexual orientation. Under the co-leadership of Cheryl White and David Denborough, the Dulwich Centre in Australia has continually addressed the oppression of women and members of the LGBT community.
Feminist Family Therapy	Feminist consciousness of alternate and diverse perspectives has infused family therapy with some of its most significant issues. In addition to helping families address issues of power and to reconsider and change gender-based roles and rules, feminists have called on the profession of family therapy to stop ignoring the social problems of family violence, cultural discrimination, ageism, poverty, race, and class, as well as discrimination against gay men and lesbians. Feminist research and therapeutic practice continually work to enlarge the focus and consciousness of family therapists, calling on us to participate in the largest social reconstruction of all.
Cognitive-Behavioral Family Therapy	When cognitive-behavioral family counselors and therapists integrate gender and cultural perspectives into their work, there are really very few limitations to this model. Normal and abnormal are then approached with gender-awareness and cultural sensitivity. When cognitions are based on gender and cultural stereotypes, the nature of both rational and irrational ideas is distorted; an understanding of gender and cultural contexts provides family practitioners with avenues for contextualizing rational responses. The same is true for assessing problem behavior and choosing behavioral goals and reinforcements for change.
Parenting	Modern parenting approaches seek the constructive involvement of both men and women in the raising of children. Gender-based stereotypes have given way to effective engagement of all parents in all areas of the child's life. The issues and processes that always have been part of women's lives—empathy; caregiving; connection; emotional support, understanding, and coaching; and involvement—are recommended for both genders in single-parent families, dual-career families, blended families, nuclear families, and extended families.

Table A.7	Techniques
Family Therapy Model	**Techniques**
Multigenerational Family Therapy	Bowen therapists believe that understanding how a family system operates is far more important than using a particular technique. They tend to use interventions such as process questions, tracking sequences, teaching, coaching, and directives with a family. They value information about past relationships as a significant context from which they design interventions in the present. Key techniques include: genogram work; asking process questions that focus on personal responsibility and differentiation; engaging clients from a stance of neutrality; detriangulation; relationship experiments; coaching; and use of I-positions and displacement stories.
Adlerian Family Therapy	Adlerians developed open-forum family counseling at the same time that they were pioneering new approaches to private family therapy. Both processes have been incorporated as part of Adlerian brief therapy. Key techniques include: Problem descriptions and goal identification; an investigation of a typical day; identifying and unlocking mistaken goals that motivate parent–child interactions; a child interview, complete with tentative goal disclosure, that aims to elicit a recognition reflex; re-orienting or re-educating the family through the use of encouragement and the application of natural and logical consequences; and getting a commitment to change coupled with an appointment for follow-up interviews.
Human Validation Process Model	Change and healing occur largely as a function of the relationship and climate created by the therapist. It is the individual family members, not the therapist, who are responsible for change. Within the therapy session, the focus of techniques is on emotional honesty, congruence, and systemic understanding. McLendon and Davis use the acronym RECIPE to remember six ingredients important to therapeutic change: resourcefulness, empowerment, congruence, inner system, pattern, and externalization. Key Satir techniques include: family maps (similar to genograms); family life-fact chronology (a listing of a family's three-generation history), family sculpting, drama, reframing, humor, touch, parts parties, and family reconstruction.
Experiential-Symbolic Family Therapy	In Whitaker's model, change must be experienced, rather than understood or designed. Families will tend to stay the same unless the therapist can disturb or frustrate family process. Within the experiential therapy session, the focus of techniques is on expressing blocked affect. Even though Whitaker relies mostly on spontaneity, some key techniques include: play especially through physical encounters of the kind we see young children enacting; acting out one's fears and negative emotions symbolically; therapeutic sharing of parts of the therapist's life without becoming the client; paradox and double messages (double binds) in the service of real intimacy; evolving a crisis; seeding the unconscious; and silence, to let therapy be, to let it percolate. Whitaker liked to be part of a co-therapy team. He felt that having a co-therapist freed him to act in whatever manner seemed to fit the situation. Furthermore, the practice afforded both therapists opportunities to have fun together, to disagree, to embellish on each other's interventions, and to model creative and productive interaction.
Structural Family Therapy	Structural family therapy aims to modify the present organization of the family with minimal exploration and interpretation of the past. Therapists join the family system they are helping, and they make interventions designed to transform the organization of that family. Key techniques include: joining, the process of building and maintaining a therapeutic alliance; negotiating the values that form the basis of problem definition, assessment, therapeutic interventions, and goal-setting; the therapist's use of self; unbalancing; accommodation; tracking sequences; enactments; intensifying; setting boundaries; restructuring (strengthening difuse boundaries and softening rigid ones); reframing; issuing directives; and family mapping.
Strategic Family Therapy	Like structural family therapists, strategic therapists tend to track sequences, reframe behavior and its contexts, assign positive connotations to problems and family interactions, and issue directives. In addition, key techniques include: joining, especially during

(Continued on next page)

Table A.7 (Contd.)

	the social (or initial) stage of therapy, and paradoxical interventions, including prescribing the symptom, restraining family change, and amplifying family difficulties.
	MRI therapists tend to assume a one-down position with families; inquire about the nature of the problem that brings people to therapy; assess problem-maintaining behaviors; set goals for treatment; use homework; and effect termination when a small but significant change has been made in the problem.
	Haley and Madanes developed ordeal therapy, which is a clinical method for working strategically with marital or family dysfunction. Strategic ordeals provide ritual challenges that are designed to be more difficult than the family problem and that facilitate a bonding among family members who go through the ordeal together. Madanes also uses humor, fantasy, and playfulness, all of which are a part of her pretend techniques.
	The Milan therapist essentially engaged in longer-term, brief therapy. Similar to the MRI therapists, the Milan group would see a family for ten sessions, but they would schedule appointments a month apart, taking almost a year to complete therapy in some cases. Similar to Haley and Madanes, they worked as a team behind a one-way mirror. About 40 minutes into the session, the entire team would meet without the family to devise an intervention. In the early years, the intervention was usually a positive connotation of the problem or a ritual designed to help the whole family act in a new way. Milan therapists also adopted a stance of neutrality. Selvini Palazzoli also experimented for a while with an invariant prescription. In the 1990s, Selvini Palazzoli retreated from strategic therapy to return to long-term therapy. Boscolo and Cecchin, after their split from the original team, used more collaborative approaches based on circular questioning.
Solution-Focused/ Solution-Oriented Family Therapy	Because clients often come to therapy in a problem-oriented state, even the few solutions they have considered are wrapped in the power of the problem orientation. Solution-focused therapists counter this client presentation with optimistic dialogues that highlight their belief in achievable, usable goals that are just around the corner. Such conversations involve reframing problems, complimenting clients, clarifying process, and linking a hypnotic-like directive to an inevitable sign of progress. Key techniques include: the miracle question, exception questions, questions of difference (signs), and scaling questions often supported by compliments, embedded messages, or summary messages.
	Solution-oriented therapists emphasize a process that includes (a) validating the experiences of the client; (b) identifying actions that are at least potentially under the client's control; and (c) developing solution-oriented actions and stories for preferred outcomes. In support of this process, solution-oriented therapists often introduce doubt about the permanence of the problem to make space for additional possibilities; normalize everyday occurrences so a problem is not construed as extreme; change the doing of the problem or by encouraging the use of solution patterns of interaction; work with the future, developing concrete goals; and use multiple-choice questions in which the answers contain embedded solutions or new possibilities.
Social Constructionism and Narrative Family Therapy	In the postmodern models, therapists do not think of themselves as applying techniques so much as adopting a decentered, not-knowing position in therapy. Therapeutic process is more about a way of being than the use of specific interventions. Still, key techniques include: Listening with curiosity; asking questions that make a difference, including circular (or relational) questions, landscape of action questions, and landscape of identity questions; deconstruction and externalization in narrative therapy; alternate stories and reauthoring in narrative therapy and telling and retelling in other models; involving reflecting teams and outside communities in therapy, most notably through definitional ceremonies; and the use of letters and documents in narrative therapy.
Feminist Family Therapy	Although feminist family therapists may incorporate any number of systemic approaches that they find congruent with feminist principles, there are certain skills and interventions that tend to be used across models. These interventions are often

(Continued on next page)

Table A.7 (Contd.)	
	chosen in relation to the developmental stage of the family and its members. Key techniques include: egalitarian relationships; consciousness-raising; gender-role and power analyses; self-disclosure; bibliotherapy; assertiveness training; and reframing and relabeling.
Cognitive-Behavioral Family Therapy	Many of the same techniques used for assessment and interventions with individuals also are applied to cognitive-behavioral family practice. When problems in the family and/or the behaviors of children become severe and extremely disturbing, cognitive-behavioral family therapists almost always rely on cognitive restructuring, as well as highly structured operant conditioning processes used in behavioral management. There are separate skills required for assessment and intervention.
	Key assessment techniques include: self-report questionnaires; assessment of cognitions interviews; assessment of interactions interviews; and behavioral observation. Key intervention techniques include: communication training; problem-solving training; challenging irrational beliefs; identifying automatic thoughts and cognitive restructuring; contracting and behavioral change agreements, including the use of shaping, reinforcements, and acting "as if."
Parenting	Two sets of interventions and techniques have been proven effective in raising children. The first set is for families in which the parents are functional partners and need to understand psychoeducational approaches to child-rearing. The second set is for families in which one or more of the children exhibit extreme and/or disturbing behaviors that threaten the development of the child as well as the overall functioning of the family. Key techniques for parents who are functional partners include: encouragement; accentuating the positive; natural consequences; logical consequences; active listening and reflection; emotion coaching; I-statements; assessing who owns the problem; giving choices; and negotiations. Key techniques for parenting difficult children essentially are derived from behavioral interventions. These techniques include: primary and social reinforcement; continuous and intermittent reinforcement; shaping; behavioral extinction; and punishment and other aversive interventions, including time-outs, dirty deeds (assigning difficult tasks), withholding privileges, and asserting the Premack principle. These interventions are supported with contracting, modeling behaviors, self-control and self-monitoring, and direct, effective communication.

References

Bitter, J. R., & Corey, G. (2005). Family systems therapy. In G. Corey, *Theory and practice of counseling and psychotherapy* (7th ed., pp. 420–459). Belmont, CA: Brooks/Cole.

Breunlin, D. C., Schwartz, R. C., & MacKune-Karrer, B. (1992/1997). *Metaframeworks: Transcending the models of family therapy*. San Francisco: Jossey-Bass. (Original work published 1992)

Haley, J., & Richeport-Haley, M. (2003). *The art of strategic therapy*. New York: Brunner Routledge.

Hare-Mustin, R. T. (1978). A feminist approach to family therapy. *Family Process, 17*(2), 181–194.

Luepnitz, D. A. (1988). *The family interpreted: Feminist theory in clinical practice*. New York: Basic Books.

McGoldrick, M. (2005). Hierarchy of power and oppression. In Milton H. Erickson Foundation, *Evolution of Psychotherapy Handout CD*. Phoenix, AZ: Author.

McGoldrick, M., Giordano, J., & Garcia-Preto, N. (Eds.). (2005). *Ethnicity and family therapy* (3rd ed.). New York: Guilford.

Rogers, C. R. (1980). *A way of being*. Boston: Houghton Mifflin.

Taggart, M. (1985). The feminist critique in epistemological perspective: Questions of context in family therapy. *Journal of Marital and Family Therapy, 11*(2), 113–126.

Glossary

(*Italics* are used to indicate words or phrases defined elsewhere in the glossary)

accommodation. The act of coordinating one's functioning to the needs of a situation or another person.

Ackerman Family Therapy Institute. Started by Nathan Ackerman in 1960 in New York City, this was one of the premier scholar-practitioner centers in the United States. Over the years, *Evan Imber-Black*, *Jorge Colapinto*, *Lynn Hoffman*, *Peggy Papp*, and *Olga Silverstein*, to name a few, have worked there.

Ackerman, Nathan. In 1960, he founded the Family Institute, now the *Ackerman Family Therapy Institute*, in New York City, a major clinical center and training ground for family therapy. His best known work is *The Psychodynamics of the Family*.

acting "as if." An intervention favored in both *Adlerian therapy* and *cognitive-behavioral family therapy* that involves practicing new behaviors and new positions or roles in the family "as if" family members were the people they wanted to be—in some cases, "as if" they were the family they wanted to be.

activating event. The A in Ellis' A-B-C theory of personality.

active commitment. The fifth stage of a *feminist identity development model* characterized by self-appreciation, personal freedom, pride in and appreciation for women in general, and even a selective appreciation for parts of the dominant culture. But most important, this stage is characterized by an understanding that the *personal is political* and that real change requires political and social activism.

active listening (reflection). A term coined by *Thomas Gordon* in *parent effectiveness training*, it means to paraphrase (or reflect) what is heard in a conversation with an emphasis on the feelings that underlie the meaning of the message.

Active Parenting. Developed by *Michael Popkin*, Active Parenting is an Adlerian-based parent-education program that teaches parents effective ways of engaging with children and adolescents.

Adler, Alfred. Founder and developer of *individual psychology* (now called *Adlerian psychology* and *therapy*).

Adlerian brief therapy. A model of *Adlerian therapy* with individuals, couples, and families. It differs only slightly from Adlerian therapy in general by focusing on interventions based on systemic and brief, time-limited strategies and by embracing a *resiliency* model.

Adlerian family counseling or therapy. *Adlerian therapy* or *Adlerian brief therapy* applied to families in either an *open forum* or in private and focusing on the *teleology* of interactions and family processes. This model employs *encouragement* and supports *democratic childrearing*, especially the use of *natural* and *logical consequences* and other effective parenting processes described in *STEP: Systematic Training for Effective Parenting* and *Active Parenting*.

Adlerian therapy. A comprehensive therapy based on the work of *Alfred Adler* and *Rudolf Dreikurs*.

ageism. The discrimination and oppression of people based on age: The presumption of privilege for those who are young or younger.

Alexander, James. A *behavioral therapist* associated with *functional family therapy*.

alignment. The ways in which some members of a family will join together. Alignments are often *coalitions* against third or other parties.

alternate story. From *narrative therapy*, a story within the family system that challenges or contradicts the *dominant family story*.

altruism. Being concerned with and doing for others; unselfishness; sharing thoughts and feelings with others and working for the common good. Similar to the Adlerian notions *community feeling* and *social interest*.

amplifying family difficulties. A strategic paradoxical intervention by which family problems are directed to increase so that the systemic needs being met by the family problem can be understood and used.

Andersen, Tom. A Norwegian psychologist who developed the use of *reflecting teams*.

Anderson, Carol. One of the first people to look at the effects that mental illness had on family systems, reversing the original systemic conceptualization that the family system maintained the illness; also a collaborator with *Monica McGoldrick* and *Froma Walsh*.

Anderson, Harlene. A colleague of the late *Harold Goolishian* who developed a *linguistic* approach to family therapy that featured the adoption by therapists of *a not-knowing position* and a privileging of *clients-as-expert*.

Ansbacher, Heinz L. Often called the Dean of Adlerian Psychology, he is the co-author with his wife Rowena of three volumes and numerous articles on Adlerian psychology.

Ansbacher, Rowena R. Co-author with her husband, Heinz, of three volumes on Adlerian psychology.

Aponte, Harry. A *structural family therapist* who developed the *ecostructural* model.

arbitrary inference. A type of cognitive distortion: A conclusion generated about an event without substantiating evidence, such as deciding your child is engaged in delinquent behavior when they come home 5 minutes late. This cognitive distortion often is noted in *cognitive-behavioral family therapy*.

assertiveness training. Learning appropriate ways of standing up for oneself. It is essential to self-esteem and to being strong, confident, and capable in the world: A skill-development intervention often used in *feminist family therapy*.

assumed disability. Another name for *Dreikurs'* fourth goal of children's misbehavior: The child, although being fully capable, adopts a position of hopelessness in an effort to get adults to leave her or him alone.

attachment. The human desire to seek closeness and care from survival beings.

attention getting. *Dreikurs'* first goal of children's misbehavior; a goal that invites parental responses of irritation, annoyance, or frustration.

authoritarian. Coming from a dictatorial position in which the designated boss rules. On the dysfunctional end of both Baumrind's and Dreikurs' parenting continuum, it is characterized by high demand (rules and order) and low responsiveness (often lacking warmth, reciprocity, or attachment).

authoritative-responsive parenting. Similar to the Adlerians' democratic parenting, *Baumrind* uses this term to describe parents who are emotionally and pragmatically responsive to their children's needs. This approach is characterized by both reasonable demands (order) and effective responsiveness (warmth, reciprocity, and attachment).

autocratic parenting. An approach to parenting based on authoritarianism.

automatic thoughts. Thoughts that are produced when triggered and that are specific applications of one's *cognitive schemas*, as discussed in *cognitive-behavioral family therapy*.

autonomy. From *principle ethics*, the valuing of individuality, independent action, and individual freedom and responsibility.

aversive control. Use of *punishment* to suppress, control, or eliminate undesirable behaviors.

aversive stimuli. Negative or punishing experiences that serve to suppress undesirable behaviors.

Avis, Judith Myers. A *feminist family therapist*.

avoidance. Staying away from or not facing something. Bitter's third supplemental goal to *Dreikurs'* model for children's misbehavior.

awareness. Conscious knowing or that to which attention is given. Part of the basic interests of Gestalt and experiential therapies.

Bandura, Albert. The developer of *social learning theory*.

Banmen, John. A *Satir* scholar and trainer, who has done extensive work in Asia.

baseline. The measurement of a behavior or set of behaviors as they currently are so that later measurements of change can be made.

Bateson, Gregory. Co-founder of the *Mental Research Institute*, and the architect of integrating *general systems theory* and family therapy.

battle for initiative. From *symbolic-experiential family therapy*, the belief that the family must win a battle with the therapist and take charge of what happens in the therapy process, including any changes that might be initiated.

battle for structure. From *symbolic-experiential family therapy*, the belief that the therapist should win the battle with the family related to the structure and ground rules for therapy, including the question of who should come to the first session and how the therapy process should proceed.

Baumrind, Diana. Developed language and research for the assessment of effective parenting. Her parenting styles (*authoritarian, authoritative-responsive, permissive,* and *neglectful*) are now in common usage.

Beck, Aaron. The founder and developer of *cognitive therapy*.

Beck, Judith. Daughter of *Aaron Beck*, and a leading contributor to *cognitive therapy*.

Becvar, Dorothy S. and Raphael J. Co-authors of *Family Therapy: A Systemic Integration*.

behavioral exchange agreements. Setting up trades in behavior in which people increase caring and love in a marriage or family.

behavioral extinction. See *extinction*.

behavioral family therapy. Family therapy focused on changing specific dysfunctional behaviors within families. Also, see *cognitive-behavioral family therapy*.

behavioral interventions. Methods derived from *behaviorism* that include *shaping, reinforcement, desensitization, rewards* and *punishment,* the *Premack principle,* etc.

behavioral observations. Assessments made by the therapist in *cognitive-behavioral family therapy* about who does what with whom: These assessments start from the moment the sessions begin.

behaviorism. Applied learning procedures based on either a *classical conditioning* model (*Pavlov*), an *operant conditioning* model (*Skinner*) or a *social learning* model (*Bandura*).

beliefs. Ideas or values that one holds strongly. The B in Ellis' A-B-C theory of personality. In Ellis' model, beliefs can be rational or irrational.

belonging. *Dreikurs* believes belonging is the main goal that all humans have.

beneficence. From *principle ethics*: To do good, to make a positive difference.

Berg, Insoo Kim. The co-developer of *solution-focused therapy*.

biased explanation. Similar to *private logic*, biased explanations are cognitive distortions in which the individual communicates to self and others a belief or viewpoint unique to the individual, lacking consensual validation, and predisposed to a given outcome.

bibliotherapy. The use of books or other written materials as a supplement to family practice.

birth order. The order in which children are born in families.

bisexual. Women or men who have a *sexual/affectional orientation* for either or both women and men.

blaming. *Satir*'s defensive communication stance, involving accusations and finger-pointing, it has a similar meaning to what *Kfir* calls the priority of *significance*.

blended family. Two families coming together by marriage or the agreement of a new couple or parental partnership.

Boscolo, Luigi. One of the Milan group who developed the *Milan model of strategic family therapy*.

Boston Family Institute. Formerly a premier family therapy training institute, founded and co-directed by *Bunny* and *Fred Duhl*, it no longer exists. *Bunny Duhl*, a close associate of *Virginia Satir*, continues to offer training throughout the world.

boundaries. Structural, emotional, and physical barriers that protect or enhance the functioning of individuals, subsystems, or families.

Bowen, Murray. The founder and developer of multigenerational family therapy.

Bowen family therapy. The multigenerational family therapy approach developed by *Murray Bowen*.

Boyd-Franklin, Nancy. A multicultural feminist who has analyzed and critiqued various models of family therapy.

brief family therapy. A model of *strategic family therapy* taught at the *Mental Research Institute* in Palo Alto, CA, this strategic approach is based on the ideas that the problem the family brings to therapy really is the problem and that everything the family has done so far has only served to maintain the problem. See also, *Fisch, Richard; Segal, Lynn; and Weakland, John*.

Brown, Laura. A *feminist therapist* who specializes in work with a diverse range of women, families, and gender-based issues.

Breunlin, Douglas C. Co-author of *Metaframeworks*.

Bumberry, William. Co-author with *Carl Whitaker* of *Dancing with the Family*, he also interviewed Whitaker on the tape *A Different Kind of Caring*.

Carlson, Jon. An Adlerian and author of numerous family therapy books and several video series featuring therapy with experts.

Carter, Betty. A *feminist Bowen family therapist* who, together with *Monica McGoldrick*, developed the *family life cycle*.

Cecchin, Gianfranco. One of the Milan group who developed the *Milan model of strategic family therapy*.

changing the doing of the problem. *O'Hanlon* and *Weiner-Davis* believe that changing the "doing" and "viewing" of the perceived problem changes the problem; that is, effective solutions have some relation to processes that counter problematic patterns.

chaos. The feeling of being disoriented; *Satir*'s third phase in the *process of change*.

Children: The Challenge. Co-authored by *Rudolf Dreikurs* and *Vicki Soltz*, this is the best selling book on parenting in the world.

Christensen, Oscar. An *Adlerian family counselor* and author of *Adlerian Family Counseling*; he is also a co-developer of *Adlerian brief therapy*.

circularity or circular causality. Systemic causality in which behaviors and interactions are understood to be recursive loops, each action influencing and being influenced by all the others.

circular questioning. A method of relational questioning developed by the *strategic therapists* in *Milan* that brings out differences among family members.

classical conditioning. A learning model based on *Pavlov*'s approach that pairs an unconditional stimulus (UCS), like meat powder on a dog's tongue, which causes an unconditioned response (UCR), like salivation, with a conditioned stimulus (CS), like a tone, until the same response (CR) occurs.

classism. Discrimination and oppression based on socioeconomic status; a privileging of the rich.

clients-as-expert. A privileging of clients' expertise, therapist power is counterbalanced by an honoring of and curiosity and interest in clients' stories.

closed system. A collective group that places a rigid boundary around itself so that it does not interact with outside agents or events.

coaching. A therapeutic stance assumed by *Bowen* and his associates in relation to helping family members differentiate. Being a coach in relation to the family team is also a position that *Whitaker* occasionally assumed.

coalition. An alliance between two people or entities, often against a third.

cognitive-behavioral family therapy. A merging of the cognitive therapies of *Ellis*, *Beck*, and their associates and behavioral interventions based on *classical* and *operant* conditioning and *social learning theory*. *Datillio* is the major developer of the cognitive-behavioral family therapy model.

cognitive distortion. A pervasive or systematic error in thinking or reasoning.

cognitive restructuring. The identification and correcting of faulty or distorted thinking.

cognitive schemas. See *schemas*.

cognitive therapy. The application of reason over emotion. This approach includes models developed by *Albert Ellis* and *Aaron Beck*.

cohesion. In *family systems* theory, the emotional bonding among family members.

Colapinto, Jorge. A *structural family therapist* who has worked and developed the model with *Salvador Minuchin*.

collaboration. An egalitarian approach to working with, including, and/or privileging client perspectives in therapy. Used in models developed by *Adlerian*, *Satir*, *solution-focused/solution-oriented*, *social constructionist*, and *feminist* therapists.

collaborative language systems. Part of *linguistic therapy*, it is a *postmodern* clinical stance in which a partnership between the therapist and the family is emphasized, and the therapist adopts a curiosity about how the family attaches meaning to their lived experiences. This stance values talking *with* rather than *to* the family.

collectivist cultures. Cultures in which one's place and relationship to the family and society are considered before one's individual needs or interests can be met.

comfort. Avoiding pain or stress: One of *Kfir's* personality priorities. It has a similar meaning to what *Satir* calls the *irrelevant* stance.

communication stances. *Satir's* concept of stress positions that she refers to as *blaming, placating, super-reasonable*, and *irrelevant*. *Congruence* is the antidote to the stress stances. Also see *personality priorities*.

communication theory. An understanding of relationships based on verbal and nonverbal interactions.

communication training. Used by family practitioners in models ranging from *Satir* to *cognitive-behavioral therapy*, effective communication includes congruent expression of thoughts and feelings, listening to and acknowledging the messages of others, giving clear directives and polite requests, setting clear and reasonable limits and expectations, and using *I-statements* in relation to personal and family needs.

community feeling. Being concerned about the well-being of others; *altruism*; Adler's term for mental health in individuals and families. The umbrella term for which *social interest* is the action line.

complaint-oriented stories. Solution-focused therapists' description of presenting problems in individual and family counseling and therapy.

complementary relationships. Different qualities or entities that fit together and enhance one another.

complementary sequence. *Structural family therapists* use this term to describe an automatic exchange of opposite kinds of behaviors (e.g., father's anger leads to an asthma attack in the daughter; such complementary sequences signal problems in the power balance of the family.

compliments. Used by *solution-focused therapists*, to be effective compliments come from a genuine appreciation of what the clients have done or have achieved. Questions of surprise and delight often are used to convey a compliment: "Wow! You really did that well. How did you do that?" Such compliments focus on strengths and direct family members toward successful interactions and interventions: solutions that already work.

confidentiality. The ethical obligation of counselors, therapists, social workers, and psychologists to protect the identities, communications, and privacy of clients, an obligation that is more difficult to maintain when the practitioner is engaged in family therapy with multiple members.

conflict induction. In structural family therapy, a technique of introducing a conflict during therapy when the family is engaged in conflict-avoidance, and the therapist wants to help the family learn to manage and resolve conflicts.

congruence. The ability to communicate clearly and effectively what one thinks and feels in a manner that is appropriate to the context in which the communication is offered. Congruence is similar to *emotional honesty*.

conjoint family therapy. The first name that *Satir* gave to her family therapy process.

consciousness-raising. A feminist therapy intervention, usually performed in groups, that allows women or men to talk with each other about what it means to them to have their *gender* identities impacted by *patriarchy* and other sociopolitical positions in society.

consequential emotions. The feelings that result from irrational thoughts or *beliefs* or distortions in cognitive *schema*. The C in Ellis' A-B-C theory of personality.

constructivism. A perspectivist model based on the subjective construction of various (multiple) realities. Reality is created through interactions with one's environment rather than having an independent, objective existence outside of the person perceiving it. Also see *social constructionism*.

contact. The way in which people interact with self, each other, and the environment; central to *Gestalt* and *experiential therapies*.

context. The situation, environment, or location in which events take place.

contextual therapy. Boszormenyi-Nagy's model of relational therapy.

contingency contracts. A behavioral agreement between family members that involves an exchange of rewards for desired behaviors.

continuous reinforcement. The application of a reinforcing *stimulus* every time a desired behavior occurs.

control. To gain power over others when power over a situation is failing; the second goal of adults faced with misbehaving children. When one of *Kfir*'s personality priorities, it denotes efforts to keep life contained, especially emotions. It has a similar meaning to what *Satir* calls the *super-reasonable* stance.

counterparadox. Originated by the *Milan strategic therapists*, a counterparadox is a directive that intends an interruption of the paradoxical family processes that keep and maintain a given problem. For example, if the family process is seen as designed to maintain a depressed individual, a counterparadox would be for the family *to not change.*

countertransference. A term that originated in *psychoanalysis*, referring to the personal or distorted feelings that arise in the counselor or therapist for the client. In family therapy, countertransference occurs when emotional reactions are triggered due to the practitioner re-experiencing *family-of-origin* issues.

courage. Facing up to one's fears; moving ahead in spite of fears.

courage to be imperfect. This is a phrase coined by Sofie Lazersfeld and used extensively by *Rudolf Dreikurs* and other *Adlerians*. This kind of courage comes from accepting ourselves as human beings who are not perfect and who make mistakes.

critical-evaluation model. Kitchener's model of ethical decision making, based on the ethical principles of *autonomy, beneficence, nonmaleficence*, and *justice*.

cross-generation coalitions. A multigenerational alliance that stands in opposition to a third member of the family.

cuing. A behavioral stimulus that initiates a behavior; for example, a family sitting down to dinner (the cue) may initiate a pleasant conversation or conflict among family members.

cultural competence. Sensitivity to and familiarity with multiple cultures and worldviews.

cultural feminists. *Feminist therapists* who believe that therapy could be an avenue for infusing society with women's values, including *altruism,* cooperation, and connectedness. They note that oppression includes the devaluing of women's strengths and that all people need a world that is more nurturing and relationally based.

cultural sensitivity. An awareness of cultural issues in families and a willingness to make these issues a central part of family practice, including an understanding of different values and beliefs, different levels of acculturation experiences, and the need to consider the marginalization, discrimination, and oppression of some cultures by the dominant culture.

culture. Shared experiences, language, and ways of being based on ethnicity, nationality, gender, age, ability, sexual/affectional orientation, and/or location.

cybernetics. How control processes work in systems, including the assessment and application of *positive* and *negative feedback loops.*

Dattilio, Frank. The foremost *cognitive-behavioral family therapist* practicing today.

decentered position. *Michael White*'s term for *narrative therapists* when they put themselves in a *not-knowing,* curious position that approaches the *client-as-expert.*

deconstruction. The breaking down of meaning or events in a manner that allows them to be re-examined: In *narrative therapy*, deconstruction often precedes the creation of space in which new meanings can be constructed.

defensive communication patterns. *Satir* identifies *blaming, placating, super-reasonable,* and *irrelevant* as defensive communication patterns.

definitional ceremonies. Based on the work of Barbara Meyerhoff and developed as a therapeutic process by *Michael White* for *narrative therapy*, definitional ceremonies call a community audience together to witness the telling of a story by an individual or family; to participate in a re-telling (or *thickening*) of the story; and to witness again the re-telling of the re-telling of the story.

demand. *Baumrind*'s word for rules, requirements, order, and expectations in families.

democratic childrearing. *Dreikurs*' description of effective parenting based on a leadership model that uses encouragement and natural and logical consequences: Similar to *authoritative-responsive* parenting.

demonstration of adequacy. The first goal of adults faced with raising children who sometimes misbehave.

demonstration of inadequacy (assumed disability). *Dreikurs*' fourth goal of children's misbehavior. A goal that invites a parental response of despair. Also, the fourth goal of *neglectful* adults faced with misbehaving children.

de-pathologize. *Feminist therapists reframe* pathology in relation to the experiences people have within a dominant culture and take away the stigma of pathology from normal reactions to dehumanizing life experiences.

desensitization (or systematic desensitization). A counter-conditioning process used by behaviorists to help people overcome fears, phobias, and anxiety.

de Shazer, Steve. The founder and co-developer of *solution-focused therapy.*

detriangulation. *Bowen*'s process for removing oneself from a negative emotional triadic relationship.

development. How individuals and families grow and change over time, including the challenges facing individuals and families at different points in life. A prominent family developmental model is called the *family life cycle*. One of the *metaframeworks*.

dichotomous thinking. A type of cognitive distortion: classifying experiences as all or nothing, always or never, complete success or failure, totally good or totally bad, absolutely right or absolutely wrong. This kind of polarization is evident when one spouse says, "I wish you would have picked up some ice cream when you went shopping," and the other spouse thinks, "Nothing I ever do is good enough."

differentiation of self. *Bowen*'s term for a functional human being who is able to use reason to overcome *emotional reactivity* and is able to remain calm and observant in an emotionally charged family atmosphere.

Dinkmeyer, Don C. An *Adlerian therapist* who wrote with *Rudolf Dreikurs* and who joined with *Gary McKay* and his son, *Don Dinkmeyer, Jr.*, in merging Adlerian childrearing principles and *parent effectiveness training* in the development of *Systematic Training for Effective Parenting* (STEP).

Dinkmeyer, Jr., Don C. An *Adlerian therapist* who co-authored with his father, *Don C. Dinkmeyer*, and *Gary McKay* the parent training program called *STEP*.

directives. Interventions used by structural, strategic, and brief therapists to assess or change systemic family processes or to interrupt problem-maintaining behaviors.

discouraged. *Adler*'s and *Dreikurs*' word for adults and children who had lost a sense of value and connectedness with others and were acting in problematic or symptomatic ways.

disengagement. Withdrawal and psychological isolation. *Structural* and *strategic therapists* believe that disengagement results from rigid boundaries established by individuals or subsystems (often while allowing more diffuse boundaries for the system as a whole). Disengaging family systems promote individuation at the expense of bonding, intimacy, support, and loyalty.

distracting. Another word for *Satir*'s *irrelevant* stance.

Dobson, James. An ultra-conservative, Christian promoter of "family values," and the author of several books and newspaper columns on parenting that include support for spanking and other aversive interventions.

dominant family story (or narrative). From *narrative therapy*, the story or narrative in which the family is stuck. Dominant family stories carry immense power and are often *problem-saturated stories*.

double bind. The experience of being locked in a significant relationship, characterized by contradictory messages and from which neither escape nor comment is possible.

downward arrow technique. Used by *cognitive-behavioral family therapists* to develop a cognitive map that leads from *automatic thoughts* to *cognitive distortions* to underlying core beliefs in the individual's private *schema*.

Dreikurs, Rudolf. A child psychologist and family counselor who developed a systematic approach to *Adlerian therapy*.

dual relationships. A situation in which a helping professional is seeing a client or family and also has another kind of relationship or contract with the client(s): Sexual or romantic relationships with clients are always harmful dual relationships, but purchasing products or services from a client may or may not be a harmful dual relationship.

Duhl, Bunny. A family therapist who focused on metaphor and sculpting—and was closely associated with *Virginia Satir*. She was one of the original founders and co-directors of the *Boston Family Institute*.

Duhl, Fred. A family therapist who was one of the original founders and co-directors of the *Boston Family Institute*. With *David Kantor*, his scholarship contributed to the development of the field of family therapy.

dyadic models. Therapeutic processes that focus on the relationship of any two people, as in couples therapy. Dyadic models seek to understand relationships based on an assessment of the interactional processes that characterize those relationships.

dyads. Any two people or entities in a relationship.

early recollections. *Adler*'s use of early memories as individual projective tests that reveal the client's *phenomenological* world.

ecostructural model. The *structural family therapy* approach developed by *Harry Aponte*. Focuses on the influences that macro-systems have on families and attempts to engage other social resources in aiding the family.

egalitarian relationships. A relationship between equals and expressed in collaborative processes.

Ellis, Albert. The founder and developer of *rational-emotive behavior therapy*.

embedded messages. *de Shazer* used embedded messages within the directives of *paradoxical interventions*. In essence, his directives would join with what the family was already doing, but would use pauses to emphasize doing something different.

embeddedness. The third stage of a *feminist identity development model* in which women endorse the value of women in general and seek women friends and colleagues. They may reject men as representing the dominant group that has oppressed them. They are female-focused, and they begin to identify with a "feminist culture."

emotional cutoff. *Bowen*'s term for fearing and rejecting emotional attachment; the other end of the continuum from *emotional fusion*; indicative of a lack of *differentiation*.

emotional fusion. *Bowen*'s term for excessive emotional involvement or connections: A contamination and blurring of psychological boundaries. The other end of the continuum from *emotional cutoff*; indicative of a lack of *differentiation*.

emotional honesty. *Satir*'s description of a communication in which the speaker's words and feelings match and are *congruent*.

emotional reactivity. *Bowen*'s term for automatic emotional responses that were learned in old experiences with one's family-of-origin and are triggered in the present by similar people or circumstances.

emotion coaching. *John Gottman*'s term for parenting that involves teaching young children the language of emotions and then listening for, acknowledging, and reflecting the feelings that arise in their children's lives. Paying attention to the emotions of hurt and anger are considered especially important.

empowerment. Interventions designed to help clients feel in charge of their own lives. A process central to the work of Adlerians, Satir, and feminists.

enactments. A *structural family therapy* directive to engage in a set of behaviors or interactions that will allow the therapist either to assess family process or work on restructuring or re-aligning the family.

encouragement. To build courage in others; to have faith in people and be able to communicate that faith in them.

enmeshment. A family structure characterized by diffuse internal boundaries with one or more family members being *emotionally reactive*, overly concerned, and overly involved in other members' lives. Paradoxically, enmeshed families are often *closed systems* in relation to other systems.

Enns, Carolyn. A *feminist family* scholar who has helped to define the continuum of *feminist therapy*.

entropy. A *systems theory* concept that suggests that change in the order of things will move toward greater disorder, randomness, and a loss of distinctive states of being.

epistemology. The study of knowledge; also used by *Bateson* to indicate worldview or beliefs.

Epston, David. A founder and developer of *narrative therapy*. Living in New Zealand, he is a collaborator with *Michael White* from Australia.

equifinality. A complex system's ability to reach a specific goal in many ways and from many different directions.

equilibrium. A steady state of a system held in balance. Similar to *homeostasis*.

equipotentiality. A *systems theory* concept that suggests different outcomes can result from similar origins.

Erickson, Milton H. A psychiatrist specializing in medical *hypnosis* and family therapy, he was the founding president of the American Society for Clinical Hypnosis and was a major influence on *strategic family therapists*, especially *Jay Haley*. His influence can also be found in the work of some *solution-focused therapists* and some *Satir* therapists too.

ethnicity. Groups who share values and customs based on common ancestry.

evolving a crisis. *Whitaker*'s term for escalating a crisis beyond what even the family is prepared to handle. If a kind of meta-event with the power of a psychological orgasm occurs within the therapy session, then stimulating it—to evolve into a full blown crisis—is one way to release the family into a greater sense of becoming.

exception questions. Questions asked by *solution-focused* or *solution-oriented therapists* about times or events that are different from normal occurrences in clients' lives.

existentialism. A philosophy of existence that stresses freedom, authenticity, and responsibility in the face of anxiety and chaos.

experience. What individuals or families do or what happens to them; central to *Satir*'s model and to *Gestalt therapy*.

experiential therapy. A term often applied to *Satir*'s *human validation process model* and *Whitaker*'s *symbolic experiential model*. It is also applicable to *Gestalt therapy* and other models with individuals and families that emphasize experience and change rather than teaching or reorganization.

experiment. Trying something out; one form of *experience*; central to *Gestalt therapy*.

extended family. Family members beyond the *nuclear family*, including aunts, uncles, cousins, grandparents, etc.

externalization. A *narrative therapy* intervention designed to name problems and locate them as outside agents working on individuals or families.

external resources. *Satir*'s concept of outside agencies or agents, perhaps including counselors, therapists, or family practitioners, who offer help to people in need.

extinction. Eliminating the reinforcement of a behavior so that it gradually ends.

facilitating change. Generally the last phase of a family therapy process in which the therapist—having *formed a relationship* with the family, conducted a *family assessment*, and offered a *hypothesis* about family process—intervenes in a variety of ways designed to support needed or desired change in the family system.

family assessment. Generally the first or second phase of a family therapy process in which the therapist attempts to understand the dynamics of the family through observation, engagement or *enactments*, *genograms*, or formal testing.

family atmosphere. An Adlerian description of the mood, feeling, or human climate maintained in the family.

family constellation. Adler's term for family system. Toman's name for birth order descriptions: It is Toman's model that was incorporated by *Bowen* in *multigenerational family therapy*.

family games. The term the *Milan strategic therapists* used for dysfunctional family patterns.

family hierarchy. A *structural family therapy* concept that addresses how the leadership and power in the family is organized. It also addresses decision making in families.

family homeostasis. Keeping the family the same; also, the tendency of families to resist change in an effort to keep things the same.

family lifecycle. Developmental stages in a family's life as proposed by *Betty Carter* and *Monica McGoldrick*, and often used as a foundation for *Bowen family therapy*. The original family life cycle began when an individual separated from her or his family, then entered into marriage, had children, grew older, entered retirement, and finally faced death.

family life-fact chronologies. *Satir*'s process for relating multigenerational family life and experiences to an individual-in-focus, as well as to historical events.

family mapping. *Satir*'s process for drawing the structural-emotional relationships in a family. *Satir*'s process is similar to *genogram* work except that she did not like to differentiate gender in her diagrams or limit people to single roles within families. Family mapping is also a process used by *structural family therapists* with a slightly different focus than the ones used by *Satir* or in genograms: *Minuchin* uses them to diagram family organization and process as they revolve around the *presenting problem*.

family myths. Family stories that are shared by all, but that are also distortions of history and reality.

family-of-origin. The original *nuclear family* of adults, including parents and *siblings*.

family-of-origin therapy. Another name for *Bowen*'s *multigenerational family therapy*.

family projection process. *Bowen*'s term for the processes by which parents pass along to their children similar levels of *differentiation of self*. Because the emotional functioning of the parents often is projected onto the children, this process explains how children become symptom-bearers. The *family projection process* also can refer to more-benign roles, values, and attributes being passed along to the next generation.

family reconstruction. *Satir*'s psychodramatic process for recreating early family-of-origin experiences and transforming them so that individuals can see them with adult eyes and experience them in a new way.

This process is designed to help individuals, especially family practitioners, gain the perspective that *Bowen* associates with a strong *differentiation of self*.

family rituals. Repeated patterns or performances within families that serve to acknowledge or celebrate given events or passages. As used within the *Milan model*, a family ritual is a prescribed performance designed to change *family rules*.

family roles. The activities and functions assumed by each member of the family.

family rules. The directives, stated or implied, that govern how family members, behave, experience, feel, interact, and communicate.

family rule transformation. *Satir* believed that *family rules* developed as a way to bring order to systemic processes, but that such rules often were communicated in impossible forms (always or never) and as lacking choice (must be done or have to be done). Her transformation process helped people to reconsider family rules in a way that added choice and possibilities.

family sculpting. Arranging the family members in physical postures that represent how each person feels and the relationship that each has to the others.

family secrets. Knowledge, beliefs, or attitudes held by one or more family members privately and kept from others; or a secret that the whole family holds against outsiders and may pass on from one generation to the next.

family structure. The organization of the family in terms of interactional patterns.

family system. The family as an organized whole, including the way the various parts of the family function together.

family triads. Any arrangement of family members in groupings of three.

family values. Therapeutically, values on which both parents agree; also a term used by social conservatives (see *James Dobson*) to indicate traditional or fundamentalist beliefs and actions.

feedback loops. From *cybernetics*, the flow of information within a system such that what is given out is processed and returned in a manner that maintains the system (*negative feedback loop*) or indicates a need for change in the system (*positive feedback loop*).

feminist ethical decision-making model. An ethical decision-making model proposed by *feminist therapists* that makes use of *participatory ethics*.

feminist family therapy. *Feminist* therapy applied to families. Major contributors to this model include, among others, *Thelma Jean Goodrich*, *Rachel T. Hare-Mustin*, and *Louise B. Silverstein*.

feminist identity development model. How women grow and develop into a full consciousness of who they are as women. One model includes five stages: (1) *passive acceptance*, (2) *revelation*, (3) *embeddedness*, (4) *synthesis*, and (5) *active commitment*.

feminist therapy and feminist therapists. A therapeutic approach that values women's voices and perspectives, and advocates for changes in patriarchal processes that affect both genders. A major contributor to this model is *Laura Brown*.

fidelity. From *principle ethics*: faithfulness, trust, confidentiality, keeping one's word.

first-order change. Changes within a system that do not change the basic organization of the system itself; changes that are temporary or superficial.

first-order cybernetics. The belief that an outside agent, such as a counselor or therapist, can observe and make changes in the system while remaining independent of the system.

Fisch, Richard. Co-author of *The Tactics of Change*, a leading theorist at the *Mental Research Institute* (MRI)

Fishman, Charles. A structural family therapist who wrote *Intensive Structural Therapy* in 1993.

Fogarty, Thomas. A *Bowen* scholar and therapist.

foreign element. The introduction of a significant difference that interrupts personal or family routines. *Satir*'s second phase in the *process of change*.

forming a relationship. The formal designation of the first stage of *Adlerian therapy*—and, in general, it is also the informal stage of almost all other family therapy approaches.

formula first-session task. At the end of the first session, *solution-focused therapists* ask families to think about what they do that they want to keep doing (or retain) as they move forward. The formula first-session task is designed to focus on family strengths and support the development of solutions.

formula tasks. Assignments given to many families, regardless of their situations, to focus them on the future, on solutions, and on improvement.

Freeman, Arthur. A *cognitive therapist* with close ties to *Adlerian therapy*.

function. Used by *strategic family therapists* to indicate role, purpose, or use within a family.

functional analysis of behavior. An assessment of specific behaviors to determine what is *cuing* them and what is *reinforcing* them. In *cognitive-behavioral family therapy*, it is an analysis of both prior and current learning experiences that contribute to current client issues.

functional family therapy. A behavioral model for functional families associated with *James Alexander*.

function of symptoms. The idea that symptoms are not simply possessed, but rather that they serve some purpose or function in the family.

fusion. See *emotional fusion*.

gay. Men who have a *sexual/affectional orientation* for other men.

gender. A consideration of different perspectives brought to life experience by each sex; one of the *metaframeworks*.

gender-awareness. A consciousness of gender issues in life and family therapy.

gender-role socialization and power analysis. How individual women and men learn to behave in stereotypic ways based on gender. As used in *feminist family therapy*, the assessment includes a consideration of how *power* is distributed within accepted roles.

gender sensitivity. An awareness of gender issues in families and a willingness to make these issues a central part of family practice, including an understanding of *patriarchy*, differential socialization processes, and the need to have both women and men choose voices and roles different from those prescribed by the dominant culture.

general systems theory. Developed by *Ludwig von Bertalanffy*, general systems theory is a biological model of living systems that maintain themselves in specific environments through continuous input and output. *Bateson* adapted general systems theory to his work at the *Mental Research Institute*.

genograms. Formal, structural maps formalized and developed by *Monica McGoldrick, Randy Gerson*, and *Sylvia Shellenberger* that are used to describe families over several generations and that code the emotional/affective and transactional relationships that exist in families.

Gerber, Jane. A Satir scholar and trainer.

Gergen, Kenneth. Author of *The Saturated Self* and a leading social philosopher/psychologist in the development of *postmodern, social constructionism*.

Gerson, Randy. Co-author with *Monica McGoldrick* and *Sylvia Shellenberger* of *Genograms: Assessment and Intervention*.

Gestalt therapy. Based on the holistic psychology of Kohler and Wertheimer, and developed in the United States by *Fritz Perls*, his colleagues, and associates, Gestalt therapy focuses on the here-and-now and the development of awareness and contact through experiments.

getting. Going after what someone wants without regard for ownership or appropriateness. Bitter's first supplemental goal to *Dreikurs*' model for children's misbehavior.

Gilligan, Carol. Author of *In a Different Voice* in 1982, she proposed an alternate moral development (to Kohlberg's) for women.

Ginott, Haim. Author of parenting books *Between Parent and Child* and *Between Parent and Teenager*, his work on communication with children is the foundation for *Gottman*'s approach to *emotion coaching*.

Goldenberg, Herbert and Irene. Co-authors of *Family Therapy: An Overview*.

Gomori, Maria. A *Satir* scholar and trainer.

Goodrich, Thelma Jean. A *feminist family therapist*, and co-author with *Louise Silverstein* of *Feminist Family Therapy: Empowerment in Social Context*.

Goolishian, Harold. A colleague of *Harlene Anderson* who developed a *linguistic* approach to family therapy that featured the adoption by therapists of *a not-knowing position* and a privileging of *clients-as-expert*.

Gordon, Thomas. A student of the late *Carl Rogers*, he wrote and developed a training model for *Parent Effectiveness Training*.

Gottman, John. A researcher from the University of Washington known for his longitudinal studies of couples and families, he is the author of *The Marriage Clinic* and *The Heart of Parenting*. His work with children focuses on *emotion coaching*.

Grey, Loren. An *Adlerian* and co-author with *Rudolf Dreikurs* of *Logical Consequences*.

Guerin, Phillip. A *Bowen* scholar and therapist.

Haley, Jay. Founder and co-developer of the Washington school of strategic family therapy.

"hanging hats." A process developed by *Satir* to help family practitioners clear their minds and hearts so that they can be present with clients. The process is an aid to counselors and therapists in dealing with *family-of-origin* issues and *countertransference*.

Hare-Mustin, Rachel T. A *feminist family therapist*; one of the first to promote *gender-awareness* in family therapy.

Hawes, Clair. An Adlerian couples and family therapist who co-developed *Adlerian brief therapy*.

here and now. Humanistic language for the present or immediate experience.

hermeneutics. Methods of assessing stories or human experiences through interpretations of meaning.

heterosexism. The discrimination and oppression of lesbian, gay, bisexual, and transgendered (LGBT) individuals; the privileges associated with and the assumption of normalcy for heterosexuals.

hierarchy. See *family hierarchy*.

Hoffman, Lynn. Family therapist, social worker, and author of foundational articles and books in family systems therapy, she started her career with *Jay Haley* and *strategic family therapy* and evolved into a leading spokesperson for *postmodern*, *social constructionist* approaches.

holism. A term developed by *Jan Smuts*, meaning an understanding of human behavior, patterns, and processes within the social contexts and interactions that support them: The goal is to understand the whole of *experience* rather than break it down into analyzed parts.

homeostasis. A steady state characterized by balance; a state of equilibrium.

homework. Homework is an out-of-session assignment that may include *bibliotherapy*, *self-monitoring*, behavioral task assignments, and activity scheduling, all important as effective methods to support changes within families.

humanism. A therapeutic approach that centralizes in therapy care for and connection with human beings. A description of self preferred by *Virginia Satir*.

human validation process model. *Satir*'s final description of her therapeutic model.

hypnosis. A form of indirect influence accomplished when the client is receptive to therapist suggestions; the most referenced form in family therapy is Ericksonian hypnosis, based on the work of *Milton H. Erickson*.

hypothesizing (shared meaning). The process in systems therapy of forming a guess about the clinical issues, family dynamics, or motivations for individual behaviors or interactions presented in family treatment. Often associated with the *Milan* group of *strategic family therapists* and *Adlerian family therapy*.

identified patient (or index person). The family member who is symptomatic and carries the problem for the rest of the family.

Imber-Black, Evan. A family therapist who addressed *family rituals, family secrets*, and families within larger systems.

individualistic cultures. Cultures or societies that focus on the rights, needs, and responsibilities of the individual independent of the needs of the collective group.

individual psychology. *Adler*'s term for his psychology and therapy. *Adler* used the term individual to focus on the person as an indivisible whole functioning within a specific social context.

informed consent. A document that clients sign acknowledging that they have been informed about the qualifications of the counselor, therapist, or family practitioner; the activities and experiences in which they are about to engage; the definitions and limits, both legal and professional, of confidentiality; and that they are entering into family counseling or therapy voluntarily.

inner system. The arrangement and use of parts within individuals.

intensifying. A *structural family therapy* process for changing family interactions by promoting strong emotions or increasing pressure on the system.

intergenerational family therapy. Another term for *Bowen*'s *multigenerational family therapy*.

intermittent reinforcement. The strongest form of reinforcement in which only some occurrences of a particular behavior are reinforced—generally on a fixed or variable ratio or time interval.

internal family systems. A systemic approach to working with the parts of individuals, developed by *Richard Schwartz*; also part of *metaframeworks*.

internal locus of control. The feeling individual's have when they believe they can direct and take charge of their own lives and the decisions that they make.

internal resources. Those parts of clients that are present but underutilized in creating solutions to problems. *Satir* focuses on internal resources when helping individuals and families through the experience of *chaos*. Internal resources also are sought in *Richard Schwartz'* work with *internal family systems*.

interpretation. Giving a specific meaning to an action, experience, event or set of events.

introducing doubt. Used by *solution-oriented therapists*, these are questions about the assumptions involved in problem-oriented stories or presentations that challenge such notions as real, permanent, or inevitable. Such doubt has the effect of making space for additional possibilities.

invariant intervention. An intervention developed by *Maria Selvini Palazzoli* that directs parents to go on a date together without informing, checking on, or taking the children. For many years, *Palazzoli* experimented with giving this prescription to every family she saw.

I-position. In *multigenerational family therapy*, the I-position is related to *Bowen's differentiation of self*: It is the ability of an individual to state a position that reflects his or her thinking and personal stance in the face of emotional pressure to be what the family wants the person to be.

irrational beliefs. See *beliefs*.

irrelevant. *Satir's* defensive communication stance, involving distracting, changing the subject, or avoiding pain or stress through side-tracking or denial of reality. It has a similar meaning to what *Kfir* calls the priority of *comfort*.

I-statements. Individual declarations (or statements) that start with the word "I," indicating that the speaker is taking ownership of both the content and the feelings included in the statement. Associated with *active listening, active parenting, STEP,* and *parent effectiveness training*.

I-thou relationship. Martin Buber's description of a real meeting and engagement of two people. This type of relationship is highly prized by *Satir* therapists.

Jackson, Don. Co-founder and developer of *Mental Research Institute* model of family therapy.

Jacobson, Neil. A behavioral therapist.

joining. A *structural family therapy* process by which the therapist accepts and accommodates the family or family members to win their confidence and sidestep resistance.

justice. From *principle ethics*: Implementing fairness to all parties involved; considering the social contexts of lives and challenging and correcting injustice.

Kantor, David. Together with *Fred Duhl*, he was a major contributor to the development of the field of family therapy.

Keith, David. A co-therapist with *Whitaker* and a scholar-practitioner of *symbolic-experiential family therapy*.

Kfir, Nira. An Israeli *Adlerian* therapist who invented personality priorities, a conceptualization similar to *Satir's communication stances*.

Krumboltz, John and Helen. *Cognitive-behavioral therapists* who applied the model to raising children. John Krumboltz is a leading scholar-practitioner who studied with *B. F. Skinner*.

labeling and mislabeling. A type of cognitive distortion: Attaching trait labels to self or others for what is essentially a single or small set of incidents, as in making a mistake and declaring oneself stupid or declaring that an adolescent's desire to watch TV rather than practice the violin as a sign of laziness or indolence.

lenses. Another word for *perspectives* or *metaframeworks* in family practice.

lesbian. Women with a *sexual/affectional orientation* for and toward other women.

lesbian feminists. *Feminist therapists* who believe that *heterosexism* is at the core of women's oppression with its insistence on male-female relationships and sexuality, its sexualized and romanticized images of women, and its almost total marginalization of strong women in same-sex relationships.

liberal feminists. *Feminist therapists* who see therapy as a means of empowering the individual woman and helping her to overcome the limits and constraints of *patriarchal* socialization. Personal fulfillment, dignity, and equality were sought as a means of negating male privilege in both social and work environments.

life tasks. An *Adlerian* concept that designates social relationships, work or occupation, and intimacy as unavoidable tasks for all human beings; used in assessment of individuals and families.

linear causality. One-way cause and effect such that the first event in a sequence causes the second or subsequent event without reciprocity.

linguistic therapy. A model of individual and family therapy developed by *Harold Goolishian* and *Harlene Anderson* that asks therapists to adopt *a not-knowing position* and that privileges *clients-as-experts*.

Lipchik, Eve. A clinical social worker who joined the Brief Family Therapy team and helped to develop solution-focused therapy. Her scholarship often centers on the relationship of theory to practice with a special emphasis on the epistemology of solution-focused therapy.

logical consequences. *Dreikurs'* term for the creation of a learning consequence by an outside agent (e.g., parent or teacher) when a *natural consequence* will not have a desired effect. Logical consequences address the needs of social situations.

Lowe, Raymond. An *Adlerian family therapist* who studied with *Rudolf Dreikurs*; for years, he ran a family education center on Saturday mornings at the University of Oregon.

Luepnitz, Deborah Ann. A *feminist family therapist* and author of *The Family Interpreted: Feminist Theory in Clinical Practice.*

MacKune-Karrer, Betty. Co-author of *Metaframeworks.*

Madanes, Cloe. Co-developer of the Washington school of *strategic family therapy.*

magnification and minimization. A type of cognitive distortion: Making more or less out of a situation or event than is warranted by the facts; an example is when an adolescent gets Bs on her report card, and her parents declare that she will never get into a good college and that she might as well go to beauty school. Later when the child's grades have improved, but are not straight As, the parents lament that the additional As didn't really help her much.

making contact. *Satir's* term for the development of a close, nurturing relationship between therapist and clients.

Malone, Thomas. An early collaborator with *Carl Whitaker.*

managed care. Modern health-care delivery in which third-party payers regulate and control the cost, quality, length, and terms of delivered services, including the regulation and control of family practice.

marginalized cultures. Cultures set aside by the dominant culture: In the United States, marginalized cultures are women; children; people of color; the aged; the poor; the disabled; lesbian, gay, bisexual, and transgendered individuals; and the non-religious and non-Christian populations.

McGoldrick, Monica. A leading family researcher and *feminist therapist* who developed, among other things, *genograms*, considerations of *culture* and ethnicity in family therapy, and the *family life cycle.*

McKay, Gary and Joyce. *Adlerians*, they co-authored and developed *STEP.*

McLendon, Jean. A *Satir* scholar and director of the Satir Institute of the Southeast in Chapel Hill, NC.

Mental Research Institute. A west-coast center in Palo Alto, CA, for the training of *brief family therapists* and *strategic family therapy.*

metacommunication or metamessages. The idea that every message or communication has both content and a comment that indicates how the content should be received. *Satir* looked at tone of voice and body language as a means of understanding metacommunications. *Strategic family therapists* look at the *directives* implied in communications as the metacommunication.

metaframeworks. The development of multiple lenses or perspectives across models in family therapy, including *internal family systems, tracking sequences, organization, development, gender,* and *multiculturalism.* This book also adds the *lenses* of a *teleology* and *process.*

Meichenbaum, Donald. A *cognitive-behavioral therapist* who made significant contributions to the practice of behavior modification techniques.

Milan model of strategic therapy. A *strategic therapy* model originally based on uses of family *paradox* and *counterparadox*; developed in Milan, Italy, by *Maria Selvini Palazzoli* and her associates.

Miller, Scott. A *solution-focused therapist* and author who did extensive work with *Insoo Kim Berg.*

mimesis. A form of *accommodation* and *joining* used in *structural family therapy*; the family practitioner mirrors or imitates the family's style, tempo, and affect.

mind reading. A type of cognitive distortion: Another arbitrary inference in which one individual believes that she or he knows what another is thinking or will do—even though nothing has been communicated verbally between the two people. Anytime spouses, parents, or children say they know what other people are going to say or do when they find out about a problem or misdeed, they are engaging in mind reading: It is a guess that more often than not is framed in the negative.

Minuchin, Salvador. Founder and developer of *structural family therapy.*

miracle question. From *solution-focused/ solution-oriented therapy*, the therapist asks clients to imagine how things would be if they woke up tomorrow and their problems were solved. Used to identify goals and desired solutions.

mirroring. Similar to *reflection* in individual therapy, the therapist expresses understanding and acceptance of the family's or family member's feeling and content.

modeling. Learning by *reinforcing* behaviors that come closer and closer to matching the behaviors set by a model; a form of learning through observation.

modernism. A belief in essences, independent reality, and the application of *the* scientific method and linear causality to understand life experiences.

monad. Any single individual or entity.

morphogenesis. The tendency of a system to change its structure.

morphostasis. The tendency of a system to maintain the same structure.

motivation. Goals or purposes that explain and direct current behaviors, feelings, and thoughts.

motivation modification. The process in *Adlerian therapy* and *Adlerian brief therapy* of changing individual and family goals so the individual and family development may continue in a functional manner.

multiculturalism. Considering and appreciating the perspectives brought to lived experience by different races, *ethnicities, cultures,* ages, abilities, *genders,* and *sexual/affectional orientations*; one of the *metaframeworks.*

multigenerational family therapy. Another name for *Bowen family therapy*; a family approach that focuses on processes involved in at least three generations of family life.

multigenerational transmission process. *Bowen's* term for the process by which poor *differentiation of self* is passed along from generation to generation. Bowen believed that people with similar levels of differentiation tend to marry with children then suffering various psychological problems.

multiple-choice questions. Used in *solution-oriented therapy*, questions about the family's problem(s) with a twist: They suggested that A-B-C answers have embedded within them solutions or directions that are new possibilities for the clients.

mystery questions. Questions used in *narrative therapy* to help clients wonder about how their problems got the best of them; a form of *externalization.*

Napier, Gus. Co-author with *Carl Whitaker* of *The Family Crucible*, and a scholar-practitioner of *symbolic-experiential family therapy.*

narrative therapy. A *postmodern, social constructionist* therapy developed by *Michael White* and *David Epston*, that includes the naming of problems, *externalization*, a search for unique events, and the development of *alternate stories*. This approach works at *thickening* client stories when clients enter therapy with often *thin* (often problem-fused) *descriptions* of themselves.

natural consequences. A consequence that automatically follows any given act; what would happen if no one intervened in a given action. *Dreikurs'* term for a consequence that occurs without outside intervention.

navel equality. *Satir's* term for human equality.

negative feedback loops. From *cybernetics*, a *feedback loop* that serves to maintain the system and set predetermined limits on how the flow of information is used.

negative reinforcement. Removal or avoidance of an aversive or unpleasant stimulus contingent on performing a desired behavior and resulting in an increase in that behavior.

negentropy. The emergence or revelation of a system's organizational pattern: The opposite or reverse of *entropy.*

neglectful. *Baumrind's* term for parents who are *discouraged* and *disengaged*, who want their children to leave them alone, and who engage in what *Adlerians* call a *demonstration of inadequacy*. Such parenting is characterized by low demand (rules or order) and low responsiveness (in the form of warmth, reciprocity, or attachment).

neutrality. The *Milan model's* term for fair and balanced acceptance of all family members.

new integration. What happens after new behaviors, interactions, or processes are practiced and have become part of people and families. The final phase of *Satir's process of change.*

new possibilities. New options that arise in people and families when they are able to connect to both *internal* and *external resources* or build on exceptions to the problems faced. The fourth phase of *Satir's process of change.*

Nichols, Michael P. Associated with structural family therapy, he is the co-author with *Richard Schwartz* of *Family Therapy: Concepts and Methods.*

Nicoll, William G. An *Adlerian family therapist* who co-developed *Adlerian brief therapy.*

nonmaleficence. From *principle ethics*: To do no harm.

normalization (or normalizing the problem). Similar to what occurs when feminists *de-pathologize* experience, both *Adlerians* and *solution-oriented* practitioners will *reframe* problems as everyday occurrences. Normalizing a problem implies that the problem is not so extreme and that it can be addressed and solved.

normalizing family experiences. Used by *Adlerians*, when families are feeling overloaded and distressed by their life experiences, normalizing is helping the clients to see that they are not alone in their situation, that other families with similar experiences would be feeling the same way, and that change is possible. Similar to the process used by *Adlerians*, the *solution-oriented therapists* often will reframe problems as normal, everyday occurrences when the family or family members have been pathologized or have begun to self-pathologize their situation.

not-knowing position. A position of interest and curiosity developed by *Harold Goolishian* and *Harlene Anderson* as a means of privileging *clients-as-expert* in the therapy process. A *not-knowing position* is greatly facilitated when family practitioners follow their clients' stories very closely and continue to ask the next, most interesting question.

nuclear family. Parents and children in a single household.

nuclear family emotional system. A *Bowen* term for a conflict that starts between the parents and evolves through *triangulation* into emotional distress or turmoil for the whole family.

nurturing triads. *Satir's* term for a positive *triadic process* in which two people join together in support of a third, as in two parents joining together to raise a child.

Nutt, Roberta. A *feminist family therapist*, and former Chair of the Psychology of Women Division of the APA.

object relations family therapy. The evolution and application of Freudian *psychoanalysis* to family systems; the model is based on attachment theory and the conceptualizations of self and others that evolve from early parent–child relationships. *David* and *Jill Savege Scharff* are the foremost scholar-practitioners of this model.

O'Hanlon, William (Bill) H. The co-developer of *solution-oriented therapy*, which he now calls *possibility therapy*.

one-down position. A paradoxical clinical stance adopted by *strategic family therapists* at the *Mental Research Institute* that aims to empower clients.

open-forum family counseling. An *Adlerian* approach to family counseling conducted in public settings and making use of an audience as an outside witness to understanding a family-in-focus and encouraging and supporting change in family interactions. This model's strongest advocate is *Oscar Christensen*.

open systems. From *general systems theory*, an open system is one that continuously exchanges feedback with its environment. In family therapy, it is a metaphor for a family's willingness to receive new information and adapt.

operant conditioning. A behavioral learning model developed by *B. F. Skinner* that emphasizes the importance of *reinforcement* in *shaping*, maintaining, and increasing desired behaviors.

ordeals. Developed by *Jay Haley* in *strategic family therapy* as a form of *paradoxical intervention*, the client(s) is directed to do something that is even harder than continuing to maintain the symptom.

ordinal birth position. Fixed attributes assigned to each birth position based solely on the order of sibling birth, as in Toman's *family constellation* model.

organization. The leadership and *hierarchy* of the family; one of the *metaframeworks*.

overfunctioning/underfunctioning relationships. A concept from *multigenerational family therapy* that describes a relationship of reciprocal roles in which one member is overly dependent, and the other member is overly responsible. Such relationships may hold the family together during periods of low stress, but in distress, both positions tend to become polarized.

overgeneralization. A type of cognitive distortion; generalizing from one or two incidents to assigning someone a consistent, ongoing attribute; an example is when one family member is late picking up another family member, and the late individual is declared to be completely unreliable.

Palazzoli, Maria Selvini. Co-founder and developer of the *Milan model of strategic family therapy*.

Papp, Peggy. Worked with *Lynn Hoffman* and others at the *Ackerman Family Therapy Institute* in New York, using a model that evolved from strategic interventions to *social constructionism*.

paradox. A self-contradictory statement or position based on equally acceptable premises.

paradoxical interventions. Associated with *strategic family therapy*; the therapist directs the family to do what appears to be the opposite of what the family needs, including *prescribing the symptom, restraining family change,* and *ordeals*.

parent effectiveness training. A model of parenting developed by *Thomas Gordon* that is based on the person-centered therapy of *Carl Rogers*; much of this model is incorporated in the parent training programs called *STEP* and *Active Parenting*.

parentification. A child is put in the role of a parent, having to care for the parents and/or other siblings.

parent value system. Values held by a single parent or individual values held by each parent.

participatory ethics. Based on a *postmodern, social constructionist* philosophy, participatory ethics is an ethical decision-making model that involves clients in conversations about what is ethical for both the family practitioner and the clients.

parts parties. *Satir's* psychodramatic process for integrating different parts of people's *inner systems*.

passive acceptance. The first stage of a *feminist identity model* in which women accept the roles and *gender* stereotypes that have been fostered by the dominant culture.

patriarchy. Patriarchy comes the Latin word *Patri* which means father. It involves the misuse of power and control by masculine authority, either individually or systemically; patriarchy discriminates against and oppresses both genders and often is manifest as male privilege and *sexism*.

pattern. Repeated behaviors, processes, or experiences to which meaning is attached.

Patterson, Gerald. A behavioral therapist who developed one of the first *behavioral* models for working with delinquent children.

Pavlov, Ivan. A Russian behaviorist who developed *classical conditioning*.

Pedesky, Christine. A *cognitive therapist* who trained with *Aaron Beck*, and who currently is an international trainer in the model.

Peller, Jane E. *Solution-focused* therapist from Chicago, she is the co-author of two books on this model.

Perls, Fritz. Founder of *Gestalt therapy* as it is practiced in the United States.

permissive parenting. A dysfunctional form of parenting in which children are allowed to do what they want. It is characterized by high responsiveness (giving in to children) and low demand (rules and order).

personal is political. A *feminist therapy* belief that one's personal way of being cannot be understood outside of the social, cultural, and political *contexts* that have impacted the person, including an understanding of *gender-role socialization*, internalized *sexism* and *patriarchy*, and socio-political norms and laws that oppress women and men. This principle values the emergent voices of women as a political statement and *consciousness-raising*.

personality priorities. Developed by *Nira Kfir*, these are *Adlerian* ways of coping with stress similar to *Satir's communication stances*.

personalization. A type of cognitive distortion; a form of arbitrary inference that occurs when someone attributes external events to oneself without sufficient evidence, such as when a comment about movie star's weight is taken to mean "She thinks I'm fat."

person-centered therapy. Developed by the humanist psychologist *Carl Rogers* in the 1940s and 1950s, this model encouraged *congruence* and self-actualization through the *active listening* and empathy of the client. Rogers approached his clients with unconditional positive regard in the present, and communicated understanding through reflections of feeling.

perspective. A certain way of seeing or experiencing that individuals bring to life events.

perspectivist model. A family systems model that relies on multiple viewpoints or lenses in *family assessment* and *tailoring* interventions.

phenomenology, (adj. **phenomenological**). A study of perceived experience(s); the theory that people behave according to their perceptions.

placating. Deferring to others and/or wanting everyone else to be happy: One of *Satir's* communication stances; similar to *Kfir's personality priority* of *pleasing*.

play. Engaging in activities that are immediately pleasurable. Used in *symbolic-experiential therapy* as a dialectical intervention; the more one can play, the greater the capacity for seriousness. Play is at the heart of what *Whitaker* considers "craziness." If one is free to be crazy, one also is free to adapt, to be sane.

pleasing. Seeking to make others happy; one of *Kfir's personality priorities*. It has a similar meaning to what *Satir* calls the *placating* stance.

Polster, Erving. A master *Gestalt therapist* and author of many books, articles, and videos on the development of the model with special attention paid to the development of self. He is the co-author (with Miriam Polster) of *Gestalt Therapy Integrated*.

Polster, Miriam. A master *Gestalt therapist* and author of many articles and several books, including *Eve's Daughter: The Forbidden Heroism of Women* and with her husband, Erving, *Gestalt Therapy Integrated*.

Popkin, Michael. An *Adlerian*, he wrote and developed a training model for *Active Parenting*.

positioning. A *strategic family therapy* intervention that paradoxically overstates the severity of the problem: When the client indicates that things are really bad, the therapist suggests that they are probably hopeless.

positive connotation. A form of *reframing*, used primarily by the *Milan* group of *strategic family therapists*, to suggest that family symptoms have a positive use.

positive feedback loops. From *cybernetics*, a *feedback loop* that serves notice to the system that change is needed and modifications in process must take place.

positive reinforcement. A pleasant stimulus that follows a desired behavior, resulting in an increase in that behavior; positive reinforcement may be applied continuously or *intermittently* on fixed or variable ratios or time intervals.

possibility therapy. The name *William O'Hanlon* now uses for *solution-oriented therapy*.

postmodern feminists. *Feminist therapists* who address *patriarchy* as one form of dominant-knowledge position, and use *deconstruction* and discourse analysis to examine how reality is socially constructed and influenced by power and hierarchical relationships.

postmodern perspective. A belief in multiple realities, and a valuing of multiple perspectives, voices, and narratives. A rejection of positivism that views knowledge as relative and co-constructed within given *contexts*. Postmodernism is the philosophical *epistemology* for *social constructionism*.

power. One's ability to influence or control situations or events.

power struggles. *Dreikurs'* second goal of children's misbehavior characterized by either active or passive fights with adults or peers; a goal which invites parental responses of anger or defensiveness and leads to feelings of being challenged or controlled.

Prata, Guiliana. One of the Milan group who developed the *Milan model of strategic family therapy*.

prediction task. A *formula task* used by *solution-focused/ solution-oriented* therapists to increase chances of success: "Today, let's predict whether your problem will be better or the same tomorrow. Tomorrow, rate the way your day goes and compare it to your prediction. What do you think made a difference in a right or wrong prediction? Do this each day until we meet again."

preferred outcomes, solutions, or stories. The *social constructionist* idea that, given an opportunity and support, clients actually can develop a life that they choose and prefer over what they have been living.

prejudice. Active discrimination against a person or group.

Premack principle. A behavioral intervention in which preferred activities are used to reinforce (or are contingent upon) behaviors that are less likely to occur.

prescribing the symptom. A *paradoxical intervention* used in *strategic family therapy* that forces clients either to give up their problem or symptom or to recognize that it is under their control.

presence. To focus on clients with interest and even fascination, bringing all of the therapist's senses to bear in meeting the people with whom she or he will work.

presenting problem. The problem or concern brought to counseling or therapy by an individual or the family. Presenting problems become a primary focus in *structural, strategic,* and *cognitive-behavioral* family therapies.

pretend techniques. A *paradoxical intervention* used in *strategic family therapy* and designed by *Cloe Madanes* that asks family members to pretend to have the problem or symptom with each other. The capacity to pretend indicates that it is really under the control of individuals or the family as a whole anyway.

primary reinforcements. *Reinforcements* that are physical in nature, such as food.

principle ethics. Ethical decision making based on the application of specific principles. Principle ethics is the underlying foundation for most ethical codes in the helping professions.

private logic. A term used by *Adler* to denote personal distortions in thinking that are at odds with common sense. The most common form of private logic would involve irrational *beliefs* or *automatic thoughts* based on distortions in cognitive *schema*, as these are described by *cognitive-behavioral therapists*.

problem-saturated stories. From *narrative therapy*, stories that individuals or families bring to therapy that are oriented around significant problems and have become dominant in the family members' lives.

problem-solving training. Used by *cognitive-behavioral family therapists*, problem-solving training is a systematic process that helps parents and families to use a series of steps to analyze an issue, identify and assess new approaches to the issue, and develop ways to implement new solutions for the issue.

process and process model (*Satir*). Considers the "how" of interaction in addition to the "content" of interactions: A process lens is an additional perspective to those proposed as *metaframeworks*. Process model is a name that *Satir* used to convey her emphasis on process over content in therapy. It is a term she used between the developments of her *conjoint family therapy* and the *human validation process model*.

process of change. *Satir*'s change model that tracks movement from a *status quo* interrupted by a *foreign element*, leading to *chaos* and a need for support from *internal* and *external resources* that may generate *new possibilities* and eventually a *new integration*. New

integrations automatically become a new *status quo*, and the process of changes starts all over again.

pseudo-hostility. A show of anger or conflict to cover up more problematic or dysfunctional aspects of the family system.

pseudo-mutuality. A show of intimacy and harmony to cover up more problematic, conflictual, or dysfunctional aspects of the family system.

pseudo-self. *Bowen*'s term for people who have a low degree of *autonomy*, are *emotionally reactive*, and unable to take a clear position on issues.

psychoanalysis or psychoanalytic theory. Of or pertaining to the model developed by Sigmund Freud. Modern neo-Freudians are called *object relations* therapists, and they are engaged in the development and use of *attachment* theory. *David* and *Jill Savege Scharff* have applied this model to couples and family therapy.

psychological disclosure. The third stage of *Adlerian therapy* in which motives or goals are disclosed to clients in a tentative manner, and clients are asked to consider and comment on the disclosure.

psychological investigation. The second stage of *Adlerian therapy*, focusing on and assessment of *family constellation* and *birth order*, *life tasks*, a *typical day*, and *early recollections*.

psychology of use. *Adler* used this term to mean that we know people by how they act or use their traits and capacities: It is the opposite of a psychology of possession (or descriptions of what they have within them).

psychosomatic families. A term used by *Minuchin* to describe families who are overly *enmeshed* with the symptom bearer. Minuchin once pinched a child and asked the father if he felt the pain: The father responded that he did. When Minuchin asked the mother if she felt the pain, she responded that she did not, but noted she had poor circulation.

punishment. A behavioral term used to describe an unpleasant stimulus that temporarily suppresses or decreases unwanted behaviors: It is a term seldom used by contemporary behaviorists today. Punishment is considered by *Adlerians* to be an imposition of *authoritarian* power: Adlerians prefer the use of *natural* and *logical consequences*.

purpose. Central to *Adlerian therapy*, it is what is intended or that which motivates, as in the goals of misbehavior in children or a discovery of the purpose of a feeling, such as anxiety.

questions of difference. An umbrella term used by *solution-focused/solution-oriented* therapists to describe questions that open up space in families to consider other possibilities and generate solutions. Questions of difference include *exception questions*, *scaling questions* and *the miracle question*.

quid pro quo. Literally, something for something. A contract for an exchange of equal value: As used by cognitive-behavioral family therapists, it is often a negotiated contract between partners in which each partner works on behaving the way the other wants.

racism. The discrimination and oppression of people of color, based on race, ethnicity, or culture: the presumption of privilege for Caucasians or the dominant race of any given country or community.

radical feminists. *Feminist therapists* who are more likely to focus on *patriarchy* and the social activism that is required to eliminate it. Within family therapy, their goals include the transformation of gender relationships; sexual, procreative, and reproductive rights; and the equalization of household chores, partnerships, parenting, and access to employment outside the home.

rational-emotive behavior therapy (REBT). REBT is a cognitive-behavioral approach to therapy developed by *Albert Ellis*.

R.E.C.I.P.E. *Jean McLendon*'s acronym for the ingredients in the Satir model that facilitate therapeutic change: *resourcefulness, empowerment, congruence, inner system, pattern,* and *externalization*.

reciprocity. Interactions between family members in which the behavior of one is complementary or dovetails with the behavior of another.

recognition reflex. *Dreikurs*' description of a child's body reflex (a twinkle in the eye and a quick smile) when a goal of misbehavior has been properly disclosed.

recursive. One part, stage, or event influencing and being influenced by every other part, stage, or event in the *system*.

reflecting team. *Tom Andersen*'s process for having a group of observers share their reactions with the family after a session. Within *social constructionism*, the reflecting team serves to provide clients with multiple perspectives and creates dialogues and dialogues about dialogues.

reframing. Relabeling individual or family behaviors, symptoms, problems, or processes to highlight the good intentions behind them or to make them more amenable to change or therapeutic intervention. Used across models, *Adlerians* tend to use it to highlight good intentions or motives; *Satir* tends to use it to generate new awareness or possibilities in communication; and *structural* and *strategic family therapists* tend to use it to describe symptoms or problems in more-human, everyday language.

reinforcements. Any stimulus that maintains or increases a given behavior. *Positive* and *negative reinforcements* are examples.

relapse prevention. Methods of helping individuals and families not fall back into old patterns after treatment is finished.

relative influence questions. From *narrative therapy*, questions designed to explore how much influence the problem has had on the client(s) versus how much influence the client(s) has/have had on the problem.

Remer, Pam. Co-author with *Judith Worrel* of *Feminist Perspectives in Therapy: An Empowerment Model for Women*.

reorientation. Re-education or re-directing clients toward a more productive way of living; the last phase of *Adlerian therapy*.

resiliency. The ability of families to bounce back from adversity and to make the most of their *internal* and *external resources*.

resistance. Clients or families having a different goal from the counselor or therapist (*Adler*); clients or families regulating contact (*Gestalt*); clients or families opposing or retarding progress in therapy.

resourcefulness. Accessing the *internal* and *external resources* needed to face life, problems, or difficulties in an effective manner. In the *Satir model*, the family practitioner is often a significant *external resource* for the client, supporting the family and its members through the process of change.

responsiveness. *Baumrind*'s term for parenting that includes warmth, effective reciprocity with children, and appropriate attachment or connectedness.

restraining family change. Originally a *paradoxical intervention* developed by the *strategic family therapists* at the *Mental Research Institute*, the family is directed not to change anything they are doing in relation to the symptom or problem, to go slowly. If the family does as they are directed to do, they discover that they have control of it. If they let go of the symptom or problem, it is over.

revelation. The second stage of a *feminist identity model* in which women begin to notice and see the impact of *patriarchy* in their lives.

revenge. *Dreikurs* third goal of children's misbehavior; a goal that invites parental responses of hurt or wanting to get even; sometimes, a goal parents use with children when they feel hurt or defeated.

reward. A *positive reinforcement* used by behaviorists. Considered by *Adlerians* to be a bribe for positive behavior, they prefer the use of *encouragement*.

Richeport-Haley, Madeline. Wife of *Jay Haley* and co-author of his last book, *The Art of Strategic Therapy*.

rituals. Repeated patterns of behavior or experience often used to mark or celebrate special occasions. As used in *strategic family therapy*, they are a set of prescribed actions designed to change *family rules*.

Robertson, Patricia E. A Feminist therapist and Chair of the Department of Human Development and Learning at East Tennessee State University.

Rogers, Carl. Developed the model known as *person-centered therapy* and was a teacher of *Thomas Gordon*, the developer of *Parent Effectiveness Training*.

Satir, Virginia M. The founder and developer of *conjoint family therapy* and the *human validation process model*.

Satir model. The complete development of the processes and interventions created by Virginia Satir, including *conjoint family therapy, family reconstruction, parts parties, process model,* and the *human validation process model*.

scaling questions. Used in *solution-focused/solution-oriented* therapies to note changes occurring in small steps. The clients are asked to rate on a 10-point scale how interested they are in finding a solution; how bad a problem is now versus last time or an earlier time; or to predict how much better the problem will be tomorrow.

scapegoat. A member of the family, usually the *identified patient* or *index person*, who is designated as the problem and who absorbs displaced conflict and is criticized by others.

Scharff, David and Jill Savege. The foremost scholar-practitioners of a model called *object relations family therapy*.

schemas. Cognitive constructions or core beliefs through which people generate perceptions and structure their experiences; underlying core *beliefs* people have about self, others, and the world (and how everything functions), they are central to the assessment and treatment processes associated with *cognitive-behavioral family therapy*.

Schwartz, Richard. The developer of *internal family systems* and co-author with *Michael Nichols* of *Family Therapy: Concepts and Methods*.

sculpting. Adapted from psychodrama by *Peggy Papp* and used by family practitioners such as *Virginia Satir* and *Bunny Duhl*, sculpting is placing family members in physical positions that depict emotional closeness and distance as well as common communications, interactions, roles, or alliances among members of the family system.

second-order change. Fundamental change in the organization and functioning of the system: The opposite of *first-order change*.

second-order cybernetics. Anyone attempting to observe or change a system is automatically part of the system.

seeding the unconscious. This refers to *Whitaker*'s process of taking a family member's inference far beyond anything the family member normally would consider. These psychological seeds suggest the forbidden, the taboo, the anxiety-provoking, and the hidden.

seed model. *Satir*'s term for a systemic worldview that answers questions about how we see ourselves (multiple roles, parts, and attributes as opposed to a fixed role); how we experience relationships (egalitarian and interdependent as opposed to hierarchical); how we view causality (*circular* and *recursive* as opposed to *linear*); and how we see change ("change *is* life" as opposed to "change is something to be resisted").

Segal, Lynn. Co-author of *The Tactics of Change*, a leading theorist at the *Mental Research Institute* (MRI).

selective abstraction. A cognitive distortion: Taking things out of *context*, paying attention to distortion-supporting details, but ignoring other important information, such as noticing your child's or spouse's mistakes, but never commenting on positive attributes or accomplishments.

self-disclosure. Sharing part of oneself or life with a client: Highly valued in feminist family therapy. Appropriate self-disclosure always involves a judgment on the part of the therapist: that sharing some aspect of the therapist's life will directly benefit the client.

self-elevation. Acting in ways that seek to make the self look better at other people's expense or at least better than one truly is. Bitter's second supplemental goal to *Dreikurs'* model for children's misbehavior.

self-monitoring. A *cognitive-behavioral* intervention that asks clients to keep a detailed, daily record of particular events or psychological reactions so that the therapist and the client can evaluate what the client is doing.

self-report questionnaires. *Cognitive-behavioral family practitioners* use questionnaires that are designed to reveal unrealistic beliefs and expectations, irrational ideas and *schemas, cognitive distortions*, and repetitive patterns of discordant behavior or interactions.

sequences of interactions. Interactions that follow one from another. One of the lenses developed as a *metaframework* that unifies the tracking processes of various systems therapies and considers sequences that are face-to-face, developmental, and cross-generational.

sexism. The discrimination and oppression of women; the presumption of privilege for men.

sexual/affectional orientation. The individual's choice and/or way of being with regard to sexual identity and affectional preferences.

shaping. Step-by-step reinforcements of small units of behavior that, taken together, add up to a larger more-complex learned behavior.

Shellenberger, Sylvia. Co-author with *Monica McGoldrick* and *Randy Gerson* of *Genograms: Assessment and Intervention*.

siblings. One's brothers and sisters.

sibling position. One's birth position in relation to brothers and sisters.

significance. *Kfir*'s personality priority in which the individual is willing to do whatever is necessary to maintain self and personal importance. Similar to *Satir*'s *communication stance* of *blaming*.

signs. See *questions of difference*.

silence. Being quiet, saying nothing, but being attentive. Whitaker uses silence to let therapy be, to let it percolate.

Silverstein, Louise B. A *feminist family therapist* and co-author with *Thelma Goodrich* of *Feminist Family Therapy: Empowerment in Social Context*.

Skinner, B. F. A behavioral psychologist who developed *operant conditioning*.

Smuts, Jan C. A former governor of South Africa and military general who wrote *Holism and Evolution*, a book that influenced *Adler, Satir, Whitaker*, and the *Gestalt* therapists.

social constructionism. A *postmodern* perspective that believes social realities and experiences are co-constructed, as is the meaning that is attached to social interactions. Social constructionism is the basis for *linguistic therapy, narrative therapy, reflecting teams*, and *solution-focused/solution-oriented therapies*. Also see *constructivism*.

social equality. The belief that all people have an equal right to be respected and valued. This concept is central to the work of *Dreikurs* and modern *Adlerians*.

social interest. The action line of having a *community feeling* (*Adler*); actively working for the betterment of others, the whole, or the community; making a contribution to life and to others.

socialist feminists. *Feminist therapists* who were the first to broaden the perspective to include the multiple discriminations based on race, socioeconomic status, national origin, and other historical biases. In therapy, their goals include an assessment of how education, work, and family roles impact the individual, and a determination to transform relationships that are socially burdened and externally imposed.

social learning theory. A behavioral learning approach that integrates social and developmental psychology with *classical* and *operant conditioning*.

social reinforcement. *Reinforcement* that occurs within a social interaction or the reinforcement that comes from being the person who administers *primary reinforcements*.

social transformation and advocacy. *Patriarchy* has such negative effects on human life that *feminist therapists* actively try to change society and to counter its influence on individuals and families. From a feminist perspective, personal liberation cannot occur without social transformation including altering the core assumptions and structures of the helping professions.

societal projection process or societal regression. *Bowen* believed that under circumstances of chronic, societal stress, public anxiety would increase and government leadership would abandon rational considerations in favor of emotionally driven decisions designed to bring about short-term relief. The most common process would involve two groups joining together to preserve their own positions at the expense of a third. Such societal projection processes tend to result in laws that do little to affect the chronic problem, bring relief to very few, and generate helplessness in many.

solid self. *Bowen's* term for people with a clarity of response marked by a broad perspective, a focus on facts and knowledge, an appreciation for complexity, and a recognition of feelings without being dominated by them.

Soltz, Vicki. Co-author with *Rudolf Dreikurs* of *Children: The Challenge*.

solution-focused therapy. A therapy that focuses on co-developing preferred solutions for clients. The model's co-developers are the late *Steve de Shazer* and *Insoo Kim Berg*.

solution-oriented therapy. A derivative of *solution-focused therapy* developed by *Bill O'Hanlon* and *Michele Weiner-Davis*; this model acknowledges problems faced by individuals and families, but uses *exception questions* to develop *new possibilities*.

Sonstegard, Manford A. An counselor educator and trainer of *Adlerian family therapists* and group counselors.

Sperry, Len. An *Adlerian*, he is the author of numerous couples and family therapy books, including a text on *family assessment*.

status quo. Familiar and routine activities that constitute normal for the person, family, or system. *Satir's* starting point in the *process of change*.

STEP: Systematic Training for Effective Parenting. Developed by *Don Dinkmeyer, Don Dinkmeyer Jr.*, and *Gary McKay*, STEP is an *Adlerian*-based parent-education program that combines the work of *Dreikurs* with the communications models of *Haim Ginott* and *Thomas Gordon*.

stepfamily. A family in which some members are related only through remarriage.

stereotype. A fixed image or perception of people, things, and places that is oversimplified, rigid, and often *prejudiced*.

stimulus. An outside agent or force working on an organism.

strategic family therapy. The application of *directives* and other techniques and strategies in an effort to realign family systems so that *presenting problems* will be resolved. There are generally three recognized schools of strategic family therapy: The *Mental Research Institute* model (*Bateson, Jackson*, and *Watzlawick*); the *Washington School* (*Haley* and *Madanes*); and the *Milan model* (*Palazzoli* and associates).

strengths perspectives. A term often associated with social work that means approaching individuals and families with the desire to identify and actualize their strengths. This perspective is central to what are called *resiliency models*.

structural determinism. In the face of disturbances, a description of how much of a change a *system* can tolerate without losing its identity and basic organization.

structural family therapy. A family therapy model founded and developed by *Salvador Minuchin* and associates; it is built on the assumption that family structures often are designed to maintain problems and that dysfunctional families lack sufficient organization to cope with external and internal problems.

structural map. A mapping process developed within *structural family therapy* that presents the organization of the family in relation to the *presenting problems* of the family.

structure. The components of a system and their relationships as it defines the organization of a *system*.

Stuart, Richard. A behavioral therapist and scholar.

subsystems. Smaller systemic groups within a larger *system*.

summary messages. Used by *solution-focused/ solution-oriented therapists*, summary messages usually come at the ends of sessions—especially the first session. The summary lets the client know what the therapist(s) has heard and understands about the family's problem, and seeks to clarify anything that the interviewer might have missed. Such a summary is followed by a compassionate expression of the emotional impact the problem has had on the couple or family coupled with *compliments* for how they have endured or what strengths have been mobilized to face the problem.

superiority. In *Adlerian* thought, *superiority* means "a better position."

super-reasonable. *Satir*'s defensive communication stance, involving a reliance on excessive reason or reasonableness in order to handle stress. It has a similar meaning to what *Kfir* calls the priority of *control*.

symbolic-experiential family therapy. The family therapy model developed by *Carl Whitaker*.

symmetrical relationship. A family relationship in which family members have relatively equal status and *power*.

symmetrical sequence. A *structural family therapist* uses this term to describe an exchange of similar behaviors in which each person assumes an absolute position in an argument from which neither can withdraw. Each part of the symmetrical sequence happens at once, leading to an almost automatic escalation of the fight.

synthesis. The fourth stage of a *feminist identity model* in which women are still female-centered and female-affirming, but they also can start to appreciate affirming men and effective parts of the dominant culture. Women begin to work closely with supportive members of the dominant culture, and they enlarge their understanding of oppression to see what it does to other groups, other cultures, and other people.

systematic desensitization. See *desensitization*.

systems. Units of interacting parts. See also *family system*.

systems theory. See *general systems theory*.

tailoring. Fitting assessments and interventions to the specific configuration, process, and needs of the family.

teleological lens. A perspective, based on *teleology*, that examines intent, purpose, and goals in individual behavior, dyadic interactions, and family life.

teleology. The study of final ends, goals, or purposes as motivation for the present. *A teleological lens* is an additional perspective to those proposed as *metaframeworks*.

termination. An ending and transition in one phase of life or work so that a new phase may begin; also, the end of counseling or therapy; a time for reorientation, summarization, discussion of future goals, and planning for follow-up events or procedures.

The Family Crucible. Co-authored by *Gus Napier* and *Carl Whitaker*, this is one of the most-referenced and most-read books in all of family therapy.

"The Question." An *Adlerian* intervention in which the client is asked, "If your problems or symptoms disappeared tomorrow, how would your life be different? What would you be doing differently?" Although "The Question" is similar in phrasing to the *miracle question*, *Adlerians* understand the answer to be an indication of what the person is avoiding by having the problem. When clients say, "Nothing would be different," the problem is probably organic or medical.

thickening. A *narrative therapy* concept that relates to deepening client stories; thickening occurs as clients' stories are met with interest and curiosity and both a telling and a re-telling of the stories are supported. Thickening stands in opposition to *thin descriptions*.

thin descriptions. A *narrative therapy* concept, describing client stories that are expressed in single words or fixed expressions (or diagnoses), such as "I'm anorexic." Thin descriptions often indicate the ways in which the person and the problem are fused; they signal a need for *externalization* and *thickening*.

time-out. A behavioral intervention for extinguishing undesirable behaviors by removing the person from situations that continue to reinforce negative behaviors.

token economy. Reward or reinforcing agents offered in exchange for earned and accumulated points (or tokens).

tracking sequences. A *structural family therapy* intervention whereby the therapist follows the evolution of content, themes, and direction that emerges in the family's communication and interactions.

transference. A term that originated in *psychoanalysis*, referring to the personal or distorted feelings that arise in the client for the counselor or therapist. In family therapy, transference occurs when emotional reactions to the family practitioner or other family members are triggered due to re-experiencing *family-of-origin* issues.

transgendered. Men or women who have been trapped in the other sex's body and/or who choose to reconnect with their correct gender.

transgenerational family therapy. Another term for *Bowen's* *multigenerational family therapy*.

transnational feminists. *Feminist therapists* who seek to link women's individual experiences to those of women throughout the world and across national boundaries. Sexual violence, prostitution, and other international processes that hurt and demean women are the focus of these global feminists.

treatment adherence. Methods for increasing the likelihood that clients will stick to treatment prescriptions until therapy is complete.

triad. Any three people or entities in relation to each other.

triadic process. The processes and interactions of any three people in relation to each other. For *Bowen*, *triangles* are two-against-one relationships and *triangulation* is a negative process that must be avoided. *Satir* recognizes that triadic process can manifest itself as two-against-one, but she also envisions the possibility that it can become two-for-one, as in two parents working to secure a happy life for a child. She refers to positive triadic process as *nurturing triads*.

triangles and triangulation. A *Bowen* conceptualization of negative *triadic process*. In *multigenerational family therapy*, triangles always result in a two-against-one experience. Triangulation is the invitation of a third member into a *dyadic* relationship for the purpose of diffusing or distorting the intensity of the pair's transactions.

tunnel vision. A *cognitive distortion* in which the individual is so focused on a single perception or belief that they can only see a given person, action, or event in one way.

typical day. An *Adlerian family assessment* process.

unbalancing. A *structural family therapy* intervention in which the therapist adds more force or emphasis to a certain behavior or role—or joins with one family member to add weight to that member's position in the family—in an effort to interfere with the *equilibrium* of the family that is maintaining the problem.

undifferentiated ego mass. *Bowen's* concept for a lack of *differentiation of self* in family members such that, under stress, there is a blurring of internal *boundaries* and often confusion related to family members' identities.

undifferentiated family ego mass. *Bowen's* term for a family that is emotionally *fused* or stuck-together—as in many schizophrenic families.

unique outcomes. *Michael White's* term for events that challenge or dispute the client's *problem-saturated* or problem-oriented *story*. *Narrative therapists* use unique events as a foundation for creating alternative stories.

unorganized families. A *structural family therapy* term, preferred by *Harry Aponte* and his *ecostructural model*, instead of the diagnosis of dysfunctional family.

veracity. From *principle ethics*; the implementation of truthfulness: It is intimately related to personal and professional integrity.

virtue. Desired qualities, traits, or attributes associated with living a good and productive life. In family practice, virtues refer to the personal qualities and ways of thinking, feeling, and being that are strongly associated with effective practice in the helping professions.

virtue ethics. Making ethical judgments based on the development and implementation of professional virtues associated with family practice.

von Bertalanffy, Ludwig. Developer of *general systems theory*.

Walsh, Froma. Author of *Normal Family Processes* and *Strengthening Family Resilience*, and a collaborator with *Monica McGoldrick* and *Carol Anderson*.

Walter, John L. *Solution-focused* therapist from Chicago, he is the co-author of two books on this model.

Washington School of Strategic Family Therapy. Founded and developed by *Jay Haley* and *Cloe Madanes*.

Watson, John Broadus. Sometimes called the father of behaviorism, he was the first to test *Pavlov's* *classical conditioning* model in the United States; he was also the author of the first best-selling book on parenting published in the United States.

Watzlawick, Paul. Theorist for the *Mental Research Institute's* approach to *strategic family therapy*.

Weakland, John. Co-author of *The Tactics of Change*, a leading theorist at the *Mental Research Institute* (MRI).

Weiner-Davis, Michele. The co-developer of *solution-oriented therapy*.

wheel of influence. *Satir's* process for diagramming significant others and the influence they have had on the individual or family. The person or family is located in the middle of a large piece of paper as the hub of the wheel; lines are drawn to significant others, suggesting spatially the closeness or separation from the person(s) in the hub. The influence of each person on the wheel is named with adjectives.

Whitaker, Carl. The founder and developer of *symbolic-experiential family therapy*.

White, Michael. A founder and developer of *narrative therapy*. Living in Australia, he is a collaborator with *David Epston* from New Zealand.

white male privilege. The idea that men in society have assigned certain unearned advantages to being white males and conferred dominance on themselves through law, custom, and tradition.

Wolpe, Joseph. A behaviorist in the *classical conditioning* tradition of *Pavlov*, Wolpe is best known for the development of *systematic desensitization* and its applications to phobias.

womanists. A preferred term for the word "feminist" by *women-of-color feminists*.

women-of-color feminists. *Feminist therapists* who note that *racism, classism, sexism*, and *heterosexism* are all interlocked and cannot be considered separately when they are all experienced together. These oppressions affect all people, and within the context of therapy, *womanists*, actualize an appreciation of women's culture, its strengths and emotional value, and seek to develop wholeness in both genders and all cultures.

working with the future. In *solution-oriented therapy*, as preferred solutions are developed, they are transformed into specific, concrete goals. In anticipation of implementing these goals, possible obstructions to success are considered and ways around those obstructions are developed.

Worrel, Judith. Co-author with *Pam Remer* of *Feminist Perspectives in Therapy: An Empowerment Model for Women*.

Name Index

A

Abbey, A., 336
Abner, A., 347
Ackerman, N., 10
Adler, A., 5, 8, 12, 13, 14, 44, 83, 97, 102, 103, 107, 114, 115, 116, 117, 259, 308, 329–330, 331
Adler, R. E., 114
Alexander, J. F., 320
Ancis, J. R., 269
Andersen, T., 10, 12, 15, 247, 248–249, 250, 255, 260, 264
Anderson, C. M., 13, 92, 270, 293
Anderson, H., 10, 12, 13, 15, 247–248, 248, 250, 252–253, 260, 264
Ansbacher, H. L., 8, 44, 104, 116, 118
Ansbacher, R. R., 104, 116, 118
Anthony, S. B., 268
Aponte, H. J., 12, 31–32, 166, 167–171, 172, 174, 175, 176, 183, 184, 186
Arciniega, M., 115
Aristotle, 44, 47
Atwood, J. D., 320, 324
Atwood, M., 281
Avis, J. M., 13

B

Baker, L., 152, 187
Baldwin, M., 31, 125, 126, 130, 138, 143, 365
Bandura, A., 13, 300, 308, 331, 345
Banmen, J., 12, 122, 138, 140, 141, 143
Bateson, G., 10, 14, 18–19, 37, 189, 197, 214, 246
Baucom, D. H., 312, 313, 320
Baumgardner, J., 281
Baumrind, D., 13, 333, 334
Beal, A. C., 347
Beaudry, G., 142
Beavers, R., 373
Beavin, J. H., 211, 214
Beck, A. T., 13, 300, 301, 308, 324
Beck, J. S., 300, 312, 320, 324
Becvar, D. S., 23, 182
Becvar, R. J., 23, 182
Berg, I. K., 10, 12, 14, 217–218, 221, 225, 231, 232, 235, 236
Bergen, L. P., 61, 63
Bernard, B., 381, 382

Bernino, J., 336
Bersoff, D. N., 51
Bitter, J. R., 6–10, 43, 45, 114, 115, 119, 129, 138, 141, 214, 255, 260, 264, 324, 350, 372, 378–379, 381
Bornstein, K., 281
Boscolo, L., 195, 200, 201, 205, 214, 223
Boszormenyi-Nagy, I., 366
Bowen, M., 8, 10, 12, 13, 25, 37, 45, 72, 81–82, 83, 84, 85–86, 87, 92, 93, 94, 95, 121, 130, 133, 139, 197, 239, 268, 364, 365
Boyd-Franklin, N., 92, 93, 183, 211
Bray, J. H., 373
Breunlin, D. C., 39, 212, 362, 363, 365, 368, 371, 380
Brown, L., 13, 279, 280, 292
Bruner, J., 253
Bubenzer, D. L., 253, 260, 264
Buber, M., 121
Bumberry, W. M., 12, 145, 160, 163
Buresh, S., 336

C

Callanan, P., 63
Carlson, J., 23, 115, 118, 379, 383, 384
Carter, B., 12, 13, 73, 76–81, 83, 87, 92, 94, 270, 368
Cass, V., 282
Cecchin, G., 195, 200, 201, 205, 214, 223
Chesler, P., 13
Christensen, O. C., 10, 12, 98, 99–101, 114, 115, 118, 120, 334
Cicero, 44, 47
Cirillo, S., 214
Ciurczak & Co., 336
Coale, H. W., 56, 63
Cohen, E. D., 51, 55, 63
Cohen, G. S., 51, 55, 63
Colapinto, J., 12, 174, 175, 184, 186
Collins, P. H., 281
Combs, G., 260, 264
Connell, G. M., 163
Corey, G., 21, 39, 63, 115, 261, 363, 378–379, 381
Corey, M. S., 63
Cormer, J. P., 347
Cormier, S., 161
Crawford, M., 281
Crowder, C. Z., 347, 349

D

Dattilio, F. M., 13, 300, 301–307, 308, 311, 312, 313, 314, 319, 320, 322, 324, 345
Davido, A., 320
Davis, B., 133, 138
DeClaire, J., 347, 349
de la Cruz, D., 138
Denborough, D., 260
Derrida, J., 267
de Shazer, S., 10, 12, 14, 217–218, 223, 225, 232, 235–236, 238
Dewey, J., 331, 333
DiCesare, E. J., 184
Dickerson, V. C., 254, 260, 265
Dinkmeyer, D., Jr., 347, 349
Dinkmeyer, D., Sr., 8, 13, 102, 114, 119, 347, 349
Disque, G., 164, 265
Dodson, L., 138
Dolan, Y., 232, 236
Downing, N. E., 278
Dreikurs, R., 8, 12, 13–14, 34, 37, 97, 104, 105, 114, 115, 117, 118, 119, 330, 331, 335, 347, 349, 350
Dubois, J. M., 51

E

Ehrenreich, B., 13, 281
Einstein, A., 240
Elizur, J., 174
Ellis, A., 13, 300–301, 308, 313, 320, 323, 324
Enloe, C. Z., 281
Enns, C. Z., 13, 269, 292
Epstein, N. B., 312, 313
Epston, D., 10, 12, 15, 224, 241, 247, 248, 249, 250, 251, 253, 254, 255, 256, 260, 263, 264, 265, 267
Erickson, M. H., 14, 189, 202, 214, 217, 225, 276
Erikson, E., 346
Ewell, S., 138

F

Faber, A., 348
Falicov, C. J., 93
Falloon, I. R. H., 320, 324
Faludi, S., 281

Fashimpar, G., 336
Fassinger, R. E., 288, 292
Fay, L. F., 94, 95
Felder, R., 163
Ferguson, A., 276
Fine, M. A., 320, 324, 347
Fisch, R., 10, 211, 214
Fishman, H. C., 12, 174, 176, 184, 186
Fogarty, T. J., 83, 94, 95, 96
Foshee, V. A., 335
Foucault, M., 241, 249, 270
Framo, J., 95
Francis, P. C., 51
Freedman, J., 260, 264
Freeman, A., 300
Freeman, S. J., 51
French, M. A., 347
Freud, S., 259, 276, 334
Friedman, S., 264

G

Gale, J. E., 232
Garcia-Preto, N., 92, 95, 182
Gerber, J., 138, 141, 143
Gergen, K. J., 10, 12, 241, 247, 260, 264
Gerson, R., 94, 177
Gilbert, R. M., 94
Gilligan, C., 13, 277, 346, 347
Ginott, H. G., 13, 331, 332, 347, 348, 350
Giordano, J., 92, 95, 182
Gladding, S. T., 63
Glasser, W., 200, 227
GlenMaye, L., 280, 287, 292
Golden, L. B., 63
Gomori, M., 138, 141, 142, 143
Goodrich, T. J., 269, 293
Goolishian, H., 10, 12, 13, 15, 247–248, 250, 252–253, 260
Gordon, T., 13, 331, 337, 338, 347, 350
Gottman, J., 13, 300, 324, 332, 335, 338, 347, 349, 350, 371
Gratz, H., 138
Grove, D. R., 214
Guerin, P. J., Jr., 84, 87, 94, 95
Guerney, B., 186

H

Haley, J., 10, 12, 14, 19, 35, 48, 189–190, 194, 198–199, 200, 201, 202, 203–204, 210–211, 213, 214, 239, 246, 365, 379
Hampson, R. B., 373
Hare-Mustin, R. T., 13, 270
Hart, B., 182, 337, 348
Hawes, C., 114
Hawkings, S., 240
Hendrickson, P., 336
Henrickson, L., 335
Herbert, M., 314
Herlihy, B., 59
Hernandez, D., 281

Hill, A., 50
Hippocrates, 48
Hoffman, E., 118–119
Hoffman, L., 10
hooks, bell, 13, 281
Horne, A. M., 320, 324
Huber, C. H., 63
Hurston, Z. N., 281

J

Jackson, C., 335
Jackson, D. D., 10, 19, 37, 189, 211, 214
Jacobson, N., 13, 300
Jensen, D., 46
Jordan, A. E., 51
Jung, C. G., 259

K

Kautto, J. G., 94, 95
Keith, D., 12, 145, 153, 154, 160, 161, 163
Kempler, W., 160
Kerr, M., 45
Kerr, M. E., 94, 95
Kfir, N., 331
Kitchener, K. S., 53
Kjos, D., 23
Kleist, D., 43
Kniskern, D. P., 163
Kohlberg, L., 277, 346
Krestensen, K. K., 141
Krumboltz, H. B., 320, 324, 331, 347, 349
Krumboltz, J. D., 300, 301, 320, 324, 331, 347, 349

L

Larsen, C. C., 56
Lazersfeld, S., 34
Lebow, J., 388
Lee, W-Y., 186
Leland, T., 163
Lewis, J. A., 118
Lipchick, E., 12, 217, 232, 236
Lorenz, S., 336
Lowe, Ray, 8
Luepnitz, D. A., 13, 139, 270, 276, 292–293

M

MacKune-Karrer, B., 39, 212, 362
Madanes, C., 10, 12, 32, 190, 194, 199, 200, 201, 203, 204, 211, 213, 214, 379
Madigan, S., 12, 241–246, 257, 261, 267
Main, F., 347, 349
Malone, T. P., 12, 145, 160, 163
Martin, A., 347
Martin, D., 13
Mathias, B., 347
Matsuyuki, M., 288
May, K. M., 293

Mazlish, E., 348
McGoldrick, M., 10, 13, 37, 73, 92, 93, 94, 95, 177, 182, 270, 293, 368, 369
McIntosh, P., 296
McKay, G., 13, 347, 349
McLendon, J. A., 12, 132–133, 138, 142
McNamee, S., 260, 264
Mead, M., 197
Meara, N. M., 51
Meichenbaum, D., 13, 300
Mendoza, M., 138
Meyerhoff, B., 255
Miller, J. B., 13
Miller, S. D., 217, 232, 235
Minuchin, P., 12
Minuchin, S., 10, 12, 14, 35, 37, 45, 152, 163, 166–167, 171, 173, 174, 175, 176, 177, 178, 182, 183–184, 186–187, 197, 204, 239, 268, 313, 364, 379
Mitten, T. J., 163
Montalvo, B., 186
Mueser, K., 320
Mullis, F., 336
Murphy, J. J., 383

N

Napier, A. Y., 12, 145, 160, 161, 163
Neill, J. R., 163
Nerin, W. F., 141
Newlon, B., 115
Nichols, M. P., 194, 205
Nicoll, W., 114, 115
Novak, S., 142
Nutt, R., 268

O

Oberst, U. E., 119
O'Hanlon, S., 226, 235
O'Hanlon, W. H., 10, 12, 14, 218, 222, 223, 226, 232, 235, 236, 251, 260

P

Padesky, C. A., 320
Papero, D. V., 95
Papp, P., 13, 92, 270
Patterson, G. R., 13, 300, 301, 311, 332, 343
Pavlov, I., 13, 307, 329
Payne, M., 264
Pedesky, C., 300
Peller, J. E., 12, 217, 218, 225, 232, 235, 236, 237
Pew, W. L., 119
Phillips, J., 269
Piaget, J., 277, 346
Pilgrim, C., 336
Plato, 44, 47
Polster, E., 9, 10, 162, 363
Polster, M., 9, 10, 162
Popkin, M., 13, 347, 349

Poussaint, A. F., 347
Prata, G., 195, 200, 205, 214
Premack, D., 345

R

Rave, E. J., 56
Rehman, B., 281
Remer, P., 13, 293
Remley, T. P., 59, 63
Richards, A., 281
Richards, H., 138
Richeport-Haley, M., 194, 210, 211
Ricker, A., 347, 349
Risley, T. R., 182, 337, 348
Roberts, A., 114
Robertson, P. E., 13, 271–276, 293
Rodriquez, G. G., 347
Rogers, C., 132, 138, 259, 331, 337
Rosen, E., 96
Rosman, B. L., 152, 186
Rourke, J., 336
Rousch, K. L., 278

S

Satir, V. M., 9, 10, 12, 14, 25, 28–29, 31,
    32, 37, 45, 83, 121–124, 125, 126, 129,
    130, 131–132, 133, 134, 137–138, 139,
    141, 142, 143, 160, 162, 197, 200, 239,
    268, 270, 279, 331, 347, 350, 363, 364,
    365, 366, 372, 379
Sayger, T. V., 320, 324
Sayles, C., 142
Schön, D., 46
Schwartz, R. C., 39, 194, 205, 212, 362, 363
Schwebel, A. I., 320, 324, 347
Segal, L., 203, 211
Selekman, M. D., 232–233
Selvini, M., 214
Selvini Palazzoli, M., 10, 12, 14, 195, 200,
    202, 205, 211, 214, 379

Selye, H., 129
Sermeno, S., 138
Sexton, T. L., 320
Shellenberger, S., 94, 177
Sherman, R., 102, 114, 119
Shoham, V., 320
Sickle, T., 320
Silverstein, L. B., 270, 271, 293
Silverstein, O., 13, 270
Simon, G. M., 186
Simon, J. B., 383
Sinacore, A. L., 269
Skinner, B. F., 13, 300, 301, 307,
    330–331
Smith, S. M., 383
Soltz, V., 104, 118, 330, 347, 349
Sonstegard, M., 8, 114, 115
Sorrentino, A. M., 214
Southern, S., 38
Spark, G., 366
Sperry, L., 115, 118, 374
Stanton, E. C., 268
Stewart, A. E., 119
Strauch, B., 347
Stuart, R., 300
Stukie, K., 61, 63
Suarez, M., 138
Sweeney, T. J., 119
Szapocznik, J., 183

T

Terner, J., 119
Thorndike, E. L., 329
Tillich, P., 151
Toman, W., 83, 84
Tong, R. P., 281

V

Van Deusen, J. M., 186
Vasquez, M. J. T., 51

Villarosa, L., 347
von Bertalanffy, L., 19

W

Walker, L., 13
Walsh, F., 13, 92, 270, 293, 382
Walter, J. L., 12, 217, 218, 225, 232, 235,
    236, 237
Walters, M., 270
Warkentin, J., 163
Watson, J. B., 13, 329, 346
Watzlawick, P., 10, 12, 189, 195, 211,
    213, 214
Weakland, J. H., 10, 12, 19, 202,
    211, 214
Webster-Stratton, C., 314
Weiner-Davis, M., 10, 12, 14, 217, 218,
    222, 223, 226, 232, 235, 236
West, J. D., 45, 253, 260, 264
Whitaker, C. A., 10, 12, 14, 35, 37, 45,
    132, 145–150, 151, 152, 153, 154–156,
    160, 161, 162, 163, 165, 239, 268,
    372, 379
White, C., 260
White, M., 10, 12, 15, 35, 224, 240,
    241, 247, 248, 249, 250, 251, 253,
    254, 255, 256, 260, 263, 264,
    264–265, 267
Wiener, N., 18
Wilcoxon, S. A., 63
Wilk, J., 222, 232
Wolf, N., 281
Wollstonecraft, M., 268
Wolpe, J., 13, 300
Woody, J. D., 63
Woody, R. H., 63
Worell, J., 13, 293

Z

Zimmerman, J. L., 254, 260, 265

Subject Index

AAMFT. *See* American Association for Marriage and Family Therapy
A-B-C model, 300, 313–314
ABCT (The Association for Behavior and Cognitive Therapies), 323
ACA. *See* American Counseling Association
Acceptance, 30
Accommodation, 173
ACQ (Areas of Change Questionnaire), 373
Acting "as if," 224, 233–234, 314
Action research, 38, 39
Activating events in A-B-C model, 300, 313–314
Active listening and reflection in parenting, 337–338
Active Parenting Today, 348
Adaptability, 31
Adaptive sequences, 366
Adlerian family therapy
    author's experience with, 8
    birth order, 102–104
    brief therapy, 107
    child interview and goal disclosure, 108
    development of, 13–14
    DVD references, 119
    emphasis and assumptions of, 239–240
    exercise for personal and professional growth, 116–117
    family atmosphere, 101–102
    family constellation, 8, 102–104
    family structure, 103
    founders and major contributors, 97–98
    further information, 114, 117–118
    gender and multicultural contributions, 115–116
    key concepts, 101–106
    mistaken goals, 97, 104–106, 330
    motivation modification, 107
    open-forum family counseling, 107, 114
    overview, 12, 114
    parenting addressed by, 107, 108–109, 328, 329–330
    parent value system, 101
    personality priorities, 364
    phenomenological approach, 116–117
    phenomenological emphasis, 103
    problem descriptions and goal identification, 107–108
    as pro-feminist, 114
    psychology of use, 8, 330
    purposefulness in, 10
    Quest family example, 109–113
    recognition reflex, 97
    recommended readings, 118–119
    reorienting and re-educating the family, 108–109
    sharing meaning, 379
    social equality, 109, 114
    techniques, 107–109
    as teleologically oriented, 31, 114, 364
    therapist's role and function, 107, 379
    therapy goals, 106–107
    therapy session examples, 98–101, 105
    typical day exploration, 108
    virtue considerations in, 44–45
Advancing Together Conference, 288
Advice, being careful with, 36
Ageism. *See* Multicultural perspectives
Albert Ellis Institute, 323
Alignment, structural aspect of families, 172
Alternate belief systems, 210
Alternate stories, 254–255, 267
Altruism, 200, 201
American Association for Marriage and Family Therapy (AAMFT)
    accreditation and, 11
    central contributors to, 94
    code of ethics, 46, 47, 50, 59
    on confidentiality and informed consent, 59
    gender consciousness, 291
    meta-analysis of effectiveness studies, 37–38
American Counseling Association (ACA)
    accreditation and, 11
    code of ethics, 46–47, 50, 53, 59
    on confidentiality and informed consent, 59
American Guidance Systems Publishing, 348
American Psychological Association (APA), 290–291
Amplifying family difficulties (paradoxical intervention), 202
Arbitrary inference (cognitive distortion), 303, 308
Areas of Change Questionnaire (ACQ), 373
The Art of Strategic Therapy (Haley & Richeport-Haley), 211
Assertiveness
    as characteristic of effective practitioner, 30
    training in feminist family therapy, 281–282
Assessment of cognitions, 312
Assessment of interactions, 312–313
Assessments. *See also* Genograms; Lenses or perspectives; *specific kinds*
    birth order, 83–84, 102–104, 117
    circular questioning, 205
    in cognitive-behavioral family therapy, 311–313, 362
    defensive communication stances, 126–129, 138, 140–141, 331
    enactments, 178
    evolving a crisis, 155
    family, 362, 373–374
    formal, 373–374
    lenses for, 362–363
    in multicultural perspective, 369–370
    ordeals, 199
    range of, 362
    tracking sequences, 184, 211–213, 365–366
    triangulation, 13, 82–83
The Association for Behavior and Cognitive Therapies (ABCT), 323
Association for Women in Psychology (AWP), 291
Assumed disability (mistaken goal), 104
Attention getting (mistaken goal), 104
Authenticity, 162–163, 165
Authoritarian parenting, 330, 333
Authoritative-responsive parenting, 107, 330, 333–336
Automatic thoughts, 301, 305, 309, 314
Autonomy
    critical-evaluation model based on, 50
    differentiation of the self and, 82
    in principle ethics, 47–48, 50, 51
AVANTA Network (The Virginia Satir Global Network), 9, 138, 142
Aversive controls, 301
Aversive interventions in parenting, 344–345
Avoidance (mistaken goal), 105
Awareness, 9, 10
AWP (Association for Women in Psychology), 291

Baseline behaviors, 301
Bay Area Family Therapy Training Associates, 263
Beavers Interactional Competence and Style (BICS) scale, 373
Beck Institute for Cognitive Therapy and Research, 323

Beginning work as a family practitioner. *See also* Integrating therapeutic systems; Personal and professional development
case conceptualization, 374, 384
family assessment, 362
finding a foundational model, 359–361
formal assessments, 373–374
forming a relationship, 361–362, 375
guidelines, 33–37
videotaping your work, 360–361
Behavioral extinction in parenting, 344
Behavioral interventions, 203
Behavioral observation, 313
Behavioral responses model, 300–301
Behaviorism, 307, 329, 354
Being is becoming belief, 151
Belonging, 152
Beneficence, 48, 50
BFTC (Brief Family Therapy Center), 217, 218
Biased explanations (cognitive distortion), 304
Bibliotherapy, 281
BICS (Beavers Interactional Competence and Style) scale, 373
Birth order, 83–84, 102–104, 117
Blaming communication stance, 127, 129, 140, 141
Blended families, 339
Borderline personality disorder, 279
Boundaries
mapping, 176–177
rigid, diffuse, and clear or healthy, 173–174
as structural aspect of families, 172
Bowen Center at Georgetown University, 94
Bowen's multigenerational family therapy
birth order, 83–84
coaching, 87
development of, 13
differentiation of the self, 82
displacement stories, 88
DVD references, 95
emotional cutoff or disengagement, 82
emphasis and assumptions of, 239–240
exercise for personal and professional growth, 93–94
family projection process, 83
founder and major contributors, 72–73
further information, 94
gender and multicultural contributions, 92–93
genogram work, 25, 86–87
I-positions, 87–88
key concepts, 81–84
multigenerational transmission, 83
neutrality of the therapist, 84
overview, 12, 72, 92
process questions, 87
pseudo-self, 82
Quest family example, 88–92
recommended readings, 94–95
relationship experiments, 87
sibling cohesion factor, 84

sibling position and power relationships, 83–84
societal applications, 84
solid self, 82
techniques, 86–88
as theory-based, 72, 81
therapist self-awareness in, 85
therapist's role and function, 85–86
therapy goals, 84–85
therapy session example, 73, 76–81
training method for therapists, 85–86
triangulation, 82–83
virtue considerations in, 45
Bread and Spirit (Aponte), 167
Brief family therapy, 14, 107, 189
Brief Family Therapy Center (BFTC), 217, 218
Burnout, avoiding, 37

CACREP (Council for Accreditation of Counseling and Related Educational Programs), 11
Caring, 30
Case conceptualization, 374, 384
Cause and effect, 17, 18
CBFT. *See* Cognitive-behavioral family therapy
CCRS (Circumplex Clinical Rating Scale), 373
Centering before meeting families, 29
Challenging irrational beliefs, 313–314
Change
contracting and behavioral change agreements, 314
developmental lens, 367–368
facilitating, 380–383, 388–389
first-order, 18, 198
inevitability of, 368
process of, 32–33, 171, 372
restraining (paradoxical intervention), 190, 191, 202
second-order, 19, 198
Changing the doing of the problem, 226
Chaos, 130–131
Characteristics of effective practitioners, 30–32
Child neglect, 50
Children: The Challenge (Dreikurs & Soltz), 330
Circular causality, 18
Circular questioning, 205
Circulation questions, 251
Circumplex Clinical Rating Scale (CCRS), 373
Classical conditioning, 307
Client-as-expert, 242, 252, 259, 267
Clinical formulation, 374
Closed systems, 18, 19
Coaching, 14, 87, 93
COAMFTE (Commission on Accreditation for Marriage and Family Therapy Education), 11
Codes of ethics, 46–47, 50, 62. *See also* Ethics
Cognitive-behavioral family therapy (CBFT)
A-B-C model, 300, 313–314
acting "as if," 314

areas of focus, 308
assessment of cognitions, 312
assessment of interactions, 312–313
assessments, 311–313, 362
assumptions germane to family life, 306
automatic thoughts, 301, 305, 309, 314
aversive controls, 301
baseline behaviors, 301
behavioral observation, 313
behavioral responses model, 300–301
behaviorism, 307, 329, 354
classical conditioning, 307
cognitive distortions, 303–304, 308–309
cognitive restructuring, 314
cognitive schemas, 301, 309
communication training, 313
contracting and behavioral change agreements, 314
downward arrow technique, 312
DVD references, 324–325
early behavioral therapy vs., 320
emphasis and assumptions of, 239–240
exercise for personal and professional growth, 321–323
founders and major contributors, 300–301
further information, 320, 323
gender and multicultural contributions, 320–321
homework assignments, 314–315
interventions, 313–315
interviews, 312–313
key concepts, 307–309
operant conditioning, 301, 307
overview, 13, 15, 319–320
parenting addressed by, 328, 329, 330–331
postmodern approaches vs., 240–241
preferred in managed-care settings, 300
private logic, 308
problem-solving training, 313
Quest family example, 315–319
recommended readings, 324
reinforcement, 307, 330–331
self-report questionnaires, 311–312
social learning theory, 308
social reinforcers, 301, 308, 331
systematic desensitization, 307, 329
techniques, 311–315
therapist's role and function, 310–311
therapy goals, 310
therapy session example, 301–307
wide acceptance of, 319
Cognitive distortions, 303–304, 308–309
Cognitive restructuring, 314
Cognitive schemas, 301, 309
Collaboration
considering collaborative practice, 35–36
facilitation and, 380
as feminist family therapy value, 45
Commission on Accreditation for Marriage and Family Therapy Education (COAMFTE), 11

Communication stances, defensive, 126–129, 138, 140–141

Communication training, 313

Community feeling, 44–45

Complaint-oriented story, 232

Compliments, 225

Conferred dominance, 296

Confidence, 30

Confidentiality, 58, 59, 114

Conflict Tactics Scale (CTS2), 373

Congruence
    in human validation process model, 9, 121, 126
    in R.E.C.I.P.E. acronym, 133

Conjoint family therapy, 121. *See also* Satir's human validation process model

Consciousness raising, 276, 280

Consequential emotions in A-B-C model, 300, 313–314

Consultant, 237

Contact, 9, 10, 29–30

Continuous primary reinforcement, 307, 330–331, 343

Contracting and behavioral change agreements, 314

Contracting in parenting, 345

Control (mistaken goal), 106

Co-therapists, 156

Council for Accreditation of Counseling and Related Educational Programs (CACREP), 11

Countertransference, 24–25

Courage, 30–31, 34

Critical-evaluation model of ethical decision making, 53–55

CTS2 (Conflict Tactics Scale), 373

Cultural diversity. *See* Multicultural perspectives

Cultural feminists, 269. *See also* Feminist family therapy

Cybernetics
    circular causality, 18
    defined, 18
    double binds, 19
    equifinality, 19
    feedback loops, 18
    first-order, 20
    first-order changes, 18
    homeostasis, 18
    importance of understanding, 17
    second-order, 20
    second-order changes, 19

DAS (Dyadic Adjustment Scale), 373

De-centered therapy, 15, 20

Deconstruction, 250, 253–254, 267

Defensive communication stances, 126–129, 138, 140–141, 331, 364

Definitional ceremonies, 255–256

Democratic child-rearing, 107

Demonstration of adequacy (mistaken goal), 106

Demonstration of inadequacy (mistaken goal), 104, 106

De-pathologizing behaviors and interactions, 279

Developing as a family practitioner. *See* Beginning work as a family practitioner; Integrating therapeutic systems; Personal and professional development

Development, personal and professional. *See* Personal and professional development

Developmental lens, 367–368

Diagnostic formulation, 374

Dialectics in symbolic-experiential family therapy, 152, 154–155

Dichotomous thinking (cognitive distortion), 303, 309

Differentiation of self
    Bowen's emphasis on, 13, 82
    in Bowen's training method for therapists, 85–86
    development by therapist, 25
    emotional cutoff vs., 82
    pseudo-self vs., 82
    Sonstegard's demonstration of, 8

Diffuse boundaries, 173

Directives in messages, 197–198, 202

Disengagement, 82

Displacement stories, 88

Distinguished Presenter Video Series (IAMFC), 23

Diversity. *See* Multicultural perspectives

Diversity feminisms, 269. *See also* Feminist family therapy

Documents and letters
    HIPPA regulations and, 267
    in narrative approach, 251, 256–257

Dominant-culture narratives, 249–250, 260–261

Double binds, 19, 155, 197

Doubt, introducing, 226

Downward arrow technique, 312

Drama, 133–134

Dual relationships, 46–47

Dulwich Centre, 263

Dulwich Centre Publications Pty Ltd., 263

DVD references
    Adlerian family therapy, 119
    cognitive-behavioral family therapy, 324–325
    feminist family therapy, 293
    human validation process model, 143
    multigenerational family therapy, 95
    parenting, 350
    postmodern and social constructionist approaches, 265
    solution-focused and solution-oriented therapies, 236
    strategic family therapy, 214–215
    structural family therapy, 187
    symbolic-experiential family therapy, 164

Dyadic Adjustment Scale (DAS), 373

Dyads, 22

Dysfunctional communication, 125–126, 139

Ebb-and-flow processes (level three sequences), 212–213, 365–366, 368

Ecostructural model of Aponte, 167, 172, 176

Egalitarian relationships, 277, 280

Embedded messages, 225

Emotional cutoff, 82

Emotional reactivity by therapist, 24–25

Emotion coaching, 338–339

Empowerment, 133, 287

Enactments, 178

Encouragement in parenting, 336

Engagement, 32

Enmeshment vs. belonging, 151

ENRICH scale, 373

Equifinality, 19

Estrangement, 82

Ethics
    codes of, 46–47, 50, 62
    common dilemmas in family practice, 58–61
    complexity of issues, 44, 46–47
    conceptualizing the client(s), 58–59
    confidentiality issues, 58
    constructivist nature of, 50
    critical-evaluation decision-making model, 53–55
    decision-making models, 53–58
    of dual relationships, 46–47
    gender and cultural issues, 60–61
    handling relational matters in individual context, 59–60
    ill-defined problems, 46
    informed consent and, 59
    Internet resources, 62
    legal issues, 44
    motivation and, 47
    as opportunities for learning and growth, 44, 47
    participatory ethics, 52, 56–57
    principle ethics, 47–51, 53–55
    virtue ethics, 51–52, 55–56

Evanston Family Therapy Institute, 263

Evolution of Psychotherapy conferences, 71

Evolving a crisis, 155

Exception questions, 218–219, 224, 231, 238

Existential therapy, 160

Experience, 9, 10

Experiential therapy, 9. *See also* Whitaker's symbolic-experiential family therapy

Extended family, cultural issues for, 60–61

Externalization
    in narrative approach, 262–263
    in postmodern and social constructionist approaches, 15, 250, 254, 267
    in R.E.C.I.P.E. acronym, 133

Externalizing questions, 250, 254, 262–263, 267

Face-to-face sequences, 212, 365

Facilitating change, 380–383, 388–389

Families and Family Therapy (Minuchin), 166

Family atmosphere, 101–102

Family constellation, 8, 102–104

Family games, 200

The Family Journal (IAMFC), 38, 94

Family life cycle, 367–368

Family life-fact chronologies, 124, 133, 366
Family mapping. *See also* Genograms
    exercise for personal and professional growth, 184–185
    in human validation process model, 124, 133
    in structural family therapy, 176–177
Family observational rating scales, 373
Family-of-origin. *See also* Personal and professional development
    in Bowen's training method for therapists, 85–86
    counseling or therapy for understanding, 27
    genogram for understanding, 25
    historical timeline for understanding, 26–27
    importance of understanding, 6, 24–25, 27
    virtue ethics and, 51–52
    wheel of influence for understanding, 26
Family Process journal, 94
Family projection process, 83
Family reconstruction, 133–134
Family resiliency, 381–383
Family sculpting, 133
Family structure
    Adlerian family therapy, 103
    ecostructural model of Aponte, 167, 172, 176
    structural family therapy, 171–172
Family systems
    in Asia, 16–17
    cybernetics and, 17–20
    family constellation (Adlerian therapy), 102–104
    gender issues avoided early on, 270
    general systems theory, 19–20
    internal, as lens, 363–364
    as open systems, 19
    overview, 16–17
    in structural family therapy, 171–174
    subsystems within, 22, 172–173
    ways of describing, 379
Family systems therapy. *See* Bowen's multigenerational family therapy
The Family Therapy Centre, 263
Family Therapy Networker journal, 94, 211
Family Therapy with the Experts videotapes (Carlson & Kjos), 23
Feedback loops, 18, 198
Feminist family therapy, 267
    assertiveness training, 281–282
    bibliotherapy, 281
    common themes in, 269–270
    consciousness raising, 276, 280
    de-pathologizing behaviors and interactions, 279
    development of, 15, 270–271
    diagnostic labels critiqued in, 279
    DVD references, 293
    egalitarian relationships in, 277, 280
    empowerment practice with women, 287

ethical decision-making model, 56–57
exercise for personal and professional growth, 289–290
feminist identity development model, 278
focus on gender issues, 15
further information, 290–292
gender and multicultural contributions, 287–289
gender-role and power analysis, 277, 280–281
heterosexual privilege, 289, 298–299
honoring women's experiences and perceptions, 276–277
key concepts, 276–277
LGBT identity, 271, 281, 282, 287, 371
male privilege, 289, 297–298
normal family critiqued in, 270, 276
overview, 13, 287
participatory ethics in, 52
patriarchy and, 269 270, 277
personal as political, 270, 277
prominent women, 296
Quest family example, 283–287
questions to consider, 271
recommended readings, 292–293
re-labeling and reframing, 282–283
self-disclosure, 281
social transformation and advocacy, 270, 277, 280
techniques, 279–283
theoretical orientations in, 268, 269
therapist's role and function, 279, 287, 379
therapy goals, 278–279
therapy session examples, 271–276, 282–283
unearned advantages and entitlements, 296
varieties of feminist stances, 268, 269
virtue considerations in, 45
white privilege, 289, 296–297
The Women's Project, 270–271
Feminist identity development model, 278
Fidelity, 48–49, 50
First-order changes, 18, 198
First-order cybernetics, 19–20
Force, 172
Formal assessments, 373–374
Formula first-session tasks, 225
Four-dimensional self, 96
Freedoms, five, 130
Functional vs. dysfunctional communication, 125–126, 139
Function of therapist. *See* Therapist's role and function
Future, working with the, 226–227

GARF (Global Assessment of Relational Functioning), 373
Gender issues. *See also* Feminist family therapy

Adlerian family therapy and, 115–116
cognitive-behavioral family therapy and, 321
effect of therapist's gender, 167–168
ethical, 60–61
gender lens, 370–371
human validation process model and, 138–139
male privilege, 289, 297–298
multigenerational family therapy and, 92–93
navel equality, 139
parenting, 348
pervasiveness of, 40
postmodern and social constructionist approaches and, 260–261
solution-focused and solution-oriented therapies and, 232–233
strategic family therapy and, 211
structural family therapy and, 183–184
symbolic-experiential family therapy and, 160, 161
Gender role socialization, 277
General systems theory, 19–20
Genograms
    defined, 73
    exercises for personal and professional growth, 93–94, 184–185, 321–322
    family-of-origin, 25
    in human validation process model (maps), 124, 133
    in multigenerational family therapy, 25, 86–87
    Quest family, 70–71, 89
    symbols and their meanings, 74 75
    Tito and Diana (blended family), 73, 76
    usefulness of, 379
Gestalt therapy, 9, 10, 160
Getting (mistaken goal), 105
Global Assessment of Relational Functioning (GARF), 373
Goals. *See* Therapy goals
Gordon Training International, 348–349
Growth, personal and professional. *See* Personal and professional development

Haley's approach. *See* Strategic family therapy
A Handmaid's Tale (Atwood), 281
"Hanging Hats" exercise, 28–30
Haworth Press, 292
The Healing Place, 142
Health Insurance Portability and Accountability Act (HIPPA), 44, 58, 65, 267
Hermeneutics, 259–260
Heterosexism. *See* Multicultural perspectives
Heterosexual privilege, 289, 298–299
Hierarchies, dysfunctional, 199, 204
Historical timeline for family-of-origin, 26–27
Holism, 31
Homeostasis, 18
Homework assignments, 203, 314–315

Honoring women's experiences and perceptions, 276–277
Humanism, 137
Human validation process model. *See* Satir's human validation process model
Humor, 35, 133
Hypothesizing and shared meaning, 378–380

IAMFC. *See* International Association of Marriage and Family Counselors
Identity questions, 250
Ill-defined problems, 46
Individual vs. systemic approaches, 20–22
Individuation vs. belonging, 152
Informed consent, 59
Inner system in R.E.C.I.P.E. acronym, 133
INS (Intimacy Needs Survey), 373
Institutionalizing Madness (Elizur & Minuchin), 174
Integrating therapeutic systems
    case conceptualization, 374, 384
    ensuring therapeutic efficacy, 384
    facilitating change, 380–383, 388–389
    family assessment, 362
    formal assessments, 373–374
    forming a relationship, 361–362, 375
    hypothesizing and shared meaning, 378–380
    lenses or perspectives, 362–373
    models of integration, 359, 379–380
    process for family therapy across models, 361–374
    Quest family example, 385–388
    reflecting and connecting, 360–361
    stages in the process, 359
    summary, 375
    tailoring treatment, 383–384
    temptations and challenges, 359
Interactions, meta-messages in, 17–18
Interest, 30
Intergenerational family therapy. *See* Bowen's multigenerational family therapy
Intermittent reinforcement, 307, 344
Internal family systems, 363–364
International Association of Marriage and Family Counselors (IAMFC)
    accreditation and, 11
    code of ethics, 46, 50, 59, 60
    on confidentiality and informed consent, 59
    Distinguished Presenter Video Series (IAMFC), 23
    The Family Journal, 38, 94
    note-taking guidelines for family therapists, 59
International Committee of Adlerian Summer Schools and Institutes, 118
Interviews, 312–313
Intimacy, 151–152
Intimacy Needs Survey (INS), 373
Introducing doubt, 226
Invariant intervention, 195–196, 205
Invitation letters, 256
Involvement, 32

I-positions, 87–88, 146
Irrational beliefs in A-B-C model, 300, 313–314
Irrelevant communication stance, 128, 129, 141
I-statements in parenting, 338
I-thou relationship, 121

Joining, 167, 176, 201
Journal keeping, 35
Journal of Feminist Family Therapy, 292
Journal of Marital and Family Therapy (AAMFT), 37–38, 94
Justice, 49, 50

Kent State University, 264

Labeling (cognitive distortion), 303, 309
Learning and Teaching Therapy (Haley), 211
Legal issues, 44, 54, 61–62
Lenses or perspectives. *See also* Gender issues; Multicultural perspectives; *specific lenses*
    in Adlerian family therapy, 114
    assessment using, 362–363
    in cognitive-behavioral family therapy, 320
    core metaframeworks, 39–40, 362–363
    developmental, 367–368
    family systems perspective, 16–20
    in human validation process model, 138
    integrative model, 380
    internal family systems, 363–364
    as metaframeworks, 16, 362–363
    models of family counseling as, 6, 16
    organization, 366–367
    overview, 362–373
    process, 371–373
    recursiveness, 39, 363
    relationship to change, 16
    sequences and patterns, 365–366
    in solution-focused and solution-oriented therapies, 231–232
    in strategic family therapy, 210
    in structural family therapy, 184
    in symbolic-experiential family therapy, 160
    teleological, 114, 364–365
    tree metaphor for, 16
    usefulness of, 363
Lesbian feminists, 269. *See also* Feminist family therapy
Letters and documents
    HIPPA regulations and, 267
    in narrative approach, 251, 256–257
Letters of invitation, 256
Letters of prediction, 256
Levels of sequences
    one (face-to-face), 212, 365
    two (routines), 212, 365
    three (ebb-and-flow processes), 212–213, 365–366, 368
    four (transgenerational), 213, 366, 368
LGBT identity, 271, 281, 282, 287, 371. *See also* Feminist family therapy

Liberal feminists, 269. *See also* Feminist family therapy
Life cycle of family, 367–368
Life-fact chronologies, 124, 133, 366
Linguistic approach to therapy, 200, 247–248
Listening
    active, in parenting, 337–338
    with an open mind, 252–253
    teleologically, 31
Locke-Wallace Marital Adjustment Scale (LWMAS), 373
Logical consequences in parenting, 337

Magnification (cognitive distortion), 303, 309
Male privilege, 289, 297–298
Mapping. *See* Family mapping; Genograms
Marginalized cultures, 182
Marital Disaffection Scale (MDS), 373
Marital Satisfaction Inventory-Revised (MSI-R) scale, 373
McMaster Clinical Rating Scale (MCRS), 373
Mental Research Institute (MRI). *See also* Strategic family therapy
    behavioral interventions, 203
    brief family therapy focus of, 14, 189
    classes of problem-maintaining solutions, 194–195
    contact information, 213
    cybernetics principles applied by, 19
    directives in messages, 197–198
    family therapy model, 194–195
    founding of, 19, 189
    homework assignments, 203
    one-down position, 203
    process and techniques, 202–203
    solution-focused model and, 217–218
    termination criteria, 203
    therapy goals, 199
Metacommunications, 9
Metaframeworks. *See also* Lenses or perspectives
    core perspectives, 39–40, 362–363
    integrative model, 380
    models of family counseling as, 16
Meta-messages, 17
Milan family therapy model. *See also* Strategic family therapy
    as bridge to postmodern approaches, 246–247
    circular questioning, 205
    family games, 200
    invariant intervention, 195–196, 205
    multiple-therapist interventions, 246
    neutrality of the therapist, 205, 246–247
    one-way mirror use, 204
    overview, 195–196
    process and techniques, 204–205
    therapy goals, 200
    therapy session example, 196–197
Milton H. Erickson Foundation, 71
Mind reading (cognitive distortion), 304, 309

Minimization (cognitive distortion), 303, 309
The Minuchin Center for the Family, 186
Minuchin's approach. *See* Structural family therapy
Miracle question
    Adlerian "The Question" compared to, 237–238
    in solution-focused and solution-oriented therapies, 224, 231, 233–235
Mislabeling (cognitive distortion), 304, 309
Mistaken goals, 97, 104–106, 330
Modeling in parenting, 345
Models of family counseling. *See also* Integrating therapeutic systems; Lenses or perspectives; *specific models*
    addressing parenting, 328, 329–332
    development of, 13–15
    family systems perspective, 16–20
    finding a foundational approach, 359–361
    finding ones that work for you, 6
    individual vs. systemic approaches, 20–22
    integration of, 39–40
    as lenses or perspectives, 6
    overview, 12–13
    process for family therapy across models, 361–374
    questions to consider, 6
    reflecting and connecting, 360–361
    virtue considerations in, 44–45
Monads, 22
Motivation, 98, 107
MRI. *See* Mental Research Institute
MSI-R (Marital Satisfaction Inventory-Revised) scale, 373
Multicultural perspectives. *See also* Feminist family therapy
    Adlerian family therapy, 115–116
    alternate belief systems, 210
    appreciating the influence of, 31
    assessments, 369–370
    cognitive-behavioral family therapy, 320–321
    dominant-culture narratives, 249–250, 260–261
    ethical issues, 60–61
    feminist family therapy, 15, 287–289
    human validation process model, 138–139
    importance in therapy, 40
    internal locus of control and, 139
    in *Journal of Marital and Family Therapy*, 38
    as lens (overview), 368–370
    marginalized cultures, 182
    multigenerational family therapy, 92–93
    parenting, 347–348
    participatory ethics and, 52
    postmodern and social constructionist approaches, 260–261
    principle ethics and, 51
    solution-focused and solution-oriented therapies, 232–233

strategic family therapy, 210–211
structural family therapy, 182–183
symbolic-experiential family therapy, 160–161
virtue and, 44
virtue ethics and, 51–52
Multigenerational family therapy. *See* Bowen's multigenerational family therapy
Multigenerational transmission, 83
Multiple-choice questions, 227

Narrative approaches to family therapy. *See* Postmodern, social constructionist, and narrative approaches to family therapy
NASAP (North American Society of Adlerian Psychology), 117–118
National Abortion and Reproductive Rights Action League (NARAL), 292
National Association for Social Workers (NASW), 46, 50, 291
National Organization for Women (NOW), 292
Natural consequences in parenting, 337
Natural systems therapy. *See* Bowen's multigenerational family therapy
Navel equality, 139
Negative feedback loops, 18, 198
Negative reinforcement, 307
Neglectful parenting, 334
Negotiations in parenting, 338
Neutrality of the therapist, 84, 205
Nonmaleficence, 48, 50
Normal family
    feminist critique of, 270, 276
    organization lens, 365–366
Normalizing a problem, 226
North American Society of Adlerian Psychology (NASAP), 117–118
Not knowing position, 15, 20, 247
NOW (National Organization for Women), 292
Nuclear family
    nurturing triads or dyads in, 130
    triangulation in, 82–83
Nurturing triads or dyads, 130

One-down position, 203
One-way mirrors, 204, 248
Open-forum family counseling, 107, 114
Open systems, 19
Operant conditioning, 301, 307
Ordinal birth order, 83–84, 102–104, 117
Organization lens, 366–367
Orientations of effective practitioners, 30–32
Overgeneralization (cognitive distortion), 303, 309
Ownership of problems, 338

Pace acronym, 9
Paradoxical interventions
    amplifying family difficulties, 202
    positioning, 190
    prescribing the symptom, 190, 202
    restraining family change, 190, 191, 202

in strategic family therapy, 190–191, 202, 204
in symbolic-experiential family therapy, 155
Parenting
    accentuating the positive, 336–337
    active listening and reflection, 337–338
    Adlerian approach, 107, 108–109, 329–330
    authoritarian approach, 330, 333
    authoritative-responsive or democratic, 107, 330, 333–336
    aversive interventions, 344–345
    behavioral extinction, 344
    blended families, 339
    chart for living in harmony, 340–343
    cognitive-behavioral approach, 329, 330–331
    communication, 345
    contracting, 345
    determining who owns the problem, 338
    difficult children, 339, 343–346
    DVD references, 350
    effective interventions, 336
    emotion coaching, 338–339
    encouragement, 336
    family homeostasis, 339
    further information, 347, 348–349
    gender and multicultural contributions, 347–348
    giving choices, 338
    history of, 329–332, 346–347
    human validation process model approach, 331–332
    I-statements, 338
    key concepts, 332–336
    logical consequences, 337
    modeling, 345
    models addressing, 328, 329–332
    natural consequences, 337
    neglectful, 334
    negotiations, 338
    overview, 13, 346–347
    parent effectiveness training, 331–332
    permissive approach, 330, 333–334
    positive techniques, 336–339
    Premack principle, 345
    punishment, 344–345, 354
    range of styles, 333–334
    reasons for addressing in this book, 328
    recommended readings, 349–350
    reinforcement, 343–344
    self-control and self-monitoring, 345
    shaping, 344
    spanking, 344, 354
    step-families, 339
    STEP: Systematic Training for Effective Parenting, 336
    techniques, 336–346
    time-outs, 344, 346
    training processes and consequences, 340–343

Parent value system, 101
Participatory ethics, 52, 56–57
Parts parties, 134
Patriarchy. *See also* Feminist family therapy;
Gender issues
critiqued by feminist family therapists,
15, 370–371
defined, 370
in dominant-culture narratives, 249
family definitions based on, 40
feminist belief about, 269–270, 277
Patterns. *See also* Sequences
family games, 200
in R.E.C.I.P.E. acronym, 133
tracking, 184, 365–366
working in, 31
Permissive parenting, 330, 333–334
Personal and professional development.
See also Beginning work as a family
practitioner
Adlerian phenomenological exercise,
116–117
Bowen's emphasis on, 13
cognitive-behavioral family therapy
exercise, 321–323
ethical issues as opportunities for, 44, 47
feminist family therapy exercise, 289–290
genogram exercises, 93–94, 184–185
human validation process model exercise,
139–141
as lifelong process, 361
multigenerational family therapy exercise,
93–94
narrative therapy exercise, 261–263
solution-focused/solution-oriented
therapy exercise, 233–235
strategic family therapy exercise,
211–213
structural family therapy exercise,
184–185
symbolic-experiential family therapy
exercise, 161–163
videotaping your work, 360–361
Personal as political, 270, 277
Personality priorities, 364
Personalization (cognitive distortion), 303,
309
Person-centered therapy, 160
Personhood vs. roles, 152
Perspectives. *See* Lenses or perspectives
Phenomenological approach, 103, 116–117
Philadelphia Child and Family Training
Center, Inc., 186
Placating communication stance, 126–127,
129, 140, 141
Positioning (paradoxical intervention),
190
Positive feedback loops, 18, 198
Possibility therapy, 218. *See also* Solution-
focused and solution-oriented therapies
Postmodern, social constructionist, and narra-
tive approaches to family therapy. *See also*
Solution-focused and solution-oriented
therapies

alternate stories, 254–255, 267
circulation questions, 251
client-as-expert in, 242, 252, 259, 267
cognitive-behavioral family therapy vs.,
240–241
deconstruction, 250, 253–254, 267
definitional ceremonies, 255–256
development of, 14–15
dominant-culture narratives, 249–250,
260–261
DVD references, 265
exercise for personal and professional
growth, 261–263
externalizing questions, 250, 254,
262–263, 267
founders and major contributors, 241,
247
further information, 260, 263–264
gender and multicultural contributions,
260–261
Gergen's social constructionism as
foundation, 241
hermeneutics emphasized by, 259–260
identity questions, 250
involving outside communities, 255–256
key concepts, 246–251
letters and documents used in, 251,
256–257, 267
linguistic approach, 200, 247–248
listening with an open mind, 252–253
Milan model as bridge to, 246–247
Milan model tied to, 200
modernist approach vs., 221, 239–240
narrative approach, 249–251
not-knowing position in, 247
one-way mirror use, 248
overview, 12–13, 239–241, 259–260
paradigm shift underlying, 241, 259
participatory ethics in, 52
problem-saturated stories, 221
Quest family example (narrative
approach), 257–259
questions that make a difference, 253
re-authoring stories, 246, 250, 254–255
recommended readings, 264–265
reflecting team in, 15, 248–249
relative influence questioning, 250
techniques, 252–257
therapist's role and function, 252, 379
therapy goals, 251–252
therapy session example (narrative
approach), 241–246
Whitaker's approach foreshadowing, 160
Postmodern feminists, 269. *See also* Feminist
family therapy
Power struggle (mistaken goal), 104
Prediction letters, 256
Prediction tasks, 225
Preferred stories, 15
Premack principle, 345
PREPARE scale, 373
Prescribing the symptom (paradoxical
intervention), 190, 202
Presence, 28–30

Pretend techniques, 204
Primary reinforcement, 343
Principle ethics
autonomy in, 47–48, 50, 51
beneficence in, 48
critical-evaluation decision-making
model, 53–55
cultural diversity and, 51
deciding among principles, 50
fidelity in, 48–49
justice in, 49
nonmaleficence in, 48
overview, 47–51
veracity in, 49–50
Private logic, 308
Problem-maintaining solutions, classes of,
194–195
Problem-saturated stories, 221
Problem-solving training, 313–314
Process lens, 371–373
Process of change
overview, 32–33, 372
process of therapy and, 372
in structural family therapy, 171
Process questions, 87
Professional development. *See* Personal and
professional development
Professional regulations, 61–62
Projection, 83, 84
Pseudo-self, 82
Psychological Care of Infant and Child
(Watson), 329
Psychology of use, 8, 330
Psychosomatic family, 173
Punishment, 344–345, 354
Purpose
in Adlerian family therapy, 10
teleology, 31, 114, 364–365
as therapeutic movement aspect, 9

Qualitative research, 38, 39
Quest family
Adlerian family therapy example, 109–113
biography, 69–70
cognitive-behavioral family therapy
example, 315–319
feminist family therapy example, 283–287
genograms, 70–71, 89
human validation process model example,
134–137
integrative therapist example, 385–388
multigenerational family therapy example,
88–92
narrative therapist example, 257–259
purpose of examples, 10, 11, 68–69
questions to consider, 68, 69
solution-oriented therapy example,
227–231
strategic family therapy example, 206–209
structural family therapy example,
178–182
symbolic-experiential family therapy
example, 156–160
Questions of difference, 218, 225

Racism. *See* Multicultural perspectives
Radical feminists, 269. *See also* Feminist family therapy
Re-authoring stories, 246, 254–255
R.E.C.I.P.E. acronym, 133
Recognition reflex, 97
Recommended readings
    Adlerian family therapy, 118–119
    cognitive-behavioral family therapy, 324
    feminist family therapy, 292–293
    human validation process model, 143
    multigenerational family therapy, 94–95
    parenting, 349–350
    postmodern, social constructionist, and narrative approaches, 264–265
    solution-focused and solution-oriented therapies, 235–236
    strategic family therapy, 214
    structural family therapy, 186–187
    symbolic-experiential family therapy, 163
    virtue, ethics, and legality, 63
Redundancy letters, 256
Reflecting and connecting, 360–361
Reflecting team, 15, 248–249
Reflection, cultivating, 35
Reflection in parenting, 337–338
Reframing
    in feminist family therapy, 282–283
    in strategic family therapy, 192, 201
    in structural family therapy, 178
    as teleologically oriented, 365–366
Reinforcement, 307, 330–331, 343–344
Re-labeling, 282–283
Relapse prevention, 384
Relationship experiments, 87
Relative influence questioning, 250
Research, 38, 39
Resiliency of families, 381–383
Resourcefulness in R.E.C.I.P.E. acronym, 133
Respect as foundation for practice, 36
Restraining change (paradoxical intervention), 190, 191, 202
Revenge (mistaken goal), 104, 106
Rigid boundaries, 173
The Robbins-Madanes Center for Strategic Intervention, 213
Rogerian or person-centered therapy, 7–8
Role of therapist. *See* Therapist's role and function
Roles vs. personhood, 152
Routines (level two sequences), 212, 365
Rules in family life, 124–125, 140, 198

Satir Institute of the Pacific, 142
Satir Professional Development Institute of Manitoba, 143
Satir's human validation process model
    author's experience with, 9
    AVANTA Network, 9
    blaming communication stance, 127, 129, 140, 141
    chaos, 130–131
    congruent communication in, 9, 121, 126

defensive communication stances, 126–129, 138, 140–141, 331, 364
development of, 14, 121–122
DVD references, 143
elements of interactions (self, others, context), 126, 127, 128
emphasis and assumptions of, 239–240
exercise for personal and professional growth, 139–141
family life-fact chronologies, 124, 133, 366
family mapping (genograms), 124, 133
family reconstruction, 133–134
family roles, 129–130
family sculpting, 133
five freedoms, 130
functional vs. dysfunctional communication, 125–126, 139
further information, 138, 142–143
gender and multicultural contributions, 138–139
internal locus of control, 139
irrelevant communication stance, 128, 129, 141
key concepts, 124–130
nurturing triads or dyads, 130
overview, 12, 121–122, 124, 137–138
parenting addressed by, 328, 331–332
parts parties, 134
placating communication stance, 126–127, 129, 140, 141
Quest family example, 134–137
R.E.C.I.P.E. acronym, 133
recommended readings, 143
rules in family life, 124–125, 140
seed model, 137–138
status quo, 130, 131
super-reasonable communication stance, 127–128, 129, 141
techniques, 132–134
therapist's role and function, 131–132, 379
therapy goals, 130–131
therapy session example, 122–124
virtue considerations in, 45
wheel of influence, 133
Whitaker's approach compared to, 132, 160
Satir Systems, 142
Satir Therapy with Jean McLendon (Allyn and Bacon tape), 142
Satisfaction in work, 32
Scales for formal assessment, 373
Scaling questions, 224–225, 231, 238
Scapegoat, 150
Schizophrenia, 19
Scholar-practitioners, 37–39, 92
Sculpting, 9
SDI (Sexual Desire Inventory), 373
Second-order changes, 19, 198
Second-order cybernetics, 20
Seeding the unconscious, 147, 155–156
Seed model, 137–138
Selective abstraction (cognitive distortion), 303, 309

Self-control and self-monitoring, 345
Self-disclosure, 161, 281
Self-elevation (mistaken goal), 105
Self-rating scales, 373
Self-Report Family Inventory (SFI), 373
Self-report questionnaires, 311–312
Sequences
    adaptive, 366
    ebb-and-flow processes (level three), 212–213, 365–366, 368
    exercise for personal and professional growth, 211–213
    face-to-face (level one), 212, 365
    routines (level two), 212, 365
    tracking in family systems therapy, 184
    tracking patterns, 365–366
    transgenerational (level four), 213, 366, 368
Session examples. *See* Quest family; Therapy session examples
Sexism. *See* Feminist family therapy; Gender issues
Sexual Desire Inventory (SDI), 373
Shaping in parenting, 344
Shared meaning and hypothesizing, 378–380
Sibling cohesion factor, 84
Sibling position (birth order), 83–84, 102–104, 117
SIDCARB scale, 373
Silence, 34–35, 156
Social constructionism. *See* Postmodern, social constructionist, and narrative approaches to family therapy
Social equality, 45, 109, 114
Social interest, 44–45
Socialist feminists, 269. *See also* Feminist family therapy
Social learning theory, 308
Social reinforcement, 343
Social reinforcers, 301, 308, 331
Social transformation and advocacy, 270, 277, 280
Societal projection process, 84
Societal regression, 84
Solid self, 82
Solution-focused and solution-oriented therapies
    acting "as if," 224, 233–234
    changing the doing of the problem, 226
    complaint-oriented story, 232
    compliments, 225
    development of, 14
    DVD references, 236
    embedded messages, 225
    exception questions, 218–219, 224, 231, 238
    exercise for personal and professional growth, 233–235
    formula first-session tasks, 225
    founders and major contributors, 217–218
    further information, 232, 235
    gender and multicultural contributions, 232–233

Solution-focused (*continued*)
  introducing doubt, 226
  key concepts, 222–223
  major tenets, 232
  miracle question, 224, 231, 233–235, 237–238
  multiple-choice questions, 227
  normalizing a problem, 226
  overview, 12, 231–232
  postmodern perspective of, 221, 232
  prediction tasks, 225
  problem-saturated stories, 221
  Quest family example, 227–231
  questions of difference, 218, 225
  recommended readings, 235–236
  review of narrative approach, 251
  scaling questions, 224–225, 231, 238
  signs, 225, 231, 238
  solution-focused vs. solution-oriented approach, 222–223
  strategic approach vs., 221
  strategic family therapy and, 217
  summary messages, 225–226
  techniques, 224–227
  therapist's role and function, 223–224
  therapy goals, 223
  therapy session examples, 218–222
  virtue considerations in, 45
  working with the future, 226–227
Spanking, 344, 354
Starting work as a family practitioner. *See* Beginning work as a family practitioner
Status quo
  family games maintaining, 200
  in human validation process model, 130, 131
  patterns maintaining, 198
Step-families, 339
STEP: Systematic Training for Effective Parenting, 336
Stereotypes, 260
Strategic family therapy. *See also* Mental Research Institute (MRI)
  behavioral interventions, 203
  circular questioning, 205
  classes of problem-maintaining solutions, 194–195
  development of, 14
  directives in messages, 197–198, 202
  double binds, 197
  DVD references, 214–215
  dysfunctional hierarchies, 199, 204
  emphasis and assumptions of, 239–240
  exercise for personal and professional growth, 211–213
  family games, 200
  feedback loops, 198
  first-order changes, 198
  further information, 211, 213
  gender and multicultural contributions, 210–211
  homework assignments, 203
  influence of, 197
  invariant intervention, 195–196, 205

  joining, 201
  key concepts, 197–199
  major contributors, 189–190
  Milan model, 195–197, 200, 204–205, 246–247
  MRI model, 194–195, 199, 202–203
  new perspectives brought by, 217
  one-down position, 203
  ordeals, 199
  organization lens, 366–367
  overview, 12, 209–210
  paradoxical interventions, 190–191, 202, 204
  prescribing the symptom, 190, 202
  pretend techniques, 204
  problem and solution approach, 209
  Quest family example, 206–209
  recommended readings, 214
  reframing, 192, 201
  restraining family change, 190, 191, 202
  rules in family life, 198
  second-order changes, 198
  solution-focused and solution-oriented therapies vs., 221
  solution-focused model and, 217
  techniques, 201–205
  termination criteria, 203
  therapist's role and function, 200–201
  therapy goals, 199–200
  therapy session examples, 190–194, 196–197
  virtue considerations in, 45
  Washington School, 194, 199–200, 203–204
Structural family therapy
  accommodation, 173
  alignment, 172
  boundaries, 172, 173–174, 176–177
  development of, 14
  DVD references, 187
  ecostructural model of Aponte, 167, 172, 176
  emphasis and assumptions of, 239–240
  enactments, 178
  exercise for personal and professional growth, 184–185
  family mapping, 176–177
  family structure, 171–172
  family subsystems, 172–173
  force, 172
  founder and major contributors, 166–167
  further information, 184, 186
  gender and multicultural contributions, 182–184
  joining, 167, 176
  key concepts, 171–174
  organization lens, 366–367
  overview, 12, 166, 182
  presenting problem, 171
  process of change, 171
  Quest family example, 178–182
  recommended readings, 186–187
  reframing, 178

  techniques, 175–178
  therapist's role and function, 175
  therapy goals, 174–175
  therapy session examples, 167–171, 172
  unbalancing, 176, 184
  underorganized families, 172
  virtue considerations in, 45
Subjective focus, 151
Summary messages, 225–226
Super-reasonable communication stance, 127–128, 129, 141
Supervision process, 323
Symbolic-experiential family therapy. *See* Whitaker's symbolic-experiential family therapy
Systematic desensitization, 307, 329
Systemic approaches. *See also* Lenses or perspectives; *specific approaches*
  emphasis and assumptions of, 239–240
  ethical issues for individuals, 58–59
  family systems perspective, 16–17
  individual approaches vs., 20–22
  postmodern approaches vs., 239–240

Tailoring treatment, 383–384
Techniques
  Adlerian family therapy, 107–109
  cognitive-behavioral family therapy, 311–315
  collaboration and, 380
  feminist family therapy, 279–283
  human validation process model, 132–134
  multigenerational family therapy, 86–88
  parenting, 336–346
  postmodern, social constructionist, and narrative, 252–257
  solution-focused and solution-oriented therapies, 224–227
  structural family therapy, 175–178
  tailoring treatment, 383–384
Teleology, 31, 114, 364–365
Tending the spirit, 31–32
Termination criteria, 203
Texas Women's University, 291–292
Theory and Practice of Counseling and Psychotherapy (Bitter & Corey), 21
Therapeutic sharing, 155
Therapist, meaning in this book, 11
Therapist's role and function
  Adlerian family therapy, 107, 379
  cognitive-behavioral family therapy, 310–311
  ensuring therapeutic efficacy, 384
  facilitating change, 380–383, 388–389
  feminist family therapy, 279, 287, 379
  human validation process model, 131–132, 379
  hypothesizing and shared meaning, 378–380
  multigenerational family therapy, 85–86
  social constructionist, 252, 379
  solution-focused and solution-oriented therapies, 223–224

strategic family therapy, 200–201
structural family therapy, 175
symbolic-experiential family therapy,
        153–154, 160
tailoring treatment, 383–384
Therapy goals
    Adlerian family therapy, 106–107
    cognitive-behavioral family therapy, 310
    feminist family therapy, 278–279
    human validation process model, 130–131
    multigenerational family therapy, 84–85
    social constructionist, 251–252
    solution-focused and solution-oriented
        therapies, 223
    structural family therapy, 174–175
    symbolic-experiential family therapy,
        153
Therapy session examples. *See also* Quest
    family
    Adlerian family therapy, 98–101, 105
    cognitive-behavioral family therapy,
        301–307
    feminist family therapy, 271–276,
        282–283
    human validation process model,
        122–124
    multigenerational family therapy, 76–81
    narrative approach to family therapy,
        241–246
    orientation of this book, 10
    questions to consider, 68
    solution-focused and solution-oriented
        therapies, 218–222
    strategic family therapy, 190–194,
        196–197
    structural family therapy, 167–171, 172
Timeline for family-of-origin, 26–27
Time-outs in parenting, 344, 346
Transgenerational family therapy. *See*
    Bowen's multigenerational family
    therapy
Transgenerational sequences (level four),
    213, 366, 368
Transnational feminists, 269. *See also*
    Feminist family therapy

Treatment adherence, 384
Treatment formulation, 374
Triads, 22, 130
Triangles
    nurturing triads, 130
    sibling cohesion factor and, 84
    in symbolic-experiential family therapy,
        149
    triangulation vs., 83
Triangulation, 13, 82–83
Tunnel vision (cognitive distortion), 304

Unbalancing, 176, 184
Underorganized families, 172
Understanding Human Nature (Adler),
    329–330
Unearned advantages and entitlements, 296
University of Kentucky, 291

Veracity, 49–50
Videotaping your work, 360–361
A Vindication of the Rights of Women
    (Wollstonecraft), 268
The Virginia Satir Global Network (formerly
    AVANTA Network), 9, 138, 142
Virtue, 43, 44–45, 51
Virtue ethics, 51–52, 55–56
Vulnerable therapist, 56–57

Washington School of Strategic Family
    Therapy. *See also* Strategic family
    therapy
    dysfunctional hierarchies, 199, 204
    founders, 194
    ordeals, 199
    paradoxical interventions, 204
    pretend techniques, 204
    process and techniques, 203–204
    therapy goals, 199–200
    therapy session example, 190–194
Wheel of influence, 26, 133
Whitaker's symbolic-experiential family
    therapy
    atheoretical, pragmatic stance, 151, 160
    authenticity in, 162–163, 165

being is becoming belief, 151
co-therapists, 156
development of, 14
dialectics of healthy families, 152
double binds, 155
DVD references, 164
emphasis and assumptions of, 239–240
evolving a crisis, 155
exercise for personal and professional
    growth, 161–163
founder and major contributors, 145
further information, 160, 163
gender and multicultural contributions,
    160–161
here-and-now focus, 145, 151
individuation vs. belonging, 152
intimacy as desired outcome, 151–152
I-positions, 146
key concepts, 151–152
overview, 12, 145, 160
paradoxical interventions, 155
play as a dialectic, 154–155
Quest family example, 156–160
recommended readings, 163
Satir's approach compared to, 132, 160
seeding the unconscious, 147, 155–156
silence in, 156
subjective focus, 151
techniques, 154–156
therapeutic sharing, 155
therapist's role and function, 153–154,
    160
therapy goals, 153
therapy session examples, 145–151,
    155, 156
virtue considerations in, 45
White privilege, 289, 296–297
Womanists, 269. *See also* Feminist family
    therapy
Women and Therapy journal, 292
Women-of-color feminists, 269. *See also*
    Feminist family therapy
Women's Interest Network, 290
The Women's Project, 270–271
Working with the future, 226–227

Credits

Photo Credits

73 Courtesy, The Bowen Center for the Study of Family; photo by Andrea Schara. **73** Courtesy the Family Institute of Westchester. **98** © Hulton Archive/Getty Images. **98** Courtesy of the ICASSI. **122** Courtesy of The Virginia Satir Global Network. **146** Courtesy, University of Wisconsin Madison Archives. **167** Courtesy, The Minuchen Center for the Family. **167** Courtesy of Dr. Harry J. Aponte. **190** Courtesy of Madeleine Richeport-Haley, Ph.D., LaJolla, CA. **195** Courtesy of the Watzlawick Collection, Don D. Jackson Archive, Mental Research Institute, Palo Alto, CA. **199** Courtesy, Chloe Madanes. **200** Courtesy of Scuola Maria Selvini. **218** Courtesy the Brief Family Therapy Center. **218** Courtesy the Brief Family Therapy Center. **249** Courtesy of Dulwich Centre, Adelaide, South Australia. **270** Courtesy of Louise Bordeaux Silverstein, PH.D. Professor of Psychology, Yeshiva University, Bronx, NY. **270** Courtesy of Dr. Thelma Goodrich. **301** Courtesy of Dr. Frank M. Dattilio. **330** Courtesy of Dr. Eva Dreikurs Ferguson.

Text Credits

This page constitutes an extension of the copyright page. We have made every effort to trace the ownership of all copyrighted material and to secure permission from copyright holders. In the event of any question arising as to the use of any material, we will be pleased to make the necessary corrections in future printings. Thanks are due to the following authors, publishers, and agents for permission to use the material indicated.

Chapter 1, pp. 21–22: From Bitter, J. R., & Corey, G. (2005). *Family systems therapy*. In G. Corey, *Theory and practice of counseling and psychotherapy* (7th ed., pp. 420–459). Belmont, CA: Brooks/Cole.

Chapter 4, pp. 73–81: From Carter, B., & McGoldrick, M. (2005). *The expanded family life cycle: Individual, family, and social perspectives* (3rd ed.). Boston: Allyn & Bacon.

Chapter 5, pp. 98–101: From Christensen, O. C. (Speaker). (1979). *Adlerian family counseling* [Educational Film]. (Available from Educational Media Corp., Box 21311, Minneapolis, MN 55421-0311.)

Chapter 6, pp. 122–124: From Golden Triad Films, Inc. (1968a). *Virginia Satir: Blended family with a troubled boy* [VT 101]. Kansas City, MO: Author.

Chapter 7, pp. 145–150: From Whitaker, C. A., & Bumberry, W. M. (1988). *Dancing with the family: A symbolic-experiential approach.* New York: Brunner-Mazel.

Chapter 8, pp. 167–171: From Aponte, H. J. (1994). *Bread and spirit: Therapy with the new poor—Diversity of race, culture, and values.* New York: Norton.

Chapter 9, pp. 190–194: From Haley, J. (1984). *Ordeal therapy: Unusual ways to change behavior.* San Francisco: Jossey Bass.

Chapter 10, pp. 218–221: From Walter, J. L., & Peller, J. E. (2000). *Recreating brief therapy: Preferences and possibilities.* New York: Norton; **pp. 221–222:** From Berg, I. K. (Speaker). (2002, December 12). Case presentations (J. Carlson, Moderator). *Brief Therapy Conference.* Orlando, FL: Milton H. Erickson Foundation.

Chapter 11, pp. 241–246: From Madigan, S. (Speaker). (1999). *Narrative therapy: Family therapy with the experts* (Moderators: J. Carlson & D. Kjos). Boston: Allyn & Bacon.

Chapter 12, pp. 271–276: With permission by Patricia E. Robertson.

Chapter 13, pp. 301–307: From Dattilio, F. M., Epstein, N. B., & Baucom, D. H. (1998). *An introduction to cognitive-behavioral therapy with couples and families.* In F. M. Dattilio (Ed.), *Case studies in couple and family therapy: Systemic and cognitive perspectives* (pp. 1–36). New York: Guilford Press.

Chapter 14, pp. 334: From Christensen, O. C. (Ed.). (2004). *Adlerian family counseling* (3rd ed.). Minneapolis, MN: Educational Media Corp.

Chapter 15, pp. 365, 366: From Breunlin, D. C., Schwartz, R. C., & MacKune-Karrer, B. (1997). Metaframeworks: *Transcending the models of family therapy.* San Francisco: Jossey-Bass. (Original work published 1992)